FIFTY YEARS OF INTERNATIONAL ENVIRONMENTAL LAW

This book explores the seminal importance of the first UN Conference on the Human Environment in Stockholm 1972 – the Stockholm Conference – for the development of international environmental law. By bringing together world leading experts from academia and legal practice, the book charts the development of international environmental law in the 50 years since 1972 in the areas of nature and biodiversity, chemicals and waste, oceans and water, and atmosphere and climate, and with respect to structures and institutions, consumption and production, and human rights and participatory rights in environmental matters. It analyses how the ideas and concepts of the Stockholm Conference have influenced this development and explores the novel ideas that have emerged since then. It describes the approaches of the developed and developing countries in this process and the relationship between international environmental law and other areas of law, such as the law of the sea and international economic law.

Jonas Ebbesson is Professor of Environmental Law, former Dean of the Faculty of Law (2012–17), and Director of the Stockholm Environmental Law and Policy Centre at Stockholm University in Sweden. He is former Chair (2011–21) and Member (2005–21) of the Aarhus Convention Compliance Committee.

David Langlet is Professor of Environmental Law at Uppsala University, former Professor of Ocean Governance Law at the University of Gothenburg in Sweden and former Research fellow at Oxford University, UK. He is the Editor-in-Chief of the *Nordic Environmental Law Journal* and Member of the Board of the Stockholm Environmental Law and Policy Centre.

Fifty Years of International Environmental Law

DEVELOPMENTS SINCE THE 1972 STOCKHOLM CONFERENCE

Edited by

JONAS EBBESSON

Stockholm University

DAVID LANGLET

Uppsala University

CAMBRIDGE
UNIVERSITY PRESS

CAMBRIDGE
UNIVERSITY PRESS

Shaftesbury Road, Cambridge CB2 8EA, United Kingdom

One Liberty Plaza, 20th Floor, New York, NY 10006, USA

477 Williamstown Road, Port Melbourne, VIC 3207, Australia

314–321, 3rd Floor, Plot 3, Splendor Forum, Jasola District Centre, New Delhi – 110025, India

Cambridge University Press is part of Cambridge University Press & Assessment, a department of the University of Cambridge.

We share the University's mission to contribute to society through the pursuit of education, learning and research at the highest international levels of excellence.

www.cambridge.org
Information on this title: www.cambridge.org/9781009445771

DOI: 10.1017/9781009445740

When citing this work, please include a reference to the DOI 10.1017/9781009445740

First published 2026

Cover image: Coral Island/Moment/Getty Images.

A catalogue record for this publication is available from the British Library

Library of Congress Cataloging-in-Publication Data
NAMES: Ebbesson, Jonas editor | Langlet, David editor
TITLE: Fifty years of international environmental law : developments since the 1972 Stockholm Conference / edited by Jonas Ebbesson, Stockholms Universitet; David Langlet, Uppsala Universitet, Sweden.
DESCRIPTION: Cambridge, United Kingdom ; New York, NY : Cambridge University Press, 2026. | Includes index.
IDENTIFIERS: LCCN 2025032327 (print) | LCCN 2025032328 (ebook) | ISBN 9781009445771 hardback | ISBN 9781009445795 paperback | ISBN 9781009445740 ebook
SUBJECTS: LCSH: Environmental law, International – History | Environmental law – Sweden – History | United Nations Conference on the Human Environment (1972 : Stockholm, Sweden)
CLASSIFICATION: LCC K3585 .F54 2026 (print) | LCC K3585 (ebook) | DDC 341.4–dc23/eng/20250724
LC record available at https://lccn.loc.gov/2025032327
LC ebook record available at https://lccn.loc.gov/2025032328

ISBN 978-1-009-44577-1 Hardback

Contents

Figures

Tables

Contributors

HARRO VAN ASSELT is the Hatton Professor of Climate Law at the Department of Land Economy and a Fellow with Hughes Hall at the University of Cambridge in the United Kingdom. He is also Professor of Climate Law and Policy at the University of Eastern Finland and an Affiliated Researcher with the Stockholm Environment Institute.

RICHARD BARNES is Professor of International Law at the University of Lincoln in the United Kingdom and Adjunct Professor of Law in the Faculty of Law at the Norwegian Centre for the Law of the Sea at the UiT – Arctic University of Norway in Tromsø, Norway.

BEN BOER is Professor Emeritus at the University of Sydney in Australia and a founder of the Australian Centre for Climate and Environmental Law. He specializes in environmental law, human rights law, and heritage law. He is a member of the Board of Governors of the International Council of Environmental Law.

JUTTA BRUNNÉE is Professor of Law and University Professor at the Henry N. R. Jackman Faculty of Law, University of Toronto. She is Fellow of the Royal Society of Canada, Member of the *Institut de droit international*, and has delivered a course at The Hague Academy of International Law (2019).

ROWENA CANTLEY-SMITH is Barrister at the Victorian Bar in Australia, an Adjunct Fellow in the Institute of Sustainable Futures at the University of Technology Sydney, and Senior Legal Consultant to the United Nations and other international organizations. She specializes in international law, climate change law, energy law and just transitions, and environmental and consumer rights.

CARL DALHAMMAR is Professor of Environmental Law at the International Institute for Industrial Environmental Economics, Lund University.

BHARAT H. DESAI is Humboldt Award Professor at Institute of Public International Law at University of Bonn, Germany, Director of the

Institute for Advanced Studies in International Law and Diplomacy, and Editor-in-Chief of *Environmental Policy and Law*. In July 2023, he gave the Summer Course at the Xiamen Academy of International Law (China) and will deliver the Winter Course in January 2028 at the Hague Academy of International Law.

JONAS EBBESSON is Professor of Environmental Law, former Dean of the Faculty of Law (2012–17), and Director of the Stockholm Environmental Law and Policy Centre at Stockholm University in Sweden. He is former Chair (2011–21) and member (2005–21) of the Aarhus Convention Compliance Committee.

ALVIN GACHIE is Legal Officer at the UN Environment Programme in Kenya and has over ten years of experience working in the UN system, in international civil society, and in the private sector. He holds a Bachelor and a Master of Laws from the University of Nairobi.

LEONIE GEENE is Environmental Law Specialist at the UN Environment Programme's Law Division in Kenya, specializing in international environmental law. She holds a Master of Laws in Public International Law from the University of Amsterdam and a Master of Arts in Environmental Policy and Planning from the Free University of Berlin.

ELLEN HEY is Emeritus Professor of Public International Law in the Erasmus School of Law at Erasmus University Rotterdam in the Netherlands and Adjunct Professor at the Norwegian Center for the Law of the Sea at UiT – Arctic University of Norway in Tromsø, Norway.

CLAUDIA ITUARTE LIMA (DR.) is an international public lawyer and scholar with over two decades of experience at the intersection of human rights, biodiversity, and climate change law and policy. She works as Thematic Lead and Senior Researcher at the Raoul Wallenberg Institute in Sweden and serves as Director of the Global Network for Human Rights and the Environment.

MACHARIA KAGURU is Teaching Fellow at Strathmore University Law School and Environmental Law and Policy Specialist at the UN Environment Programme in Nairobi, Kenya.

PATRICIA KAMERI-MBOTE is Director of the Law Division at the UN Environment Programme and Professor of Law at the University of Nairobi in Kenya. She has taught and researched diverse areas of law including environmental law for over thirty years prior to assuming her current position.

TIMO KOIVUROVA is Research Professor in the Arctic Centre at the University of Lapland in Finland. One of his areas of expertise is international environmental law. He is one of two Editors-in-Chief of the *Yearbook of International Environmental Law*.

KATHARINA KUMMER PEIRY has over thirty years' experience in international environmental policy as a government negotiator and chairperson of international meetings; as an expert advisor, a university lecturer, and author of numerous academic publications; and as a senior manager, including as Executive Secretary of the Basel Convention on the Control of Transboundary Movements of Hazardous Wastes and Their Disposal. She is now happily retired in Switzerland.

DAVID LANGLET is Professor of Environmental Law at Uppsala University and former Professor of Ocean Governance Law at the University of Gothenburg in Sweden. He is the Editor-in-Chief of the *Nordic Environmental Law Journal* and member of the board of the Stockholm Environmental Law and Policy Centre.

JAN MAINA is Advocate of the High Court of Kenya and a specialist in international environmental law. He has extensive experience in both litigation and policy development, and he has litigated and contributed to the shaping of legal frameworks on matters such as sustainability, environmental rule of law, and environmental protection in Kenya.

EVA R. VAN DER MAREL is Associate Professor of Law in the Faculty of Law at UiT – Arctic University of Norway in Tromsø, Norway, where she is associated with the Norwegian Centre for the Law of the Sea.

ELISA MORGERA is UN Special Rapporteur on Climate Change and Human Rights and Professor at Durham University Law School in the United Kingdom and at University of Eastern Finland. From 2019 to 2024, she was the Director of the One Ocean Hub (Grant no. NE/S008950/1), which pioneered inter- and transdisciplinary research on human rights at the ocean–climate nexus.

PHOEBE OKOWA is a Judge at the International Court of Justice, The Hague, the Netherlands and an Associate Member of the *Institut de droit international*. Until her election to the Court, she was Professor of Public International Law at Queen Mary University London, and a Member of the UN International Law Commission.

SEAN O'REILLY has a Bachelor of Laws from the Chinese University of Hong Kong, a Master of Laws in Public International Law from the London School of Economics, and a Bachelor of Civil Law from Oxford University. He is Barrister at Plowman Chambers in Hong Kong, China.

MARCOS ORELLANA has a Master of Laws and a Doctor of Juridical Science and is the UN Special Rapporteur on Toxics and Human Rights (2020–26). Previously, Professor Orellana has advised governments and UN agencies on sustainability issues and has also advised global civil society on global environmental justice issues. He teaches in the Washington College of Law at the American University, Washington, DC, in the United States.

JACQUELINE PEEL is a Redmond Barry Distinguished Professor at the Melbourne Law School and was the inaugural Director of Melbourne Climate Futures at the University of Melbourne in Australia. She is an Australian Laureate Fellow and Kathleen Fitzpatrick Award scholar working on corporate climate accountability. She serves as a coordinating lead author on the Intergovernmental Panel on Climate Change for its Seventh Assessment Report.

CATHERINE REDGWELL is Emerita Chichele Professor of Public International Law at the University of Oxford in the United Kingdom and Co-Director of the Oxford Martin Programmes on Sustainable Oceans and on the Future of Plastics. She is co-author of *Lyster's International Wildlife Law* (2nd ed., Cambridge University Press) and of *International Law and the Environment* (4th ed., Oxford University Press).

NICOLAS DE SADELEER is Full Professor at UCLouvain in Saint-Louis, Belgium. He is a specialist in European Union (EU) institutional law, environmental law, and comparative law, and a commentator on EU legal and political issues in the areas of trade, investment, and sustainable development. He has held several guest academic positions and has been the recipient of six international university chairs.

NICO SCHRIJVER is Professor Emeritus of International Law at Leiden University in the Netherlands, former State Councillor and Judge ad hoc at the International Tribunal for the Law of the Sea. Currently, he serves as a member of the European Union Scientific Advisory Board on Climate Change, and Rapporteur (with Jutta Brunnée) of the *Institut de droit international* on Harm Prevention Rules for the Global Environment.

DINAH SHELTON is Professor Emeritus at the George Washington University School of Law in Washington, DC, United States, and a former member of the Inter-American Commission on Human Rights.

YOSHIFUMI TANAKA is Professor of International Law with a specific focus on the law of the sea in the Faculty of Law at the University of Copenhagen, Denmark.

DIRE D. TLADI is Judge of the International Court of Justice and Distinguished Visiting Professor at the University of Johannesburg in South Africa, NRF Research Chair in International Law.

Preface

On 2–3 June 2022, the United Nations International Meeting Stockholm+50: A Healthy Planet for the Prosperity of All – Our Responsibility, Our Opportunity (Stockholm+50 Meeting) was held in Stockholm. The Stockholm+50 Meeting commemorated the United Nations Conference on the Human Environment (Stockholm Conference), also held in Stockholm fifty years earlier from 5–16 June 1972.

No other single event has had as much impact on the development of international environmental law as the 1972 Stockholm Conference.

At the occasion of the Stockholm+50 Meeting, the Stockholm Environmental Law and Policy Centre, at Stockholm University, first organized (with the Faculty of Law at Lund University, the Environmental Law Institute, and the Environmental Peacebuilding Association) the Symposium on the Law for Security and Sustainable Development as an associated event to the Stockholm+50 Meeting, and then the conference Stockholm+50: International Environmental Law in Perspective, which highlighted how international environmental law developed in different fields between 1972 and 2022. Both events related to the 1972 Stockholm Conference and the 2022 Stockholm+50 Meeting.

This edited volume builds on the presentations at the conference Stockholm+50: International Environmental Law in Perspective, and we appreciate that most speakers at the conference agreed to contribute and to develop their papers into chapters. We are also glad that Professor Nico Schrijver, who held the 2022 Stockholm Environmental Law Lecture, agreed to do the same with his lecture and publish it as part of this volume.

The contributions to *Fifty Years of International Environmental Law: Developments since the 1972 Stockholm Conference* chart the changes of international law between Stockholm 1972 and Stockholm 2022, and analyse the development of international *environmental* law as an important part of international law. They also show the impact of the 1972 Stockholm Conference on this development.

We are thankful for the financial support to the conference and the book project by the Cassel Foundation (Justitierådet Edvard Cassels stiftelse), and for the support to the conference by the Granholm Foundation (Henrik Granholms stiftelse), and the Human Science Academic Area of Stockholm University. We also appreciate the partnership with the European Society of International Law and the journal *Environmental Policy and Law* in organizing the event. Finally, we want to thank Stacy Belden for her excellent copy-editing, and Lisa Say for diligent indexing.

Abbreviations

ABNJ	areas beyond national jurisdiction
ACHR	American Convention on Human Rights
ACtHPR	African Court on Human and Peoples' Rights
APINA	Air Pollution Information Network for Africa
ASEAN	Association of Southeast Asian Nations
BAT	best available techniques
BEP	best environmental practices
BHRRC	Business and Human Rights Resource Centre
CAC	Codex Alimentarius Commission
CBAM	carbon border adjustment mechanism
CBD	Convention on Biological Diversity
CBDR	common but differentiated responsibilities
CBDRRC	common but differentiated responsibilities and respective capabilities
CEDAW	Convention on the Elimination of Discrimination against Women
CERD	Committee on the Elimination of Racial Discrimination
CFC	chlorofluorocarbon
CITES	Convention on International Trade in Endangered Species
CJEU	Court of Justice of the European Union
CMS	Convention on the Conservation of Migratory Species
COP	Conference of the Parties
CSD	Commission on Sustainable Development
CSW	Commission on the Status of Women
DELC	Division of Environmental Law and Conventions
EANET	Acid Deposition Monitoring Network in East Asia
EC	European Community
ECHR	European Convention on Human Rights

ECOSOC	Economic and Social Council
ECtHR	European Court of Human Rights
EEE	electrical and electronic equipment
EHRDs	environmental human rights defenders
EIA	environmental impact assessment
EMEP	Environmental Monitoring Program
EPR	extended producer responsibility
ESCAP	Economic and Social Commission for Asia and the Pacific
ESM	environmentally sound management
EU	European Union
FAO	Food and Agriculture Organization
FPIC	free, prior and informed consent
GATT	General Agreement on Tariffs and Trade
GDP	gross domestic product
GEF	Global Environment Facility
GHGs	greenhouse gases
GMEF	Global Ministerial Environment Forum
GMOs	genetically modified organisms
GNI	gross national income
HLPF	High-Level Political Forum on Sustainable Development
HRC	Human Rights Council
HRD	human rights defenders
IACtHR	Inter-American Court on Human Rights
IAEA	International Atomic Energy Agency
ICCM	International Conference on Chemicals Management
ICCPR	International Covenant on Civil and Political Rights
ICESCR	International Convention on Economic, Social and Cultural Rights
ICJ	International Court of Justice
ICPBS	International Commission for the Protection of the Black Sea
ICPDR	International Commission for the Protection of the Danube River
ICPR	International Commission for the Protection of the Rhine
IEG	international environmental governance
IEIs	international environmental institutions
IEL	international environmental law
ILC	International Law Commission
IMO	International Maritime Organization
INSTRAW	International Research and Training Institute for the Advancement of Women

IPCC	Intergovernmental Panel on Climate Change
ISO	International Organization for Standardization
ITLOS	International Tribunal for the Law of the Sea
IUCN	International Union for Conservation of Nature
IWC	International Whaling Commission
LCA	life cycle assessment
LMOs	living modified organisms
MDGs	Millennium Development Goals
MEAs	multilateral environmental agreements
NDCs	nationally determined contributions
NEASPEC	Northeast Asian Subregional Program for Environmental Co-operation
NGOs	non-governmental organizations
NIEO	New International Economic Order
NIMBY	not in my back yard
ODA	official development aid
OECD	Organisation for Economic Co-operation and Development
PIC	prior informed consent
POPs	persistent organic pollutants
RAPIDC	Regional Air Pollution in Developing Countries
SADC	Southern African Development Community
SAICM	Strategic Approach to Chemicals Management
SCP	sustainable consumption and production
SDGs	Sustainable Development Goals
SIDA	Swedish International Development Agency
SLAPP	strategic litigation against public participation
SRHRD	Special Rapporteur on Human Rights Defenders
TFEU	Treaty on the Functioning of the European Union
UN	United Nations
UNCCD	UN Convention to Combat Desertification
UNCLOS	UN Convention on the Law of the Sea
UNCTAD	UN Conference on Trade and Development
UNDRIP	UN Declaration on the Rights of Indigenous Peoples
UNEA	UN Environment Assembly
UNECE	UN Economic Commission for Europe
UNEP	UN Environment Programme
UNEPO	UN Environment Protection Organization
UNESCO	UN Educational, Scientific and Cultural Organization
UNFCCC	UN Framework Convention on Climate Change
UNFSA	UN Fish Stocks Agreement

UNGA	UN General Assembly
UNGP	UN Guiding Principles on Business and Human Rights
UNIFEM	UN Development Fund for Women
UNSC	UN Security Council
UNTC	UN Trusteeship Council
US	United States
VCLT	Vienna Convention on the Law of Treaties
WHO	World Health Organization
WMO	World Meteorological Organization
WTO	World Trade Organization

Introduction: Fifty Years of Shaping International Environmental Law

Jonas Ebbesson and David Langlet

I.1 STOCKHOLM 1972 AND 2022: FRAMING THE DEVELOPMENT OF INTERNATIONAL ENVIRONMENTAL LAW

Did international environmental law start with the UN Conference on the Human Environment in Stockholm (Stockholm Conference), 5–16 June 1972?[1] Both no and yes. On the one hand, important international lawmaking, case law, and jurisprudence on matters that we today perceive as environmental had developed long before 1972.[2] On the other hand, as we explain, the concept of the 'environment', as we think of it today, was hardly acknowledged in international law and governance before the Stockholm Conference. In that respect, the Stockholm Conference was the first global conference to focus on the environment in the new comprehensive, integrated, and global sense. And although it did not produce any legally binding outcome, it would indeed change international law. So, in that sense, international environmental law started with the Stockholm Conference.

As this volume reveals, the Stockholm Conference – the preparation of it and its outcome, not least the 1972 Stockholm Declaration on the Human

[1] *Report of the UN Conference on the Human Environment*, UN Doc. A/CONF.48/14/Rev.1, 16 June 1972.

[2] For reflections on the development of international law on the environment before the Stockholm Conference, see, e.g., Peter H. Sand, 'Origin and History', in Lavanya Rajamani & Jacqueline Peel (eds.), *The Oxford Handbook of International Environmental Law* (2nd ed., Oxford University Press, 2021), 56, arguing that the beginning of '"modern" international environmental law' is usually dated to the 1972 Stockholm Conference; Edith Brown Weiss, 'The Evolution of International Environmental Law' (2011) 54 *Japanese Yearbook of International Law* 1; Oscar Schacter, 'The Emergence of International Environmental Law' (1991) 44 *Journal of International Affairs* 457. On the state of international law relating to the environment around the time of the Stockholm Conference, see the various contributions in Ludwik A. Teclaff & Albert E. Utton (eds.), *International Environmental Law* (Praeger Publishers, 1974).

Environment (Stockholm Declaration)[3] – set things in motion, and it would significantly contribute to and influence international law thereafter. Fifty years later, the UN International Meeting Stockholm+50: A Healthy Planet for the Prosperity of All – Our Responsibility, Our Opportunity (Stockholm +50 Meeting), in Stockholm, 2–3 June 2022, prompts the question of how international environmental law has developed and evolved in this half-century.[4] It also begs the question of how influential the 1972 Stockholm Conference has been for this development. While the different contributions to this volume provide the detailed and lengthier answers to both questions, we disclose our short answer to the second question now: *more than any other single event*.

This volume presents advanced up-to-date reviews of the development of international environmental law from 1972 to 2022 and reflections on the impact and influence of the Stockholm Conference and the Stockholm Declaration over these fifty years. Some contributions also indicate the future relevance of Stockholm 1972. As pointed out by several contributors, fifty years later, the impact of the Stockholm Conference on international (and national) environmental law stands out in many ways, and it is still highly relevant. One important reason for this, we submit and will come back to, is that the Stockholm Conference did not reflect only the views of either the developing or industrialized countries, as they were referred to in the outcomes. It reflected the views of both of these broad categories of countries. In the negotiations of the conference outcomes, developing countries – many of them recently independent – made clear that they did not agree with the 'Northern' perception of environmental problems, which only emphasized the unintended negative effects of industrialization. Rather, they insisted that environmental issues could not be addressed without also considering much broader developmental, economic, and social concerns and inequities among states. This not only provided for a balanced approach to the environmental problems and contexts at Stockholm, but it also made the conference and its outcomes more legitimate, relevant, and adequate as a starting point for the development of international environmental law in the coming decades.

The other important feature of the 1972 Stockholm Conference, already hinted at, concerns the environment as such. The very notion of the 'environment', as understood in 2022, was still new in 1972. Yes, there were many

3 'Declaration of the United Nations Conference on the Human Environment', in *Report of the UN Conference on the Human Environment*, n. 1, 3–5 (Stockholm Declaration).

4 *Report of Stockholm+50: A Healthy Planet for the Prosperity of All – Our Responsibility, Our Opportunity*, UN Doc. A/CONF.238/9, 1 August 2022.

activities, national and international legal frameworks, and case law on the protection of nature, the use of water and other natural resources, and increasing concern with pollution (and even climate) before 1972. And, yes, the term 'environment' had long been used in daily life as well as in scientific literature. Yet the meaning of 'environment' was transformed in the decades preceding the Stockholm Conference – from being used to 'describe the *context* or background to the real subject of the story' to becoming 'a thing with its own essence that itself became vulnerable, a victim of circumstances' and even a global object.[5] In addition to capturing larger scales and linking 'the very local, or even the microscopic, to a planetary whole',[6] the environment became an integrating concept that worked across traditional scientific disciplines.[7]

This idea, which is captured by the concept and term 'environment' ('environnement', 'ambiente', 'Umweldt', 'miljö', and so on), would expand and increasingly influence the way of thinking about environmental matters from the 1940s to the 1960s. And it has been argued that at the 1972 Stockholm Conference 'the concept had reached ... the highest pinnacles of global diplomacy and prestige'.[8] Right or wrong, at least it is clear that the Stockholm Conference, unlike previous international conferences on related matters, reflects this transformed understanding of the environment. This and the key role of 'man' – used to refer to all human beings – in affecting and protecting the environment is revealed in the first preambular recital of the 1972 Stockholm Declaration:

> Man is both creature and moulder of his environment, which gives him physical sustenance and affords him the opportunity for intellectual, moral, social and spiritual growth. In the long and tortuous evolution of the human race *on this planet* a stage has been reached when, through the rapid acceleration of science and technology, man has acquired the power to transform his environment *in countless ways and on an unprecedented scale*. Both aspects of man's environment, the natural and the man-made, are essential to his well-being and to the enjoyment of basic human rights – even the right to life itself. (emphasis added)

These two features – the North-South dimension and the then quite new notion of the environment as a vulnerable entity that captures both the local

5 Paul Warde, Libby Robin & Sverker Sörlin, *The Environment: A History of the Idea* (John Hopkins University Press, 2018), 7–8 (emphasis in the original).
6 *Ibid.*, 17.
7 *Ibid.*, 15.
8 *Ibid.*, 159.

and global context – are also reflected in the principles of the Stockholm Declaration and in the Action Plan for the Human Environment (Stockholm Action Plan).[9] It has been submitted that:

> The United Nations Conference on the Human Environment, which met in Stockholm in 1972, marked a watershed in international relations . . . from the view of an earth unlimited in abundance and created for man's exclusive use to a concept of the earth as a domain of life or biosphere for which mankind is a temporary resident custodian.[10]

Although no legally binding treaty was adopted, the references to international law in the Declaration and Action Plan, as well as in the debate of the conference, reveal the presence of legal considerations in the new context: 'The Stockholm Conference underlined recognition of the environment as a holistic entity, the "biosphere", to be protected in its entirety by international law and organisations. This was a novel conception for governments.'[11]

While this volume will put these propositions to test, it is clear that the described understanding of the environment and the key role of humankind in affecting and protecting it, furthered by new notions such as 'sustainability' and 'resilience', have dominated the thinking on these matters since the 1972 Stockholm Conference. And this understanding of the environment remains essential in the concept of international environmental law today.

The contributions to this volume provide in-depth reviews, analyses, and descriptions of the developments of international environmental law in the fifty years between 1972 and 2022 with respect to the general legal principles and North-South dimensions as well as the different issue areas of human rights, participatory rights, and the rule of law; the law on waste, chemicals, consumption, and production; the law on the atmosphere, watercourses, and the sea; and the law on nature and biodiversity. In doing so, the contributors engage in the many events between 1972 and 2022 that would influence the development of international environmental law, such as the 1982 World Charter for Nature[12] and the major UN summits that took place every ten years thereafter – that is, the 1992 *UN Conference on Environment and Development* in Rio de Janeiro;[13] the 2002 *World Summit on Sustainable*

9 'Action Plan for the Human Environment', in *Report of the UN Conference on the Human Environment*, n. 1, 6–28 (Stockholm Action Plan).

10 Lynton Keith Caldwell, *International Environmental Policy: Emergence and Dimensions* (2nd ed., Duke University Press, 1990), 21.

11 Schacter, n. 2, 458.

12 UNGA Resolution 37/7 on World Charter for Nature, UN Doc. A/RES/37/7, 28 October 1982.

13 *Report of the UN Conference on Environment and Development*, UN Doc. A/CONF.151/26 (Vol. I), 12 August 1992.

Development in Johannesburg;[14] and the 2012 *Conference on Sustainable Development (Rio+20)* in Rio de Janeiro.[15] It is apparent in many contributions, that the different issue areas, just like the notion of international *environmental* law itself, are not distinct or clearly defined. Indeed, in many ways, they overlap and interlink.

In this introduction, after short presentations of the outcomes of, respectively, the 1972 Stockholm Conference and the 2022 Stockholm+50 Meeting, we highlight the key differences of international environmental law of 1972 and 2022 by some comparative snapshots. These snapshots and overview of 1972 and 2022 pertain to the following dimensions and issue areas of international environmental law:

- the North-South dimension;
- general and customary principles;
- human rights, participatory rights, and the rule of law;
- consumption and production;
- waste and chemicals;
- the atmosphere;
- water; and
- nature and biodiversity.

In these sections, we greatly benefit from, and build on, the contributions to the volume, and we extrapolate. The snapshots come with the proviso that they obviously cannot capture all of the important nuances in the complexity of international environmental law. Thus, in addition to providing brief comparisons, the snapshots should be seen as teasers to the other chapters of the volume, where the substantial descriptions and analyses of the developments of international environmental law are found.

But before looking into the different areas of international environmental law and the developments between the 1972 Stockholm Conference and 2022 Stockholm+50 Meeting, we return to the two events framing this volume and to their outcomes.

I.2 STOCKHOLM 1972: A KEY EVENT AND DOCUMENT

While the Stockholm Conference represented a new approach to international environmental governance, it built on, and related to, previous

[14] *Report of the World Summit on Sustainable Development*, Johannesburg, South Africa, UN Doc. A/CONF.199/20, 26 August–4 September 2002.

[15] UNGA Resolution 66/288 on the Future We Want, UN Doc. A/REAS/66/288, 27 July 2012.

international negotiations, conferences, and initiatives on relevant matters, including on the right for recently independent countries to exploit their natural wealth and resources.[16] In that sense, the initiative of the Swedish government to propose to the UN Economic and Social Council on 20 May 1968 that the United Nations should convene an 'international conference on the problems of human environment' did not come out of the blue.[17] On 3 December 1968, the UN General Assembly (UNGA) agreed to convene the UN Conference on the Human Environment in 1972[18] and then accepted the proposal that Sweden should host the event in Stockholm.[19]

The resolution to convene the Stockholm Conference refers to the 'need for intensified action at the national, regional and the international level in order to limit and, where possible, eliminate the impairment of the human environment and in order to protect and improve the natural surroundings in the interest of man', but it does not refer to international law or the need for legal developments. Nor are there any significant mentions of international law in the report of the UN secretary-general prepared before the conference on the activities of UN organizations and programmes relevant to the human environment.[20]

If international law was not a major concern in the preparations for Stockholm, the very understanding, or understandings, of environmental problems among developed and developing countries was key.[21] Among the many meetings preparing for the conference, the meeting of experts on environment and development held in Founex, Switzerland, in June 1971

16 For an overview of the road to Stockholm in international relations, cooperation, and policy-making, see Caldwell, n. 10, 21–54.

17 UN Economic and Social Council, *Consideration of the Provisional Agenda for the Forty-Fourth Session*, Addendum, *The Question of Convening an International Conference on the Problems of Human Environment, Letter dated 20 May 1968 from the Permanent Representative of Sweden Addressed to the Secretary-General of the United Nations*, UN Doc. E/4466/Add.1, 22 May 1968.

18 UN General Assembly (UNGA), *Problems of the Human Environment*, UN Doc. A/RES 2398 (XXIII), 3 December 1968.

19 For a concise overview of the origin and political anchoring of the process leading to the Stockholm Conference, see Lars-Göran Engfeldt, *From Stockholm to Johannesburg and Beyond: The Evolution of the International System for Sustainable Development Governance and Its Implications* (Government Offices of Sweden, 2009), 24–43.

20 UN Economic and Social Council (ECOSOC), *Question of Convening an International Conference on Problems of the Human Environment, Activities of United Nations Organizations and Programmes Relevant to the Human Environment, Report of the Secretary-General*, UN Doc. E/4553, 11 July 1968.

21 See Karin Mickelsen, 'The Stockholm Conference and the Creation of the South-North Divide in International Environmental Law and Policy', in Shawkat Alam *et al.* (eds.), *International Environmental Law and the Global South* (Cambridge University Press, 2015).

stands out as critical to bridging the different approaches to environmental problems by the North and the South and to generating support for the conference needed from developing countries.[22]

The different approaches to environmental problems – or, rather, the balance of these approaches – are well reflected in the agreed outcome of the Stockholm Conference: the Stockholm Declaration, the Stockholm Action Plan, the Resolution on Institutional and Financial Arrangements, and other resolutions adopted by the conference.[23] The broad participation of states (113 states) from all parts of the world, except from Eastern Europe and the Soviet Union (as these countries boycotted the conference because Eastern Germany was not allowed to participate), promoted the legitimacy of the Stockholm Conference and the outcomes.

The *Stockholm Declaration*, comprising a preamble of seven recitals and 26 concise principles, is the most important outcome of the Stockholm Conference for the development of international environmental law (see Annex I to this volume). Of these 26 principles, only two – Principles 21 and 22 – make explicit references to international law. Principle 21 has been subject to most discussion in literature and doctrine and will be further commented on below and in some of the contributions to this volume. It reads:

> States have, in accordance with the Charter of the United Nations and the principles of international law, the sovereign right to exploit their own resources pursuant to their own environmental policies, and the responsibility to ensure that activities within their jurisdiction or control do not cause damage to the environment of other States or of areas beyond the limits of national jurisdiction.

While Principle 21, one may say, is a fundamental assertion of what international law is, and on the rights and duties of states, the reference to international law in Principle 22 is rather about its future development as it sets out that: 'States shall co-operate to develop further the international law regarding liability and compensation for the victims of pollution and other environmental damage caused by activities within the jurisdiction or control of such States to areas beyond their jurisdiction.'

Although the input of Principle 22 on international law is not as bold as that of Principle 21, it has also rendered debate and doctrine, and developments in

22 *Ibid.*, 109–115.

23 'Resolution on Institutional and Financial Arrangements', in *Report of the UN Conference on the Human Environment*, n. 1, 29–32.

international law on liability and compensation, not least by attributing civil liability to different private actors.[24]

The lack of explicit references to law in the other principles of the Declaration do not make them legally irrelevant. They provide normative statements on the fundamental right of man (Principle 1); on safeguarding the natural environment for the benefit of present and future generations (Principle 2); on maintaining, restoring, and improving the capacity of the earth to produce vital renewable resources (Principle 3); on the special responsibility of man to safeguard wildlife (Principle 4); on employing and guarding non-renewable resources, the benefits of which are to be shared by all mankind (Principle 5); on halting the discharge of toxic and other substances to avoid serious and irreversible damage (Principle 6); and on taking steps to prevent pollution of the seas and harm to living resources and marine life (Principle 7).

The principles also set out agreed normative understandings on the importance of economic and social development for ensuring a favourable living and working condition for man and to improve the quality of life (Principle 8); on remediation of environmental deficiencies generated by the conditions of underdevelopment and natural disasters by accelerated development through the transfer of substantial quantities of financial and technological transfers to the developing countries (Principle 9); on the need of stability of prices and adequate earnings for primary commodities and raw materials for the environmental management of developing countries (Principle 10); on environmental policies that should enhance and not adversely affect the present or future development potential of developing countries nor hamper the attainment of better living conditions for all (Principle 11); and on the availability of resources to preserve and improve the environment, taking into account the circumstances and particular requirements of developing countries (Principle 12).

Furthermore, the principles push states to integrate and coordinate their development planning to improve the environment and ensure that the development is compatible with the need to protect and improve the human environment (Principle 13); to plan rationally so as to reconcile any conflict between the development and protection of the environment (Principle 14); to plan human settlements and urbanization so as to avoid adverse

[24] See, e.g., Peter Gailhofer *et al.* (eds.), *Corporate Liability for Transboundary Environmental Harm: An International and Transnational Perspective* (Springer, 2022); Alan Boyle, 'Globalising Environmental Liability: The Interplay of National and International Law' (2005) 17 *Journal of Environmental Law* 3; Elisa Morgera, *Corporate Accountability in International Environmental Law* (Oxford University Press, 2009).

environmental effects while obtaining social, economic, and environmental benefits 'for all' (Principle 15); to apply demographic policies in regions where the population growth or excessive population concentrations can have adverse effects on the environment or development (Principle 16); to entrust national institutions with the task of planning, managing, and controlling environmental resources with a view of enhancing environmental quality (Principle 17); to apply science and technology to environmental risks and solutions, thus contributing to economic and social development (Principle 18); to provide education in environmental matters 'for the younger generation as well as adults' and engage mass media in disseminating environmental information (Principle 19); and to promote scientific research and development in the context of environmental problems and make environmental solutions and technologies available to developing countries (Principle 20).

Finally, the principles in the Stockholm Declaration refer to the need to consider the applicability of standards that are valid for the most advanced countries but that may be inappropriate and of unwarranted social cost for the developing countries (Principle 23); to the cooperation of all countries through international agreements or other appropriate means to protect the environment, while taking into account the sovereignty and interest of all states (Principle 24); to the role of international organizations to protect and improve the environment (Principle 25); and to the effects of weapons of mass destruction and to the striving to reach agreement on the elimination and complete destruction of such weapons (Principle 26). This overview indicates that several principles can either be transformed into legal norms or provide legitimate grounds for the development of international treaty regimes, international case law, and international jurisprudence. As shown in the contributions to this volume, many of these principles have been used to such effects.

The *Stockholm Action Plan* is not as concise and straightforward as the Declaration. The 109 recommendations relate to the planning and management of human settlements for environmental quality (Recommendations 1–18); the environmental aspects of natural resource management, such as forests, wildlife, ecosystems, genetic resources, fishing, marine environments, marine resources, mining, and energy (Recommendations 19–69); the identification and control of pollutants of broad international significance, including climate effects, transboundary pollution, toxic substances, and marine pollution (Recommendations 70–94); the educational, informational, social, and cultural aspects of environmental issues (Recommendations 95–101); and the development and environment, including trade, financial mechanisms, and availability of environmental technologies (Recommendations 102–109). While they may not be as easily transformed into norms of international law, the recommendations have been useful for many international organizations in addressing environmental matters and pushing for action and also for governments and non-governmental organizations. Moreover, in hindsight, one can see that many of the recommendations relate to issues that would later be subject to international law and policy.

The *Resolution on Institutional and Financial Arrangements* recommends the UNGA to 'establish the Governing Council for Environmental Programs', that a 'small secretariat' be established in the UN', and that 'in order to provide for additional financing for environmental programmes' a voluntary fund be established, thus providing for the subsequent decision by the UNGA to establish the UN Environment Programme (UNEP).[25]

The other four resolutions concern the designation of an annual World Environment Day, the condemnation of nuclear weapons tests, the convening of a second UN Conference on the Human Environment, and the expression of thanks to the organizer. Interestingly, it would take another 20 years until the second conference took place in Rio de Janeiro in 1992.

1.3 STOCKHOLM 2022: WHAT KIND OF EVENT AND DOCUMENT?

In many ways, the circumstances for the Stockholm+50 Meeting were different from those of the 1972 Stockholm Conference and also from the UN conferences on environment and development of 1992, 2002, and 2012. Ambition was far lower in 2022 than in 1972; there was much less preparation; no formal declaration or action plan was adopted; and the event was not even titled 'conference'. On 24 May 2021, the UNGA decided to:

> convene the international meeting entitled 'Stockholm+50: a healthy planet for the prosperity of all – our responsibility, our opportunity', in Stockholm, on 2 and 3 June 2022, during the week of World Environment Day, *to commemorate the 50 years since the United Nations Conference on the Human Environment and its outcome documents*, as a contribution to the environmental dimension of sustainable development to accelerate the implementation of commitments in the context of the decade of action and delivery for sustainable development, including a sustainable recovery from the coronavirus disease (COVID-19) pandemic.[26]

[25] The UN Environment Programme (UNEP) was then established through UNGA, *Institutional and Financial Arrangements for International Environmental Cooperation*, UN Doc. A/RES 2997 (XXVII), 15 December 1972.

[26] UNGA Resolution 75/280 on the International Meeting Entitled 'Stockholm+50: A Healthy Planet for the Prosperity of All – Our Responsibility, Our Opportunity', UN Doc. A/RES/75/280, 25 May 2021 (emphasis added).

The intended ambition of the meeting is reflected in the same resolution when setting out that 'the international meeting will result in a summary of discussions as its outcome document'. A summary of discussions is quite different from a bold declaration or detailed action plan. Given that 2022 was also the fiftieth anniversary of UNEP, the UNGA decided 'that the international meeting should be mutually reinforcing with UNEP@50, avoiding overlap and duplication'. Soon after, the UNGA adopted yet another resolution on the Stockholm+50 Meeting,[27] this time to decide on the modalities of the meeting, to welcome the offer of Sweden to host the meeting, to set out a draft agenda and the details on the organization of work, and to present the titles and organizational arrangements for the 'leadership dialogues' that were to take place at the meeting.

The *Leadership Dialogues*, while not leading to any policy document, somehow reflect the focus of the meeting:

- Leadership Dialogue 1: Reflecting on the urgent need for actions to achieve a healthy planet and prosperity for all;
- Leadership Dialogue 2: Achieving a sustainable and inclusive recovery from the coronavirus disease (COVID-19) pandemic; and
- Leadership Dialogue 3: Accelerating the implementation of the environmental dimension of sustainable development in the context of the decade of action and delivery for sustainable development.

The *Outcome of the International Meeting*, based, inter alia, on these dialogues, is a summary of the key *Recommendations for Accelerating Action towards a Healthy Planet for the Prosperity of All* by the co-chairs (for full text, see Annex 2 to this volume):[28]

1. Place human well-being at the centre of a healthy planet and prosperity for all.
2. Recognize and implement the right to a clean, healthy, and sustainable environment.
3. Adopt a system-wide change in the way our current economic system works to contribute to a healthy planet.
4. Strengthen national implementation of existing commitments for a healthy planet.

[27] UNGA Resolution 75/326 on the Modalities for the International Meeting Entitled 'Stockholm+50: A Healthy Planet for the Prosperity of All – Our Responsibility, Our Opportunity', UN Doc. A/RES/75/326, 15 September 2021.

[28] 'Outcome of the International Meeting', in *Report of Stockholm+50*, n. 4. 25–27.

5. Align public and private financial flows with environmental, climate, and sustainable development commitments.
6. Accelerate system-wide transformations of high impact sectors, such as food, energy, water, building and construction, manufacturing, and mobility.
7. Rebuild relationships of trust for strengthened cooperation and solidarity.
8. Reinforce and reinvigorate the multilateral system.
9. Recognize intergenerational responsibility as a cornerstone of sound policy-making.
10. Take the Stockholm+50 outcomes forward.

Sure, the message in these recommendations is both relevant and important, but it does not come with much normative force. Only two months later, the UNGA recognized the right to a clean, healthy, and sustainable environment.[29] While this recognition neatly reflects Principle 1 of the 1972 Stockholm Declaration, it can hardly be credited to Recommendation 2 of the Stockholm+50 Meeting.[30]

In 1972, it was neither obvious if and how the Stockholm Conference and Stockholm Declaration would influence international law nor that it would still be so relevant fifty years later. Whatever the long-term impact of the 2022 international meeting in Stockholm (we leave that for reflections at Stockholm+100), the Stockholm+50 Meeting provides a suitable time span for taking stock of how international environmental law has changed and developed – if it has – since the 1972 Stockholm Conference.

I.4 COMPARATIVE SNAPSHOTS OF INTERNATIONAL ENVIRONMENTAL LAW IN 1972 AND 2022

I.4.1 *The North-South Dimension*

I.4.1.1 Stockholm 1972

At Stockholm 1972, the economic and social differences of the North and the South – to use this broad categorization – as well as the historic root causes to

29 UNGA Resolution 76/300 on the Human Right to a Clean, Healthy and Sustainable Environment, UN Doc. A/RES/76/300, 1 August 2022.

30 Rather, UNGA Resolution 76/300, n. 29, builds on the HRC Resolution 48/13 on the Human Right to a Clean, Healthy and Sustainable Environment, UN Doc. A/HRC/RES/48/13, 18 October 2021.

these differences and the international economic system and its institutions,[31] were at the core of international politics and law. The postcolonial North-South tensions in the international law reforms intensified in the 1960s.[32] These reforms referred to the disadvantageous situation of the South in international law and politics in general, and to the rights and permanent sovereignty of natural resources of Southern countries in particular. Much of the international economic system was in place already at the Stockholm Conference; in fact, much of that system was in place while many of the Southern countries were still under colonial rule, thus effectively denying them a say on its formation.

These North-South tensions and the experiences of 'Northern economic and political clout in Southern states' would significantly influence the Stockholm Conference and its outcome.[33] As mentioned, it was made clear already before the Stockholm Conference, not least at the 1971 Founex meeting, that the notion of the environmental problems of the North would have to be redefined so that development would become part of the concept and context, and this had to be reflected at Stockholm. So it was. The bold statement at the Stockholm Conference by Prime Minister Indira Gandhi, of India, echoes the perspective and frustration by the South on how the North perceived environmental problems:

> The environmental problems of developing countries are not the side-effects of excessive industrialisation but reflect the inadequacy of development. The rich countries may look upon development as the cause of environmental destruction, but to us it is one of the primary means of improving the environment for living, or providing food, water, sanitation and shelter, of making the deserts green and the mountains habitable.[34]

31 On these root causes, see M. Rafiqul Islam, 'History of the North-South Divide in International Law: Colonial Discourses, Sovereignty and Self-Determination', in Alam *et al.*, n. 21, 23–49. The history and shortcomings of the international economic system and its institutions is also described by Jonas Ebbesson & Ellen Hey, 'Introduction: The Sustainable Development Goals, Agenda 2030, and International Law', in Jonas Ebbesson & Ellen Hey (eds.), *The Cambridge Handbook of the Sustainable Development Goals and International Law* (Cambridge University Press, 2022).

32 Islam, n. 31, 33–38.

33 *Ibid.*, 47; see also UNGA Resolution 1803 (XVII) on Permanent Sovereignty over Natural Resources, UN Doc. A/5217 (1962), 14 December 1962.

34 Indira Gandhi, 'Address to the Plenary Session of the United Nations Conference on Human Environment, Stockholm, 14 June 1972', reprinted in Indira Gandhi, *The Years of Endeavour, Selected Speeches of Indira Gandhi August 1969–August 1972* (Government of India, 1975), 451.

The concerns of the South and references to economic and social development and the situation of the developing countries are boldly set out in the Stockholm Declaration (in Principles 1, 8, 9, 10, 11, 12, 15, 16, 20, and 23). Principles 8 and 9 reflect the point made by Gandhi in emphasizing that 'economic and social development is essential for ensuring a favourable living and working environment' and referring to the 'environmental deficiencies generated by the conditions of underdevelopment'. Principle 9 also appeals to an 'accelerated development through the transfer of substantial quantities of financial and technological assistance' to developing countries, and Principle 11 calls for the 'agreement on meeting the possible national and international economic consequences resulting from the application of environmental measures'. General economic issues, including international trade, were also addressed in the Stockholm Action Plan, and the North-South nexus framed the entire Stockholm Conference and its outcomes. Thus, we agree that, if the Stockholm Conference marked the beginning of international environmental law and policy as we know it, 'it is not much of a stretch to argue that international environmental law begins with – and needs to be understood in light of – South-North tensions'.[35]

A lesson learned from the Stockholm Conference and the international setting of that time – reflected in the Stockholm Declaration – is the multifaceted feature of the very North-South dimension in international environmental contexts. It pertains to the very notion of environmental problems and their causes, and to the different social, developmental, and economic circumstances that must be part of any initiative, negotiation, and political and legal outcome on environmental matters. Obviously, the North-South dimension in environmental contexts identified at Stockholm 1972 also refers to the differentiated responsibilities of the North and South in taking protective measures as well as to the North's responsibility to support the South by financial, technological, and other means.

I.4.1.2 Stockholm 2022

Fifty years later, it is impossible to comprehend international environmental law and governance at the global scale, let alone to agree on or develop common strategies, policies, or legal frameworks, without taking into account the described economic and social differences of states as well as the historic root causes to these differences. As put by *Jutta Brunnée*, with respect to

[35] Karin Mickelsen, 'The Stockholm Conference and the Creation of the South-North Divide in International Environmental Law and Policy', in Alam *et al.*, n. 21, 109.

international environmental law as it evolved in the wake of the Stockholm Conference, '[developing] countries remained suspicious of industrialized countries' efforts to promote international environmental cooperation. Many developing countries distrusted the underlying universalist aspirations, concerned that international environmental law was but a green variant of neo-colonialism and aimed at restricting or directing their development.'[36]

The North-South tensions that framed the 1972 Stockholm Conference have characterized international environmental law since then, and the North-South dimension remains a core element in global environmental law and governance. Accordingly, there is not one global environmental treaty, not one global important environmental policy outcome, and not one global environmental summit since Stockholm 1972 where the North-South dimension and the environment-development nexus have not been addressed. In particular, the environment-development nexus was confirmed 20 years after Stockholm by the very title of the 1992 Rio Conference on Environment and Development and by the coining of states' *common but differentiated responsibilities* and the introduction of *sustainable development* as a standard concept in international law and policy documents.

Despite the emphasis in the Stockholm Action Plan of the need of developing states for technical and financial aid when the UN secretary-general, specialized agencies, and governments take on the large number of environmental problems, international law has moved very little, if at all, in that direction. This state of affairs is largely reflected in the broader structures of international economic law. As succinctly observed by *Ellen Hey*: 'Since 1972, international economic law – in particular, international trade law and international investment law – has strengthened the position of transnational business sector actors. By the time of the Stockholm+50 Meeting, some of the 1972 Stockholm concerns of developing states had been relegated to "soft law" instruments or to exceptions in "hard law" instruments.'[37]

Although a binding treaty on sustainable development, with the implied element of solidarity, would not resolve the economic, social, and environmental inequalities right away, it is striking that such commitments are essentially asserted in soft law only. A prominent example in which the environment is a key component is the ambitious 2015 UNGA's resolution

36 Jutta Brunnée, 'Climate Protection 50 Years after Stockholm: International Law at the Precipice', in this volume, 338f (footnotes omitted).

37 Ellen Hey, 'The Missed Link between International Economic Law and Social and Environmental Issues', in this volume, 107 (footnotes omitted).

Transforming Our World: The 2030 Agenda for Sustainable Development, with the Sustainable Development Goals (SDGs), which sets out that:

> The scale and ambition of the new Agenda requires a revitalized Global Partnership to ensure its implementation. We fully commit to this. This Partnership will work in *a spirit of global solidarity*, in particular *solidarity with the poorest and with people in vulnerable situations*. It will facilitate an intensive *global engagement in support of implementation* of all the Goals and targets, bringing together Governments, the private sector, civil society, the United Nations system and other actors and mobilizing all available resources.[38]

Then what? How is this implemented, and what is the role of international law in achieving what is 'fully' committed? Despite the continued emphasis of the North-South nexus and the notion of common but differentiated responsibility in global environmental contexts, reflected in differentiated treaty obligations, the establishment of different funds (albeit with too little funding) and soft commitments on the transfer of technology, there has been no significant shift in the international economic system or in international economic law – on matters such as trade, investments, taxation, or corporate responsibility – to serve developing states. As *Ellen Hey* puts it:

> While the Stockholm Conference is remembered for inciting the development of modern international environmental law, might it have been even more fortunate if, fifty years later, it would have also been remembered for sparking the reform of international economic law or the development of development law? It is high time to fundamentally change international economic law and to take the Stockholm concerns of developing states seriously.[39]

Despite the apparent failure of resolving these issues in the fifty years since the Stockholm Conference, reforming international economic law was not at the core of the Stockholm+50 Meeting. Still, the North-South dimension in environmental contexts that was emphasized in 1972 remains equally relevant and important for the future development of international environmental law.

38 *Transforming Our World: The 2030 Agenda for Sustainable Development*, Doc. A/Res/70/1, 25 September 2015, para. 39 (emphasis added). On the message of solidarity in the 2030 Agenda and the Sustainable Development Goals in relation to international law, see Ebbesson & Hey, 'Introduction', n. 31, 2–31.

39 Hey, n. 37, 108.

I.4.2 *General and Customary Principles of International Environmental Law*

I.4.2.1 Stockholm 1972

At Stockholm 1972, according to one observation, 'general international law (or customary law) contains no rules or standards related to the protection of the environment as such'.[40] Yet some of the then established general principles of international law would certainly also apply to environmental harms, relating, for example, to territorial sovereignty and integrity, international cooperation, and equitable uses of water resources. In this section, we reflect on territorial sovereignty, integrity and no harm, precaution, international cooperation, and sustainable development, whereas equitable uses are considered in a later section.

Issues such as *territorial sovereignty*, *integrity*, and *transboundary harm* are among the most obvious candidates of a general principle and concept to be applied to transboundary environmental issue contexts. The question boils down to whether and to what extent general international law allows states to cause harm to the environment of other states. This was a key part of the environmental law discourse at the time of the Stockholm Conference, and the discussion on the scope and limits of state sovereignty was far from new at the time.

Already about a century earlier, two opposite positions on state sovereignty – adequately referred to as the 'principle of absolute territorial sovereignty' and 'the principle of absolute territorial integrity' – had been advocated in international disputes and legal doctrine.[41] The first position suggests that international law does not impose any constraint on how states use their own territories even when that gives rise to external negative impacts. If applied to environmental matters, international law would not prevent states from causing transboundary harm, for instance, through air or water pollution, by the exploitation of natural resources, or by the destruction of nature sites impacting on migratory species. A well-known expression of this position is the 1885 claim by the US Attorney General Judson Harmon in the USA-Mexico dispute over the Rio Grande.[42]

The second position implies a prohibition on actions that may cause harm to another state, at least harm above a certain level of significance. Thus, a state's sovereignty is limited due to the respect of the sovereignty of other

[40] Ian Brownlie, 'A Survey of International Customary Rules of Environment Protection' (1973) 13 *Natural Resources Journal* 179, 179.

[41] Johan G. Lammers, *Pollution of International Watercourses* (Martinus Nijhoff, 1984), 216.

[42] The case and statement are described in Lammers, *ibid.*, 268–278.

states, which would be violated if harm was caused to them without their consent. This position was set out in legal doctrine at about the same time as the 'Harmon doctrine' was coined (in fact before), suggesting that 'even within its own territory a state may not undertake or permit measures which produce a harmful effect on foreign territory so as to change the natural conditions of another state to its detriment'.[43]

While it has been questioned on good grounds whether the Harmon doctrine reflected international law by the end of the nineteenth century,[44] there is support for the latter approach on territorial integrity although with some qualification. The 1941 *Trail Smelter* arbitral award, frequently referred to in textbooks on international environmental law, shows that, also before the Stockholm Conference, international law prohibited states from causing transboundary harm of some significance: 'No State has the right to use or permit the use of its territory in such a manner as to cause injury by fumes in or to the territory of another or the properties or persons therein, when the case is of serious consequence and the injury is established by clear and convincing evidence.'[45]

The position that a state has to take the interest of other states into account when its territory is being used was also supported by the 1949 ruling of the International Court of Justice in the *Corfu Channel* case and by the 1957 *Lac Lanoux* arbitral award.[46] While acknowledging the right of each state to exploit its resources pursuant to its own environmental policies, Principle 21 of the Stockholm Declaration famously confirms the principle of territorial integrity or the *principle of no harm*, as it would later be called:

> States have, in accordance with the Charter of the United Nations and the principles of international law, the sovereign right to exploit their own resources pursuant to their own environmental policies, and the responsibility to ensure that activities within their jurisdiction or control do not cause damage to the environment of other States or of areas beyond the limits of national jurisdiction.

43 August Wilhelm Heffter, *Das Europäische Völkerrecht der Gegenwart* (Schroeder, 1873), 58: 'Selbst aus eigenem Gebiet darf kein Staat Anstalten treffen oder zulassen, welche einen schädlichen Rückschlag aus ein fremdes Territorium ausüben, dergestalt, dass dadurch die natürlichen Verhältnisse zum Nachteile des anderen Staaten verändert werben würden'; translation to English by Lammers, n. 41, 534.

44 Stephen C. McCaffrey, 'The Harmon Doctrine One Hundred Years Later: Buried, Not Praised' (1996) 36 *Natural Resources Journal* 549.

45 *Trail Smelter Award (United States v Canada)*, 11 March 1941, reprinted in (1941) 3 *Reports of International Arbitral Awards* 1911, p. 1965.

46 *Corfu Channel Case (UK v Albania)*, (1949) ICJ Reports 1; *Lax Lanoux Arbitration (France v Spain)*, reprinted in (1957) 12 *Reports of International Arbitral Awards* 281.

The rather solid ground in previous case law and jurisprudence may explain the bold provision in Principle 21. In the same vein, the quite undeveloped international law on reparation and compensation for environmental damage at the time explains why Principle 22 only asserts that states shall cooperate to further develop international law on these matters.

One of the main calls at the 1972 Stockholm Conference was the need to improve and strengthen *international cooperation* in many different respects. Still, the notion of cooperation as a legal obligation was far from new at that time. It had been elegantly and quite optimistically concluded less than a decade before the Stockholm Conference that international law applies to the traditional sphere of diplomatic existence and that

> modern needs and developments have added many new areas expressing the need for positive co-operation which has to be implemented by international treaties and in many cases permanent international institutions. This move of international society, from an essentially negative code of rules of abstention to positive rules of co-operation, however fragmentary in the present state of world politics, is an evolution of immense significance for the principles and structure of international law.[47]

International law on cooperation had developed since the late nineteenth century, and international institution building and cooperation would expand significantly in different issue areas after the Second World War, not least with the establishment of the UN organizations.

As mentioned, in the preparation of the Stockholm Conference, the UN secretary-general provided a short report outlining the work of the UN organizations and programmes relevant to the human environment, including the International Labour Organization, the Food and Agriculture Organization (FAO), the UN Educational, Scientific and Cultural Organization (UNESCO), the World Health Organization (WHO), the World Meteorological Organization (WMO), International Maritime Organization (IMO), and International Atomic Energy Agency (IAEA).[48] Although none of these institutions had the explicit mandate to deal with the environment, since the very concept of the environment was not yet established when the organizations were created, the UN secretary-general's report shows that, to some extent, many of them did work with environmental issues. Even so, and whereas international cooperation was quite developed at the time of the 1972 Stockholm Conference, international law on environmental cooperation

[47] Wolfgang Friedmann, *The Changing Structures of International Law* (Stevens & Sons, 1964), 61–62.

[48] ECOSOC, n. 20.

was not. Accordingly, there was an urgent need to increase and improve international cooperation also in relation to the environment. And, as argued by *Bharat Desai*, the Stockholm Conference became a 'major milestone for international environmental cooperation'.[49]

What about *sustainable development* and international law? Was this notion part of the thinking already in 1972? For sure, the term 'sustainable development' appears neither in international policy documents before 1972 nor in the outcome of the Stockholm Conference. Yet *Nico Schrijver* submits that

> the 1972 Stockholm Conference marked in various ways the start of an organized effort on the side of the international community to seek a balance between environmental conservation and human development and, in this way, a compromise between the industrialised world and the global South. While the very term 'sustainable development' was not yet employed, it was all there but in words.[50]

This is an important observation, yet it does not suggest that sustainable development was an established legal concept at the Stockholm Conference – it was not.

4.2.2 Stockholm 2022

Fifty years later, the mentioned principles and concepts relating to states' obligation not to cause transboundary harm, to international cooperation, and to sustainable development are still essential. The main differences compared to 1972 is that more legal principles have been developed and that some of the principles and concepts applicable in 1972 have either been more firmly confirmed or tweaked as *legal* principles. To a great extent, these developments have taken place not only through international treaty law but also through international declarations, like the 1992 Rio Declaration on Environment and Development, other soft law instruments, and the jurisprudence of international tribunals.[51]

The *principle of no harm*, expressed in Principle 21 of the Stockholm Declaration, has gained much support since the Stockholm Conference, through multilateral treaties, such as the Convention on Biological Diversity

49 Bharat Desai, 'On the International Environmental Governance Architecture: Looking Back to Look Ahead for Our Common Future', in this volume, 115.

50 Nico Schrijver, 'Stockholm 1972 and the Birth of International Sustainable Development Law', in this volume, 85.

51 'Rio Declaration on Environment and Development', in *Report of the UN Conference on Environment and Development*, n. 13 (Rio Declaration).

(CBD),[52] further policy declarations, and the jurisprudence of international courts and tribunals. It is subject to debate whether the no-harm principle implies a prohibition of transboundary harm, albeit of some significance, a due diligence obligation, or both. We submit that, slightly tweaking the relevant article of the International Law Commission's (ILC) Draft Articles on Prevention of Transboundary Harm from Hazardous Activities,[53] states must use all the means at their disposal to prevent significant transboundary harm and to minimize the risk thereof. Yet, even below this threshold, states have to act with due diligence and take positive action to prevent transboundary harm.

Almost 25 years after Stockholm, in its advisory opinion in the *Legality of Nuclear Weapons* case, the International Court of Justice confirmed that the responsibility – indeed, duty – of states not to cause transboundary harm of significance forms part of general international law: 'The existence of the general obligation of States to ensure that activities within their jurisdiction and control respect the environment of other States or of areas beyond national control is now part of the corpus of international law relating to the environment.'[54]

The due diligence element – also referred to as the *principle of prevention* – is reflected in the 1982 UN Convention on the Law of the Sea (UNCLOS),[55] the 1992 UN Framework Convention on Climate Change (UNFCCC),[56] and several other treaties of global and regional scope. It is also neatly expressed by the International Court of Justice in the *Pulp Mills* case:

> The Court points out that the principle of prevention, as a customary rule, has its origins in the due diligence that is required of a State in its territory. It is 'every State's obligation not to allow knowingly its territory to be used for acts contrary to the rights of other States' (*Corfu Channel (United Kingdom v. Albania), Merits, Judgment, I.C.J. Reports* 1949, p. 22). A State is thus obliged to use all the means at its disposal in order to avoid activities which take place in its territory, or in any area under its jurisdiction, causing significant damage to the environment of another State. This Court has established that this obligation 'is now part of the corpus of international

[52] Convention on Biological Diversity, 1992, 1760 UNTS 79, art. 3 (CBD).

[53] International Law Commission (ILC), *Draft Articles on Prevention of Transboundary Harm from Hazardous Activities*, UN Doc A/56/10, 2001, art. 3 reads: 'The State of origin shall take all appropriate measures to prevent significant transboundary harm or at any event to minimize the risk thereof.'

[54] See *Legality of the Threat or Use of Nuclear Weapons*, Advisory Opinion, 8 July 1996, (1996) ICJ Reports 226, para. 29.

[55] United Nations Convention on the Law of the Sea, 1982, 1834 UNTS 397, art. 192 (UNCLOS).

[56] UN Framework Convention on Climate Change, 1992, 1771 UNTS 107, art. 3(2) (UNFCCC).

> law relating to the environment' (*Legality of the Threat or Use of Nuclear Weapons, Advisory Opinion, I.C.J. Reports* 1996 *(I)*, p. 242, para. 29).[57]

Accordingly, a state commits an internationally wrongful act, that entails its responsibility, if it does not exercise due diligence in its performance to prevent significant harm to the environment.[58]

Another key concept of general international law in 2022 relating to the environment and to the above, which was not part of international law in 1972 – since, at that time, it had only recently been introduced in some national laws – refers to the obligation to carry out an *environmental impact assessment* (EIA). This concept is also well set out by the International Court of Justice in the *Pulp Mills* case, when referring to

> a practice, which in recent years has gained so much acceptance among States that it may now be considered a requirement under general international law to undertake an environmental impact assessment where there is a risk that the proposed industrial activity may have a significant adverse impact in a transboundary context, in particular, on a shared resource. Moreover, due diligence, and the duty of vigilance and prevention which it implies, would not be considered to have been exercised, if a party planning works liable to affect the régime of the river or the quality of its waters did not undertake an environmental impact assessment on the potential effects of such works.[59]

In practice, the requirement to undertake EIAs when there is a risk of significant transboundary harm is closely linked to the duty not to cause such harm since the assessment identifies and characterizes the harm that might be caused as well as the means for its prevention.[60] A further element to the no-harm principle and the due diligence obligation is the increasing recognition of the *precautionary principle* as part of general international law. The fact that it is frequently referred to as the *precautionary approach* does not prevent it from being construed as, or from operating as, a legal principle. In addition to the Rio Declaration,[61] the precautionary principle is reflected in the UNFCCC[62] and also in the 2023 Agreement under the United Nations Convention on the Law of the Sea on the Conservation and

57 *Case Concerning Pulp Mills on the River Uruguay*, 20 April 2010, (2010) ICJ Reports 14, para. 101.
58 *Obligations of States in Respect of Climate Change*, Advisory Opinion, 23 July 2025, (2025) ICJ Reports, para 409.
59 *Ibid.*, para. 204.
60 See also ILC, *Draft Articles on Hazardous Activities*, n. 53.
61 Rio Declaration, n. 51, principle 15.
62 UNFCCC, n. 56, art. 3(3).

Sustainable Use of Marine Biological Diversity of Areas beyond National Jurisdiction (BBNJ Agreement),[63] where it is diplomatically referred to as 'the precautionary principle or precautionary approach, as appropriate'.[64] In 2024, it was also made clear by the International Tribunal for the Law of the Sea in its advisory opinion concerning climate change and international law that: 'States must apply the precautionary approach in their exercise of due diligence to prevent, reduce and control marine pollution from anthropogenic GHG emissions.'[65]

These elements of no harm, due diligence, the EIA requirement, and precaution as part of general international law both confirm and further the part of Principle 21 that highlights the responsibility not to cause harm to the environment of other states. The other part of Principle 21 – on the sovereign right of states to exploit their resources pursuant to their own policies – is also referred to, or reflected in, legal frameworks. An obvious case is the CBD, where Principle 21 is actually copied and pasted, and given the heading 'principle'.[66] This 'bedrock principle', *Dire Tladi* reminds us, was fundamental for developing countries during the negotiations of the CBD when they were arguing that 'genetic resources could not be treated as "common heritage", and the principle of sovereignty of resources dictated control over such genetic resources and, therefore, an equitable share in the benefits arising from their exploitation'.[67]

On the notion of *cooperation* as a legal obligation under international law, we have seen that, while it was not new at the time of the Stockholm Conference, one of the key messages of the conference was the need to strengthen international cooperation in environmental matters. Since then, the duty under international law to cooperate in this area has been frequently confirmed in international treaties, policy documents, and jurisprudence by international courts. In a way, every international environmental treaty is, as such, a case of international cooperation, and just about every such treaty includes

63 Agreement under the United Nations Convention on the Law of the Sea on the Conservation and Sustainable Use of Marine Biological Diversity of Areas beyond National Jurisdiction, 2023, https://treaties.un.org/doc/Treaties/2023/06/20230620%2004-28%20PM/Ch_XXI_10.pdf (BBNJ Agreement).

64 *Ibid.*, art. 7(e).

65 ITLOS, *Request for an Advisory Opinion Submitted by the Commission of Small Island States on Climate Change and International Law*, Case no. 31, 21 May 2024, para. 242. This is confirmed by the International Court of Justice, in *Obligations of States in Respect of Climate Change*, n. 58, para 294.

66 CBD, n. 52, art. 3.

67 Dire Tladi, 'Aspirations of Developing Countries in Biodiversity Treaty-Making Processes: Dreams Deferred?' in this volume, 479.

explicit provisions on the duty to cooperate – for instance, economically – by carrying out adequate research, sharing information, or reporting on measures taken to comply with the legal requirements. *Patricia Kameri-Mbote and colleagues* show what such cooperation may involve when referring to UNEP's efforts, already in its early years, in 'developing environmental laws, assisting regions and countries in formulating environmental legislation, facilitating research, training, and expertise, and providing guidance on the implementation of the Stockholm Declaration's commitments'.[68]

So, institutionalized cooperation has expanded significantly since the Stockholm Conference, both in international organizations and through different treaty regimes, but this is not to say that existing international cooperation is sufficient or effective. Rather, as noted by *Bharat Desai*, a major challenge linked to the multiplicity of institutions is the lack of coordination of international environmental governance.[69] While this kind of institutional cooperation is essential for international environmental law and governance, the duty under international law to cooperate in environmental matters also applies more broadly with respect to transboundary harm, to include information exchange, assistance, notification, and consultation as well as the duty to prevent significant harm to the environment. This is reflected by the International Court of Justice, which in *Obligations of States in Respect of Climate Change* 'considers that the duty to co-operate for the protection of the environment forms part of customary international law and can also serve as a guiding principle for the interpretation of other rules'.[70]

Then, what about *sustainable development* and international law at the Stockholm+50 Meeting? We saw that the thinking behind the principle and concept of sustainable development can be traced back to the 1972 Stockholm Conference, and the term was used in a few international documents in the 1970s and 1980s. Even so, it was through the 1987 report by the World Commission on Environment and Development (usually referred to as the Brundtland Commission after the chair, Norwegian Prime Minister Gro Harlem Brundtland) and the 1992 Rio Conference that sustainable development became the beacon of international environmental governance.[71] Since then, it has been the key concept in the global environmental summits,

[68] Patricia Kameri-Mbote *et al.*, 'Environmental Rule of Law: From Stockholm 1972 to 2022 and Beyond', in this volume, 159.

[69] Desai, n. 49, 115.

[70] *Obligations of States in Respect of Climate Change*, n. 58, para 142.

[71] World Commission on Environment and Development, *Our Common Future* (Oxford University Press, 1987).

a reference in legal frameworks, such as the UNFCCC[72] and the CBD,[73] and referred to by international courts and tribunals, including the International Court of Justice.[74] Despite the general agreement and the legal confirmation of the concept of sustainable development, it remains vague as a normative benchmark.

On that note, since 1992, the understanding of sustainable development has itself developed. Not only has sustainable development been used in various contexts to give different relative weights and emphasis on, respectively, the environmental, social, and economic aspects of development. It has also been construed in the light of new research on, for instance, social-ecological resilience and planetary boundaries. Moreover, it has been suggested that the ambitious 2030 Agenda for Sustainable Development with the SDGs, agreed upon by the UNGA in 2015, reflects a people-centred approach, aiming at transforming our world so that no one will be left behind, and normatively expresses an innovative and bold *cosmopolitan* understanding of sustainable development. It does so by being presented as a comprehensive, far-reaching and people-centred set of universal and transformative Goals and targets, to be grounded in the Universal Declaration of Human Rights and international human rights treaties, but also by the way many of the SDGs are drafted. Accordingly, 'most, if not all, of the SDGs indeed relate to, and depend upon, international human rights law for their realization'.[75] This conclusion is supported by the 2022 UNGA's resolution recognizing the human right to a clean, healthy, and sustainable environment, which reaffirms the 2030 Agenda for Sustainable Development and the SDGs.[76]

At the Stockholm+50 Meeting, sustainable development is well rooted in international treaties, soft law instruments, and rulings by international courts and tribunals. While a coherent legal framework to incorporate sustainable

72 UNFCCC, n. 56, art. 3(4) (under the heading 'Principles').

73 CBD, n. 52, art. 8(e).

74 *Nuclear Weapons*, n. 54, para. 30 (quoting Principle 24 of the Rio Declaration, n. 51, which asserts that 'warfare is inherently destructive of sustainable development'); *Gabčíkovo-Nagymaros Project (Hungary v Slovakia)*, Judgment, 25 September 1997, (1997) ICJ Reports 7, paras. 140–141; *Pulp Mills*, n. 57, paras. 75–76, 177; *Obligations of States in Respect of Climate Change*, n. 58, para 147. WTO, *US – Import Prohibition of Certain Shrimp and Shrimp Products*, Appellate Body Report, Doc. DS58, 12 October 1998, paras. 153–154 (referring to the objective of 'sustainable development' in the preamble of the WTO Agreement when interpreting the terms 'exhaustible natural resources' in Article XX(g)) of the General Agreement on Tariffs and Trade. Agreement Establishing the World Trade Agreement, 1994, 1867 UNTS 154; General Agreement on Tariffs and Trade, 1994, 55 UNTS 194.

75 Ebbesson & Hey, 'Introduction', n. 31, 6. On the cosmopolitan reading of sustainable development, see 22–47.

76 UNGA Resolution 76/300, n. 29.

development concerns in international law is still lacking, *Nico Schrijver* concludes that

> a fascinating conceptual feature is that sustainable development functions as an integrative and guiding principle, having economic, environmental, developmental, social, and governance dimensions to such an extent that the whole is more than the sum of the parts. In this way, it has given rise to the gradual emergence of international sustainable development law, which builds both on the principles of general international law and specific principles originating in a variety of chapters of international law.[77]

I.4.3 *Human Rights, Participatory Rights, and the Rule of Law in Environmental Matters*

I.4.3.1 Stockholm 1972

At Stockholm 1972, the connection between human rights and environment protection was novel, if it existed at all.[78] Neither the 1948 Universal Declaration of Human Rights (Universal Declaration)[79] nor any of the human rights treaties adopted before 1972 – that is, the 1966 International Covenant on Civil and Political Rights (ICCPR),[80] the 1966 International Convention on Economic, Social and Cultural Rights (ICESCR),[81] the 1950 European Convention on Human Rights (ECHR),[82] and the 1969 American Convention on Human Rights (ACHR)[83] – make any reference to the environment. This is not surprising since, as mentioned, at the time of their adoption the term 'environment' was not yet used to reflect the concept of the environment of today. Among the then acknowledged human rights with a potential bearing on environment-related issues – to be shown decades

77 Schrijver, n. 50, 85.

78 On human rights and the environment, see, e.g., Alan Boyle & Michael Anderson (eds.), *Human Rights Approaches to Environmental Protection* (Oxford University Press, 1996); Ben Boer (ed.), *Environmental Law Dimensions of Human Rights* (Oxford University Press, 2015); Jonas Ebbesson, 'Getting It Right: Advances of Human Rights and the Environment from Stockholm 1972 to Stockholm 2022' (2022) 52 *Environmental Policy and Law* 79.

79 Universal Declaration of Human Rights, UN Doc. A/810/71, 10 December 1948 (Universal Declaration).

80 International Covenant on Civil and Political Rights, 1966, 999 UNTS 171 (ICCPR).

81 International Covenant on Economic, Social and Cultural Rights, 1966, 993 UNTS 3 (ICESCR).

82 European Convention for the Protection of Human Rights and Fundamental Freedoms, 1950, 213 UNTS 222 (ECHR).

83 American Convention on Human Rights, 1969, 1144 UNTS 123 (ACHR).

later – were the right to life,[84] the right to health and well-being,[85] the right to a fair trial and remedy,[86] the right to privacy and family life,[87] the right to property,[88] the right to equal protection and non-discrimination,[89] the right of opinion and expression,[90] the right to peaceful assembly and association,[91] and the right to take part in government and public affairs.[92] Importantly, as argued by *Dinah Shelton*, without explicitly mentioning the environment, the 1968 UN Conference on Human Rights in Teheran opened the door for the consideration of complex issues like the environment in relation to the established human rights, and it stimulated interest among developing states in the Stockholm Conference.[93] Still, by 1972, the then existing human rights courts, committees, and other bodies had not developed any jurisprudence on human rights and the environment based on these rights.

Nor was there any international law on participatory rights – that is, on access to information, public participation in decision-making, and access to justice – in environmental matters by 1972, except for the mentioned human rights, which were potentially applicable to environmental contexts. Rather, at that time, international law took a neutral position in regard to states' domestic governance system on environmental matters as long as states did not cause significant transboundary harm (as reflected in Principle 21 of the Stockholm Declaration), implying that it was a national matter for each sovereign state to decide on access to information and public participation.

Given this background, the provision in Principle 1 of the Stockholm Declaration, that 'man has the fundamental right to freedom, equality and adequate conditions of life, in an environment of a quality that permits a life of dignity and well-being' was bold and progressive. And ahead of its time.[94]

84 Universal Declaration, n. 79, art. 3; ICCPR, n. 80, art. 6; ECHR, n. 82, art. 2; ACHR, n. 83, art. 4.
85 Universal Declaration, n. 79, art. 25.
86 Universal Declaration, n. 79, arts. 8, 10; ICCPR, n. 80, art. 14; ECHR, n. 82, arts. 6, 13; ACHR, n. 83, art. 8.
87 Universal Declaration, n. 79, art. 12; ICCPR, n. 80, art. 17; ECHR, n. 82, art. 8; ACHR, n. 83, art. 11.
88 Protocol no. 1 to the Convention for the Protection of Human Rights and Fundamental Freedoms 1952, ETS 9, art. 1; ACHR, n. 83, art. 21.
89 Universal Declaration, n. 79, art. 7; ACHR, n. 83, arts. 24–25.
90 Universal Declaration, n. 79, art. 19; ICCPR, n. 80, art. 19; ECHR, n. 82, art. 10; ACHR, n. 83, art. 13.
91 Universal Declaration, n. 79, art. 20; ICCPR, n. 80, art. 22; ECHR, n. 82, art. 11; ACHR, n. 83, arts. 15–16.
92 Universal Declaration, n. 79, art. 21; ICCPR, n. 80, art. 25; ACHR, n. 83, art. 23.
93 Dinah Shelton, 'Litigating Human Rights and the Environment in International Tribunals 1972–2022: How Far Have We Progressed?' in this volume, 132.
94 Ebbesson, n. 78, 80.

Although Principle 1 did not reflect international law of the time, it would influence the development of constitutional provisions on the protection of the environment and the human right thereto in many countries.[95] It would also influence international law on human rights, but it would take a while. In the words of *Patricia Kameri-Mbote and colleagues*, this 'laid a crucial foundation for the flourishing of other rights, encompassing participation, access to information, and access to justice', which would become 'crucial pillars in environmental rule of law' by the time of the Stockholm+50 Meeting.[96]

Thus, while there is no mentioning of public participation or participatory rights in the Stockholm Declaration, it is clearly supported by Principle 1. In addition, Principle 19 on environmental education asserts the importance of such education 'in order to broaden the basis for an enlightened opinion and responsible conduct'. Further support for public participation is found in the 1972 Stockholm Action Plan, which recommends that 'governments and the Secretary-General provide equal possibilities for everybody, both by training and by ensuring access to relevant means and information, to influence their own environment by themselves'.[97] Interestingly, soon after the Stockholm Conference, some important advances on participatory rights were made in international law, not through common standards or agreed minimum rights but, rather, on the basis of non-discrimination in transboundary settings.

4.3.2 Stockholm 2022

Fifty years later, the adoption by the UNGA of Resolution 76/300 on the Human Right to a Clean, Healthy and Sustainable Environment neatly frames the advances of international law on human and participatory rights in relation to the environment during these years.[98] While this resolution is not as such a legally binding instrument, by 2022, there was also plenty of legal backing for such a human right, both in international and numerous national laws. Getting there from the Stockholm Conference was not straightforward but, rather, the result of several small steps, mostly in regional contexts. Soon after the Stockholm Conference, the Organisation for Economic Co-operation and

95 Stephen J. Turner, 'Introduction: A Brief History of Environmental Rights and the Development of Standards', in Stephen J. Turner *et al.* (eds.), *Environmental Rights: The Development of Standards* (Cambridge University Press, 2019), 1, 5.

96 Kameri-Mbote *et al.*, n. 68, 159.

97 Stockholm Action Plan, n. 9, Recommendation 7a. In different respects, public participation is also referred to in Recommendations 39(a) and 97.

98 UNGA Resolution 76/300, n. 29. The Resolution of the UNGA followed the approach taken by the UN Human Rights Council the year before. See HRC Resolution 48/13, n. 30.

Development (OECD) adopted recommendations on principles concerning trans-frontier pollution, including the instruction that countries should 'base their action on the principle of non-discrimination' and introduce 'a system affording equal right of hearing', thus ensuring no less favourable rights of standing in judicial and administrative proceedings.[99] In the same year, a similar regime based on non-discrimination was set out in the 1974 Nordic Convention for the Protection of the Environment.[100]

Some significant advances of the human rights and environment nexus were seen in the 1970s and 1980s – in particular, the provisions on the right to a satisfactory environment in the 1981 African Charter on Human and Peoples' Rights,[101] the (for a long time overlooked) provision on the right of everybody to live in a healthy environment in the 1988 Additional Protocol to the American Convention on Human Rights in the Area of Economic, Social, and Cultural Rights,[102] and the declaratory statements on procedural rights in the 1982 World Charter for Nature.[103] Still, as *Ben Boer and Rowena Cantley-Smith* point out, 'it was not until the UN Conference on Environment and Development in June 1992, and its Rio Declaration, that environmental access rights received universal recognition'.[104] Most likely, the geopolitical changes and the end (or pause) of the Cold War at the time helped make this possible. The Rio Conference and, in particular, Principle 10 of the Rio Declaration would have an outstanding impact on the development of international law in this field. Since then, through advances at regional and global scales, further world summits on environment and sustainable development, international treaty making on the protection of the environment and human rights, international policy documents and declarations, and remarkable jurisprudential developments, international law has developed extraordinarily with respect to the human right and environment nexus and the notion of public participation in environmental matters.

Since the 1992 Rio Conference, comprehensive jurisprudence on human rights and the environment have developed in the regional treaty regimes of Europe, Africa, and the Americas, revealing that different established human

99 OECD Recommendation on Principles Concerning Transfrontier Pollution, 14 November 1974, reprinted in OECD, *Recommendation of the Council on Principles Concerning Transfrontier Pollution*, Doc. OECD/Legal/0133, 2024.

100 Nordic Convention for the Protection of the Environment, 1974, (1974) 13 ILM 591.

101 African Charter on Human and Peoples' Rights, 1981, 1520 UNTS 217.

102 Additional Protocol to the American Convention on Human Rights in the Area of Economic, Social, and Cultural Rights, Doc. OEA/Ser. A/44, 17 November 1988.

103 UNGA Resolution 37/7, n. 12.

104 Ben Boer & Rowena Cantley-Smith, 'The Development of Environmental Access Rights and Protection of Environmental Defenders', in this volume, 183.

rights depend on the protection of the environment and also confirming the right to a clean and healthy environment as such. In parallel, new regional treaties on participatory rights have been adopted – first for Europe, Caucasus, and Central Asia through the 1998 Aarhus Convention,[105] then for Africa by the revised 2003 African Convention on the Conservation of Nature and Natural Resources,[106] and for Latin America and the Caribbean by the 2018 Escazú Agreement.[107] Still, at the time of the Stockholm+50 Meeting, there was no corresponding regional development of international law for the greater part of Asia-Pacific.

There was also no global treaty on participatory rights at Stockholm+50, but some significant steps had been taken at the global level to confirm the development of participatory rights in international law. While *no* environmental treaty of global scope adopted before the 1992 Rio Conference refers to public participation, essentially *all* environmental treaties adopted at or after the 1992 conference include provisions supporting access to information, public awareness, and public participation in decision-making.[108] In addition, the global dimension of these issues is reflected in the ICCPR, with quite similar provisions as the regional treaty regimes, in the specific guidelines on access to information, public participation, and access to justice by UNEP and in provisions adopted by the ILC.[109]

Neither the Stockholm Declaration nor the African or American treaty regimes that explicitly provide for a human right in relation to the environment are limited to the procedural or participatory aspects; rather, they assert a substantive right to a satisfactory or healthy environment. This substantive dimension was the key message also in the 2022 UNGA Resolution on the Human Right to a Clean, Healthy and Sustainable Environment, although, importantly, it also recognizes that 'the exercise of human rights, including the rights to seek, receive and impart information, to participate effectively in the conduct of government and public affairs and to an effective remedy, is vital to the protection of a clean, healthy and sustainable environment'.[110]

At Stockholm+50, the substantive and procedural dimensions of human rights in relation to the environment were increasingly confirmed also with

105 Convention on Access to Information, Public Participation in Decision-making and Access to Justice in Environmental Matters, 1998, 2161 UNTS 447.

106 African Convention on the Conservation of Nature and Natural Resources, 2003, 41550-treaty-Charter_ConservationNature_NaturalResources.pdf.

107 Regional Agreement on Access to Information, Public Participation and Justice in Environmental Matters in Latin America and the Caribbean, 2018, 3388 UNTS I-56653.

108 Jonas Ebbesson, 'Public Participation', in Rajamani & Peel, n. 2, 358.

109 *Ibid.*

110 UNGA Resolution 76/300, n. 29.

respect to climate change. While the 2015 Paris Agreement only discreetly refers to human rights in the preamble, it would soon play an unexpected role in climate litigation in national courts. In the second decennium of the twenty-first century, frustrated by the slowness of governments to tackle climate change, associations, interest groups, and individuals around the world turned to national courts and sued states and corporations for their lack of sufficient climate action.[111] In many of these cases before national courts, the plaintiffs invoked international law – in particular, the Paris Agreement and various human rights treaties. And, in many cases, the plaintiffs were successful – for instance, in Pakistan, Colombia, and the Netherlands. At Stockholm+50, climate change lawsuits had also reached international human rights tribunals. In a 2024 ruling, based on an application submitted in 2020, the European Court of Human Rights concluded that the ECHR imposes obligations on the parties to do their respective reasonable share to reduce greenhouse gas emissions and their harmful effects.[112] Importantly, the Court set out that

> it follows ... that each State has its own share of responsibilities to take measures to tackle climate change and that the taking of those measures is determined by the State's own capabilities rather than by any specific action (or omission) of any other State. ... The Court considers that a respondent State should not evade its responsibility by pointing to the responsibility of other States, whether Contracting Parties to the Convention or not.[113]

The cases before the national courts and the ruling by the European Court of Human Rights show how international law on human rights develops. They also show how international law on climate change develops, merges with other areas of international law, and applies at different scales

[111] According to the dataset of Joana Setzer & Catherine Higham, *Global Trends in Climate Change Litigation: 2024 Snapshot* (Grantham Research Institute on Climate Change and the Environment, London School of Economics and Political Science, 2024), drawing from the Sabin Center for Climate Change Law's Climate Litigation Databases, which contained 2,666 climate litigation cases in 55 different countries. Around 70 per cent of these were filed since 2015, the year the Paris Agreement was adopted. Paris Agreement on Climate Change, 2015, 3156 UNTS 79 (Paris Agreement).

[112] ECtHR, *Klimaseniorinnen Schweiz and Others v Switzerland*, Application no. 53600/20, 9 April 2024, paras. 442–444. In the same vein, a year later the International Court of Justice, in *Obligations of States in Respect of Climate Change*, n 58, concluded, in para 386, that 'the adverse effects of climate change may impair the effective enjoyment of human rights'; and, in para 393, that 'the human right to a clean, healthy and sustainable environment is inherent in the enjoyment of other human rights' and 'under international law, the human right to a clean, healthy and sustainable environment is essential for the enjoyment of other human rights.'

[113] *Ibid.*, para. 442.

simultaneously: in global as well as national contexts, and both top down through annual Conferences of the Parties of the UNFCCC and Paris Agreement, and from below through lawsuits brought by members of the public. Importantly, *Jacqueline Peel* highlights the North-South dimensions in climate litigation and concludes:

> Climate litigation as it takes off across the global South is providing an important avenue for the expression of these perspectives, presenting climate issues as one part of broader sustainable development challenges. This is an important reminder of Southern perspectives on the manifestation of the environmental challenge of climate change, even as the post-Paris implementation efforts seem to be turning towards a more universalising language of 'keeping 1.5 degrees Celsius alive' and achieving 'net zero by 2050' emissions reduction targets.[114]

Soon after the Stockholm+50 Meeting, the Inter-American Court of Human Rights was also asked to clarify, through an advisory opinion, the scope of state obligations to respond to the climate emergency within the framework of international human rights law.[115] *Dinah Shelton* concludes that 'advocates, through international litigation, have advanced Principle 1 of the Stockholm Declaration well beyond the limits that states were willing to accept fifty years ago',[116] and the human rights and participatory rights dimension probably represents one of the most profound developments of international environmental law since the Stockholm Conference.

However, focusing on the positive developments of international law from 1972 to 2022 in promoting human rights and participatory rights in environmental matters risks ignoring the constant shortcoming in enforcement and implementation, the numerous violations of these rights, and, not least, the importance of protecting those who use the asserted rights. *Ben Boer and Rowena Cantley-Smith* highlight the escalating risks and challenges facing environmental human rights defenders and others exercising their access rights, with killings and other incidents taking place around the world on a regular basis, and the increasing attention in international law and governance to protecting those who use them. Hence, the 'acknowledgement of the critical role of EHRDs [environmental human rights defenders] in promoting

114 Jacqueline Peel, 'A Southern State of Mind: From Being 'Mindful of . . . Effects on Climate' to Climate Litigation in the Global South', in this volume, 375.

115 Inter-American Court of Human Rights, *Request for an Advisory Opinion on the Climate Emergency and Human Rights Submitted to the Inter-American Court of Human Rights by the Republic of Colombia and the Republic of Chile*, 9 January 2023, www.corteidh.or.cr/docs/opiniones/soc_1_2023_en.pdf.

116 Shelton, n. 93, 155.

the full enjoyment of the right to a healthy environment ... provides a contemporary perspective on the ongoing importance of environmental access rights'.[117]

I.4.4 *Consumption and Production*

I.4.4.1 Stockholm 1972

At Stockholm 1972, resource use was a topical issue. The viability of economic growth had been increasingly questioned in the late 1960s and early 1970s. The most famous expression of this was the Club of Rome's 1972 report *Limits to Growth*, in which a group of researches paint a bleak picture of exponentially growing populations and resource use, leading to the conclusion that 'entirely new approaches are required to redirect society toward goals of equilibrium rather than growth'.[118] Although the conclusions, not least on what role technological development could play in alleviating the pressing resource challenges identified, were hotly debated, issues relating to the ability of the planet to sustain growing populations and their increasing levels of consumption were now placed on the international agenda.[119]

While recognized in principle as being relevant to international law, these issues were still controversial and divisive, and there was a general lack of legal instruments aimed at sustainably managing resource use from an environmental perspective. As reflected in Principle 21 of the Stockholm Declaration, the main legal approach to address matters relating to the environment was state centred. Developing states may have been particularly adamant to defend the right to decide on the use of their natural resources, but it was certainly not only those states who guarded states' 'sovereign right to exploit their own resources pursuant to their own environmental policies', as set out in Principle 21.

Despite the reference to states' sovereign rights in Principle 21, the focus of the Stockholm Declaration is not entirely state centred. For instance, it recognizes that achieving the environmental goals will demand 'the acceptance of responsibility by citizens and communities and by enterprises and institutions at every level' and that the world environment of the future is

117 Boer & Cantley-Smith, n. 104, 180.

118 Donella H. Meadows *et al.*, *The Limits to Growth: A Report for the Club of Rome's Project on the Predicament of Mankind* (Universe Books, 1972), 193.

119 Aik Hoe Lim, 'History of the Trade and Environment Debate at the WTO', in Panagiotis Delimatsis & Leonie Reins (eds.), *Trade and Environmental Law* (Edward Elgar, 2021), 7.

shaped by 'the sum of their actions'.[120] This could clearly pertain to consumption and production.

Given that the existing legal instruments in the early 1970s neither aimed at sustainably managing resource use from an environmental perspective nor reflected the calls from the Club of Rome, it is important, as *Timo Koivurova* observes, that 'these ideas and concerns ... found their way into the Stockholm Conference's preparations and, ultimately, into the 1972 Stockholm Declaration on the Human Environment and Action Plan'.[121] The Stockholm Declaration addresses resource management and utilization and the associated economic processes in several ways. Principle 3 holds that 'the capacity of the earth to produce vital renewable resources must be maintained and, wherever practicable, restored or improved', and, according to Principle 5, 'the non-renewable resources of the earth must be employed in such a way as to guard against the danger of their future exhaustion and to ensure that benefits from such employment are shared by all mankind'.

Obviously, at the time of the Stockholm Conference, consumption and production in the North-South context, as well as poverty and the lack of development, were at the centre of discussions. This is also reflected in the Stockholm Declaration. The preamble of the Declaration makes clear that, in the developing countries, most of the environmental problems are caused by under-development and that 'millions continue to live far below the minimum levels required for a decent human existence, deprived of adequate food and clothing, shelter and education, health and sanitation'. Hence, the *lack of ability to consume* was a core issue. While 'bearing in mind' the need to safeguard and improve the environment, developing countries should therefore direct their efforts to development.[122]

To sum up, at the time of the 1972 Stockholm Conference, concerns related to consumption and production were on the political agenda, but they were quite divisive, and the issue was not addressed in international law.

I.4.4.2 Stockholm 2022

Fifty years later, the consumption of natural resources is bigger than ever, and the growth rate shows little sign of levelling off. The energy transition away from fossil fuels has contributed to further increasing demand for several

120 Stockholm Declaration, n. 3, preambular para. 7.

121 Timo Koivurova, 'International Regulation and the Management of Mining since the 1972 Stockholm Conference: From Local to Global Concerns', in this volume, 226.

122 Stockholm Declaration, n. 3, preambular para. 4.

metals and minerals, spurring new mining operations and also creating pressure for mining to be conducted in new areas, including those beyond national jurisdiction such as the deep seabed. At the same time, the concept of sustainable consumption and production is a mainstay of international policy, and it is highlighted in the outcome of the 2022 Stockholm+50 Meeting. Among the recommendations is a call for 'a system-wide change in the way our current economic system works' by, inter alia, adopting new measures of progress and human well-being.[123] It also recognizes the special need to 'accelerate system-wide transformations of high impact sectors, such as food, energy, water, building and construction, manufacturing and mobility', inter alia, through policies to promote circularity, resource efficiency, regenerative production approaches and nature-based solutions in value chains, and transforming food systems by promoting regenerative farming and fisheries approaches.[124]

Eva R. van der Marel and Catherine Redgwell reveal the influence of the Stockholm Declaration on other international policy outcomes leading up to the Stockholm+50 Meeting:

> Emerging from early calls for more rational management of resources and development planning in the 1972 Stockholm Declaration on the Human Environment (Stockholm Declaration), SCP [sustainable consumption and production] has developed into an essential requirement for sustainable development, enshrined in Principle 8 of the 1992 Rio Declaration on Environment and Development (Rio Declaration) and in Sustainable Development Goal (SDG) 12: Responsible Consumption and Production in 2015.[125]

This is all fine, but what about international law at Stockholm+50? Although the growing use of natural resources is a main driver behind several environmental pressures, including climate change, biodiversity loss, and pollution, little concrete effort in international law has been directed at regulating consumption as such. Rather, the focus tends to be on incremental measures for reducing the environmental impact of production and consumption, including through the application of such concepts as best available technology, EIA, life cycle thinking, and circularity.

[123] Summary: Recommendations for Accelerating Action towards a Healthy Planet for the Prosperity of All, 'Outcome of the International Meeting' in *Report of Stockholm+50*, n. 4, point 3.

[124] *Ibid.*, point 6.

[125] Eva R. van der Marel & Catherine Redgwell, 'Unrealised Ambition or Unattainable Goal? Sustainable Consumption and Production in International Law', in this volume, 206 (footnotes omitted).

To the extent that these concepts appear in legal contexts, it is mainly in domestic or regional law, such as that of the European Union rather than in international treaties. The analysis of a number of multilateral environmental agreements on atmospheric pollution, chemicals, and hazardous wastes by *Eva R. van der Marel and Catherine Redgwell* shows that none of them contains reference to sustainable consumption and production as such in their text and that they 'remain considerably short of reflecting the need to think holistically about product systems in life cycle terms in order to achieve SCP'.[126] So, on that note, *Timo Koivurova* accurately concludes that, 'despite ... political debates about radically changing the way we use natural resources and, ultimately, transforming how our societies function, these topics have not been discussed in the international policy-making arena in a serious and constructive manner'.[127]

Thus, as in many fields, the discourse on consumption and production has advanced considerably compared to 1972, and the fundamental themes are clearly recognizable, but action has tended to stop short of measures needed for any actual transition in the way in which we produce and consume. Much talk, less walk.

I.4.5 *Waste and Chemicals*

I.4.5.1 Stockholm 1972

At Stockholm 1972, ten years after the publication of Rachel Carson's seminal book *Silent Spring*, pollution – in particular, pollution of the marine environment – was among the core environmental themes.[128] Still, at this time, there were few if any attempts in international law to regulate the production and handling of chemicals or the generation of waste as major sources of pollution. Existing rules and principles effectively targeted specific polluting activities or occurrences, such as oil spills or, as in the *Train Smelter* case, air emissions.[129] The handling, circulation, and recycling of waste and chemicals were not a priority at the time, as reflected in the conspicuous absence of waste and chemicals from books contemporary to the Stockholm Conference dealing with international environmental law.[130]

126 *Ibid.*, 225.
127 Koivurova, n. 121, 239.
128 Rachel Carson, *Silent Spring* (Houghton Mifflin, 1962).
129 *Trail Smelter*, n. 45.
130 See Ludwik A. Teclaff & Albert E. Utton (eds.), *International Environmental Law* (Praeger Publishers, 1974); Bo Johnsson, *International Environmental Law* (Liber Förlag, 1976).

This is also reflected in early environmental treaties adopted around that time, such as the 1972 London Dumping Convention,[131] the 1974 Paris Convention,[132] and the 1974 Helsinki Convention.[133] Although they did indeed address the very chemicals highlighted by Carson, such as DDT (and other organohalogen compounds), chemicals and wastes were essentially dealt with as constituents of emissions, and the restrictions served to directly limit their entry into the environment through specific activities.

While the Stockholm Declaration holds that both the natural and the man-made environment are essential to man's 'well-being and to the enjoyment of basic human rights – even the right to life itself', this had no bearing on the approach to chemicals or wastes at the Stockholm Conference.[134] As *Marcos Orellana* notes, 'the human rights approach did not serve as the central tenant of the conference or the main approach taken to chemicals and waste in the decades that followed. Instead, control and management for the minimization of adverse effects of these toxic and hazardous substances became the policy priority.'[135] This is the approach reflected in the Stockholm Declaration. According to its Principle 6: 'The discharge of toxic substances or of other substances and the release of heat, in such quantities or concentrations as to exceed the capacity of the environment to render them harmless, must be halted in order to ensure that serious or irreversible damage is not inflicted upon ecosystems.'

Despite the lack of a clear policy to address chemicals and wastes more directly, some traces to that effect can be found in the Stockholm Action Plan. Among other things, the plan makes reference to the FAO's 'War on Waste' in relation to the need for increased control and recycling of wastes in agriculture.[136] Recommendations are also included concerning the use of the best practicable means available to minimize the release to the environment of toxic or dangerous substances, especially persistent substances, until it has been demonstrated that their release will not give rise to unacceptable risks or unless their use is essential to human health or

[131] Convention on the Prevention of Marine Pollution by Dumping of Wastes and Other Matter, 1972, 1046 UNTS 120.

[132] Convention for the Prevention of Marine Pollution from Land-based Sources, 1974, 1546 UNTS 119 (Paris Convention).

[133] Convention on the Protection of the Marine Environment of the Baltic Sea Area, 1974, 1507 UNTS 166 (Helsinki Convention).

[134] Stockholm Declaration, n. 3, preambular para. 1.

[135] Marcos Orellana, 'The Unfinished Agenda of Stockholm 1972: A Rights-based Approach to Chemicals and Wastes', in this volume, 272.

[136] Stockholm Action Plan, n. 9, Recommendation 22.

food production, in which case appropriate control measures should be applied.[137]

In the light of these fragmented outcomes, *Katharina Kummer Peiry* concisely concludes that, at the Stockholm Conference, 'the management of wastes and chemicals was featured only marginally as it was not considered a priority issue at that time'.[138]

I.4.5.2 Stockholm 2022

Fifty years later, chemicals and waste management were central themes of international environmental law and policy, and approached in an increasingly holistic way although with many remaining shortcomings and new problems. While not specifically addressing chemicals and waste, the recommendations coming out of the Stockholm+50 Meeting refer to pollution as part of the 'triple crisis of our common environment' and calls, inter alia, for policies to promote 'circularity, resource efficiency, regenerative production approaches and nature-based solutions in value chains', thereby clearly including chemicals and waste management in the broader context of a circular and pollution free economy.[139]

Starting with guidelines and recommendations in the 1970s and early 1980s – partly drawing on the themes of the Stockholm Declaration – several international agreements on different aspects of chemicals and waste management were subsequently adopted. The first such agreement was the 1989 Basel Convention,[140] which established a requirement for prior informed consent (PIC) for shipments of hazardous waste and household waste. While it calls for measures to ensure that the generation of waste is reduced to a minimum, it is strongly focused on transboundary shipments, and the PIC procedure is largely a mechanism for enabling developing states to exercise control over their territories in relation to waste. Discontent with the lack of a ban on waste export led to the adoption of more stringent, regional waste treaties – notably, the 1992 Bamako Convention banning the import of hazardous waste into Africa.[141] An amendment to the Basel Convention, introducing a ban on the transfer of hazardous wastes

[137] *Ibid.*, Recommendation 71.

[138] Katharina Kummer Peiry, 'Chemicals and Wastes in International Environmental Policy and Law: From *Trail Smelter* to a Circular Economy', in this volume, 249.

[139] 'Summary: Recommendations for Accelerating Action towards a Healthy Planet for the Prosperity of All – Outcome of the International Meeting', in *Report of Stockholm+50*, n. 4, introduction and point 6.

[140] Convention on the Control of Transboundary Movement of Hazardous Wastes and Their Disposal, 1989, 1673 UNTS 57.

[141] Bamako Convention on the Ban of the Import into Africa and the Control of Transboundary Movement and Management of Hazardous Wastes within Africa, 1991, 2101 UNTS 177.

from, essentially, OECD to non-OECD countries was adopted in 1995, but it did not enter into force until 2019.[142]

Three global conventions focusing specifically on the control of chemicals have been adopted so far. The 1998 Rotterdam Convention applies a kind of PIC procedure for international trade in specific industrial chemicals and pesticides, although it is less stringent than the procedure in the Basel Convention.[143] The 2001 Stockholm Convention provides for the gradual phase out of production and use of the category of chemicals known as persistent organic pollutants (POPs).[144] The 2013 Minamata Convention is only concerned with mercury but aims for the regulation of the whole life cycle of that metal and also includes provisions for its gradual phase out.[145] At the time of writing, an international instrument on the management of plastics is being negotiated, which is to be based on a comprehensive approach that addresses the full life cycle of plastics.[146]

While chemicals and waste were initially addressed separately under international law, from around the turn of the millennium, attempts have increasingly been made to cluster their management so that the Basel, Rotterdam, and Stockholm Conventions now have far-reaching institutional coordination. Gradually, the perception of waste has shifted from merely a burden to be disposed of to a more nuanced one recognizing the risks as well as the potential of many categories of waste. Internationally, this is perhaps most evident in the development of management principles – notably, *environmentally sound management* – within the framework of the Basel Convention. The development and application of new concepts such as life cycle thinking and circular economy entail a necessary integration of waste and chemicals management, but they also come with new challenges. As pointed out by *Carl Dalhammar*, 'in the longer run, rules that aim to phase out substances of concern from products will support future recycling efforts, but, in the short term, they may limit the opportunities for recycling'.[147]

142 Decision III/1 of the Conference of the Parties to the Basel Convention, UN Doc. UNEP/CHW.3/35, 28 November 1995.

143 Rotterdam Convention on the Prior Informed Consent Procedure for Certain Hazardous Chemicals and Pesticides in International Trade, 1998, 2244 UNTS 337. For a comparison of the different prior-informed consent procedures and the way in which they balance various objectives, see David Langlet, *Prior Informed Consent and Hazardous Trade: Regulating Trade in Hazardous Goods at the Intersection of Sovereignty, Free Trade and Environmental Protection* (Kluwer Law International, 2009).

144 Convention on Persistent Organic Pollutants, 2006, 2256 UNTS 119.

145 Minamata Convention on Mercury, 2013, 3202 UNTS 1.

146 UNEA Resolution 5/14 on the End of Plastic Pollution: Towards an Internationally Binding Instrument, UN Doc. UNEP/EA.5/Res.14, 7 March 2022.

147 Carl Dalhammar, 'The Dynamics of International and European Union Law on Waste and Chemicals: Past, Present, and Future', in this volume, 294.

The link between toxic substances and human rights has been increasingly highlighted and even become 'institutionalized' through the establishment in 1995, by the then Commission on Human Rights, of a special rapporteur on the human rights implications of the illicit movement and dumping of toxic and dangerous products and wastes.[148] Still, *Marcos Orellana* remarks that a genuine human rights-based approach to chemicals and wastes has not been achieved. Rather than being centred on managing risks and minimizing adverse effects, such an approach would seek 'to ensure the right of every person to live in a toxic-free environment' and build on the principles of prevention and accountability as well as rights to science, information, and participation.[149]

Despite all regulatory efforts, and just a few years before the Stockholm+50 Meeting, UNEP concluded that it would not be possible to reach the global goal of minimizing adverse impacts of chemicals and waste by 2020 and that more ambitious action by all stakeholders was urgently needed.[150] On that note, *Carl Dalhammar* points to the 'need to better incentivize research on new, safer chemicals as the current rules provide a very limited driver for change',[151] and *Katharina Kummer Piery* calls for the development of a framework treaty, setting out fundamental principles on sustainable substances and materials management, covering all stages of the life cycle of substances and materials and also providing an overarching institutional framework that could integrate the existing treaties.[152]

While the thinking on, and regulatory efforts aimed at, chemicals and waste have developed considerably since 1972, huge shortcomings and challenges remain. Except for the negotiations on the plastics treaty, which offers the prospects of some genuinely constructive approaches, at the time of the Stockholm+50 Meeting and since that time, there appears to be little political appetite for more than incremental changes to the existing regulatory structures, and the existing legal frameworks are inadequate to meet the needs that lie ahead.

148 UNCHR Resolution 1995/81 on the Adverse Effects of the Illicit Movement and Dumping of Toxic and Dangerous Products and Wastes on the Enjoyment of Human Rights, Doc. E/CN.4/RES/1995/81, 8 March 1995. The title is now Special Rapporteur on the Implications for Human Rights of the Environmentally Sound Management and Disposal of Hazardous Substances and Wastes.

149 Orellana, n. 135, 281.

150 UNEP, *Global Chemicals Outlook II: From Legacies to Innovative Solutions: Implementing the 2030 Agenda for Sustainable Development*, 2019, vi.

151 Dalhammar, n. 147, 309.

152 Kummer Piery. n. 138, 263.

I.4.6 *The Atmosphere*

I.4.6.1 Stockholm 1972

At Stockholm 1972, transboundary air pollution was not a new subject. As mentioned above, it was at the core of the 1941 *Trail Smelter* award,[153] decided about thirty years earlier. While addressing transboundary air pollution, the issue was still rather local in scope; the case concerned the Trail Smelter, located in western Canada, only some fifteen kilometres north of the border to the United States, where it was causing harm to farmers.[154] In 1972, the *Trail Smelter* award – with the key message that no state has the right to use or permit the use of its territory in such a manner as to cause injury to the territory of other states – was rightly described as a 'hopeful precedent for controlling pollution in international law'.[155] And this message would be clearly set out in Principle 21 of the Stockholm Declaration. Apart from that, only some rather specific issues, like intentional weather modification and high-altitude nuclear tests, had pedigree as subjects of international law at the time. Widespread activities that cause changes in the environment inadvertently were seen as hard to address by means of international law, particularly to the extent that the effects could be seen as by-products of national economic development.[156] And, as for customary law, it was deemed to regulate 'danger which is clear and localized' but lacking capacity to 'protect against slow, accumulative global deterioration'.[157]

Yet new transboundary environmental challenges were on the horizon and would be addressed in relation to the Stockholm Conference. *Phoebe Okowa and Sean O'Reilly* note that transboundary air pollution assumed a particular prominence at the conference, largely due to the host country's efforts to highlight the growing problem of acid rain and air pollution across Europe: 'This was part of a diplomatic offensive by Sweden that aimed not only to advance its agenda on acid rain and pollution but also to position the

153 *Trail Smelter*, n. 45.

154 On the history of the *Trail Smelter* dispute, see John D. Wirth, 'The Trail Smelter Dispute: Canadians and Americans Confront Transboundary Pollution 1927–41' (1996) 1(2) *Environmental History* 34.

155 Forest Grieves, 'International Law and the Environmental Issue' (1972) 1(4) *Boston College Environmental Affairs Law Review* 826, 829.

156 Howard J. Taubenfeld, 'International Environmental Law: Air and Outer Space' (1973) 13 *Natural Resources Journal* 315, 315–316.

157 Brendan F. Brown, 'International Environmental Law and the Natural Law' (1971–1972) 18(3) *Loyola Law Review* 679, 683.

conference as a broader platform for cooperation between Eastern and Western diplomatic blocs.'[158]

Concerns for air and air pollution are reflected in the outcome of the Stockholm Conference,[159] but there is no call to start international negotiations on the matter. Somewhat surprisingly, the provisions in the Stockholm Action Plan are bolder in addressing climate change than in highlighting air pollution. Thus, governments were recommended to be mindful of activities in which there is an appreciable risk of *effects on climate*. To that end, they were asked to 'carefully evaluate the likelihood and magnitude of climatic effects and disseminate their findings to the maximum extent feasible before embarking on such activities' and to 'consult fully other interested States when activities carrying a risk are being contemplated or implemented'.[160] There is no such message regarding air pollution from the Stockholm Conference.

Still, both these cases would be subject to international law and regulations. While it would take another decade and a half until climate change was seriously on the international policy agenda, air pollution would be subject to international negotiations quite soon after Stockholm. This accords with the conclusion of the case study prepared for the conference on air pollution across national boundaries, and the impact on the environment of acid rain, that 'the deposition in any one place will be dependent on the emissions within the surrounding area with a radius of one to two thousand kilometres: The problem is thus an international one.'[161]

I.4.6.2 Stockholm 2022

Fifty years later, there are three major treaty-based regimes, which differ considerably both in terms of geographic scope and level of success, dedicated to protecting the atmosphere: on long-range transboundary air pollution, ozone layer depletion, and climate change.

One of the first treaties to regulate air pollution was the regional 1974 Helsinki Convention, which obliged the parties to counteract the introduction

158 Phoebe Okowa & Sean O'Reilly, 'Implementing Principle 21 of the Stockholm Declaration: Regional Efforts to Regulate Transboundary Air Pollution', in this volume, 316.

159 Explicit reference to air pollution is only made in the preamble of the Stockholm Declaration, n. 3, whereas principle 2 of the Declaration asserts that natural resources of the Earth, 'including the air' must be safeguarded. Air and air pollution is also referred to in the Stockholm Action Plan, n. 9, Recommendations 77, 81, 83.

160 Stockholm Action Plan, n. 9, Recommendation 70.

161 Bert Bolin *et al.*, *Air Pollution across National Boundaries: The Impact on the Environment of Sulfur in Air and Precipitation: Sweden's Case Study for the United Nations Conference on the Human Environment* (P.A. Norstedt, 1971), 87 (emphasis removed).

of, inter alia, airborne hazardous substances and to minimize airborne pollution by noxious substances into the Baltic Sea Area.[162] Still, neither the Helsinki Convention nor any other treaty adequately addressed the problem with long-range transboundary air pollution – thus, the conclusion of the time that 'with respect to the airspace environment there is not much to report from the field of international convention law'.[163]

But, quite soon, that would change. Importantly, the 1973–1975 Conference on Security and Co-operation paid attention to air pollution and resulted in recommendations concerning long-range air pollution. This, in turn, led to negotiations of a multinational treaty on the matter, and a few years later, the 1979 Convention on Long-Range Transboundary Air Pollution (LRTAP Convention) – the first international legal instrument dedicated to atmospheric pollution – saw the light of the day.[164] Administered by the UN Economic Commission for Europe with some fifty parties, the LRTAP Convention is one of the first framework conventions aimed at agreeing on the common problem and basic principles, and the building of a sound scientific base for long-term cooperation, policy-, and lawmaking. At the time of Stockholm+50, the LRTAP Convention was complemented with eight protocols, most of which specify measures to be taken in respect of different forms of air pollution, expanding from acid rain so as to also cover, for example, ground-level ozone, heavy metals, and POPs. While the LRTAP Convention can in many respects be considered a success story, the regulatory model it represents has been hard to emulate for addressing air pollution in other parts of the world. *Phoebe Okowa and Sean O'Reilly* identify various reasons for this, including a lack of scientific capacity and institutional fragmentation.[165]

Even more frequently referred to as a success story of international environmental law is the global regime on the protection of the stratospheric ozone layer, composed of the 1985 Vienna Convention and its 1987 Montreal Protocol, both on substances that deplete the ozone layer.[166] As opposed to air pollution and climate change, there were no concerns for ozone layer depletion at the Stockholm Conference. Still, with exceptional speed in global contexts, through international efforts and the agreed phase out of

162 Helsinki Convention on the Protection of the Marine Environment of the Baltic Sea Area, 1974, 1507 UNTS 166, art. 6(8).
163 Johnsson, n. 130, 70.
164 Convention on Long-Range Transboundary Air Pollution, 1979, 1302 UNTS 217.
165 Okowa & O'Reilly, n. 158, 314 and 335.
166 Vienna Convention for the Protection of the Ozone Layer, 1985, 1513 UNTS 323; Montreal Protocol on Substances That Deplete the Ozone Layer, 1987, 1522 UNTS 3.

ozone-depleting substances in the amended Montreal Protocol, as of 2022 the ozone in the upper stratosphere is expected to return to 1980 values within a few decades.[167] Important economic incentives were used to enhance the effectiveness of the Protocol. The prohibition on trading the listed ozone-depleting substances with non-parties to the Protocol, to avoid free riders, has been identified as an important means to that end. Yet, as noted by *Harro van Asselt*, 'while trade measures may have contributed to the Protocol's universal coverage, financial support for developing countries provided through the Protocol's Multilateral Fund, as well as access to technologies, have also played a major role' in making the ozone regime a success.[168] The Montreal Protocol shows the different impacts that international law can have. Not only did it define the obligations of the parties to phase out ozone-depleting substances, it also provided a common standard (the phasing out) for the private sector, thereby creating incentives for new, less harmful solutions.

The same legal model as for air pollution and ozone layer depletion – an initial framework convention to agree on the existence of a common problem and on basic principles, and to create a platform for long-term cooperation and further law-making through protocols – was used to tackle climate change. While climate change was considered already at the Stockholm Conference, the key initial steps to acknowledge it as a common concern of mankind was the 1988 UNGA Resolution on the Protection of the Global Climate,[169] and the setting up in 1988 of the Intergovernmental Panel on Climate Change (IPCC) by the WMO and UNEP.

The UNFCCC was adopted in connection with the Rio Conference[170] and supplemented by the 1997 Kyoto Protocol that specified emission reductions by percentage rates for industrialized parties.[171] While this approach was very similar to those in the regimes on air pollution and ozone layer depletion, it did not work very well for climate change. The strict distinction between developed and developing countries that provided the basis for the Kyoto Protocol's regulatory approach contributed significantly to the United States not becoming a party as well as to gradually weaning support for its regulatory model among industrialized countries. By the end of the Kyoto Protocol's

167 World Meteorological Organization, *Executive Summary: Scientific Assessment of Ozone Depletion: 2022*, GAW Report no. 278, 2022.

168 Harro van Asselt, 'Trade and Atmospheric Protection at Stockholm +50: *Plus ça Change*?' in this volume, 387 (reference omitted).

169 UNGA Resolution 43/53 on Protection of Global Climate for Present and Future Generations of Mankind, UN Doc. A/RES/43/53, 6 December 1988.

170 UNFCCC, n. 56.

171 Kyoto Protocol to the UN Framework Convention on Climate Change, 1997, 2302 UNTS 162.

2008–2012 commitment period, there was an urgent need to find a new approach that could garner wider support.

After several failed attempts, the Paris Agreement was adopted in 2015.[172] Of core significance is the agreed objective of 'holding the increase in the global average temperature to well below 2°C above pre-industrial levels and pursuing efforts to limit the temperature increase to 1.5°C above pre-industrial levels'.[173] Through the Paris Agreement, a new legal approach was adopted, based on the elaboration, communication, and regular revision of so-called nationally determined contributions (NDCs) by all parties. In the words of *Jutta Brunnée*, the Paris Agreement is 'designed not to demand and compel but, rather, to inspire and orchestrate the required shifts towards more ambitious climate action by providing common goals and principles for action as well as processes that facilitate international interaction and accountability'.[174]

This was not the only novelty of the Paris Agreement. *Jacqueline Peel* notes that, while the Southern priorities on climate effects had receded into the background since the 1992 Rio Conference, 'the 2015 Paris Agreement signalled a potential shift, with the agreement's "hybrid" approach elevating domestic policy considerations and increasing the focus on domestic enforcement action and litigation to ensure the implementation of parties' nationally determined contributions (NDCs) to the global climate change response'.[175]

Despite these promising elements, at Stockholm+50 there was considerable discrepancy between what is needed to keep within 1.5 degrees Celsius and the pledges made by states,[176] and the far-reaching transformation required in many sectors to reach the targets remains contested. This may not be so surprising given the complexity of climate change and its solutions, including the North-South dimensions. In comparing the successful outcome on the protection of the stratospheric ozone layer with the difficulties in resolving climate change, *Harro van Asselt* notes that the two issue areas share important features, including a long-time horizon, the necessity of international cooperation, and engaging major equity issues. Yet there are also important differences. Most importantly, contrary to cases such as ozone depletion where

172 Paris Agreement, n. 111.
173 See *ibid.*, art. 2.1(a).
174 Brunnée, n. 36, 354 (reference omitted).
175 Peel, n. 114, 359, referring to Lavanya Rajamani, 'From Stockholm to Johannesburg: The Anatomy of Dissonance in the International Environmental Dialogue' (2003) 12(1) *Review of European Community and International Environmental Law* 23.
176 *Nationally Determined Contributions under the Paris Agreement, Synthesis Report by the Secretariat*, Doc. FCCC/PA/CMA/2023/12, 14 November 2023; Malte Meinshausen *et al.*, 'Realization of Paris Agreement Pledges May Limit Warming Just below 2°C' (2022) 604 *Nature* 304.

technological solutions have been readily available, 'there is no silver bullet to address climate change'.[177]

While the Paris Agreement was and is significant as a normative global legal framework to set the direction for the parties and for the private sector towards a non-fossil future, it has not succeeded in pushing the parties to take sufficient measures to mitigate and adapt to climate change, and the regular Conferences of the Parties have not pushed for the needed transformation. This explains the described movement of climate lawsuits where associations, interest groups, and individuals around the world, frustrated by the slowness of governments to tackle climate change, have turned to national courts and sued states and corporations for their lack of climate action – in many cases, successfully. It is also through these advocates, rather than the discreet reference to human rights in the preamble of the Paris Agreement, that the human rights dimension in relation to climate change has been confirmed in jurisprudence both by national courts and international human rights courts. In addition, in 2022 and 2023 respectively, the International Tribunal for the Law of Sea and the International Court of Justice were asked to give advisory opinions on climate change. And they did so by explicitly confirming states' obligations to prevent climate change – thus also confirming the importance of international law for climate transition about fifty years after the Stockholm Conference.[178]

I.4.7 *Waters*

I.4.7.1 Stockholm 1972

At Stockholm 1972, the international legal order for the oceans was very much in motion. Only a few months after the conference, the UNGA requested the convening of the third UN Conference on the Law of the Sea, which commenced the following year and, after a decade, resulted in the adoption of the 1982 UNCLOS, often referred to as a constitution for the oceans.[179] Compared to most other issue areas addressed at the Stockholm

[177] Van Asselt, n. 168, 384 (reference omitted).

[178] ITLOS, *Request for an Advisory Opinion Submitted by the Commission of Small Island States on Climate Change and International Law*, advisory opinion, Case no. 31, 21 May 2024; ICJ, *Obligations of States in Respect of Climate Change*, n 58, 23 July 2025.

[179] See, e.g., Tommy T. B. Koh of Singapore, President of the Third United Nations Conference on the Law of the Sea, *Address to the 185th Plenary Session of the Third United Nations Conference on the Law of the Sea*, UN Doc. A/CONF.62/SR.185, 6 December 1982, para. 48 who states that 'the question is whether we have achieved our fundamental objective of producing a comprehensive constitution for the oceans which will stand the test of time. My answer to this question is in the affirmative.'

Conference, the management of the marine environment and its resources was less of a novelty in international law. Some aspects of the law of the sea were already fairly well established when international environmental law began to develop more generally, which, according to *Richard Barnes*, 'stymied the receptiveness of the law of the sea to wider environmental and human-centric concerns'.[180]

Already in 1958, the first UN Conference on the Law of the Sea, which took place in Geneva, succeeded in adopting four separate conventions setting out rules on the territorial sea and the contiguous zone, the high seas, fishing and the conservation of the living resources of the high seas, and the continental shelf. Still, the rules pertaining to environmental protection remained rudimentary in the law of the sea and generally focused on specific forms of pollution, such as oil discharges from ships.[181] Fundamental issues for the management of marine resources also remained unsettled, including the permissible breadth of the territorial sea and of exclusive fisheries zones. The long-held idea of the inexhaustible nature of the oceans made conservation efforts seem less pressing. As late as 1962, the oceans' renewable fisheries could be referred to as 'difficult or impossible to deplete in a degree technologically irreversible'.[182] Thus, it is not surprising that this was not addressed in international law. As for marine pollution, it was held in the year of the Stockholm Conference that such pollution had recently been recognized as a problem of global dimensions, and a legal response was only beginning to form.[183]

Another such recognition concerned protection of the marine environment in areas not covered by national jurisdiction. Two years before the Stockholm Conference, the UNGA adopted the Declaration of Principles Governing the Seabed and Ocean Floor beyond the Limits of National Jurisdiction, stating that the seabed and ocean floor, and the subsoil beyond the limits of national jurisdiction are 'the common heritage of mankind'.[184] This Declaration sets out that the area is open exclusively for peaceful purposes and that the exploration and exploitation of the resources of the area and other related

180 Richard Barnes, 'The Stockholm Declaration at Sea: Influences on the Content and Context of the Law of the Sea', in this volume, 403 (reference omitted).

181 Ludwik A. Teclaff, 'International Law and the Protection of the Oceans from Pollution' (1972) 40 *Fordham Law Review* (*FLR*) 529, 534.

182 Myres S. McDougal & William T. Burke, *The Public Order of the Oceans: A Contemporary International Law of the Sea* (Yale University Press, 1962), vii.

183 Teclaff, n. 181, 529.

184 UNGA, *Declaration of Principles, Governing the Sea-bed and the Ocean Floor, and the Subsoil Thereof, beyond the Limits of National Jurisdiction*, UN Doc. A/RES 2749(XXV), 17 December 1970.

activities shall be governed by an international regime. Importantly, according to the Declaration, states shall cooperate to adopt rules, standards, and procedures for the prevention of pollution and contamination and other hazards to the marine environment, and the 'interference with the ecological balance of the marine environment' and to protect and conserve the natural resources as well as to prevent damage to the flora and fauna of the marine environment.

At the Stockholm Conference, considerable attention was given to marine pollution and to the management of fisheries,[185] as reflected by Principle 7 of the Stockholm Declaration: 'States shall take all possible steps to prevent pollution of the seas by substances that are liable to create hazards to human health, to harm living resources and marine life, to damage amenities or to interfere with other legitimate uses of the sea.'

The Stockholm Action Plan also sets out 'general principles for assessment and control of marine pollution', which governments are recommended to endorse as guiding concepts for the upcoming Conference on the Law of the Sea,[186] and it recognizes the need for developing international legal instruments to protect species inhabiting international waters or those which migrate from one country to another.[187]

The lack of effective international regimes to preserve fish stocks at the time of the Stockholm Conference is also reflected in the critical observation in the Stockholm Action Plan that damage to fish stocks has often occurred because regulatory action is taken too slowly and in noting that 'the need for management action to be nearly unanimous' has reduced action to 'the minimum acceptable level'.[188] *Yoshifumi Tanaka* makes the important observation that, while before 1972, the environmental relation between watercourses and the oceans had not been subject to much attention, 'the inter-link between the oceans and rivers, although embryonic, was reflected already in the report of the Stockholm Conference'.[189] Thus, the Stockholm Action Plan asserts that the oceans are the ultimate recipient for wastes discharged into river systems and recommends the establishment of an exploratory programme to assess the environmental

185 For a review and overview of the impact of the Stockholm Conference on the Law of the Marine Environment, see Myron H. Nordquist, John Norton Moore & Said Mahmoudi (eds.), *The Stockholm Declaration and Law of the Marine Environment* (Kluwer Law International, 2003).

186 Stockholm Action Plan, n. 9, Recommendation 92 and Annex III.

187 *Ibid.*, Recommendation 32.

188 *Ibid.*, Recommendation 46.

189 Yoshifumi Tanaka, 'Linking International Regimes on Oceans and Fresh Water since the 1972 Stockholm Conference: The Case of Preventing Land-based Marine Plastic Pollution via International Watercourses', in this volume, 432.

effects of water management upon the oceans and define terms and estimate the costs for a comprehensive programme of action.[190]

With respect to freshwater resources, international law of 1972 was still influenced by conceptions of strong state sovereignty and a reluctance to make substantive commitments regarding the use of freshwater resources, also in transboundary settings. Although a large number of bilateral or regional treaties had been concluded, they primarily set out obligations relating to the equitable use of shared lakes and streams and on consultation with concerned states before taking actions with transboundary impacts. Around the time of the Stockholm Conference, it was held that 'no one would suggest that this is more than a modest beginning or that the treaties have achieved more than a modicum of success'.[191] While reflecting Principle 21 of the Stockholm Declaration in emphasizing 'the right of permanent sovereignty of each country concerned to develop its own resources', the Stockholm Action Plan nevertheless recommends that governments consider the creation 'of river-basin commissions or other appropriate machinery for co-operation between interested States for water resources common to more than one jurisdiction'.[192]

4.7.2 Stockholm 2022

Fifty years later, in some respects international environmental law has developed significantly with regard to the marine and freshwater environments; in others, not so much. The oceans are subject to huge pressures, including impacts of climate change, such as warming and ocean acidification. Despite a number of regional fishery management organizations, many fisheries are unsustainable. And despite regional efforts to address marine pollution, there is no general indication of progress in preventing such pollution. In addition, compared to 1972, plastic litter has emerged as a major source of marine pollution and as a major concern.

Already in 1974, two regional sea conventions for the protection of the marine environment were adopted (the Paris Convention for the North-east Atlantic,[193] and the Helsinki Convention for the Baltic Sea),[194] and UNEP had launched the Regional Seas Programme, which would result in several quite similar regional conventions – the first one in 1976 for the

190 Stockholm Action Plan, n. 9, Recommendation 55.
191 Albert E. Utton, 'International Water Quality Law' (1973) 13 *Natural Resources Journal* 282.
192 Stockholm Action Plan, n. 9, Recommendation 51.
193 Paris Convention, n. 132.
194 Helsinki Convention, n. 133.

Mediterranean.[195] At the global scale, UNCLOS was adopted in 1982, although it took until 1994 for it to enter into force.[196] While UNCLOS itself does not provide for detailed protection of the marine environment, it enshrines the fundamental principles for the management of ocean resources and the prevention of pollution. It has been seen to represent 'a sea change' by introducing the 'unqualified obligation on all states to "protect and preserve the marine environment"',[197] and it sets out active obligations to protect and preserve rare or fragile species and ecosystems. Yet, as *Richard Barnes* notes, 'although the idea of sustainable use is echoed in the provisions on fisheries conservation and management, UNCLOS does not adopt terminology used in the Stockholm Declaration such as "ecosystems", "safeguard", "careful planning", "improvement", "wise use", and "benefit sharing". … Indeed, it has been remarked that UNCLOS provides a rudimentary framework for the protection of habitats.'[198]

UNCLOS is rightly described as a living treaty,[199] evidenced, inter alia, by the adoption of the 1994 UNCLOS Part XI Agreement,[200] revising the regime for the deep seabed, and the 1995 Fish Stocks Agreement,[201] comprising, inter alia, the precautionary approach and an ecosystem-based approach.

Negotiations for the agreement on biodiversity in areas beyond national jurisdiction, which were ongoing at the time of the Stockholm+50 Meeting, were completed soon after the conference and resulted in the 2023 BBNJ Agreement. Drawing on the CBD, the BBNJ Agreement sets out rules on access to marine genetic resources in areas beyond national jurisdiction (ABNJ) and on the fair and equitable sharing of benefits arising from such resources. It also sets out elaborate requirements for environmental impact assessment in ABNJ, provides a framework for the establishment of area-based

195 Convention for the Protection of the Mediterranean Sea against Pollution, 1976, 1102 UNTS 27.

196 Since large parts of UNCLOS, n. 55, including those on protection of the marine environment, are widely considered as reflective of customary international law, the rules were applicable law before 1995 as well as in relation to non-parties.

197 David Freestone, 'Principles Applicable to Modern Oceans Governance' (2008) 23 *International Journal of Marine and Coastal Law* 385, 387 (reference omitted).

198 Barnes, n. 180, 413 (references omitted).

199 See, e.g., Jill Barrett & Richard Barnes (eds.), *Law of the Sea: UNCLOS as a Living Treaty* (British Institute of International and Comparative Law, 2016).

200 Agreement Relating to the Implementation of Part XI of the United Nations Convention on the Law of the Sea of 10 December 1982, 1994, 1836 UNTS 3.

201 Agreement for the Implementation of the Provisions of the United Nations Convention on the Law of the Sea of 10 December 1982 Relating to the Conservation and Management of Straddling Fish Stocks and Highly Migratory Fish Stocks, and Related Instruments, 1995, 2167 UNTS 3.

management tools, including marine protected areas in ABNJ, and links ocean and climate governance by clearly recognizing the role of marine management in the fight against climate change. In fact, the BBNJ Agreement is the first international agreement in which the carbon cycling of the oceans, and, thereby, a fundamental mechanism for stabilizing the climate, is explicitly referred to.[202] Still the ability of UNCLOS to deal with the pressing challenges facing the oceans can be questioned, and the Convention's perceived status as a constitution for the oceans has been described as 'a straitjacket for the regime . . . preventing the serious exploration of alternative epistemological imaginaries of the law of the sea'.[203]

In terms of basic concepts, including the preconditions for exercising jurisdiction over marine areas, the developments of international law from 1972 to 2022 have been profound. It is now established both in UNCLOS and in customary law that coastal states can claim a territorial sea of 12 nautical miles from the baseline as well as an exclusive economic zone, where they can legitimately exclude all other states from the living and non-living natural resources, for a further 188 nautical miles. As poignantly noted, the environmental law of the sea differs from most other fields of environmental law in that UNCLOS is based on a concept of 'nationalisation rather than internationalisation' of oceans.[204] Here, a general push by many states to put larger marine areas under their exclusive control has coincided with the idea that such control helps prevent the tragedy of the commons.

As mentioned, at the time of the 1972 Stockholm Conference, the UNGA had declared the area beyond national jurisdiction a 'common heritage of mankind' and that states should cooperate in the adoption and implementation of rules and procedures to prevent pollution, contamination and the interference with the ecological balance, to protect and conserve natural resources, and to prevent damage to fauna and flora in the high seas. At the time of the Stockholm+50 Meeting, we see some significant steps in this direction by the adoption of the BBNJ Agreement. On that note, *Dire Tladi*, while observing the shortcomings of the BBNJ Agreement, not least the fact that the common heritage principle is not explicitly given any operational

202 Niels Krabbe & David Langlet, 'Changing Human Uses of Marine Resources and International Law: Looking Ahead', in Niels Krabbe & David Langlet (eds.), *Marine Bioprospecting, Biodiversity and Novel Uses of Ocean Resources: New Approaches in International Law* (Hart Publishing, 2024), 233 (references omitted).

203 See Karen N. Scott, 'The LOSC: "A Constitution for the Oceans" in the Anthropocene?' (2023) 41 *Australian Year Book of International Law* 269 (with further references).

204 Geir Ulfstein, 'The Marine Environment and International Environmental Governance', in Myron H. Nordquist, John Norton Moore & Said Mahmoudi (eds.), *The Stockholm Declaration and Law of the Marine Environment* (Brill, 2003), 102.

content (which was the main issue called for by developing countries), still finds it 'remarkable that the common heritage of humankind is reflected at all when, for much of the negotiations, it had become a forgotten child'.[205]

The development of international law on freshwater since 1972 includes, in addition to different specific river-basin regimes, the adoption of two conventions of general application – the regional 1992 Water Convention[206] and the 1997 Watercourses Convention[207] of global scope – as well as the development of the ILC's Draft Articles on the Law of Transboundary Aquifers.[208] While historically strongly centred on rights of usage, environmental concerns have increasingly become a priority in freshwater law, although with a strong focus on international watercourses.[209] Despite the two conventions on international watercourses, there is still no global treaty establishing a general protective framework for the freshwater environment. And, with respect to the development of international law on the marine and freshwater nexus from 1972 to 2022, *Yoshifumi Tanaka* concludes that 'it may be said that the Stockholm Declaration constituted a forward-looking instrument. Despite the great wave of treaty making in the field of the protection of the marine and freshwater environments, however, little attention has been paid to the interaction between the marine and freshwater regimes.'[210]

Overall, the legal regime for freshwater remains fragmented. Although states are not free to pollute or destroy the ecology of shared water courses, international law on freshwater is characterized by a multitude of bilateral and regional agreements of varying nature and less clear in terms of obligations not to cause harm or to sustainably manage ecosystems, compared to the law of the sea, thus making it difficult to draw definitive conclusions concerning the legal requirements.[211]

[205] Tladi, n. 67, 488.
[206] Convention on the Protection and Use of Transboundary Watercourses and International Lakes, 1992, 1936 UNTS 269.
[207] Convention on the Law of the Non-Navigational Uses of International Watercourses, 1997, 2999 UNTS 77.
[208] ILC, Draft Articles on the Law of Transboundary Aquifers, UN Doc. A/ CN.4/ L.724, 29 May 2008.
[209] Laurence Boisson de Chazournes, *Fresh Water in International Law* (2nd ed., Oxford University Press, 2021), 8.
[210] Tanaka, n. 189, 448.
[211] Patricia W. Birnie, Alan E. Boyle & Catherine Redgwell, *International Law and the Environment* (Oxford University Press, 2009), 580.

I.4.8 *Nature and Biodiversity*

I.4.8.1 Stockholm 1972

At Stockholm 1972, the protection of wildlife already had some pedigree in international law. However, since the first treaties concerning wildlife protection were concluded in the early twentieth century, the focus had been, with a few regional exceptions, on specific species or groups of species, often ones that were seen as particularly charismatic or useful.[212] A well-known example is the 1946 Whaling Convention that was adopted with the intention of 'safeguarding for future generations the great natural resources represented by the whale stocks'.[213]

At the time of the Stockholm Conference, the focus of international law in this field started to shift, and a new generation of agreements emerged. It was widely recognized that most species – at least in the terrestrial domain – are affected more by the quality of their living environment than by hunting or other intentional targeting. This led to the safeguarding of habitats or ecosystems emerging as a cornerstone of wildlife protection. *Nicolas de Sadeleer* refers to the 1971 Ramsar Convention and the 1972 World Heritage Convention:

> Due to the irreparable loss for mankind in economic, scientific, and cultural terms caused by the disappearance of wetlands, the Ramsar Convention, for its part, sought to protect lakeland areas that were particularly threatened by human activity. The 1972 World Heritage Convention was an important step in the process of the 'heritagization' of nature. It was adopted to reconcile the protection of cultural heritage with the protection of natural heritage.[214]

The development of international law on nature protection was essentially driven by the elaboration of new treaties, and few, if any, principles of customary international law addressing conservation or biodiversity had emerged before 1972.[215]

212 See, e.g., Braulio Ferreira de Souza Dias & Kathryn Garforth, 'Historical Perspectives on the Challenge of Biodiversity Conservation', in Michael Faure (ed.), *Elgar Encyclopedia of Environmental Law* (Edward Elgar, 2017), 15; Cyrille de Klemm, in collaboration with Clare Shine, *Biological Diversity Conservation and the Law: Legal Mechanisms for Conserving Species and Ecosystems*, IUCN Environmental Policy and Law Paper no. 29 (International Union for Conservation of Nature [IUCN], 1993), 7.

213 International Convention for the Regulation of Whaling, 1946, 161 UNTS 74, preambular para. 2.

214 Nicolas de Sadeleer, 'The Influence of the Stockholm Conference on the Development of Nature Protection Law at an International Level and in Europe', in this volume, 492; Convention on Wetlands of International Importance Especially as Waterfowl Habitat, 1971, 996 UNTS 245 (Ramsar Convention); Convention for the Protection of the World Cultural and Natural Heritage, 1972, 1037 UNTS 151 (World Heritage Convention).

215 Birnie, Boyle & Redgwell, n. 211, 602.

At the Stockholm Conference itself, significant attention was given to nature as a resource to be safeguarded for present and future generations. Notably, Principle 3 of the Stockholm Declaration is concerned with the need to maintain and, wherever practicable, restore or improve the capacity of the earth to produce vital renewable resources. Somewhat less anthropocentrically, Principle 4 recognizes that man 'has a special responsibility to safeguard and wisely manage the heritage of wildlife and its habitat', which are seen as gravely imperilled, and that nature conservation, including wildlife, must receive importance in planning for economic development. The Stockholm Action Plan recommends the establishment of a programme to expand data-gathering processes so as to assess the total economic value of wildlife resources, helping to 'demonstrate to questioning nations the value of their resources'.[216] It also urges governments, with the assistance of relevant international and regional agencies, to continue the preparation of conventions required for the conservation of the world's natural resources and cultural heritage.[217]

Genetic resources get considerable attention in the Stockholm Action Plan, including through a recommendation that governments agree to an international programme to preserve the world's genetic resources and establish a global network of national and regional institutes relating to genetic resource conservation.[218] While, again, the Stockholm Conference indicated a shift in protecting nature through international law, neither the North-South nor gender dimension on these issues is reflected in the outcome of the conference. Rather, as *Claudia Ituarte-Lima* observes, 'the Stockholm Declaration has an essentialist view of "man". It lacks specification of who caused most of the social-ecological damage and, hence, obscures who bears most of the responsibility of the ecological breakdown.'[219]

I.4.8.2 Stockholm 1972

Fifty years later, there is a plethora of international – global and regional – agreements dedicated to the preservation and sustainable use of the world's biological resources, and the understanding of what is needed for the preservation of nature has evolved. In less than a decade in the 1970s, four universal conventions relating to nature conservation were adopted: the 1971 Ramsar

216 Stockholm Action Plan, n. 9, Recommendation 30.
217 *Ibid.*, Recommendation 98.
218 *Ibid.*, Recommendations 39–45.
219 Claudia Ituarte-Lima, 'Fifty Years of International Law-Making on the Environment: Women Shaping Legal Principles and Solidarity', in this volume, 512 (reference omitted).

Convention,[220] the 1972 World Heritage Convention,[221] the 1973 Convention on Trade in Endangered Species of Wild Fauna and Flora,[222] and the 1979 Convention on the Conservation of Migratory Species of Wild Animals.[223]

With the 1980s came an increased emphasis on systems perspectives and the intrinsic value of nature. The 1980 World Conservation Strategy,[224] commissioned by UNEP and prepared by (what is now) the International Union for Conservation of Nature (IUCN), called for 'a new environmental ethic' and emphasized the need for maintaining essential ecological processes and life-support systems. This was followed by the adoption by the UNGA of the 1982 World Charter for Nature,[225] according to which 'man is part of nature' while 'every form of life is unique, warranting respect regardless of its worth to man'. The World Charter also establishes that: 'Ecosystems and organisms, as well as the land, marine and atmospheric resources that are utilized by man, shall be managed to achieve and maintain optimum sustainable productivity, but not in such a way as to endanger the integrity of those other ecosystems or species with which they coexist.'

Arguably, the most significant development in this area of law is the adoption, in connection with the Rio Summit, of the 1992 CBD, with its triple objectives of 'conservation of biological diversity, the sustainable use of its components and the fair and equitable sharing of the benefits arising out of the utilisation of genetic resources'.[226] As described by *Elisa Morgera*: 'The negotiations and adoption of the CBD in the early 1990s revolutionized the international legal landscape on nature protection, with a series of regulatory innovations – new international legal concepts (biodiversity, genetic resources, ecosystems) and objectives of international regulation (sustainable use and fair and equitable benefit sharing).'[227]

The subsequent elaboration and endorsement of the ecosystem approach by the Conference of the Parties to the CBD marked a shift in the conceptualization and management of natural resources, putting emphasis on

220 Ramsar Convention, n. 214.

221 World Heritage Convention, n. 214.

222 Convention on Trade in Endangered Species of Wild Fauna and Flora, 1973, 993 UNTS 243.

223 Convention on the Conservation of Migratory Species of Wild Animals, 1979, 1651 UNTS 333.

224 IUCN, UNEP & World Wildlife Fund, *World Conservation Strategy: Living Resource Conservation for Sustainable Development*, 1980.

225 UNGA Resolution 37/7, n. 12.

226 CBD, n. 52, art. 1.

227 Elisa Morgera, 'The Progressive Development of International Biodiversity Law from the 1972 Stockholm Conference to the Synergistic Protection of Biodiversity and Human Rights, Including at the Ocean-Climate Nexus', in this volume, 456 (footnotes omitted).

integrated and long-term management based on science while also involving local populations and stakeholders and making use of their knowledge.[228] In addition, as pointed out by *Claudia Ituarte-Lima*, in contrast to the Stockholm Declaration, the CBD highlights the vital role of women in the conservation and sustainable use of biological diversity and supports the full participation of women in policy-making and implementation.[229]

Just a few months after the Stocholm+50 Meeting, the Conference of the Parties to the CBD adopted the ambitious Kunming–Montreal Global Biodiversity Framework, which sets as a target that the loss of areas of high biodiversity importance be brought close to zero by 2030 by ensuring that all areas are under 'participatory, integrated and biodiversity inclusive spatial planning and/or effective management processes'.[230] Still, in parallel with the growth and development of international law pertaining to the protection of species and ecosystems, the anthropogenic pressures on the natural environment have increased dramatically and goals relating to halting the loss of biodiversity have been repeatedly missed. As emphasized by *Nicolas de Sadeleer*,

> the existence of these agreements should not lull us into thinking that all natural components are now well protected. . . . It is mainly ignorance, lack of political will, lack of financial and human resources, and growing pressures on ecosystems as a result of the gross domestic product and demographic growth that explain the failure of international nature protection law.[231]

Although some of the concepts set out in the Stockholm Declaration have usefully guided the development of international biodiversity law since then, *Elisa Morgera* reminds us that 'the sectoral and largely incremental approach of the Stockholm Declaration is no longer fit to address the urgent triple planetary crises that we are facing'.[232]

1.5 TOWARDS STOCKHOLM+100

The contributions to this volume capture the development of international environmental law in the half-century between the 1972 Stockholm

[228] See Decision CBD V/6 CO on Ecosystem Approach, Fifth Ordinary Meeting of the Conference of the Parties to the Convention on Biological Diversity, May 2000.

[229] Ituarte-Lima, n. 219.

[230] Kunming–Montreal Global Biodiversity Framework, annexed to Decision 15/4 by the Conference of the Parties to the CBD, Doc. CBD/COP/DEC/15/4, 19 December 2022, Target 1.

[231] De Sadeleer, n. 214, 495.

[232] Morgera, n. 227, 471 (references omitted).

Conference and the 2022 Stockholm+50 Meeting. We saw in the snapshots above that in some areas of international environmental law the difference as per 1972 and 2022 is remarkable, with aspects that were not even thought of in 1972 being highly important in 2022. In other areas, essentially the same legal issues were addressed in 1972 but in quite different terms and reflecting quite different conceptions compared to 2022. And, in yet other issue areas, quite little has changed in international law over the course of fifty years. Obviously, changed circumstances in terms of increased environmental stresses and impacts, increased population (the world population just about doubled from almost four billion in 1972 to eight billion in 2022), and developments of new technologies and new scientific insights have influenced international environmental law in this period. Furthermore, some important changes in these fifty years are not the result of new scientific understandings or new or increased harm to the environment but, rather, follow from changed ideas and new conceptions and thinking.

Despite these changes, in many fundamental respects, the situation in 2022 is no less problematic or frustrating than in 1972. Rather, we are confronted with – indeed, have caused – plenty of urgent environmental problems. Among them, the United Nations now frequently refers to the triple planetary crisis of climate change, pollution, and biodiversity loss. The urgency of climate change and biodiversity loss is clearly much greater in 2022 than fifty years before, despite the elaboration of comprehensive legal regimes in international law to address them.

On a more structural level, there are still profound differences in the social and economic developments and capacities of states, and this still shapes international environmental law-making and discourse. Even so, there has been no major shift in the international economic system or in international economic law on matters such as trade, investments, taxation, or corporate responsibility so as to promote the protection of the environment.

It is difficult to assess the long-term effects of an event soon after it takes place. Still, it is not a far-fetched guess that the Stockholm+50 Meeting will achieve far less than the Stockholm Conference in influencing future policy- and law-making, and it was never intended to achieve much in that direction either. Still, more important than yet another policy document would be for such a meeting to spark off global citizens engagement and expand public participation on environmental matters around the world, as happened only a few years before the Stockholm+50 Meeting when millions of people around the world manifested for further climate action.

When looking ahead at Stockholm+50, it is easy to get cynical. The push for international cooperation and solidarity is not at its peak, the world is still affected by the aftermath of global COVID 19 pandemic, and one of the permanent members of the UN Security Council has initiated a full-scale war against a neighbouring country, thus violating one of the most fundamental rules of international law. As far as global governance and law are concerned, at the time of Stockholm+50 sustainability and environmental matters are not really 'trending' on the agenda of many political leaders. For sure, leadership for sustainable development is in short supply.

On the positive side, in 2022, the UNGA did adopt the resolution recognizing the right to a clean, healthy, and sustainable development as a fundamental human right; in 2023, the BBNJ Agreement was adopted; in 2022, a comprehensive and ambitious global biodiversity framework was agreed under the CBD; and a new global treaty on plastics may be on the horizon. And, importantly, international courts are confirming that existing treaty regimes on human rights and the law of the sea impose obligations on states to take climate action. While not surprising, the 2025 International Court of Justice advisory opinion on the obligations of states in respect of climate change is a welcome confirmation of states' obligations to prevent climate change, based on both conventional and customary international law.[233]

In addition to strengthening the protection in the many issue areas discussed in this volume, such as the protection of the marine environment and the atmosphere, some of the key tasks and challenges of international environmental law are to expand and promote the rule of law in environmental matters across state borders. Among many aspects, this includes further implementation of the human rights approach to environmental matters; the development and application of participatory rights also in transboundary contexts; and the development of legal frameworks to hold corporations to account across state borders.

Clearly, the establishment of legal structures for participation in environmental decision-making and access to courts in environmental matters, at least in a regional context, are among the most remarkable developments over the last fifty years. But, in parallel with the strengthening of participatory rights and the recognition of a human right to a healthy environment, we also witness widespread and, in some regions, accelerating harassment, persecution, and penalization – and even killing – of those who act for the protection of the environment or for local and indigenous rights.

Despite Principle 22 of the Stockholm Declaration, fifty years later little has been done in international law to prevent companies from escaping environmental responsibility and liability by hiding behind state borders and national jurisdictions. Thus far, the possibility to hold companies to account in

[233] *Obligations of States in Respect of Climate Change*, n 58.

transboundary contexts has essentially depended on the national laws of the states concerned, without any international legal framework. Still, we see some important steps in that direction. One such step is the European Union's Directive on Sustainability Corporate Due Diligence, which introduces obligations for companies 'regarding actual and potential human rights adverse impacts and environmental adverse impacts, with respect to their own operations, the operations of their subsidiaries, and the operations carried out by their business partners in the chains of activities of those companies'.[234] In addition to prescribing what corporations should do not to cause such adverse effects on human rights and the environment (and also to mitigate climate change), the Directive includes provisions on supervision and penalties. Despite its flawed provisions on civil liability, this is the first legally binding supranational framework on transboundary corporate responsibility, and it should spur similar developments in international law.

Another element of the rule of law would be to make sure that state borders do not prevent members of the public from exercising participatory rights in environmental matters. The most advanced legal frameworks on the matter – the Aarhus Convention and the Escazú Agreement – apply across state borders and make it possible for members of the public to also engage in decision-making with transboundary impacts. One pertinent illustration of this is the findings of the Aarhus Convention Compliance Committee that a Convention party must make sure that members of the public in neighbouring countries are informed about decision-making procedures and can participate effectively if they can be affected by the activity in question.[235]

Making global environmental governance and law more effective in the next fifty years will require further integration of environmental concepts, principles, and considerations with other areas of international law. As already highlighted, international economic law is one such case, which has not evolved adequately since the Stockholm Conference so as to promote fairness and equity and take states' differentiated responsibilities into account, in line with the calls in the Stockholm Declaration and the Rio Declaration to further sustainable development. Although the 2030 Agenda for Sustainable Development and the SDGs do not address these shortcomings of international economic law, they neatly show how environmental matters can be ambitiously integrated with other areas of policy-making. We see this

[234] Council Directive (EU) 2024/1760 on Corporate Sustainability Due Diligence, (2024) OJ L1764, art. 1.

[235] Aarhus Convention Compliance Committee, *Findings and Recommendations with Regard to Communication ACCC/C/2013/91 Concerning Compliance by the United Kingdom of Great Britain and Northern Ireland*, Doc. UN Doc. ECE/ MP.PP/ C.1/ 2017/, 24 July 2017, 14.

integrated approach as a way ahead in future international environmental law as well. Several SDGs explicitly refer to environmental matters, and also those that do not do so clearly have environmental repercussions. While addressed to governments and institutions, essentially all the SDGs depend on adequate implementation of international law for their achievement. International law is also essential for staying within the planetary boundaries, and, again, for the promotion of the rule of law in environmental contexts.

At the time of the Stockholm+50 Meeting, yet another important feature of international law, also pertaining to the rule of law, had achieved much attention: the notion of *ecocide* as an international criminalization of acts that may result in substantial and severe harm to the environment. Interestingly, the concern for ecocide was highlighted already at the Stockholm Conference in the statement by Olof Palme, the prime minister of the host country of the conference:

> The immense destruction brought about by indiscriminate bombing, by large scale use of bull-dozers and herbicides is an outrage sometimes described as *ecocide* which requires urgent international attention. It is shocking that only preliminary discussions of this matter have been possible so far in the United Nations and at the conferences of the International Committee of the Red Cross where it has been taken up by my country and other.[236]

Despite the described sense of shock already at the time of the Stockholm Conference that there had only been 'preliminary discussions of this matter', fifty years later the discussions on ecocide remain preliminary, but there is a strong push for including it as a defined crime in the 1998 Rome Statute of the International Criminal Court.[237] The Rome Statute defines four serious crimes: the crime of genocide, crimes against humanity, war crimes, and the crime of aggression. Although the Statute applies to certain cases of harm to the environment – for instance, in the case of war crime – it does not set out a specific crime focusing on harm to the environment. At the time of the Stockholm+50 Meeting, the growing demands of including the crime of ecocide in the Rome Statute are gaining momentum. It is difficult to see any rational argument why states who are already parties to the Rome Statute would be against including the crime of ecocide, provided that it is defined so as to be on par, in terms of seriousness and severity, with the other crimes defined by the Statute. Although some states – in particular, states that are not

236 UN Conference on the Human Environment, *Statement by Prime Minister Olof Palme in the Plenary Meeting*, 6 June 1972, https://olofpalme.arbark.se.

237 Rome Statute of the International Criminal Court, 1998, 2187 UNTS 90.

parties to the Statute – might be against including ecocide in the list of international crimes, it would be a sound development of international law that states come to an agreement of criminalizing the most serious and grave acts against the environment. And we think that it is quite likely that, long before Stockholm+100, ecocide will be included in the Rome Statute as an international crime.

It is difficult to say whether the wave of climate litigation across the globe, mentioned above, predominantly in domestic courts but also in international fora, gives an indication for the future. In many cases of climate litigation, where citizens and organizations use various legal arenas to hold states to their international and domestic commitments, the substantive matter of preventing climate change has been linked to human and participatory rights. This creates a new dynamic with the potential to transform international environmental law, by making it increasingly applicable not only in inter-state contexts but also in national cases and not only top down but also from below. In addition, the cases illustrate how different fields of international law – on climate change, human rights, and participatory rights in environmental matters – can be integrated rather than fragmented. Importantly, they also show that environmental and climate transition can take place within the framework of democracy and the rule of law. Will this also be an issue to look back on at Stockholm+100?

The emerging calls at the time of the Stockholm+50 Meeting for the recognition of rights of nature tie in with this development, and it may well have a bearing on Stockholm+100. While this can contribute to strengthening the 'voice' of those affected by destructive economic practices or technologies used without due caution, the extent to which the granting of legal personality to streams and forests is a successful environmental strategy differs between legal systems. And while it may work in certain jurisdictions, there is no indication that it would generally make environmental laws or the protection of the environment more effective than perceiving the environment as a public interest, to be invoked, referred to, and protected in decision-making by public authorities as well as by members of the public. Still, at a more profound level, acknowledging rights to nature points to a potential shift in perception, from an anthropocentric view where all non-human entities and features of the physical world are seen as resources for human convenience to the recognition of the world as a complex web where all parts are needed and deserve recognition of their value and needs.

So, perhaps, at the time of Stockholm+100, we may have come to understand the relationship between humans and the physical world in which we live differently. Such changes happen. We have seen how the new notion of the environment changed our thinking at the time of the 1972 Stockholm Conference, so as to see it not only as a background but also as a thing with its own essence, something vulnerable, where larger scales are captured and the local and even microscopic link with the planetary. And we saw how it influenced international environmental law. If, by Stockholm+100, the perception of the relationship between humans and the physical world will have changed so as to further acknowledge the intrinsic value of non-human entities and features, coming generations will have something positive to look back to and build upon. And as part of that development, environmental law – in local and global contexts – may enable us to pursue a good life and expand our knowledge of the world with a perspective of humans as stewards rather than as mere consumers of the natural world.

PART I

CONCEPTS, STRUCTURES, AND INSTITUTIONS

1

Stockholm 1972 and the Birth of International Sustainable Development Law

Nico Schrijver

1.1 INTRODUCTION

This chapter examines the UN Conference on the Protection of the Human Environment held in Stockholm in 1972 (Stockholm Conference) and the birth of international sustainable development law in the subsequent half century.[1] First, it reviews the extent to which the concerns of sustainable development were addressed by the Stockholm Conference. Second, it discusses the meaning of the concept of sustainable development. Third, it addresses the gradual incorporation of sustainable development into international law. Fourth, it examines the contours of the emerging law of international sustainable development. The chapter ends with some conclusions and reflections on the role played by the 1972 Stockholm Conference in the inception and meaning of the principle of sustainable development and international sustainable development law.[2]

1.2 THE CONTEXT OF THE 1972 STOCKHOLM CONFERENCE

1.2.1 *On the Road to Stockholm: Early Balancing between Environment and Development*

The World Meteorological Organization (WMO) declared 1957 to be an International Geophysical Year, thereby focusing much attention on the necessity of more meteorological and ozone layer research in the light of

[1] This chapter elaborates on the 2022 Stockholm Environmental Law Lecture, given at Stockholm University on 24 November 2022.

[2] Here I build on earlier work: Nico Schrijver, *The Evolution of Sustainable Development in International Law* (Martinus Nijhoff, 2008), 173–207, also published in (2007) 329(4) *Recueil des Cours* 217.

pollution of the atmosphere and climate change.[3] During the 1960s repeated reports exposed the damaging effects of the use of pesticides, overfishing, the pressures of a growing world population, and increased pollution.[4] At the UN Educational, Scientific and Cultural Organization's (UNESCO) 1968 Conference on the Conservation of the Resources of the Biosphere, the idea of a declaration came up. This idea led Sweden to propose in 1968 a UN Conference on the Human Environment.[5] Initially, the developing countries were quite suspicious of this Western concern with the state of the environment. They feared that measures in this area could lead to a further deterioration of their economic position and fewer resources being made available for development assistance.

Since the early 1960s, developing countries have assembled in the so-called Group of 77, with the UN Conference on Trade and Development (UNCTAD), established in 1964,[6] and the UN General Assembly (UNGA) serving as their main platforms to address development issues.[7] On the eve of the UN conference, the UNGA adopted, following a Brazilian initiative, a quite controversial resolution that focused on the relationship between the environment and development.[8] This resolution stressed that environmental policies should be considered in the context of economic and social development, taking into account the special needs of developing countries.[9] However, Western countries felt that this text was too concerned with the problems of developing countries and ignored the environmental problems of Western countries. In the preparatory period leading up to the Stockholm Conference, several conflicts along these lines took place, but most were resolved in time. This was made possible thanks in part to a preliminary conference held 1971 in Founex, Switzerland, which took place at the initiative of the secretary-general of

[3] See United Nations, *UN Yearbook* (1957), 487.

[4] For the first influential book on this topic, see Rachel Carson, *Silent Spring* (Houghton Mifflin, 1962), which was later followed by Paul Ehrlich, *Population Bomb* (Ballantine Books, 1971).

[5] UNGA Resolution 2398 (XXIII), 3 December 1968; see also United Nations, *UN Yearbook* (1968), 473.

[6] UNGA Resolution 1995 (XIX), 30 December 1964.

[7] See, e.g., UNGA Resolution 1515 (XV), 15 December 1960 (concerted action for economic development); UNGA Resolution 1710 (XVI), 19 December 1961 (launching the first Development Decade of the United Nations); UNGA Resolution 2542 (XXIV) on the Declaration on Social Progress and Development, 11 December 1969.

[8] UNGA Resolution 2849 (XXVII), 20 December 1971 (adopted with eighty-five votes for, two against, and thirty-four abstentions); see also United Nations, *UN Yearbook* (1971), 311.

[9] UNGA Resolution 2849 (XXVII), n. 8, para. 5.

the Stockholm Conference (Maurice Strong, who was a Canadian). Founex led to more attention for the development aspects of the environment question.[10]

1.2.2 *The 1972 UN Stockholm Conference*

The Stockholm Conference itself took place in June 1972 and was attended by 113 states. The publication of the Club of Rome report, *The Limits to Growth*, gave an added stimulus and a sense of urgency to the conference.[11] However, the conference was somewhat overshadowed by a traditional East–West conflict over the exclusion from participation of the German Democratic Republic, which resulted in most Eastern European countries staying home. On the other hand, the People's Republic of China, which, as a result of the 'ping-pong diplomacy' of Henry Kissinger, the US secretary of state, was granted the Chinese seat in the United Nations in 1971,[12] participated very actively, particularly on the issue of the relationship between the environment and development.[13]

Somewhat disappointingly, only two heads of government participated in the conference: Swedish Prime Minister Olof Palme and India's Prime Minister Indira Ghandi. Ghandi noted at the conference:

> We do not wish to impoverish the environment any further and yet we cannot for a moment forget the grim poverty of large numbers of people. Are not poverty and need the greatest polluters? For instance, unless we are in a position to provide employment and purchasing power for the daily necessities of the tribal people and those who live in or around our jungles, we cannot prevent them from combing the forest for food and livelihood; from poaching and from despoiling the vegetation. When they themselves feel deprived, how can we urge the preservation of animals? How can we speak to those who live in villages and in slums about keeping the oceans, the rivers

10 See United Nations, *Development and Environment: Report and Working Papers of a Panel of Experts Convened by the Secretary-General of the United Nations Conference on the Human Environment* (Mouton, 1972); see also Karin Mickelson, 'The Stockholm Conference and the Creation of the South-North Divide in International Environmental Law and Policy', in Swawkat Alam *et al.* (eds.), *International Environmental Law and the Global South* (Cambridge University Press, 2015), 109.

11 Dennis Meadows *et al.*, *The Limits to Growth: A Report for the Club of Rome's Project on the Predicament of Mankind* (Universe Books, 1972).

12 The UN General Assembly (UNGA) decided 'to restore all its rights to the People's Republic of China and to recognise the representative of its government as the only legitimate representative of China'. UNGA Resolution 2758 (XXVI), 25 October 1971.

13 See United Nations, *UN Yearbook* (1972), 318.

and the air clean when their own lives are contaminated at the source? The environment cannot be improved in conditions of poverty. Nor can poverty be eradicated without the use of science and technology.[14]

Highlighting the tension between environmental and developmental concerns, she stated: 'We have to prove to the disinherited majority of the world that ecology and conservation will not work against their interest but will bring an improvement in their lives.'[15]

1.2.3 *Stockholm Declaration*

The most important result of the conference was the Stockholm Declaration on the Human Environment, which is often referred to as the 1972 Stockholm Declaration. The Declaration consists of a preamble, a seven-point proclamation (part I) and 26 principles (part II).[16] The preamble refers to 'the need for a common outlook and for common principles to inspire and guide the peoples of the world in the preservation and enhancement of the human environment'. In part I, it is proclaimed that '[t]he protection and improvement of the environment is a major issue which affects the well-being of peoples and economic development, throughout the world'.[17] It is added that 'man's capability to transform his surroundings, if used wisely, can bring to all peoples the benefits of development and the opportunity to enhance the quality of life. Wrongly or heedlessly applied, the same power can do incalculable harm to human beings and the human environment.'[18] The Stockholm Conference was succinctly aware of the differentiation between developing and industrialized countries: 'In the developing countries most of the environmental problems are caused by under-development. Millions continue to live far below the minimum levels required for a decent human existence, deprived of adequate food and clothing, shelter and education, health and sanitation. ... In the industrialized countries, environmental

[14] See her speech as published in Indira Gandhi, 'The Unfinished Revolution' (1972) 28 *Bulletin of the Atomic Scientists* 35, 36.

[15] *Ibid.*, 37.

[16] 'Declaration of the United Nations Conference on the Human Environment', in *Report of the UN Conference on the Human Environment*, UN Doc. A/CONF.48/14/Rev.1, 16 June 1972 (Stockholm Declaration). For a comprehensive analysis of the debates and the text, see Louis B. Sohn, 'The Stockholm Declaration on the Human Environment' (1973) 14 *Harvard International Law Journal* 423; see also Hans Blix, 'History of the Stockholm Declaration', in Myron H. Nordquist, John Norton Moore & Said Mahmoudi (eds.), *The Stockholm Declaration and Law of the Marine Environment* (Kluwer, 2003), 15.

[17] Stockholm Declaration, n. 16, para. 2.

[18] *Ibid.*, para. 3.

problems are generally related to industrialization and technological development.'[19] The Conference also proclaims: 'To defend and improve the human environment for present and future generations has become an imperative goal for mankind – a goal to be pursued together with, and in harmony with, the established and fundamental goals of peace and of world-wide economic and social development.'[20]

Part II includes twenty-six principles expressing the common conviction of the participating states. Principle 1 states: 'Man has the fundamental right to freedom, equality and adequate conditions of life, in an environment of a quality that permits a life of dignity and well-being, and he bears a solemn responsibility to protect and improve the environment for present and future generations.' The idea of sustainable development is fully reflected in all but these two words in Principles 2 and 3, respectively: 'The natural resources of the earth, including the air, water, land, flora and fauna and especially representative samples of ecosystems, must be safeguarded for the benefit of present and future generations, through careful planning or management, as appropriate', and '[t]he capacity of the earth to produce vital renewable resources must be maintained and, wherever practicable, restored or improved'. Similarly, Principle 5 stipulates the same precaution to guard non-renewable resources against the danger of their future exhaustion.

In view of these general principles, it is only logical that careful and rational management of natural resources was subsequently addressed in several principles.[21] Among them, Principle 21 has become the most well-known, and it expresses the right of every state to sovereignty over its own natural resources but balances this with the duty to ensure that activities under its jurisdiction or control do not cause any damage to the environment of other states or of areas outside the borders of national jurisdiction. In its substance, Principle 21 confirms the key dimensions of sustainable development in the sense of promoting development and ensuring environmental protection. Yet it also relates exclusively to the transboundary effects and the impact on the areas beyond national jurisdiction and not – or, at best, cursorily – to the management of natural resources at a national level. Careful and rational national management of natural resources, however, was taken up in Principles 2–5 and in Principles 13 and 14.

19 *Ibid.*, para. 4.
20 *Ibid.*, para. 6.
21 See Nico Schrijver, *Sovereignty over Natural Resources: Balancing Rights and Duties* (Cambridge University Press, 1997; reprinted 2008), 125–127.

The relationship between development and environment is comprehensively covered in Principles 6–12. They state that economic and social development is essential for a good human environment and that the correction of environmental failings caused by underdevelopment and natural disasters requires greater financial and technical aid. Principle 10 provides that, for developing countries, price stability and good returns for raw materials are of great importance for a better management of the environment. Hence, the Stockholm Declaration also demands that environmental policy should enhance and not diminish the development potential of developing countries. Therefore, it could well be argued that many of these points from the Stockholm Declaration bear a close resemblance to texts on sustainable development that would be adopted twenty years later in Rio de Janeiro,[22] thirty years later in Johannesburg,[23] and nearly forty-five years later in the Sustainable Development Goals (SDGs).[24]

1.2.4 *Establishment of the UN Environment Programme and the Adoption of the World Charter for Nature as Follow-Ups*

Another important result of the Stockholm Conference was the foundation in December 1972 of the UN Environment Programme (UNEP) as a subsidiary organ of the UNGA.[25] The UN Environment Programme became the first UN organ whose headquarters were situated in the capital of a developing country – namely, Nairobi, Kenya. Originally, UNEP's role was supposed to be that of a coordinator and catalyst in the field of environmental policy within the UN system.[26] However, in the course of time, UNEP has also undertaken a variety of operational activities. Although criticism of UNEP has often been harsh – like that faced by UNCTAD, founded in 1964 – it has been able to achieve many results, particularly in the first decades of its existence when it had a modest budget and a relatively small staff. Important examples include the Regional Seas Programme (which now involves nearly 150 countries and 18 regional seas conventions and action plans), integrated environment and development programmes for

22 'Rio Declaration on Environment and Development', in *Report of the UN Conference on Environment and Development*, UN Doc. A/CONF.151/26 (Vol. I), 12 August 1992 (Rio Declaration).

23 *Report on the World Summit on Sustainable Development, Johannesburg, South Africa*, UN Doc. A/CONF.199/20, 4 September 2002 (adopted by consensus).

24 See *Transforming Our World: The 2030 Agenda for Sustainable Development*, UN Doc. A/RES/70/1, 25 September 2015.

25 UNGA Resolution 2997 (XXVII), 15 December 1972.

26 See Bharat D. Desai, *International Environmental Governance: Towards UNEPO* (Brill, 2014).

the catchment areas of large river systems (such as the Zambezi and Mekong rivers), and the groundwork for various multilateral and regional environment treaties including those relating to the ozone layer (1985), hazardous wastes (1989), and biological diversity (1992).[27]

A notable early normative statement on sustainable development was included in a 1975 UNEP decision: 'Environmental management implies sustainable development of all countries, aimed at meeting basic human needs without transgressing the outer limits set to man's endeavours by the biosphere.'[28] Another historic document inaugurating the international discourse on sustainable development in the aftermath of the Stockholm Conference was the 1982 World Charter for Nature, adopted following a proposal tabled by President Mobutu Sese Seko of Zaire.[29] This charter is principally concerned with the conservation and better management of living natural resources. In fact, it was prepared by the International Union for the Conservation of Nature, with the support of UNEP, the UN Food and Agriculture Organization, and UNESCO. In 1980, these organizations jointly published the World Conservation Strategy with the subtitle: 'Living Resource Conservation for Sustainable Development'.[30] The 1975 UNEP decision and the 1982 World Charter for Nature are both clearly documents building upon the Stockholm Declaration and are the first in which the term 'sustainable development' was used in so many words. It is interesting to see how these early texts were already formulating the core ingredients of the concept of sustainable development. However, it was only the work of the Brundtland Commission in 1987 and the Rio Conference in 1992 that led to the first definitions and broader political embrace of the concept of sustainable development.

[27] For an analysis of the role of the UN Environment Programme (UNEP) in the genesis and implementation of multilateral environmental agreements, see Laurence D. Mee, 'The Role of UNEP and UNDP in Multilateral Environmental Agreements' (2005) 5 *International Environmental Agreements: Politics, Law and Economics* 227.

[28] See UNEP Governing Council Decision 20(III), 2 May 1975, s. II.9(b). I owe this citation to Marc Pallemaerts, 'De opkomst van het begrip "duurzame ontwikkeling" in het internationaal juridisch en politiek discours: een conceptuele revolutie' (1995) 21 *Recht en Kritiek* 383.

[29] UNGA Resolution 37/7 on World Charter for Nature, UN Doc. A/RES/37/7, 28 October 1982; see also United Nations, *UN Yearbook* (1982), 1024; Wolfgang E. Burhenne & Will A. Irwin, *The World Charter for Nature: Legislative History and Commentary* (2nd ed., Erich Schmidt Verlag, 1986).

[30] International Union for the Conservation of Nature, UNEP, & World Wildlife Fund, *World Conservation Strategy: Living Resource Conservation for Sustainable Development* (Gland, 1980).

1.3 THE MEANING OF SUSTAINABLE DEVELOPMENT

The World Commission on Environment and Development, headed by former Prime Minister Gro Harlem Brundtland of Norway, in its report *Our Common Future*, defines sustainable development as development that 'meets the needs of the present generation without compromising the ability of future generations to meet their own needs'.[31] This is still an admirably concise description of the core of the meaning of sustainable development. This description demonstrates, first, an awareness of the finite capacity of our planet and its natural resources. From this awareness follows, second, the need to maintain sustainability and regeneration capacity. Third, it emphasizes meeting the needs of the current world population by providing an adequate living standard and development opportunities. Fourth, the definition also takes into account the interests of future generations to meet their own needs – hence, highlighting the principle of intergenerational equity.

In a way, sustainable development builds on and combines three principal chapters of international law: first, international environmental law, which is a relatively young chapter of international law;[32] second, international economic law, especially as far as it relates to development;[33] and, third, international human rights law.[34] Each of these chapters includes substantive rights relating to the conservation and protection of the environment and the promotion of social progress and development as well as procedural rights such as the participation of developing countries in international economic decision-making and citizen access to information, access to justice, and participation in environmental decision-making.

[31] World Commission on Environment and Development, *Our Common Future* (Oxford University Press, 1987), 43; see also Nico J. Schrijver, 'Development: The Neglected Dimension in the Post-Rio International Law of Sustainable Development', in Hans C. Bugge & Christina Voigt (eds.), *Sustainable Development in International and National Law* (Europa Law Publishing, 2008), 223.

[32] See Philippe Sands & Jacqueline Peel, *Principles of International Environmental Law* (4th ed., Cambridge University Press, 2018); Patricia W. Birnie, Alan E. Boyle & Catherine Redgwell, *International Law and the Environment* (4th ed., Oxford University Press, 2021); Pierre Marie Dupuy & Jorge E. Viñuales, *International Environmental Law* (2nd ed., Cambridge University Press, 2018).

[33] See Friedl G. Weiss & Nico J. Schrijver (eds.), *International Law and Sustainable Development: Principles and Practice* (Martinus Nijhoff, 2004); Sharif Bhuiyan, Philippe Sands & Nico Schrijver (eds.), *International Law and Developing Countries: Essays in Honour of Kamal Hossain* (Brill, 2014).

[34] See Danish Institute for Human Rights, *Human Rights and the 2030 Agenda for Sustainable Development. Lessons Learned and Next Steps*, 13 July 2018, www.humanrights.dk.

Seven main elements of the principle of sustainable development can be distinguished.[35] The first, and perhaps the one most firmly grounded in international law, is the sustainable use of natural resources. Many treaties now emphasize this dimension, whether in relation to fishery agreements, sustainable timber production, or preserving biological diversity. The second element, which is also very important, is sound macro-economic development and what the facilitating role of international law can be towards this end. The third element is environmental conservation, a key component of sustainable development. The fourth is equity, both between current and future generations (that is, intergenerational equity) as well as equity for and among the people living now (that is, intra-generational equity). Fifth, there is the element of time. The time dimension of sustainable development is a fascinating one, with both short- and long-term elements. This element is particularly evident in the 2015 Paris Agreement on Climate Change.[36] In the short term, the international community must act urgently now to prevent further destruction of the precious and fragile planetary climate system. But there is also a need for a sustained, long-term strategy. The Paris Agreement obliges the parties to undertake ambitious efforts so as to hold the global average temperature to well below 2°C above pre-industrial levels and to pursue efforts to limit the temperature increase to 1.5°C above pre-industrial levels.[37] The sixth element relates to respect for human rights, public participation, and justice for all. Last, the seventh element, which is perhaps the most important but, at the same time, the most complicated, is how to integrate environmental, developmental, and human rights concerns and how to blend them into a comprehensive integrated and effective international law system in the pursuance of sustainable development.[38]

1.4 THE INCORPORATION OF SUSTAINABLE DEVELOPMENT IN INTERNATIONAL LAW

Sustainable development did not come about overnight in international law in the last part of the twentieth century. The roots can be traced to some early

35 Schrijver, n. 2, 208–219.

36 Paris Agreement on Climate Change, 2015, 3156 UNTS 79.

37 *Ibid.*, art. 2, para. 1(a) and art 3.

38 See International Law Association (ILA), New Delhi Declaration of Principles of International Law Relating to Sustainable Development, UN Doc. A/57/329, 31 August 2002, principle 7 (New Delhi Declaration). The Declaration also appeared, with an introduction, as 'New Delhi Declaration of Principles of International Law Relating to Sustainable Development' (2002) 49 *Netherlands International Law Review* 299. The final report of the ILA Commission and the New Delhi Declaration were published in ILA, *Report of the 70th Conference New Delhi* (ILA, 2002), 22, 380, www.ila-hq.org.

treaties – for example, nature management treaties and anti-pollution provisions in river treaties, some of which even date back to the nineteenth century. Furthermore, we can also note the concept of the maximum sustainable yield in international fisheries law of the early part of the twentieth century.[39] Yet the concept of sustainable development was really launched through so-called soft law during the period following the establishment of the United Nations. In particular, the Stockholm Declaration and the 1992 Rio Declaration on Environment and Development have been instrumental in putting sustainable development high on the international political agenda.[40] In their track, new multilateral environmental agreements were soon concluded. Examples of follow-up treaties of the Stockholm Declaration include the 1973 Convention on International Trade in Endangered Species[41] and the 1979 Convention on Long-Range Transboundary Air Pollution.[42] Offsprings of the Rio Declaration include the 1992 UN Framework Convention on Climate Change (UNFCCC),[43] the 1992 Convention on Biological Diversity (CBD),[44] and the 1994 Convention to Combat Desertification,[45] in addition to the earlier adopted 1985 Vienna Convention and its 1987 Montreal Protocol, which has proven to be effective for the protection of the ozone layer.[46]

In addition to this intensive treaty making in various fields, there was also an increasing body of international jurisprudence, including from the International Court of Justice (ICJ).[47] The ICJ recognized sustainable development as a concept in international law for the first time in the *Danube Dam*

[39] Compare Convention on the Law of the Sea, 1982, 1833 UNTS 397, arts. 61(3), 119(1) (UNCLOS).

[40] Rio Declaration, n. 22.

[41] Convention on International Trade in Endangered Species of Wild Fauna and Flora, 1973, 993 UNTS 243.

[42] Convention on Long-Range Transboundary Air Pollution, 1979, 1302 UNTS 217.

[43] United Nations Framework Convention on Climate Change, 1992, 1771 UNTS 107 (UNFCCC).

[44] Convention on Biological Diversity, 1992, 1760 UNTS 69 (CBD).

[45] Convention to Combat Desertification in Countries Experiencing Serious Drought and/or Desertification, Particularly in Africa, 1994, 1954 UNTS 3 (Convention to Combat Desertification).

[46] Convention on the Protection of the Ozone Layer, 1985, 1513 UNTS 293; Protocol on Substances That Deplete the Ozone Layer, 1987, 1522 UNTS 28; see also Osamu Yoshida, *The International Legal Regime for the Protection of the Stratospheric Ozone Layer* (Martinus Nijhoff, 2001).

[47] See Philippe Sands, 'International Courts and the Application of the Concept of Sustainable Development' (1999) 3 *Max Planck Yearbook of UN Law* 389; Tim Stephens, 'Sustainability Discourses in International Courts: What Place for Global Justice', in Duncan French (ed.), *Global Justice and Sustainable Development* (Brill, 2010), 39.

case between Slovakia and Hungary in 1997[48] and, later, in the *Pulp Mills* case between Argentina and Uruguay in 2010[49] and in the case between Costa Rica and Nicaragua regarding *Certain Activities in the Border Area* in 2015, and – '[g]iven its continuous and uncontested universal recognition' – as a principle in the Advisory Opinion on *Obligations of States in Respect of Climate Change* in 2025.[50] Similarly, sustainable development as a general norm has been referred to in quite a few arbitral awards in international investment law.[51]

Apart from codifying and consolidating sustainable development in treaty law and judicial decisions, soft law has been instrumental in further clarifying and progressively developing the scope and meaning of sustainable development. Such is the case with the current role of the SDGs, which were adopted in 2015.[52] Their forerunners are the eight Millennium Development Goals (MDGs), adopted at the beginning of this millennium, which however did not yet employ the term 'sustainable development'.[53] In 2015, MDGs were succeeded by 17 SDGs with as many as 169 targets.[54] They are part and parcel of the wider UN World Development Agenda from 2015 to 2030.[55] These SDGs, of course, are not hard law, but they do carry some important normative value. It could well be argued that, in part, they embody 'programmatory' law and

48 *Case Concerning the Gabcikovo-Nagymaros Project (Hungary v Slovakia)*, Judgment, 25 September 1997, (1997) ICJ Reports 7.

49 *Case Concerning Pulp Mills on the River Uruguay (Argentina v Uruguay)*, Judgment, 20 April 2010, (2010) ICJ Reports 14.

50 *Certain Activities Carried Out by Nicaragua in the Border Area (Costa Rica v Nicaragua) and Construction of a Road in Costa Rica along the San Juan River (Nicaragua v Costa Rica)*, Judgment, 16 December 2015, (2015) ICJ Reports 665; *Obligations of States in Respect of Climate Change*, Advisory Opinion, 23 July 2025, (2025) ICJ Reports para. 147 (forthcoming).

51 Nico Schrijver, '2019 AIIB Law Lecture: The Rise of Sustainable Development in International Investment Law' (2020) 3 *Asian Infrastructure Investment Bank Yearbook of International Law* 297.

52 *Transforming Our World*, n. 24.

53 Millennium Declaration, UN Doc. A/RES/22/2, 8 September 2000. An extensive analysis of the substance and the state of affairs of the Millennium Development Goals is given by UN Development Programme in *Human Development Report 2003* (UN Development Programme, 2003); *Millennium Development Goals Reports* (UN Development Programme, published annually from 2001 to 2015).

54 For a general overview of the process in making the Sustainable Development Goals (SDGs), see Macharia Kamau, Pamela Chasek & David O'Connor, *Transforming Multilateral Diplomacy: The Inside Story of the Sustainable Development Goals* (Routledge, 2018); Duncan French & Louis J. Kotzé (eds.), *Sustainable Development Goals: Law, Theory and Implementation* (Edward Elgar, 2018); Jonas Ebbesson & Ellen Hey (eds.), *The Cambridge Handbook of the Sustainable Development Goals and International Law* (Cambridge University Press, 2022).

55 *Transforming Our World*, n. 24.

'aspirational' law in the sense of guidelines for the desirable future development of international law in support of sustainable development.[56]

The SDGs also have concrete targets and include monitoring, reporting, and evaluating procedures. Hence, many governments, international organizations, and non-state actors, including businesses, have subscribed to the SDGs.[57] The various elements of the concept of sustainable development, as discussed above, come clearly to the fore. For example, SDG 1 is that of poverty reduction ('leaving nobody behind'), and SDG 2 is on zero hunger; SDG 3 – of paramount interest to all of us – relates to good health; SDG 6 is on the availability and sustainable management of water and sanitation for all; SDG 13 is on combating climate change and its impacts; SDG 14 is on conserving and sustainably using the oceans, seas, and marine resources; SDG 15 is on the sustainable use of terrestrial ecosystems, forests, and biological diversity; and SDG 16 refers to promoting peaceful and inclusive societies for sustainable development, providing access to justice for all and building effective, accountable, and inclusive institutions at all levels. To achieve these goals, international cooperation is called for. Apart from article 55 of the UN Charter, such a call is amply reflected in SDG 17 on global partnership for the achievement of the global goals.[58]

In sum, we can widely note the rise of sustainable development in international law: first, in areas of direct environmental relevance, such as the management of rivers, seas, oceans, water resources, biological diversity, living and non-living natural resources, and transboundary resources. In many of these fields, there has been intensive treaty making and related international regulation. In addition, sustainable development is also on the rise in some other areas, such as trade agreements, economic cooperation treaties, international water law, the rights of Indigenous peoples, investment regulation, and the protection of the environment during armed conflict.[59]

[56] For the notion of 'programmatory' law, see René-Jean Dupuy, 'Declaratory Law and Programmatory Law: From Revolutionary Custom to "Soft Law"', in Robert Jan Akkerman, Peter J. van Krieken, & Ok Pannenborg (eds.), *Declarations on Principles: A Quest for Universal Peace* (Sijthoff, 1977), 245.

[57] See Stephen Browne & Thomas G. Weiss, *Post-2015 UN Development: Making Change Happen* (Routledge, 2014).

[58] Charter of the United Nations, 1945, 1 UNTS 15; see also *Transforming Our World*, n. 24.

[59] Daniëlla Dam-de Jong, *International Law and Governance of Natural Resources in Conflict and Post-Conflict Situations* (Cambridge University Press, 2015), 155.

1.5 THE EVOLUTION OF THE INTERNATIONAL LAW OF SUSTAINABLE DEVELOPMENT

1.5.1 *Underlying Global Values and General Principles*

It could well be argued that, currently, an identifiable international sustainable development law is evolving upon the combined basis of widely shared global values of environmental conservation, preserving the rights of future generations, a life in dignity for all, and respect for human rights: these values could also be summarized in the term 'sustainability' as a global value.[60] As such, the emergence of international sustainable development law is in direct response to urgent global needs related to combating pollution, loss of biological diversity and climate change as well as fighting poverty and realizing the human right to development and the human right to a clean, healthy, and sustainable environment. Obviously, such international law builds on longtime established general principles of international law, such as the duty to cooperate and respect for human rights.[61]

1.5.2 *Specific Legal Principles*

More specifically, some typical sustainable development-related principles have been developed. One of the first ones is the duty to ensure the sustainable use of natural resources, a principle of international law with firm roots in international fisheries law, the law of the sea, and international environmental law. This duty to ensure a sustainable use of natural resources extends both to territories under state jurisdiction[62] and to areas beyond national jurisdiction, such as the deep seabed, the high seas, Antarctica, and outer space.[63]

60 See Mohan Munasinghe & Jeffrey A. McNeely, 'Key Concepts and Terminology of Sustainable Development', in Mohan Munasinghe & Walter Shearer (eds.), *Defining and Measuring Sustainability: The Biogeophysical Foundations* (World Bank, 1995), 19; Robert Costanza & Bernard C. Patten, 'Defining and Predicting Sustainability' (1995) 15 *Ecological Economics* 193.

61 The duty to cooperate extends to international cooperation for 'international economic stability', 'general welfare of nations', 'social progress', 'development', 'environmental conservation', and 'respect for human rights', to quote from some key international instruments including the UN Charter, UNGA Resolution 2625 (XXV) on the Declaration on Principles of International Law Concerning Friendly Relations and Co-operation between States, 24 October 1970, the Stockholm Declaration, n. 16; and the Rio Declaration, n. 22.

62 Schrijver, n. 21, 324–336.

63 Nico Schrijver, 'Managing the Global Commons: Common Good or Common Sink?' (2016) 37(6) *Third World Quarterly* 1252.

A second principle of international sustainable development law is the principle of equity, with two specific offspring: intergenerational equity and intra-generational equity. Intergenerational equity implies equity between the present and future generations of humankind and is prominently recorded in the Brundtland definition of sustainable development: 'Without compromising the ability of future generations to meet their own needs.'[64] So too is intra-generational equity through the phrase 'development that meets the needs of the present generation'.[65] Especially intergenerational equity has been widely adopted as a principle in the law of the sea, outer space law, and international environmental law (for example, in the climate and biological diversity conventions). By contrast, intra-generational equity is so far hardly reflected in treaty law and has at best a soft law status in normative declarations.

A third one is the principle of common but differentiated responsibilities (CBDR), a relatively new principle of international law that gained currency in international trade law (including World Trade Organization [WTO] law), international financial law, law of the sea, and international environmental law. The contents of this principle can best be illustrated by reference to principle 7 of the Rio Declaration[66] and a WTO judgment in which the WTO Appellate Body emphasized 'the protection and conservation of sea turtles to the satisfaction of all interests involved and taking into account the principle that States have common but differentiated responsibilities to conserve and protect the environment'.[67]

A fourth principle of international sustainable development law is the human right to development. Although a new human right that is somewhat controversial, the right to development gained major impetus with the adoption of the UN Declaration on the Right of Development in 1986.[68]

64 See World Commission on Environment and Development, n. 31, 43.

65 See also Edith Brown Weiss, *In Fairness to Future Generations: International Law, Common Patrimony and Intergenerational Equity* (Transnational Publishers, 1989).

66 Rio Declaration, n. 22, principle 7 (which reads: 'In view of the different contribution to global environmental degradation, States have common but differentiated responsibilities. The developed countries acknowledge the responsibility they bear in the international pursuit of sustainable development in view of the pressures their societies place on the global environment and of the technologies and financial resources they command'). See also Stockholm Declaration, n. 16, part I, para. 4.

67 WTO, *United States Import Prohibition of Certain Shrimp and Shrimp Products: Recourse to Article 21.5 by Malaysia*, Report of the Panel, WT/DS58/AB/RW, 22 October 2001. See also *Obligations of States in Respect of Climate Change*, Advisory Opinion, n. 50, paras. 148–151. On the principle of common but differentiated responsibilities (CBDR), see Lavanya Rajamani, *Differential Treatment in International Environmental Law* (Oxford University Press, 2006).

68 See UN Declaration on the Right of Development, UN Doc. A/RES/41/128, 4 December 1986; see also International Covenant on Economic, Social and Cultural Rights, 1966, 993 UNTS 3,

First, rather than being seen as a new human right, it could be viewed as a cluster right. For the rights to a decent standard of living, including the right to food, clothing, and housing, the right to work, the right to education, the right to life, and the right to freedom of expression and organization, are a cluster of rights that together form a 'human right to development'. Second, the human right to development functions also as an integrative right in the sense that it links the three categories of human rights, sometimes referred to as the three generations. It puts civil and political rights; economic, social, and cultural rights; and the rights of peoples together since, more than any other human right, it is composed of all these three categories of human rights.[69]

A fifth principle is the human right to a clean, healthy, and sustainable environment. For a long time, the human right to an adequate environment was not part and parcel of the established human rights catalogue. Two separate developments have changed this situation. First, a tendency emerged to interpret other existing human rights, such as the right to life and the right to family life, as the basis for a human right to a healthy living environment. In the years before the UN International Meeting Stockholm +50: A Healthy Planet for the Prosperity of All – Our Responsibility, Our Opportunity (Stockholm+50 Meeting), this extensive interpretation was adopted by courts in various countries, most notably the Dutch Supreme Court in the *Urgenda* case,[70] the German *Bundesverfassungsgericht* in the *Neubauer* case, and, in 2024, the European Court of Human Rights in the *KlimaSeniorinnen* case.[71] In a similar vein, the UN Human Rights Committee noted in an authoritative commentary on the content of the right to life that

> environmental degradation, climate change and unsustainable development constitute some of the most pressing and serious threats to the ability of present and future generations to enjoy the right to life. … Implementation of the obligation to respect and ensure the right to life, and in particular life with dignity, depends, inter alia, on measures taken by States parties to

art. 11 (on the right to an adequate living standard, substantively an early version of the right to development).

69 See Nico Schrijver, 'A New Convention on the Human Right to Development: Putting the Cart before the Horse?' (2020) 38(2) *Netherlands Human Rights Quarterly* 84, 92.

70 See Dutch Supreme Court, *Hoge Raad*, Case no. ECLI:NL:HR:2019:2006, 20 December 2019.

71 German Bundesverfassingsgericht, *Neubauer et al v Germany*, 29 April 2021, http://climatecasechart.com/climate-change-litigation/wp-content/uploads/sites/16/non-us-case-documents/2021/20210429_11817_judgment-2.pdf; European Court of Human Rights, *Verein KlimaSeniorinnen Schweiz and Others v. Switzerland*, Judgment (Grand Chamber), 9 April 2024, No 53600/20.

preserve the environment and protect it against harm, pollution and climate change caused by public and private actors.[72]

Second, some standard setting with respect to the recognition of a human right to an adequate environment has taken place at both the national and international levels. Nationally, more than 100 states have incorporated either such a human right or a duty of due care for the environment in their constitutions or principal laws.[73] Furthermore, in 2022, soon after the Stockholm+50 Meeting, a breakthrough took place within the framework of the United Nations with the adoption of UNGA Resolution A/76/300 recognizing 'the right to a clean, healthy and sustainable environment' as a human right.[74] This Resolution places this human right in the broader context of the three dimensions of the pursuit of sustainable development (social, economic, and environmental protection), which forms the basis for promoting human well-being and full respect for all human rights for present and future generations.

A sixth principle relates to precaution and due diligence. There is increasing emphasis on the principle that states should not only treat the environment and natural resources in their territory with due care but should also prevent environmental harm in circumstances of scientific uncertainty. Substantively, this means that, when initiating new economic activities or infrastructural projects, the obligation always applies to prevent significant damage to the environment. Procedurally, this translates into the obligation to carry out an environmental impact assessment. In terms of principle 15 of the Rio Declaration, 'in order to protect the environment, the precautionary approach shall be widely applied by States according to their capabilities. Where there are threats of serious or irreparable damage, lack of full scientific certainty shall not be used as a reason for postponing cost-effective measures to prevent environmental degradation.'

Following its inclusion in the Rio Declaration, the precautionary principle was adopted in numerous environmental treaties in the 1990s, including the

72 UN Human Rights Committee (HRC), General Comment no. 36, UN Doc. CCPR/C/GC/35, 3 September 2019, art. 6, para. 62 (right to life).

73 John H. Knox, Report of the Special Rapporteur on the Issue of Human Rights Obligations Relating to the Enjoyment of a Safe, Clean and Sustainable Environment, UN Doc. A/73/188, 24 January 2018; John H. Knox, Right to a Healthy Environment: Good Practices, UN Doc. A/HRC/43/53, 30 December 2019.

74 UNGA Resolution A/76/300, 28 July 2022. This Resolution was an initiative of Costa Rica, supported by the Maldives, Morocco, Slovenia, and Switzerland and was adopted with 161 states in favour, none against, and eight abstentions (China, Russia, Belarus, Cambodia, Iran, Syria, Kyrgyzstan, and Ethiopia). It was a direct follow-up to an earlier, similar HRC Resolution. HRC Resolution 48/13, 8 October 2021.

UNFCCC,[75] the CBD,[76] and the 1995 Fish Stocks Agreement.[77] It has also been adopted in an unambiguous way in article 191 of the Treaty on the Functioning of the European Union, which provides: 'Union policy on the environment … shall be based on the precautionary principle and on the principles that preventive action should be taken, that environmental damage should as a priority be rectified at source and that the polluter should pay.'[78] Given the wealth of references in treaty law and general practice, it is therefore unsurprising that the ICJ recognized in *Pulp Mills* that 'it may now be considered a requirement under general international law to undertake an environmental impact assessment [EIA] where there is a risk that the proposed industrial activity may have a significant adverse impact in a transboundary context, in particular, on a shared resource'.[79] This was confirmed in *Costa Rica v Nicaragua*, where the ICJ noted that the requirement to undertake an EIA 'applies generally to proposed activities which may have a significant adverse impact in a transboundary context'.[80] It is clear that the precautionary principle and the EIA, for the time being, concern, virtually exclusively, the environmental component of sustainable development and, scarcely, the

75 UNFCCC, n. 43, art. 3(3) (which provides: 'The Parties should take precautionary measures to anticipate, prevent or minimize the causes of climate change and mitigate its adverse effects').

76 CBD, n. 44, preamble (which provides: 'Noting also that where there is a threat of significant reduction or loss of biological diversity, lack of full scientific certainty should not be used as a reason for postponing measures to avoid or minimize such a threat').

77 Agreement for the Implementation of the Provisions of the United Nations Convention on the Law of the Sea of 10 December 1982 Relating to the Conservation and Management of Straddling Fish Stocks and Highly Migratory Fish Stocks, and Related Instruments, 1995, 2167 UNTS 3, art. 6 (entitled 'Application of the Precautionary Approach'). It provides that (1) 'States shall apply the precautionary approach widely to conservation, management and exploitation of straddling fish stocks and highly migratory fish stocks in order to protect the living marine resources and preserve the marine environment.'

78 Treaty on the Functioning of the European Union, (2016) OJ C202/47, art. 191, para. 2. In 2000, the European Commission also issued an important statement elaborating its interpretation of the precautionary principle. See *Communication from the Commission on the Precautionary Principle*, Doc. COM(2000)1, 2 February 2000.

79 *Case Concerning Pulp Mills on the River Uruguay (Argentina v Uruguay)*, Judgment, 20 April 2010, (2010) ICJ Reports 14, para. 204.

80 *Certain Activities Carried Out by Nicaragua in the Border Area (Costa Rica v Nicaragua) and Construction of a Road in Costa Rica along the San Juan River (Nicaragua v Costa Rica)*, Judgment, 16 December 2015, (2015) ICJ Reports 665, para. 104; *cf. Responsibilities and Obligations of States Sponsoring Persons and Entities with Respect to Activities in the Area (Request for an Advisory Opinion Submitted to the Seabed Disputes Chamber)*, Advisory Opinion, 1 February 2011, ITLOS Case no. 17, 2011, 10, paras. 141–150 and *Obligations of States in Respect of Climate Change*, Advisory Opinion, ICJ, n. 50, paras. 295–298.

developmental and human rights aspects. Only in a few instances has the precautionary principle made its way into human rights jurisprudence.

A seventh principle is that of access to information, access to justice, and public participation, which is clearly set out in principle 10 of the Rio Declaration.[81] Indeed, this principle is not only about public participation but also about the related principles of timely access to all relevant information (as an essential precondition for participation) and the possibility of appeal procedures. This threefold principle received the clearest follow-up in the 1998 Aarhus Convention.[82] In a more general sense, the importance of the participation of individuals and Indigenous peoples had already been expressed in the 1994 Convention to Combat Desertification[83] and is also prominent in other multilateral treaties such as the 2000 Cotonou Agreement.[84]

An eighth principle is that of integration and interrelationship. This requires an integrated approach to various policy areas and their legal principles and rules. The integration principle is possibly the most important of all international law principles concerning sustainable development. As a relatively new principle, it recognizes the interrelationship between the

81 Rio Declaration, n. 22, principle 10 (which reads: 'Environmental issues are best handled with the participation of all concerned citizens, at the relevant level. At the national level, each individual shall have appropriate access to information concerning the environment that is held by public authorities, including hazardous materials and activities in their communities, and the opportunity to participate in decision-making processes. States shall facilitate and encourage public awareness and participation by making information widely available. Effective access to judicial and administrative proceedings, including redress and remedy, shall be provided').

82 Convention on Access to Information, Public Participation in Decision-making and Access to Justice in Environmental Matters, 1998, 2161 UNTS 447.

83 Convention to Combat Desertification, n. 45, art. 3 (which obliges the parties 'to ensure that decisions on the design and implementation of programmes to combat desertification and/or mitigate the effects of drought are taken with the participation of populations and local communities'); see also Kyle W. Danish, 'International Environmental Law and the "Bottom-up" Approach: A Review of the Desertification Convention' (1995) 3 *Indiana Journal of Global Legal Studies* 133 (notably, Kyle Danish calls the bottom-up approach the main characteristic of this treaty).

84 See, for example, the fundamental principle of participation in article 2 of the Partnership Agreement between the Members of the African, Caribbean and Pacific Group of States of the One Part, and the European Community and Its Member States, of the Other Part, Doc. ACP/CE/en123, 23 June 2000 (revised version, 2010) (Cotonou Agreement) (which states that the African, Caribbean and Pacific – EU partnership shall be open to 'different kinds of other actors in order to encourage the integration of all sections of society, including the private sector and civil society organisations, into the mainstream of political, economic and social life').

pursuit of poverty eradication and development, environmental protection and respect for human rights, and the integrated manner in which objectives in these areas are to be tackled. From the beginning of the discussion on sustainable development, integration has been an important theme. As principle 13 of the Stockholm Declaration already stated, 'states should adopt an integrated and co-ordinated approach to their development planning so as to ensure that development is compatible with the need to protect and improve the human environment for the benefit of their population'. In a more prescriptive sense, principle 4 of the Rio Declaration demanded that 'environmental protection shall constitute an integral part of the development process and cannot be considered in isolation from it'.

The integration principle has been expressed in a variety of treaties. For example, the UNFCCC stated that 'responses to climate change should be coordinated with social and economic development in an integrated manner with a view to avoiding adverse impacts on the latter, taking into full account the legitimate priority needs of developing countries for the achievement of sustained economic growth and the eradication of poverty'.[85] Earlier, the 1982 UN Convention on the Law of the Sea provided in its preamble that 'the problems of ocean space are closely interrelated and need to be considered as a whole'.[86] Other examples where the integration principle is reflected include the CBD, the UN Convention to Combat Desertification, the Fish Stocks Agreement, and European Union (EU) law. In EU law, the integration principle plays a very important role in seeking to achieve coherence of EU policies and cementing the European Union.[87] It is not surprising, in view of these numerous provisions, that the arbitral tribunal in the *Iron Rhine* case in 2005 observed: 'Today, both international

[85] UNFCCC, n. 43, preamble; see also the objective in art. 2: 'The ultimate objective . . . is to achieve . . . stabilization of greenhouse gas concentrations in the atmosphere at a level that would prevent dangerous anthropogenic interference with the climate system. Such a level should be achieved within a time frame sufficient to allow ecosystems to adapt naturally to climate change, to ensure that food production is not threatened at all and to enable economic development to proceed in a sustainable manner.'

[86] UNCLOS, n. 39.

[87] Treaty on European Union, (2010) OJ C83/13, art. 21(3) (which stipulates: 'The Union shall ensure consistency between the different areas of its external action and between these and its other policies'); Nele Dhondt, *Integration of Environmental Protection into Other EC Policies: Legal Theory and Practice* (Europa Law Publishing, 2003). In a similar vein, the Cotonou Agreement seeks to implement 'a comprehensive and integrated approach for a strengthened partnership', to commit all parties to 'economic, social and cultural development of the ACP states', and to establishing a 'coherent enabling framework'. Cotonou Agreement, n. 84, preamble, arts. 1, 20(1).

and EC [European Community] law require the integration of appropriate environmental measures in the design and implementation of economic development activities.' As explained by the tribunal, 'environmental law and the law on development stand not as alternatives but as mutually reinforcing, integral concepts, which require that where development may cause significant harm to the environment there is a duty to prevent, or at least mitigate, such harm'.[88]

In addition, the International Law Association's 2002 New Delhi Declaration emphasized that the integration principle brings to the fore the interrelationship of socio-economic, environmental, and human rights issues as well as those relating to the needs of present and future generations.[89] As with other principles, the Declaration emphasized that the integration principle is applicable to all sectors of (international) society and to all governmental levels, ranging from the local level to the global level.[90] This emphasis is also reflected in the 2030 Agenda for Sustainable Development and the SDGs. The 2030 Agenda for Sustainable Development specifically notes that the 'interlinkages and integrated nature of the Sustainable Development Goals are of crucial importance in ensuring that the purpose of the new Agenda is realized'.[91] It subsequently records that 'sustainable development recognizes that eradicating poverty in all its forms and dimensions, combating inequality within and among countries, preserving the planet, creating sustained, inclusive and sustainable economic growth and fostering social inclusion are linked to each other and are interdependent'.[92]

88 *Iron Rhine ('IJzeren Rijn') Railway Arbitration (Belgium v The Netherlands)*, Award of the Arbitral Tribunal, 24 May 2005, reprinted in (2008) 27 *Reports of International Arbitral Awards* 35, para. 59; see also the WTO, *Brazil – Retreaded Tyres*, Report of the Appellate Body, WT/DS332/AB/R, 3 December 2007, para. 151 ('we recognize that certain complex public health or environmental problems may be tackled only with a comprehensive policy comprising a multiplicity of interacting measures').

89 New Delhi Declaration, n. 38.

90 *Ibid.*; *cf.* ILA, Sofia Guiding Statements on Sustainable Development, 2012, Annex, 37 (noting that 'the principle of integration and interrelationship is the primary means by which courts and tribunals provide an overarching conceptual framework for sustainable development, and the expectations of standards of due process, integrative decision-making and good faith negotiations (all of which support the principle of integration) should be further strengthened'); Duncan French, 'The Sofia Guiding Statements on Sustainable Development Principles in the Decisions of International Tribunals', in Marie-Claire Cordonier Segger, with Judge Christopher G. Weeramantry (eds.), *Sustainable Development Principles in the Decisions of International Courts and Tribunals 1992–2012* (Routledge, 2017), 177.

91 *Transforming Our World*, n. 24, 2.

92 *Ibid.*, 5, para. 13.

1.6 CONCLUSIONS ON THE 1972 STOCKHOLM CONFERENCE AND SUSTAINABLE DEVELOPMENT: 'ALL THERE BUT IN WORDS'

This chapter demonstrates that the 1972 Stockholm Conference marked in various ways the start of an organized effort on the side of the international community to seek a balance between environmental conservation and human development and, in this way, a compromise between the industrialized world and the global South. While the very term 'sustainable development' was not yet employed, it was all there but in words. In subsequent decades, sustainable development has gained currency in international law relatively quickly and is by now well anchored in various sources of international law – most notably, in treaty law and in other normative instruments with often a soft law character. In addition, sustainable development is also frequently addressed in the proceedings and the decisions of international courts and tribunals. Sustainable development is in the process of being integrated in various fields of international law, ranging from international environmental law, law of the sea, and human rights law (albeit hesitantly) to international economic law and law of the EU.

However, a coherent framework to incorporate sustainable development concerns in international law is still lacking. Rather, one notes a disordered patchwork of all kinds of international norms in a wide variety of sources with an unequal status, ranging from treaties, through judicial decisions, to a host of non-binding normative guidelines. Yet a fascinating conceptual feature is that sustainable development functions as an integrative and guiding principle, having economic, environmental, developmental, social, and governance dimensions to such an extent that the whole is more than the sum of the parts.[93] In this way, it has given rise to the gradual emergence of international sustainable development law, which builds both on the principles of general international law and specific principles originating in a variety of chapters of international law, as can be noted in the evolution of, inter alia, international climate law, international natural resources law, and the law of the EU.

[93] Cf. *Obligations of States in Respect of Climate Change*, Advisory Opinion, n. 50, para. 147, where the Court 'considers that the principle of sustainable development guides the interpretation of certain treaties and the determination of rules of customary international law, including the duty to prevent significant harm to the environment and the duty to co-operate for the protection of the environment.'

It could well be argued that the Stockholm Conference in 1972 was the first ever demonstration of an awareness of the interrelatedness and interdependence of many dimensions of environmental conservation and sound macroeconomic growth and development that also aimed for an integrated approach, which are now painstakingly taking shape in international law. This means that the foundation of international sustainable development law, no matter how imperfect it still is, was rooted in Stockholm.

2

The Missed Link between International Economic Law and Social and Environmental Issues

Ellen Hey

2.1 INTRODUCTION

The UN International Meeting Stockholm+50: A Healthy Planet for the Prosperity of All – Our Responsibility, Our Opportunity (Stockholm+50 Meeting) recommended that we should 'adopt a system-wide change in the way our current economic system works to contribute to a healthy planet'. However, it failed to specify which actions should be taken. Instead, concerns that would need to be addressed were reiterated, such as 'defining and adopting new measures of progress and human well-being, supported by economic and fiscal policies that account for the value of the environment' and 'promoting the phasing-out of fossil fuels while providing targeted support to the poorest and most vulnerable, in line with national circumstances and recognizing the need for financial and technical support towards a just transition'.[1]

Considering this statement in the light of the 1972 UN Conference on the Human Environment (Stockholm Conference) prompts the question of what role the international economic system, engrained in international law,[2] played during the preparations for, and in the outcome documents of, the Stockholm Conference. The Stockholm Conference, besides marking the beginning of modern international environmental law, also marks one of the first times developing states insisted that their concerns regarding the international economic system be considered in a multilateral decision-making

[1] *Report of Stockholm+50: A Healthy Planet for the Prosperity of All – Our Responsibility, Our Opportunity*, UN Doc. A/CONF.238/9, 1 August 2022, para. 157, recommendations, para. 3.

[2] Quin Slobodian, *Globalists, The End of Empire and the Birth of Neoliberalism* (Harvard University Press, 2018).

process.[3] Their concerns focused on the need to further social and economic development as well as on the importance of an international economic system that would encourage development, also in the face of international environmental measures. The concerns of developing states resonated in the outcome documents of the Stockholm Conference, even if they did so cautiously.

However, many of these concerns still exist fifty years after the Stockholm Conference, and they have been exacerbated by COVID-19 and the war in Ukraine. These points are emphasized in the *Sustainable Development Goals Report 2022* (*SDGs Report 2022*), where António Guterres, the UN secretary-general, points out that 'creating a global economy that works for all will require bold action'.[4] However, the UN secretary-general, in his foreword to the *SDGs Report 2021*, had already noted that

> had the paradigm shift envisioned by the 2030 Agenda for Sustainable Development been fully embraced over the past six years, the world would have been better prepared to face this crisis – with stronger health systems, expanded social protection coverage, the resilience that comes from more equal societies, and a healthier natural environment. Regrettably, the SDGs [Sustainable Development Goals] were already off track even before COVID-19 emerged.[5]

This chapter first traces how the concerns of developing states emerged in the process leading up to the Stockholm Conference and were reflected in the Stockholm Conference outcome documents. It then explores how these concerns relate to developments in international economic law. Thereafter, it briefly considers how we might move forward.

2.2 THE 1972 STOCKHOLM CONFERENCE AND THE CONCERNS OF DEVELOPING STATES

2.2.1 *The Stockholm Conference Preparatory Process*

Initially, the Economic and Social Council framed the topic for a UN conference on the human environment as the state of the environment. Although developing states were mentioned, the focus was not on their specific

[3] For earlier manifestations of these concerns, see Daniel J. Whelan, '"Under the Aegis of Man": The Right to Development and the Origins of the New International Economic Order' (2015) 6(1) *Humanity* 93.

[4] United Nations, *The Sustainable Development Goals Report 2022* (United Nations, 2022), 2.

[5] United Nations, *The Sustainable Development Goals Report 2021* (United Nations, 2021), 4.

situation.[6] The subsequent 1968 UN General Assembly (UNGA) resolution, in which it was decided to convene the conference, took a similar approach,[7] even if it signalled that developing states might require some form of special attention.[8] The prevalent thinking seems to have been that developing states should aim to avoid the environmental problems faced by developed states and, through international cooperation, learn from the mistakes made by developed states.[9]

This thinking changed in 1970 when a UNGA resolution provided in its preamble that 'environmental policies should be considered in the context of economic and social development, taking into account the special needs of development in developing countries'.[10] The resolution also suggests that the agenda for preparatory meetings include 'one or more specific items relating to economic aspects in order to safeguard the interests of developing countries' and that it be ensured 'that additional resources are provided to developing countries in the context of the protection of the environment'.[11] In December 1971, the different insights of developing and developed states surfaced by way of the adoption of two UNGA resolutions. The first resolution – UNGA Resolution 2849 on Development and Environment – included the concerns of developing states.[12] It was adopted by eighty-five votes in favour, two against, and thirty-four abstentions. The United Kingdom and the United States voted against the resolution, while most developed states and many states belonging to the then Soviet bloc abstained.[13] The second resolution – UNGA Resolution 2850 – approving the provisional agenda for the Stockholm Conference, dealt with organizational matters without mentioning the special position of developing states.[14] It was adopted by 104 votes in favour, 9 votes against, and 7 abstentions. States belonging to the then Soviet

6 ECOSOC Resolution 1346 (XLV) on Question of Convening an International Conference on the Problems of the Human Environment, 30 July 1968, preamble, paras. 1, 2.

7 UNGA Resolution 2398 (XXIII) on Problems of the Human Environment, 3 December 1968, preamble, paras. 3 and 4.

8 *Ibid.*, preamble, paras. 2(b), 5, 6.

9 See, e.g., UNGA Resolution 2581 (XXIV) on United Nations Conference on the Human Environment, 15 December 1969, para. 2.

10 UNGA Resolution 2657 (XXV) on United Nations Conference on the Human Environment, 7 December 1970, preamble, para. 9.

11 *Ibid.*, paras. 2, 3.

12 UNGA Resolution 2849 (XXVI) on Development and Environment, 20 December 1971.

13 Information available at *UN Digital Library*, https://digitallibrary.un.org/record/658353?ln=en.

14 UNGA Resolution 2850 (XXVI) on United Nations Conference on the Human Environment, 20 December 1971.

bloc voted against this resolution or abstained from voting, and several developing states also abstained from voting.[15]

Clearly, between 1968 and 1971, the position of developing states with respect to the Stockholm Conference had evolved. Their position now reflected earlier resolutions adopted by the UNGA, such as the resolution on permanent sovereignty over natural resources, which was adopted in 1962.[16] This resolution focused on the role of foreign investment in developing states and the need for developing states to be able to regulate the activities of foreign investors.[17] Resolution 2849 furthermore foreshadowed the resolutions on the New International Economic Order (NIEO) that would be adopted by the UNGA in 1974.[18] The evolution of the position of developed states also directly affected the negotiations for the Stockholm Conference.

2.2.2 *The Founex Conference*

In 1971, developing states threatened to leave the Stockholm Conference's negotiating process because they found their concerns insufficiently reflected in that process.[19] This situation was a serious setback for a conference that was intended to be a world summit, but which, in the context of the Cold War, most states associated with the then Soviet bloc had decided to boycott, with the exception of Romania and Yugoslavia.[20] In this context, Maurice Strong, the secretary-general of the Stockholm Conference, organized the Founex Conference to address the concerns of developing states. The conference met 4 to 12 June 1971 in Founex, Switzerland. It was attended by twenty-seven experts from various regions of the world and representatives of UN agencies. The resulting *Founex Report*, highlights the view that development – in particular, industrialization – and a lack of development, resulting in, among other deprivations, poverty, are linked to

[15] Information available at *UN Digital Library*, https://digitallibrary.un.org/record/658354?ln=en.

[16] UNGA Resolution 1803 (XVII) on Permanent Sovereignty over Natural Resources, 14 December 1962.

[17] See section 2.3.4.

[18] UNGA Resolution 3201/S-VI on Declaration on the Establishment of a New International Economic Order, 1 May 1974; UNGA Resolution 3202/SVI on Programme of Action on the Establishment of a New International Economic Order, 1 May 1974.

[19] Claire Brighton, 'Unlikely Bedfellows: The Evolution of the Relationship between Environmental Protection and Development' (2017) 66 *International and Comparative Law Quarterly* 209, 213–15; see also *Report of the UN Conference on the Human Environment*, UN Doc. A/CONF.48/14/Rev.1, 16 June 1972, 38.

[20] UN Conference on the Human Environment, *List of Participants*, UN Doc. A/CONF.48/INF.5/Rev. 1, 21 September 1972, www.un.org/en/conferences/environment/stockholm1972.

environmental degradation.[21] The report paved the way for the participation of developing states in the Stockholm Conference and is reflected in UNGA Resolution 2849.[22]

The content of the *Founex Report* signals many of the concerns that developing states continue to face today. For example, it mentions that, in the context of adopting country-appropriate environmental policies, the question arises 'of the instruments by which environmental policies could be implemented, particularly in situations where decisions are undertaken by private investors, whether domestic or foreign, in the context of market forces'.[23] The report also provides that 'the increased cost burden arising from greater attention to environmental problems should be accompanied by a greater willingness to provide additional assistance'.[24] Moreover, the report mentions that 'if the concern for human environment reinforces the commitment to development, it must also reinforce the commitment to international aid. It should provide a stimulus for augmenting the flow of resources from the advanced to the developing countries.'[25]

While the rest of the *Founex Report* focuses on how developing states might pursue environmentally sound development, its Chapter 4 explicitly addresses international economic relations and highlights the concerns of developing states, including:

- that environmental standards might hamper exports of products – agricultural products, in particular – from developing to developed states;[26]
- that aid might be reduced or conditioned based on environmental standards;[27]
- that, if environmentally friendly technology, which might be more costly than existing technology, were transferred under tied credits, this would 'further reduce the real content of foreign assistance';[28]

21 'Founex Report on Development and Environment', *MauriceStrong.net*, 1971, especially paras. 1.2–1.5, www.mauricestrong.net/index.php?option=com_content&view=article&id=149&Itemid=75. The reason for selecting this version is because its paragraphs are numbered. The Founex Report, including an introduction by Maurice Strong, as submitted to the UN secretary-general was also published as 'Founex Report on Development and Environment Submitted by a Panel of Experts Convened by the Secretary-General of the United Nations Conference on the Human Environment, 4–12 June 1971, Founex, Switzerland' (1972) 39 *International Conciliation* 7.

22 See text accompanying n. 12 above.

23 'Founex Report', n. 21, para. 1.10.

24 *Ibid.*, para. 1.14.

25 *Ibid.*, para. 1.15.

26 *Ibid.*, para. 4.4.

27 *Ibid.*, paras. 4.8, 4.9.

28 *Ibid.*, para. 4.10.

- that polluting industries might transfer to developing states;[29] and
- that additional financial flows for developing states might need to be secured.[30]

The point about the transfer of polluting industries to developing states merits further consideration because their transfer to developing states was regarded both as a risk and an opportunity. The report states that

> there is no reason why the developing countries should permit foreign investment, … to escape more stringent environmental standards back home if it results in a high rate of remittance of profits and even a lower net transfer of resources. In any arrangement that is made, it must be ensured that (a) foreign investment is on favourable terms and conditions, (b) it adds to the net transfer of resources, and (c) it conforms to the environmental standards that the recipient country wishes to impose in the light of its own stage of development and its own cultural and social objectives. So long as these safeguards are provided, there is no reason why the developing countries should not increasingly specialize in certain industrial fields, both for home market production and export purposes, which are going to become more costly for the developed world because of their growing concern with environmental standards.[31]

Whether developing states are always in a position to ensure that foreign investment 'is on favourable terms and conditions' for them and results in the net transfers of resources to their economies has been questioned.[32] Furthermore, it is well known that developing states, on account of the protection that bilateral investment treaties and the investment chapters of multilateral trade agreements offer foreign investors,[33] are regularly not in a position to impose on foreign companies the standards they may 'wish' to implement. Moreover, the 1989 Basel Convention on the Control of Transboundary Movements of Hazardous Wastes and Their Disposal was adopted

> in response to a public outcry following the discovery, in the 1980s, in Africa and other parts of the developing world of deposits of toxic wastes imported from abroad. Awakening environmental awareness and corresponding

[29] *Ibid.*, para. 4.16.
[30] *Ibid.*, para. 4.17.
[31] *Ibid.*, para. 4.16.
[32] UN Conference on Trade and Development (UNCTAD), *Trade and Development Report 2021* (United Nations, 2021).
[33] See section 2.3.4.

> tightening of environmental regulations in the industrialized world in the 1970s and 1980s had led to increasing public resistance to the dumping of hazardous wastes – in accordance with what became known as the NIMBY (Not in My Back Yard) syndrome – and to an escalation of disposal costs. This in turn led some operators to seek cheap disposal options for hazardous wastes in Eastern Europe and the developing world, where environmental awareness was much less developed and regulations and enforcement mechanisms were lacking.[34]

Sad accounts accompanying the transfers of waste to developing states abound, involving the illegal dumping of chemicals as well as electronic waste (e-waste).[35]

2.2.3 *The Stockholm Conference's Outcome Documents*

The outcome documents of the Stockholm Conference include the 1972 Stockholm Declaration on the Human Environment (Stockholm Declaration), the Action Plan for the Human Environment (Stockholm Action Plan), and Resolution 2997 on Institutional and Financial Arrangements (Resolution on IFA).[36] The Stockholm Declaration reflects the concerns of developing states in its preamble and operative parts. The preamble provides that, in 'developing countries most environmental problems are caused by under-development', 'with millions continuing to live far below the minimum levels required for a decent human existence', and it draws the conclusion that developing states must focus on development 'bearing in mind their priorities and the need to safeguard and improve the environment'.[37] It also highlights the need 'to raise resources to

34 'Overview', *Basel Convention*, www.basel.int/TheConvention/Overview/History/Overview/tabid/3405/Default.aspx; Basel Convention on the Control of Transboundary Movements of Hazardous and Their Disposal, 1989, 1673 UNTS 126.

35 On chemical waste, see Karin van Wingerde & Lieselot Bisschop, 'Waste Away: Examining Systemic Drivers of Global Waste Trafficking Based on a Comparative Analysis of Two Dutch Cases' (2019) 12(4) *Erasmus Law Review* 80. On e-waste and electronics, see 'Overview', n. 34; Thomas Maes & Fiona Preston-Whyte, 'E-waste It Wisely: Lessons from Africa', *SN Applied Science*, 2022, https://doi.org/10.1007/s42452-022-04962-9. For a human rights perspective on the export of hazardous wastes from developed to developing states, see also Marcos A. Orellana, 'The Unfinished Agenda of Stockholm 1972: A Rights-based Approach to Chemicals and Wastes', in this volume, 267.

36 See 'Declaration of the United Nations Conference on the Human Environment', in *Report of the UN Conference on the Human Environment*, n. 19 (Stockholm Declaration); 'Action Plan for the Human Environment', in *Report of the United Nations Conference on the Human Environment*, n. 19 (Stockholm Action Plan); 'Resolution on Institutional and Financial Arrangements', in *Report of the UN Conference on the Human Environment*, n. 19.

37 Stockholm Declaration, n. 36, preamble, para. 4.

support the developing countries in carrying out their responsibilities in this field'.[38]

The operative parts of the Stockholm Declaration, besides several provisions that address the need for rational development planning,[39] reflect the concerns of developing states by way of provisions on:

- the importance of social and economic development;[40]
- the environmental consequences of underdevelopment;[41]
- the need for price stability and adequate prices for primary products and raw materials;[42]
- the need for the environmental policies of all states not to hamper development or the achievement of better living conditions for all;[43]
- the need to make available additional financial resources to cover the costs that developing states may face if they incorporate environmental consideration into their development policies;[44]
- the need for additional technical and financial assistance;[45]
- the idea that states 'in accordance with the Charter of the United Nations and the principles of international law' have the 'sovereign right to exploit their own resources pursuant to their own environmental policies';[46] and
- the notion that standards applied by developed states or agreed to internationally may not be adequate for developing states.[47]

The Action Plan contains recommendations to the UN secretary-general, specialized agencies, and governments on a large number of environmental problems, and, for each of them, it emphasizes the need of developing states for technical and financial aid.[48] It also contains a chapter devoted to 'Development and Environment'. This chapter, among other issues, provides that environmental standards should not negatively impact exports from

38 *Ibid.*, preamble, para. 7.
39 *Ibid.*, paras. 13–15.
40 *Ibid.*, principle 8.
41 *Ibid.*, principle 9.
42 *Ibid.*, principle 10.
43 *Ibid.*, principle 11.
44 *Ibid.*, principle 12.
45 *Ibid.*, principle 12.
46 *Ibid.*, principle 21.
47 *Ibid.*, principle 23.
48 On river and water management, see, e.g., Stockholm Action Plan, n. 36, recommendations 51–55.

developing states and that compensation is to be made available if the export earnings of developing states were to decline on account of environmental concerns.[49] The 1994 General Agreement on Tariffs and Trade (GATT) and its Group on Environmental Measures and International Trade are mentioned as the bodies that could further consider this concern.[50] It also points to the need to 'develop mutually acceptable common international environmental standards on products which are considered by Governments to be of significance in foreign trade', with any testing and certification procedures having to 'avoid arbitrary or discriminatory actions that might affect the trade of developing countries'.[51] Furthermore, increased support for the Codex Alimentarius Commission (CAC) is called for in order for it to develop 'standards for pollutants in food and a code of ethics for international food trade'.[52] In relation to the relocation of polluting industries, even if the term 'polluting industries' is not used, the following is provided:

> That Governments of the developing countries consider fully the new opportunities that may be offered to them to establish industries and/or expand existing industries in which they may have comparative advantages because of environmental considerations, and that special care be taken to apply the appropriate international standards on environment in order to avoid the creation of pollution problems in developing countries.[53]

With respect to the transfer of technology that may protect or improve the environment, the Action Plan provides that it is important that these technologies be used universally. Yet it basically relegates the question of how these technologies may become available to developing countries to further study by the UN secretary-general.[54] In the context of a recommendation about the Second Development Decade, which commenced on 1 January 1971,[55] it is provided that 'it should further be ensured that the preoccupation of developed countries with their own environmental problems should not affect the flow of assistance to developing countries, and that this flow should be adequate to meet the additional environmental requirements of such countries'.[56]

49 *Ibid.*, recommendation 103(b).

50 *Ibid.*, recommendation 103(c), (d); General Agreement on Tariffs and Trade, 1994, 55 UNTS 194.

51 Stockholm Action Plan, n. 36, recommendation 104.

52 *Ibid.*, recommendation 82.

53 *Ibid.*, recommendation 106(b).

54 *Ibid.*, recommendation 108.

55 UNGA Resolution 2626 (XXV) on International Development Strategy for the Second United Nations Development Decade, 24 October 1970.

56 Stockholm Action Plan, n. 36, recommendation 109.

The Resolution on IFA provides the basis for the UNGA to adopt resolutions on the establishment of the UN Environmental Programme (UNEP) and the Environmental Fund.[57] UNEP was established as a programme of the UNGA,[58] not as a UN specialized agency, which restricts its decision-making capacity, for example, to establish formal subsidiary bodies, and its financial means. The costs of UNEP's Secretariat are born by the regular budget of the United Nations, but its operational costs are dependent on voluntary contributions.[59] The Environmental Fund, a voluntary fund, was established to cover these operational costs.[60] In addition, UNEP receives voluntary earmarked contributions, which constitute its largest source of funding.[61] Developing states would have preferred mandatory funding and some might have preferred the establishment of a UN specialized agency.[62]

2.2.4 *Taking Stock of Stockholm*

What might the international community have known with respect to the international economic system and development in 1972? I suggest that, in the language of 2022, the Stockholm concerns of developing states include:

- the need to transfer finances to developing states;
- the need to transfer technology to developing states;
- the need for fair and stable commodity prices;
- the need to regulate transnational business sector actors; and
- the need for a fair international trade system, taking into account the position of developing states.

57 See UNGA Resolution 2997 (XXVII), n. 36.
58 *Ibid.*, part II.
59 *Ibid.*, part II, para. 3.
60 *Ibid.*, part III.
61 For information on how the UN Environment Programme (UNEP) is financed, see 'How UNEP Is Funded', *UNEP*, www.unep.org/about-un-environment/funding-and-partnerships/funding-facts.
62 On the history of UNEP, see Maria Ivanova, 'Designing the United Nations Environment Programme: A Story of Compromise and Confrontation' (2007) 7 *International Environmental Agreements* 337. The discussion about UNEP and its powers has continued. On the organizational structure and development of UNEP, see 'The UN Environment Programme Needs New Powers', *Nature*, 2 March 2021; see also Bharat H. Desai, 'On the International Environmental Governance Architecture: Looking Back to Look Ahead for Our Common Future', in this volume, 109.

In 2022, the following items should be added to the list:

- the need to address the debt burden accumulated by developing states, exacerbated by COVID-19 and the war in Ukraine[63] and
- the need to reform the international financial and monetary systems, including the international tax system.[64]

All of these points have been the subject of UNGA resolutions. Relevant examples include the 1962 resolution on permanent sovereignty over natural resources,[65] the 1974 resolutions on the NIEO,[66] and two resolutions entitled *Towards a New International Economic Order*, adopted in 2018 and 2020.[67] These two resolutions reflect the Stockholm concerns of developing states and highlight that, unless the international economic system and the international financial and monetary systems incorporate the concerns of developing states, public financing for eradicating poverty and improving education, health care and climate action, for example, will be endangered in developing states.[68]

Since Stockholm in 1972, the international community went to Rio in 1992, to Johannesburg in 2002, back to Rio in 2012, and returned to Stockholm in 2022. Moreover, the Millennium Development Goals were adopted in 2000 and the Sustainable Development Goals (SDGs) in 2015. While advances have been

[63] While debt accumulation by developing countries started in the 1970s, it soured in the 1990s. For further information see José Antonio Campo, 'A Brief History of Sovereign Debt Resolution and a Proposal for a Multilateral Instrument', in Martin Guzman, José Antonio Ocampo, & Joseph E. Stiglitz (eds.), *Too Little, Too Late: The Quest to Resolve Sovereign Debt Crises* (Columbia University Press, 2016), 189; Homi Kharas & Meagan Dooley, 'The Post-COVID Legacy of Debt and Debt Service in Developing Countries' (2021) 22(2) *Georgetown Journal of International Affairs* 262.

[64] See contributions to Jomo Kwame Sundaram (ed.), *Reforming the International Financial System for Development* (Columbia University Press, 2017); Imaad A. Moosa & Nisreen Moosa, *Eliminating the IMF: An Analysis of the Debate to Keep, Reform or Abolish the Fund* (Springer, 2019), in particular, Chapter 6: 'Keep, Reform or Abolish?'; Martin Hearson, *Imposing Standards: The North-South Dimension to Global Tax Politics* (Cornell University Press, 2021), in particular, Chapter 1: 'The Problem with Tax Treaties'; Marilyne Sadowsky *et al.*, 'Taxation, Taxing the Future', White Paper no. 12, July 2022, www.ilaparis2023.org/en/white-paper/taxation/.

[65] See n. 16 above.

[66] See n. 18 above.

[67] Respectively UNGA Resolution 73/240 towards a New International Economic Order, 20 December 2018; UNGA Resolution 75/225 towards a New International Economic Order, 21 December 2020. The two resolutions are identical except for the 2020 resolution includes updates and references COVID-19 in paragraphs 13 and 14 of the preamble and a new operational paragraph 13. Reference here is to Resolution 75/225. Both resolutions were adopted with most developing states voting in favour and developed states voting against or abstaining.

[68] UNGA Resolution 75/225, n. 67, para. 17.

made, including in the development of international environmental law, the concerns of developing states have largely remained unaddressed by international economic law.[69]

The Stockholm concerns of developing states could not have been resolved by international environmental law on its own or by the Stockholm Conference. However, these concerns could and should have sparked the reform of international economic law or the development of 'development law'. The term 'law' is emphasized because some of the Stockholm concerns of developing states have been relegated to 'soft law' instruments.[70] The next section summarizes how the Stockholm concerns of developing states have fared in international economic law.

2.3 INTERNATIONAL ECONOMIC LAW AND THE STOCKHOLM CONCERNS OF DEVELOPING STATES

2.3.1 *The Transfer of Financial Resources*

Already before the Stockholm Conference, in 1970, it was agreed in a UNGA resolution that developed states would transfer to developing states annually 0.7 per cent of their gross domestic product (GDP) – now 0.7 per cent of their gross national income (GNI) – as official development aid (ODA).[71] This figure was to have been met by the mid-1970s. In 1981, it was agreed that developed states would contribute 0.15 per cent of GDP – now of GNI – to least developed states, a figure that was increased to between 0.15 per cent and 0.2 per cent in 1990.[72] These commitments continue to resurface, including in the SDGs.[73]

[69] Phillipe Cullet, 'SDG 10: Reduce Inequality within and Among Countries', in Jonas Ebbesson & Ellen Hey (eds.), *The Cambridge Handbook of the Sustainable Development Goals and International Law* (Cambridge University Press, 2022), 258, 275–277.

[70] See sections 2.3.1 and 2.3.2.

[71] UNGA Resolution 2626 (XXV), n. 55, para. 43.

[72] The commitment to devote 0.15 per cent originated in the first UN Conference on the Least Developed Countries in 1981. See *Report of the United Nations Conference on the Least Developed Countries*, Doc. A/CONF.104/22/Rev.1, 28 March 1982, para. 63. The 0.2 per cent was agreed in 1990 at the second UN Conference on the Least Developed Countries. See the *Report of the Second United Nations Conference on the Least Developed Countries*, Doc. A/CONF.147/18, 1991, Programme of Action, para. 23(c).

[73] The Sustainable Development Goals (SDGs) were adopted by way of UNGA Resolution 70/1. *Transforming Our World: The 2030 Agenda for Sustainable Development*, Doc. A/Res/70/1, 23 September 2015. See SDG 17: Partnerships for the Goals; Target 17.2: Developed Countries to Implement Fully Their Official Development Assistance Commitments.

The ODA commitments have been met by very few developed states. The UN Conference on Trade and Development (UNCTAD) reports that, for 2021, overall ODA rose by 4.4 per cent, but it mentions that '[t]his rise emanated almost exclusively from donations of excess or specifically purchased vaccines for COVID-19'.[74] If the COVID-19 factor is excluded, ODA remained at 0.33 per cent of GNI, similar to what it was in 2020.[75] Moreover, according to UNCTAD, in 2020, developed states transferred 0.06 per cent of GNI to least developed states.[76] UNCTAD also reports that debt relief in ODA has increased and that, in 2020, it amounted to 0.9 per cent of ODA.[77] In other words, debt relief is counted as ODA. In addition, developed states have also channelled some of their ODA to pay for the costs of hosting refugees, amounting to 7 per cent of overall ODA in 2020. This practice might increase given that some developing agencies have suggested or decided to redirect ODA to cover the costs of hosting refugees from the war in Ukraine.[78] Thus, the amounts of ODA to be made available to developing states are commitments rather than duties on the part of developed states and are contained in 'soft law' or in policy instruments. Moreover, these commitments have not been met by most developed states.

2.3.2 *The Transfer of Technology*

'Hard law' instruments do not contain unconditioned obligations to transfer technology. Instead both 'hard' and 'soft law' instruments condition the transfer of technology by requiring 'mutual agreement'[79] or providing that the transfer be 'to the mutual advantage of the technology holders and users'.[80] This situation is intimately related to the World Trade Organization's (WTO) 1994 Agreement on Trade-Related Aspects of Intellectual Property Rights (TRIPS Agreement), which, in practice, offers the holders of intellectual property rights strong protection, despite the fact that it addresses the transfer of technology, even if in a conditioned manner,[81] and the possibility of applying for

74 See UNCTAD, *Official International Assistance: Stagnation despite Pledges and New Development Challenges*, April 2023, www.un-ilibrary.org/content/books/9789210018418c009.

75 *Ibid.*

76 *Ibid.*

77 *Ibid.*

78 *Ibid.*; see also 'Deputy UN Secretary-General's Statement on Cuts to ODA', *United Nations*, 20 May 2022, www.un.org/sg/en/content/dsg/statement/2022-05-20/deputy-secretary-generals-statement-cuts-official-development-assistance-%28oda%29.

79 See text accompanying n. 88 below and SDG 17 and its target 17.7.

80 Agreement on Trade Related Aspect of Intellectual Property Rights, 1994, 1869 UNTS 299, art. 7.

81 See text quoted at n. 80.

exemptions.[82] Adopting an exemption, known as a waiver, requires a three-quarters majority vote[83] and, in practice, consensus in the WTO.[84]

During COVID-19, it became clear how difficult obtaining a waiver under the TRIPS Agreement is, despite the 2001 Ministerial Declaration on the TRIPS Agreement and Public Health, which provides that the TRIPS Agreement 'can and should be interpreted and implemented in a manner supportive of WTO members' right to protect public health and, in particular, to promote access to medicines for all'.[85] In October 2020, India and South Africa submitted a proposal to waive intellectual property rights to the WTO for COVID-19 vaccines, diagnostics, and therapeutics.[86] In June 2022, the WTO Ministerial Conference adopted a cautious waiver for the production of vaccines but not for diagnostics and therapeutics.[87] The topic remained on the agenda of the TRIPS Council and was relegated to a stakeholder meeting. Hence, WTO law does not seem fit for the purpose of addressing a global crisis.

International environmental law is also affected by the law on intellectual property. The 1992 Convention on Biological Diversity (CBD), for example, provides that

> access to and transfer of technology referred to in paragraph 1 above to developing countries shall be provided and/or facilitated under fair and most favourable terms, including on concessional and preferential terms *where mutually agreed*, and, where necessary, in accordance with the financial mechanism established by Articles 20 and 21. In the case of technology subject to patents and other intellectual property rights, such access and transfer shall be provided on terms which recognize and are consistent with the adequate and effective protection of intellectual property rights.[88]

82 Marrakesh Agreement Establishing the World Trade Organization, 1994, 1867 UNTS 154, art. IX(1), (3), (4) (WTO Agreement).

83 *Ibid.*

84 On the transfer of technology, see Andria Naudé Fourie, 'SDG 9: Building Resilient Infrastructure, Promote Inclusive and Sustainable Industrialization and Foster Innovation', in Ebbesson & Hey, n. 69, 231, 243–247.

85 Declaration on the TRIPS Agreement and Public Health, Doc. WT/MIN(01)/DEC/2, 20 November 2001, para. 4; see also Stéphanie Dagron, 'SDG3: Ensure Healthy Lives and Promote Well-Being for All at All Ages', in Ebbesson & Hey, n. 69, 95.

86 Communication from India and South Africa, *Waiver from Certain Provisions of the TRIPS Agreement for the Prevention and Containment and Treatment of* COVID-19, WTO Doc. IP/C/W/669, 2 October 2020.

87 *Ministerial Decision on the Trips Agreement*, WTO Doc. WT/MIN(22)/30, WT/L/1141, 22 June 2022.

88 Convention on Biological Diversity, 1992, 1760 UNTS 79, art. 16(2) (emphasis added).

The text of the 2015 Paris Agreement, the 1992 UN Framework Convention on Climate Change (UNFCCC), and the 1997 Kyoto Protocol do not contain this type of language.[89] However, in 2010, the Conference of the Parties (COP) to the UNFCCC decided that action on the acceleration of technology development and transfer would be: '*consistent with international obligations*, at different stages of the technology cycle, including research and development, demonstration, deployment, diffusion and transfer of technology . . . in support of action on mitigation and adaptation'.[90]

The COP thereby provided a basis for subjecting the transfer of technology within the climate change regime to international intellectual property law. Furthermore, the commitment, adopted in 2009, that developed states contribute $100 billion annually by 2020 to climate projects in developing states has not been met.[91] In 2021, it was extended to 2025.[92] Its non-realization has been linked to objections by developed states and private sector actors to sharing technology outside existing intellectual property regimes.[93] The transfer of technology then is grounded in exceptions to the TRIPS regime or based on conditioned commitments in other instruments, such as the CBD and the decision of the COP in the climate change regime. As a result, the implementation of these agreements in developing states has not been optimally facilitated.

2.3.3 *Commodity Prices*

Commodities are products such as oil, ore, and agricultural products, including soy produced to feed cattle. Commodity prices tend to be volatile, which is a problem especially for developing states because they are often heavily

89 Paris Agreement on Climate Change, 2015, 3156 UNTS 79; UN Framework Convention on Climate Change, 1992, 1171 UNTS 107; Kyoto Protocol to the UN Framework Convention on Climate Change, 1997, 2303 UNTS 162.

90 *Report of the Conference of the Parties on Its Sixteenth Session, Held in Cancun from 29 November to 10 December 2010, Addendum Part Two: Action Taken by the Conference of the Parties at Its Sixteenth Session*, Doc. FCCC/CP/2010/7/Add.1, 15 March 2011, para. 115 (emphasis added).

91 *Copenhagen Accords: Report of the Conference of the Parties on Its Fifteenth Session, Held in Copenhagen from 7 to 19 December 2009 Addendum Part Two: Action Taken by the Conference of the Parties at Its Fifteenth Session*, Doc. FCCC/CP/2009/11/Add.1, 30 March 2010, para. 8.

92 *Glasgow Climate Pact: Report of the Conference of the Parties on Its Twenty-sixth Session, Held in Glasgow from 31 October to 13 November 2021 Addendum Part two: Action Taken by the Conference of the Parties at Its Twenty-sixth Session*, Doc. FCCC/CP/2021/12/Add.1, 8 March 2022, paras. 25–27.

93 Stuart Bruce & Jorge E. Viñales, 'SDG 7: Ensure Access to Affordable, Reliable, Sustainable and Modern Energy for All', in Ebbesson & Hey, n. 69, 187, 203.

dependent on one or a few commodities for their export earnings.[94] A state is considered to be 'a commodity-dependent state' if more than 60 per cent of its merchandise export consists of commodities.[95] One hundred and one states were commodity dependent during the period of 2018–19, and only four of them were developed states (Australia, Iceland, New Zealand, and Norway).[96] Commodity dependence has been linked to lower gross national income per capita in developing states.[97]

In order to control the volatility of commodity prices, commodity agreements were established, beginning in 1953 with the International Sugar Agreement.[98] The aim of commodity agreements was to stabilize and raise market prices by controlling market supply by way of export quotas and buffer stock interventions.[99] During the 1990s, commodity agreements failed for various reasons, including because commodity price controls did not correspond with the market-based logics that emerged at the time.[100] Although commodity agreements still exist, they focus on exchanging information and consultations, not on the regulation of prices, with the exception of the Organization of the Oil Exporting Countries.[101]

Commodity prices remain volatile. For developing states that are exporters of commodities, this means fluctuating export earnings, which affect their budgets and the income of those involved in the production of commodities. While several market mechanisms are available to avoid the risks of price volatility, these may not be readily available to developing states or to the producers of commodities in developing states.[102] Diversification of exports by investing in technology and innovation seems to be the logical answer.[103] However, it raises the question whether developing states will be able to access the necessary financial resources and technical know-how to engage in such

94 UNCTAD, *Managing Commodity Price Risk in Commodity Dependent Developing Countries*, Note by the UNCTAD Secretariat, Doc. TD/B/C.I/MEM.2/46, 4 February 2019.

95 UNCTAD, *The State of Commodity Dependence* (United Nations, 2021), v.

96 *Ibid.*, 4–5.

97 *Ibid.*, 14.

98 International Sugar Agreement, 1953, 258 UNTS 153. On the history of commodity agreements, see Christopher L. Gilbert, 'International Commodity Agreements: An Obituary Notice' (1996) 24(1) *World Development* 1, 2.

99 *Ibid.*, 3–5.

100 *Ibid.*, 16.

101 See the activities of the listed commodity bodies at 'International Commodity Bodies', *UNCTAD*, https://unctad.org/topic/commodities/international-commodity-bodies.

102 See UNCTAD, n. 94.

103 *Ibid.*, 14; UNCTAD, *Escaping from the Commodity Dependence Trap through Technology and Innovation: Commodity and Development Report 2021* (United Nations, 2021).

a process.[104] Since 1972, volatile commodity prices continue to be a fact, even though they were recognized as being problematic for developing states at that time. Moreover, to the extent that there are mechanisms available to control prices, these mechanisms are driven by the market, with international law playing a limited role.

2.3.4 *Regulating Transnational Business Sector Actors*

The concern of developing states that they, as host states, needed to be able to regulate foreign investment and transnational business sector actors was implicit in Principle 21 of the Stockholm Declaration[105] and was highlighted in the *Founex Report*.[106] Transnational business sector actors, especially since the 1990s, have been shielded from host state regulation by bilateral investment treaties and, more recently, by the investment chapters of various multilateral trade agreements.[107] These agreements protect foreign investments through their stabilization clauses, requiring that the value of the investment not decline due to an action by the host state and their arbitration clauses, enabling the investor to take the host state to arbitration in case the value of the investment declines due to an action of the host state. These clauses have been used to bring claims against host states for adopting more stringent environmental measures or adopting new labour standards, and some of those claims have been successful.[108] While more sustainable investment treaties have been developed, these treaties have not entered into force, and doubts have been raised as to the enforceability of their social and environmental provisions.[109] In addition, developing states also have limited their ability to tax transnational business sector actors by entering into bilateral tax treaties, resulting in a loss of public revenue in those states.[110]

During the 1970s, initiatives were taken in the United Nations to develop a Code of Conduct for Transnational Corporations. These initiatives failed due to opposition from developed states, even though the UNGA adopted the

[104] See UNCTAD, *From Recovery to Resilience: The Development Dimension: Trade and Development Report 2021* (United Nations, 2021).

[105] See text accompanying n. 46 above.

[106] See text accompanying n. 23 above.

[107] Alessandra Arcuri & Francesco Montanaro, 'Justice for All: Protecting the Public Interest in Investment Treaties' (2018) 59(8) *Boston College Law Review* 2791; Alessandra Arcuri & Enrico Partiti, 'SDG 12: Ensuring Sustainable Consumption and Production', in Ebbesson & Hey, n. 69, 304, 314–317.

[108] *Ibid.*

[109] Arcuri & Partiti, n. 107, 317.

[110] Hearson, n. 64; Sadowsky *et al.*, n. 64.

1974 Charter of Economic Rights and Duties of States.[111] This Charter, after reaffirming the principle of permanent sovereignty over natural resources,[112] sets out the following, among other things:

Each State has the right:

(a) To regulate and exercise authority over foreign investment within its national jurisdiction in accordance with its laws and regulations and in conformity with its national objectives and priorities. No State shall be compelled to grant preferential treatment to foreign investment;

(b) To regulate and supervise the activities of transnational corporations within its national jurisdiction and take measures to ensure that such activities comply with its laws, rules and regulations and conform with its economic and social policies. Transnational corporations shall not intervene in the internal affairs of a host State. Every State should, with full regard for its sovereign rights, co-operate with other States in the exercise of the right set forth in this subparagraph.[113]

However, decision-making on the regulation of transnational business sector actors has remained controversial.

A step forward was made in 2011 with the adoption of the UN Guiding Principles on Business and Human Rights (UNGP) by the Human Rights Council.[114] The UNGP set out responsibilities for home states and host states and for the businesses themselves, including transnational business sector actors.[115] The UNGP are a 'soft law' instrument. Human rights treaty bodies have started to develop standards that home and host states should apply to business sector actors operating transnationally. For example, the Committee on Economic, Social and Cultural Rights adopted General Comment no. 26 on Land and Economic, Social and Cultural Rights.[116] It develops both the responsibilities of home and host states. Yet if host states act on these standards, the question remains whether the UNGP and General Comment no. 26 will be able to trump international investment law. Moreover, where home states act on these standards, they seem to translate into market-access regulation, at

[111] UNGA Resolution 3281 (XXIX) on Charter of Economic Rights and Duties of States, 12 December 1974.

[112] *Ibid.*, art. 2(1).

[113] *Ibid.*, para. 2(2).

[114] HRC Resolution 17/4 on Human Rights and Transnational Corporations and Other Business Enterprises, 16 June 2011.

[115] For further information, see 'OHCHR and Business and Human Rights', *United Nations*, www.ohchr.org/en/business-and-human-rights.

[116] Committee on Economic, Social and Cultural Rights, *General Comment no. 26 (2022) on Land and Economic, Social and Cultural Rights*, Doc. E/C.12/GC/26, 22 December 2022.

least for the European Union.[117] Such standards may be easier to meet by transnational business sector actors and are not always applied consistently to all states to which they apply.[118]

Attempts to regulate transnational business sector actors remain rooted in 'soft law' instruments. In the meantime, transnational business sector actors continue to enjoy the protection offered by bilateral investment treaties and the investment chapters of various trade agreements as well as the free trade rule, which is discussed below.

2.3.5 *A Fair International Trade System*

International trade law also did not develop in ways that reflected the Stockholm concerns of developing states. This section focuses on how the concerns expressed by developing states at the Stockholm Conference fared in WTO law. International trade law was significantly strengthened by the adoption of the 1994 Marrakesh Agreement Establishing the WTO,[119] leading to the further liberalization of international trade. As argued elsewhere, the free trade rule that is at the basis of WTO law tele-connects producers anywhere in the world to consumers anywhere in the world if producers can access the market.[120] The free trade rule, furthermore, functions as a default rule.[121] This situation implies that the free trade rule applies unless an exception is part of WTO law, such as Article XX of the GATT; is agreed to in the WTO, such as for COVID-19 vaccines;[122] or perhaps if the state in question is a party to a multilateral environmental agreement that is open to all WTO member states,[123] such as the 1987 Montreal Protocol on Substances that

117 Anu Bradford, *The Brussels Effect: How the European Union Rules the World* (Oxford University Press, 2020); Johannes Jarlebring, '"Regime Vetting": A Technique to Exercise EU Market Power' (2022) 29(4) *Journal of European Public Policy* 530.

118 Johannes Jarlebring, 'Backlisting and the EU as Global Regulator: The Institutionally Predisposed Norm Breaker' (2023) 61(4) *Journal of Common Market Studies* 1007; Jamile Bergamaschine Mata Diz & Hélio Eduardo de Paiva Araújo, 'Extraterritoriality and the Impact of EU Regulatory Authority: Environmental Protection as Soft Power', in Nuno Cunha Rodrigues (ed.), *Extraterritoriality of EU Economic Law* (Springer, 2021), 319.

119 WTO Agreement, n. 82.

120 Ellen Hey, 'International Law, Planetary Boundaries and Teleconnections', in Duncan French & Louis Kotzé (eds.), *Research Handbook on Law, Governance and Planetary Boundaries* (Edward Elgar, 2021), 167.

121 *Ibid.*, 173–175.

122 See text accompanying n. 85 above.

123 WTO, *United States – Measures Concerning the Importation, Marketing and Sale of Tuna and Tuna Products*, Report of the Appellate Body, WT/DS381/AB/R, 6 May 2012, para. 399.

Deplete the Ozone Layer.[124] Qualification of the free trade rule also happens by way of internationally agreed product standards such as those adopted by the International Organization for Standardization and, for food products, the CAC. In these organizations, developing states have been found to be under-represented, and producers – in particular, large transnational companies – have been found to have significant influence.[125] As a result, developing states and their producers – in particular, smaller-scale producers – find it difficult to access the international market. In addition, producers in developing states find it difficult to move up the global value chain unless they liaise with transnational private sector actors.

International trade law also does not account for the environmental or social consequences of the production of goods. This means that the environmental or social consequences of the production of soy in Brazil, for example, is not included in the price of meat in Europe or China.[126] Doing so unilaterally would enhance the price of soy from Brazil and might not be in Brazil's interest. Yet sustainability would be fostered if it were agreed internationally that the environmental and social costs are to be reflected in the price of products, provided, of course, that higher earnings trickle down to the poor and that business sector actors, including transnational business sector actors, are properly taxed and regulated.

The default nature of the free trade rule, like the rules on the protection of intellectual property rights, then, has been problematic when it comes to attaining social and environmental sustainability in developing states. It has strengthened the position of transnational business sector actors that are able to access the international market. But, given the uncertain future of the WTO,[127] the question arises whether preferential trade agreements, and the

[124] Montreal Protocol on Substances That Deplete the Ozone Layer, 1987, 1522 UNTS 3.

[125] Panagiottis Delimatsis, 'Global Standard Setting 2.0: How the WTO Spotlights ISO and Impacts the Transnational Standard-Setting Process' (2018) 28 *Duke Journal of Comparative and International Law* 273; Alessandra Arcuri, 'The Coproduction of the Global Regulatory Regime for Food Safety Standards and Limits of a Technocratic Ethos', EUI Working Papers no. RSCAS 2014/97, 25 September 2014.

[126] Edward Challies, Jens Newig, & Andrea Lenschow, 'What Role for Social-ecological Systems Research in Governing Global Teleconnections' (2014) 27 *Global Environmental Change* 32; Andrea Leschow, Jens Newig, & Edward Challies, 'Globalization's Limits to the Environmental State? Integrating Telecoupling into Global Environmental Governance' (2016) 12 *Environmental Politics* 136.

[127] Donald McRea, 'The Development of the Regulation of International Trade: The Past and the Future', in Daniel Bethlehem *et al.* (eds.), *The Oxford Handbook of International Trade Law* (2nd ed., Oxford University Press, 2022), 7; Daniel Bethlehem & Donald McRea, 'The International Trading System: Looking to 2100', in Bethlehem *et al.*, *ibid.*, 1065.

market access regulation that seems to be replacing it, will enable developing states to fair better.

2.4 CREATING AN ECONOMIC SYSTEM THAT WORKS FOR ALL

Since 1972, international economic law – in particular, international trade law and international investment law – has strengthened the position of transnational business sector actors. By the time of the Stockholm+50 Meeting, some of the 1972 Stockholm concerns of developing states had been relegated to 'soft law' instruments or to exceptions in 'hard law' instruments. Add to that the debt burden and the problematic tax situation that developing states face as well as the unequal participation of developed and developing states in international standard-setting institutions and international financial institutions, it seems high time to fundamentally change international economic law.

The *SDG Report 2022* does not spell out what the required 'bold actions' referred to by António Guterres, the UN secretary-general, might entail.[128] However, his 2020 Nelson Mandela Annual Lecture provides insight into what Guterres might be suggesting. In his lecture,[129] Guterres underlined that 'inequality defines our times' and the 'legacy of colonialism still reverberates', and he fundamentally criticized the international economic system. Amongst other things, he pointed out that COVID-19 has exposed fallacies and falsehoods such as 'the lie that free markets can deliver healthcare for all' and 'the myth that we are all in the same boat'. Guterres also mentions that 'the vision and promise of the United Nations is that food, healthcare, water and sanitation, education, decent work and social security are not commodities for sale to those who can afford them, but basic human rights to which we are all entitled'. He also noted that the legacy of colonialism is discernible 'in the global trade system' because 'economies that were colonized are at greater risk of getting locked into the production of raw materials and low-tech goods – a new form of colonialism'. These and other considerations led Guterres to propose a New Social Contract and a New Global Deal. If a New Social Contract or Global Deal is to be realized, international economic law will need to change fundamentally in order to support the cosmopolitan view of

[128] See text accompanying n. 4 above.

[129] António Guterres, 'Tackling the Inequality Pandemic: A New Social Contract for a New Era', Nelson Mandela Lecture, 18 July 2020, www.nelsonmandela.org/news/entry/annual-lecture-2020-secretary-general-guterress-full-speech.

sustainable development reflected in the SDGs[130] or, as formulated by Guterres, 'the paradigm shift envisioned in the SDGs'.[131]

2.5 CONCLUSION

That the Stockholm concerns of developing states have not been acted on is evidenced by the dire state of implementation of the SDGs. While the Stockholm Conference is remembered for inciting the development of modern international environmental law, might it have been even more fortunate if, fifty years later, it would have also been remembered for sparking the reform of international economic law or the development of development law? It is high time to fundamentally change international economic law and to take the Stockholm concerns of developing states seriously. International trade law, international investment law, and international tax law need to be reformed to also serve developing states. In addition, the ways of overcoming commodity dependence and the debt burden need to be found. Furthermore, the transfer of technology should not be relegated to exceptions to default rules in the WTO regime or to conditioned commitments in other regimes, and commitments to transfer ODA on the part of developed states should be lived up to. In his Mandela Lecture, Guterres points the way forward.

Participants at the Stockholm+50 Meeting in 2022 agreed to recognize and implement the human right to a clean, healthy, and sustainable environment.[132] Implementing this right will require bold action to reform international economic law in order to address the myth that we are all in the same boat. While we are floating on the same sea, 'it's clear that some are in superyachts while others are clinging to drifting debris'.[133]

130 Jonas Ebbesson & Ellen Hey, 'Introduction to the Sustainable Development Goals, Agenda 2030, and International Law', in Ebbesson & Hey, n. 69, 22.

131 Guterres, n. 129; see also text accompanying n. 5 above.

132 'Key Recommendations for Accelerating Action towards a Healthy Planet for the Prosperity of All', *Stockholm +50 Conference*, www.stockholm50.global/resources/stockholm50-recommendations-and-actions-renewal-and-trust. This right was adopted by HRC Resolution A/HRC/RES/48/13 on the Human Right to a Clean Healthy and Sustainable Environment, 8 October 2021, para. 1; UNGA Resolution A/RES/76/300 on the Human Right to a Clean, Healthy and Sustainable Environment, 28 July 2022, para. 1.

133 Guterres, n. 129.

3

On the International Environmental Governance Architecture: Looking Back to Look Ahead for Our Common Future

Bharat H. Desai

3.1 INTRODUCTION

In many respects, the hub of international environmental governance (IEG) architecture – the UN Environment Programme (UNEP) – was established by the UN General Assembly (UNGA) in 1972 as a follow-up to the first UN Conference on Human Environment (Stockholm Convention) in order to meet the 'urgent need for a permanent institutional arrangement within the United Nations system for the protection and improvement of the environment'.[1] Since then, there has been momentous growth in the corpus of international institutions engaging with environmental matters.

A closer scrutiny of the sovereign states' quest for institution-building in the field of environmental governance reveals a remarkable effort to balance the idealistic notions of institutionalized international cooperation with the practical constraints arising from the national interests of states. This process has kept pace with the changing needs of the international community to regulate its affairs, especially through the means of institutional structures.[2] Designing these human institutions has not been easy. They also reflect the egos of the humans who run them and have undergone numerous twists and turns as well as suffering from problems of hierarchy, rivalry, and conflicts due to the crossing of invisible limits of their boundaries. As a result, the institution-building process and its functional jurisdiction have been mired in complexities with respect to the prevailing circumstances of the time.

[1] *Report of the United Nations Conference on the Human Environment*, UN Doc. A/CONF.48/14/Rev.1, 16 June 1972.

[2] For a detailed study, see Bharat H. Desai, *Institutionalizing International Environmental Law* (Transnational Publishers, 2004).

The prognosis of the global environmental *problematique* since the time of the 1972 Stockholm Conference on the Human Environment[3] to the UN International Meeting Stockholm+50: A Healthy Planet for the Prosperity of All – Our Responsibility, Our Opportunity (Stockholm+50 Meeting)[4] and beyond shows the workings of a marathon global environmental regulatory enterprise. After more than fifty years, the nature, content, quality, and actual workings of the legal instruments are worrisome. In a state-centric global order, we need an honest introspection on the architecture of IEG. In order to understand the process at work through intergovernmental efforts, one needs to examine issues such as sovereignty, membership, legal personality, internal law, coordination, contribution of respective states as well as the decision-making process that plays a key role in the evolution of the institutions.[5] These international institutions have provided useful forums for international cooperation on a variety of issues. Their 'constitutional problems' in the wake of 'organizing' were foreseen by some scholars even at the advent of the 1945 UN Charter.[6] The growth of functional international organizations (specialized agencies), functional commissions, and regional commissions as well as other programmes within the UN system provide a living testimony of the craving for the institutionalization of international cooperation.[7]

This web of institutionalization has been slowly but steadily spreading in the last five decades (1972–2022) in the field of international environmental law. In fact, the international lawmaking process in the environmental field is generally moulded by international institutions, which act as catalysts, stimulators, and active participants in the process, notwithstanding the fact that the final call is taken by the sovereign states. As a corollary, the international environmental lawmaking process underlies a remarkable symbiosis between the development of law and the various institutions in the field. The mosaic of IEG architecture provides an interesting picture of a web of institutionalization at work (see Figure 3.1).[8] In fact, the growing corpus of

3 *Report of the United Nations Conference on the Human Environment*, n. 1.

4 *Report of Stockholm+50: A Healthy Planet for the Prosperity of All – Our Responsibility, Our Opportunity*, UN Doc. A/CONF.238/9, 1 August 2022; UNGA Resolution 75/326 on Modalities, 10 September 2021.

5 *Report of Stockholm+50*, n. 4, 17–62.

6 C. Wilfred Jenks, 'Some Constitutional Problems of International Organizations' (1945) 22 *British Yearbook of International Law* 11; Charter of the United Nations, 1945, 1 UNTS 15 (UN Charter).

7 Jenks, n. 6.

8 For a comprehensive exposition on international environmental governance (IEG), see Bharat H. Desai, *International Environmental Governance: Toward UNEPO* (Brill Nijhoff, 2014).

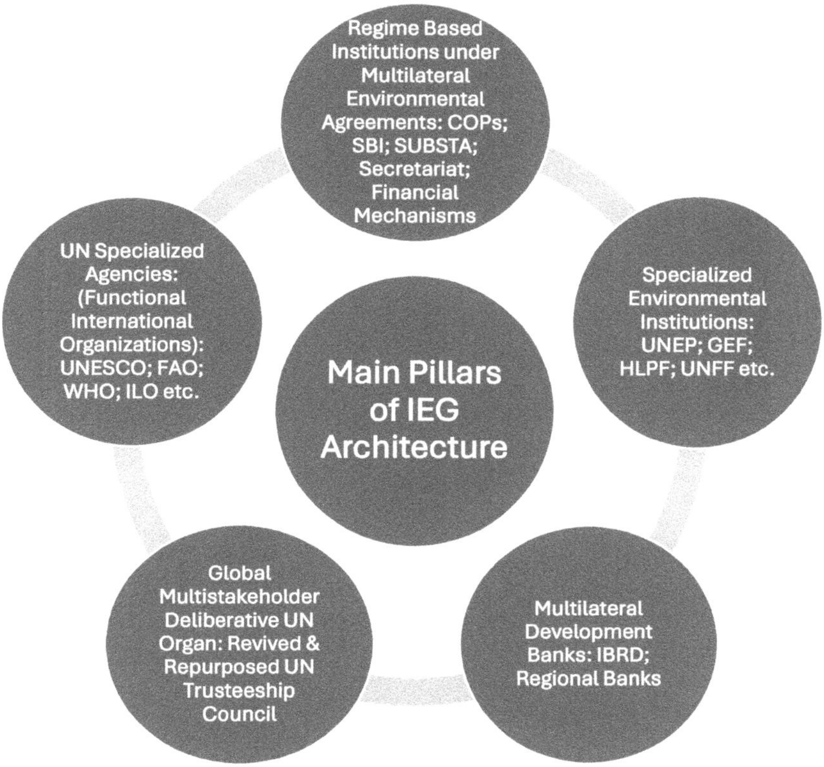

FIGURE 3.1 The main pillars of the architecture of IEG: present and future, including (from the top, clockwise) (1) UN specialized agencies – functional international organizations (UNESCO, FAO, WHO, ILO, and so on); (2) regime-based institutions under MEAs (COPs, SBI, SUBSTA, Secretariat, Financial Mechanisms); (3) specialized environmental institutions (UNEP, GEF, HLPF, UNFF, and so on); (4) multilateral development banks (IBRD and regional banks); and (5) global multi-stakeholder deliberative organ – revived and repurposed UN Trusteeship Council.[9]

9 Figure 3.1 encapsulates the entire corpus of this author's works on international environmental governance: Desai, n. 2; Desai, n. 8; Desai, n. 9; Bharat H. Desai, Ed., *Our Earth Matters: Pathways to a Better Common Environmental Future* (IOS Press, 2021); Bharat H. Desai, Ed., *Envisioning Our Environmental Future: Stockholm+50 and Beyond* (IOS Press, 2022); Bharat H. Desai, Ed., *Regulating Global Climate Change: From Common Concern to Planetary Concern* (IOS Press, 2023). Bharat H. Desai, Ed., *Perspectives of Women Scholars on International Environmental Law* (IOS Press, 2024)

multilateral environmental agreements (MEAs)[10] has significantly contributed to the proliferation of sector-specific institutions that cater to regulatory requirements.[11] As compared to these regime-specific institutions, several specialized international environmental institutions (IEIs) like the UN Environment Program (UNEP),[12] the High-Level Political Forum on Sustainable Development (HLPF),[13] which replaced the Commission on Sustainable Development (CSD),[14] and the UN Forum on Forests[15] have been constituted by the political organs of the United Nations (the UNGA and the Economic and Social Council [ECOSOC]).

The Global Environment Facility (GEF) also came into being, and its unique instrumentality lacks legal personality per se.[16] The GEF was set up in 1991 by the World Bank, which continues to serve as the GEF Trustee, administering the GEF Trust Fund. The UN secretary-general's 2021 report *Our Common Agenda* brought to the fore a long pending quest[17] for the revival and repurpose of the UN Trusteeship Council.[18]

[10] For a detailed examination of the phenomenon of multilateral environmental agreements (MEAs), see Bharat H. Desai, *Multilateral Environmental Agreements: Legal Status of the Secretariats* (Cambridge University Press, 2010).

[11] *Ibid.*

[12] 'Resolution on Institutional and Financial Arrangements', in *Report of the UN Conference on the Human Environment*, n. 1.

[13] UNGA Resolution 67/290 on Forum and Organizational Aspects of the High-level Political Forum on Sustainable Development, 9 July 2013.

[14] UNGA Resolution 47/191 on Institutional Arrangements to Follow up the United Nations Conference on Environment and Development, 22 December 1992.

[15] ECOSOC Resolution 35, 18 October 2000, para. 3(a), http://daccessdds.un.org/doc/UNDOC/GEN/N01/487/49/IMG/N0148749.pdf?OpenElement.pdf. Paragraph 18 of ECOSOC Resolution 35 provides that the establishment of the UN Forum on Forests was not to be 'construed as constituting a precedent'.

[16] The Global Environment Facility was launched as a pilot project just prior to the 1992 Rio Conference on Environment and Development. However, due to issues concerning democratic structure and transparency, it led to its restructuring in 1994. See Global Environment Facility, 'Instrument for the Establishment of the Restructured Global Environment Facility', *Report of the GEF Participants Meeting*, 14–16 March 1994, https://documents1.worldbank.org/curated/en/282361492622558487/pdf/Instrument-for-the-establishment-of-the-restructured-Global-Environment-Facility-GEF.pdf.

[17] For a detailed account, see generally Bharat H. Desai, 'The Repurposed UN Trusteeship Council for the Future' (2022) 52 *Environmental Policy and Law* (*EPL*) 223; Desai, *Our Earth Matters*, n. 15, 189–202; Bharat H. Desai, 'A New Mandate for the Revived UN Trusteeship Council' (2021) 51 *EPL* 97; Bharat H. Desai, *International Environmental Governance: Toward UNEPO* (Brill Nijhoff, 2014), 213–218; Bharat H. Desai, 'Revitalizing International Environmental Institutions: The UN Task Force Report and Beyond' (2000) 40(3) *Indian Journal of International Law* 498.

[18] United Nations, *Our Common Agenda: Report of the Secretary-General* (United Nations, 2021), 77, para. 125.

3.2 DESIGNING THE ARCHITECTURE OF IEG

The advent of MEAs and other IEIs, especially during the 1972–2022 period, shows persistent growth in institutional actors – and the clogging of this space – in the environmental field. However, there does not seem to be any coherent long-term strategy at work for the purpose under a single or unified institutional umbrella. This situation has contributed to making the environmental institutional scenario highly complex. In turn, it presents significant challenges in addressing issues of institutional coordination, interlinkages as well as synergy.[19] As a plenary organ of the United Nations, the UNGA has played a crucial role in designing the institutions. The UNGA has marshalled the technique of 'global conferencing', and it has become popular and is here to stay.[20] During the five decades from the Stockholm Conference to the Stockholm+50 Meeting (1972–2022), the UNGA has shown intense engagement in the global environmental arena (see Figure 3.2). The UNGA has acted as a 'conductor of a grand orchestra', providing political guidance to states,[21] notwithstanding the built-in Charter limitation that it can only make recommendations through its principal instrumentality of resolutions (Article 11).[22]

The UNGA has adopted, often without a vote, resolutions comprising constituent instruments of specialized environmental institutions such as UNEP, the CSD, the HLPF, and the UN Forum on Forests. In this context, an analytical study of the design of IEIs with a focus on the CSD and its replacement with the HLPF (pursuant to UNGA Resolution 67/290) is a good example of the changing character and trend of institutional design at work.[23]

19 Desai, n. 2, 6.

20 See generally Peter M. Haas, 'UN Conferences and Constructivist Governance of the Environment' (2002) 8 *Global Governance* 73.

21 Desai, n. 2, 144.

22 There has been a great debate concerning the nature and legal effect of the resolutions of the UN General Assembly (UNGA). It has been observed that the records of the UN Conference on International Organization in San Francisco do not provide an authoritative interpretation of what exactly was envisaged by the use of the word 'recommendations' in Articles 10–14 of the UN Charter. See F. Blaine Sloan, 'The Binding Force of a "Recommendation" of the General Assembly of the United Nations' (1948) 25 *British Yearbook of International Law* 7, 10; see also Rosalyn Higgins, 'The Development of International Law by the Political Organs of the United Nations' (1965) 59 *ASIL Proceedings* 117; Wolfgang Friedmann, 'Preface', in Obed Y. Asamoah (ed.), *The Legal Significance of the Declarations of the General Assembly of the United Nations* (Martinus Nijhoff, 1966), v; Stephen M. Schwebel, 'The Effect of Resolutions of the UN General Assembly on Customary International Law' (1979) 73 *American Society of International Law (ASIL) Proceedings* 301.

23 UNGA Resolution 67/290, 9 July 2013.

FIGURE 3.2 UNGA's role in global environmental conferencing, 1972–2022.

3.3 RESOLVING THE IEG PUZZLE

The first decades of the 2000s saw the creation of the Committee of Permanent Representatives, the Environment Management Group, the Global Ministerial Environment Forum (GMEF), the HLPF, and, in 2013, the UN Environment Assembly (UNEA),[24] as well as the unmaking of institutions such as the Environmental Coordination Board, the UNEP Governing Council, the GMEF, and the CSD on the IEG chessboard. The role played by these institutions has often resulted in overlapping jurisdictions, working at

[24] Bharat H. Desai, 'The Advent of the United Nations Environment Assembly' (2015) 19(2) *ASIL Insights*, https://asil.org/insights/volume/19/issue/2/advent-united-nations-environment-assembly.

cross-purposes, turf wars, and the wastage of resources.[25] Cumulatively, they have not helped in efficiently and effectively realizing the goal of institutionalized international environmental cooperation. At the same time, the multiplicity of institutions has also made the task of coordination very difficult. In fact, a lack of coordination has emerged as one of the major challenges of IEG. Some studies have underscored that the system of IEG that has developed since the Stockholm Conference is 'not only too complicated, but it is also steadily getting worse'.[26]

In view of this situation, the current state of the architecture of IEG shows a lack of interest in crafting *de novo* remedial institutions and the effects of sheer fatigue and a rudderless navigation prevailing at various levels. Clearly, some concrete and least-cost solutions are in order. These 'low-hanging fruits' could galvanize global institutional responses to the environmental challenge. In turn, they could pave the way for reorienting the global environmental regulatory framework for the future. In this chapter, some immediate goals for redesigning the architecture of IEG are suggested.

3.3.1 *UNEP*

As noted above, UNEP was established as a follow-up to the Stockholm Conference. The 1972 conference became a major milestone for international environmental cooperation. It came out with a charter of principles in the form of the Stockholm Declaration on Human Environment as well as an Action Plan for the protection of the environment, comprising 109 recommendations on a wide array of issues.[27] At UNEP's twenty-fifth anniversary, the Governing Council responded to declining resources and eroding authority by seeking to reassert the program's pre-eminence in the field of the environment. With the adoption of the 1997 Nairobi Declaration by the Governing Council, serious efforts were launched to 'revitalize' UNEP.[28]

[25] Bharat H. Desai, 'Strengthening International Environmental Governance: Some Reflections', in Smitu Kothari, Imtiaz Ahmed, and Helmut Reifeld (eds.), *The Value of Nature: Ecological Politics in India* (Rainbow Publishers, 2000), 221.

[26] UN University, *International Sustainable Development Governance: The Question of Reform: Key Issues and Proposals*, Final Report no. 10 (UN University, 2002), 10.

[27] 'Declaration of the United Nations Conference on the Human Environment', in *Report of the UN Conference on the Human Environment*, n. 1; 'Action Plan for the Human Environment', in *Report of the United Nations Conference on the Human Environment*, UN Doc. A/CONF.48/14/Rev.1, 16 June 1972.

[28] Nairobi Declaration on the Role and Mandate of the United Nations Environment Programme, UN Doc. UNEP/GC/DEC/19/1, 7 February 1997.

The debate concerning the 'revitalization' of UNEP has taken many shapes, twists, and turns and culminated in the 2013 rejig of the Governing Council as the UNEA (pursuant to UNGA Resolution 67/251).[29] The first UNEA meeting witnessed approximately 1,200 participants, 170 national delegations, 80 ministers, and 40 events during the 5-day event, which took place in Nairobi from 23 to 27 June 2014.[30] The UNEA now provides a global platform for biennial sessions of environment ministers to set priorities for global environmental policies and to adopt decisions on simmering global environmental challenges. The advent of the UNEA with universal membership (all 193 UN members) has effectively jettisoned the Governing Council (with 58 members elected by the UNGA), which held sway for 40 years (1972–2012).[31]

The new body, with its broad mandate as well as its composition, has increased its political weight, compared to the Governing Council. This is especially relevant to the extent to which it can present a strong voice for the environment. Hence, it could provide more room for UNEP to contribute, mainly through its Law Division, to the development of international environmental law. The Law Division could work out concrete arrangements with MEA secretariats, several of which operate under UNEP. UNEP may even seek to procure legal capacity for itself through a concerted 'creeping' process under an IEG agenda.[32] It may become a stepping-stone to finally elevate UNEP to the level of a UN 'specialized agency'.[33] Such an entity would have better standing and organizational clout as 'global environmental authority'[34] to protect and improve the global environment. It may also provide a strong forum for international environmental lawmaking and institution building processes within the UN system. Interestingly, the international lawmaking process in the environmental field is, generally, moulded by international institutions that not only push the process further but also participate actively in shaping and reshaping the law. In this context, in the present form, the UNEA would help UNEP to play a modest law enabling role amidst multiple environmental institutions.

The Governing Council hosted its final twenty-seventh session in its new incarnation with universal membership. The new structure obviated the need

29 UNGA Resolution 67/251, 13 March 2013. For a detailed exposition into the process of 'revitalization', see Desai, 'Revitalizing', n. 17; Bharat H. Desai, 'UNEP: A Global Environmental Authority?' (2006) 36(3–4) *EPL* 137; Bharat H. Desai, 'The Quest for a United Nations Specialized Agency for the Environment' (2012) 101(2) *The Round Table* 167.

30 Desai, n. 24.

31 *Ibid.*

32 Desai, n. 8, 9.

33 Desai, 'Quest', n. 29.

34 Desai, 'UNEP', n. 29.

for any formal role by the UNGA to elect members for UNEP's new plenary body, now designated as the UNEA. It became a symbolic snapping of the umbilical cord with the UNGA, of which UNEP still technically remains a subsidiary organ. As mandated by the UNGA, the UNEA has assumed the elevated status of a plenary body akin to the plenary organs of the seventeen 'specialized agencies' of the United Nations. Despite universal membership as well as a high-level ministerial segment to bolster decision-making, the UNEA remains a subsidiary organ of UNEP, which is itself a subsidiary organ of the UNGA. This means that decisions of the UNEA need to be reported to the UNGA unlike decisions taken by plenary organs of the specialized agencies of the UN. Since UNEP has been upgraded both with universal membership and the change of name from 'Governing Council' to 'Environmental Assembly', there was no need for the artificial and temporary construct of the GMEF. Hence, the GMEF ended abruptly after a life span of twelve years. Instead, the UNEA will now 'normally hold one regular session every two years'.[35]

The UNEP restructuring process seems to be *ad hoc* and hortatory and reflects the lack of political will of the major actors for a long-term treaty-based 'functional' international organizational structure as a final salvation. In institutional terms, UNEP, with the universal membership of the UNEA, could formally emerge as a global environmental forum that could act as a global environmental authority and reflect the wishes and expectations of all the UN members. The advent of the UNEA's universal membership was a landmark development in the incremental process of UNEP's 'upgradation'. It has provided UNEP with the virtual trappings of an international organization without formally declaring it to be so. Thus, UNEP has been moved closer to being a unique proto-specialized agency under the UN system, thus underscoring its *sui generis* legal status.

This reform, coupled with adequate, stable, and predictable funding from the regular UNGA annual budget, could provide, in due course, a basis for UNEP's final elevation to the level of a UN 'specialized agency'. This would be a pragmatic course of action compared to the creation of a *de novo* (new) organization with a new bureaucracy to replace UNEP. Such an approach, favoured by some due to a deep disdain for its location in Nairobi (being the only important UN institution located in a developing country), would amount to throwing the baby out with the bathwater and, hence, prove to be

35 United Nations Environment Assembly, 'Rules of Procedure', *UNEP*, 2016, rule 1, www.unep.org/environmentassembly/general-unea/un-environment-assembly-rules-procedure?%2Fun-environment-assembly-rules-procedure=.

counterproductive. In this context, the UNEA heralds fresh hope for UNEP as it gradually limps towards attaining the status of a 'specialized agency' for the environment.

At the Stockholm+50 Meeting in 2022 – and the UNEP@50 Conference, also in 2022[36] – the UNEA still had the trappings of a functional agency without formally being one. This is due to many reasons, including the lack of a treaty to provide its constitution, the status of the UNEP's executive director in the UN hierarchy, its reporting mechanism to the UNGA, and the fact that it is part of the UN Office in Nairobi without its own independent headquarters. Though called, hyperbolically, a 'game changer', the UNEA may be just the proverbial old wine in a new bottle. This step remains a far cry from upgrading UNEP to the status of an UN 'specialized agency' (which can be designated as UN Environment Protection Organization),[37] which is a necessary prerequisite to address the planetary scale of the current environmental challenges.

3.3.2 *High-Level Political Forum on Sustainable Development*

The establishment of the CSD was seen as one of the main outcomes of the 1992 Rio Conference on Environment and Development (Rio Conference), especially since it was agreed that the follow-up activities would be vital for sustainable development. However, there was concern regarding the ability of the CSD to fulfil its mandate to follow up on Rio's sustainable development agenda.[38] Even within the UN parlance, it was widely felt for some time that the CSD was a 'talk shop' as well as a waste of time and resources. This disenchantment of the member states and stakeholders with respect to the working of the CSD finally led to its termination after a twenty-year-long journey that started with the 1992 Rio Conference and ended with the 2012 Rio Conference on Sustainable Development (Rio+20 Conference).[39] It seems that the CSD provided a good perch for sovereign states to 'talk' about sustainable development as the agenda came under sharp focus during the 2002 Johannesburg World Summit on Sustainable Development. By the time

36 'Marking 50 Years of the UN Environment Program', *UNEP*, 2022, www.unep.org/50-years/.

37 See Desai, 'IIEL' (Chapter 6, pp.262-265) n.2, 'IEG' (Chapters 4-7) n.8, 17, 'Quest' n. 29; see also UNGA, 58th Session, 23 September 2003, www.un.org/webcast/ga/58/statements/fraeng030923.htm (which discussed the French President Jacques Chirac's recommendation to the UNGA for a UN Environment Organization (UNEO)).

38 Desai, 'Quest', n. 29.

39 United Nations, *Report of the United Nations Conference on Sustainable Development*, UN Doc. A/CONF.216/16, 22 June 2012, https://digitallibrary.un.org/record/737074?ln=en&v=pdf.

of the Rio+20 Conference, it had outlived its symbolic utility even as a 'talk shop' to those who sought to bring the CSD into being, even at the cost of undermining the authority of UNEP, the United Nations' 'environmental conscience'.[40] However, the advent of the HLPF in 2013 brought down the curtain on an uneventful phase of the CSD (1992–2012) in addressing the global sustainability agenda.

The creation of the HLPF was spelled out in the outcome document of the 2012 Rio+20 Conference, *The Future We Want*.[41] In carving out a new institutional structure, states have derived lessons from the past experiences of international institutions. The HLPF was expected to start its work from where the CSD left off in 2012 – understanding what went wrong with the CSD in fulfilling the Rio Conference's mandate? The making and unmaking of institutions have become a logical process in the quest for meeting the expectations of states and addressing the challenge. There have been rising financial commitments in terms of funding contributions for IEIs as well as obligations to implement these commitments at the national level. It remains very important that the HLPF, as a successor UN entity to the CSD, will be able to stand up to the challenge of the 2015 UNGA's resolution *Transforming Our World: The 2030 Agenda for Sustainable Development*, with the Sustainable Development Goals,[42] drawing lessons from the CSD's experience.

The HLPF had its first inaugural session in 2013.[43] And it has been expected that this new forum would face some teething troubles in its formative years. The significance attached by sovereign states to this new political forum underscores its legitimacy and has provided it with the necessary impetus to carry forward the 2030 SDG agenda. Meanwhile, issues such as inadequate funding, limited technical capabilities, complex scientific assessments, weak institutions, as well as the participation and understanding of the marathon environmental lawmaking process remain perennial challenges. The utility of the new structures would make sense only if they could provide impetus to the demands of the UN member states to actually bring about substantive change in the lives of millions of people in all parts of the world.

40 *Ibid.*

41 UNGA Resolution 66/288, 11 September 2012, 1–53, www.un.org/en/development/desa/population/migration/generalassembly/docs/globalcompact/A_RES_66_288.pdf.

42 *Transforming Our World: The 2030 Agenda for Sustainable Development*, Doc. A/Res/70/1, 25 September 2015.

43 United Nations, *Summary of the First Meeting of the High-Level Political Forum on Sustainable Development: Note by the President of the General Assembly*, UN Doc. A/68/588, 13 November 2013.

The inaugural meeting of the HLPF in 2013 presented an opportunity to open a new chapter in sustainable development governance.[44] With the participation of presidents, prime ministers, and vice presidents, it did become a 'high-level' meeting.[45] It also appeared as a change from the CSD since environment ministers were not the only ones in the room. Speakers included ministers of foreign affairs, development cooperation, multilateral affairs, irrigation and water resources management, social development, and trade, which led to more of a balance between the three dimensions of sustainable development. It was in this context that the introduction of the new institutional structure of the HLPF as a replacement for the older CSD provided an interesting scenario amidst scepticism on the role of multiple IEIs in the same arena. However, the birth of the HLPF with its special mandate could be a product of the 'compelling force of circumstances'[46] or the 'evident need' arising from institutionalized international environmental cooperation.[47] The shape of such an international institution generally reflects the balance of power and the realities of international life.[48] The HLPF is a hybrid body that will operate under the auspices of both the ECOSOC and the UNGA. In envisaging the establishment of the HLPF, the report drafted at the Rio+20 Conference stated: 'We decide to establish a universal intergovernmental high-level political forum, building on the strengths, experiences, resources and inclusive participation modalities of the Commission on Sustainable Development, and subsequently replacing the Commission. The high-level political forum shall follow up on the implementation of sustainable development and should avoid overlap with existing structures, bodies and entities in a cost-effective manner.'[49]

Hence, the HLPF was expected to draw upon the strengths, experiences, resources, and inclusive participation modalities of its predecessor, the CSD.[50] And it was created to address 'the shortcomings of the current system'. The HLPF was expected to operate at the highest possible political level. As a corollary, it was convened at the level of heads of state and government every

44 *Ibid.*

45 'Summary of the First Meeting of the High-Level Political Forum on Sustainable Development' (2013) 33(1) Earth Negotiations Bulletin 9, www.iisd.ca/hlpf/hlpf1/.

46 James L. Brierly, *The Law of Nations: An Introduction to the International Law of Peace* (4th ed., Clarendon Press, 1949), 94.

47 Derek W. Bowett, *The Law of International Institutions* (4th ed., Stevens & Sons, 1982), 1.

48 *Ibid.*

49 UNGA Resolution 66/288 on the Future We Want, 27 July 2012; 'Rio Declaration on Environment and Development', in *Report of the UN Conference on Environment and Development*, UN Doc. A/CONF.151/26 (Vol. I), 12 August 1992, para. 84 (Rio Declaration).

50 Rio Declaration, n. 49, preamble, para. 3.

four years under the aegis of the UNGA, and its participation is universal in comparison to the fifty-three-member CSD. In the intervening years, the HLPF will be convened for eight days under the auspices of the ECOSOC and include a three-day ministerial segment.[51] Thus, it also seems that the HLPF does not have any independent capacity (like the CSD). On the contrary, it has two masters – the UNGA and ECOSOC – that will control its agenda. This hybrid organizational structure has thrown up some procedural and governance issues. There have been concerns that the HLPF could become an obstacle in giving coherent and focused treatment to the agenda for sustainable development. A universal model of high-level decision-making has the advantage of widespread legitimacy, but it also has a limited capacity for deliberation and diffuses peer pressure. The limited frequency of high-level meetings raises the challenge of addressing new and current issues as well as having a dynamic agenda. As such, the HLPF will need to balance its mandate to 'provide political leadership' and 'agenda setting' that could provide an independent high-level voice for sustainable development with its close organizational and political relationship to the ECOSOC and the UNGA.[52]

The mandate of the HLPF comprises 'other relevant stakeholders'.[53] It implies that stakeholders other than those mentioned in Agenda 21, adopted at the Rio Conference,[54] could now participate in the meetings of the HLPF. Moreover, the constitutive UNGA resolution has emphatically laid down that major groups and other stakeholders will be allowed to (1) attend all official meetings of the forum; (2) have access to all official information and documents; (3) intervene in official meetings; (4) submit documents and present written and oral contributions; (5) make recommendations; and (6) organize side events and round tables.[55] The more inclusive language in the HLPF's mandate highlights the challenge of ensuring inclusive and fair access and the need to engage and attract the widest possible range of relevant stakeholders if the HLPF is to attain legitimacy and provide effective leadership in the field.

51 *Ibid.*

52 Steven Bernstein, 'The Role and the Place of the High-Level Political Forum in Strengthening the Global Institutional Framework for Sustainable Development', September 2013, https://sustainabledevelopment.un.org/content/documents/2331Bernstein%20study%20on%20HLPF.pdf.

53 UNGA Resolution 67/290 on the Format and Organizational Aspects of the High-Level Political Forum on Sustainable Development, 9 July 2013, para. 16.

54 Agenda 21, UN Doc. A/CONF. 151/26, 13 June 1992.

55 UNGA Resolution 67/290, n. 53, para. 15.

3.4 REPURPOSED TRUSTEESHIP COUNCIL

In the run-up to the 2022 Stockholm+50 Meeting, António Guterres, the UN secretary-general, suggested in his report entitled *Our Common Agenda* that the UN Trusteeship Council (UNTC) be repurposed as a deliberative forum on behalf of succeeding generations:

> The activities of the Trusteeship Council have been suspended since 1994. Previous commissions and secretaries-general, along with some Member States, have proposed a repurposing of the Council to enhance the governance of the global commons. Building on these ideas and as part of the follow-up to Our Common Agenda, I invite States to consider making the Council available as a multi-stakeholder body to tackle emerging challenges and, especially, to serve as a deliberative forum to act on behalf of succeeding generations. Among other tasks, it could issue advice and guidance with respect to long-term governance of the global commons, delivery of global public goods and management of global public risks.[56]

In 2022, soon after the Stockholm+50 Meeting, this author published an ideational proposal entitled: 'The Repurposed UN Trusteeship Council for the Future'.[57] The proposal holds significance in view of a flurry of initiatives taken by Guterres, including the report of '*Our Common Agenda*'.[58] The revival and repurpose of the UNTC has hitherto remained a taboo for scholars, sovereign states, other institutional actors, and civil society groups etc. The UNTC's repurpose has been endorsed in another report titled *Our Common Agenda and the Road to 2023* to 'improve governance of the global commons, including the high seas, Antarctica, the atmosphere, and outer space', which requires going beyond the reconfigured body's proposed 'advice and guidance' role.[59] In 2022, the UN secretary-general formed the High-Level Advisory Board for Effective Multilateralism as a sequel to his 2021 report *Our Common Agenda* as well as the statement to the seventy-fifth session of the UNGA in September 2021. It was a prelude to the UN secretary-general's

56 United Nations, n. 18, 77, para. 125.

57 Desai, 'Repurposed', n. 17.

58 United Nations, n. 18. The proposal for 'repurposed UNTC' was originally mooted by this author in an invited talk dated 15 January 1999 at the Legal Department of the World Bank, Washington, DC as well as presented at the Max-Planck Institute for Comparative Public Law and International Law (Heidelberg) on 09 March 1999, and published in Desai, 'Revitalizing', n. 17.

59 Madeleine Albright & Ibrahim Gambari, *Our Common Agenda and the Road to 2023*, 21 October 2021, www.project-syndicate.org/commentary/un-summit-of-future-reform-strategy-by-madeleine-albright-and-ibrahim-gambari-2021-10.

proposals for the Special Envoy on Future Generations and the 2024 Summit of the Future.[60]

The UN secretary-general's endorsement for repurposing the UNTC provided a fresh impetus for the revival and repurpose/restructuring of the council[61] at the same time that the world was getting ready to celebrate the fiftieth anniversary of the 1972 Stockholm Conference.[62] The UNGA adopted Resolution 75/280 and Resolution 75/326 on modalities, which set the stage for convening the Stockholm+50 Meeting from 2 to 3 June 2022.[63] Following the Stockholm+50 Meeting, it was an opportune time to think aloud and ahead with respect to the new international legal instruments and new international institutions required to meet the changed needs of the era of a planetary crisis . The UN secretary-general's 2021 report brought into focus the quest for 'repurposing' the UNTC as one of the principal UN organs that has remained dormant since 1994. How can the UNTC be 'repurposed' in a new context and with a new mandate?

The UNTC suspended its operation on 10 November 1994 after the independence of the last trust territory of Palau.[64] On the basis of Resolution 2199 (LXI), the UN Security Council (UNSC) adopted Resolution S/RES/956 in 1994.[65] The tasks of the UNTC were to supervise the dependent territories, and the concept of a 'sacred trust' for the purpose of hand-holding and care for the chosen territories, remained a cardinal principle.[66] Since it had completed its mandated task, the UNTC amended its rules of procedure by a resolution on 25 May 1994 and agreed to drop the obligation to meet annually. It was agreed to meet as occasion required. However, the elections are periodically carried

60 UNGA Resolution 76/307 on Modalities for the Summit of the Future, 8 September 2022.

61 Desai, 'Repurposed', n. 17; Desai, *Our Earth Matters*, n. 15, 189–202; Desai 'New Mandate', n. 17, 97–109; Desai, 'Revitalizing', n. 17, 498–503.

62 See n. 1 above.

63 UNGA Resolution 75/280, 24 May 2021; UNGA Resolution 75/326, n. 4.

64 'Trusteeship Council', *United Nations*, www.un.org/en/about-us/trusteeship-council.

65 Resolution 2199 (LXI), 25 May 1994; UNSC Resolution 956 on Termination of the Status of Palau as a Trust Territory, UN Doc. S/RES/956 10 November 1994 ('satisfied that the people of Palau have freely exercised their right to self-determination in approving the new status agreement in a plebiscite observed by a visiting mission of the Trusteeship Council and that, in addition to this plebiscite, the duly constituted legislature of Palau has adopted a resolution approving the new status agreement, thereby freely expressing their wish to terminate the status of Palau as a Trust Territory; Taking note of resolution 2199 (LXI) of the Trusteeship Council of 25 May 1994; Determines, in the light of the entry into force on 1 October 1994 of the new status agreement for Palau, that the objectives of the Trusteeship Agreement have been fully attained, and that the applicability of the Trusteeship Agreement has terminated with respect to Palau').

66 Sherman S. Hayden, 'The Trusteeship Council: Its First Three Years' (1951) 66(2) *Political Science Quarterly* 226.

out, as done at its seventy-fourth session in 2023.[67] The 'repurpose' can be a decision of the UNTC, a decision of its president, or a decision of the majority of its members or the UNGA or the UNSC. It's doable, practical, no-cost step and 'low-hanging fruit' for restructuring of one of the principal organs of the UN that remains dormant since 1994.

The UN secretary-general's 2021 report imparted much needed relevance for the revival and repurposing of the UNTC. So, again, how can the UNTC be restructured with a new mandate in a new context? In a restructured UNTC, the composition of the organization, as set out in Article 86 of the UN Charter, could range from fifteen members, at the minimum, to fifty-four, at the maximum. The UNGA would elect members for a period of three years, with one-third of the members retiring every year. The allocation of seats would be on the basis of an equitable geographical distribution. Unlike the earlier incarnation of the UNTC, no trust areas would be assigned to it. No member of the revived and repurposed Council would be assigned any special role or conferred with any veto or special or privileged voting rights. The function of the Council would be democratic on the basis of the one-state–one-vote principle, which is the same as outlined for the UNGA in Article 18 of the UN Charter.[68]

If retained in its present form, UNEP, or its possible future upgrade into a UN 'specialized agency' that may be called UN Environment Protection Organization (UNEPO),[69] would have to work out a special 'relationship agreement' with the ECOSOC. If this were to happen, UNEPO, as a *specialized agency*, would report directly to the UNTC and, through it, to the UNGA. Of course, the UNTC would be able to avail the assistance of the ECOSOC and other UN specialized agencies in regard to matters with which they are respectively concerned, according to Article 91 of the UN Charter. The new mandate for the revived UNTC could be 'repurposed/restructured' as follows in the UN Charter:

> ***Article** 87*: The General Assembly and, under its authority, the Trusteeship Council, in carrying out their functions, may:

a. examine progress in reversing global environmental deterioration in consultation with the UN Environment or (its future upgrade into a UN specialized agency) United Nations Environment Protection Organization (UNEPO; or known by any other nomenclature);

[67] See *United Nations*, https://press.un.org/en/2023/tr2436.doc.htm.
[68] UN Charter, n. 6.
[69] Desai, 'IIEL' (Chapter 6, pp. 262–265) n.2, 'IEG' (Chapters 4–7) n.8, 17, 'Quest' n. 29.

b. consider reports submitted by the UN Environment or UNEPO as well as relevant multilateral environmental agreements (preferably climate change, biological diversity, desertification, which have universal membership and were crystallized through the UNGA mandated law-making processes) duly sanctioned by their respective Conferences of Parties on the basis of relationship agreements with the Trusteeship Council;
c. review the status of each of the designated global commons keeping in view the overall interest of all the inhabitants of the planet earth, in consultation with decision-making organs of their respective regulatory regimes through relationship agreements and provide a mandate for further law-making processes as deemed most appropriate;
d. adopt appropriate decisions and other actions, as deemed proper, from time to time, consistent with the respective international agreements, arrangements and mechanisms.[70]

Article 88: The Trusteeship Council shall prepare the form and modalities for submission of periodic reports by each of the regulatory regime of multilateral environment agreement as well as the global commons areas placed under its supervision. The decision-making organs of the respective regimes shall provide an annual report to the Trusteeship Council and, through it, to the General Assembly.[71]

The UN secretary-general's 2021 report has firmly placed the revival and restructuring of the UNTC on the global agenda. Thus, it seems that the restructure of the UNTC is an idea whose time has come even as humankind faces a planetary-level crisis.[72] In principle, it will necessitate an amendment process under Article 108 of the UN Charter, or it could be part of the larger process (as and when it happens) under Article 109 (general conference for a review of the UN Charter). Since both routes appear to be difficult at the present juncture, the UNGA (as a plenary organ) could trigger the process,

[70] Desai, 'Repurposed', n. 17.

[71] Desai, *Regulating*, n. 15.

[72] Bharat H. Desai, 'The Sleepwalking into a Planetary Crisis: Invoking International Law', *SIS Blog*, 29 March 2023, https://sisblogjnu.wixsite.com/website/post/blog-special-i-the-sleepwalking-into-a-planetary-crisis-invoking-international-law (part 1) and https://sisblogjnu.wixsite.com/website/post/blog-special-ii-the-sleepwalking-into-a-planetary-crisis-invoking-international-law (part 2); see also Bharat H. Desai, 'The Audacity of Hope for People and Planet: Rescue Plan for 2030 Sustainable Development Goals', *Green Diplomacy*, 5 September 2023, www.greendiplomacy.org/article/the-audacity-of-hope-for-people-and-planet-rescue-plan-for-2030-sustainable-development-goals/; Bharat H. Desai and Jay B. Desai, 'Ideating on the Planetary Future: Prognosis and Prospects', Environmental Policy and Law 54 (4–6) 2024 205–221; Ideating on the Planetary Future: Prognosis and Prospects.

through its resolution, and by entrusting a new mandate (repurpose/restructure) and authorize the convening of regular sessions of the UNTC to give effect to it.

Through this mandate, the UNTC would reflect a genuine trusteeship, with a responsibility for the planetary trust of present and future generations. Its duty would shift from territory to the rights and welfare of the 'peoples' (to walk-the-talk of the opening line of the preamble to the UN Charter). It would essentially serve as a guardian of the 'planetary concerns'[73] as well as of the 'common heritage of humankind'. Thus, its primary mandate would constitute the global environment and the global commons (planetary concerns). Thus, in essence, the UNTC would be entrusted as the principal instrument with the responsibility for the 'trusteeship of the planet'.[74]

The evolution of the idea of trust in the global domain underscores that there are places, territories, and areas that require special and careful nurturing. Hence, the practice has been to place them under the tutelage of a sovereign state or an international institution that can supervise their well-being. At this juncture, global supervision of environmental protection and the global commons (planetary concerns) assumes significance since they hold special value for present and future generations on the entire planet earth.[75] As the UN practice shows, any proposal for an amendment of the UN Charter is generally treated cautiously. There has been much effort to push for the expansion of the UNSC's membership and to review the veto power itself; however, this has not yet materialized. It is feared that it would open up a Pandora's box for review of the whole UN Charter as many member states feel strongly that the UNSC is not fully representative and the UN Charter does not reflect the realities of the twenty-first-century world. Any such restructuring of the United Nations would need to be reflective of the aspirations of the 'peoples' in whose name the Charter was adopted on 26 June 1945. Therefore, if there is a consensus on the revival and repurpose of the UNTC in this new context, an appropriate mandate would need to constitute a 'trusteeship of the planet' (planetary concern). The governance of the global commons in this new context forms a significant part of the larger architecture of IEG for securing our planetary future.

73 Bharat H. Desai, 'Regulating Global Climate Change: From Common Concern to Planetary Concern', EPL 52 (5–6) 2022, 331–447.
74 Desai, 'Sleepwalking', n 72; Desai, 'Audacity', n. 72; Desai, 'Ideating', n. 72.
75 *Ibid*.

3.5 CONCLUSION

Within the limits of this chapter, effort has been made to put forward a future roadmap for much needed overhauling of the existing IEG architecture. It needs to comprise the three key structures that have been discussed in this chapter. These organs could be duly revitalized and repurposed as well as marshalled for addressing the current planetary-level crisis. After all the twists and turns over the last more than fifty years, UNEP needs to be elevated as a 'specialized agency' in the shape of UNEPO. It can be done through a treaty-based constituent instrument. In essence, UNGA Resolution 2997 (1972) can be reformulated and updated in changed circumstances as a constituent instrument for a functional (specialized) UN environmental agency. The instrument can be tagged as an annex to a UNGA resolution and adopted by the UN member states. It can provide a renewed mandate, structure, nomenclature (UNEPO), and identity as a UN 'specialized agency' without creating a *de novo* organization. Similarly, the HLPF needs to be strengthened (to be accountable both to the UNGA and ECOSOC) as a deliberative forum for the environment and sustainable development. Finally, the restructured UNTC (especially 'repurposed' with a new mandate for environment, global commons and planetary concerns), as one of the principal UN organs, could carry much of the necessary legitimacy and authenticity for resolute engagement in securing the common future of humankind on the planet. It is a 'low-hanging' fruit with no cost and attainable in the near future.

The UN secretary-general has sounded the alarm bells that 'global well-being is in jeopardy, in large part because we have not kept our promises on the environment'.[76] Hence, we need to work on a priority basis as the UN secretary-general identified the 'triple planetary crisis' of climate change, nature, and biodiversity loss, and pollution and waste at the Stockholm+50 Meeting. The message of 'depleting time itself' presents a planetary challenge for the protection of nature and human civilization on earth.[77] Abdulla Shahid, the president of the seventy-sixth UNGA, stated 'that the policies we implement today, will shape the world we live in tomorrow'.[78] This could be implemented by translating new scholarly ideas into effect without any fear or

76 'Secretary-General's Remarks to the Stockholm+50 International Meeting', *UN Secretary-General*, 2 June 2022, www.un.org/sg/en/content/sg/statement/2022-06-02/secretary-generals-remarks-stockholm50-international-meeting-delivered.

77 Nicholas A. Robinson, 'Depleting Time Itself: The Plight of Today's 'Human' Environment', in Desai, *Envisioning*, n. 15, 3–11.

78 'Stockholm+50 Issues Call for Urgent Environmental and Economic Transformation', *United Nations*, 3 June 2022, https://news.un.org/en/story/2022/06/1119732.

favour. It is imperative that we develop timely concrete solutions for the 'world *problematique*', which remains as real as it was in 1972.[79] Thus, urgent action needs to be taken now, especially through the overhaul of the existing architecture of IEG as there is 'no planet B'.[80] One only hopes that wiser counsels will prevail for securing our planetary future before the rapidly depleting time itself runs out.

79 Club of Rome, *The Limits to Growth* (Universe Books, 1972), 10, foreword, https://collections.dartmouth.edu/content/deliver/inline/meadows/pdf/meadows_ltg-001.pdf.

80 'Secretary-General's Remarks at the UN Biodiversity Conference – COP15', *United Nations*, 6 December 2022, www.un.org/sg/en/content/sg/speeches/2022-12-06/secretary-generals-remarks-the-un-biodiversity-conference-—-cop15.

PART II

HUMAN RIGHTS, PARTICIPATORY RIGHTS, AND THE RULE OF LAW

4

Litigating Human Rights and the Environment in International Tribunals 1972–2022: How Far Have We Progressed?

Dinah Shelton

4.1 LINKING HUMAN RIGHTS AND ENVIRONMENTAL PROTECTION

The 1972 Stockholm Conference on the Human Environment (Stockholm Conference) was one of the first international meetings to conclude with a text, the 1972 Stockholm Declaration on the Human Environment (Stockholm Declaration), which recognized the inextricable link between human rights and environmental protection.[1] Although it did not fully accept a right to a safe and healthy environment, lawmakers in many countries, perhaps in recognition of the linkages, drafted constitutional and legislative provisions after the conference setting forth the right to an environment of a specified quality, such as 'healthy', 'safe', 'secure', 'clean', and 'ecologically sound'.[2] The UN General Assembly (UNGA) adopted a resolution acknowledging this right only in mid-2022, soon after the UN International Meeting Stockholm+50: A Healthy Planet for the Prosperity of All – Our Responsibility, Our Opportunity (Stockholm+50 Meeting),[3] citing the work

[1] See 'Declaration of the United Nations Conference on the Human Environment', in *Report of the UN Conference on the Human Environment*, UN Doc. A/CONF.48/14/Rev.1, 16 June 1972 (Stockholm Declaration).

[2] Examples include Angola ('all citizens shall have the right to live in a healthy and unpolluted environment' (art. 24–1); Argentina ('all residents enjoy the right to a healthy, balanced environment which is fit for human development' (art. 41); Azerbaijan ('everyone has the right to live in a healthy environment' (art. 39); Brazil ('everyone has the right to an ecologically balanced environment, which is a public good for the people's use and is essential for a healthy life' (art. 225). See Alan E. Boyle & Michael R. Anderson (eds.), *Human Rights Approaches to Environmental Protection* (Clarendon Press, 1996); James R. May & Erin Daly, *Environmental Constitutionalism* (Edward Elgar, 2016).

[3] See *Report of Stockholm+50: A Healthy Planet for the Prosperity of All – Our Responsibility, Our Opportunity*, UN Doc. A/CONF.238/9, 1 August 2022.

at the Stockholm Conference fifty years earlier as a precursor event.[4] Two regional human rights treaties independently have expressly affirmed this right.[5] In fact, as far as litigation and jurisprudence is concerned, most of the developments have occurred in the human rights field; fewer advances have taken place in international environmental law.

Human rights law at the time of the 1972 Stockholm Conference provided the only international legal recourse available to individuals seeking to remedy environmental harm. International environmental law was undeveloped then, although environmental issues had clearly emerged on the global agenda.[6] Significantly, preparations for the Stockholm Conference coincided with the United Nations convening the 1968 Teheran Conference on Human Rights,[7] marking the twentieth anniversary of the adoption of the Universal Declaration of Human Rights.[8] The Teheran Conference, overcoming a long-standing political debate that led to the adoption of two human rights covenants,[9] proclaimed that all human rights are interdependent and indivisible, opening the door for consideration of complex issues like environmental rights. The Teheran Conference also addressed concerns about economic development and human rights, proclaiming the interdependence of peace, development, and human rights. This agenda stimulated interest among developing states in the Stockholm Conference. It also contributed to scepticism among the same group of states about a global human rights approach to environmental protection.

4 UNGA Resolution A/RES/76/300 on the Human Right to a Clean, Healthy and Sustainable Environment, 28 July 2022. At the 1972 Stockholm Conference, a proposal by the US delegation to include a right to environment was rejected. The proposal was supported by non-governmental organizations, but participating states preferred the formulation of what became the oft-quoted Principle 1 of the final Declaration. It sees human rights as a fundamental goal and environmental protection as instrumental to achieve the 'adequate conditions' for the guaranteed 'life of dignity and well-being'.

5 American Convention on Human Rights, 1969, 1144 UNTS 123 (ACHR); Additional Protocol to the American Convention on Human Rights in the Area of Economic, Social and Cultural Rights, 1988, 28 ILM 156 (1989), art. 11 (Protocol of San Salvador); African Charter on Human and Peoples' Rights, 1981, 1520 UNTS 217, art. 24 (African Charter).

6 In particular, developments in the law of the sea had begun to be concerned with marine pollution and conservation of marine living resources.

7 See *Final Act of the International Conference on Human Rights, Teheran, 22 April–13 May 1968*, UN Doc. A/CONF. 32/41, 1968, 3.

8 Universal Declaration of Human Rights, UN Doc. A/810/71, 10 December 1948 (Universal Declaration).

9 The two covenants divide human rights into categories of civil and political rights, on the one hand, and economic, social, and cultural rights, on the other hand. International Covenant on Civil and Political Rights, 1966, 999 UNTS 171 (ICCPR); International Covenant on Economic, Social and Cultural Rights, 1966, 993 UNTS 3.

The advances in human rights law have shown that it is possible to formulate a new human right to an environment whose quality is not defined in purely anthropocentric terms – an environment that is safe not only for humans but one that is ecologically balanced and sustainable in the long term. International success finally attended the many efforts undertaken in this direction with the adoption of the 2022 UNGA Resolution 76/300, cited above, which referred to the Stockholm Declaration and declared the human right to a clean, healthy, and sustainable environment. It was approved with no dissents and eight abstentions.[10]

In this chapter, I review how the link between human rights and environment protection has developed through litigation at the international level between 1972 and 2022. This pertains both to the substantive and procedural dimensions of human rights in environmental matters.

4.2 ENVIRONMENTAL PROTECTION IN INTERNATIONAL HUMAN RIGHTS LAW

In general, fifty years after Stockholm, the human rights community views environmental protection as an appropriate part of the human rights agenda and the legal protection of human rights through international litigation as an accepted means to achieve that end. An applicant normally cannot choose between bringing an international human rights complaint or an international environmental case because almost no forum exists for the latter.[11] Human rights tribunals thus provide the main international venues to challenge government action or inaction respecting environmental protection. International courts and treaty bodies have expanded or reinterpreted their guarantees in the light of environmental concerns, despite the lack of explicit reference to environmental rights in most global human rights instruments.

As discussed in the following parts, the UN Human Rights Council, the UN Human Rights Committee, the European Court of Human Rights, the Inter-American Commission and Court of Human Rights, and the African Commission and Court of Human Rights have all developed a jurisprudence that recognizes and enforces rights linked to environmental protection. The regional inter-American system and the African human rights bodies have been particularly important in recognizing and enforcing the right to a safe and healthy environment.

[10] Belarus, Cambodia, China, Ethiopia, Iran, Kyrgyzstan, Russia, and Syria abstained.

[11] An exception is the Aarhus Convention with its individual communications procedure. Convention on Access to Information, Public Participation in Decision-making and Access to Justice in Environmental Matters, 1998, 2161 UNTS 447 (Aarhus Convention).

4.2.1 *Global Human Rights Treaty Bodies*

The UN Human Rights Committee supervises state implementation of, and compliance with, the 1966 International Covenant on Civil and Political Rights (ICCPR), primarily through a system of state reporting.[12] The committee may make comments and recommendations to the state individually or issue General Comments to all state parties. The Human Rights Committee also may hear individual complaints against a state party to the ICCPR if the state has also accepted the first 1996 Optional Protocol to the Covenant that creates the procedure.[13]

The Human Rights Committee has received several complaints concerning environmental matters addressing violations of one or more civil and political rights,[14] particularly from Indigenous groups seeking to protect their land and culture from environmental degradation. The Committee has interpreted Article 27 on the right to enjoy culture in a broad manner to encompass resource and land rights, including environmental rights. The Committee has stated that measures whose impact amounts to a denial of the right to culture are incompatible with the ICCPR, but more limited measures can be acceptable. In *Ilmari Länsman et al. v Finland*, the Committee held that Article 27 was not violated by stone quarrying permitted by Finland in the traditional lands of the Sami.[15] The Committee specifically noted that the state complied with the procedural human rights; the community was consulted; and their views were taken into account. Moreover, the Committee determined that the state took measures to minimize the impact on reindeer herding activity and on the environment.[16]

12 ICCPR, n. 9.

13 Optional Protocol to the International Covenant on Civil and Political Rights, 1966, 999 UNTS 171.

14 First, in Human Rights Committee, *EHP v Canada*, Communication no. 67/1980, 21 July 1980, a group of Canadian citizens alleged that the storage of radioactive waste near their homes threatened the right to life of present and future generations. The Committee found that the case raised 'serious issues with regard to the obligation of states parties to protect human life' but declared the case inadmissible due to failure to exhaust local remedies. See Human Rights Committee, Selected Decisions of the Human Rights Committee, vol. 2, 1990, 20.

15 Human Rights Committee, *Ilmari Länsman et al. v Finland*, Communication no. 511/1992, 26 October 1994. See *Final Decisions*, Doc. CCPR/C/57/1, 1996, 74.

16 Other cases involving Sami reindeer breeders include Human Rights Committee, *O.S. et al. v Finland*, Communication no. 431/1990, 23 March 1994; Human Rights Committee, *Jouni E. Länsman et al. v Finland*, Communication no. 671/1995, 30 October 1996.

The balance between minority rights and the protection of marine living resources was at stake in *Apirana Mahuika et al. v New Zealand*.[17] New Zealand made efforts to regulate fishing after a dramatic growth in the fishing industry. The government and the Maori, whose rights are guaranteed by the Treaty of Waitangi, executed a deed of settlement in 1992 to regulate all fisheries issues between the parties. Various tribes and subtribes objected to the settlement, contending that they had not been adequately informed and that the negotiators did not represent them. The Human Rights Committee held for the government. It emphasized 'that the acceptability of measures that affect or interfere with the culturally significant economic activities of a minority depends on whether the members of the minority in question have had the opportunity to participate in the decision-making process ... and whether they will continue to benefit from their traditional economy'.[18] The process of consultation undertaken by the government complied with this requirement because the government paid special attention to the cultural and religious significance of fishing for the Maori.

Another UN human rights body – the Committee on the Elimination of Racial Discrimination (CERD) – has one reported case, *Ågren et al. v Sweden*, that addressed environmental matters. The case was brought by members of a traditional Sami reindeer herding community against Sweden and concerned mining concessions granted on Sami traditional lands.[19] The petitioners submitted that they have their own culture, livelihoods, and language, distinct from the cultures of non-Sami populations. On the merits, the CERD Committee emphasized the rights to consultation and prior informed consent without mentioning the environment explicitly. Instead, it focused on the right to lands, territory, and resources in international human rights law.[20] The Committee decided that independent and competent environmental and social impact studies should be part of the consultation, prior to the awarding of a concession for any development or investment project affecting traditional territories. These consultations must be held from the early stages, and they

17 Human Rights Committee, *Apirana Mahuika et al. v New Zealand*, Communication no. 547/1993, 2000.

18 *Ibid.*, para. 9.8.

19 Committee on the Elimination of Racial Discrimination, *Ågren et al. v Sweden*, Communication no. 54/2013, 18 December 2020.

20 The Inter-American Court of Human Rights (IACtHR) has acknowledged in several cases that Indigenous peoples' rights are indeed protected within the framework of communal property. The same principles are recognized in the African human rights system. See IACtHR, *Centre for Minority Rights Development (Kenya) and Minority Rights Group (on Behalf of Endorois Welfare Council) v Kenya*, Case no. 276/03, 2009; IACtHR, *African Commission on Human and Peoples Rights v Republic of Kenya*, Application no. 006/2012, 2017.

must involve constant communication between the parties. In the light of all the above, the Committee concluded that Sweden had violated the petitioners' right to own property alone as well as in association with others, without discrimination under Article 5(d)(v) of the 1965 Convention on Racial Discrimination.[21] It recommended that Sweden provide an effective remedy to the Sami reindeer-herding community by effectively revising the mining concessions after an adequate process of free, prior, and informed consent.

UN treaty bodies have been limited in how much they can treat issues of human rights and the environment, given the lack of textual references to the environment in their underlying treaties. In addition, the Human Rights Committee has maintained its view that the right of self-determination is non-justiciable through the individual complaint procedure, further limiting the litigation options. The CERD addressed the rights of Indigenous peoples in the progressive *Ågren* decision, although it has mostly followed the case law of regional tribunals.

4.2.2 *Regional Human Rights Treaty Bodies*

4.2.2.1 Litigation before European Treaty Bodies

THE AARHUS CONVENTION AND COMPLIANCE COMMITTEE International human rights bodies in Europe, the Americas, and Africa have all examined cases alleging violations of human rights due to environmental harm. Among international efforts to promote procedural rights, states in the UN Economic Commission for Europe concluded a landmark regional agreement, the 1998 Aarhus Convention, guaranteeing rights to environmental information, public participation, and access to justice.[22] The Aarhus Convention builds on prior texts, especially Principle 1 of the Stockholm Declaration and Principle 10 of the 1992 Rio Declaration on Environment and Development (Rio Declaration).[23] The preamble of the Rio Declaration expressly states that 'every person has the right to live in an environment adequate to his or her

[21] Convention on the Elimination of All Forms of Discrimination against Racial Discrimination, 1965, 660 UNTS 195.

[22] Aarhus Convention, n. 11. The Convention was sponsored by the UN Economic Commission for Europe (UNECE) and is open for signature by all members of the UNECE, which includes all of Europe as well as the United States, Canada, and states of the former Soviet Union. According to Article 19(3), upon approval by the Meeting of the Parties, the Aarhus Convention is open for accession also by UN member states that are not members of the UNECE.

[23] *Report of the UN Conference on Environment and Development*, UN Doc. A/CONF.151/26 (Vol. I), 12 August 1992, Annex I (Rio Declaration).

health and well-being, and the duty, both individually and in association with others, to protect and improve the environment for the benefit of present and future generations'. This is also reflected in Article 1 of the Aarhus Convention.

The right to access to information in Article 4 mirrors many other human rights treaties, although, as pointed out in notes 40–42, Article 10 of the 1950 European Convention on Human Rights (ECHR) guarantees only 'the freedom to receive information'.[24] Public participation in decision-making, as guaranteed by Articles 6–7 of the Aarhus Convention, shall be ensured for all decisions on whether to permit or renew permission for industrial, agricultural, and construction activities listed in an annex to the Convention, and other activities that may have a significant impact on the environment as well as for decisions on plans, policies, and programmes. According to Article 8, the parties shall also strive to promote public participation in the preparation of executive regulations and other generally applicable legally binding rules that may have a significant effect on the environment. The provisions of Article 9 on access to justice follow many other human rights texts in requiring proceedings before an independent and impartial body established by law.

Based on Article 15 of the Aarhus Convention, the Meeting of the Parties decided to establish a Compliance Committee, which allows not only submissions by state parties but also communications from members of the public on matters related to the Convention. The Aarhus Convention Compliance Committee marks an important step in promoting the effectiveness of international environmental agreements. The Compliance Committee began hearing cases and issuing decisions in 2005.[25] Since that time, it has issued close to one hundred findings, often combined with recommendations on communications submitted to it, alleging violation of one or more rights guaranteed by the Convention. While only a few cases have been submitted by state parties to the treaty, more cases have been brought by individuals, and the overwhelming majority of communications have come from non-governmental organizations (NGOs). The alleged violations are quite varied, ranging from complaints about a lack of consultation and information about mining activities, industrial and hydroelectric projects,[26] and the imposition

[24] Convention for the Protection of Human Rights and Fundamental Freedoms, 1950, 213 UNTS 222 (ECHR).

[25] See *Compilation of Findings of the Aarhus Convention Compliance Committee, adopted 18 February 2005 to date*, 14 December 2021.

[26] *Findings and Recommendations with Regard to Communication* ACCC/C/2009/37 *Concerning Compliance by Belarus (adopted by the Compliance Committee on September 24, 2010)*, Doc. ECE/MP.PP/2011/11/Add.2, 12 May 2011.

of excessive costs preventing access to justice.[27] A significant number of cases have challenged procedures for approval or extension of licenses for nuclear power plants.[28] Another group of cases object to wind energy farms. Land use planning permission is also a frequent subject of litigation. One feature of this procedure, unlike proceedings before other human rights tribunals, is how frequently the process is invoked for nature protection.[29] There is no need to have an impact on human well-being for an applicant to have standing.

Many of the early cases before the Compliance Committee concerned countries in Central and Eastern Europe, but soon numerous communications were submitted regarding Western Europe as well. Importantly, cases have also been brought against the European Union, some of them successfully – for instance, with respect to the access of members of the public to the Court of Justice of the European Union. On access to justice, in another case concerning fees in domestic court proceedings, the Compliance Committee spoke not only about the importance of access to justice but also about the important role of NGOs, and it emphasized that

> the rights granted to the public by the Convention and its three pillars aim not only at the protection of the individual right to a healthy environment, but also at improving the environment (preambular para. 7) and enhancing the quality and the enforcement of environmental decisions (preambular para. 9). The Convention explicitly recognizes the importance of the role that environmental NGOs can play in environmental protection (preambular para. 13). The Committee also considers that, in keeping with the objective set out in preambular paragraph 7 and article 1 to protect and improve the environment for the benefit of present and future generations, concomitant implementation of the rights under the Convention, in general, should be strengthened over time.[30]

27 See, e.g., Communication ACCC/C/2008/33, Doc. ECE/MP.PP/C.1/2010/6/Add.3, 2 June 2010 (United Kingdom).

28 *Findings and Recommendations of Compliance Committee with Regard to Communication ACCC/C/C/2009/44 Concerning Compliance by Belarus*, Doc. ECE/MP.PP/C.1/2011/6/Add.1, 28 September 2011 (Belarus); *Findings and Recommendations with Regard to Communication ACCC/C/2012/71 Concerning Compliance by Czechia*, Doc. ECE/MP.PP/C.1/2017/3, 13 September 2016 (Czech Republic).

29 See, e.g., *Report by the Compliance Committee, Addendum, Compliance by Denmark with Its Obligations under the Convention*, Doc. ECE/MP.PP/2008/5/Add.4, 8 March 2008 (Denmark) (the communicant claims that Danish law does not provide him with any means to challenge the alleged failure of Denmark to correctly implement the Council Directive (EEC) 79/409 on the Conservation of Wild Birds); see also *Findings and Recommendations with Regard to Communication ACCC/C/2008/35 Concerning Compliance by Georgia*, Doc. ECE/MP.PP/C.1/2010/4/Add.1, 8 February 2011 (forestry law in Georgia).

30 *Findings and Recommendations Concerning Communication* ACCC/C/2011/57, Doc. ECE/MP.PP/2008/5/Add.4, 16 July 2012, para. 46 (Denmark) (findings and recommendations adopted 30 March 2012).

In the first interstate case, *Romania v Ukraine*,[31] the Compliance Committee found that, by failing to provide for public participation as required by the Aarhus Convention, Ukraine was not in compliance with its obligations. In another interstate case, *Lithuania v Belarus*,[32] the Compliance Committee held similarly that, in cases subject to a transboundary procedure under an international treaty, the party of origin is also responsible under the Aarhus Convention for the adequate, timely, and effective notification of the public concerned in the affected country.[33] The Committee had already found Belarus to be in non-compliance with Article 6(6) of the Convention for failing to inform the Belarusian public in a timely manner of the possibility of examining the full environmental impact assessment report.[34] Since Belarus provided the Lithuanian public with notice at an even later stage, and thus provided less favourable treatment to the Lithuanian public regarding access to information relevant to the decision-making, Belarus also violated the principle of non-discrimination, as set out in Article 3(9) of the Aarhus Convention.

The Compliance Committee has also examined several cases on access to justice and expressed its views on what it requires. On this matter, the Committee has emphasized that judicial independence, both individual and institutional, is one of the preconditions in ensuring fairness in the access-to-justice process.[35] The Compliance Committee has developed a substantial

[31] *Findings and Recommendations with Regard to Request ACCC/M/2021/5 Concerning Compliance by the Republic of Moldova*, ACCC/S/2004/01, and *Findings and Recommendations with Regard to Compliance by Ukraine with the Obligations under the Aarhus Convention in the Case of Bystre Deep-water Navigation Canal Construction, Submission ACCC/S/2004/01 by Romania and Communication ACCC/C/2004/03 by Ecopravo-Lviv (Ukraine)*, Doc. ECE/MP.PP/C.1/2005/2/Add.3, 18 February 2005.

[32] *Findings and Recommendations with Regard to Submission ACCC/S/2015/2 Concerning Compliance by Belarus* ACCC/S/2015/2, Doc. ECE/MP.PP/C.1/2021/13, 23 July 2021.

[33] *Findings and Recommendations with Regard to Communication ACCC/C/2012/71 Concerning Compliance by Czechia*, Doc. ECE/MP.PP/C.1/2017/3, 13 September 2016, para. 72.

[34] *Ibid.*, para. 80.

[35] See, e.g., *Findings and Recommendations with Regard to Compliance by Kazakhstan with the Obligations under the Aarhus Convention in the Case of Access to Justice in the Court of Medeuski Region of Almaty (Communication ACCC/C/2004/06 by Ms. Gatina, Mr. Gatin and Ms. Konyushkova (Kazakhstan))*, Doc. ECE/MP.PP/C.1/2006/4/Add.1, 16 June 2006, para. 36. In a case against Belgium, the Compliance Committee recalled that 'the Parties must take the necessary legislative, regulatory and other measures to establish and maintain a clear, transparent and consistent framework to implement the provisions of the Convention. . . . The independence of the judiciary, which is indeed presumed and supported by the Convention, cannot be taken as an excuse by a Party for not taking the necessary measures. In the same vein, although the direct applicability of international agreements in some jurisdictions may imply the alteration of established court practice, this does not relieve a Party from the duty to take the necessary legislative and other measures.' *Findings and*

jurisprudence on the three procedural rights. It has broadly interpreted words and phrases in the Aarhus Convention to make it more effective.[36] It has also reinforced jurisprudence of the European Court of Human Rights (ECtHR) on the protection of environmental defenders and activists when finding arrests and detentions of members of the public to constitute harassment, penalization, and persecution in non-compliance with Article 3(8) of the Convention.[37] As part of its mandate, in each case where the Compliance Committee found a party non-compliant, it gave recommendations to the party concerned on how to get in compliance. In many cases, this has had the positive effect of encouraging the parties to change their laws.[38]

THE EUROPEAN COURT OF HUMAN RIGHTS For its part, the ECtHR has applied a restrictive approach to Article 10 of the ECHR (right to information) in environmental cases.[39] In *Guerra et al. v Italy*,[40] the applicants asserted the

Recommendations with Regard to Compliance by Belgium with Its Obligations under the Aarhus Convention in Relation to the Rights of Environmental Organizations to Have Access to Justice (Communication ACCC/C/2005/11 by Bond Beter Leefmilieu Vlaanderen VZW (Belgium)), Doc. ECE/MP.PP/C.1/2006/4/Add.2, 16 June 2006, para. 43 (Belgium).

36 One of many examples is the case involving mining in Romania, in which '[t]he Committee recalls that the definition of "environmental information" in article 2, paragraph 3(c), includes, inter alia, any information in any material form on "cultural sites and built structures." The archaeological study in question contained information on the state of "cultural sites and built structures" (i.e., the Roman ruins), which may be affected by activities or measures, including administrative measures. The Committee noted that art. 2(3)(a) of the Convention stipulates that "elements of the environment" includes soil, landscape and natural sites. Exploration/exploitation of ore is an activity affecting or likely to affect the state of these elements, within the definition of art. 2(3) (b). The Committee found that the licenses and other mining-related information requested, including the quantities of ore that could be extracted under those licenses were clearly "environmental information" within the scope of Convention art. 2(3). Thus, Romania could not refuse access to this information on the ground that it was not "environmental information".' *Ibid.*, paras. 50–52.

37 *Findings and Recommendations with Regard to Communication ACCC/C/2014/102 Concerning Compliance by Belarus*, Doc. ECE/MP.PP/C.1/2017/1, 18 June 2017, paras. 70–72 (Belarus) (citing the ECHR, n. 24, for shifting the burden of proof to the state once the applicants have made a *prima facie* case of harassment).

38 This has been done since the first communication, in which the Committee made recommendations and also requested that the party concerned submitted 'a strategy, including a time schedule, for transposing the Convention's provisions into national law and developing practical mechanisms and implementing legislation that would set out clear procedures for their implementation'. *Findings and Recommendations with Regard to Compliance by Kazakhstan with the Obligations under the Aarhus Convention in the Case of Construction of High-voltage Power Lines (Communication ACCC/C/2004/02 by Green Salvation (Kazakhstan))*, Doc. ECE/MP.PP/C.1/2005/2/Add.1, 18 February 2005 (Kazakhstan).

39 See Stefan Weber, 'Environmental Information and the European Convention on Human Rights' (1991) 12 *Human Rights Law Journal* 177.

40 ECtHR, *Guerra and Others v Italy*, Application no. 116/1996/735/932, 19 February 1998.

government's failure to inform the public of the risks and the measures to be taken in case of a major accident, measures prescribed by the domestic law transposing the (then) European Community's 'Seveso' Directive.[41] The Court did not rule on a violation of Article 10 on freedom of expression but found a violation of Article 8 on the right to respect for private and family life. The Court reaffirmed an earlier holding that Article 10 generally only prohibits a government from interfering with the ability of a person to receive information that others wish, or may be willing, to impart. According to the Court, 'that freedom cannot be construed as imposing on a State, in circumstances such as those of the present case, positive obligations to collect and disseminate information of its own motion'.[42]

Regarding other matters, neither the ECHR nor any of its protocols mention the environment. Consequently, those who have suffered from environmental harm have most often complained that the resulting conditions violate Article 8, according to which 'everyone has the right to respect for his privacy, his home and his correspondence'. The ECtHR has held that environmental harm attributable to state action or inaction that has significant injurious effect on a person's home or private and family life constitutes a breach of Article 8, although the harm may be excused if it results from an authorized activity of economic benefit to the community in general, as long as there is no disproportionate burden on any particular individual – that is, the measures must have a legitimate aim, be lawfully enacted, and be proportional. States enjoy a margin of appreciation in determining the legitimacy of the aim pursued. Decisions of the ECtHR overtly balance the competing interests of the individual and the community, with considerable deference to the state's conclusions.

Lopez-Ostra v Spain was the first major ruling by the ECtHR on pollution as a breach of the right to private life and the home.[43] In the case, a waste treatment plant operating without a required license and without having followed the procedure to obtain such a licence caused health problems and nuisance to people living in the district. Despite this, the authorities allowed the plant to resume partial operation. The Court noted that severe environmental pollution may affect individuals' well-being and prevent them from enjoying their homes in such a way as to affect their private and family life adversely, without, however, seriously endangering their health. It reiterated

[41] Council Directive (EEC) 82/501 on the Major Accident Hazards of Certain Industrial Activities, (1982) OJ L230.

[42] *Guerra and Others*, n. 40, para. 53; see also ECtHR, *Bladet Tromsø A/S and Stensaas v Norway*, Application no. 21980/93, 20 May 1999 (on the application of Article 10 to prosecutions for defamation in the dissemination of environmental information).

[43] ECtHR, *Lopez-Ostra v Spain*, Application no. 16798/90, 7 August 1994.

that the determination of whether this violation had occurred should be tested by striking a fair balance between the interest of the town's economic well-being and the applicant's effective enjoyment of her right to respect for her home and her private and family life. Based on that balance, the Court concluded that Spain had violated Article 8.

The ECtHR further explained the *Lopez Ostra* standard in *Fadayeva v Russia*, noting that because 'no right to nature preservation is as such included among the rights and freedoms guaranteed by the Convention', the adverse effects of environmental pollution must attain a certain minimum level if it is to fall within the scope of Article 8.[44] It is enough if there are serious risks posed. In *Fadayeva*, the applicant succeeded on her claim because she was made more vulnerable to various diseases, even though quantifiable harm to her health was deemed to be not proven; in addition, the Court found that her quality of life at her home was adversely affected.

In *Guerra et al v Italy*, the ECtHR reaffirmed that Article 8 can impose positive obligations on states to ensure respect for private or family life.[45] The Court again stated that 'severe environmental pollution may affect individuals' well-being and prevent them from enjoying their homes in such a way as to affect their private and family life'.[46] In finding that Italy had violated Article 8, the Court noted that the individuals had not been able to access essential information 'that would have enabled them to assess the risks they and their families might run if they continued to live at Manfredonia, a town particularly exposed to danger in the event of an accident at the factory'.[47] The ECtHR has often been deferential to the state's claim that it is acting to protect the environment. In *Chapman v United Kingdom*, the ECtHR considered whether planning restrictions imposed to preserve natural areas conflicted with Article 8.[48] The Court ruled that prohibiting a family to occupy its own land in its caravans did not violate Article 8 of the ECHR and held that the individual's preference as to their place of residence cannot override the general interest.

Many of the European privacy and home cases have involved noise pollution, particularly from airports; they have generally been settled or decided against the applicants.[49] In contrast, Article 1 of the 1952 Protocol no. 1 to the

44 ECtHR, *Fadayeva v Russia*, Application no. 55723/00, 9 June 2005.
45 *Guerra and Others*, n. 40.
46 *Ibid.*, para. 60.
47 *Ibid.*, para. 62.
48 ECtHR, *Chapman v United Kingdom*, Application no. 27238/95 (GC), 18 January 2001.
49 See, e.g., *Arrondale v United Kingdom*, 7889/77 (settled); *Baggs v United Kingdom* (1985) 44 D. & R. 13 (settled); *Hatton and Others v United Kingdom*, Application no. 36022/97, 8 July 2003) (overturning the Chamber decision and holding for the government).

ECHR ensures that 'every natural or legal person is entitled to the peaceful enjoyment of his possessions'.[50] The former European Commission accepted that pollution or other environmental harm may result in a breach of Article 1 of Protocol no. 1 but that only where such harm results in a substantial reduction in the value of the property, and where this reduction is not compensated by the state, is it treated, in effect, as an issue of expropriation. In *Pialopoulos and Others v Greece*, which concerned planning restrictions that prevented applicants from building a shopping centre on their land, the ECtHR accepted that the impugned measures aimed at environmental protection but held that the applicants were entitled to compensation because their property rights were violated.[51]

Cases on environmental matters before the ECtHR may also concern a lack of access to justice. In *Zander v Sweden*, the applicants complained that they had been denied judicial review of a drinking water decision.[52] Finding that the applicants had a right to clean water under Swedish law, the Court held that the lack of judicial review violated Article 6 of the ECHR on the right to a fair trial.[53] In later cases, the ECtHR has given effect to various human rights linked to environmental protection by reference to international environmental principles, standards, and norms. In addition, it has emphasized the importance of giving effect to national environmental rights provisions. In so doing, it has given substantive content to environmental rights and corresponding state obligations. In *Öneryildiz v Turkey*,[54] the Court referred to the 1993 Convention on Civil Liability for Damage Resulting from Activities Dangerous to the Environment and the Convention on the Protection of the Environment through Criminal Law despite the fact that the majority of member states, including the respondent State, had neither signed nor ratified the two Conventions.[55] In *Taşkin and Others v Turkey*, the ECtHR built on its case law concerning Article 8 of the Convention in matters of environmental

[50] Protocol no. 1 to the Convention for the Protection of Human Rights and Fundamental Freedoms, 1952, ETS 9.

[51] ECtHR, *Pialopoulos and Others v Greece*, Application no. 37095/97, 15 February 2001.

[52] ECtHR, *Zander v Sweden*, Application no. 14282/88, 25 November 1993.

[53] See also ECtHR, *Karin Andersson et al. v Sweden*, Application no. 29878/09, 25 September 2014 (where Sweden was found to have violated Article 6 since 'the applicants were not able, at any time of the domestic proceedings, to obtain a full judicial review of the authorities' decisions, including the question whether the location of the railway infringed their rights as property owners. Thus, . . . they did not have access to a court for the determination of their civil rights in the case.'

[54] ECtHR (GC), *Oneryildiz v Turkey*, Application no. 48939/99, 30 November 2004.

[55] Convention on Civil Liability for Damage Resulting from Activities Dangerous to the Environment, 1993, ETS no. 150.

protection, largely on the basis of principles enshrined in the Aarhus Convention, even though Turkey had not signed the treaty.[56]

In deciding the merits of admissible cases, the ECtHR has cited other instruments that refer to environmental quality. *Taşkin and Others v Turkey'* involved challenges to the development and operation of a gold mine, which the applicants alleged caused environmental damage to the detriment of people in the region. In reviewing the applicable legal framework, the Court referred to Principle 10 of the Rio Declaration and the Aarhus Convention as they set forth procedural rights. In addition, the Court quoted from a resolution by the Parliamentary Assembly of the Council of Europe on environment and human rights that was relevant to the substantive issues in the case.[57] The Court found Article 8 applicable 'where the dangerous effects of an activity to which the individuals are likely to be exposed have been determined as part of an environmental impact assessment procedure in such a way as to establish a sufficiently close link with private and family life'.[58] The Court held that this broad reading was necessary to ensure the effectiveness of the right and found that, by depriving the procedural guarantees available to the applicants of any useful effect, Turkey had violated Article 8 of the ECHR.

The ECtHR's application of environmental standards reached a new level of protection in the case of *Tatar v Romania*.[59] The case arose after an ecological disaster at a gold mine in Romania, which resulted in high levels of sodium cyanide and heavy metals being released into local freshwaters. As in other cases, the Court made note of the right to a healthy and balanced environment under the Romanian Constitution and of the domestic law implementing this right. It focused in large part on the procedural rights to information, public participation, and redress, but it also considered the substantive obligations of the government under international environmental standards. The Court relied on findings by the UN Environmental Programme about the causes and consequences of the accident as well as determinations by the World Health Organization about the health consequences of exposure to sodium cyanide, placing heavy reliance on them in the absence of adequate domestic fact-finding.

Interestingly for the focus of this chapter, the ECtHR also referred to international standards on best practices for the mining industry and, significantly, quoted extensively from the Stockholm Declaration, the Rio

[56] ECtHR, *Taşkin and Others v Turkey*, Application no. 49517/99, 27 May 2003, paras. 99, 119.
[57] Parliamentary Assembly Recommendation no. 1614 (2003), 27 June 2003.
[58] *Taşkin and Others*, n. 56, para. 113.
[59] ECtHR, *Tatar v Romania*, Application no. 67021/01, 27 January 2007 (in French only).

Declaration, and the Aarhus Convention. Two of its conclusions were particularly significant. First, the Court declared in this case that the precautionary principle had become, on the European level, a juridical norm with content to be applied. This meant government should adopt reasonable and adequate measures capable of respecting the rights of individuals against serious risks to their health and well-being, even where scientific certainty is lacking. Second, the Court recalled to Romania the obligation under Stockholm Principle 21 and Rio Principle 14 to prevent significant transboundary harm, noting that both Hungary and Serbia were affected by the mining accident. These international norms, the Court found, should have been applied by the Romanian government.

In its jurisprudence on human rights and environment protection, the ECtHR requires at a minimum that a state should comply with its domestic environmental standards. The issue of compliance with domestic law is particularly important when there is a domestic constitutional or legislative right to environmental protection. This is shown in *Okyay and Others v Turkey*,[60] which concerned the failure of Turkish authorities to enforce constitutional rights and statutory environmental laws. The applicants explicitly argued that the Turkish Constitution guaranteed them the right to live in a healthy and balanced environment. Importantly, the Court agreed and concluded that this amounted to a civil right under the ECHR. It also held that the applicants' rights to a fair trial under Article 6 of the Convention had been violated due to the failure of the Turkish authorities to comply in practice and within a reasonable time with the domestic court's judgments.

Finally, the ECtHR has ruled on the responsibility of states with respect to risks, which is relevant also for the protection of the environment. The case of *Budayeva and Others v Russia* concerned governmental knowledge of risks and the responsibility when failing to act upon that knowledge.[61] The applicants pleaded violations of Article 2 on the right to life and Article 1 of Protocol no. 1 on the right to property. The Court held that the government was responsible for the loss of life and placed special emphasis on the need to adopt regulations covering the licensing, setting up, operation, security, and supervision of activities, particularly with regard to the level of the potential risk to human life. In cases of such risks, the state has a positive obligation to do everything within the authorities' power to protect the right to life. The Court found Russia had violated Article 2 because the government's measures were

60 ECtHR, *Okyay v Turkey*, Application no. 36220/97, 12 July 2005.
61 ECtHR, *Budayeva and Others v Russia*, Application no. 15339/02, 20 March 2008.

too limited and that there was no justification for the failure to act regarding foreseeable risks.

In comparison, the Aarhus Convention's Compliance Committee has been assertive in enforcing the obligations of states under the provisions of the Convention. It helps that the treaty is rather detailed in the obligations it contains, more so than human rights treaties generally are. It is closer to environmental agreements in its specificity, which may have aided the Compliance Committee. The ECtHR, by way of contrast, has a treaty that mentions neither the environment nor nature, and it has rejected claims that are not plausibly grounded in one of the limited set of rights it guarantees. In recent years, it has been assisted by the growing number of national provisions guaranteeing an environment of a specified quality. It has also made use of developments like the recognition of the precautionary principle to advance environmental protection in cases submitted to it.

4.2.2.2 Litigation before Inter-American Treaty Bodies

The inter-American system is built on the 1969 American Convention on Human Rights and related agreements.[62] Recently, it added a convention modelled on the Aarhus Convention, the Escazu Agreement for Latin America and the Caribbean.[63] Adopted by the Economic Commission for Latin America and the Caribbean on 4 March 2018, it has been accepted by fifteen states, and it elected its first Compliance Committee member in the spring of 2023. Its preamble refers both to Stockholm Declaration and to the Rio Declaration. In the inter-American system, the Inter-American Commission already in the mid-1980s established a link between environmental quality and the human right to life in response to a petition brought on behalf of the Yanomami Indians of Brazil.[64] Brazil constructed a highway through Yanomami territory and authorized the exploitation of the territory's resources.[65] The Commission found violations of numerous rights. Since that

62 ACHR, n. 5.

63 Regional Agreement on Access to Information, Public Participation and Justice in Environmental Matters in Latin America and the Caribbean, Doc. LC/PUB.2018/8/Rev.1, 4 March 2018.

64 The petition alleged that the government violated the American Declaration of the Rights and Duties of Man. American Declaration on the Rights and Duties of Man, OAS Resolution XXX, 2 May 1948, reprinted in (1949) 43 *American Journal of International Law Supplement* 133 (American Declaration).

65 The Inter-American Commission on Human Rights found that the government had violated the Yanomami rights to life, liberty, and personal security guaranteed by Article 1 of the American Declaration as well as the right of residence and movement (Article VIII) and the

decision, the inter-American human rights bodies have developed a unique jurisprudence that gives prominence to the collective and individual rights of Indigenous peoples, centring on a broadly interpreted right to property, defined in cultural and religious as well as economic terms, as guaranteed by the 1948 American Declaration on the Rights and Duties of Man (American Declaration)[66] and the 1969 American Convention.[67] In 2004, in *Maya Indigenous Community of the Toledo District v Belize*, the Commission affirmed that states must effectively demarcate Indigenous peoples' lands.[68]

The Inter-American Commission and Court on Human Rights (IACtHR) have similarly emphasized the importance to Indigenous peoples of their lands and resources. In the 2001 case of *Mayagna (Sumo) Awas Tingni Community v Nicaragua (Awas Tingni)*, the Court, relying on the right to property in the American Convention, looked to the Indigenous groups' own system of allocating land as a source of law.[69] Even in the absence of 'real title', Indigenous peoples' customary law of land tenure could give rise to property rights pursuant to the Convention. The Court applied Article 27 of the ICCPR and the International Labour Organization's 1989 Convention no. 169 as *lex specialis*, based on provisions of the American Convention, to imply that international law guarantees rights specific to the needs of Indigenous people.[70] The judgment recognized that the collective land rights of Indigenous peoples extend to the resources on that land and that a government's failure to act to protect Indigenous rights may be as much a violation as direct governmental action.

In line with the 2007 UN Declaration on the Rights of Indigenous Peoples (UNDRIP), decisions of the Inter-American Commission and IACtHR suggest that Indigenous peoples are subject to special human rights protections with respect to their traditional lands and resources.[71] These decisions require

right to the preservation of health and well-being (Article XI). Inter-American Commission on Human Rights, Case 7615, Doc. OEA/Ser.L/V/II.66, 5 March 1985 (Brazil).

66 American Declaration, n. 64. The American Declaration is utilized as a source of international legal obligations for member states of the Organization of American States by both the Commission and the Court. See Inter-American Commission on Human Rights, 'Basic Documents Pertaining to Human Rights in the Inter-American System: Introduction', www.cidh.oas.org/basicos/english/Basic1.%20Intro.htm.

67 ACHR, n. 5.

68 Inter-American Commission on Human Rights, *Maya Indigenous Community of the Toledo District v Belize*, Case no. 12.053, Doc. OEA/Ser.L/V/II.122, 12 October 2004.

69 Inter-American Court of Human Rights, *Case of the Mayagna (Sumo) Awas Tingni Community v Nicaragua*, Judgment of August 31, 2001, Ser. C, No. 79.

70 Convention no. 169 Concerning Indigenous and Tribal People in Independent Countries, 1989, 1650 UNTS 383.

71 UN Declaration on the Rights of Indigenous Peoples, UN Doc. A/61/49, 13 September 2007 (UNDRIP).

that states recognize Indigenous peoples' distinct land tenure systems and guarantee the permanent use and enjoyment of the lands they have used and occupied, together with the resources that have sustained them. These rights in turn give rise to a requirement of prior informed consultation or consent whenever the state seeks to engage in activities impacting Indigenous peoples' lands and resources.

The 2016 American Declaration on the Rights of Indigenous Peoples codifies to a large extent the judgments of the IACtHR on this issue by confirming the right of Indigenous peoples to maintain and strengthen their distinctive relationship to their lands, territories, and resources.[72] States must give legal recognition and protection to these relationships, with due respect to the customs, traditions, and land tenure systems of the Indigenous peoples concerned. Exploitations of subsurface and surface resources on Indigenous lands are activities that are especially destructive of the environment, and they have been repeated sources of complaints by Indigenous peoples because the property systems of many Latin American countries vest subsurface mineral rights in the state regardless of private land ownership. Litigation efforts have focused on procedural rights, especially the principle of free, prior, and informed consent. UNDRIP and the American Declaration both require 'free, prior, and informed consent' from affected Indigenous peoples prior to actions being undertaken by the state or others operating under state concessions.[73]

The case law of the inter-American human rights system has contributed considerably to recognizing the right to a safe and healthy environment, through a groundbreaking advisory opinion and a subsequent court judgment. In its *Advisory Opinion OC 23/17 of November 15, 2017, Requested by the Republic of Colombia*, the IACtHR deemed human health to be the bridge between human rights and environmental protection, being a primary objective of both areas of regulation. Among the prerequisites for health are safe environmental milieu – that is, air, water, and soil. The Court observed the potentially conflicting emphases of human rights law and environmental law, as the essential concern of human rights law is to protect individuals and groups alive today, while the purpose of environmental law is to sustain life globally by balancing the needs and capacities of present generations of all species with those of the future. The two bodies of law thus have placed

72 American Declaration on the Rights of Indigenous Peoples, Doc. AG/RES.2888, 15 June 2016 (ADRIP).

73 UNDRIP, n. 71, art. 19; ADRIP, n. 72, art. XXIII.

emphasis on different components of environmental protection. Summing up this point, the Court found that

> owing to the close connection between environmental protection, sustainable development and human rights, currently (i) numerous human rights protection systems recognize the right to a healthy environment as a right in itself, particularly the Inter-American human rights system, while it is evident that (ii) numerous other human rights are vulnerable to environmental degradation, all of which results in a series of environmental obligations for States to comply with their duty to respect and to ensure those rights. Specifically, another consequence of the interdependence and indivisibility of human rights and environmental protection is that, when determining these State obligations, the Court may avail itself of the principles, rights and obligations of international environmental law, which, as part of the international *corpus iuris* make a decisive contribution to establishing the scope of the obligations under the American Convention in this regard.[74]

The IACtHR noted that the right to a healthy environment is established expressly by Article 11 of the 1988 Protocol of San Salvador.[75] The Court also considered that this right is included among the economic, social, and cultural rights protected by Article 26 of the American Convention. The Court further underscored that the right to a healthy environment is recognized in the domestic laws of several states of the region as well as in some provisions of the international *corpus iuris*. In its advisory opinion, the Court expanded on several important issues on human rights and environment protection. First, the Court determined that the human right to a healthy environment is understood as a right that has both individual and collective connotations. In its collective dimension, the right to a healthy environment constitutes a universal value that is owed to both present and future generations. In its individual dimension, its violation may have a direct and an indirect impact on the individual owing to its connectivity to other rights, such as the rights to health, personal integrity, and life. In sum, 'environmental degradation may

74 IACtHR, *State Obligations in Relation to the Environment in Relation in the Context of the Protection and Guarantee of the Rights to Life and to Personal Integrity: Interpretation and Scope of Articles 1(1) and 2 of the American Convention on Human Rights*, Advisory Opinion OC-23/17, November 2017, para. 55.

75 Protocol of San Salvador, n. 5. The Protocol guarantees the right to a healthy environment in Article 11 ('(1) Everyone shall have the right to live in a healthy environment and to have access to basic public services. (2) The States Parties shall promote the protection, preservation, and improvement of the environment.'). Article 11 is not, however, one of the rights in the Protocol that is subject to the petition procedure established by the American Convention. See Dinah Shelton, 'Environmental Rights', in Philip Alston (ed.), *Peoples' Rights* (Oxford University Press, 2001), 185.

cause irreparable harm to human beings; thus, a healthy environment is a fundamental right for the existence of humankind'.[76]

Second, the IACtHR identified the following five state obligations stemming from the right to a healthy environment: (1) guaranteeing everyone, without any discrimination, a healthy environment in which to live; (2) guaranteeing everyone, without any discrimination, basic public services; (3) promoting environmental protection; (4) promoting environmental conservation; and (5) promoting improvement of the environment.

Third, the Court stressed that, as an autonomous right, the right to a healthy environment protects the components of the environment, such as forests, rivers, and seas, as legal interests in themselves, even in the absence of the certainty or evidence of a risk to individuals. This means that it protects nature and the environment not only because of the effects that their degradation may have on rights, such as health, life, or personal integrity but also because their importance to other living organisms also merits protection.

Fourth, the Court considered that the rights that are particularly vulnerable to environmental impact include the rights to life, personal integrity, private life, health, water, food, housing, participation in cultural life, property, and the right to not be forcibly displaced.

Fifth, the Court expanded on states' obligation to avoid transboundary environmental damage that can affect the human rights of individuals outside their territory. The Court concluded that the obligation to prevent transboundary environmental damage or harm is an obligation recognized by international environmental law, under which states may be held responsible for any significant damage caused to persons outside their borders by activities originating in their territory or under their effective control or authority, whether the activities are lawful or not.

Sixth, noting that the precautionary principle has been included in various international treaties on environmental protection, the Court considered that, in the context of the protection of the rights to life and to personal integrity, states must act in keeping with the precautionary principle. Therefore, even in the absence of scientific certainty, they must take 'effective' measures to prevent severe or irreversible damage.

Seventh, the Court highlighted the procedural obligations related to: (1) access to information; (2) public participation; and (3) access to justice in relation to environmental protection obligations. The Court considered that states have the obligation to respect and ensure access to information concerning possible environmental impacts. This obligation must be ensured to every

76 IACtHR, n. 74, para. 59.

person subject to their jurisdiction in an accessible, effective, and timely manner, without the person requesting the information having to prove a specific interest. Furthermore, in the context of environmental protection, this obligation involves providing both the mechanisms and procedures for individuals to request information and the active compilation and dissemination of information by the state.

The IACtHR called public participation 'one of the fundamental pillars of instrumental or procedural rights because it is through participation that the individual exercises democratic control of the state's activities and is able to question, investigate and assess compliance with public functions'.[77] The Court considered that the obligation to ensure the participation of persons in decision-making and policies that could affect the environment, without discrimination and in a fair, significant, and transparent manner, is derived from the right to participate in public affairs, and, to this end, states must have previously ensured access to the necessary information.

With respect to access to justice, the Court had indicated previously that this amounts to a peremptory norm of international law. States parties to the American Convention are obliged to provide effective judicial remedies to the victims of human rights violations (Article 25), and remedies must be substantiated in accordance with the rules of the due process of law (Article 8(1)). This applies to all persons subject to their jurisdiction (Article 1(1)). Accordingly, states must guarantee that the public have access to remedies to contest any provision, decision, act, or omission of the public authorities that violates or could violate obligations under environmental law; to ensure the full realization of the other procedural rights (that is, the right of access to information and to public participation); and to redress any violation of their rights as a result of failure to comply with obligations under environmental law.

This innovative and comprehensive opinion was followed in 2020 with a judgment in the case of the *Indigenous Communities of the Lhaka Honhat (Our Land) Association v Argentina*, in which the Court for the first time applied its advisory opinion on the right to a healthy environment.[78] The Court reiterated its long-standing jurisprudence on the right to Indigenous communal property before turning to the rights to movement and residence, the right to a healthy environment, and the related rights to food, water, and to take part in cultural life.

[77] *Ibid.*, para. 226.

[78] IACtHR, Case of the Indigenous Communities of the Lhaka Honhat Association (Our Land) v Argentina (Merits, Reparations and Costs), 6 February 2020.

The IACtHR has moved the furthest in linking environmental protection and human rights. In 2023, the Court received a joint request by Colombia and Chile for an advisory opinion on the scope of state obligations to respond to the climate emergency within the framework of international human rights law, which will test the limits of the Court's approach to these issues. Its opinions and judgments have been largely welcomed among advocates and activists in the southern hemisphere.

4.2.2.3 Litigation before African Treaty Bodies

On the regional level, the 1981 African Charter on Human and Peoples Rights, being adopted after the 1972 Stockholm Conference, was the first international human rights instrument to contain an explicit guarantee of environmental quality (Article 24).[79] Still, the cases in the African system addressing environmental matters have invoked other rights, such as the right to health (Article 16) under the African Charter rather than the right to the environment contained in the same document.[80] The African Commission on Human and Peoples' Rights was the first international human rights body to decide a contentious case involving a violation of the right to a general satisfactory environment. *Social and Economic Rights Action Center (SERAC) and Center for Economic and Social Rights (CESR) v Nigeria* was a landmark case not only in this respect but also in the African Commission's articulation of the duties of governments in Africa to monitor and control the activities of multinational corporations.[81] The Commission found that Nigeria had breached its obligations to respect, protect, promote, and fulfil rights guaranteed by the African Charter. These obligations apply to all rights and entail a combination of negative and positive duties.

79 African Charter, n. 5.

80 In Communications no. 25/89, 47/90, 56/91, and 100/93 against Zaire, the African Commission on Human and Peoples' Rights held that failure by the government to provide basic services such as safe drinking water constitutes a violation of article 16. More recently, applicants have successfully alleged violations of the right to environment. On the development of international human rights in environmental matters in Africa, see, e.g., Dinah Shelton, 'Pursuing Environmental Sustainability in Africa: Procedural Obstacles to Environmental Litigation Based on Human Rights Law', in Jean-Claude N. Ashukem & Semie M. Sama (eds.), *Human Rights and the Environment: A Research Companion* (Routledge, 2023), 136–158; Jonas Ebbesson, 'International Participatory Rights and Environment Protection in Africa – Powerful Tools or "Sleeping Rights?"', in Ashukem & Sama, *ibid.*, 97–115.

81 African Commission on Human and Peoples' Rights, *Social and Economic Rights Action Center (SERAC) and Center for Economic and Social Rights (CESR) against Nigeria*, Case no. 155/96, 13–27 October 2001.

Among other violations were the right of peoples to freely dispose of their wealth and natural resources (Article 21 of the African Charter) and the right of peoples to a 'general satisfactory environment favorable to their development' (Article 24). The African Commission found that the right to a general satisfactory environment imposes clear obligations upon a government, requiring the state to take reasonable and other measures to prevent pollution and ecological degradation, to promote conservation, and to secure an ecologically sustainable development and use of natural resources. The suggestion of a broadly justiciable right to environment is reinforced by the Commission's final comment that all rights in the Charter may be applied and enforced.

In another case with environmental dimensions, the *Endorois*, the African Commission relied on the developing consensus on the relationship between the identity of Indigenous peoples and their unique association with a specific territory that is relevant to their survival.[82] Although the case was mostly about Indigenous peoples' rights, it also touched on environmental conditions important to their well-being and survival. In general, regional and global jurisprudence could be characterized 'as representing a bold and creative attempt at interpreting traditional human rights norms through the lens of historically excluded and marginalized groups'.[83]

In a third case with environmental repercussions, the case of the *Commission v Kenya*, the African Commission asked the African Court on Human and Peoples' Rights (ACtHPR) to order Kenya to halt the eviction of the Indigenous Ogiek from the East Mau Forest and refrain from harassing, intimidating, or interfering with the community's traditional livelihoods.[84] Like the *Endorois* case, this one dealt with environmental rights in relation to lands, livelihoods, and natural resources. The Commission also asked the Court for an order to recognize the Ogiek's historic land, and an order that the state be required to pay compensation to the community for all the injuries

82 See African Commission on Human and Peoples' Rights, *Centre for Minority Rights Development (Kenya) and Minority Rights Group International on behalf of Endorois Welfare Council v Kenya*, Case no. 276/2003, 4 February 2010 (right to culture, Indigenous land rights); African Commission on Human and Peoples' Rights, *Free Legal Assistance Group et al. v Zaire*, Communications no. 25/89, 47/90, 56/91,100/93, 11 October 1993 (right to water and sanitation); Chidi Odinkalu, 'Analysis of Paralysis or Paralysis of Analysis? Implementing Economic, Social, and Cultural Rights under the African Charter on Human and Peoples' Rights' (2001) 23 *Human Rights Quarterly* 327.

83 Korir Sing'Oei & Jared Shepherd, 'In Land We Trust: The Endorois' Communication and the Quest for Indigenous Peoples' Rights in Africa' (2010) 16 *Buffalo Human Rights Law Review* 57.

84 ACtHPR, *African Commission HPR v Republic of Kenya*, Application no. 006/201, 26 May 2017.

they suffered through the loss of their property, development, natural resources and also freedom to practise their religion and culture.

The ACtHPR ordered that Kenya compensate the Ogiek for the material and moral prejudice suffered. On restitution of their lands, the Court held that, in international law, granting Indigenous people privileges such as mere access to land is inadequate to protect their rights to land. The Court held that, in order to make the protection of the Ogiek's right to property meaningful, there must be more than an abstract or juridical recognition of the right to property. The Court further ordered that Kenya commence dialogue and consultations between the Ogiek and/or their representatives and the other concerned parties for purposes of reaching an agreement on whether they can be allowed to continue their operations and to either compensate the concerned third parties and return the land to the Ogiek or agree on appropriate compensation for the Ogiek.

4.3 CONCLUSION

As has been shown, between 1972 and 1992, international law on environmental rights developed in significant ways. From a focus primarily on procedural rights (access to information, public participation, and access to justice), human rights law has articulated broad substantive rights, most importantly, with the recent adoption of a human right to a safe, healthy, and sustainable environment. Most of the advances in litigation have occurred at the regional level – in the regional courts and commissions – not only in contentious cases but also in advisory opinions. However, it was at the global level, in the UN General Assembly, that the crucial declaration on the human right to a healthy environment was adopted. Thus, the value of both global and regional institutions in taking action to protect the environment and human rights has been demonstrated.

The interrelationship between human rights and environmental protection is today undeniable. Human rights depend upon environmental protection, and environmental protection depends upon the exercise of existing human rights such as the right to information and the right to political participation. Despite this common core, the two topics remain distinct. Environmental protection probably cannot be wholly incorporated into the human rights agenda without deforming the concept of human rights and distorting its program. In addition, some human rights are not directly affected by environmental considerations – for example, the right to a name or to be free from *ex post facto* laws.

Even without the link of property or privacy, health, conscience, or association, international treaty bodies and human rights tribunals, especially the Aarhus Convention's Compliance Committee and the regional courts, have begun to move more broadly into nature protection. Scenic areas, flora and fauna, and the general ecological balance are increasingly viewed as part of the rights to which humans are entitled as part of the recognition of the right to a safe and healthy environment. No doubt, debate will continue over whether this recognition serves to enhance environmental protection or simply to further the anthropocentric, utilitarian view that the world's resources exist solely to further human well-being. What is clear is that advocates, through international litigation, have advanced Principle 1 of the Stockholm Declaration well beyond the limits that states were willing to accept fifty years ago.

Probably the biggest change in focus and litigation starting in the years preceding the Stockholm+50 Meeting is the emergence of global climate change as the overriding concern. From the UN Committee on the Rights of the Child,[85] to the International Tribunal on the Law of the Sea[86] and regional courts,[87] climate change matters have dominated recent litigation and other actions.[88] While some of the cases have been declared inadmissible, others remain pending and may further develop the law relating to human rights and the environment. It also appears that the issue has largely crowded other matters off the agenda for at least the time being. This is quite a remarkable development given that climate change was scarcely on the agenda during the 1972 Stockholm Conference. We can only hope that courts and other tribunals are up to the challenge.

85 See UN Committee on the Rights of the Child, *Chiara Saachi et al. v Argentina/Germany et al.*, Communication no. 104/2019, 23 September 2019.

86 ITLOS, *Request for an Advisory Opinion Submitted by the Commission of Small Island States on Climate Change and International Law*, Case no. 31, 21 May 2024.

87 See, e.g., CJEU, *Armando Carvalho et al. v Parliament and Council*, Case no. C-565/19 P, 25 March 2021 (Sixth Chamber); IACtHR, Request for an Advisory Opinion on the Climate Emergency and Human Rights Submitted to the Inter-American Court of Human Rights by the Republic of Colombia and the Republic of Chile, 9 January 2023.

88 See the Committee on the Elimination of Discrimination against Women, Committee on Migrant Workers, Committee on Economic, Social and Cultural Rights, Committee on the Rights of the Child, Committee on the Rights of People with Disabilities, *Joint Statement on Human Rights and Climate Change*, 16 September 2019.

5

Environmental Rule of Law: From Stockholm 1972 to 2022 and Beyond

Patricia Kameri-Mbote, Alvin Gachie, Leonie Geene, Macharia Kaguru, and Jan Maina

5.1 INTRODUCTION

Normative desirability of the rule of law as a political ideal of organizing democratic societies is well settled.[1] While its precise conceptual parts are contested,[2] as a functional governance tool, it is generally accepted that it is an indispensable tool against arbitrariness.[3] Further, there is a general agreement that the rule of law requires legal predictability, impersonal rules, prospectivity, accountability, equality, and clear and determinate rules.[4] For the United Nations (UN), the rule of law is upheld through the formulation of legal norms that align with fundamental rights, the inclusive development of laws, and the fair enforcement of these laws with accountability as a crucial element.[5]

While the rule of law is traditionally regarded as an organizing concept applied in public law, its normative universal acceptance has led to its application in nuanced legal fields. Consequently, scholars and policymakers are actively transplanting the foundational principles of the concept into other fields of law, including public international law[6] and the international law of

This article was prepared by the authors in their personal capacity. The views and opinions expressed in this article are the authors' own and do not reflect the view of the United Nations.

1 Clement Fatovic, 'Emergencies and the Rule of Law', in Eric Stern (ed.), *Oxford Research Encyclopedia of Politics* (Oxford University Press, 2019).

2 Patricia Kameri-Mbote, *Contending Norms in a Plural Legal System: The Limits of Formal Law* (School of Law, University of Nairobi, 2021).

3 Brian Z. Tamanaha, 'The History and Elements of the Rule of Law' [2012] *Singapore Journal of Legal Studies* 232.

4 Clement Fatovic, 'Emergencies and the Rule of Law', in Stern, n. 1, 2.

5 UN Environment Programme (UNEP), *Environmental Rule of Law: First Global Report*, 24 January 2019.

6 See, e.g., Robert McCorquodale, 'Defining the International Rule of Law: Defying Gravity?' (2016) 65(2) *International and Comparative Law Quarterly* (*ICLQ*) 277.

oceans,[7] to address special contexts. In environmental law, the concept of environmental rule of law has emerged over time as a formal framework that employs holistic rule of law principles within the context of environmental law.[8]

While there is currently no formally internationally agreed-upon definition, the United Nations Environment Programme (UNEP) defines environmental rule of law as 'the principles of rule of law applied in the environmental context'.[9] This concept harmonizes essential environmental needs with the core principles of the rule of law, serving as a foundation for reforming environmental governance.[10] Developed to address the absence of the concept of the rule of law in environmental law discourses,[11] environmental rule of law plays a crucial role in ensuring the implementation, compliance, and enforcement of environmental laws.[12] This concept allows for a targeted focus on these aspects, broadening the interpretation of environmental problems into rule of law issues. Moreover, it acknowledges that there are unique rule of law considerations that are specific to environmental law, requiring contextual application. This approach enables a broader range of stakeholders, including the judiciary, political class, and communities to actively participate in environmental law discourses.[13]

Although the current conceptual depth of environmental rule of law may not have existed at the time of the 1972 Stockholm Conference on the Human Environment (Stockholm Conference), certain foundational principles were already emerging, albeit sporadically, indicating an evolving conceptual depth. Following the 1992 Rio Conference on Environment and Development (Rio Conference), these principles gained prominence, marking a significant enhancement in the recognition and emphasis on environmental rule of law.[14] As environmental law reached early adulthood in the

[7] See, e.g., Froukje MariaPlatjouw & Alla Pozdnakova (eds.), *The Environmental Rule of Law for Oceans: Designing Legal Solutions* (Cambridge University Press, 2023).

[8] UNEP, n. 5, 28.

[9] UNEP, Environmental Rule of Law: Tracking Progress and Charting Future Directions, 22 November 2023.

[10] UNEP, n. 5, 8; see also UNEP, *Environmental Rule of Law: Critical to Sustainable Development*, 29 May 2015.

[11] See generally Elizabeth Barratt Ristroph, 'The Role of Philippine Courts in Establishing the Environmental Rule of Law' (2012) 42(9) *Environmental Law Reporter* 10866; UNEP, n. 9, 15.

[12] UNEP, n. 5, 28.

[13] UNEP, n. 9, 17.

[14] The Rio Declaration had more explicit and comprehensive provisions on environmental rule of law, including public participation and access to justice, among others. 'Rio Declaration on Environment and Development', in *Report of the UN Conference on Environment and Development*, UN Doc. A/CONF.151/26 (Vol. I), 12 August 1992 (Rio Declaration).

early 2000s, the focus shifted from environmental law formulation to implementation. This shift created a demand for a holistic and harmonized framework to address the rule of law in environmental law.[15] This momentum saw the concept formally recognized in an international forum by UNEP's Governing Council in 2013.[16] Since then, environmental rule of law has surged in recognition with an evolving understanding and has mobilized stakeholders. Its application in domestic courts is also gaining traction. However, its developmental journey is incomplete. Emerging concepts, such as the core content of the right to a clean, healthy, and sustainable environment, environmental rule of law beyond national jurisdictions, environmental rule of law in emergencies and crises, and environmental rule of law with respect to technology continue to evolve.

5.2 STOCKHOLM CONFERENCE TO RIO CONFERENCE: SPORADIC ENVIRONMENTAL RULE OF LAW PRINCIPLES EMERGE

Following the United Nations General Assembly (UNGA) resolution to convene the Stockholm Conference, the Secretary-General invited member states to submit reports on environmental problems and proposed measures.[17] During the conference's preparatory stage, intense contention over the balance between development and environmental protection ensued. Developing countries viewed the introduction of environmental considerations into the development plans of developing countries sceptically as it was perceived to potentially limit progress in eradicating poverty and addressing pressing human needs.[18] After the Founex seminar in 1971, it was agreed that environmental preservation and development were compatible. This understanding became an important organizing principle at the Stockholm Conference. This crucial compromise paved the way for the recognition that man (sic) has a right to adequate conditions of life in an environment of quality and a corresponding responsibility to protect it.

15 A review of the Montevideo Programme reports shows a significant increase in implementation efforts within the UN system after recognition that adequate effort had been spent in the formulation of laws. Efforts have since shifted to implementing the already existing laws. UNEP, *Montevideo Programme for the Development and Periodic Review of Environmental Law*, 2 February 1982, https://wedocs.unep.org/bitstream/handle/20.500.11822/20587/Montevideo-Programme-I.pdf?sequence=1&amp%3BisAllowed= (Montevideo Programme I).

16 UNEP Governing Council, Decision 27/9 on Advancing Justice, Governance and Law for Environmental Sustainability, 22 February 2013.

17 Lena Joos, '"Only One Earth": Environmental Perceptions and Policies before the Stockholm Conference, 1968–1972' (2023) 18(2) *Journal of Global History* 281.

18 *Ibid.*, 285.

The first principle articulated in the 1972 Stockholm Declaration on the Human Environment (Stockholm Declaration)[19] represents an early manifestation of the right to a clean, healthy, and sustainable environment, which was formally recognized by the UNGA in 2022.[20] The Stockholm Declaration intricately linked environmental exploitation with human rights. This significant development bore witness to the emergence of environmental constitutionalism, the gradual integration of diverse sectors of society with the environment, and domestic courts' interpretation of fundamental rights – such as the right to life and health – as inherently connected and contingent upon a clean environment.[21] This evolution laid a crucial foundation for the flourishing of other rights, encompassing participation, access to information, and access to justice. By the time of the UN International Meeting Stockholm +50: A Healthy Planet for the Prosperity of All – Our Responsibility, Our Opportunity, these rights had become crucial pillars in environmental rule of law.

The Stockholm Conference was instrumental in establishing the legal, institutional, and financial architecture of UNEP as the principal advocate for environment issues within the UN system.[22] This marked a significant step towards coordinating international efforts to safeguard the environment. While the founding mandate of UNEP in 1972 was not restrictive, its priorities and action points were guided by the Stockholm action points, focusing on three pillars: Earthwatch, environmental management, and support measures.[23] A review of UNEP's Governing Council resolutions during its early years reveals, understandably, that its efforts in the realm of environmental law predominantly involved developing environmental laws, assisting regions and countries in formulating environmental legislation, facilitating research, training, and expertise, and providing guidance on the implementation of the Stockholm Declaration's commitments.[24] However, as early as

19 'Declaration of the United Nations Conference on the Human Environment', in *Report of the UN Conference on the Human Environment*, UN Doc. A/CONF.48/14/Rev.1, 16 June 1972 (Stockholm Declaration).

20 UN General Assembly (UNGA), *The Human Right to a Clean, Healthy and Sustainable Environment*, UN Doc. A/76/L.75, 26 July 2022.

21 David R. Boyd, *The Environmental Rights Revolution: A Global Study of Constitutions, Human Rights, and the Environment* (UBC Press, 2012); James R. May & Erin Daly, *Global Environmental Constitutionalism* (Cambridge University Press, 2014).

22 UNGA Resolution 2997 (XXVII), 15 December 1972.

23 Donald Kaniaru, *Environmental Law and Diplomacy* (Strathmore University Press, 2022).

24 The Governing Council held its first session with universal membership in February 2013, where countries agreed to rename the Governing Council as the UN Environment Assembly of the UNEP. See the UNEP Governing Council Decision 27/2: Implementation of

1973, UNEP's Governing Council urged states to establish robust institutions aimed at raising public awareness and disseminating information to enhance the public's understanding of environmental concerns.[25]

In 1978, UNEP's Governing Council adopted Draft Principles of Conduct in the Field of the Environment for the Guidance of States in the Conservation and Harmonious Utilization of Natural Resources Shared by Two or More States.[26] These draft principles mandated participatory environmental impact assessments and information sharing between states prior to the commencement of projects affecting shared resources. Additionally, the principles stipulated that any person harmed by environmental damage resulting from such utilization should have equal access to the same administrative and judicial proceedings, irrespective of nationality.

Outside of UNEP, early environmental conventions, both regional and multilateral, incorporated certain environmental rule of law principles. For instance, the 1974 Convention on the Protection of the Environment (Nordic Convention)[27] and the 1977 Recommendation of the Council for the Organisation for Economic Co-operation and Development's (OECD) for the Implementation of a Regime of Equal Right of Access and Non-Discrimination in Relation to Transfrontier Pollution (OECD Recommendation)[28] were formulated to regulate and reduce transboundary pollution. The foundational principles of the Nordic Convention and the OECD Recommendation – non-discrimination, equal rights of access, and information obligation – are crucial environmental rule of law principles. Another regional example of the early manifestation of environmental rule of law principles is the 1981 African Charter on

Paragraph 88 of the Outcome Document of the United Nations Conference on Sustainable Development, 22 February 2013.

25 UNEP Governing Council, Decision 1/1: Action Plan for the Human Environment: Programme Development and Priorities, 22 June 1973.

26 UNEP, Draft Principles of Conduct in the Field of the Environment for the Guidance of States in the Conservation and Harmonious Utilization of Natural Resources Shared by Two or More States, 25 May 1977, https://wedocs.unep.org/bitstream/handle/20.500.11822/17274/77_05_GC5_Report_K7703225.pdf?sequence=5&isAllowed=y.

27 Convention on the Protection of the Environment, 1974, 1092 UNTS 279. See an analysis of the principles of the convention in Marcelo Gutierrez-Bustamante & Leonardo Espinosa-Leal, 'Natural Language Processing Methods for Scoring Sustainability Reports: A Study of Nordic Listed Companies' (2022) 14(15) *Sustainability* 9165.

28 Organisation for Economic Co-operation and Development, *Recommendation of the Council for the Implementation of a Regime of Equal Right of Access and Non-Discrimination in Relation to Transfrontier Pollution*, Doc. OECD/LEGAL/0152, 17 May 1977. The Recommendation was abrogated on 8 November 2023.

Human and Peoples' Rights, which recognized, along with other rights, the right to participate in decision-making as well as access to justice.[29]

In 1980, the International Union for Conservation of Nature (IUCN), in collaboration with other stakeholders, prepared the World Conservation Strategy, incorporating key environmental rule of law principles. In this strategy, it was acknowledged that environmental laws, up to that point, had witnessed haphazard development trajectories, a lack of public participation, and conflicting agency mandates, among other challenges.[30] As a remedy, the strategy recommended that states should enhance the clarity of mandates between agencies, provide information to members of the public, and enhance public participation in the planning, decision-making, and management of resources.

As UNEP institutionalized its activities and initiated different programmes, its Governing Council, at the recommendation of the Executive Director, prioritized the development of environmental law, formulating general principles, and standardizing guidelines.[31] In 1982, UNEP's Governing Council passed a resolution to establish the Montevideo Programme for the Development and Periodic Review of Environmental Law (Montevideo Programme), which lasted for ten years.[32] This programme was aimed at the development and periodic review of environmental law and its implementation. In the resolution, UNEP was tasked with developing guidelines, principles, and agreements to meet agreed objectives and strategies, including legal and administrative prevention and redress mechanisms and environmental impact assessments. Additionally, UNEP was mandated to lead in the harmonization and encouragement of an integrated approach to environmental concerns and the implementation and codification of the law. Furthermore, it was mandated to provide assistance to develop strong institutions, education, training, and information sharing regarding environmental law. This programme was instrumental in assisting in the conclusion of regional and global multilateral agreements as well as domestic laws in

29 African Charter on Human and Peoples' Rights, 1981, 1520 UNTS 217.

30 International Union for Conservation of Nature (IUCN), UNEP & World Wildlife Fund, *World Conservation Strategy: Living Resource Conservation for Sustainable Development*, 5 March 1980, https://portals.iucn.org/library/efiles/documents/wcs-004.pdf.

31 See UNEP Governing Council resolutions beginning 1975, e.g., Governing Council Resolution 35 on Environmental Law, 2 May 1975; Resolution 13/18 on Environmental law, 24 May 1985.

32 Montevideo Programme I, n. 15. For a quick summary of the main programmes under the Montevideo Programme since inception, see International Institute for Sustainable Development (IISD), *Montevideo Programme Bulletin*, June 2021, https://enb.iisd.org/sites/default/files/2021-06/montevideo_programme_summary_0.pdf.

a harmonized and integrated manner, a key requirement in the implementation of environmental laws.[33]

Cognizant of the need for further guidance on the relationship between development and the environment, the UNGA appointed the Brundtland Commission to study and propose guidance on the issue. Alongside the 1987 Brundtland Commission's report was the Expert Group of Environmental Law of the World Commission on Environment and Development's Proposed Legal Principles for Environmental Protection and Sustainable Development.[34] The principles proclaimed the fundamental right of all human beings to an 'environment adequate for [their] health and well-being' and called for adequate environmental standards while monitoring their dissemination, access to justice, public consultation prior to carrying out projects, non-discrimination, and equal access and treatment in judicial and administrative proceedings. These principles formed an important basis in formulating the 1992 Rio Declaration on Environment and Development (Rio Declaration).[35]

5.3 RIO CONFERENCE AND BEYOND

In 1992, following the Brundtland report, the Rio Conference was convened in Rio de Janeiro, Brazil. Its aim was to develop strategies and initiatives fostering development in an environmentally conscious world. This marked the apex of global endeavours to merge environmental conservation and development as harmonious principles and served as an evaluative milestone, commemorating twenty years since the Stockholm Conference. The Rio Declaration, adopted at the Rio Conference, further entrenched environmental rule of law principles. For instance, Principle 10 emphasized that public participation is central to resolving environmental issues. It called on states to facilitate access to information and public participation and to create awareness among the public. Further, it provided for effective access to judicial and administrative proceedings, including redress and remedy. On the other hand, Principle 11 required states to pass effective legislation, including aligning objectives with standards, while Principle 20 called for more inclusion of women in environmental management.

[33] Gonzalo Biggs, 'The Montevideo Environmental Law Programme' (1993) 87(2) *American Journal of International Law* 328.

[34] Brundtland Commission, *Our Common Future: Report of the World Commission on Environment and Development*, 20 October 1987, Annexe 1, https://sustainabledevelopment.un.org/content/documents/5987our-common-future.pdf.

[35] Rio Declaration, n. 14.

The Rio Conference was transformative and significantly shaped the environmental rule of law principles.[36] First, there was a burgeoning association between human rights and the environment, sparking discussions on the necessity of recognizing a stand-alone right to a clean and healthy environment. National judicial bodies also increasingly acknowledged the crucial role of the environment in human life, forming the basis for the enjoyment of other human rights.[37] At this stage, the debate centred on whether there should be a stand-alone right to a clean and healthy environment or if it should be integrated within the existing separate frameworks of human rights law on one side or environmental law on another side. Increasingly, the significance of merging these two spheres became apparent.[38]

Second, conventions and model laws completed after the Rio Conference were comprehensive, integrated, and incorporated facets of environmental rule of law. In addition to its role in treaty-making, UNEP, in conjunction with other stakeholders, also made significant efforts to harmonize laws and accelerated its function in soft law-making. In contrast to the Montevideo Programme I, which ran from 1982 to 1992, the Montevideo Programme II, which was adopted in 1993, sharply reoriented UNEP's legal engagements from developing 'new law' to the effective implementation of multilateral environmental agreements (MEAs), guidelines, and domestic laws as well as the strengthening of environmental institutions, public participation, and access to justice.[39] Relatedly, UNEP initiated training programmes for judicial officers on environmental law to build capacity within courtrooms.[40] In formulating Montevideo Programme III, the implementation of environmental laws was one of the three main themes for UNEP in the following ten years.[41]

[36] Foo Kim Boon, 'The Rio Declaration and Its Influence on International Environmental Law' [1992] *Singapore Journal of Legal Studies* 347.

[37] May & Daly, n. 21; Lael K. Weis, 'Environmental Constitutionalism: Aspiration or Transformation?' (2018) 16(3) *International and Comparative Law Quarterly* 836; Boyd, n. 21.

[38] Pau de Vilchez & Annalisa Savaresi, 'The Right to a Healthy Environment and Climate Litigation: A Game Changer?' (2021) 32(1) *Yearbook of International Environmental Law* 3.

[39] Biggs, n. 33; see, e.g., Model Law on International Trade in Wild Fauna and Flora, 11 October 2021, https://cites.org/sites/default/files/projects/NLP/E-Model_law-revised_Oct.2021.FINAL.DRAFT.pdf; UNEP, *Guidelines on Compliance with and Enforcement of Multilateral Environmental Agreements*, adopted in Governing Council Decision SS.VII/4: Compliance with and Enforcement of Multilateral Environmental Agreements, 15 February 2002, https://wedocs.unep.org/bitstream/handle/20.500.11822/17018/UNEP-guidelines-compliance-MEA.pdf?sequence=1&isAllowed=y.

[40] Donald Kaniaru, *Environmental Law and Diplomacy* (Strathmore University Press, 2022).

[41] IISD, *Environmental Law Programme to Identify Priorities for Legal Responses*, 8 June 2022, https://sdg.iisd.org/commentary/policy-briefs/environmental-law-programme-to-identify-priorities-for-legal-responses/.

By 2002, considerable effort had been directed towards lawmaking and local commitments to align national action with international instruments.[42] Rather than generating new international commitments, the emphasis shifted to fulfilling the existing ones.[43] In sustaining implementation efforts, various initiatives and efforts focused on implementing international environmental law. UNEP took the lead in promoting implementation by formulating guidelines, highlighting innovations, and carrying out capacity building in national institutions and agencies. The 2012 Rio+20 Conference, which was organized to commemorate twenty years since the Rio Conference, reiterated the need for focusing on the implementation of existing environmental laws. The Rio+20 outcome document emphasized that 'strong institutions, access to information and justice, and the political will to implement and enforce environmental law' were central to achieving sustainable development, paving the way for the elaboration of the concept of environmental rule of law.[44]

5.4 FORMALIZATION OF ENVIRONMENTAL RULE OF LAW IN ENVIRONMENTAL LAW IN 2013

While the term 'environmental rule of law' had previously been used by non-governmental organizations (NGOs), 2013 marked the first time the term was used in a decision of an intergovernmental body.[45] UNEP's Governing Council, in Decision 27/9, requested the Executive Director of UNEP to lead in the 'development and implementation of environmental rule of law'.[46] This resolution emphasized the need to mutually support governance features, including information disclosure, public participation, implementable and enforceable laws, and mechanisms for implementation and accountability. Subsequently, the United Nations Environment Assembly (UNEA) – the successor of UNEP's Governing Council – in its Resolution 1/13 adopted in 2014, urged countries to 'work for the strengthening of environmental rule of law' at all levels.[47]

Since 2013, the term 'environmental rule of law' has gained prominence. In 2016, the first World Environmental Law Congress was organized by the IUCN in collaboration with UNEP, and it adopted the 2016 World

42 UNEP, n. 5.
43 Carl Bruch & John Pendergrass Jr, 'Type II Partnerships, International Law, and the Tragedy of the Commons' (2003) 15 *Georgetown International Environmental Law Review* 855.
44 UNEP, n. 5, 27.
45 *Ibid.*
46 *Ibid.*
47 UNEP Governing Council, n. 16.

Declaration on the Environmental Rule of Law.[48] In 2019, UNEP published its first Global Environmental Rule of Law report, raising awareness on acceptance of environmental rule of law as an important concept.[49] The environmental rule of law is now part of the vision of Montevideo Programme V, which was adopted in 2019. Furthermore, in 2022, UNEA adopted a political declaration of the Special Session of UNEA, recognizing 'the importance of fostering environmental rule of law for addressing biodiversity loss, climate change, and desertification and land degradation'.[50] Additionally, the rule of law is an important pillar in Sustainable Development Goal 16 (Peace, justice and strong institutions).

5.5 UNIFYING ENVIRONMENTAL RULE OF LAW PRINCIPLES: A HOLISTIC FRAMEWORK

The formal recognition of environmental rule of law and the UNEP Governing Council's request that the UNEP Executive Director lead in the development and implementation of environmental rule of law provided an important grounding for UNEP's Law Division. Since 2013, in collaboration with scholars, policy-makers, and stakeholders, UNEP has led efforts to create a holistic framework of environmental rule of law by consolidating the conceptual meaning and identifying and clarifying the development of salient features.[51] Furthermore, stakeholders have been working on strengthening environmental rule of law programmes and actions in national jurisdictions.[52] In the next section, the chapter highlights the essential elements of the environmental rule of law, as set out in UNEP's report on the environmental rule of law.

5.5.1 *Fair, Clear, and Implementable Laws*

Environmental laws can only achieve desired goals if they are fair in their formulation, implementation, and enforcement.[53] Fairness, a foundational

48 IUCN, *World Declaration on the Environmental Rule of Law*, 29 April 2016.
49 UNEP, n. 5, 28.
50 UNGA Resolution 73/333, 30 August 2019, preamble.
51 See generally UNEP, n. 5; UNEP, n. 9.
52 See, e.g., European Union, *Strengthening Environmental Rule of Law through Effective Fight against Environmental Crime*, 7 June 2023, https://covenant-of-companies.ec.europa.eu/events/strengthening-environmental-rule-law-through-effective-fight-against-environmental-crime-2023-06-07_en; see also European Commission, *New Environmental Crime Directive Comes into Force*, 20 May 2024, https://environment.ec.europa.eu/news/new-environmental-crime-directive-comes-force-2024-05-20_en.
53 UNEP, n. 5, 7.

principle in legal systems, guarantees equal treatment before the law and decisions based on objective and impartial criteria. Fairness in environmental rule of law requires accountability to the law and transparency in administration. Given the differentiated impacts that environmental problems present to various categories of people, this principle seeks to ensure that all persons bear equitable and fair responsibilities in complying with environmental laws.[54]

Just like the cardinal principle of the rule of law in general, environmental laws must be objective and clear.[55] They should unambiguously outline the different roles of right holders, duty bearers, and enforcers. Often, environmental considerations are pervasive and cut across several institutions. Any ambiguity as to which of these multiple institutions enforces specific environmental law provisions creates an incentive for reluctance, relaxed enforcement, and blame games among the enforcers.[56] This is detrimental to the environment and sustainable development. In the early years of environmental law development, countries hurriedly enacted environmental laws by transplanting them from other jurisdictions.[57] However, environmental governance and its regulation require a contextual economic, social, institutional, technological, and cultural application. Thus, a nuanced approach to environmental laws at the designing stage guarantees easier enforcement and acceptability and reduces implementation costs. Environmental rule of law, therefore, calls for the formulation of laws capable of being enforced in the contexts to which they apply. Absent this, environmental laws risk being violated to the detriment of the environment and those most vulnerable.

5.5.2 *Access to Information, Public Participation, and Access to Justice*

Public participation allows the public to shape how public authority is exercised and is a critical factor in sustainable development.[58] In many societies, the environment has a multitude of meanings, including cultural, religious, and social interpretations. Further, the environment is crucial for existence, for the sustenance of livelihoods, and for the well-being of people. Thus, there is a heightened incentive for people's engagement in designing, implementing, complying with, and enforcing environmental laws. Active engagement of

54 *Ibid.*
55 *Ibid.*
56 *Ibid.*
57 *Ibid.*
58 Juan R. Palerm, 'Public Participation in Environmental Decision Making: Examining the Aarhus Convention' (1999) 1(2) *Journal of Environmental Assessment Policy and Management* 229.

the people reduces implementation costs and incentivizes compliance.[59] As the overall target of environmental laws is the well-being of the people, environmental rule of law requires constant engagement with the people if the benefits of environmental laws are to be optimized.

There cannot be meaningful public engagement without access to relevant information. In environmental rule of law, effective implementation, enforcement, and compliance are greatly dependent on the availability of information about environmental problems and impacts in an easily accessible manner. Once availed, the public is able to determine what actions are allowable, when violations have taken place, and how to take steps towards enforcement, including approaching judicial and administrative bodies for redress.

Inextricably linked to public participation and access to information is access to justice. This basic principle guarantees that people can exercise and enforce their rights against alleged violations before an impartial decision-maker. It is also a means of holding decision-makers and duty bearers to account. Access to justice is particularly important in environmental rule of law given the non-discriminative and transboundary nature of environmental harms, the accrual of benefits to all, and, often, the reluctance and belittling of environmental concerns by governments. Traditionally, members of the public, NGOs, community organizers, and justice defenders, either on their own behalf or on behalf of the most vulnerable, have been the biggest petitioners against environmental harms. Thus, guaranteeing access to impartial courts and tribunals provides an important impetus to holding people and the state accountable.

5.5.3 *Accountability and Integrity of Institutions and Decision-Makers*

Strong, accountable, and transparent institutions supporting good governance are indispensable for upholding the environmental rule of law.[60] Strengthening institutional capacity involves not only having well-educated, informed, and skilled personnel but also establishing clear mandates, allocating adequate financial resources, ensuring sufficient authority, and promoting effective coordination among institutions across sectors and jurisdictional

[59] Ané du Plessis, 'Public Participation, Good Environmental Governance and Fulfilment of Environmental Rights' (2008) 11(2) *Potchefstroom Electronic Law Journal/Potchefstroomse Elektroniese Regsblad* 1–34.

[60] Arnold Kreilhuber & Angela Kariuki, 'Environmental Rule of Law in the Context of Sustainable Development' (2019) 32 *Georgetown Environmental Law Review* 591.

levels.[61] Empowering institutions, such as courts, tribunals, law enforcement agencies, auditing bodies, and other stakeholders at the national, subregional, regional, and international levels,[62] positions them as key actors in the implementation of environmental rule of law.

It should not be lost on us that, in societies that are rich with natural resources, corruption in environmental concerns can be a challenge.[63] Corruption allows people to violate environmental laws. Unfortunately, those who engage in corruption often possess adaptive capabilities that greatly jeopardize the lives of the most vulnerable. Thus, it is important that environmental institutions and decision-makers are empowered, exercise their roles objectively in a transparent manner, and uphold integrity. Confidence in institutions and decision-makers cultivates a compliance culture for the common good. This serves as an important driver of environmental rule of law.

Environmental rule of law is vital in guiding decision-making that protects human health and the environment, particularly in the face of uncertainty and data gaps.[64] It underscores intergenerational equity and adopts the concept of sustainability, treating the earth and its resources not merely as an investment opportunity but also as a trust passed from one generation to the next for the benefit of both today's and tomorrow's generations.[65] These unique environmental characteristics require independent decision-making on behalf of the people.

5.5.4 *Clear and Coordinated Mandates and Roles across and within Institutions*

The environment is ubiquitous in diverse societal sectors. It is thus natural to have different departments and agencies playing a role in environmental governance in the course of their diverse operations. This reality, however, presents fertile ground for lowering the guard in the rule of law as conflicting, underlapping, and overlapping roles create confusion, blame games, and lax enforcement.[66] Given this reality, environmental rule of law dictates that responsibilities must be clearly demarcated. Should there be a requirement to cooperate, coordination arrangements must be clear across sectors and jurisdictional levels.

61 UNEP, n. 5.
62 UNEP, n. 10.
63 Paltseva, n. 59.
64 Kreilhuber & Kariuki, n. 60.
65 *Ibid.*, 595.
66 UNEP, n. 10.

5.5.5 *Accessible, Fair, Impartial, Timely, and Responsive Adjudication*

In vibrant democratic societies, the availability of an impartial means of resolving controversies guarantees legal certainty and accountability and protects the rights and liberties of all. In environmental law, this element is critical given the nature, circumstances, and incentives relating to resolving environmental disputes. As noted, environmental resources attract the high and mighty and can also be a good breeding ground for corruption. Environmental institutions in some countries are weak, are relegated to inferior positions in government, are poorly funded, and have inadequate capacity.[67] Thus, in some countries, environmental protection through adjudicatory means is primarily a citizen-driven process with the vulnerable taking on powerful government entities and those with means.

Against this background, environmental rule of law requires a legal system to establish and maintain dispute resolution mechanisms that are fair, impartial, and responsive. Legal hurdles including costs, legal standing, and technicalities undermine environmental conservation efforts.[68] Environmental disputes, especially disputes that try to prevent environmental law violations, tend to be time sensitive, and, given that some environmental violations may have irreversible consequences, the expeditious resolution of disputes is critical. To build public confidence in adjudicative tribunals and to guarantee that environmental concerns will be resolved in a timely manner not only incentivizes compliance but also encourages people to approach courts and tribunals for adjudication of claims.

5.5.6 *Specific Criteria for the Interpretation of Environmental Law*

Environmental conservation efforts including laws are made in two unique circumstances. First, environmental laws are heavily dependent on science. In line with the precautionary principle, some environmental laws are made in the face of uncertainty and data gaps.[69] Second, the encompassing and cross-sectional nature of environmental conservation necessitates formulation of environmental laws in broad principles and terms.[70] This affords significant discretion to authorities. While, ideally, certainty discourages broad authority and discretion, these two features are important in environmental law to allow

67 UNEP, n. 5, viii.

68 Gayatri Sarathy, 'Costs in Environmental Litigation: Venn v Secretary of the State for Communities and Local Government' (2015) 27(2) *Journal of Environmental Law* 313.

69 Kreilhuber & Kariuki, n. 60.

70 UNEP, n. 5, viii.

'interpretive tailoring of laws to fit changing scientific understanding and circumstances'.[71] To confront this reality, environmental rule of law emphasizes certainty by requiring the enactment of laws that are as clear as possible. Even when exercising discretion, environmental rule of law demands interpretative consistency from implementing agencies.[72] Thus, implementing authorities should provide clarity on priorities, explanatory notes, guidance notes, and guidelines on how the laws are to be interpreted or implemented. This not only creates certainty for duty bearers but also enables right holders to hold agencies and people accountable so they can know, with significant certainty, how the laws are to be interpreted.

5.5.7 *Recognition of the Relationship with Rights*

The profound influence of environmental factors on the ability to enjoy fundamental human rights is now a recognized reality.[73] The relationship between human rights and the environment is intricate and interdependent. Many of the rights enshrined in international human rights law inherently encompass an environmental protection dimension. This understanding has led to the recognition of the right to a clean, healthy, and sustainable environment as a human right.[74] While the right to a clean, healthy, and sustainable environment was first internationally recognized in 2021 by the United Nations Human Rights Council (HRC) and, in the following year, by the UNGA,[75] its manifestation is old. While elements of it appeared in the 1972 Stockholm Declaration, it is the following years that had a profound impact. The Stockholm Conference linked environmental exploitation to human rights, leading to the recognition of environmental rights and environmental constitutionalism, and the linkage of fundamental rights to a clean environment in domestic laws, regional treaties, and human rights treaties. For example, while there was no environmental right recognition in any constitution in the world in 1968, between 1971 and 1982, twenty-eight countries included environmental protection provisions in their constitutions, and, by

71 *Ibid.*

72 *Ibid.*

73 Philippe Cullet, 'Definition of an Environmental Right in a Human Rights Context' (1995) 13(1) *Netherlands Quarterly of Human Rights* 25.

74 UN Human Rights Council (UNHRC), Report of the Independent Expert on the Issue of Human Rights Obligations Relating to the Enjoyment of a Safe, Clean, Healthy and Sustainable Environment, by John H. Knox, 24 December 2012, www.ohchr.org/sites/default/files/Documents/HRBodies/HRCouncil/RegularSession/Session22/A-HRC-22-43_en.pdf.

75 UNHRC Resolution 48/13, 8 October 2021; UNGA Resolution 76/300, 28 July 2022, https://digitallibrary.un.org/record/3982508?ln=en.

1992, another forty-four countries had environmental protection rights in their constitutions.[76] Even among those without constitutional provisions, there was a notable increase in environmental rights protection provisions in legislation.[77]

Even in countries without formal recognition of environmental rights, courts have increasingly interpreted environmental rights as an essential aspect of guaranteeing other fundamental rights. Thus, to enjoy the right to life, dignity, and freedom, among others, a clean environment has been a requirement. Governments have made efforts, with varying degrees of success, to respect, protect, fulfil, and promote environmental rights and to link environmental rights with other rights as a basis for laying claims.[78] Adopting a human rights approach to environmental problems has had many benefits. In a constitutional context, the 'constitutionalization' of an issue in a state's supreme law communicates its fundamental importance to a society.[79] This removes the issue from majoritarian political debate and provides significant protection. Phrasing environmental issues in human rights contexts heightens 'legal and moral authority to environmental violations as well as open additional avenues for addressing those violations'.[80] Environmental rule of law emphasizes the interlinkage and derivative nature of rights to the environment as an essential tool for the implementation, compliance, and enforcement of environmental laws. Not only do the rights become claim rights against the state as a duty bearer, but they also extend to private entities and all members of the public, allowing widespread compliance efforts. Armed with this context of rights, members of the public can approach state administrative agencies and courts to enforce such rights.

Risking oversimplification, environmental rights may be broadly categorized into two categories: procedural rights and substantive rights. While procedural rights rarely mention the environment, they ensure that, in making

76 David R. Boyd, *The Status of Constitutional Protection for the Environment in Other Nations* (David Suzuki Foundation, 2014), 4.

77 *Ibid.*

78 UNEP, n. 5.

79 Macharia Kaguru, 'The Undelivered Promise: Constitutional Environmental Rights and Judicial Redress in Kenya and South Africa' (2024) 8(2) *Strathmore Law Journal* 23.

80 UNEP, n. 5, 25. A human rights approach to climate change petitions has gained prominence and is seen by many as a 'game changer' in climate change policy-making and court decisions. See, e.g., UNEP, n. 10; de Vilchez & Savaresi, n. 38, 3–19 (in this article, the authors demonstrate that a human rights approach has allowed some courts, especially the Asian and many other global South courts, to recognize even an unwritten right to a clean environment, basing it on the foundational nature of the environment to the achievement of other rights).

decisions on environmental matters, people's views are incorporated. These 'access rights' were recognized in Principle 10 of the Rio Declaration and reaffirmed in the Rio+20 Conference's 2012 outcome document.[81] The cornerstone of environmental decision-making lies in the fundamental rights to information and participation in shaping decisions that will impact the environment. To this end, numerous countries have not only adopted but also strengthened laws that guarantee transparency and public involvement, with the majority of legal frameworks globally ensuring the right to access environmental information.[82] Many states have enshrined procedural requirements within their environmental legislation, mandating government agencies to inform, consult, and meaningfully engage with individuals and communities affected by environmental decisions.[83]

Public participation in environmental rule of law is enabled through participatory procedures essential for the democratic legitimacy of decision-making procedures and their ensuing outcomes.[84] On a global and regional scale, legal instruments are in place to reinforce the right to participate in public affairs, including matters of the environment. Notably, Articles 6, 7, and 8 of the 1998 Aarhus Convention obligate its signatory parties to facilitate public participation in environmental matters.[85] Furthermore, the 2018 Escazú Agreement guarantees the full enjoyment of these access rights in environmental decision-making processes.[86] The Aarhus Convention and Escazú Agreement build on Principle 10 of the Rio Declaration, focusing on the key procedural tenets of environmental governance such as access to information, public awareness, public participation, and access to judicial remedies. As of 2025, the Aarhus Convention has forty-eight Parties and remains open for ratification by other states. Presently, twenty-four countries have signed the Escazú Agreement, of which eighteen have ratified it. Similarly, the revised 2003 Maputo Convention provides for procedural environmental rights.[87]

81 UNGA Resolution 66/288 on the Future We Want, UN Doc. A/REAS/66/288, 27 July 2012.

82 UNEP, n. 5, 7.

83 *Ibid.*, 116.

84 Chiara Armeni, 'Participation in Environmental Decision-making: Reflecting on Planning and Community Benefits for Major Wind Farms' (2016) 28(3) *Journal of Environmental Law* 418.

85 Convention on Access to Information, Public Participation in Decision-making and Access to Justice in Environmental Matters, 1998, 2161 UNTS 447, art. 3.

86 Regional Agreement on Access to Information, Public Participation and Justice in Environmental Matters in Latin America and the Caribbean, 2018, 3397 UNTS 195.

87 African Convention on the Conservation of Nature and Natural Resources, 2003, https://au.int/sites/default/files/treaties/41550-treaty-Charter_ConservationNature_NaturalResources.pdf. For

With respect to substantive environmental rights, the main human rights treaties do not contain a stand-alone environmental right.[88] Substantive elements of environmental rights have traditionally been based on other related rights already acknowledged and recognized in international and national law, including the rights to life, health, food, water, and land. Still, the right to a clean, healthy, and sustainable environment as a stand-alone right is contained in many national constitutions and statutory laws. The differences among countries lie in the phraseology of the adjectives appearing before 'environment', such as clean, healthy, sustainable, prudent, and good in various laws.[89]

After decades of lobbying for the recognition of the right to environment as a fundamental human right, the HRC acknowledged this right in Resolution 48/13 in 2021, setting the stage for its recognition by the UNGA.[90] On 28 July 2022, the UNGA adopted a resolution recognizing the right to a clean, healthy, and sustainable environment as a human right, providing the much-needed legal basis.[91] While resolutions such as this are soft law instruments, this is a major achievement in solidifying the connection between human rights and the environment at the international level. This resolution not only acknowledged the vital significance of this right but also emphasized its role in protecting and enhancing human lives, especially those of marginalized and vulnerable populations.[92] It provides another important development of international environmental law, holding immense potential in promoting the environmental rule of law.

States bear the obligation to promote, protect, and fulfil the right to a clean, healthy, and sustainable environment.[93] Remarkably, more than 150 countries have incorporated environmental protection or the right to a healthy environment into their national constitutions.[94] This legal

a detailed analysis, see Jonas Ebbesson, 'International Participatory Rights and Environment Protection in Africa: Powerful Tools or "Sleeping Rights?"' in Jean-Claude N. Ashukem & Semie M. Sama (eds.), *Human Rights and the Environment in Africa: A Research Companion* (Routledge, 2023), 97.

88 For many years, the debate among scholars and policy-makers was on whether to formulate and recognize a standalone right to a clean and healthy environment or 'green' human rights. See, e.g., de Vilchez & Savaresi, n. 38.

89 Kaguru, n. 79.

90 UNHRC Resolution 48/13, n. 75.

91 UNGA, n. 20.

92 *Ibid.*

93 UN Human Special Procedures, *Right to a Healthy Environment: Good Practices*, UN Doc. A/HRC/37/59, 24 January 2018, 9 https://wedocs.unep.org/bitstream/handle/20.500.11822/32450/RHE.pdf.

94 UNEP, n. 5.

recognition has played a vital role in addressing various environmental challenges. The right to a clean, healthy, and sustainable environment extends to social protection in environmental matters, providing avenues to address the needs of the most vulnerable, including women, children, Indigenous Peoples, and local communities, who often rely heavily on the land and natural resources for their livelihoods.[95] Social protection measures aimed at overcoming the structural obstacles faced by the most vulnerable require coordination with broader human rights-based development strategies, including those regarding the right to health, equality, social protection, and the environment.[96]

While some regional MEAs provide for the protection of human rights, including for the most vulnerable, the 2015 Paris Agreement stands out as a global MEA that recognizes climate change as a human rights issue, acknowledging its disproportionate impact on vulnerable groups, including minorities, and Indigenous Peoples.[97] Various stakeholders in the process of negotiating a legally binding instrument on plastic pollution, including in the marine environment, have indicated the importance of providing for human rights considerations in the treaty's text.[98] Such recognition underscores the interdependence of human rights and environmental protection.

UNEP is mandated to promote the right to a healthy environment, thereby contributing towards achieving sustainability for both people and the planet.[99] In collaboration with the Office of the High Commissioner for Human Rights and other stakeholders, UNEP is actively supporting the promotion, protection, and respect of the right to a clean, healthy, and sustainable environment.[100] For instance, UNEP has worked closely with the Committee of the Rights of the Child to develop guidance on children's rights

95 International Labour Organization, *Social Protection for Indigenous Peoples*, April 2018, 6, www.ilo.org/wcmsp5/groups/public/–ed_protect/–protrav/–ilo_aids/documents/publication/wcms_626564.pdf.

96 *Ibid.*, 7.

97 Paris Agreement on Climate Change, 2015, 3156 UNTS 79. The Paris Agreement states in its preamble: 'Acknowledging that climate change is a common concern of humankind, Parties should, when taking action to address climate change, respect, promote and consider their respective obligations on human rights, the right to health, the rights of indigenous peoples, local communities, migrants, children, persons with disabilities and people in vulnerable situations and the right to development, as well as gender equality, empowerment of women and intergenerational equity.'

98 'A Human Rights-based Approach to Preventing Plastic Pollution', *Sea Circular*, Issue no. 1, 2023, https://wedocs.unep.org/bitstream/handle/20.500.11822/40520/SEA_brief1_human_rights.pdf?sequence=3&isAllowed=y.

99 UNEP, *Medium-Term Strategy 2022–2025*, Doc. UNEP/EA.5/3/Rev.1, 17 February 2021.

100 *Ibid.*, 40.

and the environment, with a particular focus on climate change. Additionally, UNEP has incorporated gender considerations into its mandate to ensure a more inclusive approach to environmental protection.

The recognition of the right to a clean, healthy, and sustainable environment underscores that environmental considerations are at the same level as other human rights. It underlines the imperative of the protection of human rights in environmental matters. member states and international organizations now have a clear and solid basis to implement this right in their legal and regulatory frameworks. In doing so, member states and international organizations can contribute to promoting, protecting, and respecting this right, alongside other human rights. This recognition reaffirms the interconnectedness of human well-being and environmental integrity and stands as a landmark development in the field of international environmental law.

5.6 THE FUTURE OF ENVIRONMENTAL RULE OF LAW

Significant progress has been made in shaping environmental rule of law. The triumphant journey started from once scattered principles lacking institutional standing to international recognition, to the establishment of a robust and cohesive holistic framework, and to the formation of a key pillar in Montevideo Programme V.[101] Yet the journey is far from complete; much remains to be done, nuances demand elucidation, and critical issues persist in their evolution. Although the right to a clean, healthy, and sustainable environment has existed in legal documents for over fifty years, its more recent recognition as a fundamental right demands a harmonized interpretation. Different national constitutions use differing phraseology ranging from 'clean', 'healthy', 'sound', and 'favourable', among others. These differences may lead to differentiated interpretation in national contexts. Whereas the fundamental aspect of all these variations is the preservation of rights,[102] there is a need for a harmonized understanding. A compliance committee akin to those set under other human rights instruments would provide a good basis to harmonize the practices and develop a holistic and concrete application.

[101] UNEP, *Delivering for People and the Planet: Fifth Montevideo Programme for the Development and Periodic Review of Environmental Law*, adopted through UN Environment Assembly Resolution 4/20, 15 March 2019, https://wedocs.unep.org/bitstream/handle/20.500.11822/35875/K2100501-e.pdf (environmental rule of law forms a key pillar in the Montevideo Programme V's medium-term strategy).

[102] Yann Aguila, *The Right to a Healthy Environment* (IUCN, 2021), www.iucn.org/news/world-commission-environmental-law/202110/right-a-healthy-environment.

The right as phrased adopts an anthropocentric character. While this is a step forward, there is a significant movement that adopts an ecocentric perspective to environmental law. This perspective has to contend with states, especially African and Latin American countries, that place nature rather than human beings at the centre. This divergent appreciation of the right requires continued elaboration and discussion to arrive at the most optimizing level of environmental conservation. Relatedly, there is a growing movement to recognize the rights of nature independent from human beings.[103] Although certain countries and regions have acknowledged the rights of nature within their domestic legal frameworks, the global recognition and integration of these principles into international law and treaties remain topics of ongoing discussion. Expanding these principles within the domain of environmental rule of law is an area for further development, especially in the face of escalating biodiversity loss and environmental degradation.

Another important environmental rule of law issue is the continued emphasis on the rights of future generations. While some countries have recognized the interests of future generations without explicitly granting rights, the issue is currently under scholarly and policy interrogation. Indeed, children, and young people, have made their mark as suitable climate change litigation petitioners among climate change communities due to the ability to create a life causation of today's emissions that would affect their future lives given their expectancy in fifty to seventy years to come.

In another area, UNEP has led the way in assessing the environmental rule of law status. It has also provided key indicators for measuring environmental rule of law. However, since environmental rule of law is focused on implementation, compliance, and enforcement, there is a need to continuously develop stronger mechanisms to track, report, and enforce compliance with environmental rule of law.

To improve compliance with environmental laws, harnessing technology becomes increasingly essential. This encompasses the deployment of satellite monitoring systems, geographic information systems, and remote sensing to monitor environmental changes and potential violations. For instance, satellite imagery can be instrumental in identifying illegal deforestation, monitoring air and water quality, and detecting unauthorized mining activities. Blockchain technology can also offer a means to create transparent and tamper-proof records of environmental commitments and transactions, ensuring accountability and traceability.

[103] David R. Boyd, 'Recognizing the Rights of Nature: Lofty Rhetoric or Legal Revolution?' (2018) 32(4) *Natural Resources and Environment* 13.

The application of environmental rule of law in the international and regional context and in transboundary circumstances is another important area requiring further research and development. This would apply to oceans and shared resources, particularly in the promotion of environmental rule of law in relation to binding treaty obligations. In these regions, there are overlapping claims and interests, including disputes regarding the control, use, and protection of shared resources.

As we look to the future, addressing these unfinished business matters is paramount for the enhancement of environmental rule of law, the fortification of environmental law, and the assurance of effective environmental protection. These challenges mirror the evolving nature of environmental governance in general, demanding adaptation and progress to tackle intricate global environmental issues. They underscore the urgency of continued discussions and cooperation in transforming these concerns into actionable actions.

5.7 CONCLUSION

This chapter has underscored the extensive journey of environmental rule of law, transitioning from a sporadic and haphazard application of principles to the formalization and institutionalization of a holistic framework at the international level. It traces the evolution of its normative content and character, demonstrating a trajectory of fifty years, from Stockholm in 1972 to 2022 and beyond. Various countries have put in place national framework environmental laws, established institutions on the environment, provided for human rights in environmental matters, safeguarded civic engagement and participation, and advocated for the protection of access to justice. As environmental rule of law matures and is applied robustly, efforts must continue to strengthen its core elements for an effective outcome.

This journey is far from complete, and there remain ample opportunities to enhance accountability, promote institutional governance, and bolster the implementation of environmental laws. As the world grapples with increasingly complex and interconnected environmental challenges, it is paramount to harness the full potential of environmental rule of law. Looking ahead, environmental rule of law remains an important concept that can catalyse environmental protection efforts. Its development and nuanced application must continue for optimal results. The future of environmental law hinges on promoting environmental rule of law. Strengthening institutions, enhancing stakeholder engagement, and fostering collaboration among governments, scientists, and civil society are pivotal. As we look ahead, it is a shared responsibility to reinvigorate global commitments to environmental protection, ensuring that current and future generations are protected. By embracing these principles and taking collective action, a future where environmental, social, and economic conditions surpass the initial vision set at the 1972 Stockholm Conference can be achieved. It is a future where generations to come will inherit a world that is not only ecologically sound but also equitable and just.

6

The Development of Environmental Access Rights and Protection of Environmental Defenders

Ben Boer and Rowena Cantley-Smith

6.1 INTRODUCTION

In 1972, the Stockholm Declaration drew attention to the indivisible nature of the relationship between the environment and the enjoyment of human rights.[1] In 1992, Principle 10 of the 1992 Rio Declaration laid down the three fundamental environmental access rights – namely, access to information, opportunity to participate in decision-making processes, and access to justice, including redress and remedy.[2] Fifty years after Stockholm, in 2022, the UN General Assembly (UNGA) expressly recognized the human right to a clean, healthy, and sustainable environment and observed that the exercise of the 'rights to seek, receive and impart information, to participate effectively in the conduct of government and public affairs and to an effective remedy, is vital to the protection of a clean, healthy and sustainable environment'.[3] Forming a critical element of the

This chapter draws on publications prepared by the authors for the UN Environment Programme (UNEP), including UNEP, *Human Rights and the Environmental Rule of Law*, Issue Brief SDG 16:1, March 2021; UNEP, *Environmental Rule of Law and Human Rights in Asia Pacific: Supporting the Protection of Environmental Human Rights Defenders*, Working Paper, February 2023; UNEP, *Strategic Litigation against Public Participation (SLAPP)*, July 2023; UNEP, *Free, Prior and Informed Consent (FPIC)*, July 2023. However, the legal and policy views expressed here do not purport to reflect or represent the views of UNEP.

1 'Declaration of the United Nations Conference on the Human Environment', in *Report of the UN Conference on the Human Environment*, UN Doc. A/CONF.48/14/Rev.1, 16 June 1972 (Stockholm Declaration), para 1.

2 'Rio Declaration on Environment and Development', in *Report of the UN Conference on Environment and Development*, UN Doc. A/CONF.151/26 (Vol. I), 12 August 1992, Annex I, Principle 10; see also UNCHR Resolution 1994/65 on Human Rights and the Environment, UN Doc. E/CN.4/RES/1994/65, 9 March 1994.

3 UNGA Resolution 76/300 on the Human Right to a Clean, Healthy and Sustainable Environment, UN Doc. A/RES/76/300, 28 July 2022, Preamble, recital 14 (access rights) and recital 16, and Operative para. 1 (right to a healthy environment) see also HRC Resolution 48/13 on the Human Right to a Clean, Healthy and Sustainable Environment, UN Doc. A/HRC/

maintenance of 'civic space' and the environmental rule of law, environmental access rights are fundamental to the implementation of sustainable development. These rights have been recognized in two international treaties: the 1998 Aarhus Convention[4] and the 2018 Escazú Agreement.[5]

In 2015, the Sustainable Development Goals (SDGs) assigned targets to all three environmental access rights in SDG 16: Peace, Justice, and Strong Institutions.[6] Accompanying advancements in the normative legal framework of environmental access rights has been the growing recognition, by the United Nations and others, of the important role of environmental human rights defenders (EHRDs).[7] EHRDs, through peaceful, legitimate actions, strive to promote and protect the environment and the full enjoyment of environmental rights, especially 'when the exercise of those rights is being threatened'.[8] Acknowledgement of the critical role of EHRDs in promoting the full enjoyment of the right to a healthy environment thus provides a contemporary perspective on the ongoing importance of environmental access rights. Even so, EHRDs are facing escalating risks and challenges, with killings and other physical violence, as well as judicial harassment, intimidation, doxing, and other incidents taking place around the world on a regular basis.[9] To date, the Escazú Agreement includes the first, and only, treaty provision that expressly recognizes EHRDs.[10]

RES/48/13, 8 October 2021, Preamble, recital 12 (access rights) and recital 14 and Operative para. 1 (right to a healthy environment).

4 Convention on Access to Information, Public Participation in Decision-Making and Access to Justice in Environmental Matters, 1998, 2161 UNTS 447 (Aarhus Convention).

5 Regional Agreement on Access to Information, Public Participation and Justice in Environmental Matters in Latin America and the Caribbean, 2018, 3397 UNTS 195 (Escazú Agreement).

6 'The 17 Goals', *Sustainable Development Goals*, https://sdgs.un.org/goals (see Targets 16.10, 16.7, 16.3); see also Table 6.1 in this chapter.

7 See, e.g., UNGA Resolution 53/144 on the UN Declaration on the Right and Responsibility of Individuals, Groups and Organs of Society to Promote and Protect Universally Recognized Human Rights and Fundamental Freedoms, UN Doc. A/RES/53/144, 9 December 1998 (Declaration on HRDs); HRC Resolution 40/11 on Recognizing the Contribution of Environmental Human Rights Defenders to the Enjoyment of Human Rights, Environmental Protection and Sustainable Development, UN Doc. A/HRC/RES/40/11, 21 March 2019; UNEP, *Environmental Rule of Law and Human Rights in Asia Pacific: Supporting the Protection of Environmental Human Rights Defenders*, Working Paper, February 2023, https://wedocs.unep.org/20.500.11822/42048.

8 UNEP, *Promoting Greater Protection for Environmental Defenders: Policy*, 2018, https://wedocs.unep.org/handle/20.500.11822/22769.

9 *Roots of Resistance*, Global Witness, September 2025, https://globalwitness.org/en/campaigns/land-and-environmental-defenders/roots-of-resistance/; see also Mary Menton & Philippe Le Billon (eds.), *Environmental Defender: Deadly Struggles for Life and Territory* (Routledge, 2021).

10 Escazú Agreement, n. 5, art. 9. However, the authors note that the Aarhus Convention, n. 4, art. 3(8), nevertheless implicitly recognizes a specific group of environmental human rights

This chapter first traces the development of environmental access rights, tracking the background of key international human rights instruments and the growing recognition of the symbiotic nature of the human-environment relationship. It draws on key markers between the Stockholm Conference in 1972 and the UN International Meeting Stockholm+50: A Healthy Planet for the Prosperity of All – Our Responsibility, Our Opportunity in 2022.[11] It then provides an overview of the normative framework supporting the role of EHRDs, the challenges and the risks that they are increasingly being subjected to around the world, and the urgent need to protect EHRDs through international and regional law responses. As the demand increases for coordinated action concerning what is described as the global environmental crisis,[12] the legal and political restrictions on the ability of civil society to express the need for action must also be addressed. The chapter concludes that, despite advances in the acceptance of environmental access rights in general, more robust strategies and actions are required to promote the full enjoyment of environmental access rights and to ensure greater protection for those seeking to exercise those rights.

6.2 DEVELOPMENT OF ENVIRONMENTAL ACCESS RIGHTS

6.2.1 *Overview*

Environmental access rights, which are sometimes referred to as participatory or procedural rights, comprise the right of access to environmental information, the right to public participation in environmental decision-making, and the right of access to environmental justice and effective remedies. The present-day, almost universal, recognition of environmental access rights is evidenced by a wide range of international instruments, national constitutions, and environmental laws. This is a vastly different situation from what it was in 1972, when such rights were generally of little concern. International human rights law provides the foundations of the normative framework of

defenders (EHRDs) (that is, those parties exercising the Convention's environmental access rights, and states' obligation to protect them).

11 *Report of Stockholm+50: A Healthy Planet for the Prosperity of All – Our Responsibility, Our Opportunity*, UN Doc. A/CONF.238/9, 1 August 2022.

12 The global environmental crisis is seen as encompassing climate change, biodiversity loss, land degradation and desertification, pollution and waste, and their intersections; see UNEP, *Global Environmental Outlook, A Future We Choose*, 663. Elements of the crisis are also reflected in Resolution 48/13, n. 3, preamble recital 13; Resolution 76/300, n. 3, preamble, recital 12, 14.

both environmental access rights and the right to a healthy environment. The 1948 Universal Declaration on Human Rights and the 1966 International Covenant on Cultural and Civil Rights set down fundamental rights and freedoms that underpin contemporary environmental rights.[13] These include the rights to freedom of expression, to peaceful association and assembly, to freely receive and impart information, to participate in public affairs, and to access justice and effective remedies.

The evolutionary normative foundational pathway of environmental access rights is also grounded in the progressive advancement of environmental law. As Catherine Redgwell has observed, influential developments include 'the rise of environmental awareness in the 1960s which led to the flourishing of domestic, regional, and international environmental law' and 'changes in governance, both nationally and internationally, with an enhanced role for non-state actors in decision-making procedures'.[14] The Stockholm Declaration expresses the essential role of the environment in ensuring human 'well-being and to the enjoyment of basic human rights – even the right to life itself'.[15] As Jonas Ebbesson has noted, the Declaration was 'ahead of its time' in one notable regard – namely, 'the *notion of a fundamental and basic human right to the environment*'.[16] Alexandre Kiss and Dinah Shelton have stated that, since 1972, a 'growing number of international, constitutional and statutory provisions', creating or recognizing 'rights relating to environmental protection', have shaped 'environmental protection generally, and the particular role of the courts in implementing such protection'.[17] The Stockholm Declaration itself was largely silent concerning environmental access rights,[18] but its associated Action Plan contained more specific 'access' provisions.[19] Although demand for such rights

[13] Universal Declaration of Human Rights, UN Doc. A/810/71, 10 December 1948; International Covenant on Civil and Political Rights, 1966, 999 UNTS 171.

[14] Catherine Redgwell, 'Access to Environmental Justice', in Francesco Francioni (ed.), *Access to Justice as a Human Right, Collected Courses of the Academy of European Law* (Oxford University Press, 2007), 153.

[15] Stockholm Declaration, n. 1, para. 1.

[16] Jonas Ebbesson, 'Getting It Right: Advances of Human Rights and the Environment from Stockholm 1972 to Stockholm 2022' (2022) 52 *Environmental Policy and Law* 79, 80 (emphasis in original).

[17] Alexandre Kiss & Dinah Shelton, *Judicial Handbook on Environmental Law* (UNEP, 2004), 26.

[18] But note recognition of the need to defend the environment in the Stockholm Declaration, n. 1, para. 6; see also Principle 19 ('disseminate information … on the need to protect and improve the environment') and Principle 20 (recognition of the need to support and facilitate 'the free flow of up-to-date scientific information').

[19] 'Action Plan for the Human Environment', in *Report of the United Nations Conference on the Human Environment*, n. 1, ch. 2, recommendations 7(a), 39(a), 97.

grew slowly but steadily between the 1970s and the 1990s, it was not until the UN Conference on Environment and Development in June 1992, and its Rio Declaration, that environmental access rights received universal recognition.[20] Nowadays, these three environmental access rights are integral elements of the environmental rule of law, as set out in the UN Environment Programme's (UNEP) 2019 *Environmental Rule of Law* report.[21] Based on UNEP's contemporary explanation of the rights and core elements of the Environmental Rule of Law, we clarify the relationship between the access rights in Figure 6.1.

According to UNEP, these 'three pillars of civic engagement build responsiveness and accountability' that are 'essential to environmental rule of law'.[22] Indeed, the relationship between environmental access rights and environmental rule of law is seen as a mutually reinforcing one, 'whereby environmental law relies on procedural rights to protect substantive rights that depend on the environment'.[23] More specifically, environmental access rights and other environmental rights further support the environmental rule of law by providing the requisite cause of action to enable rights holders to seek effective remedies for rights violations.[24]

6.2.2 *From Soft Law to Treaty Rights*

The journey of environmental access rights over the past five decades has been complex and detailed. Significant advancements of these rights are set out in Table 6.1.[25] While by no means intended to be comprehensive, the various

20 Ebbesson, n. 16, 81–82 (who provides more detail on the development of procedural and substantive rights at the regional and international levels between 1972 and 1992), 83–87 (from 1992 onwards at the regional level), 87–92 (at the global level).

21 The text of each box in Figure 6.1 has been quoted directly by the authors from the UNEP, *Environmental Rule of Law: First Global Report*, 2019, 21, para 1.3.2 'Access to Information, Public Participation, and Access to Justice'. See also Patricia Kameri-Mbote, Alvin Gachie, Leonie Geene, Macharia Kaguru, and Jan Maina, 'Environmental Rule of Law: From Stockholm 1972 to 2022 and Beyond', in this volume, 156.

22 UNEP, *Environmental Rule of Law: First Global Report*, n. 21, 89; see also 'Civic Engagement', in UNEP, *Environmental Rule of Law: Tracking Progress and Charting Future Directions*, 2023, 60 and passim.

23 *Ibid.*

24 *Ibid.*

25 The authors note that there are examples of access rights from other regions, including those contained in the North American Agreement on Environmental Co-operation, 1993, 32 ILM 1480 (1993), and in the revised African Convention on the Conservation of Nature and Natural Resources (revised version), 2003, https://au.int/sites/default/files/treaties/41550-treaty-Charter_ConservationNature_NaturalResources.pdf. However, each of these documents suffers from a range of practical obstacles – for example, complaints that may lead to trade sanctions that cannot be initiated by the public under the former; a lack of institutional backing diminishes the effect of the latter. See, e.g., Steve Charnovitz, 'The NAFTA Environmental Side Agreement: Implications for Environmental Cooperation, Trade Policy, and American Treatymaking'

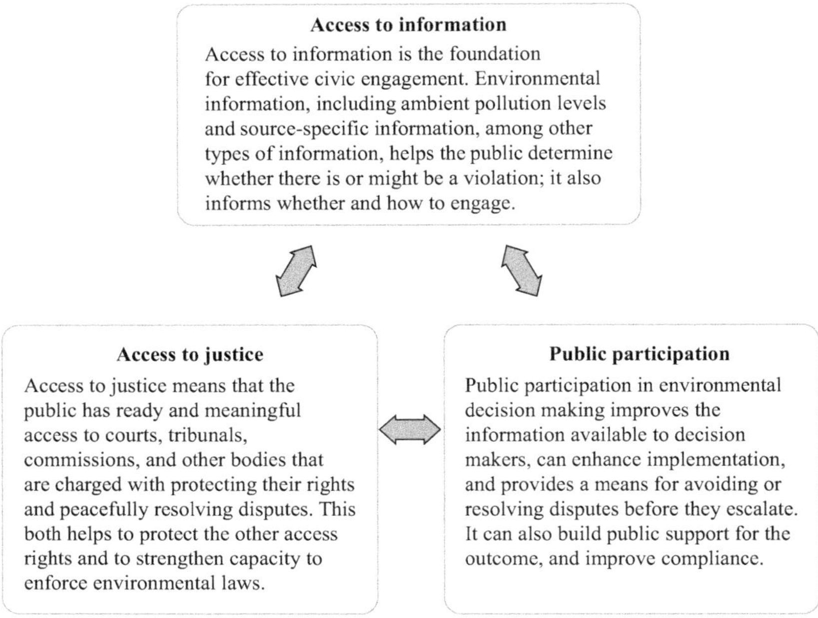

FIGURE 6.1 Access rights and environmental rule of law.

articulations of such rights are drawn from both soft and hard sources of international law. Collectively, they provide a clear picture of the international community's consistent approach to environmental access rights and their importance more generally. The UNGA's 1982 World Charter for Nature supported the application of access rights to environmental matters in several of its provisions, especially paragraph 23, which can be seen as a precursor to Principle 10 of the Rio Declaration.[26] Even so, another decade passed before Principle 10 laid down what is now regarded as the cornerstone of contemporary environmental access rights and the corresponding duties of states. Although not referred to in Table 6.1, public participation and access to information also formed an integral part of Agenda 21, with its focus on the

(1994) 8 *Temple International and Comparative Law Journal* 257; Jonas Ebbesson, 'International Participatory Rights and Environment Protection in Africa – Powerful Tools or "Sleeping Rights?"', in Jean-Claude Ashukem & Semie Sama (eds.), *Human Rights and the Environment in Africa: A Research Companion* (Routledge, 2023), 97–115.

26 UNGA Resolution 73/7 on World Charter for Nature, UN Doc. A/RES/37/7, 28 October 1982, paras. 16, 18, 23; Ebbesson, n. 16.

TABLE 6.1 *Environmental access rights in international law: 1972–2022*

Year	Instrument	Access to information	Public participation	Access to justice
1982	World Charter for Nature	Article 21: 'States and, to the extent they are able, other public authorities, international organizations, individuals, groups and corporations shall: (a) Co-operate in the task of conserving nature through common activities and other relevant actions, including information exchange and consultations.'	Article 23: 'All persons, in accordance with their national legislation, shall have the opportunity to participate, individually or with others, in the formulation of decisions of direct concern to their environment, and shall have access to means of redress when their environment has suffered damage or degradation.'	
1992	Rio Declaration	Principle 10: 'Environmental issues are best handled with the participation of all concerned citizens, at the relevant level. At the national level, each individual shall have appropriate access to information concerning the environment that is held by public authorities, including information on hazardous materials and activities in their communities, and the opportunity to participate in decision-making processes. States shall facilitate and encourage public awareness and participation by making information widely available. Effective access to judicial and administrative proceedings, including redress and remedy, shall be provided.'		
1998	Aarhus Convention	Article 4(1): 'Each Party shall ensure that . . . public authorities, in response to a request for environmental information,	Article 7(1): 'Each Party shall make appropriate practical and/or other provisions for the public to participate during the	Article 9 (1) and (2): 'Each Party shall ensure that "any person who considers that his or her request for information" has not been

(continued)

TABLE 6.1 (*continued*)

Year	Instrument	Access to information	Public participation	Access to justice
		make such information available to the public.' Article 5(2): 'Each Party shall ensure that . . . the way in which public authorities make environmental information available to the public is transparent and that environmental information is effectively accessible.'	preparation of plans and programmes relating to the environment, within a transparent and fair framework, having provided the necessary information to the public.'	dealt with appropriately, and members of the public concerned who have "a sufficient interest" or maintain an "impairment of a right", "have access to a review procedure before a court of law or another independent and impartial body established by law".'
1998	Declaration on Human Rights Defenders	Article 6: 'Everyone has the right, individually and in association with others: (a) To know, seek, obtain, receive and hold information about all human rights and fundamental freedoms, including having access to information as to how those rights and freedoms are given effect in domestic legislative, judicial or administrative systems.'	Article 8(1): 'Everyone has the right, individually and in association with others, to have effective access, on a non-discriminatory basis, to participation in the government of his or her country and in the conduct of public affairs.'	Article 9(1): 'In the exercise of human rights and fundamental freedoms, including the promotion and protection of human rights as referred to in the present Declaration, everyone has the right, individually and in association with others, to benefit from an effective remedy and to be protected in the event of the violation of those rights.'

(continued)

2015	SDG 16 Targets	Article 16.10: 'Ensure public access to information and protect fundamental freedoms, in accordance with national legislation and international agreements.'	Article 16.7: 'Ensure responsive, inclusive, participatory and representative decision-making at all levels.'	Article 16.3: 'Promote the rule of law at the national and international levels and ensure equal access to justice for all.'
2018	Escazú Agreement	Article 5(1): 'Each Party shall ensure the public's right of access to environmental information in its possession, control or custody, in accordance with the principle of maximum disclosure.'	Article 7(1): 'Each Party shall ensure the public's right to participation and, for that purpose, commits to implement open and inclusive participation in environmental decision-making processes based on domestic and international normative frameworks.'	Article 8(1): 'Each Party shall guarantee the right of access to justice in environmental matters in accordance with the guarantees of due process.'

practical 'integration of environmental and development concerns' and the achievement of sustainable development.[27]

The first transition from soft law into treaty rights was relatively rapid, taking only six years for environmental access rights to gain international treaty status in the Aarhus Convention. Negotiated through the UN Economic Commission for Europe, Article 19(3) provides that the Aarhus Convention is nevertheless open to all states throughout the world. This ground-breaking instrument 'goes to the heart of the relationship between people and government'.[28] Unlike most international environmental conventions, which 'cover obligations that Parties have to each other, the Aarhus Convention covers obligations that Parties have to the public'.[29] The Aarhus Convention does so by vesting rights in the public and imposing comprehensive mandatory obligations on all signatory states and public authorities 'regarding access to information and public participation. It backs up these rights with access to justice provisions that go some way towards putting teeth into the Convention'.[30] In addition to linking environmental and human rights, the Convention acknowledges intergenerational obligations and recognizes that the engagement of all stakeholders is critical to the realization of sustainable development.[31]

Following the adoption of the Aarhus Convention, states continued to reaffirm their political commitment to sustainable development and the Rio Principles.[32] Of note are two outcomes of the 2012 Rio+20 Conference: states' agreement to draft a set of SDGs[33] and the first steps towards the establishment of a new environmental access rights treaty,[34] the latter resulting in the adoption of the Escazú Agreement in 2018. That Agreement 'addresses key aspects of environmental management and protection from a regional perspective, regulating access rights to information, public participation and justice in matters as important as the sustainable use of natural resources,

27 *Agenda 21*, UN Doc. A/CONF. 151/26, 13 June 1992, paras. 1.1, 23.2. https://sdgs.un.org/publications/agenda21.

28 Jonas Ebbesson *et al.*, *The Aarhus Convention: An Implementation Guide* (2nd ed., UN Economic Commission for Europe [UNECE], 2014), 15.

29 *Ibid.*

30 *Ibid.*

31 *Ibid.*

32 See, e.g., UN Conference on Sustainable Development (Rio+20), Rio de Janeiro, 20–22 June 2012, https://sustainabledevelopment.un.org/rio20. A key outcome of Rio+20 was UNGA Resolution 66/288 on the Future We Want, UN Doc. A/REAS/66/288, 27 July 2012, paras. 42–55, 99 (which recognizes the important role of environmental access rights).

33 UNGA Resolution 66/288, n. 32, paras. 245–251, especially para. 246.

34 As recorded in the Declaration on the Application of Principle 10 of the Rio Declaration on Environment and Development, Doc. A/CONF.216.13, 27 June 2012, 3.

biodiversity conservation, the fight against land degradation and climate change, and building resilience to disasters'.[35] Table 6.1 illustrates the similarities between the Escazú Agreement and the Aarhus Convention. The Escazú Agreement reaffirms the Aarhus Convention's environmental access rights and responsibilities regime by providing detailed recognition of the relationship between human rights, the environment, and sustainable development.

Similar to the Aarhus Convention, the Escazú Agreement's preamble emphasizes the interrelated and interdependent relationship between the three access rights, highlights the need for 'each and every one of them' to 'be promoted and implemented in an integrated and balanced manner', and expresses a firm conviction that 'access rights contribute to the strengthening of, *inter alia*, democracy, sustainable development and human rights'.[36] In addition, the Agreement's twofold objective is described in terms of guaranteeing the full and effective implementation of all three environmental access rights as well as protecting 'the right of every person of present and future generations to live in a healthy environment and to sustainable development'.[37] However, the Agreement goes beyond the Aarhus Convention by specifically defining the terms 'access rights', 'persons or groups in vulnerable situations', and states' obligation to guarantee everyone the right to live in a healthy environment.[38] Between them, both the Aarhus Convention and the Escazú Agreement offer opportunities to support the environmental rule of law, environmental access rights, and the right to a healthy environment. They also offer greater protections for EHRDs, discussed later in this chapter.

Other articulations of environmental access rights set out in Table 6.1 warrant brief consideration. The three targets of SDG 16 express the important role of public participation and access to information and justice in states' ability to realize sustainable development and secure the many associated economic, environmental, and social benefits. Likewise, the UN Human Rights Council's (HRC) Resolution 48/13 in 2021 and the UNGA Resolution 76/300 in 2022 have reaffirmed the pivotal role of environmental access rights in securing everyone's right to a clean, healthy, and sustainable environment and addressing the current challenges presented by what has become known as the global environmental crisis.[39] Several of the 2018 *Framework Principles on Human Rights and*

35 Alicia Bárcena, 'Preface', in ECLAC, *Regional Agreement on Access to Information, Public Participation and Justice in Environmental Matters in Latin America and the Caribbean* (Santiago, 2018) 8.

36 Escazú Agreement, n. 5, preamble, recitals 3–4.

37 *Ibid.*, art. 1.

38 *Ibid.*, arts 2(a), (e), 4(1).

39 See Resolution 48/13, n. 3; Resolution 76/300, n. 3.

the Environment provide a contemporary illustration of the broadening international recognition and expanding relevance of environmental access rights to the achievement of the right to a healthy environment.[40]

6.3 ENVIRONMENTAL HUMAN RIGHTS DEFENDERS

Having briefly explored the historical development of environmental access rights from Stockholm to the present decade, we now turn to consider whether the mechanisms to implement these access rights require further attention with regard to the situation of EHRDs. While a specific description of EHRDs had not yet emerged in the 1970s, the Stockholm Declaration implicitly recognized their role, with Principle 1 advising of the 'solemn responsibility' of humans 'to protect and improve the environment for present and future generations'. Nowadays, this 'solemn responsibility' is carried out by EHRDs, described by the United Nations as '[i]ndividuals and groups who, in their personal or professional capacity and in a peaceful manner, strive to protect and promote human rights relating to the environment, including water, air, land, flora and fauna'.[41] This journey – from implicit to express international recognition – is framed by considerable advancements in international law, several of which are considered here.

6.3.1 A *Universal Right to Be an Environmental Human Rights Defender*

In 1998, fifty years after the Universal Declaration of Human Rights, the UNGA adopted the Declaration on Human Rights Defenders (Declaration on HRDs).[42] The Declaration recognized the critical role of those seeking to promote and protect human rights around the world. It sought to legitimize the peaceful activities of human rights defenders (HRDs), including participation in meetings and non-governmental organizations (NGOs), associations or groups, communicating with non-governmental or intergovernmental organizations, freely discussing, publishing, or disseminating information and knowledge on all human rights

[40] UN Human Rights Council (UNHRC), *Report of the Special Rapporteur on the Issue of Human Rights Obligations Relating to the Enjoyment of a Safe, Clean, Healthy and Sustainable Environment*, UN Doc. A/HRC/37/5, 24 January 2018, principles 7, 9, 10 (*Framework Principles*).

[41] UNGA, *Report of the Special Rapporteur on the Situation of Human Rights Defenders*, UN Doc. A/71/281, 3 August 2016, para. 7 (*SRHRD Report*); see also 'Who Are Environmental Defenders?', *UNEP*, www.unep.org/topics/environmental-law-and-governance/who-are-environmental-defenders.

[42] Declaration on HRDs, n. 7.

and fundamental freedoms, as well as providing effective remedies and protection where these and other rights are violated.[43]

6.3.2 *Who Are EHRDs?*

Since 1998, the various categories of HRDs have broadened to specifically include women HRDs,[44] cultural rights defenders,[45] and land and environmental rights defenders.[46] Terms used to describe EHRDs in the HRC's report on the situation of HRDs include 'land and environmental rights defenders', 'environmental rights defenders', and 'environmental activists'.[47] Nowadays, all such defenders can be defined inclusively as EHRDs on the basis of what they do – namely, the exercise of environmental rights and the protection of the environment. In consequence, the provisions of the Declaration on HRDs should be seen as being applicable to these different groups of HRDs.[48] The Special Rapporteur on Human Rights Defenders (SRHRD) has explained states' obligations *vis-à-vis* EHRDs as follows:

> It is the duty of the State to respect the right of everyone to promote and protect a safe, clean, healthy and sustainable environment, necessary for the enjoyment of a vast range of human rights. The State has a parallel duty to protect environmental human rights defenders from violations committed by both State and non-State actors. Nevertheless, international human rights law makes it clear that business enterprises, the media and other non-State actors are obliged to respect human rights obligations and refrain from contributing to or committing violations.[49]

The HRC's broad definition makes it clear that EHRDs are, first and foremost, recognized by what they do, including 'actions to protect environmental and land rights' undertaken on behalf of themselves and/or others.[50] As stated by David Boyd, EHRDs can be 'environmentalists, farmers, women

43 *Ibid.*, arts 5–9.
44 UNHRC, *Situation of Women Human Rights Defenders*, UN Doc. A/HRC/40/60, 10 January 2019.
45 UNHRC, *Cultural Rights Defenders*, UN Doc. A/HRC/43/50, 20 January 2020.
46 *SRHRD Report*, n. 41.
47 *Ibid.*
48 *Ibid.*, para. 3.
49 *SRHRD Report*, n. 41, para. 3.
50 *Ibid.*, para. 8; see also Special Rapporteur on the Situation of Human Rights Defenders (SRHRD), *About Human Rights Defenders*, www.ohchr.org/en/special-procedures/sr-human-rights-defenders/about-human-rights-defenders; Business and Human Rights Resource Centre, *Business and Human Rights Defenders in Southeast Asia*, 2022, www.business-humanrights.org/en/from-us/briefings/business-and-human-rights-defenders-in-southeast-asia/; *Roots of Resistance*, n. 9.

leaders, indigenous peoples, lawyers, scientists, community leaders, journalists, and social media activists'.[51] They can be individuals or groups of 'ordinary citizens exercising their rights', NGOs, or specific groups, such as Indigenous peoples and local communities 'who are defending their lands, and access to the natural resources their communities depend on for survival and livelihoods'.[52] Regardless of the exact nature of their motivation, EHRDs have several features in common. First, they all 'have a stake in protecting the environment and in ensuring respect for environmental rights',[53] and they are all pursuing a common goal: making 'the world a more just and sustainable place'.[54] Second, EHRDs engage in peaceful, legitimate activities concerning environmental protection and/or promoting, protecting and redressing violations of environmental rights. This includes peaceful participation in online and in-person protests concerning global and local issues such as climate change, biodiversity loss, forest destruction, mining and other resource extractive activities, as well as deep-seabed mining, and marine pollution. Third, EHRDs, individually or collectively, often speak 'truth to power'.[55] Through their various activities, EHRDs regularly challenge government, public authorities', and corporations' decisions and actions that harm the environment and threaten or violate the human rights of individuals and communities. Such decisions and actions frequently involve large-scale natural resource exploitation activities that underpin governments' national development and economic objectives but, at the same time, can breach a wide array of rights, including access rights.[56] Such activities include violations of rights over ancestral lands, territories, natural resources, property, culture, and resource management and conservation. Under existing international environmental and human rights law treaties, actions by defenders constitute acts of public participation, which constitute the legitimate exercise of fundamental environmental human rights. The serious harm to which EHRDs are subjected as a

[51] David Boyd, UN Special Rapporteur on Human Rights and the Environment, *Reclaiming the Narrative* (Asia Pacific Network of Environment Defenders and Commission for Environmental Cooperation, 2021), foreword, 1–2.

[52] *SRHRD Report*, n. 41, para. 7.

[53] 'Who Are Environmental Defenders?', n. 41.

[54] Boyd, n. 51.

[55] *SRHRD Report*, n. 41, para. 1.

[56] See UNEP, *Human Rights and the Environmental Rule of Law*, Issue Brief SDG 16:1, March 2021, https://www.unep.org/resources/factsheet/human-rights-and-environmental-rule-law; UNEP, n. 7; UNEP, *Strategic Litigation against Public Participation (SLAPP)*, July 2023, https://wedocs.unep.org/items/5624f8de-d97d-4ec4-a6bc-f24ed1ba8ce5; UNEP, *Free, Prior and Informed Consent (FPIC)*, July 2023, https://wedocs.unep.org/items/3f76cd89-744a-419d-870a-3bb8047a31ea.

result of 'what they do' are considered further in section 6.3.5, below. Before turning to that discussion, relevant treaty provisions in the Aarhus Convention and Escazú Agreement and institutional responses relating to EHRDs are briefly considered.

6.3.3 *Protections in the Aarhus Convention and the Escazú Agreement*

Given that the Declaration on Human Rights Defenders was adopted by the UNGA in the same year as the 1998 Aarhus Convention, it is not surprising that it contains the access rights provisions noted in Table 6.1. The Convention's definitions under Article 2 are important to note: 'the public' means 'one or more natural or legal persons, and, in accordance with national legislation or practice, their associations, organizations or groups'. With regard to EHRDs, this broad definition can include a very wide range of individuals as well as any type of either legally or informally constituted bodies. However, the words 'in accordance with national legislation or practice' can severely limit the range of bodies that might claim the right to participate in environmental decisions. 'The public concerned' is also a crucial definition, meaning 'the public affected or likely to be affected by, or having an interest in, the environmental decision-making; for the purposes of this definition, non-governmental organizations promoting environmental protection and meeting any requirements under national law shall be deemed to have an interest'. While it is a broad definition, the words 'and meeting any requirements under national law' may give rise to narrow drafting of regulatory frameworks by states.[57]

While these definitions in the Aarhus Convention were important steps in recognizing environmental access rights, the Aarhus Convention does not explicitly recognize EHRDs. However, Article 3(8) nevertheless obliges state parties to ensure that members of the public are not harassed, persecuted, or penalized when exercising their participatory rights.[58] It is of course hardly surprising that provisions expressly recognizing and articulating terms such as 'environmental rights defenders' or 'human rights defenders' and related rights and duties are not a formal part of the Convention's language given that, as noted earlier, much of this terminology entered the international law dialogue after 1998. The most significant advancement since the 1990s is the Escazú

57 See further Ebbesson *et al.*, n. 28, 57–58.

58 It should be recorded here that the mandate and functions of the Special Rapporteur on Environmental Defenders appointed under the Aarhus Convention was based on article 3(8). See UNECE, *Mandate and Functions of the Special Rapporteur*, https://unece.org/environment-policy/public-participation/mandate-and-functions-special-rapporteur.

Agreement's explicit inclusion (in the words of its Secretariat) of the 'world's first binding provision on human rights defenders in environmental matters in a region where sadly they are all too often subject to attacks and intimidation'.[59] The addition of specific rights and duties to the international law concerning EHRDs via Article 9 of the Escazú Agreement is thus notable indeed. These obligations articulate the internationally recognized human rights-based duties of states in the environmental context, but they extend them further, as provided in Article 9(2):

> Each Party shall take adequate and effective measures to recognize, protect and promote all the rights of human rights defenders in environmental matters, including their right to life, personal integrity, freedom of opinion and expression, peaceful assembly and association, and free movement, as well as their ability to exercise their access rights, taking into account its international obligations in the field of human rights, its constitutional principles and the basic concepts of its legal system.[60]

6.3.4 *Growing Concerns and Institutional Responses*

Concerns over the situation of human rights defenders have been considered by numerous UN organs and specialist bodies for many years. In 1984, the UN Commission on Human Rights established an open-ended working group to draft the Declaration on HRDs.[61] Thirteen years later, the UNGA finally adopted this Declaration by consensus.[62] In so doing, it issued a clear message about the commitment of states 'to acknowledge, promote and protect the

59 Bárcena, n 35, 8.

60 See further Sarah Dávila A., 'The Escazú Agreement: The Last Piece of the Tripartite Normative Framework in the Right to a Healthy Environment' (2023) 42(1) *Stanford Environmental Law Journal* 63.

61 UN Commission on Human Rights (UNCHR), Decision 1984/116 on Question of the Violation of Human Rights and Fundamental Freedoms in Any Part of the World, with Particular Reference to Colonial and Other Dependent Countries and Territories, Doc. E/1984/14&E/CN.4/1984/77, 1984, and subsequent actions. See, e.g., Resolution 1995/84 on Question of a Draft Declaration on the Right and Responsibility of Individuals, Groups and Organs of Society to Promote and Protect Universally Recognized Human Rights and Fundamental Freedoms, Doc. E/CN.4/RES/1995/84, 1995; *Drafting of a Declaration on the Right and Responsibility of Individuals, Groups and Organs of Society to Promote and Protect Universally Recognized Human Rights and Fundamental Freedoms*, Reports of the Working Group, Doc. E/CN.4/1994/81, 1994, and Doc. E/CN.4/1995/93, 1995; *Draft Declaration on the Right and Responsibility of Individuals, Groups and Organs of Society to Promote and Protect Universally Recognized Human Rights and Fundamental Freedoms: Consolidated Text*, Doc. E/CN.4/1987/WG.6/WP.9, 1987.

62 Declaration on HRDs, n. 7.

work and rights of human rights defenders around the world'.[63] In the interim years, and those following the adoption of the Declaration, concerns over the 'threats, harassment and insecurity' faced by HRDs 'because of their activities in favour of the recognition, promotion and defence of human rights' have been raised regularly by various organs and specialist bodies of the UN, NGOs, and other civil society members.[64]

In 2011, attention was drawn in the SRHRD's annual report to the precarious position of HRDs 'working on land and environmental issues'.[65] Five years later, the SRHRD's thematic report focused specifically on the situation of EHRDs,[66] drawing international attention to 'the shocking rate of killings, as well as threats, harassment and intimidation, of environmental human rights defenders'.[67] Even so, the SRHRD made it clear that the reported killings and other threats were the 'tip of the iceberg' and that the reported figures 'underestimate the true extent of threats and risks facing environmental human rights defenders'.[68] Official attention on EHRDs dramatically increased in 2018 when UNEP published a policy entitled *Promoting Greater Protection for Environmental Defenders*.[69] In the same year, the UNGA approved the Framework Principles on Human Rights and the Environment,[70] of which principle 4 is of particular significance in this context: 'States should provide a safe and enabling environment in which individuals, groups and organs of society that work on human rights or environmental issues can operate free from threats, harassment, intimidation and violence.'

63 UNCHR, *Promotion and Protection of Human Rights: Human Rights Defenders: Report of the Special Representative of the Secretary-General on HRDs*, UN Doc. E/CN.4/2001/94, 26 January 2001, paras. 1, 2.

64 See, e.g., UN Sub-Commission on Prevention of Discrimination and Protection of Minorities, *Resolution 1995/25 on the Protection by Competent Authorities of Everyone against Threats, Retaliation, Pressure or Any Other Arbitrary Action as a Consequence of Legitimate, Peaceful and Non-Violent Exercise of the Right to Strive for the Protection of Human Rights*, UN Doc. E/CN.4/Sub.2/RES/1995/25, 23 October 1995; UN Sub-Commission on the Promotion and Protection of Human Rights Resolution 1999/3 on Violations of the Rights of Human Rights Defenders in All Countries, UN Doc. E/CN.4/Sub.2/RES/1999/3, 10 November 1999; UNCHR Resolution 2000/61 on Human Rights Defenders, UN Doc. E/CN.4/RES/2000/61, 26 April 2000; *Declaration on the Right and Responsibility of Individuals, Groups and Organs of Society to Promote and Protect Universally Recognized Human Rights and Fundamental Freedoms*, UN Doc. A/RES/64/163, 18 December 2009.

65 Margaret Sekaggya, Human Rights Council, *Report of the Special Rapporteur on the Situation of Human Rights Defenders*, UN Doc. A/HRC/19/55, 21 December 2011, especially para. 27.

66 *SRHRD Report*, n. 41.

67 *Ibid.*, para. 2.

68 *SRHRD Report*, n. 41, paras. 2–3.

69 UNEP, n. 8.

70 *Framework Principles*, n. 40.

In 2019, the HRC unanimously passed a resolution recognizing the contribution of EHRDs,[71] while UNEP initiated the Environmental Rights Initiative.[72] UNEP also concluded a memorandum of understanding with the Office of the United Nations High Commissioner for Human Rights in the areas of human rights and the environmental rule of law, including a focus on the protection of EHRDs.[73] In 2022, Michel Forst, previously the UN Special Rapporteur on Human Rights Defenders, was appointed as Special Rapporteur on Environmental Defenders under the Aarhus Convention. He noted that, in order to adequately implement environmental rights and protect the environment, it is necessary to recognize and protect EHRDs:[74]

> The individuals, groups, communities, movements, and organisations that are standing up for the enjoyment of the right to a clean, healthy and sustainable environment as recognized by the UN General Assembly need to be better protected and supported. … Climate change, pollution and biodiversity loss cannot be addressed without guaranteeing that those who stand up against this triple environmental emergency can safely exercise their fundamental freedoms of expression, association and assembly to do so.[75]

6.3.5 *Escalating Challenges and Risks Facing EHRDs*

Several recent reports provide sobering insights into the escalating risk facing EHRDs around the world. Sadly, death has become a dangerous reality for them. According to Global Witness's 2025 report, *Roots of Resistance*, EHRDs

[71] HRC Resolution 40/11, n. 7.

[72] 'Environmental Rights Initiative Fact Sheet', *UNEP*, www.unep.org/resources/factsheet/environmental-rights-initiative-fact-sheet.

[73] The cooperation on EHRDs includes the 'development of advocacy or communication tools and resources, the convening of joint meetings for environmental human rights defenders, and the strengthening of networks of environmental human rights defenders'. *Memorandum of Understanding Concerning Cooperation between the UN Environment Programme (UNEP) and the UN Office of the High Commissioner for Human Rights (OHCHR)*, 2019, para. 2(j), https://wedocs.unep.org/items/35c21f96-c9ea-4b26-8639-6cb5480d5725.

[74] UNECE, Decision VII/9 on a Rapid Response Mechanism to Deal with Cases Related to Article 3 (8) of the Convention on Access to Information, Public Participation in Decision-making and Access to Justice in Environmental Matters, UN Doc. ECE/MP.PP/2021/2/Add.1, 21 October 2022; see also 'Special Rapporteur on Environmental Defenders under the Aarhus Convention', *UNECE*, https://unece.org/env/pp/aarhus-convention/special-rapporteur.

[75] 'UN Special Rapporteur on Environmental Defenders Presents His Vision for Mandate to Ensure Protection under the Aarhus Convention', *UNECE*, 22 November 2022, https://unece.org/media/press/373361; see also Ebbesson, n 25, 113, who notes that the African Commission Resolution 345 on the Situation of Human Rights Defenders in Africa also pays attention to human rights defenders 'working on land and environmental issues'.

have been killed in every region of the globe.[76] During the 12-year period from 2012 to 2024, Global Witness reported the killing or disappearance of 2253 EHRDs (on 2024 figures). In September 2025, Global Witness recorded the murder or disappearance of 146 EHRDs in 2024, an average of 3.5 cases per week.[77] It also observed that seven of the ten most dangerous countries in which to be an EHRD are in Latin America – namely, Brazil, Columbia, Mexico, Honduras, Guatemala, Nicaragua, and Peru.[78] Two are in Asia Pacific, being the Philippines and India, and one is in Africa, the Democratic Republic of Congo.[79] Global Witness also reports that, according to 2024 statistics, of 146 cases, around one third of EHRDs murdered or disappeared were indigenous (48) or Afro-descendent (2), while another third (54) were small-scale farmers. It recorded that in total, 10 percent of all murdered (13) or disappeared (one) defenders in 2024 were women, including five from Mexico.

Attacks on all types of HRDs in the context of the private sector has regularly been reported on by the Business and Human Rights Resource Centre (BHRRC). In 2022, the BHRRC stated that 'attacks against human rights and environmental defenders occur in every region of the world'.[80] Specifically, between January 2015 and March 2023, the BHRRC tracked more than 4,700 attacks against HRDs and raised serious concerns over harmful business practices associated with these violations. Moreover, since the centre began tracking in 2015, 'Latin America and Asia and the Pacific have consistently been the most dangerous regions; with the most vulnerable group of defenders being EHRDs – around 70 percent of targeted defenders being land and environmental defenders'. Like the SRHRD, the BHRRC makes the point that its data refers to reported incidents involving businesses and, as such, do not present a full picture of the level of risks faced by EHRDs.

6.3.6 *Civic Space and EHRDs*

According to the United Nations, 'civic space is the environment that enables people and groups to participate meaningfully in the political, economic, social, and cultural life of their societies'.[81] This statement accords with the

76 *Roots of Resistance*, n. 9.
77 *Ibid.*
78 *Ibid.*
79 *Ibid.*
80 BHRRC, *Human Rights Defenders and Business in 2022: People Challenging Corporate Power to Protect Our Planet*, 2023.
81 United Nations, *Guidance Note on the Protection and Promotion of Civic Space*, September 2020, 3.

basic tenets of environmental access rights. The shrinking of civic space is a worrying trend reported on by UN bodies and others. In its 2021 annual review, Civicus reported a 'continuing deterioration of civic rights around the world' and a corresponding downgrading of '13 more countries in its annual rankings on civic space'.[82] In its 2023 *State of Civil Society Report*, Civicus observed that legitimate acts of public participation, such as peaceful protests against environmental harm, are under rising threat, 'even in longstanding democracies':

> The right to protest is under attack all over the world, whether people are mobilising to seek economic justice, democracy, human rights and environmental action or articulate other demands. . . . All kinds of states are repressing protests. Protesters are being criminalised in democracies such as Australia and the UK for demanding climate action, even when governments claim to take climate change seriously.
>
> Although international human rights law makes clear people have a right to peaceful protest – and the vast majority of protests throughout the year were indeed peaceful – many governments are deploying a wide range of tactics to crack down on peaceful protests and using the occasional violent protest event as an excuse to restrict all protests. Frequent tactics include disproportionate violence, all the way up to lethal violence, and harassment, arbitrary detention and criminalisation of protesters. There's increasing use of facial recognition technology and other forms of pervasive surveillance enabled by artificial intelligence. Journalists covering protests are often targeted too. There's widespread impunity for violations of protest rights.[83]

The marginalization and violation of basic environmental rights such as those relating to public participation and access to justice has far-reaching adverse ramifications for civil society. This trend is problematic in the light of global-wide attempts to mitigate the global environmental crisis. As Civicus reports, 'civil society is engaging on every front possible: responses to mitigate the worst impacts of climate change and practical projects to improve adaptation, street protest and direct action, and advocacy, legal action and international-level engagement. All the urgency to prevent the worst impacts of the crisis continues to come from civil society.'[84] However, the ability of civil society to engage in meaningful dialogue and action to address aspects of

[82] 'People Power under Attack 2021: Findings from the Civicus Monitor', *Civicus*, 2022, https://shorturl.at/mrFTI.

[83] 'State of Civil Society Report 2023', *Civicus*, March 2023, 6, www.civicus.org/documents/reports-and-publications/SOCS/2023/state-of-civil-society-report-2023_en.pdf; see also 'State of Civil Society Report', *Civicus*, https://publications.civicus.org/publications/2025-state-of-civil-society-report/download-report/.

[84] State of Civil Society Report 2023, n. 83, 60.

the global environmental crisis is severely diminished by shrinking civic space. In many such contexts, 'taking to the streets is the only means available to express dissent and try to influence decision-making'.[85] This is especially the case with respect to the restricting or closing down of legitimate 'protest space' and the resulting restriction on the exercise of basic rights and fundamental freedoms, including environmental access rights.[86]

This shrinking of civic space around the world presents a considerable threat to EHRDs.[87] Moreover, as Boyd notes, in some of the 'most biologically diverse nations on Earth, with an extraordinary abundance of wild species', rather than EHRDs being celebrated and their vital work being honoured, these 'courageous individuals are subjected to harassment, intimidation, violence, and criminalization. Governments are weaponizing the law, shrinking civic space, and at least tacitly endorsing extrajudicial killings. Large corporations collude with government, putting private interests ahead of public interests and profit ahead of people'.[88] In 2023, UNEP released a working paper entitled *Environmental Rule of Law and Human Rights in Asia Pacific: Supporting the Protection of Environmental Human Rights Defenders*[89] as well as two associated briefs entitled *Strategic Litigation against Public Participation* and *Free, Prior and Informed Consent*.[90] Drawing on a number of sources, including the analysis of the situation of EHRDs in selected countries across the Asia Pacific region, the reports found that EHRDs are regularly subjected to a wide range of violence, intimidation, and harassment that commonly includes gender-based violence, extrajudicial killings, beatings, torture, arbitrary arrests and detention, enforced or involuntary disappearances, surveillance, social isolation and 'red-tagging', land grabbing, and forced displacement.

Other common challenges include the failure by powerful state actors and businesses to obtain free, prior, and informed consent of Indigenous peoples and local communities, inadequate or non-existent environmental impact assessments, and corruption and lack of accountability and/or impunity of government and private sector interests. Another concerning trend is the use of legal systems to harass and victimize EHRDs. States, often including the military, and other powerful actors such as corporations, are increasingly employing a range of legal strategies and procedures to impede or prevent legitimate environmental and other 'human rights work, restrict civic space, and repress dissenting

85 State of Civil Society Report 2023, n. 83, 6.
86 *Ibid.*
87 Boyd, n. 51.
88 *Ibid.*, 1–2.
89 UNEP, n. 7.
90 UNEP, *Strategic Litigation*, n. 56; UNEP, *Free, Prior and Informed Consent*, n. 56.

voices'.[91] Of particular concern is the growth in strategic litigation against public participation (SLAPP). According to the EU Directive of 2024, 'such court proceedings are not initiated for the purpose of access to justice, but to silence public debate and prevent investigation of and reporting on breaches of Union and national law, typically using harassment and intimidation.[92] The targets of SLAPP include individuals, representatives of Indigenous peoples and local communities, journalists and independent media networks, academics, civil society, and a range of environmental human rights NGOs.[93]

6.4 PROMOTING AND PROTECTING ENVIRONMENTAL RIGHTS

As a result of the growing demand for participatory mechanisms concerning environment matters over the fifty years since 1972, the world community has come a fair distance with the procedural rights of access to information, public participation, and justice. We have also seen an increase in the importance of established and emerging principles associated with the environmental rule of law that underlie the now globally recognized human right to a clean, healthy, and sustainable environment. However, it has become obvious that the right to a clean, healthy, and sustainable environment as well as the implementation of the environmental rule of law will continue to have much less traction if environmental access rights are not able to be effectively implemented and enforced, with the result that EHRDs will not be adequately protected against reprisals. Without these access tools, challenging decisions of government becomes virtually impossible, and the trampling of the rights of EHRDs will consequently persist.

It is clear from the evidence that the practical implementation of environmental access rights is manifestly failing with respect to the legitimate activities of EHRDs in many jurisdictions. As noted in this chapter, over the last two decades at least, a range of rights are being regularly breached with impunity by administrative officials, the military, and the police. Frequently, private sector actors are also involved in acting against EHRDs, sometimes with the encouragement or connivance of officials and elected representatives. Laws

91 See, e.g., BHRRC, SLAPPed but Not Silenced: Defending Human Rights in the Face of Legal Risks, June 2021, www.business-humanrights.org/en/from-us/briefings/slapped-but-not-silenced-defending-human-rights-in-the-face-of-legal-risks/.

92 Directive (EU) 2024/1069 of the European Parliament and of the Council of 11 April 2024 on protecting persons who engage in public participation from manifestly unfounded claims or abusive court proceedings ('Strategic lawsuits against public participation'), preamble, recital 14; see also definition of 'Abusive Court Proceedings against public participation' (Article 4(3).

93 See further UNEP, *Strategic Litigation*, n. 56.

meant to protect those rights, both in general and in the environmental realm, are being narrowed with regard to civic freedoms, wrongly interpreted, or, perhaps worst, simply ignored. Sadly, in a small number of jurisdictions where judicial independence is not the norm, courts and their judges are also implicated in these matters – for example, through their failure to enforce or through selective enforcement when it is politically convenient. In some jurisdictions, corruption is rife across the national institutional and governmental spectrum with regard to decisions concerning environmental protection and the exploitation of natural resources. Thus, despite the many positive legal and policy developments at the international level and, to a lesser extent, at the regional level, national governments often fall short of the widely-accepted standards expected of them in the international human rights and environmental law instruments to which they have agreed.

A fundamental question then is what international regional and national legal responses are required to substantially enhance the public participatory processes in environmental decision-making in general, as well as specifically to expand the civic freedoms that EHRDs should enjoy, in particular, when it comes to environmental protection and promoting, protecting and enjoying their environmental rights. A range of suggested legal and policy responses have been set out in several UNEP publications.[94] These include recommendations for strengthening and protecting public participation, safeguarding civic space, and guaranteeing access to justice at the international, regional, and national levels. Suggested measures include urging states to implement the recommendations in UNEP's policy on the protection of EHRDs[95] and, where national laws are silent, to enact constitutional and legal provisions consistent with the HRC's and the UNGA's resolutions on the right to a clean, healthy, and sustainable environment; incorporate the principle of free, prior, and informed consent as a fundamental provision in their environmental and natural resources laws; enact laws with specific provisions included on the recognition and protection of EHRDs; and introduce anti-SLAPP and anti-criminalization provisions for legislative enactment or introduction by supreme courts. States are also urged to negotiate agreements for environmental access rights and the protection of EHRDs between jurisdictions in regions where such agreements are not yet in place. The Aarhus Convention and Escazú Agreement could act as models for such agreements.

94 UNEP, n. 7; UNEP, *Human Rights*, n. 56; UNEP, *Strategic Litigation*, n. 56; UNEP, *Free, Prior and Informed Consent*, n. 56.

95 UNEP, n. 8.

6.5 CONCLUSION

This chapter has shown that, despite the legal recognition and development of environmental access rights since Stockholm 1972, fifty years later, the shrinking of civic space and restrictions on the exercise of environmental access rights is growing. As a result, EHRDs around the world are facing an increasing range of risks and threats. These risks and threats have serious adverse ramifications not only for the EHRDs themselves but also for all of society in so far as they prevent the full enjoyment of everyone's environmental rights, including the right to a clean, heathy, and sustainable environment. Further, the capacity of states to realize the environmental rule of law and achieve sustainable development is also severely constrained by these growing threats. In seeking to exercise their rights, EHRDs continue to come into direct conflict with government and private sector interests. The situation of EHRDs has highlighted the contradictions between what governments have committed to with respect to their SDG obligations and their actual responses on the ground. This is so especially concerning the three targets set out in SDG 6.3 (Progress on Wastewater Treatment; SDG 16.7, Ensure Responsive, Inclusive and Representative Decision-making; and SDG 16.10, Public Access to Information and Protect Fundamental Freedoms). The implementation of the environmental rule of law itself is also made much more difficult.

In the light of the above, we conclude that the exercise of environmental access rights must be much more robustly supported. There is a need to put into place a range of strategies and actions to strengthen the full enjoyment of environmental access rights and to ensure greater protection for those seeking to exercise these rights. At a broader level, as greater awareness of the need to take coordinated global action to respond to the global environmental crisis identified by the United Nations, the legal and political restrictions on the ability of civil society to express that need must also be more specifically and actively addressed. Without more determined and stronger legal and policy responses to facilitate access rights, the significant achievements in addressing global environmental issues in the past half-century will continue to be eroded.

PART III

CONSUMPTION, PRODUCTION, CHEMICALS, AND WASTE

7

Unrealized Ambition or Unattainable Goal? Sustainable Consumption and Production in International Law

Eva R. van der Marel and Catherine Redgwell

7.1 INTRODUCTION

Fifty years after the 1972 UN Conference on the Human Environment (Stockholm Conference) produced a first set of agreed global environmental principles,[1] states held a commemorative international meeting from 2 to 3 June 2022 entitled the UN International Meeting Stockholm+50: A Healthy Planet for the Prosperity of All – Our Responsibility, Our Opportunity (Stockholm+50 Meeting)[2] to take stock of the state of the human environment and discuss the way forward.[3] A key recommendation that emerged from this meeting was the need 'to adopt system wide change in the way our current economic system works to contribute to a healthy planet', inter alia, through 'investing in infrastructure, developing effective policy and encouraging a global dialogue to promote sustainable consumption and production'.[4] This concern for promoting sustainable consumption and production (SCP)[5] highlights an important evolution in the sustainable development agenda over fifty years.

[1] *Report of the UN Conference on the Human Environment*, UN Doc. A/CONF.48/14/Rev.1, 16 June 1972.

[2] Convened pursuant to UNGA Resolution 75/280 on International Meeting Entitled 'Stockholm+50: A Healthy Planet for the Prosperity of All – Our Responsibility, Our Opportunity', UN Doc. A/RES/75/280, 24 May 2021.

[3] International Institute for Sustainable Development, 'Stockholm+50' (2022) 13(14) *Earth Negotiations Bulletin* 1, https://enb.iisd.org/stockholm50.

[4] 'Key Recommendations', *Stockholm+50*, www.stockholm50.global/resources/stockholm50-recommendations-and-actions-renewal-and-trust.

[5] Policy documents and their commentaries vary between using the expressions 'sustainable consumption and production' (for example, in Sustainable Development Goal [SDG] 12: Responsible Consumption and Production) and 'sustainable production and consumption' (for example, in Principle 8 of the Rio Declaration). 'Rio Declaration on Environment and Development', in *Report of the UN Conference on Environment and Development*, UN Doc. A/CONF.151/26 (Vol. I), 12 August 1992 (Rio Declaration).

Emerging from early calls for more rational management of resources and development planning in the 1972 Stockholm Declaration on the Human Environment (Stockholm Declaration),[6] SCP has developed into an essential requirement for sustainable development, enshrined in Principle 8 of the 1992 Rio Declaration on Environment and Development (Rio Declaration)[7] and in Sustainable Development Goal (SDG) 12: Responsible Consumption and Production in 2015.[8]

Indeed, it was the 1992 Rio Conference on Environment and Development, with its emphasis on both consumption and production,[9] that placed SCP squarely on the international environmental policy agenda. Principle 8 of the Rio Declaration explicitly declares that, 'to achieve sustainable development and a higher quality of life for all people, States should reduce and eliminate unsustainable patterns of production and consumption and promote appropriate demographic policies', and aspects of SCP are also addressed in the accompanying Agenda 21.[10] Subsequent

6 'Declaration of the United Nations Conference on the Human Environment', in *Report of the UN Conference on the Human Environment*, n. 1 (Stockholm Declaration). Though there is no express reference to sustainable consumption and production (SCP) in the Stockholm Declaration and accompanying Stockholm Action Plan, the key tenet of SCP of 'doing more with less' is detectable in the Declaration (for example, on the management of natural resources, the call for pollution prevention from toxic and other substances, and the linking of development needs and environmental protection and improvement) and the Stockholm Action Plan (reducing the harmful impacts of production in key economic sectors, minimizing the release of polluting substances, including through greater transparency over chemicals throughout their life cycle, and the possible substitution of synthetic products). 'Action Plan for the Human Environment', in *Report of the United Nations Conference on the Human Environment*, n. 1 (Stockholm Action Plan).

7 Rio Declaration, n. 5, Annex I.

8 See *Transforming Our World: The 2030 Agenda for Sustainable Development*, UN Doc. A/Res/70/1, 25 September 2015; see also generally Jonas Ebbesson & Ellen Hey (eds.), *The Cambridge Handbook of the Sustainable Development Goals and International Law* (Cambridge University Press, 2022). There are interlinkages between the SDGs, with SCP providing a framework of reference for decoupling economic growth from environmental degradation in SDG 8: Decent Work and Economic Growth. See UN Economic and Social Council, *Progress Report on the 10-Year Framework of Programmes on Sustainable Consumption and Production Patterns*, UN Doc. E/2023/72, 11 July 2023.

9 For the earlier emphasis on 'cleaner production', see discussion in UN Environment Programme (UNEP), *Sustainable Consumption and Production: A Handbook for Policymakers* (UNEP, 2015); see also Livia Bizikova & Lynn M. Wagner, 'Sustainable Consumption and Production', in Noha Shawki (ed.), *International Norms, Normative Change, and the UN Sustainable Development Goals* (Lexington Books/Fortress Academic, 2016).

10 Agenda 21, UN Doc. A/CONF. 151/26, 13 June 1992, Annex II. See, in particular, ch. IV on changing consumption patterns and sector-specific chapters on energy, transportation, wastes, economic instruments, and the transfer of technology. In her authoritative commentary on Principle 8, Christina Voigt characterizes this shift in emphasis to encompass consumption as 'a significant change in environmental policymaking'. Christina Voigt, 'Principle 8', in

international environmental policies have built on the foundations laid at the Rio Conference, through the subsequent 2002 World Summit on Sustainable Development in Johannesburg[11] and the 2012 Conference on Sustainable Development in Rio de Janeiro (Rio+20 Conference),[12] to the adoption of the SDGs in 2015[13] and a new Global Strategy for Sustainable Consumption and Production (2023–30).[14] The UN General Assembly (UNGA) recognizes that 'fundamental changes in the way societies consume and produce are indispensable for achieving global sustainable development',[15] with SCP thus both 'a prerequisite and a sub-goal with respect to sustainable development' more generally.[16] The targets and indicators for SDG 12 also demonstrate how SCP may be conceptualized in more contemporary terms, referring to both its end goals (for example, resource efficiency and a reduction in [food] wastes) and operational elements (for example, reporting by businesses, informing consumers, monitoring, encouraging sustainable public procurement, developing country support, phasing out harmful and inefficient fossil fuel subsidies that encourage wasteful consumption, and developing environmentally sound management [ESM] of wastes and chemicals).

It is clear from this brief sketch that SCP has been developed by and through international policy instruments, where it has gradually been given increasing prominence, triggering action at the international, national, and

Jorge E. Viñuales (ed.), *The Rio Declaration on Environment and Development: A Commentary* (Oxford University Press, 2015), 250.

11 Johannesburg Declaration and Johannesburg Plan of Implementation, in *Report of the World Summit on Sustainable Development, Johannesburg, South Africa, 26 August–4 September* 2002, UN Doc. A/CONF.199/20, 2002, Annex (including a chapter dedicated to consumption and production, which encouraged the development of the 10-Year Framework of Programmes (10YFP) in support of regional and national initiatives to accelerate the shift towards SCP among states and stakeholders).

12 UNGA Resolution 66/288 on the Future We Want, UN Doc. A/RES/66/288, 27 July 2012 (which also adopted the 10YFP and, with a recent extension to 2030, is now a part of realising the 2030 Agenda for Sustainable Development. *Transforming Our World*, n. 8. For an overview of the 10YFP, see Voigt, n. 10.

13 *Transforming Our World*, n. 8.

14 UNGA Resolution 76/202 on Promoting Sustainable Consumption and Production Patterns for the Implementation of the 2030 Agenda for Sustainable Development, Building on Agenda 21, UN Doc. A/RES/76/202, 5 January 2022. The Global Strategy was welcomed by the UN General Assembly (UNGA) in Resolution A/RES/77/162, December 2022.

15 UNGA Resolution 66/288, n. 12.

16 Martin Führ & Julian Schenten, 'Sustainable Production and Consumption (SPC)', in Ludwig Krämer & Emanuela Orlando (eds.), *Principles of Environmental Law* (Edward Elgar, 2018), 129.

industry/private level. What is less clear is exactly what the principle of SCP brings to the table at the time of the Stockholm+50 Meeting and how it relates to existing concepts such as environmentally sound waste and chemicals management, resource efficiency, life cycle thinking, and circular economy approaches. Its development has not been without many challenges, not least of which is that SCP has been considered a multidimensional, open-ended, and continuously reinterpreted concept, which moreover is defined differently in different countries and across different sectors.[17] Nonetheless, a widely relied upon definition of SCP is 'the use of services and related products, which respond to basic needs and bring a better quality of life while minimizing the use of natural resources and toxic materials as well as the emissions of waste and pollutants over the life cycle of the service or product so as not to jeopardize the needs of further generations'.[18] It can presently be understood as doing more (better quality of life) with less (lower negative environmental and health impacts, taking into account the whole life cycle of a service or a product, from the efficient use of resources through to minimizing pollution from waste).[19] A recent and increasingly prevalent approach is to envisage a more circular economy,[20] which can be defined as an economy in which the value of products, materials, and other resources is maintained for as long as possible[21] and which 'entails decoupling economic activity from the consumption of finite resources'.[22]

17 See Bizikova & Wagner, n. 9, 161, 166.

18 UNEP, Global Outlook on Sustainable Production and Consumption Policies. Taking Action Together, 2012, 19, referencing the Oslo Symposium on Sustainable Consumption, hosted by the Norwegian Ministry of Environment, 19–20 January 1994. This definition is widely referenced in the literature.

19 See, in particular, Voigt, n. 10, 247.

20 UNEA Resolution 5/11 on Enhancing Circular Economy as a Contribution to Achieving Sustainable Consumption and Production, Doc. UNEP/EA.5/Res.11, 7 March 2012; UNEA Resolution 4/1 on Innovative Pathways to Achieve Sustainable Consumption and Production, UN Doc. UNEP/EA.4/Res.1, 28 March 2019; UNEP, *Innovative Solutions for Environmental Challenges and Sustainable Consumption and Production: Report of the Executive Director*, UN Doc. UNEP/EA.4/17, 19 December 2018.

21 See, e.g., European Commission, *Closing the Loop: An EU Action Plan for the Circular Economy*, Doc. COM(2015) 614 final, 2 December 2015, 2. Note, however, the many different definitions of 'circular economy' in both literature, policy documents, and law. For an overview, see Julian Kirchherr, Denise Reike, & Marko Hekkert, 'Conceptualizing the Circular Economy: An Analysis of 114 Definitions' (2017) 127 *Resources, Conservation and Recycling* 221, in particular, the supplementary materials, Table 3 'Definitions of the Circular Economy'.

22 'Circular Economy Glossary', *Ellen MacArthur Foundation*, www.ellenmacarthurfoundation.org/topics/circular-economy-introduction/glossary; see also Kirchherr, Reike & Hekkert, n. 21.

Despite its prominence in policy, however, there exists little in terms of international law to support these required changes in global production and consumption, which instead focuses more on end-of-pipe solutions (pollution control, waste management, and so on). Further development is of course always possible – for example, SCP plays a primary role in the negotiations on a new legally binding instrument on plastics pollution, which is among other things intended 'to promote sustainable production and consumption of plastics, through, among other things, product design, and environmentally sound waste management, including through resource efficiency and circular economy approaches'.[23] As for existing international law, section 7.4 of this chapter considers the (limited) international legal tools that have been developed over the years that support SCP, mapping the mechanisms and principles that have been developed across multilateral environmental agreements (MEAs) on atmospheric pollution, chemicals, and hazardous wastes.[24] Whilst acknowledging the importance of trade and investment tools in ensuring SCP in the global economy – trade restrictions being one feature of the MEAs that we examine, for example – these areas are not the focus of this chapter.[25] This MEA analysis is preceded by the next section, which critically evaluates the key substantive and procedural aspects of the concept of SCP as it should be understood today, identifying underlying principles as well as remaining uncertainties about its scope. The chapter concludes with the identification from these case studies of key gaps between what it is that SCP requires and the legal tools presently available to support this goal.

7.2 CONCEPTUALIZING SCP

The overarching goal of SCP in international policy is, first and foremost, 'doing more with less' by decoupling human well-being and economic growth, on the one hand, and resource use and environmental degradation,

[23] UNEA Resolution 5/14 on End Plastic Pollution: Towards an International Legally Binding Instrument, UN Doc. UNEP/PP/OEWG/1/INF/1, 10 May 2022, 4, para. 3(b).

[24] These are also the 'case studies' most frequently relied on in the literature discussing the normative impact of SCP. See, e.g., UNEP, *The Global Outlook on SCP Policies*, 2012 (which focuses on hazardous materials and toxic chemicals in the 10YFP); see also Voigt, n. 10. The registration, evaluation, authorization, and restriction of chemicals (REACH) is the example of choice in the discussion in Führ & Schenten, n. 16.

[25] For a focus on trade and investment regimes, see Alessandra Arcuri & Enrico Partiti, 'SDG 12: Ensure Sustainable Consumption and Production Patterns', in Ebbesson & Hey, n. 8, 304.

on the other hand.[26] In addition, some authors have argued that SCP should entail a reduction in overall consumption levels, although what level could be considered sustainable remains indistinct.[27] Indeed, greater efficiency is often overcompensated by a growth in consumption.[28] The latest SDG process reports observe that, although fewer materials now appear to be required to produce a unit of output, domestic material consumption per capita and in absolute terms is steadily growing globally (from 2000 to 2019, total domestic material consumption rose by more than 65 per cent globally), with consequences in terms of both resource depletion and associated environmental impacts.[29] A number of scholars argue that, to achieve sustainable consumption (and, consequently, production), increased efficiency in consumption should be accompanied by a general reduction in consumption volumes in absolute terms, though this discussion has not featured significantly in international policy discussions.[30] Instead, discussions have centred on consumption and production patterns,[31] although an increase in consumption is something to avoid.[32] This lack of emphasis on reducing consumption may be in acknowledgement that large parts of the world suffer from under-consumption and do

26 Voigt, n. 10, 248; see also UNEP, *Towards a Green Economy: Pathways to Sustainable Development and Poverty Eradication* (UNEP, 2011).

27 See Doris A. Fuchs & Sylvia Lorek, 'Sustainable Consumption Governance: A History of Promises and Failures' (2005) 28 *Journal of Consumer Policy* 261, 282 (though they are writing specifically about consumption); Thomas Princen, 'Principles for Sustainability: From Cooperation and Efficiency to Sufficiency' (2003) 3(1) *Global Environmental Politics* 33; Joachim H. Spangenberg & Sylvia Lorek, 'Environmentally Sustainable Household Consumption: From Aggregate Environmental Pressures to Priority Fields of Action' (2002) 43 *Ecological Economics* 127.

28 See Fuchs & Loreck, n. 27, 262, referring, *inter alia*, to Lorna A. Greening, David L. Greece & Carmen Difiglio, 'Energy Efficiency and Consumption – The Rebound Effect: A Survey' (2000) 28 *Energy Policy* 389.

29 High-level Political Forum on Sustainable Development, '2018 HLPF Review of SDGs Implementation: SDG 12', *Sustainable Development*, 2, https://sustainabledevelopment.un.org/content/documents/196532018backgroundnotesSDG12.pdf; 'The Sustainable Development Goals Report 2022', *United Nations*, 50, https://unstats.un.org/sdgs/report/2022/The-Sustainable-Development-Goals-Report-2022.pdf.

30 See, e.g., Fuchs & Loreck, n. 27, 262; Princen, n. 27, 49.

31 See also James Salzman, 'Sustainable Consumption and the Law' (1997) 27(4) *Environmental Law* 1267 (who demonstrates that national laws have indeed mostly addressed patterns rather than levels of consumption – for example, by regulating product composition and performance, environmentally conscious public procurement, and labelling requirements).

32 See also UNEP, *Sustainable Consumption and Production: A Handbook for Policymakers*, 2015, 125 (which guards 'against the re-bound effect, where efficiency gains are cancelled out by resulting increases in consumption'). The handbook also highlights the dangers related to over-consumption.

not have their basic needs met[33] and that the 'political reality in democratic societies is such that it will be much easier to change consumption patterns than levels of consumption, although both issues need to be addressed'.[34]

Both the biggest contribution and challenge of SCP is the growing emphasis on procedural expectations: the need to think holistically about product systems in life cycle terms. Life cycle thinking is mentioned throughout Agenda 21 with regard to production, in general, and chemicals and waste management, in particular,[35] and it has become a staple of SCP since then.[36] Although the various policy references to 'taking into account' the life cycle of products/chemicals/wastes and so on are not usually defined, life cycle thinking can be explained as 'a broad concept that helps conceptualize environmental problems as a system-level issue', whereby 'all environmental aspects from cradle to grave are considered and possibilities for environmental improvement of products and services are found along their life cycles'.[37] It finds practical application for industry in the form of a life cycle assessment (LCA), which was standardized in 2006 by the International Organization for Standardization (ISO).[38] Arguably, not only environmental but also other types of information should be gathered. Martin Führ and Julian Schenten highlight that 'a meaningful application of life cycle thinking in the context of Sustainable Development requires a truly holistic approach, taking into account not only all environmental aspects, but also social and economic negative impacts and benefits, to facilitate [SCP] decision-making',[39] by reference to the UN-developed concept of life cycle sustainability assessment.[40]

33 See Agenda 21, n. 10, Annex II, paras. 4.4, 4.5; Johannesburg Plan of Implementation, n. 11, para. 14.

34 Norwegian Ministry of Environment, *Outcomes of the Oslo Roundtable Conference on Sustainable Production and Consumption*, 10 February 1995, para. 1.2, https://enb.iisd.org/consume/oslo000.html.

35 Agenda 21, n. 10, paras. 9.18(e), 19.44, 19.49, 19.50, 21.4 (specifying that the environmentally sound management (ESM) of wastes 'implies the application of the integrated life cycle management concept, which presents a unique opportunity to reconcile development with environmental protection').

36 Norwegian Ministry of Environment, n. 34; Johannesburg Plan of Implementation, n. 11, paras. 15, 23 (renewing the Agenda 21 commitment to sound management of chemicals throughout their life cycle and hazardous wastes); UNGA Resolution 66/288, n. 12, para. 7; see also UNEP, n. 32; UNEA Resolution 4/1, n. 20; Resolution 5/11, n. 20.

37 Oksana Mont & Raimund Bleischwitz, 'Sustainable Consumption and Resource Management in the Light of Life Cycle Thinking' (2007) 17 *European Environment* 59, 60.

38 See, e.g., International Organization for Standardization (ISO) no. 14044 (2006), section 3.1 (definition of life cycle).

39 Führ & Schenten, n. 16, 131.

40 UNEP, *Towards a Life Cycle Sustainability Assessment*, 2011.

The ISO notes that 'the depth and the breadth of LCA can differ considerably depending on the goal of a particular LCA'.[41] This last point is important also for when governments engage in life cycle thinking more broadly: what should be its depth and breadth, and what should be its goal for SCP? Life cycle thinking is not an outcome in and of itself but, rather, a tool that can be used differently for different purposes.[42] It provides relevant information based on which particular decisions can be made, but it does not tell us what the modalities should be for life cycle thinking at the government (or even at the global) level nor what to do with the information that is obtained. In the context of SCP, life cycle thinking broadly serves to improve the environmental performance of a product system.[43] However, the question remains whether the growing attention given to life cycle thinking masks a persistent lack of clarity over what important trade-offs are to be made (and by whom) on the basis of such life cycle thinking as well as a general unwillingness to look beyond optimizing current economic activities. It is likely that this should now also be understood in the context of transitioning to a more circular economy, which has gained growing traction as a viable model among states and international (non-)governmental organizations alike.

With this critical understanding of the criteria for ensuring SCP in mind, we now turn to examine how SCP is animated or is reflected across key MEAs (atmospheric pollution, chemicals, and hazardous wastes).

7.3 SCP IN INTERNATIONAL LAW

7.3.1 *Life Cycle Thinking through Best Available Techniques, Best Environmental Practices, and Environmentally Sound Management*

Chemicals and waste management are an important element of many SCP priority sectors (construction, food systems, consumer information, and so on).

[41] ISO, n. 38.

[42] See Führ & Schenten, n. 16, 128 (explaining that life cycle thinking is a scientific rationale for operationalizing the conflicting objectives of SCP). Exploring the role of life cycle thinking in law, see Carl Dalhammer, 'The Application of "Life Cycle Thinking" in European Environmental Law: Theory and Practice' (2015) 12(2) *Journal for European Environmental and Planning Law* 97.

[43] As part of the European Union's integrated product policy, see European Commission, *Communication on the Integrated Product Policy Building on Environmental Life-Cycle Thinking*, Doc. COM/2003/0302 final, 18 June 2003 (which, however, is 'not aimed at achieving a reduction in the consumption of products' but, rather, at 'better products', as noted by Rosalind Malcolm, 'Life Cycle Thinking as a Legal Tool: A Codex Rerum' (2019) 5(2) *Law, Environment and Development Journal* 208, 214).

They are inextricably linked to resource efficiency and decoupling economic growth from natural resource use and environmental impacts,[44] and are therefore of key relevance to achieving SCP,[45] as reflected in SDG 12.[46] The main MEAs that regulate the chemicals and waste sectors are the 1989 Basel Convention,[47] the 1998 Rotterdam Convention,[48] and the 2001 Stockholm Convention[49] (collectively known as the BRS Conventions) – each through a slightly different set of principles and mechanisms.

A key feature of the Basel Convention is that wastes that fall within its scope (controlled wastes) are subject to ESM, a concept that predates and is not unique to the Basel Convention, but which has been given specific meaning in its context of waste management.[50] The Basel Convention defines ESM as 'taking all practicable steps to ensure that [wastes that fall within the scope of the Convention] are managed in a manner which will protect human health and the environment against the adverse effects which may result from such wastes'.[51] ESM is expressed through, and incentivised by, the Basel Convention's key mechanisms. For example, states shall take the appropriate measures to ensure that the generation of wastes is 'reduced to a minimum',[52]

44 UNEP, *Global Chemicals Outlook II: From Legacies to Innovative Solutions: Implementing the 2030 Agenda for Sustainable Development*, 2019, 11.

45 See, e.g., Johannesburg Plan of Implementation, n. 11; UNGA Resolution 66/288, n. 12; UNEA Resolution 4/7 on Environmentally Sound Management of Waste, UN Doc. UNEP/EA.4/Res.7, 28 March 2019; UNEA Resolution 4/8 on the Sound Management of Chemicals and Wastes, UN Doc. UNEP/EA.4/Res.8, 28 March 2019 (drawing the link between waste management and the use of hazardous substances in material cycles, on the one hand, and adapting production and consumption models, on the other hand).

46 See also the Johannesburg Plan of Implementation, n. 11 (which states: (i) that the ratification and implementation of relevant international instruments on chemicals and waste should be promoted; (ii) that partnerships aimed at enhancing ESM of chemicals and hazardous waste should be fostered; and (iii) that countries should be encouraged to implement a globally harmonised system for the classification and labelling of chemicals).

47 Basel Convention on the Control of Transboundary Movements of Hazardous Wastes and Their Disposal, 1989, 1673 UNTS 126 (Basel Convention).

48 Convention on the Prior Informed Consent Procedure for Certain Hazardous Chemicals and Pesticides in International Trade, 1998, 2244 UNTS 337 (Rotterdam Convention).

49 Stockholm Convention on Persistent Organic Pollutants, 2001, 2256 UNTS 119 (Stockholm Convention).

50 UNEP, *Cairo Guidelines and Principles for the Environmentally Sound Management of Hazardous Wastes*, Decision 14/30, 17 June 1987 (whose adoption fed into the preparatory work to the Basel Convention).

51 Basel Convention, n. 47, art. 2(8).

52 *Ibid.*, art. 4(2)(a). The importance of waste minimization has been progressively reaffirmed in Conference of the Parties (COP) meetings, including through the adoption of the Cartagena Declaration and guidance on prevention and minimization. See Report of the Conference of the Parties to the Basel Convention on the Control of Transboundary Movements of Hazardous Wastes and Their Disposal on its tenth meeting UN Doc. UNEP/CHW.10/28,

adequate disposal facilities must be in place for the ESM of wastes whose generation cannot be prevented, and states are to prevent and minimize any pollution from their waste management.[53] Increasingly detailed guidance has been developed by the Basel parties to give substance to these general obligations to ensure ESM, with implications for production and consumption more generally.[54] Although these guidelines are non-binding, it can be noted that they are prepared by experts and subsequently adopted by the Conference of the Parties (COP), by way of consensus (normally).[55] This gives them 'persuasive force as a basic standard for countries to meet in fulfilling their obligations'.[56]

Already in the early days following the Rio Conference, one of the key environmental principles identified in guidance on ESM that would 'merit consideration' is the 'Integrated Life-cycle Principle, by which substances and products should be designed and managed such that minimum environmental impact is caused during their generation, use, recovery and disposal'.[57] Subsequent guidance on ESM (both general framework guidance and technical guidelines on specific waste streams) has repeated this call for life cycle thinking, as have indications for the direction of decision-making following such thinking – namely, to adopt measures in line with the

2011, Annex IV 'Cartagena Declaration on the Prevention, Minimization and Recovery of Hazardous Wastes and Other Wastes'; *Guidance to Assist Parties in Developing Efficient Strategies for Achieving the Prevention and Minimization of the Generation of Hazardous and Other Wastes and Their Disposal*, UN Doc. UNEP/CHW.13/INF/11/Rev.1, 11 August 2017 (adopted with Decision BC-13/3 at COP-13 in 2017); see also Juliette Voinov Kohler, 'Chapter V.32: The Basel Convention on the Control of Transboundary Movements of Hazardous Wastes and Their Disposal 1989', in Michael Faure (ed.), *Elgar Encyclopaedia of Environmental Law* (Edward Elgar, 2015), 335.

53 Basel Convention, n. 47, art. 4(2)(b), (c).

54 *Ibid.*, art. 4(8), 10(e); 'Environmentally Sound Management (ESM) Toolkit', *Basel Convention*, www.basel.int/Implementation/CountryLedInitiative/EnvironmentallySoundManagement/ESMToolkit/Overview/tabid/5839/Default.aspx.

55 *Report of the First Meeting of the Conference of the Parties to the Basel Convention*, UN Doc. UNEP/CHW.1/24, 5 December 1992, Annex III, Decision BC-1/1 on Rules of Procedure, Rule 40(1).

56 See generally Alan Boyle & Catherine Redgwell, *Birnie, Boyle and Redgwell's International Law and the Environment* (4th ed., Oxford University Press, 2021), 495.

57 *Guidance Document on the Preparation of Technical Guidelines for the Environmentally Sound Management of Wastes Subject to the Basel Convention*, 1994, para. 10 (adopted at COP-2); see *Report of the Second Meeting of the Conference of the Parties to the Basel Convention*, UN Doc. UNEP/CHW.2/30, 25 March 1994, Annex: Decision BC-2/13: Technical Guidelines for the Environmentally Sound Management of Wastes Subject to the Basel Convention. The Guidance Document itself is available online at www.basel.int/Implementation/TechnicalMatters/DevelopmentofTechnicalGuidelines/TechnicalGuidelines/tabid/8025/Default.aspx.

waste hierarchy.[58] The waste hierarchy is a widely supported priority order for waste management options, and it includes the following: prevention, minimization, reuse, recycling, other recovery systems including energy recovery, and final disposal.[59] The Basel Convention's general ESM framework guidance, moreover, explains that reuse, recycling, and recovery techniques should be encouraged to deliver the 'best overall environmental outcomes' in accordance with the best available techniques (BAT), the best environmental practices (BEP), and a life cycle approach.[60]

The procedural prerequisite of life cycle thinking has become an integrated part not only of the waste regime but also of international chemicals management under the Stockholm Convention. By cross-referencing to the Basel Convention for cooperation over the ESM of wastes contaminated by persistent organic pollutants (POPs), such wastes have also become relevant for parties to the Stockholm Convention.[61] Life cycle thinking has moreover become part of the Stockholm regime through its reference to best available techniques (BATs) and best environmental practices (BEPs) for measures to reduce or eliminate releases from unintentional production.[62] Guidance has been developed under the Stockholm Convention on both BATs and BEPs[63]

58 *Follow-up to the Indonesian-Swiss Country-led Initiative to Improve the Effectiveness of the Basel Convention: Framework for the Environmentally Sound Management of Hazardous Wastes and Other Wastes*, UN Doc. UNEP/CHW.11/3/Add.1/Rev.1, 4 June 2013, Annex: Framework for the Environmentally Sound Management of Hazardous Wastes and Other Wastes, 2011, para. 11, 9 (*ESM Framework*); see *Report of the Conference of the Parties to the Basel Convention on the Control of Transboundary Movements of Hazardous Wastes and Their Disposal on Its Tenth Meeting*, UN Doc. UNEP/CHW.10/28, 1 November 2011, Annex I: Decision BC-10/2 on Strategic Framework for the Implementation of the Basel Convention for 2012–2021, para. 3.

59 UNEP, *Global Waste Management Outlook* (UNEP, 2015), 31, n. 24 (though also noting that 'the hierarchy can be stated in many different ways, and the specifics of the generalized priority order are themselves hotly debated' as it 'refers only to environmental aspects and not to public or occupational health, financial or other considerations such as materials criticality').

60 *ESM Framework*, n. 58.

61 Stockholm Convention, n. 49, art. 6(2) (which provides that, for managing stockpiles of persistent organic pollutants (POP)-contaminated wastes, parties shall 'collaborate closely with the appropriate bodies of the Basel Convention'). As a consequence, the Basel Convention has adopted general and specific technical guidelines on POPs, and whenever a POP is listed by decisions of the COP to the Stockholm Convention, existing technical guidelines are updated or newly established under the Basel Convention (as referred to in the Stockholm Convention's 'Guidelines on best available techniques and guidance on best environmental practices [2019/2021 updates]').

62 Stockholm Convention, n. 49, art. 5, Annex C.

63 Report of the Conference of the Parties of the Stockholm Convention on Persistent Organic Pollutants on the work of its third meeting, UN Doc. UNEP/POPS/COP.3/30, 4 May 2007,

that, inter alia, identifies the potential relevance of environmental principles, including that of sustainable consumption[64] and life cycle management.[65]

Through the concept of ESM and the guidance that has been progressively developed as a result, the Basel Convention not only contributes to the substantive elements of SCP (the reduction of waste and pollution from production and consumption) but, together with the Stockholm Convention, also promotes indirectly the core procedural element of life cycle thinking that is a prerequisite of SCP. This can be contrasted with the Stockholm Convention's additional mechanism to restrict some of the substances that go into the production process from the very beginning. Similar to the ozone regime, this eliminates altogether particularly harmful substances from production processes, as discussed next.

7.3.2 *Minimizing Key Pollutants from Production Cycles*

The elimination of the consumption and production of harmful ozone-depleting substances is the ultimate objective of the ozone regime. While the 1985 Vienna Convention[66] was largely an empty framework, requiring further action by parties who in 1985 were unable to agree on proposals for more specific control measures,[67] the 1987 Montreal Protocol[68] represents

Annex I: Decision SC-3/5 on Guidelines on Best Available Techniques and Provisional Guidance on Best Environmental Practices, adopting the Draft Guidelines on Best Available Techniques and Provisional Guidance on Best Environmental Practices Relevant to Article 5 and Annex C**, UN Doc. UNEP/POPS/COP.3/INF/4, 13 April 2007.

64 Defined by reference to the Oslo Symposium, n. 18.

65 Defined as 'an integrated concept for managing the total life cycle of goods and services towards more sustainable production and consumption, building on the existing procedural and analytical environmental assessment tools and integrating economic, social and environmental aspects' by reference to UNEP (website no longer in use, but see www.unep.org/explore-topics/resource-efficiency/what-we-do/life-cycle-initiative).

66 Vienna Convention for the Protection of the Ozone Layer, 1985, 1513 UNTS 323.

67 UNEP, Ad Hoc Working Group on the Ozone Convention, Revised Draft Protocol Concerning Measures to Control, Limit, and reduce the Emissions of CFCs for the Protection of the Ozone Layer, 14 November 1983, UN Doc. UNEP/WG.94/9. This is not to say that the Vienna Convention was without significance in the development of international environmental law. See further Boyle & Redgwell, n. 56, ch. 6(3)(1).

68 Montreal Protocol on Substances That Deplete the Ozone Layer, 1987, 1522 UNTS 3 (Montreal Protocol); Ad Hoc Working Group of Legal and Technical Experts, *Draft Report of the Ad Hoc Working Group on the Work of Its First Session*, Doc. UNEP/WG, 15 January 1987.151/L.4; Ad Hoc Working Group of Legal and Technical Experts, *Report of the Ad Hoc Working Group on the Work of Its Second Session*, Doc. UNEP/WG 167/2, 4 March 1987; Ad Hoc Working Group of Legal and Technical Experts, *Report of the Ad Hoc Working Group on the Work of Its Third Session*, Doc. UNEP/WG 172/2, 8 May 1987. See

a much more significant agreement.[69] Unlike the vague 'appropriate measures' approach of the Vienna Convention, the Montreal Protocol sets firm targets for reducing and eliminating consumption and production[70] of a range of ozone-depleting substances.[71] These targets were supported particularly strongly by the United States, which referred to the need to err on the side of caution and to recall the well-being of future generations, as well as by the executive director of the UN Environment Programme (UNEP), whose efforts ensured that a consensus emerged among the scientific experts on predicting the rate of ozone depletion and the regulatory measures needed to protect human health and the environment.

Following scientific evidence that demonstrated that the standards adopted in 1987 would not be effective in reducing ozone depletion, however, additional substances were included by the amendments adopted in 1990 and 1992, and the timetable for complete elimination was revised and brought forward to 1996.[72] These changes were made possible by the development of new technology and alternative substances,[73] although, in some cases, these substitutes may still have an ozone-depleting potential and others are greenhouse gases. Limited allowance was made for increases in the production of ozone-depleting substances to meet domestic needs and to facilitate industrial rationalization. Control of consumption and production was necessary in

Richard Benedick, *Ozone Diplomacy: New Directions in Safeguarding the Planet* (Harvard University Press, 1998).

69 '[A] landmark international environmental agreement, providing a precedent for new regulatory techniques and institutional arrangements, and the adoption and implementation of innovative financial mechanisms.' Philippe Sands & Jacqueline Peel, *Principles of International Environmental Law* (4th ed., Cambridge University Press, 2018), 280. In 2009, the Montreal Protocol became the first treaty of any kind in the UN system to achieve universal participation.

70 Each is defined in article 1 of the Montreal Protocol, n. 68 (as amended): '"Production" means the amount of controlled substances produced, minus the amount destroyed by technologies to be approved by the Parties and minus the amount entirely used as feedstock in the manufacture of other chemicals. The amount recycled and reused is not to be considered as "production"' (art. 1(5)). '"Consumption" means production plus imports minus exports of controlled substances' (art. 1(6)).

71 *Ibid.*, art. 2, for example, adopts limitation and reduction requirements on the consumption and production of all Annex A substances (for example, chlorofluorocarbons [CFCs] and halons) and through subsequent amendments for other controlled substances.

72 For amendments and adjustments, see UNEP, *Handbook for the Montreal Protocol on Substances That Deplete the Ozone Layer* (13th ed., UNEP, 2019) and subsequent updates. Decisions of the parties will also be found there.

73 Substitutability of substances being one reason attributed for the Montreal Protocol's overall success, with the phasing out of existing cheaper CFCs paving the way for more costly alternatives to be developed and marketed. Stephen Andersen & Madhava Sarma, *Protecting the Ozone Layer: The United Nations History* (Routledge, 2002), 361–362.

order to protect the interests of producers and importers by deterring price inflation or overproduction in the interim period until the eventual phase-out of these gases.[74]

Controls on ozone-depleting substances have been strengthened at successive meetings of the parties, new substances have been added, and the supervisory institutions have evolved. Without the Montreal Protocol and successive adjustments, ozone depletion would be ten times greater than it is currently.[75] The level of compliance in developed states appears to have been high, with most phasing out the major ozone-depleting substances by 1996 as required by the accelerated timetable set by the Protocol's amendments. The obligation of developing states parties to phase out production and consumption only began to take effect in 1999, so that, by 1996, the world's main chlorofluorocarbon (CFC) producers, apart from Russia, were India and China. Thereafter, the data show that consumption in a majority of developing countries had begun to fall significantly, and some parties, including China,[76] had accelerated the phase out.[77]

Faced with the relatively straightforward task of eliminating production and consumption of ozone-depleting substances, the Vienna Convention and the Montreal Protocol have been a success. Provided the Protocol is fully adhered to, global ozone losses and the Antarctic ozone hole should have recovered by around 2050.[78] For SCP, the practical effect of measures taken has been to require interventions across consumption and production chains for a number of goods and, through the multilateral fund, in particular, to promote the conversion to cleaner and more sustainable products and technology. The Montreal Protocol has also encouraged resort to substitute substances,[79] some

74 Mostafa K. Tolba, *Explanatory Note by the Executive Director of UNEP* (UNEP, 1987).

75 Andersen & Sarma, n. 73, 346.

76 However, in 2019, it became apparent that significant emissions of ozone-depleting substances were still occurring in China. Matthew Rigby *et al.*, 'Increase in CFC-11 Emissions from Eastern China Based on Atmospheric Observations' (2019) 569 *Nature* 546.

77 UNEP, *Report of 10th Meeting of Parties*, UN Doc. UNEP/OzL.Pro.10/9, 1998, paras. 72ff.

78 Scientific assessments showed that, in its original 1987 form, the Montreal Protocol would not have halted an accelerating level of ozone-depleting substances in the stratosphere. However, subsequent revisions were predicted to result in a gradually diminishing level after the year 2000, when increases attributable to past emissions were due to stabilize. World Meteorological Organization, *Scientific Assessment of Ozone Depletion* (World Meteorological Organization, 2018). Other problems could affect the success of the Protocol, including new ozone-depleting substances that it does not cover but that are the subject of research and ongoing review.

79 UNEP, n. 72.

of which are also greenhouse gases included in the climate regime, necessitating coordination between the two regimes.[80]

In a similar vein to the Montreal Protocol, the Stockholm Convention builds on a further priority of Agenda 21 in the Rio Declaration – namely, that of reducing risks for toxic chemicals through measures such as the phasing out or banning of chemicals 'that pose an unreasonable and otherwise unmanageable risk to the environment or human health and those that are toxic, persistent and bio-accumulative and whose use cannot be adequately controlled'.[81] Unlike the Rotterdam Convention, discussed below, it explicitly refers to the precautionary approach[82] and spells out different sets of obligations in relation to the production of different lists of chemicals (namely, to prohibit or eliminate their production or to restrict production and use).[83] The Convention also contains screening criteria that must be taken into account when states assess new or existing chemicals so as to identify (and prevent the emergence of) chemicals that exhibit the characteristics of POPs.[84]

Whereas the Rotterdam Convention suffers from major difficulties in listing new substances, the listing of substances under the Stockholm Convention can be adopted as a last resort by a three-fourths majority (though it may be subject to subsequent opting out).[85] Where the Rotterdam Convention is 'nearly vacuous' on precaution, the Stockholm Convention is merely 'thin';[86] although it does explicitly mention a precautionary approach, the critique has been voiced that a lack of scientific certainty has prevented certain chemicals from being listed.[87] The Stockholm Convention, moreover, is relatively adaptive in so far as it makes use of BATs and BEPs, as highlighted above. It contains a clear social dimension through public information and

80 See, for example, hydrofluorocarbons, which are included in Annex A of the Kyoto Protocol, and now covered by the 2016 amendment of the Montreal Protocol, underscoring the evident need for coordination of these two regimes.

81 Agenda 21, n. 10, ch. 19, 'Environmentally Sound Management of Toxic Chemicals', paras. 19.44, 19.49(b).

82 Stockholm Convention, n. 49, preamble, art. 1.

83 *Ibid.*, art. 3 (note that some exemptions apply, such as that listed chemicals may be imported for their environmentally sound disposal [art. 6(1)] or for a use or purpose that is explicitly permitted for that party by the Convention [art. 4]).

84 Stockholm Convention, n. 49, art. 3(3)–(4), Annex D. However, the Convention does not oblige state parties to put in place regulatory and assessment schemes for new or existing chemicals where such schemes do not already exist. For a general overview and appraisal, see Boyle & Redgwell, n. 56.

85 Stockholm Convention, n. 49, art. 21.

86 David VanderZwaag, 'The Precautionary Approach and the International Control of Toxic Chemicals: Beacon of Hope, Sea of Confusion and Dilution' (2011) 33(3) *Houston Journal of International Law* 605, 616, 618.

87 Notwithstanding the Stockholm Convention, n. 49, art. 8(7); see Boyle & Redgwell, n. 56.

participation requirements on POPs and their alternatives, including by specific reference to 'women, children and the least educated', though the impact of this provision is somewhat mitigated by the fact that the modalities for doing so (information centres, safety data sheets, reports, and so on) are left to the discretion of the parties.[88] This means that the Convention addresses not only the production of POPs but also their consumption, to the extent that consumers would indeed have access to alternatives in practice.

7.3.3 *Controlling Life Cycles in a Global Economy*

In an increasingly global economy, trade plays a key role in ensuring SCP across the different stages of the life cycle of a product.[89] One problem that arises, therefore, is how to ensure that the non-participation of key states does not undermine these efforts. A familiar technique to address the problem of non-parties in the MEAs discussed in this chapter is their ban on trade with such states, such as under the Basel Convention (with the exception of when parties have an agreement that requires at least the same level of ESM)[90] and under the Montreal Protocol[91] (which also discourages the export of CFC production technology).[92] Even with parties to the same MEA, trade control remains an important tool for ensuring SCP in a global economy.

88 Stockholm Convention, n. 49, art. 10.

89 See also Arcuri & Partiti, n. 25, 309 (on the relevance of trade and investment regimes for SCP).

90 Basel Convention, n. 47, art. 11. On the scope of this provision, see Pierre-Marie Dupuy & Jorge E. Viñuales, *International Environmental Law* (Cambridge University Press, 2017), 224–225.

91 Montreal Protocol, n. 68, art. 4, as revised in 1990 and 1997. To take only one example, Korea was thus forced to participate if it wished to continue to export cars and fridges. Andersen & Sarma, n. 73, 353.

92 During the 1987 negotiations, the question of the trade law compatibility of this article was raised. Ad Hoc Working Group of Legal and Technical Experts, Second Session, n. 68, 22; Ad Hoc Working Group of Legal and Technical Experts, Third Session, n. 68, 18. Since the measures proposed were neither arbitrary nor unjustifiable and did not discriminate against non-parties as such, but could only be applied against those not following the Montreal Protocol's control measures, it was concluded that article 4 would be in accordance with article 20(b) of the General Agreement on Tariffs and Trade, 1994, 55 UNTS 194, concerning protection of human, animal, or plant life, or health, although the final judgment in the event of a bilateral dispute would rest with the World Trade Organization. In any event, there were already precedents for controls on trade with non-parties in the Convention on Trade in Endangered Species of Wild Fauna and Flora, 1973, 993 UNTS 243, and under resolutions of the parties to the International Convention for the Regulation of Whaling, 1946, 161 UNTS 72, for example. On the use of trade bans for ozone-depleting substances, see Harro van Asselt, 'Trade and Atmospheric Protection at Stockholm+50: Plus ça Change?' in this volume, 377.

A well-known mechanism (though criticized for its lack of effectiveness) is that of prior informed consent (PIC).[93] Under the Basel Convention, parties may decide not to consent to certain categories of waste imports altogether, and where transboundary movement does take place, consent must still be sought for individual shipments.[94] What is more, parties to the Basel Convention may only export controlled wastes to other parties when they cannot themselves dispose of the waste in an environmentally sound and efficient manner[95] or if the wastes in question are required as a raw material for recycling or recovery industries in the country of import.[96] This constitutes both a reality check for states' differing capacities for waste management and an acknowledgement of the commercial value of some wastes for the global economy (such as recoverable metals, in particular, at the time of the negotiations). Moreover, exports of Basel-controlled waste are conditional on their ESM abroad;[97] similarly, parties to the Stockholm Convention must prohibit the import and export of listed chemicals and only import them for the purpose of their environmentally sound disposal,[98] which invites a critical reflection on what role the country of export can and should play in ensuring their ESM abroad.[99]

The Rotterdam Convention builds on the Basel Convention's PIC model as well as UNEP's Guidelines for the Exchange of Information on Chemicals and International Trade[100] and the Food and Agriculture Organization's International Code of Conduct on the Distribution and Use of Pesticides,[101] both of which were amended in 1989 to include a (voluntary) PIC procedure. The overarching objective of the Rotterdam Convention is 'to promote shared responsibility and cooperative efforts among Parties in the international trade

93 See David Langlet, *Prior Informed Consent and Hazardous Trade: Regulating Trade in Hazardous Goods at the Intersection of Sovereignty, Free Trade and Environmental Protection* (Wolters Kluwer, 2009).

94 On the development of prior informed consent (PIC) in the Basel Convention, see Katharina Kummer, *International Management of Hazardous Wastes: The Basel Convention and Related Legal Rules* (Oxford University Press, 2000), 55; Boyle & Redgwell, n. 56, ch. 8.

95 Basel Convention, n. 47, art. 4(9)(a).

96 *Ibid.*, art. 4(9)(b).

97 *Ibid.*, art. 4(2)(e).

98 Stockholm Convention, n. 49, art. 3(2).

99 See, e.g., Eva van der Marel, 'Trading Plastic Waste in a Global Economy: Soundly Regulated by the Basel Convention?' (2022) 34(3) *Journal of Environmental Law* 477, 493ff.

100 UNEP, *London Guidelines for the Exchange of Information on Chemicals in International Trade, as amended by Decision 15/30 of the Governing Council of UNEP*, 25 May 1989.

101 Food and Agriculture Organization (FAO), *International Code of Conduct on the Distribution and Use of Pesticides*, 1985 (subsequently amended to include provisions for PIC at the twenty-fifth session of the FAO Conference in 1989).

of certain hazardous chemicals in order to protect human health and the environment'.[102] Prior informed consent is required for those hazardous chemicals that are listed under Annex III, whereby listing triggers an obligation on states to decide whether to consent to import.[103] Further information requirements exist on the exporting state for chemicals that it has itself banned or severely restricted.[104]

The Rotterdam Convention, moreover, encourages the exchange of information for chemicals that fall within its scope, including relevant safety data such as (eco)toxicological test results.[105] In so doing, the Convention helps improve transparency over certain hazardous chemicals and pesticides in international trade, closing the knowledge gap between state parties (and, in particular, between developing and developed countries). This not only gives states agency over their trade, but greater transparency also allows state parties to carry out a more informed risk assessment and decide on how to manage the risks. It thus enables states to regulate the production of products that contain such hazardous chemicals and pesticides, if they so wish. However, the Rotterdam Convention has been critiqued for its non-precautionary and cumbersome procedures for listing new substances under Annex III,[106] which, inter alia, requires the support of parties in at least two regions and consensus by the COP.[107]

7.4 CONCLUSIONS: KEY GAPS REMAIN

Despite the progressive combined contribution of the MEAs to SCP, discussed above, they predominantly help reduce the negative impacts of current economic activities and only with regard to narrowly listed categories of substances and wastes. This is so even with respect to the oft-cited 'success story' of the Montreal Protocol; the way in which the Rotterdam and Stockholm Conventions regulate chemicals, in particular, is conceptually limited. Whether for the purpose of sharing information as part of their international trade or in order to eliminate them, chemicals are conceptualized as 'risky objects' rather than part of a process that can be shaped and designed differently.[108] Apart from limited references to BATs and BEPs in the

102 Rotterdam Convention, n. 48, art. 1.
103 *Ibid.*, art. 10.
104 *Ibid.*, arts. 5, 12, 13.
105 *Ibid.*, art. 14.
106 See VanderZwaag, n. 86, 617; Arcuri & Partiti, n. 25, 309. For a general overview and appraisal, see Boyle & Redgwell, n. 56.
107 Rotterdam Convention, n. 48, art. 22(5).
108 On different ways of constructing chemicals as regulatory objects, see further Elizabeth Fisher's thought-provoking reflections in Elizabeth Fisher, 'Chemicals as Regulatory

Stockholm Convention, the guidance on which makes reference to life cycle thinking more generally, neither the Stockholm nor the Rotterdam Conventions regulate the chemicals sector holistically.

This can be contrasted with UNEP's efforts to promote green and sustainable chemistry through principles that have been developed by chemists themselves[109] to 'challenge chemists and other scientists to consider inherent properties of chemical molecules at the design stage'.[110] These efforts to encourage holistic chemicals design by infusing sustainability into the chemicals sector have gradually been developing since the 1990s, and UNEP now notes that 'many countries around the world have engaged the creation of green chemistry networks and adopted green chemistry policy statements'.[111] What the green and sustainable chemistry agenda arguably does, and what the chemicals regime put into place by the Rotterdam and Stockholm Conventions does not, is to condition the chemicals sector on environmental considerations and life cycle thinking, key elements in ensuring SCP. It brings attention to the relevance of design at the very early stages of molecular production when the building blocks of key materials and subsequent products are formed. Design has been identified as one of the most impactful stages in the life cycle of many products and services, where much of its environmental impact is already decided.[112] However, no international design standards currently exist (neither for products nor materials).[113] Nor is there global

Objects' (2014) 23(2) *Review of European, Comparative and International Environmental Law* 163.

109 Paul Anastas and John Warner's twelve principles of green chemistry, which gained widespread traction and have since been complemented by the twelve principles of green engineering. See Paul Anastas & John Warner, *Chemistry: Theory and Practice* (Oxford University Press, 1998), 30; Paul Anastas & Julie Zimmerman, 'Design through the 12 Principles of Green Engineering: Sustainability requires Objectives at the Molecular, Product, Process, and System Levels' (2003) 37(5) *Environmental Science and Technology* 94. For an overview and discussion, see UNEP, *Green and Sustainable Chemistry: Framework Manual* (UNEP, 2021).

110 UNEP, n. 109, 15; see also Julie Zimmerman *et al.*, 'Designing for a Green Chemistry Future' (2020) 367(6476) *Science* 397.

111 UNEP, n. 109, 20; see also Fisher, n. 108 (who refers to the Californian Green Chemistry Initiative, which has developed as a specific legal manifestation of this broader international discourse about green chemistry).

112 An oft-repeated claim (with uncertain origins) is that the design of a product is said to determine 80 per cent of its environmental impact. See, e.g., 'Recycling and the Circular Economy: What's the Difference?' *Ellen McArthur Foundation*, www.ellenmacarthurfoundation.org/articles/recycling-and-the-circular-economy-whats-the-difference; Barbara Pollini & Valentina Rognoli, 'Early-stage Material Selection Based on Life Cycle Approach: Tools, Obstacles and Opportunities for Design' (2021) 28 *Sustainable Production and Consumption* 1130.

113 Proposing a series of common principles for the appropriate use of resources and production methods in the plastics sector, for example, see Fernando Vidal *et al.*, 'Designing a Circular Carbon and Plastics Economy for a Sustainable Future' (2024) 626(7997) *Nature* 45.

agreement over the (environmental) trade-offs that should be made at these early stages of design, except that particularly hazardous chemicals, as listed under the Stockholm Convention, are to be phased out altogether. This leaves much potential for further and more holistic regulation.

Moreover, for life cycle thinking to become possible at a global scale, there is a need for closer synergies between the chemicals and waste regimes, particularly if the aim is to transition to a more circular economy. After many years of being addressed separately (beyond the Stockholm Convention's cross-reference to the Basel Convention for measures regarding the environmentally sound disposal of POP-contaminated wastes), there is a growing realization that the chemicals and waste agendas overlap.[114] In a circular economy, developments in the one sector can impede or promote developments in the other. For example, the range of end-of-life options available for a particular waste stream depends on various factors, including the different types of waste in question and the (known) presence of hazardous chemicals and other types of contamination.[115] Efforts are therefore being made to bring the international chemicals and waste agendas closer together and to link this back to SCP.[116] Actions under the BRS Conventions, for instance, are subject to increased cooperation and coordination, and, today, the BRS COPs are being hosted jointly. Furthermore, waste has been increasingly addressed as part of UNEP's efforts to promote green and sustainable chemistry.[117]

Ultimately, however, these are all, relatively, 'baby steps' in the challenge of implementing 'the multi-dimensional, open-ended and continuously reinterpreted concept of SCP', discussed at the outset of this chapter, which is an appropriate enough analogy given that 'the movement towards sustainable production and consumption is still in its infancy'.[118] To be sure, the challenge is immense with 'unsustainable practices ... woven deeply into the fabric of

[114] UNEP, n. 44, 12 (noting that Agenda 21 addresses chemicals and wastes in different chapters).

[115] See, e.g., Ina Vollmer *et al.*, 'Beyond Mechanical Recycling: Giving New Life to Plastic Waste' (2020) 59 *Angewandte Chemie, International Edition* 15402; see also European Commission, *Communication to the European Parliament, the Council, the European Economic and Social Committee, and the Committee of the Regions on the Implementation of the Circular Economy Package: Options to Address the Interface between Chemical, Product and Waste Legislation*, Doc. COM(2018)32 final, 16 January 2018.

[116] See UNEP, *Strengthening the Sound Management of Chemicals and Wastes in the Long Term*, UN Doc. UNEP/EA.1/5/Add.2, 27 June 2014, Annex I (the outcome document of the country-led consultative process on the challenges to and options for further enhancing cooperation and coordination within the chemicals and wastes cluster in the long term).

[117] UNEP, n. 44.

[118] See, e.g., Voigt, n. 10, 254.

modern life'.[119] While the policy goals for SCP have undoubtedly proliferated since 1972 (see, for example, the Rio Declaration's Principle 8 and SDG 12), the same cannot be said of international law developments to support the changes necessary in global consumption and production. The analysis of MEAs on atmospheric pollution, chemicals, and hazardous wastes – none of which contains reference to SCP as such in their text – reveals that their focus has remained more on end-of-pipe solutions (for example, pollution control, waste management) than on restraining or eliminating unsustainable patterns of consumption and production. They remain considerably short of reflecting the need to think holistically about product systems in life cycle terms in order to achieve SCP. The plastics treaty currently being negotiated provides a fresh opportunity for the international community to do just that, and some of the proposals on the table – for example, to restrain plastic consumption and production to sustainable levels, including through global sustainability criteria and standards for plastics – appear to be moving in this direction.[120] Therefore, there is reason to hope that Stockholm+100 might reach a more optimistic conclusion about the state of international law on SCP.

119 Secretary-General Kofi Annan, *Address to the World Summit on Sustainable Development*, UN Press Release nos. SG/SM/8358, AFR/468, ENV/DEV/693, 3 September 2002.

120 See the three strategic goals and list of deliverables being advocated by the High Ambition Coalition to End Plastics Pollution. 'End Plastic Pollution by 2040', *High Ambition Coalition to End Plastics Pollution*, https://hactoendplasticpollution.org/.

8

International Regulation and the Management of Mining since the 1972 Stockholm Conference: From Local to Global Concerns

Timo Koivurova

8.1 INTRODUCTION

The mining of minerals and metals encountered many environmental and other challenges long before the 1972 Stockholm Conference on the Human Environment. For instance, mining often requires trees and other vegetation as well as the topsoil to be cleared. There is a risk that the chemicals and other harmful substances used to process ores will enter rivers and the surrounding environment. There are also issues associated with mining waste. It can be toxic and thus presents a risk to the surrounding environment and human communities. Given the comprehensive impact that mining has on the surrounding environment, it is not surprising that mining has been a target of environmental movements and non-governmental organizations. Increasingly, mining has been recognized as not only a local activity but also a global issue. Already at the time of the Stockholm Conference, policy discussions were taking place on whether humanity might exhaust its non-renewable resources, including metals and minerals, due to population and economic growth. The Club of Rome's well-known *Limits to Growth* report, which was released in 1972, contained a warning that, at the current pace of development, we will run out of non-renewable resources.[1]

These ideas and concerns also found their way into the Stockholm Conference's preparations and, ultimately, into the 1972 Stockholm Declaration on the Human Environment and the Stockholm Action Plan.[2]

1 Donella H. Meadows *et al.*, *The Limits to Growth: A Report for the Club of Rome's Project on the Predicament of Mankind* (Universe Books, 1972).

2 'Declaration of the United Nations Conference on the Human Environment', in *Report of the UN Conference on the Human Environment*, UN Doc. A/CONF.48/14/Rev.1, 16 June 1972 (Stockholm Declaration); 'Action Plan for the Human Environment', in *Report of the United Nations Conference on the Human Environment*, *ibid.* (Stockholm Action Plan).

The Stockholm Action Plan also focused on accumulating knowledge and information on the environmental conditions of mining sites, the action taken with respect to the environment, and the positive and negative environmental repercussions of mining and mineral processing. It was even suggested that such a body of information could be used to determine 'where certain kinds of mining should be limited, where reclamation costs would be particularly high, or where other problems would arise'.[3] The Stockholm Declaration also addressed the challenges created by all non-renewable resource use, including mining minerals, in principle 5: 'The non-renewable resources of the earth must be employed in such a way as to guard against the danger of their future exhaustion and to ensure that benefits from such employment are shared by all mankind.'[4] It is also important to mention principle 21 here, which affirmed the sovereign right of states to exploit their own resources pursuant to their own environmental policies, yet with the corresponding responsibility to ensure that such activities did not cause damage to the environment of other states or of areas beyond the limits of national jurisdiction. As will be shown, most mining activities have been largely regulated by national laws, and they are increasingly regulated at the international level as well.

Mining is a major challenge for humanity as it contributes to humankind's transgression of the planetary boundaries.[5] One of the reasons that mining is a concern even at the global scale is the transition to a low-carbon economy that was agreed upon to achieve the climate targets set out in the 2015 Paris Agreement.[6] To gradually decrease and ultimately end our dependence on fossil fuels, we need vast amounts of metals and minerals; hence, the green transition, digitalization, and urbanization are pushing us to accelerate our mining efforts on land and also in frontier areas, such as marine areas. There is an increasing awareness that we need to manage the increasing demand for minerals and metals and to ensure that they are used efficiently and sustainably.

This chapter will focus on two questions. First, why does mining require international regulation at all? For much of the last fifty years, the challenges associated with mining have been perceived to impact only a certain locality

3 Stockholm Action Plan, n. 2, recommendation 56(c).

4 For an analysis, see Louis Sohn, 'The Stockholm Declaration on the Human Environment' (1973) 14 *Harvard International Law Journal* 423.

5 Vanessa Schenker, Viktoras Kulionis, Christopher Oberschelp, & Stephan Pfister, 'Metals for Low-carbon Technologies: Environmental Impacts and Relation to Planetary Boundaries' (2022) 372 *Journal of Cleaner Production* 133620.

6 Paris Agreement on Climate Change, 2015, 3156 UNTS 79.

and, thus, have focused on the various local environmental, social, and cultural impacts of the mining operation. While mining has been regulated mostly by national and subnational law, the intention here is to focus on international regulatory efforts, which have increased considerably over time since 1972. Two sub-questions will also be addressed: why and when was it perceived as being important to take international policy and legal action over the environmental concerns of mining and what type of hard and soft law international regulatory action has been taken and for what reason? Second, based on the answers to these questions, the chapter explores how the international regulation of mining has evolved in the fifty years between the 1972 Stockholm Conference and the UN International Meeting Stockholm+50: A Healthy Planet for the Prosperity of All – Our Responsibility, Our Opportunity (Stockholm+50 Meeting). Which policy and legal actions have reduced the environmental and other impacts of mining, understood in a broad manner, and which, by and large, have failed or at least not adequately addressed the identified problems?

While specific mining operations have long been covered by national law and, increasingly, by international law, there are other aspects of mining that present environmental challenges. The growing demand for various industrial minerals and metals is leading to discussions about the current and future intensity of natural resource extraction. Thus, it is vital to ask whether international law and policy can generally tackle unsustainable resource extraction on a global scale and, if so, how? In examining this question, this chapter will focus on industrial minerals and metals that are in high demand – in particular, those in the 'critical mineral' and 'critical raw material' categories.[7] Still, most of the arguments presented here also apply to mined energy minerals (for example, coal or uranium) and minerals used mostly for domestic consumption or the so-called development minerals.

The chapter first explores how we extract and consume natural resources, in general, and industrial minerals and metals, in particular. It then reviews, in a general manner, how international regulation of mining has progressed over the fifty years since the Stockholm Conference. This part is divided into developments in international law and policy related to mining operations and developments related to natural resource extraction in general. The final

[7] For instance, in its critical raw materials legislation, the European Union (EU) evaluates the criticality of a raw material by studying how important a certain mineral is for the EU and its supply risks. In its critical raw materials policy, the EU has identified critical raw materials since 2011. *Communication from the Commission to the European Parliament, the Council, the European Economic and Social Committee and the Committee of the Regions: Tackling the Challenges in Commodity and on Raw Materials*, Doc. COM (2011) 25 final, 2 February 2011.

part contains concluding thoughts on where progress has been made in the international regulation of mining as well as on which areas require further development.

8.2 OUR USE OF NATURAL RESOURCES, PARTICULARLY INDUSTRIAL MINERALS AND METALS

As noted above, while most of the concerns about mining have referred to its local environmental and social impacts, mining is increasingly perceived as part of the larger problem of overconsumption of natural resources (not only in developed states but also in emerging economies). This situation has already resulted in humankind exceeding some of the planetary boundaries, and the road ahead looks bleak. More specifically, according to the 2019 International Resource Panel's Outlook, in the previous fifty years, the global population doubled, the extraction of materials tripled, and the gross domestic product quadrupled.[8] The extraction and processing of natural resources has accelerated over the last twenty years and accounts for more than 90 per cent of our biodiversity loss and water stress and approximately half of our climate change impacts. In addition, over the last fifty years, we have not once experienced a prolonged period of stabilization or a decline in global demand for material.

The International Resource Panel also projected that, without drastic changes to our production and consumption patterns, global material use would more than double between 2015 and 2060, ultimately reaching up to 190 billion tons. In its Global Material Resources Outlook to 2060, the Organisation for Economic Co-operation and Development (OECD) outlined a challenge of similar magnitude.[9] This increase reflects not only growth in the global economy and population but also a rising middle class. The growing use of natural resources is the root cause of some of the most urgent environmental pressures, including the triple planetary crisis identified at the Stockholm+50 Meeting – that is, climate change, biodiversity loss, and pollution (waste).[10]

[8] United Nations Environment Programme (UNEP) & International Resource Panel, *Global Resources Outlook 2019: Natural Resources for the Future We Want*, 2019, https://wedocs.unep.org/20.500.11822/27517.

[9] Organisation for Economic Co-operation and Development (OECD), *Global Material Resources Outlook to 2060: Economic Drivers and Environmental Consequences* (OECD Publishing, 2019).

[10] See *Report of Stockholm+50: A Healthy Planet for the Prosperity of All – Our Responsibility, Our Opportunity*, UN Doc. A/CONF.238/9, 1 August 2022, para. 34.

The extraction and processing of metals and industrial minerals alone is responsible for around 10 per cent of greenhouse gas emissions and has grown significantly during the fifty years since the Stockholm Conference. Projections indicate that the demand for industrial minerals and metals will increase very quickly due to the growth in green energy technologies (for example, wind and solar technologies and zero/low-emission vehicles). This much-needed transition to a low-carbon future will require more mining all over the world; the World Bank Group projects increases of almost 500 per cent for some metals, depending on how ambitious societies are in moving towards carbon neutrality.[11] The demand for mined materials is also necessitated by major drivers of global change, such as digitalization and urbanization, and the needs of the aerospace and defence industries. Most media attention has focused on the implications of the transition away from fossil fuels, which requires enormous amounts of various critical metals. This has led to new discussions about the concern that was raised during the 1972 Stockholm Conference – namely, that we may exhaust our non-renewable resources such as minerals. A 2021 study suggested that, if states are to live up to their long-term climate promises, we may well run out of many critical metals in one generation.[12]

8.3 INTERNATIONAL REGULATION OF MINING: EFFORTS MADE BETWEEN 1972 AND 2022

Since the time of the 1972 Stockholm Conference, mining has been viewed mostly as a local and land-based activity, and these local dimensions and aspects continue to be the focus of mining policy and law. Thus, most attention has been given to the impact of mining on the surrounding environment and the people living in the immediate vicinity. This explains why environmental and other matters related to mining are mainly regulated by national and subnational laws and policies. However, international laws and policies on land-based mining operations have gradually developed over time. High-quality mineral deposits in easily accessible areas are becoming exhausted, and this has resulted in lower quality ore being mined. In addition,

[11] Kirsten Hund *et al.*, *Minerals for Climate Action: The Mineral Intensity of the Clean Energy Transition World Bank Group*, 2020, https://documents.worldbank.org/en/publication/documents-reports/documentdetail/099052423172525564/p166278o6f5aa4005o8f8cobdcbao878a3e.

[12] Simon Michaux, *Assessment of the Extra Capacity Required of Alternative Energy Electrical Power Systems to Completely Replace Fossil Fuels*, GTK Open File Work Report no. 42/2021, 2021, www.gtk.fi/en/research/time-to-wake-up/downloads/.

mining activities are moving to new frontier areas, such as the Arctic, including areas beyond national jurisdiction.

8.3.1 *International Law and Policy on Local Mining Operations in Areas within National Jurisdiction*

The starting point for the governance of many local mining activities is stated in principle 21 of the Stockholm Declaration: each state will govern how its mineral resources are explored and exploited, while ensuring that mining activities do not cause damage to the environment of other states or of areas beyond the limits of national jurisdiction. This norm has now gained customary international law status and thus applies worldwide.[13] Even though the 1972 Stockholm Action Plan included special policy recommendations on mining, as mentioned above, the real international policy on mining emerged much later. It was only by the end of the 1990s, and especially around the time of the 2002 Johannesburg Summit on Sustainable Development and the development of the 2002 Johannesburg Plan of Implementation, that mining was emphasized as being part of sustainable development policy.[14] International sustainable development action was then geared specifically towards mining through the establishment of two international bodies: the International Council on Mining and Metals (ICMM), and the Intergovernmental Forum on Mining, Minerals, Metals and Sustainable Development.[15] Both entities have produced a range of international soft-law and good-practice guidance documents covering various aspects of local mining operations.[16]

It is also worth noting that local mining and the management of mining operations have been increasingly influenced by international law – for example, through developments in international environmental law and

[13] *Case Concerning Pulp Mills on the River Uruguay (Argentina v Uruguay)*, Judgment, 20 April 2010, (2010) ICJ Reports 14, para. 101.

[14] *Plan of Implementation of the World Summit on Sustainable Development*, Doc. A/CONF.199/20, 2022, para. 46.

[15] See *International Council on Mining and Metals*, www.icmm.com/; *Intergovernmental Forum on Mining, Minerals, Metals and Sustainable Development*, www.igfmining.org/.

[16] Intergovernmental Forum on Mining, Minerals, Metals and Sustainable Development (IGF), *Mining Policy Framework: Mining and Sustainable Development*, 2023, www.iisd.org/system/files/2023-12/igf-mining-policy-framework-en.pdf; IGF, *Guidance for Governments; Environmental Management and Mining Governance*, May 2021, www.iisd.org/system/files/2021-05/igf-guidance-governments-environmental-management-mining-en.pdf; International Council on Mining and Metals, *The Global Industry Standard on Tailings Management*, 2020, www.icmm.com/website/publications/pdfs/environmental-stewardship/2020/global-industry-standard-on-tailings-management.pdf.

human rights law – of which a brief overview is here provided. One of the main legal developments relevant to the local management of mining operations has been the requirement for mining companies to conduct an environmental impact assessment (EIA) (and a social impact assessment) during the planning stage of each mining operation.[17] Environmental impact assessment procedures are now found in national laws and regulations worldwide, with countries adopting regulatory mechanisms proven to be successful in other countries. International regulatory influence and lending institutions requiring EIA reports for projects that they fund are also driving factors. Conducting EIAs in cases of transboundary harm has also been endorsed by the International Court of Justice.[18] An EIA must not only evaluate the environmental and social impacts of the mining operation but also identify various alternatives for the implementation of the proposed activity, including mitigation options, and involve relevant experts and civil society in public discussions – a trend that has been reinforced by normative instruments requiring public input on environmental matters.[19]

The transboundary impacts of a proposed industrial activity, including a mining operation, have also been subjected to international regulation. The UN Economic Commission for Europe's 1991 Convention on Environmental Impact Assessment in a Transboundary Context (Espoo Convention) expanded the scope of domestic EIA systems so as to also include the environmental impacts on neighbouring states.[20] The strategic environmental assessment (SEA) process is also relevant to mining. SEAs are conducted to identify the environmental, health, and social impacts of plans, programmes, and policies. This enables a more holistic way of projecting the

17 The emphasis on taking onboard the social challenges in mining has led to concepts such as social licence to operate. In the EU-funded Mining and Metallurgy Regions in Europe, the concept of a social licence to operate was examined in a mining context. The project entitled 'Social License to Operate Guidelines for Europe' stated that social licence to operate may be a misleading term as 'no actual licence is granted by anyone. Terms such as "social acceptance" or "social performance" might in fact better describe the underlying concept'. See Michael Tost *et al.*, *Social Licence to Operate: Guidelines for Europe*, Doc. D4.3, 28 February 2021, https://mireu.eu/sites/default/files/2021-05/D%204.3.pdf.

18 *Pulp Mills*, n. 13, para. 204; see also Tseming Yang, 'The Emergence of the Environmental Impact Assessment Duty as a Global Legal Norm and General Principle of Law' (2019) 70 *Hastings Law Journal* 525; Governing Council of UNEP, *Goals and Principles of Environmental Impact Assessment*, Decision 14/25, 17 June 1987; International Law Commission, *Draft Articles on Prevention of Transboundary Harm from Hazardous Activities*, 2001, https://legal.un.org/ilc/texts/instruments/english/commentaries/9_7_2001.pdf.

19 See, e.g., Convention on Access to Information, Public Participation in Decision-Making and Access to Justice in Environmental Matters, 1998, 2161 UNTS 447.

20 Convention on Environmental Impact Assessment in a Transboundary Context, 1991, 1989 UNTS 309.

overall impacts of various developments in each area, thereby making it at least possible to mitigate the environmental impacts in a more effective manner. Unfortunately, SEAs are not as widely used as EIAs, and conducting a SEA is not yet recognized as a duty of general international law.[21]

The fight against global environmental problems, which are deemed in the respective international conventions as common concerns of humankind, has also influenced how mining operations should be conducted. Gradually, national regulations, especially the requirement for an EIA, have pressed mining companies to also consider the impact of their operations on biological diversity and climate change.[22] Current research has shown that, even if a mining activity is restricted to a rather confined area, it can still have direct and indirect impacts on biodiversity within a 50-kilometre radius.[23] In a similar vein, it has been calculated that mining operations globally are responsible for around 10 per cent of climate change, and this climate footprint is increasing. This is still a fairly recent phenomenon, and it is difficult to estimate the proportion of EIA procedures that include assessments of the impact on biological diversity and climate change. It is also interesting to observe that the globally applicable 2013 Minamata Convention on Mercury, which recognized that mercury is a global concern due to its long-range atmospheric transport, banned new mercury mines.[24]

A related important global regulatory development was the establishment of laws relating to Indigenous peoples, which largely developed as part of the human rights regime; the ICMM has issued many guidelines and recommendations in this area.[25] In particular, the negotiations of the 2007 UN Declaration on the Rights of Indigenous Peoples (UNDRIP) clearly influenced the requirements for mining activities.[26] Even though the UNDRIP is a non-legally binding instrument, it carries legal weight in various ways, especially because it was directly negotiated between Indigenous peoples

21 See Hussein Abaza, Ron Bisset, & Barry Sadler, *Environmental Impact Assessment and Strategic Environmental Assessment: Towards an Integrated Approach* (UNEP, 2004). https://wedocs.unep.org/bitstream/handle/20.500.11822/8753/Environmental_impact_assessment.pdf?sequence=3&amp%3BisAllowed=.

22 European Commission, Directorate-General for Environment, *Guidance on Integrating Climate Change and Biodiversity into Environmental Impact Assessment* (Publications Office, 2013), https://data.europa.eu/doi/10.2779/11735.

23 Sebastian Luckeneder *et al.*, 'Surge in Global Metal Mining Threatens Vulnerable Ecosystems' (2021) 69 *Global Environmental Change* 102303.

24 Minamata Convention on Mercury, 2013, 3202 UNTS 220.

25 See, e.g., ICMM, *Indigenous Peoples and Mining: Position Statement*, 2013, www.icmm.com/website/publications/pdfs/mining-principles/position-statements_indigenous-peoples.pdf?cb=59899.

26 UN Declaration on the Rights of Indigenous Peoples, UN Doc. A/61/49, 13 September 2007.

and states. The set of principles that were considered to be emerging principles at the time of the conclusion of UNDRIP have undergone rapid regulatory development and are now increasingly being considered strong candidates for customary international law, such as the principle of free, prior, and informed consent.[27] This principle also requires mining companies to conduct serious negotiations with Indigenous peoples and is based on the idea that Indigenous peoples need to provide consent for mining enterprises to proceed in their ancestral areas.

Another international regulatory development grounded in human rights and good governance principles highlights accountability and transparency, which is particularly relevant in situations where transnational enterprises from developed countries plan to conduct mining in developing states.[28] For instance, minerals sourced from conflict areas have provoked soft-law guidance from the OECD and legislative efforts from, for example, the United States and the European Union (EU).[29] Yet another broad legal development is the introduction of due diligence regulations, originating in part from the UN Guiding Principles on Business and Human Rights, and these have been developed in some European countries, the OECD, and the EU.[30] The idea behind some of these international guiding principles and domestic laws has been to force mining and other transnational companies to observe due diligence over their entire supply chains, ensuring that human rights and sustainability are considered. This regulatory approach, which applies to mining and other transnational enterprises throughout their global supply chains, reflects the fact that a tremendous amount of mining occurs in the global South. The due diligence approach, the pioneer of which has been the

27 See, e.g., Emily McCulloch, 'Free, Prior, and Informed Consent: A Struggling International Principle' (2021) 44 *Public Land and Resources Law Review* 241.

28 See, e.g., the Extractive Industries Transparency Initiative to which over 50 countries are committed. *Extractive Industries Transparency Initiative*, https://eiti.org/.

29 See, e.g., OECD, *Due Diligence Guidance for Responsible Supply Chains of Minerals from Conflict-Affected and High-Risk Areas* (3rd ed., OECD Publishing, 2016), http://dx.doi.org/10.1787/9789264252479-en; Dodd–Frank Wall Street Reform and Consumer Protection Act, 2010, 124 Stat. 1376, s. 1502 (conflict minerals); Council Regulation (EU) 2017/821 Laying Down Supply Chain Due Diligence Obligations for Union Importers of Tin, Tantalum, Tungsten, Their Ores and Gold Originating from Conflict-Affected and High-Risk Areas, (2017) OJ L130.

30 Human Rights Council, *Guiding Principles on Business and Human Rights: Implementing the United Nations 'Protect, Respect and Remedy' Framework*, Doc. A/HRC/17/31, 21 March 2011. For an analysis, see Justine Nolan & Robert McCorquodale, 'The Effectiveness of Human Rights Due Diligence for Preventing Business Human Rights Abuses', UNSW Law Research Paper no. 22–23, 2022, https://ssrn.com/abstract=4219908.

OECD and its soft-law guidance,[31] is now being developed by the EU for all major transnational companies headquartered or having major operations in the EU. EU Directive 2024/1760 on Corporate Sustainability Due Diligence is intended to ensure that major transnational companies observe major human rights and environmental treaty obligations throughout their supply chains.[32] There have also been global negotiations for a treaty to guarantee that victims of transnational enterprises have access to justice in the enterprise's home states.[33] Importantly, these initiatives ensure that transnational enterprises observe due diligence throughout their supply chains, particularly in terms of all human rights (including the right to a decent environment) and environmental considerations. Yet, contrary to the earlier-mentioned EU legislation, it does not seem likely that such a convention will become a reality, and, even if it does, it is not expected to be widely ratified by developed states.[34]

8.3.2 *Regulating Mining in Areas beyond National Jurisdiction*

International regulatory efforts are also directed at mining in areas beyond national jurisdiction. The notion of the deep seabed as part of the common heritage of humankind started to gain traction at the end of the 1960s, was recognized by the UN General Assembly in 1970,[35] and influenced the negotiations of the 1982 Convention on the Law of the Sea (UNCLOS) that commenced in 1973 and were concluded in 1982.[36] Part XI of UNCLOS (on

31 OECD, *OECD Due Diligence Guidance for Responsible Business Conduct*, 2018, https://web-archive.oecd.org/2018-11-27/485071-OECD-Due-Diligence-Guidance-for-Responsible-Business-Conduct.pdf.

32 Council Directive (EU) 2024/1760 on Corporate Sustainability Due Diligence, (2024) OJ L1760.

33 'Open-ended Intergovernmental Working Group on Transnational Corporations and Other Business Enterprises with Respect to Human Rights', *UN Human Rights Commission*, www.ohchr.org/en/hr-bodies/hrc/wg-trans-corp/igwg-on-tnc. This is not the first of its kind. In fact, there have been three rounds of international negotiations between states over the duties of transnational enterprises. See Radu Mares, 'Regulating Transnational Corporations at the United Nations: The Negotiations of a Treaty on Business and Human Rights' (2022) 26(9) *International Journal of Human Rights* 1522.

34 Joe Zhang, *Breakthrough in Business and Human Rights Binding Treaty Negotiation but Be Prepared for a Bumpy Road Ahead*, 20 December 2021, www.iisd.org/itn/en/2021/12/20/breakthrough-in-business-and-human-rights-binding-treaty-negotiation-but-be-prepared-for-a-bumpy-road-ahead/.

35 UN General Assembly, *Declaration of Principles Governing the Sea-Bed and the Ocean Floor, and the Subsoil Thereof, beyond the Limits of Nations Jurisdiction*, Doc. A/RES/2749(XXV), 17 December 1970.

36 Convention on the Law of the Sea, 1982, 1833 UNTS 397 (UNCLOS). As Louis Sohn argues, principle 5 of the Stockholm Declaration was influenced by the developments related to the

the Area), as modified by the 1994 Implementation Agreement, states that all 'rights in the resources of the Area are vested in mankind as a whole',[37] and the International Seabed Authority (ISA) was tasked with regulating the prospecting, exploration, and exploitation of mineral resources. Even though deep-seabed mining has not yet progressed to exploitation, exploration is already taking place at many sites across the world's oceans. Given the vast increase in demand for minerals and metals, it is expected that the earth's oceans will be the next frontier of mining, not only the seabed beyond national jurisdiction but also the marine areas under the jurisdiction of coastal states.[38] While states are negotiating exploitation regulations, the adoption of such regulations may prove to be difficult since many states are calling for a moratorium on deep-sea mining.[39]

Due to the projected resource scarcity and issues associated with mining on the earth, the feasibility of conducting mining operations in space has also been considered. While space mining, especially on near-earth asteroids, has enormous potential for supplying humanity with many critical minerals, it would require overcoming huge challenges – for example, research missions have only been able to bring back minimal amounts of materials to earth.[40] Nevertheless, a regulatory framework for this future economic activity is being developed. The basis has been formed, as for all activities in space, by the 1967 Outer Space Treaty, which states in Article 1 that 'Outer space, including the moon and other celestial bodies, shall be free for exploration and use by all

deep-sea bed regime, which is manifested in the latter part of the principle: 'The non-renewable resources of the earth must be employed in such a way as to guard against the danger of their future exhaustion and to ensure that benefits from such employment are shared by all mankind.' See Sohn, n. 4, 461.

37 UNCLOS, n. 36, art. 137(2); Agreement on the Implementation of Part XI of the United Nations Convention on the Law of the Sea of 10 December 1982, 1994, 1836 UNTS 3.

38 A good example is Norway, which has opened its marine areas for mining, see Kathryn Miller, Kevin Bridgen, David Santillo *et al.*, 'Challenging the Need for Deep Seabed Mining from the Perspective of Metal Demand, Biodiversity, Ecosystems Services, and Benefit Sharing' (2021) 8 *Frontiers in Marine Science*, 706161. Some countries, like Norway, are opening their continental shelves for mining. See 'Seabed Minerals: Substantial Resources on the Norwegian Shelf', *Norwegian Offshore Directorate*, www.npd.no/en/whats-new/news/general-news/2023/seabed-minerals-substantial-resources-on-the-norwegian-shelf/.

39 At the time of writing, over twenty states have taken a negative stance to opening deep-sea mining, either advocating a ban, a moratorium, or precautionary pause. See 'Voices Calling for a Moratorium', *Save the High Seas*, https://savethehighseas.org/voices-calling-for-a-moratorium-governments-and-parliamentarians/.

40 Shriya Yarlagadda, 'Economics of the Stars: The Future of Asteroid Mining and the Global Economy', *Harvard International Review*, 8 April 2022.

States'.[41] By the end of the 1970s, the 1979 Agreement on the Moon and Other Celestial Bodies was also concluded, which states in Article 4(1) that 'the exploration and use of the moon shall be the province of all mankind and shall be carried out for the benefit and in the interests of all countries, irrespective of their degree of economic or scientific development'.[42] This resembles the agreement that the international community reached on deep-seabed resources. Yet this agreement has not been ratified by major space-faring nations. In addition, it has been argued that this agreement has been contested by the so-called 2020 Artemis Accords, whereby the United States and the other Accord signatories aim to advance the possibility of extracting moon and asteroid resources.[43]

Soon after the conclusion of UNCLOS, negotiations commenced to regulate mining in Antarctica. These negotiations led to the 1988 Convention on the Regulation of Antarctic Mineral Resources, which would allow the relevant states to open Antarctica to mining, provided that it was conducted according to the strict rules of the Convention.[44] However, this process came to a halt when two of the original signatories – France and Australia – stated that mining cannot be permitted in Antarctica. This in turn led to new negotiations and ultimately to prohibiting all mining in Antarctica via the 1991 Madrid Protocol on Environmental Protection.[45] Under the provisions of this Protocol, the prohibition can be reviewed fifty years after its entry into force, which is 2048.

8.4 EFFORTS TO CURTAIL THE USE OF NATURAL RESOURCES, INCLUDING MINERALS AND METALS

Many policy actions have been implemented by international organizations to address the overconsumption of the earth's natural resources, including minerals and metals. The most relevant initiative has been the Sustainable Development Goals (SDGs) by the United Nations in 2015.[46] Of particular

41 Treaty on Principles Governing the Activities of States in the Exploration and Use of Outer Space, Including the Moon and Other Celestial Bodies, 1967, 610 UNTS 205.

42 Agreement Governing the Activities of States on the Moon and Other Celestial Bodies, 1979, 1363 UNTS 3.

43 For an analysis, see Rossana Deplano, 'The Artemis Accords: Evolution or Revolution in International Space Law?' (2021) 70(3) *International and Comparative Law Quarterly* 799.

44 Convention on the Regulation of Antarctic Mineral Resource Activities, 1988, (1988) 27 ILM 859.

45 Protocol on Environmental Protection to the Antarctic Treaty, 1991, (1991) 30 ILM 1461.

46 *Transforming Our World: The 2030 Agenda for Sustainable Development*, Doc. A/Res/70/1, 25 September 2015. For an overview of the Sustainable Development Goals in relation to

relevance is SDG 12: Responsible Consumption and Production, which is to ensure sustainable consumption and production patterns, and target 12.2: 'By 2030, achieve the sustainable management and efficient use of natural resources.'[47] Progress towards this target is to be measured via material footprint, material footprint per capita, and domestic material consumption (DMC). As stated in the SDGs indicator metadata, 'DMC and Material Footprint (MF) need to be looked at in combination, as they cover the two aspects of the economy, production and consumption. The DMC reports the actual amount of material in an economy, MF the virtual amount required across the whole supply chain to service final demand'.[48] Measuring the material footprint is important as it enables us to attribute global material extraction to the domestic final demand of a country. Hence, it is a good proxy for understanding how much biomass, fossil fuels, metal ores, and non-metal ores are needed to sustain current consumption levels in a given country and globally. Our global material footprint is rising steeply, as stated in the *Sustainable Development Goals Report*:

> The global material footprint rose from 43 billion metric tons in 1990 to 54 billion in 2000, and 92 billion in 2017 – an increase of 70 per cent since 2000, and 113 per cent since 1990. The rate of natural resource extraction has accelerated since 2000. Without concerted political action, it is projected to grow to 190 billion metric tons by 2060. What's more, the global material footprint is increasing at a faster rate than both population and economic output.[49]

Despite increasing awareness of the overconsumption of natural resources, it is clear that it will not be politically easy to achieve SDG target 12.2 (that is, sustainable management and efficient use of natural resources by 2030). The most ambitious way forward will likely involve the development of a global international agreement that, over time, specifies the amounts of natural resources that countries are allowed to consume.[50] However, there do not seem to be any real policy drivers currently for such an ambitious undertaking. Within the EU, a policy document has been released that outlines a desire to

international law, see Jonas Ebbesson & Ellen Hey (eds.), *The Cambridge Handbook of the Sustainable Development Goals and International Law* (Cambridge University Press, 2022).

47 *Transforming Our World*, n. 46.

48 'SDG Indicator Metadata', *United Nations*, 46, https://unstats.un.org/sdgs/metadata/files/Metadata-12-02-02.pdf.

49 *Sustainable Development Goals Report*, 2019, https://unstats.un.org/sdgs/report/2019/.

50 See Colette van der Ven, *An International Agreement on Natural Resource Management: An Overview of the Opportunities and Challenges: Study Commissioned by the Public Waste Agency of Flanders (OVAM)*, February 2022.

'consider initiating discussions on an international agreement on the management of natural resources', but no further details are available.[51]

At the Stockholm+50 Meeting, there were interesting debates, which have a long pedigree, about new ways to measure progress and human well-being beyond gross domestic product and its focus on economic growth.[52] Despite such political debates about radically changing the way we use natural resources and, ultimately, transforming how our societies function, these topics have not been discussed in the international policymaking arena in a serious and constructive manner. Yet there are important international policy developments underway to increase resource efficiency, an area of policy that is very relevant when addressing the consumption of minerals and metals, given that many of these can be reused and recycled. This is much more politically acceptable because it does not require any system-wide changes in the way in which societies operate but, rather, encourages relatively minor tweaking of how current economies function. Resource efficiency is now being addressed, for example, by the EU under the Group of Seven (Alliance for Resource Efficiency) and Group of Twenty (Alliance for Resource Efficiency) and by the OECD.[53] These and other initiatives have increased our understanding of the possibilities and limitations associated with increasing resource efficiency (for example, via the introduction of good practices) and offer a path to economic growth that does not degrade the environment.

The development of due diligence regulations, particularly in Europe, as discussed above, is also relevant to curtail the use of natural resources. Some national laws are designed to ensure that mining and other transnational companies exercise due diligence in terms of their entire supply chains and that human rights and sustainability are considered more widely.[54] Notably, this approach has gained traction in the EU but has not been widely applied elsewhere. And, still, fifty years after the Stockholm Conference, there is no international treaty on corporate due diligence and corporate responsibility.

[51] *Communication from the Commission to the European Parliament, the Council, the European Economic and Social Committee and the Committee of Regions: A New Circular Economy Action Plan*, Doc. COM(2020)98 final, 2020, ch. 7.

[52] *Report of Stockholm+50*, n. 10.

[53] For a good overview of these processes, see Ralph Bodle, Stephan Sina, Lena Donat, *et al.*, *Options under International Law to Increase Resource Efficiency* (German Environment Agency, 2021).

[54] The work in France, Germany, and the Netherlands has advanced furthest in this respect. See 'Corporate Sustainability Due Diligence', *European Parliament*, 2023, www.europarl.europa.eu/RegData/etudes/BRIE/2022/729424/EPRS_BRI(2022)729424_EN.pdf.

8.5 WHAT HAVE WE ACHIEVED THROUGH FIFTY YEARS OF POLICY AND LEGAL DEVELOPMENTS SINCE THE 1972 STOCKHOLM CONFERENCE?

The 1972 Stockholm Conference is considered a starting point for both national and international environmental protection. We have learned a lot since then. For example, fifty years after Stockholm we are considerably more knowledgeable about how ecological systems function, how environmental problems develop, and how we can better manage those environmental problems. In these fifty years, a huge number of policies, laws, declarations, action programmes, guidelines, and international environmental agreements have been adopted, many of which affect mining. Even if it is difficult to give any clear answers to the question posed above – which policy and legal actions have reduced the environmental and other impacts of mining, understood in a broad manner, and which have failed, by and large, or at least not adequately addressed the identified problems – it is possible to contemplate what we have achieved in international regulation of mining and its impacts.

8.5.1 *How Have Regulations Related to Mining Operations Evolved?*

At the 1972 Stockholm Conference, guidelines for mining were approved, even if these guidelines did not at the time lead up to any follow-up efforts. This was still an extraordinary step at the time as mining was primarily regulated nationally, and there were hardly any international rules. Still, fifty years later, despite the international efforts mentioned above, mining is mainly regulated by national laws, and specific international hard-law instruments on mining are conspicuously absent. The exceptions are the deep seabed regime, and one proposal for a comprehensive regulatory framework for mining in 2020.[55] Regulations designed to protect the environment and promote human rights also affect how mining is conducted. Since the early 2000s, as noted above, there have been intergovernmental and international mining industry cooperation processes in place, which focus on mining and provide soft guidance on how mining should be undertaken. As mentioned earlier, as humanity's demand for minerals and metals increases, mining is projected to spread beyond states' areas of jurisdiction to the bottom of the deep sea and into space.

[55] International Resource Panel, *Mineral Resource Governance in the 21st Century: Gearing Extractive Industries towards Sustainable Development* (UNEP, 2020).

As was also noticed above, there has been a significant evolution of the international laws and policies that influence local mining operations, which used to be managed primarily at the national and subnational levels. With the increasing awareness of the extent of the environmental and social impacts of mining, conscious decisions have been made to implement international policy measures to improve local mining operations all over the world. Yet most international policy and law measures have not been developed specifically with mining in mind, such as EIA obligations or treaties on climate change or biodiversity loss. Nevertheless, such instruments instil legal obligations on mining operators. Mining operations are today influenced by numerous regulations of international law. Due to the increasing demand for minerals and metals and the fact that easily accessible mining deposits will become exhausted, mining is moving to areas beyond national jurisdiction. In response, international law has been developed to either prohibit (for example, in Antarctica) or regulate mining operations in such areas. It seems fair to say that there has been significant regulatory attention directed to mining in such areas. A good topical example is deep-sea mining. While such mining has not even commenced yet, there is a heated debate about whether full-blown mining should be permitted at all. Negotiations on exploitation regulations have divided the community of states into those who are against deep-sea mining and those who advocate for its strict regulation under the International Seabed Authority.

Considering the lessons learned and the knowledge gained since Stockholm 1972, are we better able to manage the negative effects of local mining on the environment and on local communities fifty years later? In a broad sense, it seems that our ability to manage mining has improved. Our scientific understanding of the environmental impacts of mining has grown. The technologies used in mining have improved and have enabled solutions, in principle, that have resulted in reduced environmental burdens. For a long time, we have been developing better mining governance models internationally, and, consequently, our capacity to reduce the negative effects of local mining operations has improved. The number of international soft- and hard-law guidance documents continues to grow, and as they penetrate national systems, there is improvement observed in the capacity to better manage mining operations around the world. In addition, an EIA is usually required for any mining operation proposed by a company, wherever it is planned to take place. In many cases, mining companies must also assess the effects of any proposed operations on biodiversity, climate change, and/or the Indigenous peoples of the area.

8.5.2 *How Have Policies on Sustainable Use of Natural Resources Evolved?*

As indicated, mining not only burdens local environments, but it also has global consequences. Increasing the volume of mining operations has the combined effect of depleting the earth's mineral resources. Around the time of the 1972 Stockholm Conference, it was feared that we would exhaust the earth's non-renewable natural resources in a relatively short time; for this reason, principle 5 of the Stockholm Declaration focused on managing these resources. Today, we are more concerned with how quickly we will exhaust all of the earth's natural resources, not just the non-renewable resources. At the time of Stockholm+50 we have the scientific capacity to estimate our consumption of natural resources and whether we are using them in a sustainable manner.[56] At the international level, we have also set the policy goal of managing our natural resources sustainably and efficiently by 2030. Whether we can meet this challenge is a different matter.

The international community is working to find international solutions to this huge challenge in diverse ways. As mentioned above, the international community is aiming to increase the efficiency of resource use and establish circular economies to tackle unsustainable resource use. Another way to address this is to place obligations directly on companies. For example, major multinational companies could be obligated to ensure that throughout their entire supply chains, all the operators commit to principles of environmental and human rights stewardship, as in the EU Directive on Corporate Sustainability Due Diligence, which is applicable to major companies headquartered or conducting major operations in the EU. Such measures can be developed to align with the overall global regulatory system that we have created and continue to maintain.

Around the time of the 1972 Stockholm Conference, the international community was just recognizing the various transboundary environmental problems. At the time of Stockholm+50, we face many global environmental problems. Our increased scientific capacity also enables us to understand how intertwined these environmental problems – and their root causes – are. Combating climate change requires that we move away from fossil fuels by investing in clean technologies. Paradoxically, this green transition increases the demand for minerals and metals extracted from either the earth's crust or potentially the deep seabed. Although our capacity to manage individual mining projects has increased since 1972, the challenges associated with

56 See, for example, how to compute data related to SDG target 12.2. 'SDG Indicator Metadata', n. 48.

accelerating the global output of mining have grown since then. We understand better how the increasing amount of mining contributes to the overconsumption of natural resources, the root causes of which are extremely difficult to tackle from a political perspective. We also know that overconsumption of natural resources is a key contributing factor of these interdependent global environmental problems. The policy measures that have been implemented to enhance sustainable resource management are clearly not enough to address the current and imminent issues. Thus, we need transformative changes, which are difficult to agree on in a world of almost 200 states.

8.6 CONCLUDING REMARKS

The most general normative guidance available for sustainable development is the 2030 Agenda for Sustainable Development, with its seventeen SDGs and their sub-goals.[57] The mining industry has been very vocal about its active role in achieving these global goals. Mining is an important contributor to economic growth and helps meet economic needs; however, it is vital to balance social development with economic development and to ensure that all mining is undertaken in an environmentally responsible manner. All seventeen SDGs interface with mining in multiple ways, and it can be argued that responsible mining can indeed contribute to sustainable local and national development.

However, mining operations – which are likely to increase due to growing demand – have a considerable impact on the environment. The related SDG target 12.2 sets us the challenge of ensuring that we use our natural resources sustainably and efficiently by 2030. As we continue to measure the progress, if any, towards this target, our consumption of natural resources is glaringly obvious, especially that of the developed world (and emerging economies) and so is our consumption of industrial minerals and metals. The accumulating data allow us to learn more about the big picture as well as the root causes of environmental problems rather than isolated activities that only impact certain environments. Thus, we can use this information to focus our efforts on addressing the key factors contributing to environmental problems.

Ultimately, it is difficult to be optimistic about whether we can sustainably manage our natural resources with the existing fairly minimal policy and regulatory actions. Ideally, we need to be able to influence how the drivers of the overconsumption of natural resources develop. Compared to 1972, at the time of Stockholm+50 global population is double, we extract three times as many materials, and the combined national product of our economies has

57 *Transforming Our World*, n. 46.

quadrupled. Mining has accelerated over the past fifty years and is predicted to grow even faster in the coming years. Minerals and metals are needed to satisfy the demands of our urbanizing and digitizing world. We need a new and elevated level of ambition to sustainably manage our natural resources. This ambition was manifested, at least at the idea level, during the stocktaking at the Stockholm+50 Meeting. Underlying this conference was a call to recognize that we are facing a triple planetary crisis of climate change, biodiversity loss, and pollution (waste).[58] The participants discussed how to measure progress in human societies in more sustainable ways than we do today and even the need to think of degrowth as a viable way of development. Much attention was paid to building economies in new ways, based on circular economy principles – an observation that is truly relevant for minerals and metals. It was generally acknowledged that the right to a decent environment is part of the corpus of international human rights, that the rights of nature are making incremental progress in various countries, and that climate litigations are already affecting policy changes.

The ten recommendations issued at the Stockholm+50 Meeting call for serious action to achieve demonstrable outcomes and transform the way in which our societies and economies function. It was agreed during the conference that we cannot celebrate the success of our international environmental actions given the enormity of the existing environmental problems. This is obvious for managing mining, which is a significant contributor to the excessive use of natural resources and thus causes many environmental problems. We have the normative ideas needed to transform our societies, as shown by the output of the Stockholm+50 Meeting. What we need is to transfer these ambitious ideas into reality, which is still built on the ideology of growing economic outputs and higher living standards. To change this is a tall order; yet we must do everything in our power to try to effect such change.

58 'Stockholm+50', www.stockholm50.global/; 'Presidents' Final Remarks to Plenary: Key Recommendations for Accelerating Action towards a Healthy Planet for the Prosperity of All', *United Nations*, www.stockholm50.global/presidents-final-remarks-plenary-key-recommendations-accelerating-action-towards-healthy-planet.

9

Chemicals and Wastes in International Environmental Policy and Law: From Trail Smelter *to a Circular Economy*

Katharina Kummer Peiry

9.1 CHEMICALS AND WASTES: SCOPE

My chemistry teacher in high school had a favourite saying when introducing his subject area to a class of new students: 'What is chemistry? Everything is chemistry!' Indeed, chemicals are everywhere. Their many benefits for industry, food production, and health care have contributed significantly to the emergence of modern societies. A broad range of international legal instruments address their potentially problematic effects – including chemical weapons, occupational health, and drug trafficking; the chemical pollution of the air, watercourses, and the oceans; and the deleterious effects of chemicals on the global climate and the ozone layer – in addition to the legal and policy instruments specifically addressing the management of potentially hazardous chemicals as well as wastes, on which this chapter will focus.

Traditionally, environmental damage caused by chemicals and wastes was addressed through the concept of pollution as defined by the Organisation for Economic Co-operation and Development (OECD) in 1974: 'Pollution means the introduction by man, directly or indirectly, of substances or energy into the environment, resulting in deleterious effects of such a nature as to endanger human health, harm living resources and ecosystems, and impair or interfere with amenities and other legitimate uses of the environment.'[1] Since the 1970s, the evolving discipline of international environmental law has addressed pollution by the emission of chemicals into the atmosphere, the oceans, and continental waterways under the heading of the protection of the relevant spheres. The containment of the hazardous properties of chemicals

[1] *Recommendations of the OECD Council on Principles Concerning Transfrontier Pollution*, Doc. C74(224), 14 November 1974; Katharina Kummer, *International Management of Hazardous Wastes: The Basel Convention and Related Legal Rules* (Oxford University Press, 1999), 13ff.

that are not released into the environment as by-products of human activity but that have an intrinsic value – being traded and used in production processes – emerged as a separate topic in the 1980s, as did the containment of hazardous properties of materials that had come to the end of their useful lives. Both these activities can and often do lead to pollution. The present analysis, while focusing on the management of chemicals and wastes, will also consider regimes devoted to the protection of the different spheres of the environment from chemicals where relevant.

The clustering of the management of chemicals and wastes emerged around the early 2000s. International environmental policy in the 1980s and 1990s addressed the two issues separately,[2] as did older textbooks on international environmental law,[3] both giving greater attention to wastes. This prioritization was due to the public outcry following the dumping of toxic wastes from the industrialized world in developing countries in the 1980s, placing waste in the spotlight and prompting international action.[4] The so-called synergies process between the 1989 Basel, 1998 Rotterdam, and 2001 Stockholm Conventions,[5] which was concluded in 2011, reinforced the perception of chemicals and waste management as a single area of international environmental law. Aimed at achieving greater efficiency by building on the synergies between the three conventions, this process resulted in joint activities and coordinated implementation as well as institutional and administrative streamlining.[6]

The clustering of chemicals and waste management is understandable given the hazardous properties of all the substances addressed and their

[2] UN Environment Programme (UNEP), *Montevideo Programme for the Development and Periodic Review of Environmental Law*, UNEP Governing Council Decision 10/21, 31 May 1982; Agenda 21, UN Doc. A/CONF. 151/26, 13 June 1992.

[3] See, e.g., Alexandre Kiss, *Droit international de l'environnement* (Pedone, 1989); Astrid Epiney & Martin Scheyli, *Umweltvölkerrecht* (Stämpfli Verlag AG, 2000); Patricia Birnie & Alan Boyle, *International Law of the Environment* (2nd ed., Oxford University Press, 2002).

[4] Kummer, n. 1, chs 1, 2; Katharina Kummer, 'International Management of Chemicals and Wastes', in Malgosia Fitzmaurice, Marcel Brus, & Panos Merkouris (eds.), *Research Handbook on International Environmental Law* (2nd ed., Edward Elgar, 2021), 441ff.

[5] Basel Convention on the Control of Transboundary Movements of Hazardous and Their Disposal 1989, 1673 UNTS 126 (Basel Convention); Convention on the Prior Informed Consent Procedure for Certain Hazardous Chemicals and Pesticides in International Trade, 1998, 2244 UNTS 337 (Rotterdam Convention); Stockholm Convention on Persistent Organic Pollutants 2001, 2256 UNTS 119 (Stockholm Convention). The three conventions are discussed in section 9.2.5.

[6] Katharina Kummer Peiry, 'The Chemicals and Waste Regime as a Basis for a Comprehensive International Framework on Sustainable Management of Potentially Hazardous Materials?' (2014) 23(2) *Review of European Community and International Environmental Law (RECIEL)* 175.

negative effects on human health and the environment. However, there is a significant difference between the two: chemicals have a useful life for their holder, whereas wastes are substances to be discarded. This means that, while many of the management concepts and principles that have evolved since the 1972 UN Conference on the Human Environment (Stockholm Conference) apply to both areas, some apply to one only. This will be taken into account when discussing the relevant approaches.

9.2 THE EVOLUTION OF INTERNATIONAL LAW AND POLICY ON CHEMICALS AND WASTE MANAGEMENT

9.2.1 *Industrialized World: Early Cases and Policy*

Damage caused by chemical substances – in this case, through air pollution – famously appeared on the horizon long before the birth of international environmental law at the 1972 Stockholm Conference. It was at the centre of the *Trail Smelter* arbitration in 1941, in which an arbitration tribunal awarded damages to the United States for transboundary pollution caused by a smelter located in Canada, near the common border, and set out obligations to contain further damage.[7] Together with the *Corfu Channel* case,[8] it is widely acknowledged to have established the customary law rule that every state has the obligation to ensure that activities within its area of jurisdiction or under its control do not cause serious harm to other states.[9] In the following three decades, chemical pollution of different spheres of the environment was one of the first forms of environmental damage to be recognized, initially at the national level in the industrialized world. From the 1960s, developed countries began adopting policy and law to address it. This was followed by national policy and legislation on the management of chemicals and wastes. The transnational effects of trade in these substances were rapidly recognized, leading to efforts of cooperation within the (then) European Community and the OECD.[10]

7 *Trail Smelter Case (United States v Canada)*, Judgment, 16 April 1938 and 11 March 1941, reprinted in 3 *Reports of International Arbitral Awards* 1905; Phoebe Okowa & Sean O'Reilly, 'Implementing Principle 21 of the Stockholm Declaration: Regional Efforts to Regulate Transboundary Air Pollution', in this volume, 313.

8 *Corfu Channel Case (United Kingdom v Albania)*, Judgment, 9 April 1949, (1949) ICJ Reports 4.

9 Birnie & Boyle, n. 3, 109; Kummer, n. 1, 17.

10 Marc Pallemaerts, *Toxics and Transnational Law* (Hart Publishing, 2003), 7–8.

9.2.2 *Stockholm Conference on the Human Environment*

The 1972 Stockholm Conference, convened by a UN General Assembly (UNGA) decision on the initiative of the government of Sweden,[11] constitutes the first effort at global cooperation on environmental protection and is generally perceived as having given birth to international environmental law as a discipline. At that time, environmental protection was considered an issue that concerned mostly industrialized states. Developing countries were reluctant to accept any measures that might impede the economic development that they considered their priority. The resulting differences between the two groups of countries influenced the discussions at Stockholm and continued to do so in the following fifty years.

The two outcome documents – the Stockholm Declaration and the Stockholm Action Plan for the Human Environment[12] – provided the basis for the evolution of international environmental policy and law in the following decades, including on pollution control and, to a lesser extent, on the management of hazardous chemicals and wastes. Several of the twenty-six principles set out in the Stockholm Declaration helped lay the groundwork for policy and law addressing these issues. Principle 6 called for halting 'the discharge of toxic substances or of other substances and the release of heat, in such quantities or concentrations as to exceed the capacity of the environment to render them harmless'. It may be seen as a precursor to the OECD's 1974 definition of pollution.[13] Principle 7 advocated the prevention of pollution of the marine environment. Principle 21 codified the rule established by the *Trail Smelter* arbitration, developing it further:

> States have, in accordance with the Charter of the United Nations and the principles of international law, the sovereign right to exploit their own resources pursuant to their own environmental policies, and the responsibility to ensure that activities within their jurisdiction or control do not cause damage to the environment of other States or of areas beyond the limits of national jurisdiction.

[11] UNGA Resolution 2398 (XXIII), 8 January 1970; Eric Paglia, 'The Swedish Initiative and the 1972 Stockholm Conference: The Decisive Role of Science Diplomacy in the Emergence of Global Environmental Governance', *Nature Journal*, 5 January 2021, www.nature.com/articles/s41599-020-00681-x.

[12] 'Declaration of the United Nations Conference on the Human Environment', in *Report of the UN Conference on the Human Environment*, UN Doc. A/CONF.48/14/Rev.1, 16 June 1972 (Stockholm Declaration); 'Action Plan for the Human Environment', in *Report of the United Nations Conference on the Human Environment, ibid.* (Stockholm Action Plan).

[13] Robert E. Stein, 'The OECD Guiding Principles on Transfrontier Pollution' (1976) 6 *Georgia Journal of International and Comparative Law* 245.

In this form, the rule subsequently became recognized as customary international law. The Stockholm Action Plan devoted one chapter each to pollution in general and to marine pollution.[14] The management of wastes and chemicals was featured only marginally as it was not considered a priority issue at that time.

9.2.3 *Successor Conferences*

The UN Conference on Environment and Development, convened in Rio de Janeiro twenty years after the Stockholm Conference, was the first to embrace the concept of sustainable development, which had been developed by the Brundtland Commission in 1987 and subsequently became recognized as the key to balancing environmental protection with other important human aspirations.[15] The Rio Conference adopted a declaration and a plan of action.[16] A number of principles of the Rio Declaration again applied to chemicals and waste management: Principle 2 reiterated Principle 21 of the Stockholm Declaration; Principle 18 required states to notify emergencies likely to affect the environment of other states; and Principle 19 advocated prior notification and consultation in good faith before undertaking activities that may have significant adverse transboundary environmental effects.[17] Agenda 21, the ambitious action plan for sustainable development in the twenty-first century, contains a chapter each on chemicals, hazardous wastes, solid wastes and sewage, and radioactive wastes.[18] The chapters address risk reduction in chemicals management and waste prevention, containing recommendations to both governments and industry. They cover a broad range of actions and set out the means of implementation, including financing.[19] The Johannesburg Plan of Implementation, adopted by the first successor conference ('Rio+10') in 2002, set the goal to achieve the sound management of chemicals throughout their life cycle, and the sound management of hazardous wastes, by

[14] Kummer, n. 1, 16–18; Stockholm Action Plan, n. 12.

[15] Duncan French, 'Sustainable Development', in Fitzmaurice, Brus & Merkouris, n. 4, 130–50.

[16] 'Rio Declaration on Environment and Development', in *Report of the UN Conference on Environment and Development*, UN Doc. A/CONF.151/26 (Vol. I), 12 August 1992 (Rio Declaration).

[17] Birnie & Boyle, n. 3, 105.

[18] Agenda 21, n. 2; Michael Keating, *The Earth Summit's Agenda for Change: A Plain Language Version of Agenda 21 and the Other Rio Agreements* (4th ed., Centre of Our Common Future, 1995).

[19] Kummer Peiry, n. 6, 172.

2020.[20] This was reaffirmed at the second successor conference ('Rio+20'), held again in Rio de Janeiro in 2012.[21]

The other UN mega-conferences of the new millennium that encompassed environment and development tended to address overarching issues rather than specific aspects of environmental protection. The Millennium Declaration,[22] adopted at the UN Millennium Summit in 2000, contains a section entitled 'Protecting our common environment', explicitly mentioning neither pollution control nor the management of chemicals and wastes. The seventh of the UN Millennium Development Goals, 'Ensure Environmental Sustainability', encompasses all efforts towards environmental protection without specifically addressing any of them.

Of the 17 Sustainable Development Goals (SDGs) and the related targets adopted by the UNGA in 2015,[23] SDG 12:Responsible Consumption and Production encompasses chemicals and waste management as well as pollution in Target 12.4, expanding on the Rio+10 and Rio+20 goals and advocating a comprehensive approach to the reduction and management of the relevant substances: 'By 2020, achieve the environmentally sound management of chemicals and all wastes throughout their life cycle, in accordance with agreed international frameworks, and significantly reduce their release to air, water and soil in order to minimize their adverse impacts on human health and the environment.'

Finally, the outcomes of the UN International Conference: A Healthy Planet for the Prosperity of All – Our Responsibility, Our Opportunity (Stockholm+50), held in June 2022, the first such global summit without a negotiated outcome document, were summarized in a report by the co-presidents.[24] The report highlighted agreement on the urgent need to address the triple planetary crisis – climate change, biodiversity loss, and pollution – and recommended ten actions to this end. By this time, the triple planetary crisis had already been widely discussed within the UN system.[25]

20 Johannesburg Plan of Implementation, in *Report of the World Summit on Sustainable Development*, Johannesburg, South Africa, 26 August–4 September 2002, UN Doc. A/CONF.199/20, 2002, para. 23.

21 *Report of the United Nations Conference on Sustainable Development*, Rio de Janeiro, Brazil, 20–22 June 2012, Doc. A/CONF.216/16, 2012, paras. 213–23 (*Report on Sustainable Development*).

22 Millennium Declaration, UNGA Resolution A/RES/55/2, 18 September 2000.

23 *Transforming Our World: The 2030 Agenda for Sustainable Development*, Doc. A/Res/70/1, 25 September 2015.

24 *Report of Stockholm+50: A Healthy Planet for the Prosperity of All – Our Responsibility, Our Opportunity*, UN Doc. A/CONF.238/9, 1 August 2022.

25 UN University, *Beyond Opportunism: The UN Development System's Response to the Triple Planetary Crisis*, 2021, https://i.unu.edu/media/cpr.unu.edu/attachment/4977/UNUTriplePlanetaryCrisis2021.pdf.

9.2.4 *Non-binding Policy Instruments*

Although not a priority in international law and policy in the 1980s, chemicals management was addressed at the technical level through efforts such as the inception of the International Programme on Chemical Safety, the Intergovernmental Forum on Chemical Safety, the UN Environment Programme's (UNEP) International Register of Potentially Toxic Chemicals, and the Inter-Organization Programme for the Sound Management of Chemicals.[26] Between 1985 and 1987, guidelines were adopted by both UNEP and the UN Food and Agriculture Organization (FAO) on the management of hazardous wastes and on hazardous chemicals and pesticides in international trade.[27] Their objective was to provide advice and guidance to governments on the management of these substances, with a focus on the international dimension of the trade and the responsibilities of states towards each other in this respect.

In 2006, the Strategic Approach to Chemicals Management (SAICM) was adopted by the International Conference on Chemicals Management as a mechanism to meet the Johannesburg target of significantly reducing the negative effects of chemicals by 2020.[28] It constituted a non-binding overarching policy framework, providing guidance on the management of chemicals throughout their life cycle. Due mostly to a lack of funding and political support, it did not prove very effective.[29] In 2022, the UN Environment Assembly decided to establish a science-policy panel on pollution prevention and the management of chemicals and wastes to complement the work of the equivalent panels already in operation for the two other elements of the triple planetary crisis.[30] In 2023, the International Conference on Chemicals

[26] Jim Willis, International Institute for Sustainable Development, Chemicals and Waste Policy and Practice, A *Brief Historical Perspective on International Progress in the Sound Management of Chemicals and Wastes*, 28 March 2014.

[27] Food and Agriculture Organization, *Code of Conduct on the Distribution and Use of Pesticides*, FAO Conference Resolution 10/85, 28 November 1985; UNEP, *London Guidelines for the Exchange of Information on Chemicals in International Trade*, UNEP Governing Council Decision 14/27, 17 June 1987; UNEP, *Cairo Guidelines and Principles for the Environmentally Sound Management of Hazardous Wastes*, UNEP Governing Council Decision 14/30, 17 June 1987.

[28] UNEP, *SAICM Texts and Resolutions of the International Conference on Chemicals Management*, www.saicm.org.

[29] Kummer Peiry, n. 6, 175; Franz Xaver Perrez, 'The Strategic Approach to International Chemicals Management: Lost Opportunity or Foundation for a Brave New World?' (2009) 15(3) *RECIEL* 254.

[30] UN Environment Assembly (UNEA), Resolution 5/8 on Science-Policy Panel to Contribute Further to the Sound Management of Chemicals and Waste and to Prevent Pollution, UN Doc. UNEP/EA.5/Res.8, 7 March 2022.

Management adopted the Global Framework on Chemicals, intended as a more robust follow-up to SAICM working strategically with the science-policy panel.[31]

9.2.5 *Treaties*

Between 1989 and 2013, four global treaties were adopted to address the management of hazardous wastes and different aspects of chemicals management. The 1989 Basel Convention,[32] negotiated under the auspices of UNEP, built on the relevant UNEP guidelines and on previous efforts by the (then) European Community and the OECD. While the Convention's cornerstone is a system of prior informed consent for transboundary movements of hazardous wastes, it also sets out obligations related to waste minimization and environmentally sound management and assigns responsibility for illegal traffic and for movements that cannot be completed as intended. A 1995 amendment introducing a ban on the transfer of all types of hazardous wastes for any purpose from OECD to non-OECD countries entered into force in 2019.[33]

Both before and after the adoption of the Basel Convention, a series of regional treaties on transboundary movements of hazardous wastes were adopted, mostly with the objective of preventing wastes from outside the relevant region entering the territories of the contracting parties. The European Union (EU) and the OECD also adopted legislation to take account of the Basel Convention.[34] Two global treaties address specific aspects of chemicals management. The first is the 1998 Rotterdam Convention,[35] which was negotiated under the joint auspices of UNEP and FAO and builds on the relevant guidelines, setting up a system of prior informed consent for international trade in the chemicals and pesticides listed in its annexes.[36] The second treaty is the 2001 Stockholm Convention,[37] which was negotiated under UNEP's auspices, building in part on the 1998 Aarhus Protocol to the

31 Global Framework on Chemicals, www.unep.org/global-framework-chemicals.

32 Basel Convention, n. 5.

33 Decision III/1 of the Conference of the Parties to the Basel Convention, UN Doc. UNEP/CHW.3/35, 28 November 1995.

34 Kummer, n. 1, chs. 3, 4; see also Katharina Kummer, *International Management of Hazardous Wastes: The Basel Convention and Related Legal Rules* (rev. ed., Oxford University Press, 1999), preface.

35 Rotterdam Convention, n. 5.

36 Katharina Kummer, 'Prior Informed Consent for Chemicals in International Trade: The 1998 Rotterdam Convention' (1999) 8(3) *RECIEL* 322.

37 Stockholm Convention, n. 5.

1979 Convention on Long-Range Transboundary Air Pollution,[38] and providing for the gradual phase out of the production and use of chemicals known as persistent organic pollutants (POPs). The negotiation of the 2013 Minamata Convention[39] under the auspices of UNEP was prompted by increasing scientific understanding of the highly hazardous effects of methyl mercury on brain development in humans and animals.[40] It addresses the management of mercury throughout its life cycle and provides for its gradual phase out. The latest global treaty related to chemicals and wastes was expected to materialize pursuant to the 2022 UN Environment Assembly's decision to negotiate an international instrument on the management of plastics throughout their life cycle.[41] However, the negotiations collapsed for the second time in August 2025, with no decision or plan to resume.

9.3 EVOLUTION SINCE STOCKHOLM: VIEWING CHEMICALS AND WASTE MANAGEMENT THROUGH CHANGING LENSES

I would like to equate the evolving perception of chemicals and waste management, as part of the overall topic of environmental protection and sustainable development, to the use of lenses through which the issue is viewed – not only by policy-makers and lawyers but also by those who influence them: scientists, politicians, academics, the media, pressure groups, and, last but not least, the general public.[42]

9.3.1 *From Insignificance to Mainstream*

In general, at the time of the 1972 Stockholm Conference, environmental protection (including chemicals and waste management) was seen through the lens of insignificance. Environmentalists constituted a small group of

38 Aarhus Protocol on Persistent Organic Pollutants to the UNECE Convention on Long-Range Transboundary Air Pollution, 2022, 2230 UNTS 79; Convention on Long-Range Transboundary Air Pollution, 1979, 1302 UNTS 217.

39 Minamata Convention on Mercury, 2013, 3202 UNTS 220.

40 Kummer, 'International Management', n. 4.

41 UNEA Resolution 5/14 on the End of Plastic Pollution: Towards an Internationally Binding Instrument, UN Doc. UNEP/EA.5/Res.14, 7 March 2022; *Report of the Intergovernmental Negotiating Committee to Develop an International Legally Binding Instrument on Plastic Pollution, Including in the Marine Environment, on the Work of Its Second Session*, UN Doc. UNEP/PP/INC.2/5, 6 July 2023; Eva van der Marel & Catherine Redgwell, 'Unrealised Ambition or Unattainable Goal? Sustainable Consumption and Production in International Law', in this volume, 205.

42 Kummer, 'International Management', n. 4; Kummer Peiry, n. 6, 172.

idealists who were not taken seriously by mainstream policy. If noticed at all, they were seen as a nuisance, as intending to sabotage economic development and human well-being. By the time of the Stockholm+50 Conference in 2022, environmental protection, as one of the three pillars of sustainable development, had emerged as a key public preoccupation, with climate change at the forefront. Every political party embraces sustainability, every major company has a sustainability strategy, and banks promote sustainable investment. Sustainability foundations abound, and sustainability prizes are awarded. In 1972, this would have been beyond anyone's imagination. In part, this shift is certainly due to the degradation of the environment over the last fifty years, which is now visible to even the non-specialist – not only the extreme weather patterns attributed to climate change but also issues such as the rampant loss of biodiversity and natural habitats and plastic pollution of the oceans.

Within the environmental agenda, chemicals and waste management was for a long time seen as even more insignificant than other aspects of environmental protection. Any attention and resources attributed to the environment were directed at climate change, with biological diversity lagging far behind. As late as 2010, one of my favourite sayings was that I had yet to learn of a candidate for political office anywhere in the world promising better waste management if they were elected. Waste management was left to underfunded and understaffed local authorities. With the endorsement of the concept of the triple planetary crisis from the early 2020s, biodiversity loss and pollution (including by chemicals and wastes) have entered the mainstream. Not least due to some lens changes evolving in the first decade of the new millennium, which are discussed below, chemicals and waste management as a source of pollution have attracted considerable interest from that time onward.

9.3.2 *From Transboundary to Global*

The *Trail Smelter* arbitration symbolizes the 'transboundary' lens traditionally used when it comes to pollution, including through chemicals and waste management. This lens shows a perpetrator and a victim, which are seen in international law as two states with rights and responsibilities towards each other. The 'transboundary' lens determined the customary law rule derived from the Stockholm Declaration's Principle 21 as well as other customary norms such as the obligations of mutual information and cooperation in good faith with a state affected by a harmful activity.[43] The 'transboundary' lens dominated the negotiations of the first two global treaties on chemicals and

43 Kummer, n. 1, ch. 1K.

wastes – the Basel and Rotterdam Conventions. It led to the development of the concept of prior informed consent, which is the cornerstone of both of these conventions, and features also in the Minamata Convention.[44]

While the 'transboundary' lens continued to be used at the time of the Stockholm+50 Conference, a 'global' lens was increasingly used in parallel over the previous decades. Through this lens, the effects of environmental degradation and pollution, including by chemicals and wastes, are seen as affecting the planet as a whole, independently of national borders. When using this lens, it is evident that our priority must be a holistic approach to preventing – or at least minimizing – damage. Interestingly, the use of the 'global' lens was evident already in the Stockholm Declaration, through Principles 6 and 7 on pollution. The customary law rule that was derived from the *Trail Smelter* arbitration was modified by Principle 21 in accordance with this lens to encompass an obligation on states to refrain from activities within their territory that result in serious harm to the environment, regardless of whether another state is directly affected.[45] Many of the soft law instruments on chemicals and waste management that were developed in the 1980s and 1990s used the 'global' lens, as did the negotiations of the treaty systems on the protection of the ozone layer, climate change, and biological diversity. With respect to chemicals and wastes, the 'global' lens dominated the negotiations of the 2001 Stockholm Convention and the 2013 Minamata Convention, both of which have as their ultimate objective the phase out of the substances they address, thus preventing harm caused by their production and use independently of national borders.

9.3.3 *From Reactive to Preventive*

Through the 'reactive' lens, we see harm that has already occurred, and we thus develop rules to deal with the consequences. This is the lens traditionally used in international law, including in the area of chemicals and waste management. It led to the development of the rules on state responsibility and liability as well as customary law rules such as the obligation to negotiate in good faith with a state that has been affected by a harmful activity and, more recently, the polluter pays principle. Conversely, the use of the 'preventive' lens allows anticipation of harm and, accordingly, the development of rules that prevent it from materializing. Over the past decades, this lens was

44 Katharina Kummer Peiry, 'Prior Informed Consent', in *Max Planck Encyclopedia of International Law* (Oxford University Press, 2007).

45 Kummer, n 1, ch. 1F.

increasingly used in international environmental law, in general, and applied to chemicals and waste management, in particular. At the time of the Stockholm+50 Conference, the preventive approach had become widely accepted as a customary law rule. Other concepts that reflect this approach have solidified since the 1990s, including the precautionary principle and extended producer responsibility.[46] The objective of the Stockholm and Minamata Conventions to phase out hazardous substances to prevent further harm is also in line with the preventive approach, as is the requirement of prior informed consent in the Basel, Rotterdam, and Minamata Conventions.

9.3.4 *From Sectoral to Comprehensive*

A 'sectoral' lens shows us each set of problems separately and, accordingly, leads to the development of rules for each issue without taking account of the wider context. This lens dominated the early approach to chemicals and wastes: many of the rules that were developed in the years following the Stockholm Conference aim at a particular group of substances, a particular stage in their life cycle, and a particular aspect of their management.[47] The Basel Convention addresses the downstream management of a specific group of substances once they no longer have a useful life for their holder. The Rotterdam Convention addresses a set of chemical products in international trade, covering only the exchange of information on national measures regarding these substances. The Stockholm Convention addresses only the chemicals known as POPs and sets out measures to achieve their phase out.

The 'comprehensive' lens permits us to see the management cycle of chemicals and wastes as a whole. It has resulted in the adoption of a life cycle or cradle-to-grave approach to chemicals management, which was advocated in the 2002 Johannesburg Plan of Implementation, in the outcome document of the Rio+20 Conference, and in SDG 12. It is reflected in concepts such as life cycle management and assessment. The newest of the chemicals and waste treaties, the Minamata Convention, is the only one to cover the entire life cycle of the substance it addresses. Interestingly, this Convention embraces a sectoral approach at the same time in that it addresses only a single substance. The negotiations on the plastics agreement, which was intended to address the entire life cycle of plastics in accordance with the 2022

46 Nicolas de Sadeleer, 'The Principles of Prevention and Precaution in International Law: Two Sides of the Same Coin?' in Fitzmaurice, Brus & Merkouris, n. 4, 151–187; Nicole C. Kibert, 'Extended Producer Responsibility: A Tool for Achieving Sustainable Development' (2004) 19(2) *Journal of Land Use and Environmental Law* 503.

47 Kummer, n. 1, chs 1J, 5.

decision of the UN Environment Assembly,[48] failed in 2025 due to opposition by a group of states to this very concept. The overall approach to chemicals and waste management thus remains sectoral. The best effort at a comprehensive approach so far was the SAICM. We can hope that its successor, the 2023 Global Framework on Chemicals, will move the comprehensive approach forward. The synergies process between the Basel, Rotterdam, and Stockholm Conventions is a limited practical version of a comprehensive approach to implementation.

9.3.5 *From Prohibition and Control to Environmentally Sound Management*

Using a lens that focuses on environmental damage caused by chemicals and wastes, the traditional reaction is to prohibit or at least minimize their release into the environment. Most pollution control treaties set emission limits, while the Stockholm and Minamata Conventions have as their objective the phase out of the substances they address. The prior informed consent system, which appears in three of the four chemicals and waste conventions, prohibits the export and import of the substances they address unless expressly authorized in advance by the importing state.[49] The Ban Amendment to the Basel Convention reinforces the focus on prohibition and control.[50]

From the 1990s, in accordance with the life cycle approach, a lens showing the beneficial as well as the harmful effects of chemicals and wastes began to be used. This resulted in the introduction of management principles as a means to avoid environmental damage from potentially hazardous substances while allowing their use for beneficial purposes. Such principles include cleaner production, life cycle management and assessment, best available techniques (BAT) and best environmental practices (BEP), and the waste hierarchy, which details an order of priority of the ways in which to deal with materials that no longer have a useful life. Some of these principles have been embodied in guidelines and similar instruments adopted by international organizations and the conferences of the parties to the chemicals and waste treaties. The move from mere control and prohibition to also adopting management principles is

48 Potential options for elements towards an international legally binding instrument, based on a comprehensive approach that addresses the full life cycle of plastics as called for by UNEA Resolution 5/14, Note by the Secretariat, Doc. UNEP/PP/INC.2/4, 13 April 2023.

49 David Langlet, *Prior Informed Consent and Hazardous Trade: Regulating Trade in Hazardous Goods at the Intersection of Sovereignty, Free Trade and Environmental Protection* (2nd ed., Kluwer Law International, 2009).

50 Decision III/1: Amendment to the Basel Convention, Decisions adopted by the Third Meeting of the Conference of the Parties to the Basel Convention, Doc UNEP/CHW.3/35, 28 November 1995.

perhaps most evident in the Basel Convention. While setting out a general obligation to ensure environmentally sound waste management, the main aim of the Convention as it was adopted focused on control and prohibition, later reinforced by the Ban Amendment. From 1994, the adoption of detailed technical guidelines on the environmentally sound management of priority waste streams reflected the emerging use of the new lens, a move supported by the adoption of the 1999 Basel Declaration on Environmentally Sound Waste Management.[51] Under the Stockholm and Minamata Conventions, guidelines on BAT/BEP that are relevant to some of the substances covered were adopted by the conferences of the parties.[52]

9.3.6 *Wastes: From Problem to Resource*

For a long time, wastes were viewed, first and foremost, through a lens showing them to be a problem: a source of pollution, a hazard to human health and the environment, useless, and costly. Accordingly, international rules focused on their reduction and control and, from the 1980s, on the protection of developing countries from the dumping of hazardous wastes from the industrialized world. In the decades following the Stockholm Conference, new ways of looking at wastes and, accordingly, new concepts gradually entered international environmental law. Starting with the (then) European Community's policy in the mid-1970s, the waste hierarchy categorized ways of dealing with wastes – from the most desirable to the least desirable in terms of environmental protection – including prevention, preparing for reuse, recycling, other recovery (including energy recovery), and disposal.[53]

From the early 2000s, Japan promoted the concept of the 3Rs (reduce, reuse, recycle) of waste management.[54] While recycling had already been

[51] Basel Declaration on Environmentally Sound Waste Management, reprinted in *Report of the Fifth Meeting of the Conference of the Parties to the Basel Convention*, Document Doc. UNEP/CHW.5/29, 10 December 1999, Annex II; Kummer, 'International Management', n. 4, 447.

[52] 'BAT and BEP Guidance', *Stockholm Convention*, http://chm.pops.int/Implementation/BATandBEP/Guidance/Overview/tabid/5121/Default.aspx; 'Guidance on Best Available Techniques and Best Environmental Practices', *UN Environment Programme*, September 2019, www.mercuryconvention.org/en/resources/guidance-best-available-techniques-and-best-environmental-practices.

[53] Council Directive (EC) 2008/98 on Waste, (2008) OJ L312 (first adopted in 1975); Ana Pires & Graça Martinho, 'Waste Hierarchy for a Circular Economy in Waste Management' (2019) 95 *Waste Management* 298, www.sciencedirect.com/science/article/abs/pii/S0956053X19303927; Kummer, n. 1, ch. 4.

[54] 'Environmental Performance Reviews: Japan 2010', *OECD*, 2010, part II, ch. 6, https://read.oecd-ilibrary.org/environment/oecd-environmental-performance-reviews-japan-2010/waste-

recognized as a desirable way of dealing with wastes, the issue was increasingly being viewed through the lens of wastes as a valuable resource or a secondary raw material, capable of providing economic opportunities and creating jobs. Waste-to-resource and waste-to-energy evolved as new concepts. In the first decade of the new millennium, e-wastes became a showcase for this notion as it was calculated that one ton of e-waste could yield roughly 350 grams of gold compared to five grams yielded by a ton of virgin ore.[55] E-waste recycling was referred to as 'urban mining', with a modified version of the 3R concept: repair, refurbish, reuse, recycle. This was linked to a growing perception of possible monetary value that might be derived from wastes. E-waste recycling subsequently gained additional significance as a means of reducing dependence on those countries where primary resources such as rare earth metals occur naturally. Nonetheless, in international environmental policy, viewing the issue through this new lens initially met with opposition from environmental pressure groups and developing countries, who saw it as an attempt to undermine control and prohibition and, thus, to weaken the protection of vulnerable countries against waste imports. Under the Basel Convention, a paradigm shift occurred at the tenth Conference of the Parties in 2011 with the formal recognition of the concept of wastes as a resource.[56] The relevant decisions of the Conference of the Parties to the Basel Convention were subsequently endorsed explicitly by the Rio+20 Conference.[57]

9.3.7 *Anthropocentric Approach*

The notion of the environment requiring protection in order to serve humans has not changed between 1972 and 2022. Expressed by the reference to the human environment in the title of the Stockholm Conference, it was further developed in subsequent decades through concepts such as ecosystem services. It was confirmed by the 2022 UNGA resolution recognizing

management-and-the-3rs-reduce-reuse-recycle_9789264087873-7-en#page1 (on waste management and the 3Rs [reduce, reuse, recycle]).

55 Katharina Kummer Peiry, Rita Khanna & Veena Sahajwalla, 'Resource and Energy Recovery from Wastes: Perspectives for a Green Economy' (2012) 42(6) *Environmental Policy and Law* 344.

56 Cartagena Declaration on the Prevention, Minimization and Recovery of Hazardous Wastes and Other Wastes, Decision BC-10/2, Doc. UNEP/CHW.10/28, 1 November 2011; Juliette Voïnov Kohler, 'A Paradigm Shift under the Basel Convention on Hazardous Wastes', in Katharina Kummer Peiry, Andreas R. Ziegler, & Jorun Baumgartner (eds.), *Waste Management and the Green Economy: Law and Policy* (Edward Elgar, 2016), 80–94.

57 *Report on Sustainable Development*, n. 21, para. 219; Kummer Peiry, Khanna & Sahajwalla, n. 55.

a human right to a clean, healthy, and sustainable environment, which encompasses freedom from pollution and management of chemicals and wastes in a way that avoids harm to humans.[58] As yet, with the notable exception of the Antarctic Treaty System,[59] there has been no shift to a lens that focuses not merely on the value of the environment for humans but on its intrinsic value, despite lip service paid to the concept. This is something that might be considered by future generations.

9.3.8 *Problem-by-Problem Approach*

In line with the use of the 'reactive' and 'sectoral' lenses, international policy and law on chemicals and waste management has taken the approach of responding to any issue that comes to public attention – for example, due to scientific findings on the harmful effects of a substance or due to a scandal publicized through environmental pressure groups and the media – by negotiating a treaty to address it. The Stockholm and Minamata Conventions are examples of the first of these triggers, the Basel Convention is an example of the second. The result is a system resembling a Swiss cheese: rather than providing a comprehensive regulatory framework based on systematic considerations, it addresses only those operations and only those substances that came on the radar of public attention at any given time. This approach has not changed since the 1972 Stockholm Conference: an example is the UN Environment Assembly's 2022 decision to negotiate a treaty on plastic pollution. The problem-by-problem approach also led to a categorization of the legal instruments that is not necessarily logical. As noted in section 9.1 above, only a small number of treaties dealing with chemicals are classified as chemical treaties; others come under the heading of the sphere of the environment that they are intended to protect. This is due to the fact that environmental policy traditionally addressed the negative effects of chemicals on each sphere of the environment separately as they came to public attention, and responded with measures to protect that sphere, an approach that continued with the ozone and climate treaty systems.[60]

58 UNGA Resolution A/76/L.75, 26 July 2022.

59 Antarctic Treaty, 1980, 402 UNTS 71, and related agreements.

60 Kummer Peiry, n. 6, 172ff; Kummer, 'International Management', n. 4, 447; Pallemaerts, n. 10, 11.

9.4 NEW OVERARCHING CONCEPTS: GREEN ECONOMY AND CIRCULAR ECONOMY

Since the second decade of the new millennium, international policy and law on chemicals and waste management, and, in particular, the changing lenses through which these issues were viewed, have become embedded in a new way of looking at the interface of environmental protection and the economy. Through a traditional lens, these had been seen as implacably opposed, with discussions in policy and academia focusing on which should be given precedence over the other.[61] In environmental treaty negotiations in the 1980s and 1990s, the inclusion of a provision stating that the treaty would not affect the rights and obligations of the parties under other international legal instruments was hotly debated. Whereas some wanted to give priority to the environmental concerns addressed by the new treaty, others wanted to prioritize trade interests and the right to economic development. Compromise language was usually included in the preamble to reflect the different viewpoints while not resolving the question of priority.[62]

The concept of a green economy built on the well-established concept of sustainable development. It was initially promoted mainly by UNEP, which defined it as 'an economy that results in improved human well-being and social equity, while significantly reducing environmental risks and ecological scarcities'.[63] It was formally recognized by the Rio+20 Conference in 2012. At the time of the Stockholm+50 Conference, it had largely been bypassed in the policy discussion by the concept of a circular economy, which first emerged in China and later became universally embraced. It denotes an economy in which waste products re-enter the production process rather than being discarded.[64] It enjoyed broad support at the time of the Stockholm+50 Conference, being recognized as a baseline for policy and law on waste and chemicals management. Prominent examples include the 2021 EU Circular Economy Action

61 Molly Scott Cato, *Environment and Economy* (2nd ed., Routledge, 2021); Jonathan Krueger, *International Trade and the Basel Convention* (Earthscan, 1999), ch. 1.

62 Such preambular language was included in the Rotterdam and Stockholm Conventions as well as in the UN Framework Convention on Climate Change, 1992, 1171 UNTS 107, and in the Convention on Biological Diversity, 1992, 1760 UNTS 79, and its Cartagena Protocol on Biosafety, 2000, 2226 UNTS 208; Christoph Bail, Robert Falkner, & Helen Marquard (eds.), *The Cartagena Protocol on Biosafety: Reconciling Trade in Biotechnology with Environment & Development?* (Earthscan, 2002), 467 (ch. 49, Thomas Cottier); Kummer, n. 36.

63 Vera Weick, 'Green Economy and Sustainable Development', in Kummer Peiry, Ziegler & Baumgartner, n. 56, 121–146.

64 Martin Geissdörfer, Paulo Savaget, Nancy M.P. Bocken, & Erik Jan Hultink, 'The Circular Economy: A New Sustainability Paradigm?' (2017) 143 *Journal of Cleaner Production* 757.

Plan,[65] and the 2030 Agenda for Sustainable Development,[66] referencing the circular economy in nine of the 17 SDGs.

9.5 LOOKING TOWARDS THE FUTURE

As the above overview shows, the changes of lenses between 1972 and 2022 have mostly been gradual: rather than replacing the old with the new, both the traditional lenses – the transboundary, the reactive, the sectoral, the prohibition-oriented, and the problem-oriented lenses – and the innovative ones – the global, the preventive, the comprehensive, the management-oriented, and the resource-oriented lenses – were being used in parallel at the time of the Stockholm+50 Conference. This is quite often justified: it is not always necessary to replace the old with the new; a valid option can be to retain the old and improve it. For example, with respect to the international waste trade, control and prohibition are still needed despite the move towards environmentally sound management principles. The different lenses are interconnected and build on each other: a reactive approach is linked to a sectoral and problem-by-problem approach, while a global approach is linked to a comprehensive and preventive approach. The emergence of the concepts of a green economy and a circular economy supports the use of the innovative lenses and sets them into a broader context.

The addition of innovative lenses to the traditional ones between 1972 and 2022 has broadened the policy approach to chemicals and waste management. The new perspectives have led to the regulation of aspects not addressed at the time of the Stockholm Conference, thus filling some of the gaps in the international regulatory framework. However, due to the continued predominance of the problem-by-problem approach, the fundamental problem has not been solved: we still have a set of legal and policy instruments that collectively address only parts of the management cycle of chemicals and wastes. SDG Target 12.4, the environmentally sound management of chemicals and wastes throughout their life cycle by 2020, has not been met.[67] The ultimate objective and challenge remains the creation of an international regulatory system that is capable of integrating the existing pieces in a way that provides the comprehensive regulation of chemicals and waste management in line with the circular economy.

65 European Commission, *A New Circular Economy Action Plan for a Cleaner and More Competitive Europe*, Doc. COM/2020/98 final, 11 March 2020.

66 *Transforming Our World*, n. 23.

67 As acknowledged by UNEA Resolution 5/7 on the Sound Management of Chemicals and Wastes, Doc. UNEP/EA.5/Res.7, 7 March 2022, para. 1.

9.5.1 *A Framework Treaty on Sustainable Substances and Materials Management*

One way of achieving a comprehensive regime would be the development of a global framework convention on substances and materials management, which could build on and complement the existing instruments on chemicals and wastes. As is typical of framework treaties, it could set out fundamental principles while leaving detail regulation to specialized treaties. Accordingly, it could determine commonly agreed environmental management principles for potentially hazardous substances and materials in line with the circular economy and set out baseline provisions on each stage of the life cycle of substances and materials, including production, use, transportation, storage, reuse, recovery, and disposal, and could mandate the phase-out of those materials the dangers of which significantly outweigh the benefits. It could also establish an overarching institutional framework and streamlined procedures, which could integrate those of the existing treaties, as well as a financial mechanism or strategy. The existing chemicals and waste treaties that deal with specific substances and specific aspects of their management could operate in its framework, and additional protocols could be adopted to address in more detail individual substances or operations. This would be an important move away from the fragmented system produced by the use of the problem-by-problem lens. It would also ensure institutional and procedural economy and provide flexibility, as states could adhere to the framework treaty and to individual protocols in accordance with their individual national priorities and positions.

This approach could build an overarching treaty system with a core treaty, legally independent but substantively related treaties, and protocols, similar to the Antarctic Treaty System. The objective of the framework treaty could be defined as protecting human health and the environment from the adverse effects of potentially hazardous substances and materials while ensuring sustainable management throughout their life cycle of those that have recognized benefits for human activity. It could build on the widely supported concepts and principles incorporated in the existing treaties and soft law instruments on chemicals and waste management and thus broaden their scope of application. The framework treaty could feature a general definition of 'potentially hazardous substance or material' and criteria to distinguish the hazardous from the non-hazardous and wastes from non-wastes. By broadening the scope from 'chemicals and wastes' to 'substances and materials', the framework treaty could also encompass things that are not considered either a chemical or a waste, such as used electronics. In order to reflect a circular economy approach, its structure could roughly follow that of the Minamata Convention.[68]

9.5.2 *Introduction of New Concepts through Soft Law*

Given the magnitude of the task, the negotiation of a framework treaty as described above is unlikely to obtain the necessary political support in the foreseeable future. Indeed, a similar proposal was discussed by the Governing Council of UNEP in 1999, but it failed to obtain agreement.[69] As an alternative, an attempt could be made to improve the existing international chemicals and waste management system, introducing the innovative lenses set out above and using the circular economy as a reference framework. One option could be the development of a non-binding framework that would enhance and support the current sectoral treaties, as was intended by the negotiators of the SAICM. This framework could redefine the current area of 'chemicals and wastes' as 'sustainable substances and materials management' and set out the key elements proposed for the framework agreement.

Another option, which might be considered in parallel with a non-binding framework, could be the introduction of these new approaches into the existing chemicals and waste treaties. Rather than through formal amendments that entail the lengthy and cumbersome process of negotiation, adoption, and ratification, this might in some cases be more easily achieved through informal instruments such as guidelines, action programmes, partnerships, strategic frameworks, and work programmes adopted through conference decisions, declarations, and resolutions. In fact, changes in focus of environmental treaties throughout their lifetime often do take place not through amendment but, rather, through decisions adopted by their conferences of the parties. Such an approach would be feasible to the extent that any changes remain within the defined scope of the treaty, and that they do not require formal amendment. As is already being done under the synergies process of the Basel, Rotterdam, and Stockholm Conventions, this approach could include the adoption of joint work programs and joint implementation activities.

The change in focus of the Basel Convention described in subsections 9.3.5 and 9.3.6 has taken place through the type of informal instruments that are proposed above. A further move in the direction of contributing to a circular

68 Kummer Peiry, n. 6 (who elaborates on this proposal).
69 Perrez, n. 29; Kummer, n. 36.

economy could be to strengthen the Convention's capacity to prevent undesirable operations (the shipment of wastes to countries that are not equipped to handle them) while allowing desirable ones (the shipment of wastes for the purpose of extraction of valuable resources – for example, rare earth metals – in specialized facilities). This could be done by reforming the prior informed consent procedure to generally make it less cumbersome and to provide different levels of control in accordance with the level of hazardousness of the material. In addition, the current distinction between developed countries to which hazardous wastes may be shipped and developing countries to which shipment is prohibited might be replaced with detailed criteria for countries to receive shipments of specific types of wastes – for example, a requirement that the material be treated in a facility certified to an internationally recognized standard. Similar shifts in focus could be initiated for the chemical treaties.

9.5.3 *Practical Issues*

Some practical considerations are in my view crucial if significant progress is to be achieved regarding how international environmental law addresses chemicals and waste management. First, the negotiation techniques, patterns, and constellations used in UN bodies when developing any type of international legal instrument – treaty and soft law alike – have not evolved since the Stockholm Conference. The approach commonly used does not feature real problem-solving methods but mostly consists of lengthy series of statements in a plenary setting, similar proceedings in smaller working groups, and negotiations behind the scenes. The imperative of consensus in environmental negotiations often leads to a 'lowest common denominator' approach and enables small groups of states (or even individual states if they are powerful enough) to block agreement. This is perfectly illustrated by the collapse of the negotiations on a plastics agreement: A group of fossil fuel producing states vehemently opposed the inclusion of plastic production in the treaty's scope as determined by the negotiating mandate, which would have rendered the treaty worthless in the view of the majority.

In the world outside the United Nations, modern negotiation techniques have been developed and are being used to have large groups of people look at a problem and arrive at solutions that are acceptable to all. Examples include the World Café and Open Space methods.[70] The use of such techniques

[70] For an overview, see 'World Café Method'. *World Café*, https://theworldcafe.com/key-concepts-resources/world-cafe-method/; 'What Is Open Space Technology'. *Open Space World*, https://openspaceworld.org/wp2/what-is/.

could significantly contribute to progress in the directions outlined above. In my experience, however, this is a change that will be extremely difficult to achieve. As the traditional UN negotiation rules are firmly established and strongly adhered to, considerable resistance to any change must be expected.

Second, mechanisms for consulting specialists or specialist bodies familiar with the practical aspects of the management of specific substances should be used so as to ensure that an approach envisaged by government negotiators is feasible in practice. Third, any negotiation process depends on funding, which is usually to a large extent extra-budgetary. In practice, it is often the same small group of industrialized countries that provide the funds. If an issue is not of sufficient interest to any of this group of donors, the negotiation will not take place. In order to ensure a more sustainable approach, it would be important to develop and use appropriate funding mechanisms.

9.6 CONCLUSIONS

While the *Trail Smelter* case in 1941 represented a milestone for addressing the negative effects of chemicals long before the birth of international environmental law – arguably, making chemicals the very first environmental issue to come to international attention – it was not until the 1972 Stockholm Conference that an international regime for chemicals and waste management began to emerge. This regime was shaped by the Stockholm Conference and its successor conferences as well as by non-binding policy instruments and treaties. It was influenced by the changing lenses through which chemicals and waste management was viewed over five decades. These shifts were reinforced by the emergence of new concepts – in particular, the circular economy. However, despite significant progress, the existing international regime for chemicals and waste management remains a piecemeal affair. In order to regulate all stages of the management cycle of potentially hazardous substances and materials in accordance with a circular economy, the existing sectoral legal instruments should be embedded in an overarching management regime, either through a framework treaty complemented with protocols on management aspects not yet addressed or through a soft law regime offering guidance on the management of the substances throughout their life cycle. If there is to be a real chance of this materializing, the outdated negotiating techniques and patterns used in the UN system would need to be replaced with the modern solution-oriented negotiation techniques developed in the decades since Stockholm. Given the tradition-oriented mindset prevalent in the world of international diplomacy, I would however expect a shift in this direction to require at least another fifty years.

10

The Unfinished Agenda of Stockholm 1972: A Rights-Based Approach to Chemicals and Wastes

Marcos A. Orellana

10.1 INTRODUCTION

In 1972, at the Stockholm Conference on the Human Environment (Stockholm Conference), states and interested stakeholders came together to steer a new era of international environmental law. The Stockholm Conference catalysed the creation of a myriad of instruments for environmental protection, including on the management of chemicals and wastes. Yet half a century after the Stockholm Conference, the impacts of hazardous substances and wastes on people and the environment have grown in scale and intensity. Scientific evidence reveals how humanity is exceeding the planetary boundary for chemical pollution.[1]

One of the lasting legacies of the 1972 Stockholm Conference is its acknowledgement of the inextricable link between environmental protection and human rights. However, multilateral environmental agreements (MEAs) on chemicals and wastes centre on minimizing adverse effects through regulating toxic and hazardous substances, and they lack an explicit inclusion of a human rights-based approach. This design feature limits the effectiveness of these instruments. While these environmental harms would be even more dire without MEAs in the chemicals and waste field, these instruments have been unable to reverse the toxification of the planet.

A human-rights based approach to MEAs is indispensable to effectively address the deleterious impacts of toxics on human rights and the environment. International environmental law needs to change course and embrace a human-rights based approach.[2] It can no longer continue to

[1] Lina Persson *et al.*, 'Outside the Safe Operating Space of the Planetary Boundary for Novel Entities' (2022) 56 *Environmental Science and Technology* 1510.

[2] Elisa Morgera, 'The Progressive Development of International Biodiversity Law from the 1972 Stockholm Conference to the Synergistic Protection of Biodiversity and Human Rights, including at the Ocean-Climate Nexus', in this volume, 451.

focus on simply attempting to minimize harm since that technique is leading to, and even legalizing, the gradual destruction of the planet. Rather, international environmental instruments and practice need to be inspired by, and give effect to, the right to a clean, healthy, and sustainable environment, whose roots and inception can be traced to the Stockholm Conference.

10.2 THE 1972 STOCKHOLM CONFERENCE

The Stockholm Conference was the first global conference to focus on transnational environmental issues, including pollution and sustainability. For the first time, humanity's damage to the environment garnered international attention and brought stakeholders together to consider concrete solutions.

The formulation of the Stockholm Conference resulted from a Swedish government proposal, transmitted to the UN secretary-general in 1968, for the General Assembly of the United Nations to convene 'an international conference on the problems of the human environment'.[3] When Sweden recommended the convening of a conference in 1968, it requested urgent attention for the changes that modern agriculture and industry had made to the environment and human health.[4] Pollution, chemicals, and wastes were key issues. Sweden specifically stated that 'problems such as air and water pollution, erosion, and/or depletion of the soil, excessive and uncontrollable use of biocides, problems of waste … and the disturbance of ecological balance' deserved international attention.[5]

In 1968, the General Assembly, in its resolution 2398 (XXIII), decided 'to convene in 1972 a United Nations Conference on the Human Environment'.[6] The General Assembly noted, 'the continuing and accelerating impairment of the quality of the human environment caused by such factors as air and water pollution, erosion and other forms of soil deterioration, waste, noise and the secondary effects of biocides', and expressed concern about 'the consequent effects on the condition of man, his physical, mental and social well-being, his

3 UN Economic and Social Council, *The Question of Convening an International Conference on the Problems of Human Environment: Letter dated 68/05/20 from the Permanent Representative of Sweden Addressed to the Secretary-General of the United Nations*, Doc. E4466Add.1, 22 May 1968.

4 *Ibid.*

5 *Ibid.*

6 UNGA Resolution 2398 (XXIII), 03 December 1968, 2.

dignity and his *enjoyment of basic human rights*, in developing as well as developed countries' (Emphasis added).

The Stockholm Conference's success can be credited to extensive and detailed preparation. Most concepts were agreed to prior to the conference's start.[7] The UN General Assembly entrusted the secretary-general with the responsibility of organizing and preparing the conference, and it established a Preparatory Committee composed of over two dozen government representatives to advise the secretary-general.[8] The Preparatory Committee set up an Intergovernmental Working Group to prepare a draft declaration on the human environment.

Human rights were not absent from the Stockholm Conference. Already in presenting its proposed draft declaration, the Intergovernmental Working Group's chairman acknowledged how human rights were integral to the construction of the draft: 'The draft prepared by the Group was based on the recognition of the rights of individuals to an adequate environment, the responsibility of States for damage to the environment of other States, or of areas beyond the limits of national jurisdiction resulting from activities within their own jurisdiction, and the particular interests of developing countries.'[9] Yet human rights were not the only narrative inspiring the conference. In preparation for the conference, various approaches and concepts were considered on how to handle environmental issues, including with regard to the exploitation of natural resources.

At odds were national sovereignty versus international regulation. Two delegations expressed concerns that the proposed Stockholm Declaration on the Human Environment should not dictate policies to sovereign states.[10] One delegation, supported by several others, confirmed states' right to sovereignty and proposed to extend that right to include the right of non-interference by other states on its environment. Other delegations strongly disapproved of this connection between territorial sovereignty and the right of a state to protect its environment.[11] The debate on development versus the environment also played an outsized role.[12] Delegations generally agreed that

7 Louis B. Sohn, 'The Stockholm Declaration on the Human Environment' (1973) 14 *Harvard International Law Journal* 423, 424.

8 UNGA Resolution 2581 (XXIV), 15 December 1969, 44.

9 Sohn, n. 8, citing *Report of the Preparatory Committee for the United Nations Conference on the Human Environment*, UN Doc. A/CONF.48/PC/17, 1972, para. 77.

10 UN General Assembly, *Preparatory Committee for the United Nations Conference on the Human Environment: Report of the Intergovernmental Working Group on the Declaration on the Human Environment*, UN Doc. A/CONF.48/PC.12, 14 June 1972.

11 *Ibid.*, paras. 58–64.

12 *Report of a Panel of Experts Convened by the Secretary-General of the United Nations Conference on the Human Environment (Founex, Switzerland, 4–12 June 1971)*, UN Doc. A/CONF.48/10, 22 December 1971.

environmental protections should not become an obstacle to development.[13] Still, many delegations were concerned that developing nations should first bridge the gap in poverty, malnutrition, and illiteracy while incorporating environmental regulations to prevent environmental harms during development. Another major theme regarding development was the management of the exploitation of resources and how to prevent environmental harms.

By its end, the Stockholm Conference had produced several important outcomes that progressed international environmental law. The conference's report included the 1972 Stockholm Declaration on the Human Environment, an Action Plan for the Human Environment, and a Referral to Governments of Recommendations for Action at the National Level.[14] The conference also served as the impetus for the creation of the UNEP.[15] Other resolutions were also adopted on the designation of World Environment Day and the cessation of nuclear weapons testing.[16]

The Stockholm Conference has been key to the emergence of the human right to a clean, healthy, and sustainable environment. It has helped catalyse what is known as the 'Environmental Rights Revolution' in which states began adopting laws and establishing institutions to protect the environment or including environmental protections in the formulation of state constitutions.[17] Today, over one hundred states include an explicit protection of the right to a healthy environment in their constitutions or domestic legislation.[18]

In this process, the 1972 Stockholm Declaration on the Human Environment has played a very important role.[19] The Declaration is a set of principles on international environmental norms, policy goals, and objectives. It sets out a normative vocabulary for the emerging international dialogue on

[13] *Report of the UN Conference on the Human Environment*, UN Doc. A/CONF.48/14/Rev.1, 16 June 1972, paras. 44–50.

[14] 'Declaration of the United Nations Conference on the Human Environment', in *Report of the UN Conference on the Human Environment*, n. 12 (Stockholm Declaration); 'Action Plan for the Human Environment', in *Report of the United Nations Conference on the Human Environment*, n. 13 (Stockholm Action Plan).

[15] UNGA Resolution 2997 (XXVII), 15 December 1972, 43.

[16] Stockholm Declaration, n. 14, 29–31.

[17] See David R. Boyd, *The Environmental Rights Revolution: A Global Study of Constitutions, Human Rights, and the Environment* (UBC Press, 2012), 12.

[18] See Human Rights Council, *Right to a Healthy Environment: Good Practices, Report of the Special Rapporteur on the Issue of Human Rights Obligations Relating to the Enjoyment of a Safe, Clean, Healthy and Sustainable Environment*, 30 December 2019, UN doc. A/HRC/43/53, Annex II.

[19] Stockholm Declaration, n. 14.

environmental sustainability. Perhaps the most progressive insight of the Stockholm Conference and Declaration was the inclusion of human rights into its principles. The Declaration proclaims that 'both aspects of man's environment, the natural and the man-made, are essential to his well-being and to the enjoyment of basic human rights – even the right to life itself'. Principle 1 uses explicit human rights language, asserting that 'man has the fundamental right to freedom, equality, and adequate conditions of life, in an environment of a quality that permits a life of dignity and well-being, and he bears solemn responsibility to protect and improve the environment for present and future generations'.

Concerning chemicals and waste, Principles 6 and 7 acknowledge the detriment of pollution on human health and state obligations to prevent and protect people from these harms. Principle 6 asserts that the discharge of toxic and other pollution that might inflict serious or irreversible damage upon ecosystems must be halted. Principle 7 also requires states to 'take all possible steps to prevent pollution of the seas by substances that are liable to create hazards to human health, to harm living resources and marine life, to damage amenities or to interfere with other legitimate uses of the sea'. While the Stockholm Declaration established a connection between human rights and the environment, the recommendations in the Stockholm Action Plan translated this vision through the lens of planning and management, albeit without an explicit human rights focus.[20] In regard to chemicals and wastes, many of the relevant recommendations are framed under the 'identification and control of pollutants of broad international significance'. Recommendation 71 is illustrative of the management approach. It advises that governments 'use the best practicable means available to minimize the release to the environment of toxic or dangerous substances, especially if they are persistent substances'.

Similarly, recommendation 22 emphasizes 'control and recycling of wastes in agriculture, such as from crop residues and animal wastes, agro-industrial waste, and waste from fertilizers'.[21] With respect to waste in oceans, recommendation 48 advises governments and the UN Food and Agriculture Organization (FAO) to take action to control and regulate the 'discharge of toxic chemicals, heavy metals, and other wastes [that] may affect even high-seas resources'.[22] Issues of management and control in the Action Plan also

20 The Stockholm Action Plan's framework separated the recommendations into three broad types of actions: '(a) the global environmental assessment programme (Earthwatch); (b) Environmental management activities; (c) International measures to support the national and international actions of assessment and management'. Stockholm Action Plan, n. 14, 6–28.

21 Stockholm Declaration, n. 14.

22 *Ibid.*

relate to issues concerning environmental standards. In this regard, the differentiation of environmental standards according to levels of development also received prominent attention, and Principle 23 calls for the consideration of the extent of the 'applicablity of standards which are valid for the most advanced countries but which may be inappropriate and of unwarranted social cost for the developing countries.'[23] Still today, industrialized countries often export to developing countries hazardous and toxic substances banned for use in their own territories, externalizing the detrimental human rights and environmental impact of these toxics.[24]

To sum up, from its inception, the 1972 Stockholm Conference envisaged the relevance of a human rights-based approach to international environmental law. The General Assembly, in convening the 1972 Stockholm Conference, explicitly referred to human rights when expressing concern about the effects of the impairment of the quality of the human environment. The preparation and debates demonstrated that human rights were a considered, deliberate part of the conference's approach to the human environment and addressing environmental harms. The Stockholm Declaration highlighted human rights in its very first preambular paragraph and in its Principle 1. Yet it is also clear that the human rights approach did not serve as the central tenant of the conference or the main approach taken to chemicals and waste in the decades that followed. Instead, control and management for the minimization of adverse effects of these toxic and hazardous substances became the policy priority.

10.3 EMERGENCE OF CHEMICALS AND WASTE INSTRUMENTS

Flowing from the Stockholm Conference and its resulting Stockholm Declaration were international legal instruments that address a range of environmental issues. Through the decades after the conference, over eleven hundred binding and non-binding international legal instruments appeared concerning the environment or included environmental provisions.[25] In the chemicals and waste cluster, agreements came about ad hoc to address more narrow chemicals and waste management issues. Over the next several decades, the 1989 Basel, 1998 Rotterdam, 2001 Stockholm, and 2013 Minamata

[23] *Ibid.*, 3–5.

[24] See, e.g., *Mandate of the Special Rapporteur on the Implications for Human Rights of the Environmentally Sound Management and Disposal of Hazardous Substances and Wastes*, Doc. OL OTH 203/201, 21 June 2021.

[25] Edith Brown Weiss, 'The Evolution of International Environmental Law' (2011) 54 *Japanese Yearbook of International Law* 1, 6.

Conventions were negotiated, along with non-binding instruments such as the Strategic Approach to International Chemicals Management (SAICM) and the International Code of Conduct on Pesticide Management.[26] These documents address policies and practices such as the transboundary movement of waste and prior informed consent and target specific dangerous chemicals and wastes that affect human health and the environment. These instruments share a common objective to protect human health and the environment. However, they do not integrate an explicit human rights approach into their texts or implementations.

10.3.1 *Basel Convention*

The international community rallied around the creation of the 1989 Basel Convention after several disasters revealed that industrialized nations sent their hazardous waste to developing countries.[27] As a result, many viewed the international treaty as a contribution to environmental justice by addressing the disproportionate harms of 'toxic colonialism' in which developed countries and businesses sent waste abroad to drive profits and reduce their burden.[28] The Basel Convention's preamble provides a bridge to the rights to health and a clean, healthy, and sustainable environment. It recognizes the damage to human health and the environment caused by hazardous wastes and affirms state responsibility 'for the fulfilment of their international obligations concerning the protection of human health and protection and preservation of the environment'. The Basel Convention applies to materials it defines as 'hazardous wastes' and certain types of 'other wastes' and focuses on controlling the export and import of these materials through a prior informed consent procedure. It also features several general obligations

26 Basel Convention on the Control of Transboundary Movements of Hazardous and Their Disposal, 1989, 1673 UNTS 126 (Basel Convention); Convention on the Prior Informed Consent Procedure for Certain Hazardous Chemicals and Pesticides in International Trade, 1998, 2244 UNTS 337 (Rotterdam Convention); Stockholm Convention on Persistent Organic Pollutants 2001, 2256 UNTS 119; Minamata Convention on Mercury, 2013, 3202 UNTS 220; Strategic Approach to International Chemicals Management, reprinted in *Report of the International Conference on Chemicals Management on the Work of Its First Session*, Doc. SAICM/ICCM.1/7, 2006; World Health Organization (WHO) & Food and Agriculture Organization (FAO), *International Code of Conduct on Pesticide Management* (WHO & FAO, 2014).

27 Basel Convention, n. 26.

28 Christina A. Lucier & Brian J. Gareau, 'Obstacles to Preserving Precaution and Equity in Global Hazardous Waste Regulation: An Analysis of Contested Knowledge in the Basel Convention' (2016) 16 *International Environmental Agreements* 493, 496.

related to the minimization and environmentally sound management of wastes.

Yet the Basel Convention's adoption met criticism and pushback from developing countries and environmental groups because the final text did not include an export ban, except to Antarctica.[29] The African group of countries even negotiated a regional treaty – the 1991 Bamako Convention, to prevent the import of hazardous waste into the African continent.[30] Continued pressure from developing nations and civil society for a global ban led to the second Conference of the Parties to adopt a decision in 1994 prohibiting hazardous waste exports from developed countries to developing countries.[31] At the time, Australia, Canada, Japan, New Zealand, South Korea, and the United States pushed back hard against this decision.[32]

Against this backdrop, the Conference of the Parties adopted an amendment to the Basel Convention in 1995 prohibiting the transboundary movement of hazardous waste from member states of the European Union, the Organisation for Economic Co-operation and Development, and Liechtenstein to all other countries.[33] After nearly two-and-a-half decades, in December 2019, the Basel Ban Amendment entered into force, when enough states parties had ratified it.[34] The ban aims to reduce the toxic contamination that affects human health and the environment in developing nations, better protecting the rights to life and health of the most vulnerable populations. Yet gaps in the Basel Convention remain. Priority waste streams under the Convention, such as plastic and electronic waste, have motivated amendments that clarify and expand the Convention's regulation of these wastes.[35] However, the Convention also allows an exception for electrical

29 Cyril Uchenna, *Toxic Waste and Human Rights* (Authorhouse, 2010).

30 Convention on the Ban of the Import into Africa and the Control of Transboundary Movement and Management of Hazardous Wastes within Africa, 1991, 2102 UNTS 177; Basel Action Network (BAN) & International Pollutants Elimination Network (IPEN), *The Entry into Force of the Basel Ban Amendment: A Guide to Implications and Next Steps*, 2020, 17.

31 UNEP, *Report of the Second Meeting of the Conference of the Parties to the Basel Convention on the Control of Transboundary Movements of Hazardous Wastes and Their Disposal Decision II/12*, UN Doc. UNEP/CHW.2/30, 1994.

32 BAN & IPEN, *supra* n. 30, at 17.

33 UNEP, *Decision III/1 Adopted by the Third Meeting of the Conference of the Parties to the Basel Convention*, UN Doc. UNEP/CHW.3/35, 1995, 5 December 2019.

34 *Ibid.*

35 UNEP, *Report of the Conference of the Parties to the Basel Convention on the Control of Transboundary Movements of Hazardous Wastes and Their Disposal*, UN Doc. UNEP/CHW.14/28, 2019, 58–63; 'Basel Convention E-Waste Amendments', *Basel Convention*, www.basel.int/Implementation/Ewaste/EwasteAmendments/Overview/tabid/9266/Default.aspx.

and electronic equipment to be exported for reuse. Furthermore, it lacks clarity on what is e-waste and what will truly be exported for reuse. Many argue that there is no effective sanction or enforcement mechanism in cases of non-compliance.[36]

In 2022, the Conference of the Parties adopted amendments to the Basel Convention's Annexes to bring all e-waste under the prior informed consent (PIC) procedure. This will require states to consent to the import of e-waste.[37] However, since most e-waste shipments are nominally for reuse, the amendments may not suffice to prevent human rights or environmental harms.

10.3.2 *Rotterdam Convention*

In the 1980s, there were growing concerns about the inadequate infrastructure for monitoring imports and exports of hazardous chemicals and pesticides. UNEP and the FAO led a process to create voluntary information exchange programmes.[38] The FAO developed the International Code on the Distribution and Use of Pesticides, and UNEP created the London Guidelines for the Exchange of Information on Chemicals in International Trade. Calls for a binding agreement resulted in the 1998 Rotterdam Convention by which the parties hoped to instil shared responsibility over particularly damaging chemicals.[39] The Rotterdam Convention incorporated elements used in the Basel Convention, particularly the PIC procedure. States must receive the prior informed consent of importing states before exporting chemicals or pesticides listed in the agreement. Given the various exceptions and limitations of the Rotterdam's Convention PIC procedure, however, it has been questioned whether it can be called a 'consent requirement'.[40] Also, rather than addressing specific management or regulatory requirements for these substances, the Rotterdam Convention lays out specific reporting mechanisms for import and export.

The Rotterdam Convention is largely outdated in its approach and lacks explicit human rights language and approaches. The right to information is treated as a right of states in this instrument, but it is also an essential human

36 Gulzharzira Ilyassova *et al.*, 'Prospects of Legal Regulation in the Field of Electronic Waste Management in the Context of a Circular Economy' (2020) 21 *International Environmental Agreements* 367, 371–374.

37 'Basel Convention E-Waste Amendments', n. 35.

38 'History of the Negotiations of the Rotterdam Convention', *Rotterdam Convention*, www.pic.int/TheConvention/Overview/History/Overview/tabid/1360/language/en-US/Default.aspx.

39 Rotterdam Convention, n. 26; European Commission, *Assessment for the Continued Effectiveness of the Rotterdam Convention*, Doc. Env/07.0201/512.723161/ETU/A.3, 2017, 3.

40 See David Langlet, *Prior Informed Consent and Hazardous Trade* (Kluwer, 2009), 145–148.

right of individuals and communities that may be affected by the import of toxics. The right to information in this context should encompass access to information on what is being imported, to what regions of the state, and the potential effects of those imports. The PIC procedure has also not kept up with other normative developments, such as the 2006 UN Declaration on the Rights of Indigenous Peoples.[41] This Declaration recognizes the right of Indigenous peoples to free prior and informed consent of activities on or affecting their land. The PIC procedure has yet to adapt to this human rights requirement or provide guidance or policies on requesting free prior and informed consent from Indigenous peoples that may be affected by imports of toxic and hazardous substances.[42]

Additionally, the need for effective translation of scientific evidence into adequate protections is an integral element of the human right to science.[43] In this regard, while the Rotterdam Convention has a platform for the interface between science and policy – that is, the Chemical Review Committee – the Conference of the Parties to the Rotterdam Convention has failed to act on its recommendations to list certain hazardous substances, such as asbestos and paraquat.[44] This gap between science and policy results in limited coverage of chemicals under the Convention, which limits its effectiveness and undermines the right to science.[45]

10.3.3 *Stockholm Convention*

The Stockholm Convention was adopted in 2001 to eliminate/restrict the production and use of persistent organic pollutants (POPs). The Convention served as the international community's response to public concerns in the 1990s about the serious risks posed by POPs. POPs can bioaccumulate, travel up the food chain, and spread across great distances. With the discovery of POPs in the territories of the Arctic Indigenous peoples, debates centred on

41 UN Declaration on the Rights of Indigenous Peoples, UN Doc. A/61/49, 13 September 2007.

42 See Victor A. Lopez-Carmen *et al.*, 'United States and United Nations Pesticide Policies: Environmental Violence against the Yaqui Indigenous Nation' (2022) 10 *Lancet Regional Health – Americas* 1, 10.

43 On the right to science, see section 10.4.4 in this chapter.

44 UN Human Rights Council (UNHRC), *Right to Science in the Context of Toxic Substances: Report of the Special Rapporteur on the Implications for Human Rights of the Environmentally Sound Management and Disposal of Hazardous Substances and Wastes*, UN Doc. A/HRC/48/61, 26 July 2021, para. 71.

45 See 'Promoting the Effectiveness of the Rotterdam Convention: Ways Forward and Procedural Implications', *Center for International Environmental Law*, 2017, www.ciel.org/wp-content/uploads/2017/11/RCEffectiveness_legal-implication-analysis_Final.pdf.

the need for protections of human health and environment.[46] The Stockholm Convention articulates the connection between human rights and the environment in its preamble:

> *Aware of* the health concerns, especially in developing countries, resulting from local exposure to persistent organic pollutants, in particular impacts upon women and, through them, upon future generations,
>
> *Acknowledging* that the Arctic ecosystems and indigenous communities are particularly at risk because of the biomagnification of persistent organic pollutants and that contamination of their traditional foods is a public health issue.

The Stockholm Convention, like the Basel and Rotterdam Conventions, did not incorporate more specific or explicit elements of human rights into its text. It focuses on the management of POPs and does not fully secure rights to information, participation, and remedies to affected individuals and communities.

In recent years, the Basel, Rotterdam, and Stockholm Conventions have enhanced cooperation between them and their respective governance mechanisms. These synergies have resulted, inter alia, in an implementation programme on gender.[47] But other groups that may be in vulnerable situations – such as children or Indigenous peoples – lack the same specific focus.

10.3.4 *Strategic Approach to International Chemicals Management*

In 2006, the first International Conference on Chemicals Management (ICCM-1), which was convened under the auspices of UNEP and hosted by the United Arab Emirates, debated how to achieve the goal articulated at the World Summit on Sustainable Development: the sound management of chemicals by 2020.[48] ICCM-1 adopted the non-binding SAICM, including several documents as annexes: the 2006 Dubai Declaration on International Chemicals Management, the 2006 Overarching Policy Strategy, and the 2006 Global Plan of Action.[49] The priority was to ensure that by 2020 states would

46 Pia M. Kohler, *Science Advice and Global Environmental Governance: Expert Institutions and the Implementation of International Environmental Treaties* (Anthem Press, 2020), 74.

47 'Gender: Overview', *Basel/Rotterdam/Stockholm Conventions*, www.brsmeas.org/Implementation/Gender/Overview/tabid/3651/language/en-US/Default.aspx.

48 See United Nations, *Report of the World Summit on Sustainable Development, Johannesburg, South Africa, 26 August–4 September 2002*, UN Doc. A/CONF.199/20, 4–26 August 2002, 119–134.

49 International Conference on Chemicals Management, Dubai Declaration on International Chemicals Management, 6 February 2006; International Conference on Chemicals Management Overarching Policy Strategy, February 2006; International Conference on Chemicals Management, Global Plan of Action of the Strategic Approach, 2006.

no longer produce or use chemicals that pose unreasonable or unmanageable risk to human health and the environment and minimize the unintended release of these chemicals.[50]

Following ICCM-1, there was an acknowledgement of the intricate connection between toxics and human rights. The Dubai Declaration specifically included a commitment to 'respecting human rights and fundamental freedoms'.[51] The Dubai Declaration includes a pledge to 'facilitate public access to appropriate information and knowledge on chemicals throughout their life cycle, including the risks that they pose to human health and the environment'. The document infuses commitments to alleviate poverty, prevent disproportionate effects on vulnerable populations and developing countries, and protect human health and the environment. The Overarching Policy Strategy recognized that local populations lack access to clear, timely information and that there was a need to improve risk reduction for groups in particularly vulnerable situations such as children, pregnant women, and the elderly. The Strategy also includes an objective to promote meaningful participation for civil society in decision-making on chemical safety, specifically women, workers, and Indigenous peoples.

The SAICM's attempt and effort to meet the global goal of achieving the sound management of chemicals by 2020, as set out at the 2002 World Summit on Sustainable Development in Johannesburg, did not come to fruition.[52] While progress was made in many areas, implementation and regulations failed to grasp the volume and hazards of the chemicals used globally, focusing on managing a narrow set of chemicals and substances while the global industry grew at a fast pace.[53]

In 2023, the fifth session of the International Conference on Chemicals Management (ICCM-5), organized by UNEP and hosted by Germany, faced the challenge of crafting a post-2020 framework for the management of chemicals and waste. During the preparatory works of this conference, several voices proposed a high-level declaration to build on the promises of the Dubai Declaration and strengthen a human rights-based approach centred on participation, transparency, accountability, and protection of populations at risk.[54] In

[50] International Conference on Chemicals Management, *Report of the International Conference on Chemicals Management on the Work of Its First Session*, Doc. SAICM/ICCM.1/7, 4–6 February 2006, 19.

[51] *Ibid.*, 13–15.

[52] UN Environment Programme (UNEP), *Global Chemicals Outlook II: From Legacies to Innovative Solutions: Implementing the 2030 Agenda for Sustainable Development* (UNEP, 2019), vi–vii.

[53] *Ibid.*

[54] 'Comments by the Special Rapporteur on Toxics and Human Rights ICCM-5 and Its High-Level Declaration', *OHCHR*, www.ohchr.org/sites/default/files/SR_toxics_letter_ICCM5_F

the end, ICCM-5 adopted the 2023 Bonn Declaration, which recalls the UN General Assembly's resolution that recognizes the right to a clean, healthy, and sustainable environment.[55] ICCM-5 also adopted the 2023 Global Framework for Chemicals.[56] The Bonn Declaration serves a critical role in setting the vision for the Global Framework for Chemicals, and this vision in turn may be key to injecting a human-rights based approach in the implementation of the framework.

10.3.5 *Minamata Convention*

The Minamata Convention regulates the use and trade of mercury globally. Mercury is highly toxic for people and the environment, requiring widespread regulation of a single substance. The preamble of the Minamata Convention takes note of 'the particular vulnerabilities of Arctic ecosystems and indigenous communities because of the biomagnification of mercury and contamination of traditional foods', and the Convention's parties are 'concerned about indigenous communities more generally with respect to the effects of mercury'. The Convention calls for the phase out of primary mercury mining; the reduction, and elimination where feasible, of mercury use in artisanal and small-scale gold mining; reduced mercury emissions to the atmosphere and release to land and water; the management of contaminated sites; and the protection of vulnerable populations from the exposure to mercury.

While the Minamata Convention is proving successful in certain phase-outs and control of emissions and releases, it has major gaps regarding mercury use. The increase in small-scale gold mining is particularly concerning. Such mining uses mercury to separate the gold from the ore. It is the largest emitter of mercury to the environment. By 2018, this method of extracting gold contributed to 37 per cent of all mercury emissions.[57] Yet mercury trade for, and use in, small-scale gold mining is allowed in the Minamata Convention,[58] with the exception of mercury from primary

EB_2021.pdf; see also 'Statement by UN Experts on the Fifth Session of the International Conference on Chemicals Management', *OHCHR*, 20 September 2023, www.ohchr.org/sites/default/files/documents/hrbodies/special-procedures/statements/20-sep-2023-ICCM5-SPs-full-Statement.pdf.

55 Bonn Declaration for a Planet Free of Harm from Chemicals and Waste, Resolution V/1, Annex I, Doc. SAICM/ICCM.5/4, 2023.

56 Global Framework for Chemicals for a Planet Free of Harm from Chemicals and Waste, Resolution V/1, Annex II, September 2023.

57 UNEP, *Global Mercury Assessment 2018* (2018), 15.

58 Minamata Convention, Article 2 (k).

mercury mining, which shall not be used in artisanal and small-scale gold mining.[59] Moreover, phasing out mercury use in small-scale gold mining poses unique challenges due to the informal or illegal character of the activity. The Convention also allows primary mercury mining to continue for up to fifteen years from its entry into force in 2017, despite the known severe consequences of mercury.

The allowance of mercury for use and export in small-scale gold mining suggests that gold profits are a priority over the major toll on human health and the proliferation of contaminated sites. People in vulnerable situations suffer disproportionate impacts. Such is the case for miners and their families that are exposed to mercury and the Indigenous peoples who rely on fish for subsistence lifestyles.[60] Under the Minamata Convention, parties with a significant amount of small-scale gold activity in their territory must submit a national action plan. The Convention's Conference of the Parties has updated its guidance on national action plans, calling on states to engage with Indigenous peoples and local communities in their elaboration. However, it has yet to elaborate on specific guidelines on how to do so.[61] The Conference of the Parties has also called on parties and other stakeholders to obtain free, prior, and informed consent from Indigenous peoples regarding artisanal and small-scale mining in their territories.[62]

10.3.6 *Preliminary Conclusions on Chemicals and Waste MEAs*

The cursory overview in the preceding subsections reveals certain key points:

- MEAs contain preambular language that refers to elements of a human rights-based approach, such as references to human health and the environment, future generations, and Indigenous peoples. But there is no explicit human rights language in the agreements.

59 *Ibid*, Article 3.4.

60 UNHRC, *Mercury, Small-Scale Gold Mining and Human Rights: Report of the Special Rapporteur on the Implications for Human Rights of the Environmentally Sound Management and Disposal of Hazardous Substances and Wastes*, UN Doc. A/HRC/51/35, 8 July 2022, paras. 55–65.

61 United Nations, *Conference of the Parties to the Minamata Convention on Mercury Fourth Meeting: Report of the Conference of the Parties to the Minamata Convention on Mercury on the Work of Its Fourth Meeting – In Person Segment*, UN Doc. UNEP/MC/COP.4/28/Add.1, 8 April 2022, 33.

62 'Conference of the Parties to the Minamata Convention on Mercury Fifth Meeting', *Earth Negotiations Bulletin*, 3 November 2023, https://enb.iisd.org/minamata-convention-mercury-cop5-summary.

- MEAs reflect a horizontal design of state-to-state relations and do not explicitly incorporate vertical or diagonal obligations regarding the rights of individuals, groups, or peoples.
- The agreements contain certain elements on information and participation, but these elements are not framed as enforceable human rights.
- The agreements are generally lacking in mechanisms for accountability and effective remedies for individuals and groups that may suffer harms from non-compliance or human rights violations resulting from exposure to hazardous substances.
- Science-policy interface platforms have been undermined by economic interests of states parties and private actors.

Against this background, it is useful to see what a human rights-based approach could look like for the MEAs in the chemicals and waste cluster.

10.4 A HUMAN RIGHTS-BASED APPROACH TO CHEMICALS AND WASTES

The agenda of the 1972 Stockholm Conference remains unfinished; its implementation is missing a human rights-based approach to chemicals and wastes. By contrast to an approach centred on managing risks and minimizing adverse effects, a human rights-based approach seeks to ensure the right of every person to live in a toxic-free environment. To this effect, the principles of prevention and accountability are paramount, alongside rights to science, information, and participation, among others. A human rights-based approach provides a clear framework of rights holders and duty bearers. States have a duty to prevent, address, and remedy exposure to toxic and hazardous substances. This includes implementing the rights to science, information, participation, and an effective remedy in the management of chemicals and wastes. States also have duties of protection where business activity may result in toxic pollution and infringe on the effective enjoyment of human rights. Where states fail on these duties and cause human rights violations, they should be held accountable. This section explores certain key elements of the human rights-based approach as it is applied to chemicals and wastes.

10.4.1 *Right to a Clean, Healthy, and Sustainable Environment*

After decades of discussion and normative developments, the UN General Assembly recognized the human right to a clean, healthy, and sustainable environment soon after the UN International Meeting Stockholm+50: A Healthy Planet for the Prosperity of All – Our Responsibility, Our Opportunity.[63,64] The UN Human Rights Council had recognized the right in 2021.[65] In 2025, the International Court of Justice, in its advisory opinion on Obligations of States in Respect of Climate Change, recognized the human right to a clean, healthy and sustainable environment under international law, noting that the right is 'inherent' and 'essential' for the enjoyment of other human rights.[66]

The right to a healthy environment can be described as an umbrella right that brings together the acquis of jurisprudence and doctrine on the human rights and environment linkage.[67] Its scope and content have been elaborated since the 1972 Stockholm Declaration. The right exhibits characteristics of civil, cultural, economic, political, and social rights, all of which have a bearing on its normative content. The right includes procedural elements, such as access to environmental information, public participation in decision-making and access to justice, as well as substantive elements, including clean air, safe climate, healthy and sustainably produced food, access to safe water and adequate sanitation, healthy ecosystems and biodiversity, and a non-toxic environment in which to work, live, and play.[68]

A major consequence of the failure to protect the right to a clean, healthy, and sustainable environment is the proliferation of sacrifice zones. These areas are heavily contaminated and polluted, and they cause severe human health and environmental harms.[69] Following the recognition of the right to a healthy environment at the global level is the challenge of implementation. Multilateral environmental agreements are a key tool in this regard.

63 See *Report of Stockholm+50: A Healthy Planet for the Prosperity of All – Our Responsibility, Our Opportunity*, UN Doc. A/CONF.238/9, 1 August 2022.

64 UNGA Resolution 76/300, 7 July 2022.

65 HRC Resolution 48/13, 18 October 2021.

66 ICJ Advisory Opinion, *Obligations of States in Respect of Climate Change*, 23 July 2025, para 393.

67 Marcos Orellana, 'Human Rights and International Environmental Law', in Erika Techera, Jade Lindley, Karen N. Scott, and Anastasia Telesetsky (eds.), *Routledge Handbook of International Environmental Law* (2nd ed., Routledge, 2020), 341, 342.

68 David R. Boyd, *Human Rights Obligations Relating to the Enjoyment of a Safe, Clean, Healthy, and Sustainable Environment*, UN Doc. A/74/161, 15 July 2019, para. 43.

69 See UNHRC, *The Right to a Clean, Healthy and Sustainable Environment: Non-Toxic Environment: Report of the Special Rapporteur on the Issue of Human Rights Obligations Relating to the Enjoyment of a Safe, Clean, Healthy and Sustainable Environment*, UN Doc. A/HRC/49/53, 12 January 2022, paras. 21–46.

10.4.2 *Right to Information*

The right to information on toxics is vital for understanding the risks and harms involved in chemicals and adopting adequate protections.[70] People have the right not to be exposed to substances that can affect their health and the environment. Information must be accessible without discrimination, functional, and culturally specific. This includes information on the effects of toxics on people that may be in particularly vulnerable situations, such as women, children, and workers.[71] The right to information is particularly important for Indigenous peoples, who have the right to offer or withhold their free, prior, and informed consent on activities on or affecting their lands and territories.[72] Consent hinges on access to all available information on toxic and hazardous substances and their potential adverse effects, including when the effects are unknown and potentially dangerous.[73]

States have a duty to generate, collect, assess, and update information; effectively disseminate information and identify and inform those at risk of disproportionate impacts; ensure confidentiality claims are legitimate; and engage in international cooperation to help make information available and accessible.[74] Businesses, in turn, must identify and assess adverse impacts and effectively communicate information. Protecting human rights requires chemical and waste MEAs to promote the right to information, including the responsibility of states to make information available. A good practice can be found in the 2003 Kyiv Protocol on Pollutant Release and Transfer Registers, which requires parties to collect and publish information on pollution from industrial facilities.[75]

70 UNHRC, *Right to a Healthy Environment: Good Practices: Report of the Special Rapporteur on the Issue of Human Rights Obligations Relating to the Enjoyment of a Safe, Clean, Healthy and Sustainable Environment*, UN Doc. A/HRC/43/53, 30 December 2019, paras. 14–21; see also UNHRC, *Report of the Special Rapporteur on the Implications for Human Rights of the Environmentally Sound Management and Disposal of Hazardous Substances and Wastes*, UN Doc. A/HRC/30/40, 8 July 2015.

71 UNHRC, *Right to a Healthy Environment*, n. 69, paras. 22–31; UNGA, *The Impact of Toxic Substances on the Human Rights of Indigenous Peoples*, UN Doc. A/77/183, 28 July 2022, para. 55.

72 Inter-American Commission on Human Rights, *Centre for Minority Rights Development (Kenya) and Minority Rights Group International on Behalf of Endorois Welfare Council v Kenya*, Case no. 276/2003, 2010, 77, para. 291; ACtHPR, *African Commission on Human and Peoples' Rights v Republic of Kenya*, Case no. 006/2012, 2017, 47, para. 144; IACtHR, *Saramaka People v Suriname*, Series C, no. 172, 28 November 2007, para. 129.

73 UNHRC, *Report of the Special Rapporteur*, n. 70, paras. 27–28.

74 *Ibid.*

75 Kyiv Protocol on Pollutant Release and Transfer Registers, Decision 2006/61/EC, 21 May 2003; UNHRC, *Right to Science in the Context of Toxic Substances: Report of the Special Rapporteur on the Implications for Human Rights of the Environmentally Sound Management and Disposal of Hazardous Substances and Wastes*, UN Doc. A/HRC/48/61, 26 July 2021, para. 44.

10.4.3 *Right to Participation*

Information is not enough to secure effective protections against the risks and harms of chemicals. The right to participation ensures that individuals and groups can use information on toxics to meaningfully engage in decision-making. This right also lies at the heart of sustainable development as a process of informed societal dialogue to confront environmental threats.[76] Yet language barriers, discrimination, and poor dissemination of information are some of the barriers preventing individuals and groups affected by toxics from participating in decision-making at the national and international levels. The right to participation requires equitable and non-discriminatory access to the meetings, decision-making, and compliance mechanisms of MEAs. States must provide access for rights holders to engage in the decision-making process.[77] In this regard, MEAs concerning chemicals and waste can integrate this principle by mirroring standards and good practices from international instruments regarding the implementation of environmental rights, such as the 2018 Escazú Agreement and the 1998 Aarhus Convention.[78]

10.4.4 *Right to Science*

The right to enjoy the benefits of scientific progress is recognized by several international and regional human rights instruments.[79] Essential to toxics policy is the alignment of policy to the best available science.[80] Effective science-policy interfaces are vital to turn science into concrete measures of protection for people and the environment at the domestic and international levels. Practice with science-policy interface mechanisms includes bringing in independent, credible, and recognized experts with diverse technical expertise; the review of

[76] See Antonio Augusto Cançado Trindade (ed.), *Human Rights, Sustainable Development and Environment* (Inter-American Institute of Human Rights and Inter-American Development Bank, 1995).

[77] See 'United Nations Sustainable Development Cooperation Framework – Internal Guidance', *UN Sustainable Development Group*, 3 June 2019, para. 18, https://unsdg.un.org/sites/default/files/2022-06/UN%20Cooperation%20Framework%20Internal%20Guidance%20–%201%20June%202022.pdf.

[78] See Regional Agreement on Access to Information, Public Participation and Justice in Environmental Matters in Latin America and the Caribbean, 2018, 3397 UNTS 195; Convention on Access to Information, Public Participation in Decision-making and Access to Justice in Environmental Matters, 1998, 2161 UNTS 447; see generally Emily Barritt, 'Global Values, Transnational Expression: From Aarhus to Escazú', *TLI Think!*, November 2019.

[79] UNHRC, *Report of the Special Rapporteur*, n. 75, paras. 31–48.

[80] *Ibid.*, paras. 51–60.

scientific evidence as it evolves to better protect human health and the environment against toxics; and the implementation of recommendations illuminated by the best available scientific evidence.[81] When gaps in knowledge or uncertainties exist, the precautionary principle will enable states to take measures to avoid potential harms to health and the environment.

The right to science includes the right to access scientific methodologies and findings on the harms and risks of exposure to toxic and hazardous substances. States and business often try to elude their responsibility for toxic contamination by spreading disinformation on the scientific evidence. Scientists are often targeted and harassed when they speak out on the harms of toxic and hazardous substances.[82]

In 2022, UN Environmental Assembly (UNEA) passed a resolution in support of the creation of a science-policy interface platform on chemicals, waste, and pollution.[83] After several years of work, in June 2025 UNEP convened an Intergovernmental Meeting that established a science-policy panel to contribute further to the sound management of chemicals and waste and to prevent pollution.[84] This panel may raise awareness of the toxification of our planet, complement similar mechanisms that exist in MEAs, assess the body of scientific evidence concerning chemicals and wastes, and raise early warnings on chemicals and waste issues of special concern. Effective safeguards against conflict of interest are essential for its legitimacy and credibility.

10.4.5 *Right to Remedy*

The right to effective remedy is codified in many international human rights instruments and is necessary for guaranteeing the full enjoyment of human rights.[85] States must investigate allegations, take appropriate actions, bring

81 *Ibid.*, paras. 67–73.
82 *Ibid.*, paras. 84–85.
83 UNEP Resolution 5/8, 7 March 2022.
84 Draft report of the intergovernmental meeting to establish a science-policy panel to contribute further to the sound management of chemicals and waste and to prevent pollution, 20 June 2025, UNEP/SPP-CWP/IM/L.1. See also, Draft Decision to establish the Panel, 19 June 2025, UNEP/SPP-CWP/IM/2. See generally, https://enb.iisd.org/oewg3-2-science-policy-panel-contribute-sound-management-chemicals-waste-prevent-pollution-summary
85 See Human Rights Council, *Report of the Special Rapporteur on the implications for human rights of the environmentally sound management and disposal of hazardous substances and wastes, Marcos Orellana, Guidelines on access to justice and effective remedies in the context of toxics*, A/HRC/60/34 (2025); Theo van Boven, 'Victims' Rights to a Remedy and Reparations: The New United Nations Principles and Guidelines', in Carla Ferstman and Mariana Goertz

justice to those responsible, and redress human rights violations. Reparations for violations can include restitution, compensation, rehabilitation, satisfaction, guarantees of non-repetition, including changes in relevant laws and practices, as well as bringing to justice the perpetrators of human rights violations.[86] Emphasis should be placed on the need for remedies to be effective for the specific violation or affected community and can include one or all forms of reparation.

The 2011 Guiding Principles on Business and Human Rights highlight the need for adequate remedies and grievance mechanisms to foster the participation of affected groups in the presentation of alleged violations.[87] States are recommended to take 'appropriate steps to prevent, investigate, punish and redress' business-related human rights abuses within their territory and/or jurisdiction.[88] Additionally, the Guiding Principles propose three types of mechanisms to provide access to an effective remedy in business-related human rights abuses: 'state-based judicial mechanisms, state-based non-judicial grievance mechanisms, and non-state-based grievance mechanisms'.[89] Generally, states can improve access to an effective remedy for toxics by removing barriers for the affected communities' standing to sue, statute of limitations, economic barriers, and lack of judicial expertise in environmental matters.[90]

10.4.6 *Principle of Accountability*

Accountability requires that states and businesses comply with their international obligations regarding the prevention of exposure to toxic and hazardous substances. The United Nations describes accountability as possessing three dimensions: 'obligation of those in authority to take responsibility for their actions, to answer for them to those affected, and to be subject to some form of enforceable sanction if their conduct or

(eds.), *Reparations for Victims of Genocide, War Crimes, and Crimes against Humanity* (Brill, 2009), 22.

86 UNHRC, *The Human Right to an Effective Remedy: The Case of Lead-Contaminated Housing in Kosovo*, UN Doc. A/HRC/45/CRP.10, 4 September 2020, para. 6.

87 UNHRC, *Guiding Principles on Business and Human Rights: Implementing the United Nations 'Protect, Respect and Remedy' Framework*, Doc. A/HRC/17/31, 21 March 2011.

88 *Ibid.*, 4.

89 Working Group on Business and Human Rights, 'Access to Remedy', www.ohchr.org/en/special-procedures/wg-business/access-remedy.

90 UNHRC, *Right to a Healthy Environment*, n. 70, para. 30.

explanation is found wanting'.[91] Guarantees of the rights to information and meaningful participation buttress these principles as they enable rights holders to engage in decision-making and challenge the actions of those responsible.[92] A human rights-based approach to chemicals and waste provides substantive responsibilities and avenues to provide specific redress for violations.

The current system of compliance committees used by the chemicals and wastes MEAs helps parties meet their obligations under these treaties.[93] These mechanisms are meant as transparent, non-confrontational, and non-binding preventive measures. Missing, however, is a complaint procedure for civil society to bring forward state violations of the conventions. As a result, the rights of the affected communities are largely absent from these mechanisms. Compliance committees are not a substitute for affected communities' right to access effective remedies. States have an obligation to redress human rights violations resulting from exposure to toxic pollution. This obligation includes setting up effective mechanisms to ensure redress in cases where international human rights obligations are breached. Accordingly, MEAs should establish a mechanism to hear grievances and provide remedies in cases where the breaches of an agreement result in harm to human rights or the environment.

To sum up, the protection of the right to a non-toxic environment requires chemical and waste MEAs to infuse a human rights-based approach. A human rights-based approach places an emphasis on prevention of exposure and on accountability where harms occur. It involves meaningful and informed participation in decision-making on the life cycle of chemicals and wastes. This approach also centres on the protection of persons and groups in most vulnerable situations, including children, women and girls, persons living in poverty, workers, persons with disabilities, older persons, migrants, and Indigenous peoples.[94]

91 UN Office of the High Commissioner for Human Rights, *Who Will Be Accountable? Human Rights and the Post-2015 Development Agenda*, UN Doc. HR/PUB/13/1/Add.1, May 2013, ix.

92 *Ibid.*, 14.

93 See 'Implementation and Compliance Committee: Mandate', *Basel Convention*, www.basel.int/TheConvention/ImplementationComplianceCommittee/Mandate/tabid/2296/Default.aspx; 'Compliance Committee', *Rotterdam Convention*, www.pic.int/TheConvention/ComplianceCommittee/Overview/tabid/8446/language/en-US/Default.aspx.

94 UNGA Resolution 76/300, n. 64; UNHRC, *Report of the Special Rapporteur on the Implications for Human Rights of the Environmentally Sound Management and Disposal of Hazardous Substances and Wastes*, UN Doc. A/HRC/36/41, 20 July 2017, para. 24.

10.5 A NEW PLASTICS TREATY: AN OPPORTUNITY FOR A HUMAN RIGHTS-BASED APPROACH

The negotiations for a new binding agreement on plastic pollution, initiated about fifty years after the 1972 Stockholm Conference, present an opportunity to incorporate a human rights-based approach.[95] The UNEA's resolution 'End Plastics Pollution: Towards a Legally Binding Instrument' requires that the agreement be based on a comprehensive approach to plastics at every stage of its cycle.[96] This mandate opens the door for a human rights-based approach to protect the full enjoyment of human rights affected by plastics pollution. Integral to this approach is the right to information and participation, which allows civil society and affected populations to have meaningful input in decision-making without discrimination. For example, consumers often lack access to information on the chemical additives in plastic products and the human health and environmental harms posed by them. Similarly, disinformation campaigns tout recycling as a viable solution to the plastics crisis when only 9 per cent of all plastics produced have been recycled.[97]

Consumers and affected communities must have complete, accurate, and understandable information on the volumes of plastic products, the toxic additives used, and the human health and environmental impacts of each stage of the plastics cycle. Toxic chemical additives in plastics pose one of the greatest threats to environmental health, and they also undermine efforts at creating a chemically safe circular economy. Accordingly, toxic chemical additives in plastics should be controlled effectively. Also, effective provisions on remedies are key for holding states and business accountable for the harms people suffer resulting from each stage of the plastics cycle. Principles of prevention and precaution, polluter pays, and just transition are crucial in protecting affected individuals, groups, and communities adversely impacted by plastic pollution. These provisions also equip states with tools to transition to a chemically safe circular economy.

95 UN General Assembly, *Report of the Special Rapporteur on the Implications for Human Rights of the Environmentally Sound Management and Disposal of Hazardous Substances and Wastes, Marcos Orellana – The Stages of the Plastics Cycle and Their Impacts on Human Rights*, UN Doc. A/76/207, 22 July 2021.

96 UNEP, *End Plastics Pollution: Towards a Legally Binding Instrument*, UN Doc. UNEP/EA.5/Res.14, 7 March 2022.

97 UN General Assembly, n. 95, para. 22.

In August 2025, the Intergovernmental Negotiating Committee (INC) tasked with negotiating the new international treaty on plastic pollution, was expected to finalize negotiations and deliver a treaty text, based on a draft which included explicit human rights language in the preamble; but it did not. At the time of writing, it is not clear if and how the negotiations will continue.[98]

10.6 CONCLUSION

The 1972 Stockholm Conference was a turning point. For the first time in history, humanity came together to look at the planet as our shared home. The conference succeeded in raising awareness on the need to protect the human environment. Our collective consciousness and imagination were forever marked by the ideas and images of unity and interconnectedness of life on the planet. Its vision on the linkage between human rights and the environment planted the seeds for the emergence of the human right to a clean, healthy, and sustainable environment. Yet national environmental laws and international agreements on chemicals and waste have largely followed a path that is focused not on preventing, but, rather, on minimizing and managing, impacts. This path has contributed to legalizing exposure to hazardous substances. The legal contamination has resulted in widespread suffering of countless individuals and species.

The current focus of chemicals and waste instruments on managing and minimizing impacts has been incapable of reversing the toxification of the planet. The global goal articulated by the international community at the World Summit on Sustainable Development, where states committed to achieving the sound management of chemicals by 2020, has failed. This has had serious adverse consequences for the effective enjoyment of the rights to life, personal integrity, health, and a clean, healthy, and sustainable environment, among others. Infusing a human rights-based approach into the texts and implementation of chemicals and waste agreements is necessary to strengthen the tools to confront the toxification of humanity and our

[98] https://resolutions.unep.org/incres/uploads/chairs_revised_draft_text_proposal_-_15.08.25_at_00.482.pdf. During the negotiation, the United Nations Special Rapporteur on toxics and human rights and the United Nations Special Rapporteur on human rights and environment had outlined how human rights could be introduced into the agreement; see OTH 70/2024, 12 April 2024, available here: https://spcommreports.ohchr.org/TMResultsBase/DownLoadPublicCommunicationFile?gId=28969.

planet. A human rights-based approach prioritizes action to protect persons and groups in vulnerable situations. A rights-based approach also prioritizes accountability, transparency, and participation. These are key principles to empower society in confronting environmental threats and preventing environmental harm.

11

The Dynamics of International and European Union Law on Waste and Chemicals: Past, Present, and Future

Carl Dalhammar

11.1 INTRODUCTION

The state of the environment fifty years after the 1972 Stockholm Conference on the Human Environment is deeply problematic,[1] with all major ecological trends going in the wrong direction.[2] Looking at the challenges facing mankind, including not only environmental issues but also social development and health matters, the need for effective international environmental agreements (IEAs) is greater than ever. Yet most existing agreements tend to suffer from well-known problems, including poor implementation and insufficient funding, national interests that undermine negotiations, 'treaty congestion' and a lack of coordination between related regimes, limited financial support for capacity building, and, in some cases, limited environmental effects.[3] The level of international cooperation does not match the need for increased collaboration on sustainability and social issues.[4] At the same time, future international agreements must focus more on justice[5] and on how we can ensure a fairer distribution of resources and a fair 'consumption space'.[6]

1 *Report of the UN Conference on the Human Environment*, UN Doc. A/CONF.48/14/Rev.1, 16 June 1972.

2 UN Environment Programme (UNEP), *Making Peace with Nature: A Scientific Blueprint to Tackle the Climate, Biodiversity and Pollution Emergencies* (UNEP, 2021); Carl Folke, Stephen Polasky, Johan Rockström, *et al.*, 'Our Future in the Anthropocene Biosphere' (2021)50 *Ambio* 834.

3 See, e.g., Joyeepta Gupta, Courtney Vegelin & Nicky Pouw, 'Lessons Learnt from International Environmental Agreements for the Stockholm+50 Conference: Celebrating 20 Years of INEA' (2022) 22 *International Environmental Agreements* 229.

4 *Ibid.*

5 *Ibid.*

6 See, e.g., Lewis Akenji *et al.*, *1.5-Degree Lifestyles: Towards a Fair Consumption Space for All* (Hot or Cool Institute, 2021); Sivan Kartha *et al.*, *The Carbon Inequality Era: An Assessment of the Global Distribution of Consumption Emissions among Individuals from 1990 to 2015 and Beyond* (Stockholm Environment Institute and OXFAM, 2020); Kate Raworth, *Doughnut*

There are also new tendencies emerging in environmental governance, such as an increased proliferation of bilateral trade agreements with sustainability elements,[7] not least in agreements by the European Union (EU),[8] and new types of governance mechanisms emerging. For instance, the EU is known to be a strong champion of IEAs, but many corporations and governments around the world are also adopting EU rules and standards due to economic and political reasons, without any need to integrate them into international agreements – the so-called 'Brussels effect'.[9] The EU has also shown a willingness to complement its role as a supporter of IEAs and sustainability concerns in trade agreements with a more 'direct' approach to affecting practices outside the EU. As an example, the 2022 Corporate Sustainability Reporting Directive requires EU-based companies to report on social and environmental issues in their supply chains.[10] Likewise, the EU's 2023 Carbon Border Adjustment Mechanism,[11] which requires importers of certain goods to pay for carbon emissions outside the EU, is an example of an act with 'extraterritorial' implications.

This chapter reviews the historical developments for laws related to chemicals and waste in IEAs and EU law. In the 1972 Stockholm Declaration on the Human Environment,[12] the issue of toxic substances was on the agenda, and principle 6 states that 'the discharge of toxic substances or other substances and the release of heat, in such quantities or concentrations as to exceed the capacity of the environment to render them harmless, must be halted'. In the

Economics: Seven Ways to Think Like a 21st-Century Economist (Chelsea Green Publishing, 2018).

7 Clive George, 'Environment and Regional Trade Agreements. Emerging Trends and Policy Drivers', Organisation for Economic Co-operation and Development (OECD), Trade and Environment Working Paper no. 2014/02, 2014; National Board of Trade, *Implementation and Enforcement of Sustainable Development Provisions in Free Trade Agreements: Options for Improvement* (Kommerskollegium, 2016).

8 Jana Titievskaia, *Sustainability Provisions in EU Free Trade Agreements: Review of the European Commission Action Plan* (European Parliamentary Research Service, 2021).

9 *Cf.*, Anu Bradford, *The Brussels Effect: How the European Union Rules the World* (Oxford University Press, 2020). Anu Bradford differentiates between a 'de facto' Brussels effect, where corporations voluntarily comply with European Union (EU) regulations, most notably to secure access to the EU's internal market, and a 'de jure' effect, where jurisdictions outside the EU adopt similar laws or legal requirements as the EU due to expected benefits or EU rules setting a 'good example'.

10 Council Directive (EU) 2022/2464 as Regards Corporate Sustainability Reporting, (2022) OJ L322/15.

11 Council Regulation (EU) 2023/956 Establishing a Carbon Border Adjustment Mechanism, (2023) OJ L130/52.

12 'Declaration of the United Nations Conference on the Human Environment', in *Report of the UN Conference on the Human Environment*, n. 1 (Stockholm Declaration).

five decades since then, several IEAs have been devoted to toxic substances. The EU and/or its member states have also been signatories of these IEAs, and, in many cases, EU laws related to toxic substances 'mirror' the IEAs. However, in some cases, EU laws have also gone beyond the IEAs – most notably, in the case of toxic substances in products as well as through the remarkable reform of EU chemicals law through the 2006 REACH Regulation,[13] as will be discussed later in this chapter in section 11.3.2.

In relation to waste, the 1972 Stockholm Declaration does not specifically use the term 'waste', though several of its principles refer to the preservation and proper management of resources.[14] Most notably, principle 21 of the Declaration states that the activities of a state should not harm other states, and this principle has been very important as a basis for regulating and banning the export of dangerous waste.[15] After 1972, the increasing levels of waste, and the problems associated with exporting waste to poorer countries and regions with insufficient capabilities to deal with it, mandated a policy response.[16] This resulted in several IEAs. These developments were also reflected in EU waste law, but the EU has gone much further than the IEAs in relation to waste and resource issues, addressing intra-EU waste trade and developing new legal innovations like extended producer responsibility (EPR) schemes. Fifty years after the Stockholm Conference, the EU is trying to move from a 'waste' to a 'resource' focus with its circular economy policies.[17] In the area of waste law, we can also notice how the Organisation for Economic Co-operation and Development's (OECD) policy has strongly influenced the developments of IEAs and EU law.

When reviewing the legal developments and reflecting on how these legal systems have influenced each other, the aim of this chapter is not only to look back at the developments but also to look forward. There are some key reasons why it makes sense, at this stage in time, to look at the regimes on waste and

[13] Council Regulation (EC) 1907/2006 Concerning the Registration, Evaluation, Authorisation and Restriction of Chemicals Establishing a European Chemicals Agency, (2006) OJ L396/1 (REACH Regulation).

[14] The related Action Plan for the Human Environment issued at the 1972 Stockholm Conference, however, does use the term 'waste'. 'Action Plan for the Human Environment', in *Report of the United Nations Conference on the Human Environment*, n. 1.

[15] See Ved Nanda & George Pring, *International Environmental Law and Policy for the 21st Century* (Martinus Nijhoff, 2013), 463–464.

[16] For an analysis of waste export from a human rights perspective, see Marcos A. Orellana, 'The Unfinished Agenda of Stockholm 1972: A Rights-based Approach to Chemicals and Wastes', in this volume, 267.

[17] For an overview of EU policy and law developments, see Leonidas Milios, 'Policy Framework for Material Resource Efficiency: Pathway towards a Circular Economy' (PhD dissertation, Lund University, 2020).

chemicals in an integrated analysis, and why it is relevant to look at IEAs and EU legal developments in an integrated way. First, there are clear signs that the two regimes – related to hazardous substances and waste respectively – are on a collision course, at least to some extent. There is a push, supported by the emerging circular economy discourse, to recycle more materials, support practices like remanufacturing, and support markets for recycled materials. However, when rules on chemicals, such as persistent organic pollutants (POPs), are strengthened, limiting the legally allowed levels of chemicals in new products, this means that recycled materials may not comply with the regulations for new products with respect to substance-limit levels.[18] In the longer run, rules that aim to phase out substances of concern from products will support future recycling efforts, but, in the short term, they may limit the opportunities for recycling.

Second, many legal frameworks – most notably, the 1989 Basel Convention in the case of IEAs[19] – aim at reducing exports of toxic waste from richer to poorer countries. Unfortunately, despite these efforts, these practices continue.[20] At the same time, in the circular economy discourse, the importance of increasing the lifetime of products and components is stressed in order to save resources, and the importance of reuse, repair, and refurbishment and remanufacturing as practices is emphasized to support this objective. Waste from electrical and electronic components is often highlighted as a potential toxic waste stream and, therefore, subject to export restrictions both within the EU and internationally. At the same time, in the case of electrical and electronic equipment (EEE), such as laptops and cell phones, there are large environmental gains from prolonging the lifetime through, for example, reuse activities.[21] Further, reuse could allow people in poorer regions of the world to access better products at a lower cost. There is mounting evidence that both EU rules and Basel Convention rules impede some beneficial reuse activities.[22] The question is

18 The most striking example is probably plastics and to what extent plastics with additives can be recycled. See, e.g., Swetlana Wagner & Martin Schlummer, 'Legacy Additives in a Circular Economy of Plastics: Current Dilemma, Policy Analysis, and Emerging Countermeasures' (2020) 158 *Resources, Conservation and Recycling* 104800.

19 Basel Convention on the Control of Transboundary Movements of Hazardous Wastes and Their Disposal, 1989, 1673 UNTS 125 (Basel Convention).

20 See, e.g., 'States Must Stop Exporting Unwanted Toxic Chemicals to Poorer Countries, Says UN Expert', *United Nations*, 9 July 2020, www.ohchr.org/en/press-releases/2020/07/states-must-stop-exporting-unwanted-toxic-chemicals-poorer-countries-says-un.

21 See, e.g., Carl Dalhammar, Leonidas Milios & Jessika Luth Richter, *Increasing the Lifespan of Products: Policies and Consumer Perspectives* (Swedish Energy Agency, 2021), ch. 7.

22 See Natalia Milovantseva & Colin Fitzpatrick, 'Barriers to Electronics Reuse of Transboundary E-Waste Shipment Regulations: An Evaluation Based on Industry

whether we can develop a more 'targeted' approach to these issues in order to support the objectives of the circular economy while still ensuring that exports do not lead to increased risks from toxic waste?

Third, rules on chemicals can be a barrier for remanufacturing[23] and repairs,[24] not least if they block the reuse of spare parts or components or if a remanufactured product is considered a 'new' product and may have to comply with rules for chemical substances in new products. In several cases, the EU rules on chemicals have made exemptions for spare parts and remanufactured products. Remanufacturing of medical devices can be very beneficial for health-care services in developing countries,[25] and remanufacturing of products like cars and information and communication technology can also have great environmental benefits, so it is crucial that rules on chemicals are not a major barrier for such practices. Fourth, the existing rules on chemicals and waste are a 'patchwork' in that only some wastes and chemicals – and related practices – are regulated, and there is no comprehensive approach to waste and chemicals management.[26] There has been some interesting developments, however, related to cooperation between the IEA regimes on chemicals and waste transport – most notably, official cooperation between the Basel Convention,[27] the 1998 Rotterdam Convention,[28] and the 2001 Stockholm Convention.[29] Fifth, the emergence of

Experiences' (2015) 102(C) *Resources, Conservation and Recycling* 170; Josh Lepawsky, 'Are We Living in a Post-Basel World?' (2025) 47(1) *Area* 7; Josh Lepawsky, Joshua Goldstein & Yvan Schulz, 'Criminal Negligence?' *Discard Studies Online*, 24 June 2015, https://discardstudies.com/2015/06/24/criminal-negligence/.

23 Note that there is still some confusion over the terminology in the case of 'remanufacturing', 'reconditioning', and 'refurbishment'. This is an area where there is a great need for both legal definitions and standardization efforts. See Niclas Gustavsson *et al.*, *Regulatory Mapping for Remanufacturing of Products under EU Law* (Swedish Chemicals Agency, 2021); Dalhammar, Milios & Richter, n. 21.

24 Sahra Svensson-Hoglund *et al.*, 'Barriers, Enablers and Market Governance: A Review of the Policy Landscape for Repair of Consumer Electronics in the EU and the US' (2021) 288 *Journal of Cleaner Production* 125488.

25 Solomon Eze, Winifred Ijomah & Andy T. C. Wong, 'Remanufacturing: A Potential Sustainable Solution for Increasing Medical Equipment Availability' (2020) 10 *Journal of Remanufacturing* 141.

26 Katharina Kummer Peiry, 'The Chemicals and Waste Regime as a Basis for a Comprehensive International Framework on Sustainable Management of Potentially Hazardous Materials?' (2014) 23(2) *Review of European and Comparative International Environmental Law* 172; Philippe Sands *et al.*, *Principles of International Environmental Law* (4th ed., Cambridge University Press, 2018), ch. 12.

27 Basel Convention, n. 19.

28 Convention on the Prior Informed Consent Procedure for Certain Hazardous Chemicals and Pesticides in International Trade, 1998, 2244 UNTS 337 (Rotterdam Convention).

29 Stockholm Convention on Persistent Organic Pollutants, 2001, 2256 UNTS 119 (Stockholm Convention).

the circular economy as a key policy area in environmental governance challenges existing regimes. In international law and policy, there is an evident need to coordinate standards, definitions, and various regimes such as trade and waste regimes.[30] In the EU, the need to harmonize the regulatory frameworks for products, waste, and chemicals is urgent.[31]

The following parts highlight the developments in waste law and rules on dangerous substances respectively.

11.2 DEVELOPMENTS IN WASTE LAW

11.2.1 *International Law*

Several international legal frameworks were developed in the 1980s in response to increasing waste flows in international trade and problems with dumping. The concerns were also increasingly reflected in relevant documents, such as the report by the Brundtland Commission[32] and the 1992 Rio Declaration on Environment and Development,[33] which highlighted the waste problems, dumping, and externalities associated with waste treatment and pollution. Most adopted IEAs, however, were bilateral or regional in nature, reflecting the fact that it is hard to agree on international laws that are acceptable for many countries and reflecting the 'political' nature of waste movements and treatments.[34] The many different IEAs – bilateral or regional in nature – and the many national laws with a mostly national focus, combined with the fact that the EU has developed its own waste policies (discussed in section 11.2.2), have made it hard to get a good picture of the state of international law on waste. That said, a more coherent regime, where the export of certain wastes is increasingly banned – some past IEAs have seemed to promote such exports – is emerging.[35] Meanwhile, we have also seen import bans in some countries, with China's ban on the import of plastics being

[30] Mattias Lindahl & Carl Dalhammar, *The Circular Economy: Towards a New Business Paradigm with Support from Public Policy* (Stockholm Environment Institute, 2022).

[31] See, e.g., Joonas Alaranta & Topi Turunen, 'How to Reach a Safe Circular Economy?: Perspectives on Reconciling the Waste, Product and Chemicals Regulation' (2021) 33(1) *Journal of Environmental Law* 113.

[32] Brundtland Commission, *Report of the World Commission on Environment and Development: Our Common Future*, 1987.

[33] 'Rio Declaration on Environment and Development', in *Report of the UN Conference on Environment and Development*, UN Doc. A/CONF.151/26 (Vol. I), 12 August 1992 (Rio Declaration).

[34] See Nanda & Pring, n. 15, s. 12.1.

[35] *Ibid.*, 465.

perhaps the most well-known example.[36] The emergence of the Basel Convention and various OECD rules and guidelines have supported these developments, especially the management of the export of hazardous wastes.

The 1989 Basel Convention is still the only truly global treaty on waste, though not all major nations are parties. OECD decisions, guidelines, and technical support are also very important for the development of national practices, and OECD measures have helped pave the way for the Basel Convention.[37] This Convention is built upon the principle of the sound management of waste. It introduces a scheme of prior informed consent where authorities of the state importing waste must receive information about the nature of a planned export of waste to their country in advance and agree to it in writing before it is allowed to take place. Since these requirements do not guarantee that toxic waste is not exported from developed to developing countries, the 1995 Basel Ban Amendment was agreed to but did not enter into force until 2019.[38] Accordingly, member states of the OECD and the EU, and Liechtenstein, are not allowed to export hazardous wastes – as defined by the Basel Convention – to other countries.[39] While the Basel Convention suffers from several weaknesses, it does focus on the right issues and is considered a 'step in the right direction'.[40] That said, the Convention mainly deals with waste management and has no mechanisms to support waste prevention and quantitative target setting for such purposes. Thus, the international law on waste does not provide incentives for waste prevention and thus fails to stop practices where disposal problems are shifted from one medium to another.[41]

The OECD has addressed waste issues since the 1970s and has taken more concrete steps to regulate the problems of waste import and export since 1984.[42] Its various decisions and guidelines also paved the way for the Basel Convention.[43] The OECD has also been crucial for developing waste statistics

36 Zongguo Wen *et al.*, 'China's Plastic Import Ban Increases Prospects of Environmental Impact Mitigation of Plastic Waste Trade Flow Worldwide' (2021) 12 *Nature Communications* 425.

37 Basel Convention, n. 19.

38 Decision III/1 Amendment to the Convention, Doc. UNEP/CHW. 3/35, 28 November 1995 (Basel Ban Amendment).

39 For a discussion on the Basel Ban Amendment, see Basel Action Network /The International Pollutants Elimination Network (BAN/IPEN), *The Entry into Force of the Basel Ban Amendment: A Guide to Implications and Next Steps* (BAN/IPEN, 2020).

40 Sands *et al.*, n. 26, 620.

41 *Ibid.*, at 571.

42 See, e.g., Nanda & Pring, n. 15, 466.

43 OECD, *Celebrating 40 Years of the OECD Environment Policy Committee 1971–2011* (OECD, 2011), 52.

and technical guidelines.[44] Its various technical guidelines have been very influential, and it has also worked to promote principles like the producer pays principle and EPR in waste policy and law.[45] Laws promoting EPR aim to extend producers' responsibilities for their products to the post-consumer phase by making them responsible for collecting, sorting, and recycling. In the case of EPR, the OECD has promoted the concept through various activities that have helped shape the concept and how it has been successfully implemented, often in cooperation with EU member states.[46]

11.2.2 *Developments in EU Law*

The 1972 Paris Summit, held after the 1972 Stockholm Conference, is considered to have kickstarted the EU's development of environmental policy and law.[47] Waste policy was on the agenda already in 1972, and the first Environmental Action Program of the EU discussed the need for EU laws on waste and intra-EU harmonization of laws.[48] EU waste law has since developed in magnitude and scope, encompassing a number of laws related to waste handling, transport, and storage. EU rules on the shipment of waste was first adopted in 1984, through a directive, which has since been replaced through a series of waste shipment regulations.[49] EU law on waste shipment implements the Basel Convention and is also influenced by OECD rules and guidelines, but, in some cases, it goes further when addressing risks.[50] In the 1970s and 1980s, the issue of 'waste dumping' was also relevant within the EU, not least as a lot of waste was landfilled in Wallonia, leading to the famous 'Wallonia waste cases'.[51] The outcome of the cases was that the import of waste

[44] Nanda & Pring, n. 15, 466.

[45] Extended producer responsibility (EPR) can be considered a concrete way to promote the polluter pays principle in waste policy.

[46] Thomas Lindhqvist, 'Extended Producer Responsibility in Cleaner Production: Policy Principle to Promote Environmental Improvements of Product Systems' (PhD dissertation, Lund University, 2001).

[47] Christoph Knill & Duncan Liefferink, 'The Establishment of EU Environmental Policy', in Andrew Jordan & Camilla Adelle (eds.), *Environmental Policy in the EU* (3rd ed., Routledge, 2012).

[48] See discussion in Ludwig Krämer, *EU Environmental Law* (8th ed., Sweet & Maxwell, 2016), s. 10–01.

[49] The current one is Regulation (EU) 2024/1157 of the European Parliament and of the Council of 11 April 2024 on shipments of waste (2024) OJ L 2024/1157.

[50] See, e.g., David Langlet, *Prior Informed Consent and Hazardous Trade. Regulating Trade in Hazardous Goods at the Intersection of Sovereignty, Free Trade and Environmental Protection* (Kluwer Law International, 2009), 279.

[51] For a detailed review, see Daniel Simcox, 'The Future of Europe Lies in Waste' (1995) 28(3) *Vanderbilt Journal of Transnational Law* 543.

could be restricted for environmental protection reasons, and, thus, waste was not like other 'goods' – it cannot always be allowed to flow freely within the EU. Still, while the EU member states can stop the import of waste for landfilling, and also import for recycling under certain circumstances, there has always been a willingness to support waste transport within the EU for material recycling and energy recovery in order to stimulate recycling and keep costs of waste management low.

Thus, historically, the EU has also promoted trade of waste destined for recovery and recycling more than trade in waste for landfilling. This is reflected in Article 16 of the 2008 Waste Framework Directive, which outlines the principles of proximity and self-sufficiency.[52] The principle of proximity implies that waste should generally be managed as near as possible to its place of production; however, in Article 16, it is stressed that not all EU member states must possess the full range of final recovery facilities. The principle of self-sufficiency requires that most waste should be treated or disposed of within the region in which it is produced. Yet, Article 16 stresses that the EU, as a whole, should strive for self-sufficiency in this respect. The way in which recycling works today, cost-effective recycling processes often require large volumes, and, thus, for many waste streams, it would be most effective to focus on recycling at certain hubs in the EU.

Compared to international law, the EU has a more elaborate set of rules to cover various types of waste, and various practices, such as landfilling and incineration. The EU has a couple of advantages when it comes to legal developments, compared to international law. First, it has been able to set important laws related to products, which support recycling. This includes not only laws on producer responsibility but also rules on toxic substances in products. The REACH Regulation provides a horizontal approach to address these issues, but there are also laws that relate to specific product groups like toys, electronics, cars, and packaging. An example is the 2011 RoHS Directive, which has led to the phase out of certain substances in EEE and this phase out supports recycling since – typically – toxics like brominated flame retardants make it difficult to recycle plastics.[53] Second, the EU has introduced new legal concepts like the waste management hierarchy that provides a legal basis for diverting waste from landfills to upper levels of the hierarchy like material recycling.[54] This general obligation has been supplemented by EPR rules for

52 Council Directive (EC) 2008/98 on Waste, (2008) OJ L312/3.

53 Council Directive (EU) 2011/65 on the Restriction of the Use of Certain Hazardous Substances in Electrical and Electronic Equipment (recast), (2011) OJ L174/88.

54 See Council Directive 2008/98 on Waste, n. 52, art. 4.

products groups like cars, EEE, and packaging, mandating producers to collect and recycle these waste streams. Third, many EU countries have devoted significant resources to monitor waste and transport and thus have more resources for such practices compared to developing countries. Fourth, the EU has been able to somewhat change the 'framing' of the waste issue. Originally, it was mainly about managing the risks of waste.

From the 1980s and onwards, policy objectives related to increased recycling and reduced landfilling led to legal developments such as EPR schemes. Increasingly, the discourse has shifted towards the 'resource challenge' and access to critical raw materials, and, since 2015, when the first circular economy action plan was adopted,[55] the circular economy discourse has become the dominant one.[56] This discourse aims to more clearly prevent waste and stresses that recycling may not be as great as we previously thought as it often degrades materials (downcycling). The key is to keep material value high, for example, by prolonging the lifetime of products, and it is important that the recycling that takes place should be of high quality, and not – as is currently often the case – only focus on large material streams and neglect other materials. This change is also reflected in the 2022 Environmental Action Program, where one priority objective is to advance 'towards a well-being economy that gives back to the planet more than it takes and accelerating the transition to a non-toxic circular economy, where growth is regenerative, resources are used efficiently and sustainably, and the waste hierarchy is applied'.[57] However, while the circular economy discourse is emerging, in practice, old waste rules in the EU, and in various IEAs – which are often built on a risk management approach – can block desired practices like repair and remanufacturing.[58] Even EPR rules that support material recycling can be barriers for remanufacturing and reuse if producers mainly aim to fulfil legal obligations through recycling systems that do not promote reuse.[59] Thus, there are shortcomings in how the legal framework can support a 'move upwards' in alignment with the waste hierarchy and move from material recycling to reuse, repair, remanufacturing, and longer product lifetimes.

55 European Commission, *Closing the Loop: An EU Action Plan for the Circular Economy*, Doc. COM(2015) 614 final, 2 December 2015.

56 For an overview of EU policy developments, see Milios, n. 17, 5.

57 Council Decision (EU) 2022/591 on a General Union Environment Action Programme to 2030, (2022) OJ L114/22, art. 2.

58 Lindahl & Dalhammar, n. 30.

59 Carl Dalhammar *et al.*, 'Enabling Reuse in Extended Producer Responsibility Schemes for White Goods: Legal and Organisational Conditions for Connecting Resource Flows and Actors' (2021) 1 *Circular Economy and Sustainability* 671, 674.

The EU focus on prevention, however, has started to result in some interesting legal developments. The most striking example concerns EU proposals to stop destruction of unsold products. Many products that are produced today – especially clothes and electronics – are never used; due to increasing customer returns in e-commerce and overproduction, and the high costs associated with labour to ensure the products are sold, a lot of goods are destroyed.[60] In the Ecodesign for Sustainable Products Regulation (ESPR), the EU has adopted a partial ban on of the product destruction of textiles and footwear, and is likely to introduce similar provisions and/or reporting requirements on destruction practices for additional product groups.[61] Another apparent trend in EU law and policy is to try and develop digital solutions for environmental law purposes. According to the ESPR, proposal, 'digital product passports' can be used on products.[62] This can help keep track of products and support waste management practices as recyclers will have more data on product design and content. Hopefully, it can also support measures to stop illegal waste transport. Interestingly, in the 2021 proposal for a shipment regulation, the European Commission envisions more use of digital solutions for EU waste transport.[63] It remains to be seen if such development can support better control and less illegal trade.

11.2.3 *Integrated Analysis of International and EU Laws on Waste*

Here, we discuss general developments, making references to some key international and EU laws.[64] In the case of the shipment of waste, EU laws have been very much influenced by the OECD decisions and recommendations and, later, by the Basel Convention. The OECD framework was also very influential when the Basel Convention was designed.[65] In the communication

60 For an overview of the issue and policy responses, see Hedda Roberts *et al.*, 'Product Destruction: Exploring Unsustainable Production-Consumption Systems and Appropriate Policy Responses' (2023) 35 *Sustainable Production and Consumption* 300.

61 Regulation (EU) 2024/1781 of the European Parliament and of the Council of 13 June 2024 establishing a framework for the setting of ecodesign requirements for sustainable products (2024), OJ L, 2024/1781, art. 23-26.

62 *Ibid.*, arts. 9-15.

63 *Proposal for a Regulation of the European Parliament and of the Council on Shipments of Waste and amending Regulations (EU) no 1257/2013 and (EU) no 2020/1056*, Doc. COM/2021/709 final, 17 November 2021.

64 Here, we only provide examples of key laws. For a more detailed overview, see e.g., Malgosia Fitzmaurice, Meagan Wong & Joseph Crampin, *International Environmental Law* (Edward Elgar, 2022), ch. 14.

65 For more details, see Katharina Kummer, *International Management of Hazardous Wastes: The Basel Convention and Related Legal Rules* (Oxford University Press, 2000), ch. 4.

that accompanied the proposals for a new EU Shipment Regulation, the European Commission states the need for the EU to take more responsibility for treating its own waste; to stop shipments outside the EU to countries that do not explicitly notify the EU of their willingness to receive EU waste exports and demonstrate their ability to treat this waste in an environmentally sustainable manner; to require EU exporting companies to show that their exports are sustainable; and to establish clear criteria to prevent waste from being falsely exported as 'used goods'.[66] The Commission states its support for working with the Basel Convention and the OECD to support new rules and guidelines and especially states that '[the] EU is supporting specific work carried out in the Basel Convention to improve the management of a series of waste streams, especially household waste, plastic waste, ewaste, waste batteries or waste containing persistent organic pollutants'.[67]

The OECD has had significant influence over EU law. In some cases, such as the rules on hazardous wastes, there is even historical evidence of parallel developments. A difference is that OECD binding rules tend to primarily establish principles, whereas many detailed rules are instead set through recommendations; the EU has more binding, detailed rules. Another example of interactions between OECD and EU developments is the development of EPR as a guiding strategy or principle of waste policy and law. Extended producer responsibility was originally proposed in a Swedish governmental report, and it was first introduced as a policy for packaging waste in Germany.[68] The OECD was a strong supporter of EPR and initiated several projects and guidance reports related to EPR as well as evaluations of EPR policies.[69] The EU has adopted EPR as a guiding principle in waste law and also introduced several EU directives that mandate the set-up of EPR schemes in the EU – for example, for vehicles, packaging, and EEE. This has been supported by several stakeholder events organized to spread the ideas and best practices.

When comparing international law and EU law on waste from 1972 until today, we can see that both international and EU laws have developed into

66 See European Commission, *Our Waste, Our Responsibility: Waste Shipments in a Clean and More Circular Economy*, Doc. COM(2021) 708 final, 17 November 2021; see also European Commission, *Proposal for a Regulation on Shipments of Waste*, Doc. COM(2021) 709 final, 17 November 2021.

67 *Ibid.*, 7.

68 See OECD, n. 43, 51. For a historical review of EPR laws, see, e.g., Lindhqvist, n. 46. For more information on the current status of EPR and its implementation in Europe, see Carl Dalhammar, 'Extended Producer Responsibility', in Ludwig Krämer & Emanuela Orlando (eds.), *Principles of Environmental Law* (Edward Elgar, 2018).

69 For an overview, see Lindhqvist, n. 46.

a more coherent system of laws to address waste. However, international law is still fragmented with mostly bilateral agreements, and the Basel Convention is still the only truly international treaty of global scope, and it mainly deals with waste transport. There are, however, regional waste treaties like the 1991 Bamako Convention in Africa.[70] This means that the issue of waste has gone from being almost a 'non-issue' in international law in 1972 to a highly important issue today. Still, the primary focus is on the transport, import, or export of waste, and there is little in terms of rules that prevent the generation of waste. The Basel Ban Amendment, and some of the waste import restrictions applied by developing countries or countries in transition, could have positive outcomes as they may force waste-exporting countries to deal with their own waste and develop better waste treatment systems. This does not mean that the 'last word' has been said, as existing rules may also stop the export of valuable waste to developing economies, like used batteries in electric vehicles. However, this is less of a problem than the rules stopping products that can be repaired or remanufactured and used in developing economies. Such practices can help poorer people getting access to televisions, medical equipment, and so on, and support longer product lifetimes, which is desired from a circular economy perspective. Still, fifty years after the Stockholm Conference, the rules are quite general in nature and may stop desired exports. This could be addressed by setting up better solutions for the licensing of importers who will take better care of products, but, of course, it also opens the door to 'loopholes' and therefore needs to be carefully designed.

It is hard to envision how IEAs on waste will develop in the near future. The chances of adopting truly global agreements such as the Basel Convention seem limited, meaning bilateral agreements may continue to be the way forward. It is also possible that EU laws will strongly affect countries outside the EU. In the EU's law on waste, the direction seems clear: place more focus on keeping the value of resources, avoid downcycling, and move towards a circular economy rather than a narrow focus on waste management and risk mitigation. However, there is a mismatch between the vision and the practice as there are still large volumes of waste that are hard to recycle and may contain toxic substances, meaning that rules dealing with risks associated with waste transport and handling are still necessary. The EU has clearly indicated that it will prefer to work through international rules and follow

70 Bamako Convention on the Ban of the Import into Africa and the Control of Transboundary Movements and Management of Hazardous Wastes within Africa, 1991, 2101 UNTS 177.

the Basel regime, but we can also see that the EU is moving ahead with its own agenda, with a strong focus on product regulation.[71]

11.3 DEVELOPMENTS IN LAWS ON HAZARDOUS SUBSTANCES

11.3.1 *International Law*

The first international regime to control hazardous substances was the 1998 Rotterdam Convention.[72] It promotes the open exchange of information and calls on exporters of hazardous chemicals to use proper labelling and directions on safe handling and to inform purchasers of any known restrictions or bans. Signatory states can decide whether to allow or ban the importation of chemicals listed in the treaty, and exporting parties must ensure that producers within their jurisdiction comply. The Rotterdam Convention, if compared to the Basel Convention, is less trade intrusive and builds less on the absolute ban of exports.[73] The 2001 Stockholm Convention addresses POPs.[74] It requires parties to introduce bans and restrictions, respectively, for various POPs and to safely handle stockpiles of POPs, and it also mandates developed countries to provide new and additional financial resources and measures to eliminate production and use of intentionally produced POPs, eliminate unintentionally produced POPs where feasible, and manage and dispose of POPs wastes in an environmentally sound manner. The 2013 Minamata Convention applies to mercury only.[75] Its provisions include a ban on new mercury mines, the phase out of existing ones, the phasing out or down of mercury use in a number of products and processes, and control measures on emissions to air and on releases to land and water. The Convention also addresses the interim storage of mercury and its disposal (as waste), sites contaminated by mercury, and health issues.

Other relevant international developments concern good standards and soft law instruments, such as the Food and Agriculture Organization's (FAO) 2014 International Code of Conduct for Pesticides[76] and the FAO/World Health

[71] See the discussion in Carl Dalhammar, 'Making Sustainable Products the Norm on the Internal Market: An Assessment of the Proposal for a New Ecodesign Regulation' (2023) 1 *Europarättslig Tidskrift* 43.

[72] Rotterdam Convention, n. 28. For an overview, see Langlet, n. 50.

[73] *Ibid.*, 280.

[74] Stockholm Convention, n. 29.

[75] Minamata Convention on Mercury, 2013, 3202 UNTS 220.

[76] *International Code of Conduct on Pesticide Management*, Doc. WHO/HTM/NTD/WHOPES/2014.1, 2014, www.fao.org/fileadmin/templates/agphome/documents/Pests_Pesticides/Code/CODE_2014Sep_ENG.pd.

Organization's Codex Alimentarius initiative.[77] The international law on toxic substances is often characterized as a patchwork, where issues have been regulated when there is awareness of certain environmental impacts, though they are often lacking a holistic, life-cycle perspective on how to deal with substances in a more comprehensive way.[78] Another concern is the extent to which rules are binding on corporations' subsidiaries in developing countries.[79] That said, there are some promising signs. Philippe Sands and colleagues point out that the Minamata Convention takes a more comprehensive approach to mercury than has traditionally been the case and covers emissions, storage, waste, and contaminated sites.[80] The Stockholm Convention can also be considered to be an example of a more precautionary approach where the science-policy interactions can be considered quite successful.[81]

11.3.2 *EU Law*

The early inceptions of the EU (the European Economic Community and the European Community) had, in its first decades, limited legal mandate to adopt environmental laws. Still, trade-oriented rules related to chemicals could be implemented if they were needed to avoid the distortion to trade, such as 1967 Directive on Classification, Packaging and Labelling of Chemicals.[82] The United States was the main leader of standard setting in the 1970s, including for toxic substances, but the EU started to catch up in the 1980s, and, in the early 1990s the EU had surpassed the United States as the leader in setting progressive standards to protect human health and the environment, including on chemicals.[83] The EU *acquis* on substances at the time of the UN International Meeting Stockholm+50: A Healthy Planet for the Prosperity of All – Our Responsibility, Our Opportunity (Stockholm+50 Meeting) covers a range of issues, including pesticides and biocides, ozone-depleting substances, and various forms of labelling of relevance (including

77 See 'About Codex', *Codex Alimentarius*, www.fao.org/fao-who-codexalimentarius/about-codex/en/.

78 See, e.g., Sands *et al.*, n. 26, 570.

79 *Ibid.*, 571.

80 *Ibid.*, 571.

81 *Ibid.*, 581–583.

82 Council Directive (EEC) 67/548 on the Approximation of Laws, Regulations and Administrative Provisions Relating to the Classification, Packaging and Labelling of Dangerous Substances, (1967) OJ L196/1 (no longer in use).

83 See David Vogel, *The Politics of Precaution: Regulating Health, Safety, and Environmental Risks in Europe and the United States* (Princeton University Press, 2012).

rules for labelling genetically modified organisms, recyclable packaging, and organic farming).[84] In many cases, these EU rules also go much further than international law.

Most notably, the EU has much legislation in place on substances in products, especially dealing with packaging, batteries, vehicles, and EEE. This legislation has strong impacts also outside the EU – for instance, the RoHS Directive has transformed the global production chains for EEE to phase out a number of substances.[85] Regarding dangerous substances, many EU laws 'mirror' the IEAs. But the main 'flagship' of EU law is of course the REACH Regulation, often considered to be the EU's attempt to revolutionize chemicals policy.[86] It sets up a regime that goes way beyond any measures in the IEAs. The key elements of the REACH Regulation include the placing of 'the burden of proof' on manufacturers and importers of chemicals, who must identify and manage the risks linked to the substances they manufacture and market in the EU. They have to demonstrate to the European Chemicals Agency how the substance can be safely used and must communicate the risk management measures to the users. If the risks cannot be properly managed, authorities can restrict the use of substances in different ways, including through bans.

While the REACH Regulation suffers from well-known implementation problems – most notably, that corporations that provide insufficient information can still use the chemicals, that there are issues in addressing chemicals produced in small volumes, and that there is limited progress in banning or restricting the use of dangerous chemicals – it is still a success in many ways, and many other jurisdictions have also used it as a model for their national laws.[87] Another main flaw in EU law – and, most notably, with the REACH Regulation – is the shortcomings in promoting innovation (of new, safer chemicals) – that is, 'green chemistry' – and in driving the substitution of dangerous chemicals with safer ones.[88] Simply put, producers make money on old, existing chemicals, and it is expensive to develop alternatives. The

84 For an overview, see, e.g., Krämer, n. 48, ch. 6.

85 Bradford, n. 9.

86 For a discussion on this, and a more detailed analysis of the REACH Regulation, n. 13, see Steven Vaughan, *EU Chemicals Regulation: New Governance, Hybridity and REACH* (Edward Elgar, 2015).

87 See, for example, India's proposal for an India REACH Regulation; *Draft Chemicals (Management and Safety) Rules, 20xx*. For more information, see 'About India REACH (CMSR)', https://indianchemicalregulation.com/india-reach/?cn-reloaded=1.

88 Carl Dalhammar, 'Policies Promoting Green Chemistry: Substitution Efforts in Europe', in Sanjay Sharma & Ackmez Mudhoo (eds.), *Green Chemistry for Environmental Sustainability* (Taylor & Francis, 2010); Wood and Lowell Center for Sustainable Production, *Chemicals*

European Commission has identified this as a weak spot, and the 2020 EU Chemicals Strategy has set out actions to address this issue.[89] However, the proposed measures seem to provide rather limited incentives given the major barriers.

11.3.3 *Interactions between International and EU Law*

International environmental agreements and various international cooperation mechanisms have had a great influence on EU laws, which in some cases 'mirror' the IEAs. This applies to substances such as POPS. Further, the EU's 2008 Classification, Labelling and Packaging Regulation is based on the United Nations' Globally Harmonised System.[90] More generally, the European Commission has stated in several documents that the Strategic Approach to International Chemicals Management (SAICM) is very influential for EU chemical law and policy, and the Commission has made efforts to show how the SAICM principles are realized through EU law and policy.[91]

Looking back to 1972, we can see an impressive development in international law on substances, which has often been triggered by new research showing that existing substances are dangerous to human health and the environment. The emergence of the precautionary principle in international law,[92] and not least in EU law, has supported these developments,[93] and the fact that the principle is increasingly recognized in international law is an achievement in itself. It is hard to predict how international law on toxic substances will emerge in the future. Currently, the key issue of attention concerns the use of plastics, and especially micro plastics, where we have seen significant legal developments in the last couple of years before the Stockholm +50 Meeting. In the EU, the 2022 proposal for a chemicals strategy seems to

Innovation Action Agenda: Transition to Safer Chemicals and Technologies (European Commission, 2019).

89 European Commission, *Chemicals Strategy for Sustainability towards a Toxic-Free Environment*, Doc. COM (2020) 667 final, 2020.

90 Council Regulation (EC) 1272/2008 on Classification, Labelling and Packaging of Substances and Mixtures, (2008) OJ L353/1.

91 The Strategic Approach to International Chemicals Management (SAICM) is a framework to promote chemical safety, based upon five key strategies. For more information on the SAICM, see 'Strategic Approach to International Chemicals Management', www.saicm.org/. See discussions in European Commission, n. 89.

92 First codified in international law in principle 15 of the Rio Declaration, n. 33, and later applied in some international environmental agreements, not least related to biodiversity protection.

93 Poul Harremoës *et al.*, *Late Lessons from Early Warnings: The Precautionary Principle 1896–2000* (European Environment Agency, 2001).

represent more of an evolution than a revolution, mainly aiming at strengthening existing laws and mechanisms.[94]

11.4 THE WAY FORWARD: HOW DO WE SUPPORT A TOXIC-FREE CIRCULAR ECONOMY?

Looking at international law developments since 1972, the main achievements include an increasing number of IEAs addressing toxic substances and waste. The IEAs related to toxic substances address an increasing number of substances, and some recent IEAs also address them in a more 'holistic' way than older conventions. Substances that were not considered to be very problematic in the 1970s – such as POPS and plastics – are now in the spotlight. The EU has – through the REACH Regulation – taken additional steps in chemicals policy to require that chemicals are evaluated before being put on the market, with the 'burden of proof' that chemicals are safe being the responsibility of the producers. As many other jurisdictions increasingly model their chemical legislation on the REACH Regulation, some of its principles may over time be more commonly applied in international law.

Regarding waste law, the advancements in international law are probably less substantial, but progress has been made not least through the Basel Convention. The Basel Ban Amendment will hopefully be very important as it will force richer countries to deal with their own waste streams.[95] This trend has been reinforced by national bans on waste imports of certain waste streams (such as plastics) in some countries. EU waste law is more advanced than international law as it has introduced rules on producer responsibility that mandate the collection and recycling of used products. More important is the development of the vision of a circular economy, and related policies, as it can support the shift from simply focusing on how to deal with waste to actually trying to keep the value of materials in the economy longer – for instance, by supporting longer product lifetimes.

Despite these advances, at the time of the Stockholm + 50 Meeting, the global governance system for waste and chemicals was characterized by fragmentation, deficient information management systems and obligations, insufficient funding, and limited compliance, and the indicators used under SAICM have limited usefulness.[96] Despite calls for a new, simplified, but

94 See European Commission, n. 89.

95 Basel Ban Amendment, n. 38.

96 Tuula Honkonen & Sabaa Khan, *Chemicals and Waste Governance beyond 2020: Exploring Pathways for a Coherent Global Regime* (Nordic Council of Ministers, 2017).

comprehensive legal framework,[97] it is questionable if such developments can be expected in the near term. Rather, it is possible that future international agreements on topics like micro plastics and nanotechnology will deliver an even more fragmented law and policy landscape. When it comes to the relation between international and EU law, the European Commission has repeatedly stated its preference for international rules through international agreements where the EU can be a signatory, but it seems very likely that, in the absence of global agreements, the EU will continue to set its own rules. These rules will – through the 'Brussels effect' – influence other jurisdictions; whether this situation is positive or negative lies in the eye of the beholder.[98]

The EU seems better equipped than the international community to adopt a comprehensive future legal framework to support the vision of a circular economy for several reasons. First, the EU has adopted two circular economy action plans and has a rather strong institutional support for this vision. The circular economy concept is increasingly discussed also in international law, but it is not the subject of specific policies. Second, the EU has the potential to address several relevant fields of environmental law – including laws on products, waste, and toxic substances – in an integrated manner. Further, the appetite for regulation is still strong in the EU, though there are voices calling the EU to slow down and stop adopting too many laws aimed at industries and instead focus on legal compliance.[99]

Looking to the future, both international and EU law need to better incentivize research on new, safer chemicals as the current rules provide a very limited driver for change. But effective mechanisms for this goal would probably include a policy mix with quite controversial measures, such as bans on an increasing number of substances and the use of market drivers – for example, public procurement – to provide economic incentives for change. Such measures are costly and controversial and likely to be met with strong resistance from industries. In the future, it is likely that the debate on the advantages and disadvantages of waste export will continue, and several lines of arguments are likely to become more prominent. Proponents of the Basel Ban Amendment have used a number of arguments in favour of the ban,

97 *Ibid.*

98 The positive and negative aspects are discussed in Bradford, n. 9. We can notice how environmental non-governmental organizations in developing countries are often rather positive towards the extraterritorial reach of the EU's policies as it influences industries outside the EU to adopt more sustainable practices.

99 See, e.g., 'Macron's Calls for "Regulatory Pause" in EU Environmental Laws Wink at Conservatives', *Politico*, 2023, www.politico.eu/article/emmauel-macron-the-eu-sophies-choice-moment-juggling-growth-and-the-environment/.

including that the rules of the Basel Convention constitute a 'noble but failed' attempt to control waste flows from developed to developing countries.[100] There are also valid arguments against the ban – for instance, that it starves developing nations of necessary materials for industrial developments, constitutes a trade barrier, and restricts useful recycling efforts.[101] Obviously, no legal regime can get the balance perfectly right: restricting trade in waste can be the right approach even if it has some negative implications.

While there is good reason to control hazardous waste, there is mounting evidence that the Basel Convention impedes beneficial reuse activities.[102] The current rules are quite 'blunt' in this respect. The question is whether a better balance can be struck? Natalia Milovantseva and Colin Fitzpatrick have provided some proposals on how a better balance can be struck between the objectives of controlling dangerous waste flows and allowing export for reuse and reconditioning. They propose streamlining and changing existing laws to better support transport for reuse, establishing a comprehensive international legislative database to help harmonize variations in e-waste regulations among different countries, and developing a 'green channel' whereby regulated destinations and logistics channels that are independently audited to be operating to best practices get a 'green light' to import certain wastes.[103]

Is this realistic? It is possible, especially in the near future if the digitalization of waste transport can increase. The EU stresses the need for digital solutions, though primarily for supporting the tracking of waste shipments among OECD states. But being able to track waste shipments in international trade would also allow for better monitoring and thus open the door for more exemptions to the Basel rules. Another key issue for the future is to ensure that developing countries have the right systems, laws, and competencies in place to deal with toxic substances and waste. Thus, a justice perspective, where issues related to waste and toxic substances are addressed coherently, is called for. Hopefully, the vision of a fair circular economy, where the world's resources are more evenly divided, and problematic substances and waste flows are not exported to regions ill-equipped to handle them, will be guiding future developments.

[100] Nanda & Pring, n. 15, 474.
[101] *Ibid.*, 473–474.
[102] Milovantseva & Fitzpatrick, n. 22.
[103] *Ibid.*

PART IV

THE ATMOSPHERE

12

Implementing Principle 21 of the Stockholm Declaration: Regional Efforts to Regulate Transboundary Air Pollution

Phoebe Okowa and Sean O'Reilly

12.1 INTRODUCTION: EXPANDING THE NOTION OF TRANSBOUNDARY AIR POLLUTION AND THE LEGAL RESPONSE

The 1972 Stockholm Conference on the Human Environment was a watershed moment for global efforts to protect the environment.[1] A core part of the Stockholm Conference's legacy is the regulation of long-range transboundary air pollution. The influential scientific reports on acid rain presented at the conference showed that transboundary air pollution was not limited to local contexts, as in the *Trail Smelter Arbitration* delivered some thirty years earlier but stretched over huge areas and many national jurisdictions.[2] These insights sparked the negotiation of what would become a significant achievement, the 1979 Convention on Long-Range Transboundary Air Pollution (LRTAP Convention) and its protocols or, together with its protocols, the Air Pollution Treaties), applicable to the UN Economic Commission for Europe (UNECE) region – that is, Europe, North America, Caucasus, and Central Asia.[3] Now, at the time of UN International Meeting Stockholm+50: A Healthy Planet for the Prosperity of All – Our Responsibility, Our Opportunity, the UNECE Air Pollution Treaties are still

[1] See, e.g., Nico Schrijver, 'Stockholm 1972 and the Birth of International Sustainable Development Law', in this volume, 65.

[2] *Trail Smelter Arbitration (United States v Canada)*, Award, 16 April 1938 and 11 March 1941, reprinted in (1950) 3 *Reports of International Arbitral Awards* 1905.

[3] Convention on Long-Range Transboundary Air Pollution, 1979, 1302 UNTS 217 (LRTAP Convention). Among its related protocols are: Helsinki Protocol on the Reduction of Sulphur Emissions or Their Transboundary Fluxes by at Least 30%, 1985, 1480 UNTS 215; Protocol to the 1979 Convention on Long Range Transboundary Air Pollution on Further Reduction of Sulfur Emissions, 1994, 2030 UNTS 122; Protocol to the Convention on Long-Range Transboundary Air Pollution on Persistent Organic Pollutants, 1998, 2237 UNTS 4; Protocol Concerning the Control of Emissions of Nitrogen Oxides, 1988, 1593 UNTS 287; Protocol on the Reduction of Volatile Organic Compounds, 1991, 2001 UNTS 187.

widely praised as an exemplar of international co-operation in the protection of the environment. Less attention has been paid, however, to the question of whether the model established by the UNECE Air Pollution Treaties can be successfully replicated in other parts of the world.

This chapter will critically examine the relevance of the UNECE Air Pollution Treaties to the global South, with particular attention on the regulation of transboundary air pollution in Asia and Africa. State practice from these regions, including Southern Africa as well as Northeast and Southeast Asia, demonstrate that the framework of UNECE Air Pollution Treaties' cannot be directly transplanted into other contexts. Legal liability for transboundary air pollution is rarely adopted as a model (not even in the UNECE Air Pollution Treaties themselves), with the notable exception of Singapore, where it was adopted in response to the persistent haze from fires in Southeast Asia. It is therefore not surprising that the specific proclamation in both the *Trail Smelter Arbitration* and in principle 21 of the 1972 Stockholm Declaration on the Human Environment for state responsibility has not been interpreted as necessarily requiring the imposition of liability.[4] Regional legal frameworks like the UNECE Air Pollution Treaties are also surprisingly uncommon, again with the exception of Southeast Asia. The development of multilateral treaty regimes comparable to the UNECE Air Pollution Treaties is often hampered by regional factors that require tailored approaches before further cooperation is possible. In Southern Africa, for example, lack of data collection and low state capacity has stalled cooperation in tackling transboundary air pollution. Northeast Asia suffers from the opposite problem, where the proliferation of overlapping regional bodies and initiatives fosters scientific cooperation but impedes the gathering of momentum for states to commit to binding multilateral pollution-reduction agreements.

Overall, while the UNECE Air Pollution Treaties are no doubt an exemplar in international environmental governance, they do not represent a one-size-fits-all model for states in the global South. That does not mean that the Stockholm Conference's legacy for states in the global South is irrelevant, however. What this chapter shows is that these regions do aspire to cooperation in regulating transboundary air pollution in the manner of the UNECE Air Pollution Treaties and their success in tackling the problem. But the factors preventing the replication of the UNECE Air Pollution Treaties' success vary. Northeast and Southeast Asia, for instance, both possess coordinating bodies

4 'Declaration of the United Nations Conference on the Human Environment', in *Report of the UN Conference on the Human Environment*, UN Doc. A/CONF.48/14/Rev.1, 16 June 1972 (Stockholm Declaration).

similar to the UNECE and yet cannot progress beyond scientific cooperation. In the case of Southern Africa, coordination among states would not be sufficient to overcome their lack of development and inability to monitor, or define the scope of, the air pollution problem. This context creates stronger arguments for international (and not just regional) cooperation and assistance.

Section 12.2 of this chapter serves as an introduction to the historical context of the Stockholm Conference and its principle 21 as well as its impact on international environmental law. It will then move to an examination of the model created by the UNECE Air Pollution Treaties and the factors that contributed to their success in regulating transboundary air pollution in section 12.3. Section 12.4 will consider the regulation of transboundary air pollution in Africa beginning with an overview of the current challenges facing the continent with respect to air pollution and its transboundary effects. Presently, while air pollution is a pressing threat across Africa, both international and regional cooperation remains embryonic. This section will then analyse current state practice in Southern Africa with respect to transboundary air pollution. Despite the accumulation of regional policy frameworks, the regulation of transboundary air pollution in Southern Africa is hampered by a lack of objective data and poor state capacity to engage in data collection and monitoring. Section 12.5 explores the regulation of transboundary air pollution in Asia, contrasting the experiences of Northeast Asia and Southeast Asia as case studies. It describes the significant threat that air pollution poses to populations across Asia, including Northeast and Southeast Asia. Although industry and power generation are significant contributors to air pollution across the continent, Southeast Asia is particularly affected by haze from forest fires and land clearing, while Northeast Asia is also afflicted by dust storms. This part then analyses the state practice addressing those issues in their respective regions. Sections 12.6 and 12.7 conclude with reflections on the legacy of the Stockholm Conference and the UNECE Air Pollution Treaties for regulating air pollution in the global South.

12.2 THE HISTORICAL CONTEXT OF THE STOCKHOLM CONFERENCE AND PRINCIPLE 21 OF THE STOCKHOLM DECLARATION

The Stockholm Conference, despite being forward-looking in many ways, was also firmly a product of its time and was thus not immune to great power politics or the competing interests and objectives of its participants. This chapter cannot cover in detail the fraught diplomatic road to the Stockholm Conference, but it will emphasize two areas of relevance before moving to principle 21. The first is that the question of transboundary air pollution and the appropriate responses to it assumed a particular prominence at the Stockholm Conference.[5] This was in large part due to Sweden's efforts to highlight the growing problem of acid rain and air pollution across Europe.[6] Scandinavian states, in particular, were deeply concerned by acid rain's effect on the environment, and scientific consensus was building that acid rain was bringing deleterious effects to lakes, fisheries, and forests across Europe. Sweden's 1971 scientific case study, entitled *Air Pollution across National Boundaries: The Impact on the Environment of Sulphur in Air and Precipitation*, was thus instrumental in setting the tone of the Stockholm Conference.[7] This was part of a diplomatic offensive by Sweden that aimed not only to advance its agenda on acid rain and pollution but also to position the conference as a broader platform for cooperation between Eastern and Western diplomatic blocs.[8]

This intent by Sweden proved a prescient one as the United States and the Soviet Union, after a period of worsening relations following, among other incidents, the Korean War (1950–1953), the Cuban Missile Crisis (1962), and the ongoing Vietnam War (1955–1975) were exploring potential off-ramps that could lead to a further détente.[9] In fact, the United States and the Soviet Union had concluded, a year prior to the Stockholm Conference, their own bilateral agreement on cooperation in environmental protection.[10] Scandinavian diplomats had keenly observed that there was potential for both Eastern and Western blocs, despite their political differences, to negotiate a binding agreement on acid rain.[11] It was estimated at the time, for example, that the damage to agriculture throughout the western regions of the Soviet Union (now Belarus, Lithuania, Latvia, and Estonia) amounted to US $150 million per year.[12] Similarly, the acidification of fresh water systems in Scandinavia (as well as in Canada) had been a matter of serious scientific

5 *Ibid.*

6 See generally Eric Paglia, 'The Swedish Initiative and the 1972 Stockholm Conference: The Decisive Role of Science Diplomacy in the Emergence of Global Environmental Governance' (2021) 8(2) *Humanities and Social Sciences Communications* 1.

7 Bert Bolin *et al.*, *Air Pollution across National Boundaries: The Impact on the Environment of Sulfur in Air and Precipitation: Sweden's Case Study for the United Nations Conference on the Human Environment* (P.A. Norstedt, 1971).

8 Lars-Goran Engfelt, 'The United Nations and the Human Environment: Some Experiences' (1973) 27(3) *International Organisation* 393.

9 UN Economic Commission for Europe (UNECE), *Clearing the Air: 25 Years of the Convention on Long-Range Transboundary Air Pollution*, UN Doc. ECE/EB.AIR/84, 2004, 21.

10 Agreement on Cooperation in the Field of Environmental Protection between the United States of America and the Union of Soviet Socialist Republics, 1972, 846 UNTS 105.

11 UNECE, n. 9, 9.

12 *Ibid.*, 9.

study since at least the 1960s.[13] Cooperation between Eastern and Western blocs would only manifest later, however, as the Soviet Union and other Eastern bloc states (except Romania) boycotted the Stockholm Conference due to diplomatic controversy over the status of East Germany.

The second important consideration was the participation of states from the global South in the Stockholm Conference, which proved to be a major point of contention. Rather than being concerned about transboundary air pollution, developing states were concerned with the perceived posturing by developed states, and some viewed the Stockholm Conference as either ignoring the importance of development or using environmental protection as a guise with which to continue established patterns of exploitation.[14] This tension was perhaps best encapsulated by the speech given by Indira Gandhi at the Stockholm Conference's plenary session where she memorably asked: 'Are not poverty and need the greatest polluters?'[15] The scepticism of developing states, however, was met by genuine efforts not just by the Stockholm Conference's Secretariat but also by participating developed states to cement the link between development and the environment.[16] The influential Founex report in 1971 placed development firmly on the Stockholm Conference's agenda, concluding that 'the major environmental problems of developing countries . . . are predominantly problems that reflect the poverty and very lack of development in their societies'.[17] As will be seen, development and environmental protection remain recurring themes in addressing environmental protection and transboundary air pollution to this day.

The major product of the Stockholm Conference – the highly influential Stockholm Declaration – contained twenty-six principles stated to be the 'common conviction' of participating states.[18] Most pertinently for this chapter is principle 21, which provides that '[s]tates have [. . .] the Sovereign right to exploit their own resources pursuant to their own environmental policies, and

[13] *Ibid.*, 17, 61; Lars Björkbom, 'Negotiations over Transboundary Air Pollution: The Case of Europe' (1999) 4 *International Negotiation* 389, 392, n. 3 (and the case studies cited therein); Nuria Castells, 'Science and Policy in International Environmental Agreements: Lessons from the European Experience on Transboundary Air Pollution' (2001) 1 *International Environmental Agreements: Politics, Law and Economics* 405, 406.

[14] Engfelt, n. 8, 402.

[15] Peter Sand, 'Origin and History', in Lavanya Rajamani & Jacqueline Peel (eds.), *The Oxford Handbook of International Environmental Law* (Oxford University Press, 2021), 56; Sumudu Atapattu, 'Global South Approaches', in Rajamani & Peel, *ibid.*, 189.

[16] Engfelt, n. 8, 400.

[17] United Nations, *Development and Environment: Report and Working Papers of a Panel of Experts Convened by the Secretary General of the United Nations Conference on the Human Environment (Founex, Switzerland, June 4–12, 1972)*, 1972, 6.

[18] Stockholm Declaration, n. 4.

the responsibility to ensure that activities within their jurisdiction or control do not cause damage to the environment of other States or of areas beyond the limits of national jurisdiction'.[19] The immediate familiarity of this formulation indicates that the Stockholm Conference did not proceed on the basis of a *tabula rasa* but recognized that environmental problems, including transboundary air pollution, were governed by law. The responsibility of states was thereby concretized as a foundational principle (albeit without the consequences of making such a move expressly spelled out).

Principle 21 was an explicit nod to the *Trial Smelter Arbitration* where the tribunal observed that, under the principles of international law, 'no State has the right to use or permit the use of its territory in such a manner as to cause injury by fumes in or to the territory of [other states], when the case is of serious consequence and the injury is established by clear and convincing evidence'.[20] The Stockholm Declaration's preambular provisions established the objectives of the principles contained therein as being to 'inspire and guide the peoples of the world in the preservation and enhancement of the human environment'.[21] But, if so, what sort of regime did it anticipate? Would it be one where liability and compensation for environmental harm would take centre stage? Responsibility in this formulation would represent the traditional positivist model of damages awarded in response to a concrete identifiable breach of an existing legal right. Or would it envisage a model of responsibility capable of balancing competing values, such as the economic or social value of the polluting activity?[22] Interestingly, principle 22 of the Stockholm Declaration provides that states 'shall ... co-operate to develop further the international law regarding liability and compensation for the victims of pollution'.[23] This would indicate a tendency towards some form of liability regime. While examples can be seen in other areas of environmental law – for example, marine pollution[24] – principle 22 did not appear to have much effect on transboundary air pollution. When assessing the international law on the protection of the atmosphere, the International Law Commission focused its attention when considering principle 21, on obligations of prevention and the

[19] *Ibid.*, principle 21.

[20] *Trail Smelter*, n. 2, 1965.

[21] United Nations, n. 17, 3.

[22] Russell Miller, 'Surprising Parallels between *Trail Smelter* and the Global Climate Change Regime', in Rebecca M. Bratspies & Russell A. Miller (eds.), *Transboundary Harm in International Law: Lessons from the Trail Smelter Arbitration* (Cambridge University Press, 2006).

[23] Stockholm Declaration, n. 4, principle 22.

[24] International Convention on Civil Liability for Oil Pollution Damage, 1969, 973 UNTS 3.

need to conduct environmental impact assessments (albeit leaving the door open for a residual compensation regime in the event of harm).[25]

12.3 REGULATING TRANSBOUNDARY AIR POLLUTION IN THE UNECE REGION

While the idea of a multilateral convention to control transboundary air pollution had been put forward at the Stockholm Conference, its realization would only come to fruition a few years later; the Soviet Union and other Eastern bloc states had boycotted the Stockholm Conference, making cooperation difficult. The efforts by Scandinavian states for a transboundary air pollution convention continued at the Conference on Security and Co-operation, which took place from 1973 to 1975 in both Helsinki and Geneva (Helsinki Conference).

During this brief thaw in the Cold War, the 'Final Act' of the Helsinki Conference officially reopened the door to environmental cooperation between the two great powers and, with them, other states in Western and Eastern Europe. The 'Environment' was the subject of its own section of the Final Act as a matter for 'Co-Operation in the Field of Economics, of Science and Technology and of the Environment'. Echoes of principle 21 are visible in the preamble to the Final Act's section on the environment, albeit couched in the amicable terms of 'the spirit of co-operation'.[26] Most pertinently, one of the Final Act's 'recommendations on specific measures' was 'to develop through international co-operation an extensive programme for the monitoring and evaluation of the long-range transport of air pollutants, starting with sulphur dioxide'.[27] With the stage having been set, it was a proposal from the Soviet Union in 1976 (relayed via Norway and Sweden to make it more palatable) that the subject of the multilateral convention be acid rain.[28]

Following several years of arduous negotiations, the LRTAP Convention was adopted by thirty-two states at a high-level meeting in November 1979 and subsequently entered into force on 16 March 1983.[29] The original participants were confined to Europe and North America, although, since 2011, there have been concerted efforts to involve other states in Central Asia and the Caucuses

[25] Shinya Murase, *Third Report on the Protection of the Atmosphere*, UN Doc. A/CN.4/692, 25 February 2016.

[26] Conference on Security and Co-Operation in Europe (Helsinki, 30 July 1975–1 August 1975), Final Act.

[27] *Ibid.*

[28] UNECE, n. 9, 10; Björkbom, n. 13, 396.

[29] LRTAP Convention, n. 3, art. 16(1).

but with only limited success.[30] The adoption of the LRTAP Convention's protocols across the UNECE (which now counts fifty-six states among its members) has been scattered.[31] What today comprises the UNECE Air Pollution Treaties is the LRTAP Convention along with eight protocols that were entered into between (some, not all) states parties from 1984 to 1999.[32] These protocols, together with decisions of its Executive Body (which effectively functions as a Conference of the Parties), set out in detail the institutional and substantive framework that establishes the normative content of the LRTAP Convention's obligations. While the LRTAP Convention in its original form appeared skeletal, hindsight teaches us that it represents a successful (and one of the first) example of a 'framework convention'. Framework conventions are those international treaties whose body text contains broad commitments that are subsequently built out by protocols, amendments, or decisions of subsidiary bodies established under the treaty.[33] As such, the LRTAP Convention serves as a worthy prototype for arriving at a consensus in the face of both scientific uncertainty and competing priorities among states parties. As an aside, it is certainly a testament to the UNECE Air Pollution Treaties' influence that both the 1987 Montreal Protocol – touted as one of the most successful environmental agreements of all time – and the 1992 UN Framework Convention on Climate Change share these same normative features.[34]

A large part of the consensus that made the LRTAP Convention possible was that it and its protocols were negotiated under the auspices of the UNECE. The UNECE acting as the coordinating body allowed it to foster both negotiations between the parties and ongoing review of the scientific basis for the LRTAP Convention's obligations.[35] As will be suggested further below in sections 12.4 and 12.5, the absence of equivalent similarly equipped institutions may explain the relative lack of progress in other regions.

[30] Adam Byrne, 'Trouble in the Air: Recent Developments under the 1979 Convention on Long Range Transboundary Air Pollution' (2017) 26(3) *Review of European Comparative and International Environmental Law* (*RECIEL*) 210. Formally, in addition to most countries in Europe, Russia, Turkey, Canada, and the United States, some states in the Caucasus and Central Asia – Armenia, Georgia, Azerbaijan, Kazakhstan, and Kyrgyzstan – are involved as parties to the LRTAP Convention, n. 3.

[31] Byrne, n. 30.

[32] See n. 3 above.

[33] Another notable example in international environmental law is the UN Framework Convention on Climate Change, 1992, 1771 UNTS 107 (UNFCCC).

[34] Montreal Protocol on Substances That Deplete the Ozone Layer, 1987, 1522 UNTS 3; UNFCCC, n. 33, arts. 2–4.

[35] See, e.g., Gregory Wetstone, 'Long-Range Transboundary Air Pollution: Executive Body, First Session' (1983) 11 *Environmental Policy and Law* 26.

Supplementing the coordinating role of the UNECE was the Independent Environmental Monitoring Program (EMEP).[36] The EMEP and its steering body were what provided a strong scientific foundation for the policy work that continued to inform the evolution of the UNECE Air Pollution Treaties.[37] The involvement of scientific research and information sharing in the treaty-making process is widely seen as one of the LRTAP Convention's successes.[38]

The key provisions in the LRTAP Convention contain substantive obligations of means. States parties are required to achieve specified reductions in emissions levels, but they are left a wide margin of appreciation in how they achieve this objective. States parties are only required to 'endeavour to limit and, as far as possible, gradually reduce and prevent air pollution including long-range transboundary air pollution'.[39] Article 3 then envisions that this obligation would be realized through successive processes of information exchange, consultation, research, and monitoring (implemented by the EMEP and its various working groups).[40] The core of the treaty, Article 6, contains an early form of the now well-known 'due diligence' obligation – parties are exhorted to 'develop the best policies and strategies including air quality management systems and, as part of them, control measures ... in particular by using the best available technology'.[41] The concept of 'best available technology' was sufficiently flexible to be developed in the LRTAP Convention's subsequent protocols and fit neatly into its science and technology-driven framework.[42] This development, too, took time. The LRTAP Convention's first protocol on sulphur emissions, for example, was not backed by any technological guidance because it was not envisaged that technological cooperation would materialize; as political conditions improved, these were added to the treaty regime.[43]

Conspicuously absent from the LRTAP Convention is the liability model of transboundary pollution restated in principle 21. In fact, far from cautiously acknowledging principle 21, as the Final Act of the Helsinki Conference did, the LRTAP Convention controversially eschewed liability altogether (in

36 See LRTAP Convention, n. 3, arts. 9–10; Protocol to the LRTAP Convention on the Long-term Financing of the Co-operative Programme for Monitoring and Evaluation of the Long-Range Transmission of Air Pollutants in Europe, 1984, 1491 UNTS 167.

37 Castells, n. 13, 409.

38 Noelle Eckley, 'Dependable Dynamism: Lessons for Designing Scientific Assessment Processes in Consensus Negotiations' (2002) 12 *Global Environmental Change* 15, 17.

39 LRTAP Convention, n. 3, art. 2.

40 *Ibid.*, art. 3.

41 *Ibid.*, art. 6.

42 UNECE, n. 9, 143.

43 *Ibid.*, 112.

a footnote no less).[44] The footnote was attached to Article 8(f) of the LRTAP Convention, which is a provision concerning the exchange of 'data relating to the effects of long-range transboundary air pollution and the extent of the damage which these data indicate can be attributed to long-range transboundary air pollution'. The footnote was specifically inserted on the insistence of the United Kingdom, which did not want the duties pertaining to the exchange of information to be linked to the idea of responsibility.[45] While it is questionable whether the footnote to Article 8(f) is sufficient as a matter of international law to exclude state responsibility, it is likely that such principles were beyond the intentions of the negotiating states, especially in the light of the political tensions of that era.[46] A previous Nordic proposal to insert liability provisions into the LRTAP Convention was rejected by the parties, and,[47] to date, there appears to have been no attempts to evoke state responsibility for any alleged breaches of the LRTAP Convention. Even as the political conflicts that marked the beginning of the convention melted away, there was still no shift towards a liability and compensation model as envisaged by Principle 21. Even placing cooperation aside, this is likely explicable by the significant causal complexity posed by long-range transboundary air pollution. Regulating emissions of various airborne pollutants across UNECE states is far removed from the simple bilateral cases envisaged by the *Trail Smelter Arbitration*.[48] The complex and highly technical nature of modern air pollution regulation called for pragmatism rather than litigation. By many accounts, it appears that this approach was ultimately successful in reducing air pollution across Europe.[49]

Given the core features of the UNECE Air Pollution Treaties explored in sections 12.1–12.3 of this article, has this model successfully been replicated in other parts of the world and, if not, why not? The following two sections of this chapter will outline the regulation of air pollution in both Africa and Asia. Before exploring the frameworks in question, each section will begin with an overview of the threat caused by air pollution in each region.

[44] See LRTAP Convention, n. 3, art. 8(f).

[45] *Report of the High-Level Meeting within the Framework of the ECE on the Protection of the Environment, Geneva, 13–15 November 1979*, UN Doc. ECE/HLM.1/2/Add 1, Annex IV, 1979, 104.

[46] See generally Phoebe Okowa, *State Responsibility for Transboundary Air Pollution* (Oxford University Press, 2000), ch. 2.

[47] Marc Pallemaerts, 'International Legal Aspects of Long-range Transboundary Air Pollution' (1988) 1 *Hague Yearbook of International Law* 189, 216.

[48] Okowa, n. 46, 10–11.

[49] Byrne, n. 30.

12.4 REGULATING TRANSBOUNDARY AIR POLLUTION IN AFRICA

12.4.1 *The Problem of Air Pollution on the African Continent*

Africa is a large and diverse continent, and it would be reductive to offer a uniform simplistic explanation that largely hinges on its relative state of underdevelopment. It is in fact a continent of unique regions and over fifty states at various stages of development. That said, a lack of granular data regarding air pollution means that this issue can only be approached at a high level of abstraction. What is clear, however, is that air pollution represents a significant threat to populations and vulnerable individuals across Africa. In 2019, it was estimated that air pollution was responsible for 1.1 million deaths across the continent, representing 16.3 per cent of all deaths caused by air pollution globally.[50] Those most susceptible to deaths caused by air pollution are children and the elderly.[51]

The sources of air pollution across Africa vary based on geographic conditions and particular states. However, the largest threat posed by air pollution is in fact household air pollution, primarily from the use of solid fuels in cooking. Approximately 77 per cent of households in Africa use solid fuels (biomass fuels, wood, charcoal, and so on) for both cooking and heating.[52] While this is predominantly a rural phenomenon, around 80 per cent of urban households across Africa use charcoal as their primary cooking fuel.[53] It is not surprising, therefore, that household air pollution was the most significant cause of death (697,000 out of 1.1 million) compared to other sources of air pollution across Africa.[54] Rapid growth across the continent, and greater access to technology, is decreasing the impact of household air pollution, however.[55] Unfortunately, urbanization and industrialization are causing a concomitant rise in deaths and health impacts attributable to outside air pollution.[56] In urban areas, the burning of waste and refuse and emissions from vehicle exhausts are significant contributors to outdoor air pollution.[57] A recent study in 2020 found that emissions from

50 Samantha Fisher *et al.*, 'Air Pollution and Development in Africa: Impacts on Health, the Economy, and Human Capital' (2021) 5 *Lancet Planetary Health* e681.

51 Patrick Katoto *et al.*, 'Ambient Air Pollution and Health in Sub-Saharan Africa: Current Evidence, Perspectives and a Call to Action' (2019) *Environmental Research* 173, 174–188.

52 *Ibid.*

53 Leo Zulu & Robert Richardson, 'Charcoal, Livelihoods, and Poverty Reduction: Evidence from Sub-Saharan Africa' (2013) 17(2) *Energy for Sustainable Development* 127.

54 Fisher *et al.*, n. 50.

55 *Ibid.*

56 *Ibid.*

57 Eleanne Van Vliet & Patrick Kinney, 'Impacts of Roadway Emissions on Urban Particulate Matter Concentrations in Sub-Saharan Africa: New Evidence from Nairobi, Kenya' (2007) 2(4) *Environmental Research Letters* 045028.

the open burning of refuse in Addis Ababa was contributing to particulate matter (PM 2.5) readings that were 8.6 times higher than the World Health Organization's (WHO) recommended guidelines.[58] Similar research that took place in informal settlements in Nairobi also found that residents were exposed to particulate matter (PM 2.5) levels far above what is recommended by the WHO as safe.[59]

Besides the sources mentioned above, air pollution in Africa also originates from desert dust, fires, and burning biomass as well as emissions from power generation and industry.[60] Pausing here, one observation becomes immediately obvious. The dominance of household air pollution as a cause of death and negative health impacts indicates that air pollution across Africa manifests as a public health concern rather than as an ecological one. Similarly, household air pollution alone does not implicate interstate relations and is not amenable to being rectified via international agreements as opposed to targeted interventions (and greater economic development) at the domestic level. The African context thus presents the opposite of that faced by Eastern and Western Europe in the 1970s. As mentioned, the studies that brought acidification to states' attention were centred on, among other things, the damage from sulphur emissions to lakes, rivers, and forests. The source of these emissions was heavy industry across Europe. Africa, by contrast, is at present the least industrialized continent on Earth.[61] At first glance, this would weigh strongly against an uncritical importation of the LRTAP Convention's framework into the African context. However, transboundary air pollution from outdoor sources has received some (limited) attention in Africa, and it is to these frameworks that we now turn.

12.4.2 *Regional Efforts to Regulate Transboundary Air Pollution in Africa*

As discussed, Africa should not be viewed reductively as a continent without considering the contexts of specific regions and states. While policy initiatives with respect to air pollution vary across the continent, this section will focus particularly on Southern Africa, which has seen the most regional cooperation between states and the greatest successes (so far) in implementing

58 Tadesse Weyuma Bulto, 'Impact of Open Burning Refuse on Air Quality: In the Case of "Hidar Sitaten" at Addis Ababa, Ethiopia' (2020) *Environmental Health Insights* 14.

59 Thaddaeus Egondi *et al.*, 'Exposure to Outdoor Particles (PM2.5) and Associated Child Morbidity and Mortality in Socially Deprived Neighborhoods of Nairobi, Kenya' (2018) 9(9) *Atmosphere* 351.

60 Susanne Bauer *et al.*, 'Desert Dust, Industrialization, and Agricultural Fires: Health Impacts of Outdoor Air Pollution' (2019) 124 *Africa Journal of Geophysical Research* 4104.

61 Landry Signé & Chelsea Johnson, *The Potential of Manufacturing and Industrialisation in Africa* (Brookings Africa Growth Initiative, 2018).

international measures to reduce air pollution. At present, there is no continent-wide air pollution treaty in the vein of the UNECE Air Pollution Treaties. It is notable that perhaps the earliest efforts to create regional and interstate air pollution initiatives in Africa bears a direct connection to the LRTAP Convention and the Stockholm Conference. Inspired by the successes of its environmental diplomacy, the Swedish International Development Agency (SIDA) began funding programmes to foster air pollution regulation on a regional basis in the Global South – Regional Air Pollution in Developing Countries (RAPIDC).[62] RAPIDC's purpose was explicitly to 'facilitate the development of agreements and/or protocols to implement measures which prevent and control air pollution through promoting international cooperation and developing scientific information for the policy process'.[63] Its focus in Africa was in the south of the continent, primarily those states that would later go on to form and/or join the Southern African Development Community (SADC) (that is, Botswana, Malawi, Tanzania, Zambia, South Africa, and Mozambique).[64]

RAPIDC's first initiative in Southern Africa was the Air Pollution Information Network for Africa (APINA) in 1997. APINA functioned as a network of scientists who would cooperate in gathering data and fostering policy developments around air pollution in Africa. Following shortly after was a policy dialogue in 1998 held under the auspices of the SADC, which led to the Harare Resolution on the Prevention and Control of Regional Air Pollution in Southern Africa and Its Likely Transboundary Effects (Harare Resolution).[65] The Harare Resolution saw an African vision of the recognition of the problem of transboundary air pollution, with emphasis being placed on the importance of balancing economic development, and also the threat to health posed by air pollution.[66] The Harare Resolution's ultimate objective was a call to request the SADC Council of Ministers to develop a binding protocol on regional air quality and atmospheric emissions.[67]

62 John Magne Skjelvik & Haakon Vennemo, *Regional Air Pollution in Developing Countries (RAPIDC) 1998–2007* (Swedish International Development Agency, 2008).

63 *Ibid.*, 5.

64 Treaty of the Southern African Development Community,1992, 3062 UNTS 331 (SADC Treaty). Note that the SADC Treaty calls for the achievement of sustainable utilization of natural resources and the effective protection of the environment.

65 Harare Resolution on the Prevention and Control of Regional Air Pollution in Southern Africa and Its Likely Transboundary Effects, 1998, cited in RAPIDC, *Air Pollution in Asia and Africa: Approaches to the RAPIDC Programme*, Proceedings of the First Open Seminar on Regional Air Pollution in Developing Countries, 4 June 2002, 19.

66 *Ibid.*, fifth perambulatory paragraph.

67 *Ibid.*, final paragraph.

The Harare Resolution itself was of course a soft law instrument reiterating the conclusions of the 1998 policy dialogue and did not create binding obligations on the SADC member states. However, this did not dent its ambitions. Likely owing to SIDA's influence, the Harare Resolution expressly stated that 'international agreements that have successfully addressed air pollution in industrialized regions, such as the [LRTAP Convention] might provide useful guidance for developing appropriate legislation for Southern Africa'.[68] Interestingly, the Harare Resolution drew even deeper from the corpus of international environmental law by 'reiterating' principle 21 in its preamble.[69] But the direct lineage to the UNECE Air Pollution Treaties and principle 21 did not guarantee that Southern African efforts to create a multilateral air pollution framework would meet the same success.

After the Harare Resolution, the SADC member states continued to meet with policy support from APINA and build momentum for the regulation of transboundary air pollution. Following the second policy dialogue, the parties adopted the 2003 Maputo Declaration, which revisited similar themes as the Harare Resolution, including reiterating principle 21.[70] The Maputo Declaration was more focused, identifying specific sources of outdoor air pollution (industry, transport, wildfires, domestic fuel, and waste burning) and recommending that the SADC member states, among other things, analyse the causes of air pollution and harmonize national legislation and monitoring standards.[71] This was built on even further in the 2008 Lusaka Agreement, which contained a detailed list of over sixty actions to be taken by SADC member states across the areas highlighted by the Maputo Declaration and more.[72] The Lusaka Agreement established agendas for cooperation, data collection, the harmonization of national laws, and encouraged emission reductions across several sectors. The stage appeared to be set for an African framework convention to follow in the footsteps of the UNECE Air Pollution Treaties.

68 *Ibid.*, eighth perambulatory paragraph.

69 *Ibid.*, second perambulatory paragraph.

70 Maputo Declaration on the Prevention and Control of Regional Air Pollution in Southern Africa and Its Likely Transboundary Effects, 2003, www.sei.org/wp-content/uploads/2021/05/final-circulated-lusaka-agreement.pdf.

71 *Ibid.*, first perambulatory paragraph.

72 Southern African Development Community (SADC) Regional Policy Framework on Air Pollution, 2008, www.sei.org/wp-content/uploads/2021/05/final-circulated-lusaka-agreement.pdf (Lusaka Agreement). The Lusaka Agreement was adopted by the SADC ministers at their ministerial session on 7 March 2008. There is no treaty registered at the UN depository matching the Lusaka Agreement.

And, yet, those ambitions never seemed to bear fruit. The Lusaka Agreement, the SADC's most ambitious initiative on air pollution at the time, did not take the form of an international treaty. Despite being termed an 'agreement', it was, in reality, a regional policy framework – namely, a further and more elaborate soft law instrument to set the stage for further cooperation.[73] Sometime thereafter, the SADC did include transboundary air pollution in its 2014 Protocol on Environmental Management for Sustainable Development, which is binding on all the SADC member states.[74] Article 5 of the Protocol provides that states parties 'shall take measures to manage and control the transboundary effects of air pollution' through the elaboration of national frameworks, 'managing and reducing emissions', and promoting low-carbon development. While binding, there appears to be little information concerning the SADC member states' implementation of the protocol as well as the previous soft law declarations. Without comprehensive information, it is difficult to evaluate the effectiveness of this nascent framework or whether it is being implemented within the SADC at all. To the best of our research, progress on transboundary air pollution cooperation in Southern Africa has mostly stalled.

The next concern, therefore, is whether this failure to implement a form of regional air pollution control beyond basic cooperation is due to flaws inherent in the UNECE Air Pollution Treaties' model or a failure to properly modify the model to the African context. The answer is likely the latter. At present, the clearest failure is a lack of objective data, which makes monitoring and tackling reductions in air pollution exceedingly difficult, especially in a coordinated manner. Therefore, even binding commitments would be meaningless without objective measures of air pollution in Southern Africa. As explored earlier in this chapter, the scientific foundations of the UNECE Air Pollution Treaties were instrumental to its success, and this element appears to be lacking in Southern Africa, even with the assistance from APINA. There is an overall lack of air quality data across Africa, making compiling air pollution information difficult.[75] The issue is likely down to state capacity as most SADC member states (except South Africa) only have

[73] *Ibid.*

[74] Protocol on Environmental Management for Sustainable Development, 2014, www.veritaszim.net/sites/veritas_d/files/Protocol%20on%20Environmental%20Management%20for%20Sustainable%20Development.pdf.

[75] Stephen Simukanga *et al.*, *The Air Pollution Information Network for Africa: Activities Promoting Regional Co-Operation on Air Pollution Issues in Southern Africa*, 2003, www.umad.de/infos/cleanair13/pdf/full_292.pdf.

a limited number of air quality monitoring stations.[76] Therefore, without international assistance, the SADC states, or even African states generally, would be unable to generate sufficient data to define the problems of transboundary pollution for a future convention. Without this fundamental precondition being fulfilled, it is unlikely that the LRTAP Convention model will succeed.

12.5 REGULATING TRANSBOUNDARY AIR POLLUTION IN ASIA

As a contrast to the background of the LRTAP Convention and the embryonic attempts to regulate transboundary air pollution in Africa, this part will explore the legal frameworks concerning transboundary air pollution in Asia. Again, Asia is too large a continent to be reduced to a single metric. The parts that follow will contrast the cases of Northeast Asia (Japan, China, and South Korea) with Southeast Asia. This part will again begin with an overview of the threats caused by air pollution in the region before examining whether states in those regions have adopted solutions that are similar to those seen in the UNECE Air Pollution Treaties.

12.5.1 *Air Pollution in Northeast and Southeast Asia*

While there are common determinants of pollution across Asia, as there are anywhere in the world, the geographic circumstances of Northeast and Southeast Asia make them each vulnerable to certain types of air pollution. China, South Korea, and Japan will be considered together as their geographic proximity and climatic continuity have them functioning as a single ecological community.[77] In Northeast Asia, pollution mostly comes from industry and power generation, including from coal-fired power plants. China, Japan, and South Korea have all struggled with air pollution in the previous decades given their high rates of industrialization and rapid economic growth. The major air pollution source across all three states is industry,[78] which echoes the conditions that Europe faced prior to the entry into force of the LRTAP Convention. In particular, all three states exhibit high levels of, among other

76 See, e.g., Modupe Akinola *et al.*, 'Air Quality Management in Botswana' (2017) 27(1) *Clean Air Journal* 43; Harold Mapoma *et al.*, 'State of Air Quality in Malawi' (2013) 4(11) *Journal of Environmental Protection* 1258.

77 Reinhard Drifte, Transboundary Pollution as an Issue in Northeast Asian Regional Politics, London School of Economics Asia Research Centre Report no. 12, 2005, 2.

78 Organisation for Economic Co-operation and Development (OECD), *Enhancing Air Quality in North East Asia: Regulatory Frameworks, Enforcement and Co-operation*, 2019.

things, sulphur dioxide and nitrogen dioxide emissions.[79] The region's most pervasive form of transboundary air pollution is acid rain, with regional winds serving as powerful vectors for acid deposition caused by sulphur dioxide and nitrogen dioxide emissions generated in all three countries.[80]

By far the largest source of air pollution in Northeast Asia is China, owing to its heavy reliance on coal-fired power plants and gigantic production base. Around half of all installed power generation in China currently is still based on coal.[81] This contributes heavily to its emission of air pollution that is then dispersed across Asia, including Northeast Asia.[82] South Korea and Japan, both downwind of China, can experience significant haze and pollution when exacerbated by weather patterns.[83] South Korea, as another manufacturing powerhouse, is also a significant generator of air pollution, as is Japan.[84] Besides air pollution arising from industry and power generation, Northeast Asia sees significant pollution from dust originating in Mongolia and China's Inner Mongolia, which is then periodically dispersed over the region.[85] All three states thus share responsibility for, and the experience of, the deleterious effects of transboundary air pollution. Theoretically, this would generate strong reasons in favour of cooperation and mitigation on the part of each state. However, as is discussed next, cooperation between China, South Korea, and Japan has not yet progressed beyond scientific and technical cooperation.

Southeast Asia presents a different set of challenges caused by transboundary air pollution. While pollution from industry and deforestation is significant (including long-range transboundary air pollution from other parts of Asia), it has not received as much attention as the haze pollution that plagues Southeast Asia.[86] While originating in several states across Southeast Asia, including Vietnam, Thailand, and Malaysia, smoke from fires in Indonesia are the main drivers of haze pollution in Southeast

79 OECD, n. 78; Drifte, n. 77, 2.

80 Drifte, n. 77, 2.

81 'Coal Still Accounted for Nearly 60% of China's Electricity Supply in 2023: CEC', *S&P Global*, 31 January 2024, https://shorturl.at/qVH75.

82 Xinming Du *et al*., 'Transboundary Air Pollution from Coal-Fired Power Generation' (2020) 270 *Journal of Environmental Management* 110862.

83 OECD, n. 78, 29.

84 *Ibid*.

85 Laura Henry *et al*., 'From Smelter Fumes to Silk Road Winds: Exploring Legal Responses to Transboundary Air Pollution over South Korea' (2012) 11 *Washington University Global Studies Law Review* 565.

86 Qinqin Chen & David Taylor, 'Transboundary Atmospheric Pollution in Southeast Asia: Current Methods, Limitations and Future Developments' (2018) 48 *Critical Reviews in Environmental Science and Technology* 997.

Asia.[87] Agriculture practices in Indonesia, including for rice paddies and land near forests, involves the cycling of land, which, while fallow, becomes overgrown with wooded vegetation. The cheapest and most convenient method to clear this land is by burning, which when conducted across Indonesia's vast territory generates significant haze pollution.[88] Indonesia is also home to rich peat lands, which, when burned for agriculture, cause haze pollution; peat fires are the main cause of the haze pollution that emanates from Indonesia.[89] The level of haze pollution created by these burnings across Southeast Asia can be exacerbated by regional weather patterns such as El Niño.[90] For instance, the large fires in 2015 led to the destruction of over 600,000 hectares of peat land in Indonesia and blanketed the region in haze.[91]

12.5.2 *Comparing Regional Efforts to Regulate Transboundary Air Pollution in Asia*

Dealing first with Northeast Asia, it appears as if it suffers from the opposite problem from Southern Africa. There is a large amount of technical cooperation and scientific data collection and sharing among China, Japan, and Korea. But, ironically, cooperation is split over a multiplicity of initiatives and bodies that have overlapping mandates. Instead of building momentum towards the creation of a binding framework, this duplication of efforts may have stifled it instead. At present, as with Africa, there is no regional agreement covering transboundary air pollution akin to the UNECE Air Pollution Treaties. The overarching tendency among China, Japan, and South Korea is for environmental matters to be dealt with via direct diplomacy on a case-by-case basis rather than through multilateral conventions.[92]

87 See generally Paruedee Nguitragool, 'Negotiating the Haze Treaty Rationality and Institutions in the Negotiations for the ASEAN Agreement on Transboundary Haze Pollution' (2002) 51(2) *Asian Survey* 356.

88 Chen & Taylor, n. 86.

89 Shawkat Alam & Laely Nuridayah, 'The International Law on Transboundary Haze Pollution: What Can We Learn from the Southeast Asia Region?' (2017) 26 *RECIEL* 243.

90 María José Rodríguez Vásquez *et al.*, 'Estimating Greenhouse Gas Emissions from Peat Combustion in Wildfires on Indonesian Peatlands, and Their Uncertainty' (2021) 35(2) *Global Biogeochemical Cycles* 1.

91 Chen & Taylor, n. 86.

92 Esook Yoon, 'Cooperation for Transboundary Pollution in Northeast Asia: Non-binding Agreements and Regional Countries' Policy Interests' (2007) 22(2) *Pacific Focus* 77; Inkyoung Kim, 'Messages from a Middle Power: Participation by the Republic of Korea in Regional Environmental Cooperation on Transboundary Air Pollution Issues' (2014) 14 *International Environmental Agreements* 147.

The first point to note is that each of the three states have already entered into bilateral agreements with each other for cooperation on environmental matters, including air pollution. In 1993, South Korea and China signed an agreement on environmental cooperation and established a joint committee thereunder to launch projects aimed at improving environmental protection in China, including projects related to air pollution.[93] Japan and South Korea also signed an environmental cooperation treaty that same year.[94] Subsequently, in 1994, Japan and China signed their own bilateral agreement on environmental cooperation and conservation.[95] Japan's agreement with China also included significant development aid and technical assistance to promote green technology. Japan, for example, appears to prefer engaging with China on environmental protection via their existing bilateral treaty and development projects.[96] Furthermore, all three states have exhibited high degrees of cooperation in other areas of environmental protection, including entering into binding agreements.[97] Transboundary air pollution, however, continues to remain a stubborn outlier.

One major factor inhibiting the formation of a binding agreement on air pollution is the overlap and duplication of efforts between different agencies and regional initiatives (see Table 12.1). One of the first initiatives in the region was the Acid Deposition Monitoring Network in East Asia (EANET) in 1998, which did not contain any binding obligations but was formed as a cooperative framework to create a common understanding among states on the problem of acid deposition and provide policy inputs through data collection.[98] As part of its work, EANET included yearly intergovernmental meetings to discuss progress on its objectives and continually update scientific and monitoring standards.[99] EANET would also publish reports periodically outlining its progress on studying acid deposition for use by member states.[100] EANET's membership counts thirteen states from all across Asia.[101] China, Japan, and

93 Agreement on Environmental Cooperation, 1993, 1767 UNTS 71.
94 Agreement on Cooperation in the Field of Environmental Protection, 1993, 1752 UNTS 131, art. 4.
95 Agreement between the Government of the People's Republic of China and the Government of Japan on Environmental Protection Cooperation, 1994, art. 2(1), www.fao.org/faolex/results/details/en/c/LEX-FAOC139759/ (which explicitly mentions acid rain).
96 Drifte, n. 77, 4.
97 Henry *et al.*, n. 85, 587.
98 Acid Deposition Monitoring Network in East Asia (EANET), *The Fourth Periodic Report on the State of Acid Deposition in East Asia, Part III: The Executive Summary*, 2021, 1–3.
99 See, e.g., Decision 1/IG12 on Strengthening the Work of the EANET, 23–24 November 2010.
100 See generally EANET, n. 98.
101 EANET members are the Russian Federation, China, Japan, South Korea, Mongolia, Cambodia, Indonesia, Laos, Malaysia, Myanmar, Philippines, Thailand, and Vietnam.

TABLE 12.1 *Asian cooperative frameworks on air pollution*

	EANET	NEASPEC	LTP	TEMM
North Korea	No	Yes	No	No
Russia	No	Yes	No	No
China	Yes	Yes	Yes	Yes
Japan	Yes	Yes	Yes	Yes
South Korea	Yes	Yes	Yes	Yes
Mongolia	Yes	Yes	No	No
Cambodia	No	No	No	No
Indonesia	Yes	No	No	No
Laos	Yes	No	No	No
Malaysia	Yes	No	No	No
Myanmar	Yes	No	No	No
Philippines	Yes	No	No	No
Thailand	Yes	No	No	No
Vietnam	Yes	No	No	No

South Korea have two initiatives between them on environmental cooperation. The first is their Annual Meeting of Environment Ministers (TEMM) and the second is the Joint Research Project on Long-range Transboundary Air Pollutants in Northeast Asia (LTP),[102] the latter being an initiative of the Northeast Asian Subregional Program for Environmental Co-operation (NEASPEC).[103]

NEASPEC is perhaps the closest to crystallizing a framework for building a multilateral convention on air pollution in Northeast Asia. At its twenty-second meeting of the states parties in 2018, member states launched the North-East Asia Clean Air Partnership, a voluntary framework that will gradually strengthen national policies around the mitigation of, among other things, sulphur dioxide and nitrogen dioxide emissions.[104] However, its voluntary nature makes it questionable whether it can translate into the necessary political will to create a framework convention akin to the LRTAP Convention. As mentioned, the greatest difficulty is managing the overlapping bodies and initiatives whose work focus and geographical scope make coordination difficult (see Table 12.1). Northeast Asia is also coordinated by the

102 Drifte, n. 77, 12.

103 Economic and Social Commission for Asia and the Pacific, *Review of Programme: Planning and Implementation in Item 5(a) Transboundary Air Pollution in Northeast Asia*, UN Doc. NEASPEC/SOM(22)/1, 6 January 2016. NEASPEC's membership includes North Korea, the Russian Federation, and Mongolia in addition to China, Japan, and South Korea.

104 *Ibid.*

United Nations' Economic and Social Commission for Asia and the Pacific (ESCAP).[105] However, ESCAP (or NEASPEC, for that matter) have not been able to cut the gordian knot and coordinate (or leap over) the diverse actors in this region to put forward a workable framework.

Southeast Asia, then, presents an intriguing contrast. It is a region with a legally binding multilateral agreement regulating haze pollution – the Agreement on Transboundary Haze Pollution (Haze Treaty) – but one that is roundly criticized as being ineffective at addressing the cause of transboundary air pollution.[106] Created under the umbrella of the Association of Southeast Asian Nations (ASEAN),[107] the Haze Treaty was signed by all ASEAN member states in June 2002 before entering into force the following year.[108] Indonesia, one of the main sources of haze pollution, only ratified the Haze Treaty in 2015.[109] The Haze Treaty operates very similarly to a framework convention like the LRTAP Convention in that it has general commitments by states parties and provisions for a Conference of the Parties and subsequent amendments to build out measures taken under the Treaty.[110] The Treaty also establishes a coordination centre for haze pollution control facilitating coordination of the monitoring of haze pollution in Southeast Asia.[111] The core obligation under the Haze Treaty is to 'co-operate in developing measures to prevent and monitor transboundary haze pollution as a result of land and/or forest fires which should be mitigated'.[112]

The main criticism levelled at the Haze Treaty is that its obligations are not stringent enough or are too 'soft'. While Article 3(1) of the Haze Treaty nods to principle 21, the Haze Treaty does not create a liability regime.[113] This was explicitly rejected at early conferences during the drafting of the agreement as

105 Henry *et al.*, n. 85.

106 Agreement on Transboundary Haze Pollution, 2002; Daniel Heilmann, 'After Indonesia's Ratification: The ASEAN Agreement on Transboundary Haze Pollution and Its Effectiveness as a Regional Environmental Governance Tool' (2015) 34(3) *Journal of Current Southeast Asian Affairs* 95; Tim Forsyth 'Public Concerns about Transboundary Haze: A Comparison of Indonesia, Singapore, and Malaysia' (2014) 25 *Global Environmental Change* 76; Laely Nurhidayah *et al.*, 'Regional Environmental Governance: An Evaluation of the ASEAN Legal Framework for Addressing Transboundary Haze Pollution' (2014) 15(1) *Australian Journal of Asian Law* 1.

107 The ASEAN Declaration (Bangkok Declaration), 1967, reprinted in (1967) 6 *International Legal Materials* 1233.

108 Agreement on Transboundary Haze Pollution, 2002, https://asean.org/wp-content/uploads/2021/01/ASEANAgreementonTransboundaryHazePollution-1.pdf (Haze Treaty).

109 Heilmann, n. 106, 96.

110 Haze Treaty, n. 108, arts. 18, 21–22.

111 See the annex to the Haze Treaty, *ibid.*

112 *Ibid.*, art. 4(1).

113 *Ibid.*, art. 3(1).

being contrary to the 'ASEAN way', which is characterized by non-interference in the domestic affairs of other member states.[114] Its critics argue, therefore, that there is no means by which to enforce the commitments in the Treaty.[115] This may be an unduly narrow view of the importance of legal bindingness (which is itself a spectrum) in international environmental law.[116] While Indonesia has brought itself into the fold and adopted a 'zero burning policy' in line with the Haze Treaty, compliance at the domestic level (including by corporations operating in Indonesia but owned by Malaysian and Singaporean interests) appears to remain low.[117]

There is one notable exception to the 'ASEAN way' with respect to haze pollution and that is Singapore's 2014 Transboundary Haze Pollution Act.[118] This piece of domestic legislation explicitly adopts the liability approach and provides for extraterritorial liability of companies and individuals who, as a result of acts or omissions, are responsible for fires in another state that cause transboundary air pollution in Singapore.[119] The Haze Pollution Act also empowers Singaporean authorities to issue arrest warrants and penal notices to those suspected of committing a wrong under the Haze Pollution Act.[120] The passage of the Haze Pollution Act in Singapore was understandably met with concern by Indonesia, which pointed out that the invasive extraterritorial powers of the Haze Pollution Act violated its sovereignty. Singaporean legal experts also questioned whether the Haze Pollution Act would be effective if the evidence it relied on would only be obtainable via Indonesia's cooperation with the investigations in Indonesia.[121] To date, no case in Singapore appears to have gone to trial over the Haze Pollution Act, although the Singaporean authorities have issued multiple penal notices and one arrest warrant for suspects under the Haze Pollution Act.[122] The lack of further enforcement nearly ten years after its passing (with little improvement in transboundary haze) indicates that the Haze Pollution Act may have been

[114] Roda Mushkat, *International Environmental Law and Asian Values: Legal Norms and Cultural Influences* (UBC Press, 2004), 122; Heilmann, n. 106, 114.

[115] Heilmann, n. 106.

[116] Consider the arguments put forward in Lavanya Rajamani, 'The 2015 Paris Agreement: Interplay between Hard, Soft and Non-Obligations' (2016) 28(2) *Journal of Environmental Law* 337.

[117] Mahdev Mohan, 'A Domestic Solution for Transboundary Harm: Singapore's Haze Pollution Law' (2017) 2(2) *Business and Human Rights Journal* 325.

[118] Transboundary Haze Pollution Act 2014 (Singapore).

[119] *Ibid.*, ss. 4–6.

[120] *Ibid.*, s. 17.

[121] Mohan, n. 117, 332.

[122] *Ibid.*, 331.

part of Singapore's attempt to force greater compliance from Indonesia or to perhaps bypass the Haze Treaty's non-adoption of state responsibility. Ultimately, it does not appear to have succeeded, especially considering that this goes far beyond what was envisaged by principle 21. Therefore, both the 'hard' and the 'soft' approach to solving the transboundary haze problem have led to few results.

12.6 COMPARATIVE REFLECTIONS AND CONCLUSIONS

The core conclusion from this chapter is that, while the legacy of the UNECE Air Pollution Treaties is commendable, they may not represent a one-size-fits-all model that can be directly transplanted into different contexts without modification. Nor does a model of liability and compensation appear to be the norm. This is especially true for the global South. The experience from Southern Africa demonstrates that there must be a solid foundation of technical cooperation before further progress is possible. Where technical cooperation cannot take place due to a lack of state capacity, it strengthens the case for global (and not just regional) attention on the issue of transboundary air pollution. Applying the model of the UNECE Air Pollution Treaties in Asia presents a different set of challenges. Northeast Asia, like Europe, is highly industrialized and ripe for a convention like the LRTAP Convention. However, cooperation is too fragmented to coalesce into a binding instrument, despite ESCAP attempting to perform a similar coordinating role to the UNECE. Southeast Asia, on the other hand, has reached a binding agreement on transboundary air pollution but one that is regarded as ineffective. Further cooperation within the Haze Treaty is likely the only path forward given that Singapore's example (the most aggressive implementation of principle 21 seen thus far) has failed to increase compliance.

The 1972 Stockholm Conference, as the progenitor of international law's transboundary air pollution regimes, thus enjoys a considerable influence over international environmental law, including in the global South. Indeed, it was the success of the Stockholm Conference and the LRTAP Convention that it inspired, which brought about the attempts to replicate it in the global South. The difficulties faced with doing so, particularly in Africa, demonstrate that transboundary air pollution must become a problem of international concern – with sufficient assistance provided to developing states – for the legacy of the Stockholm Conference to continue well into the future.

13

Climate Protection Fifty Years after Stockholm: International Law at the Precipice

Jutta Brunnée

Consider human history as a grand journey through the wilderness. There are wrong turns and times of hardship, but also times of sudden progress and heady views. In the middle of the twentieth century we came to a high mountain pass and found that the only route onward was a narrow path along the cliff-side: a crumbling ledge on the brink of a precipice. Looking down brings a deep sense of vertigo. If we fall, everything is lost. We do not know just how likely we are to fall, but it is the greatest risk to which we have ever been exposed.

Toby Ord, *The Precipice: Existential Risk and the Future of Humanity* (*Hachette Books*, 2020), 31.

13.1 INTRODUCTION

From around 1950 onwards, human impacts on the environment have accelerated and globalized to such an extent that the socio-economic system and the biophysical earth system are now inextricably linked.[1] Through this 'great acceleration', human activity has pushed the earth to a series of tipping points, and the world is said to have entered a new geologic epoch – the Anthropocene.[2] Alas, we find ourselves not only in a time where humanity has become a 'planetary-scale geologic force'[3] but also at a 'precipice', as

[1] Will Steffen *et al.*, 'The Trajectory of the Anthropocene: The Great Acceleration' (2015) 2(1) *The Anthropocene Review* 81, 93; see also Eva Lövbrand, Malin Mobjörk & Rickard Söder, 'One Earth, Multiple Worlds: Securing Collective Survival on a Human-dominated Planet', in Eva Lövbrand & Malin Mobjörk (eds.), *Anthropocene (In)securities: Reflections on Collective Survival 50 Years after the Stockholm Conference* (Oxford University Press, 2021), 3.

[2] Steffen *et al.*, n. 1.

[3] *Ibid.*

Oxford philosopher Toby Ord puts it in a recent book. Humanity, he argues, is at a point where 'it is at high risk of destroying itself'.[4]

Standing at the precipice ought to be clarifying, bringing into focus 'the defining challenge of our time', which is nothing less than 'safeguarding humanity's future'.[5] But, as Ord also tells us, looking into the abyss is a dizzying experience. What is more, humanity has lacked 'the maturity, coordination and foresight necessary to avoid making mistakes from which we would never recover'.[6] That this should be so is sobering, seeing as the signs of impending crisis have been all around us for some time, and, indeed, we have been warned. Both the challenge and the task ahead were laid out for us with remarkable clarity fifty years ago in the 1972 Stockholm Declaration on the Human Environment.[7] The degree to which the Stockholm Declaration foreshadows the situation in which we now find ourselves is striking. It is worth quoting some of the key passages:

> In the long and tortuous evolution of the human race on this planet a stage has been reached when, through the rapid acceleration of science and technology, man has acquired the power to transform his environment in countless ways and on an unprecedented scale.[8]
>
> In the developing countries most of the environmental problems are caused by underdevelopment. ... Therefore, the developing countries must direct their efforts to development ... [while] the industrialized countries should make efforts to reduce the gap between themselves and developing countries.[9]
>
> Through ignorance or indifference we can do massive and irreversible harm to the earthly environment on which our life and well-being depend. ... To defend and improve the human environment for present and future generations has become an imperative goal for mankind.[10]
>
> A growing class of environmental problems ... will require extensive co-operation among nations and action by international organizations in the common interest.[11]
>
> The natural resources of the earth ... must be safeguarded for the benefit of present and future generations.[12]

4 Toby Ord, The Precipice: Existential Risk and the Future of Humanity (Hachette Books, 2020), 33.

5 *Ibid.*, 3.

6 *Ibid.*, 3–4.

7 'Declaration of the United Nations Conference on the Human Environment', in *Report of the UN Conference on the Human Environment*, UN Doc. A/CONF.48/14/Rev.1, 16 June 1972 (Stockholm Declaration).

8 *Ibid.*, art. 2, corr. 1, proclamation 1.

9 *Ibid.*, proclamation 4.

10 *Ibid.*, proclamation 6.

11 *Ibid.*, proclamation 7.

12 *Ibid.*, principle 2.

> [Defending] ... the human environment for present and future generations ... will demand the acceptance of responsibility by citizens and communities and by enterprises and institutions at every level, all sharing in common efforts.[13]

The Stockholm Conference put environmental protection firmly on the international agenda.[14] At the same time, it cast a spotlight on the need to engage development concerns and the legacies of colonialism. For some observers, it is precisely due to the effort to give the linkages between environment and development pride of place and grapple with the postcolonial South-North tensions that the Stockholm Declaration marks 'the beginning of international environmental law and policy in a true sense'.[15]

Colonialism entailed the exploitation and often ravaging of natural resources in the global South,[16] precipitating environmental decline and entrenching conditions of economic disadvantage or even incapacity.[17] It also underpinned and reinforced the economic rise of wealthy industrialized countries.[18] Unsurprisingly, newly independent and developing countries sought to defend the hard-won sovereignty over their natural resources.[19] And, as modern international environmental law began to evolve in the wake of the Stockholm Conference, these countries remained suspicious of industrialized countries' efforts to promote international environmental cooperation.[20] Many developing countries distrusted the underlying universalist aspirations,[21] concerned that international environmental law was but

13 *Ibid.*, proclamations 6, 7.

14 See Peter H. Sand, 'Origin and History', in Lavanya Rajamani & Jacqueline Peel (eds.), *The Oxford Handbook of International Environmental Law* (2nd ed., Oxford University Press, 2021), 56.

15 See Karin Mickelson, 'The Stockholm Conference and the Creation of the South-North Divide in International Environmental Law and Policy', in Shawkat Alam *et al.* (eds.), *International Environmental Law and the Global South* (Cambridge University Press, 2015), 109.

16 See Usha Natarajan & Ki Khoday, 'Environment', in Jean d'Aspremont & John Haskell (eds.), *Tipping Points in International Law: Commitment and Critique* (Cambridge University Press, 2021), 137.

17 See, e.g., M. Rafiqul Islam, 'History of the North-South Divide in International Law: Colonial Discourses, Sovereignty, and Self-Determination', in Alam *et al.*, n. 15, 30.

18 See Natarajan & Khoday, n. 16; see also Cocoyoc Declaration, Mexico, 8–12 October 1974, reprinted in UN Environment Programme, *In Defence of the Earth: The Basic Texts on Environment: Founex – Stockholm – Cocoyoc*, 1981, 109.

19 See Islam, n. 17, 34, 47–48.

20 See Malavika Rao, 'A TWAIL Perspective on Loss and Damage from Climate Change: Reflections on Indira Gandhi's Speech at Stockholm' (2022) 12 *Asian Journal of International Law* 63.

21 See Lövbrand, Mobjörk & Söder, n. 1, 2.

a green variant of neo-colonialism and aimed at restricting or directing their development.[22] Meanwhile, industrialized states demanded that developing nations cooperate in protecting the global environment while, at the same time, resisting recognition of historical responsibility for environmental degradation. This North-South tension remains inscribed in international environmental law and policy to this day.[23]

Notwithstanding these enduring challenges, the Stockholm Conference did help ignite the growth of international environmental law into what, today, is a dynamic and continuously evolving field.[24] Whereas customary law in the field has seen only modest development,[25] numerous multilateral environmental agreements (MEAs), dealing with regional and global issues, have been negotiated since the 1970s.[26] In the context of the protection of the atmosphere, some international regimes have been quite successful. By contrast, fifty years after the Stockholm Conference, international climate protection efforts still fall short, which is both deeply troubling and unsurprising – troubling because the climate crisis is one of the existential risks flagged by Ord that is emblematic of human development pushing against planetary boundaries and to the precipice.[27] And yet the challenges of international lawmaking in relation to climate change are unsurprising, given the sheer complexity of this multifaceted, intergenerational crisis[28] and the starkly unequal distributions in development, contributions to the crisis, and exposure to harmful impacts.[29]

In this chapter, I explore the progress of international climate law since the Stockholm Conference. Although climate change as such was not on the agenda of the conference,[30] the Stockholm Action Plan it adopted does make

22 See Natarajan & Khoday, n. 16, 138. These concerns also found expression in the Stockholm Declaration, n. 7, see, e.g., Principle 1.

23 See, e.g., Björn-Ola Linnér & Henrik Selin, 'Geopolitics and the United Nations Conference on the Human Environment', in Lövbrand & Mobjörk, n. 1, 30, 33.

24 See Lavanya Rajamani & Jacqueline Peel, 'International Environmental Law: Changing Context, Emerging Trends, and Expanding Frontiers', in Rajamani & Peel, n. 14, 2.

25 See section 13.2 in this chapter.

26 See section 13.3 in this chapter.

27 Ord, n. 4, 103–13. Ord defines 'existential risk' as 'a risk that threatens the destruction of humanity's longterm potential', stressing that the concept applies 'only to threats against the whole of humanity' (37, 39).

28 See, e.g., Richard Lazarus, 'Super Wicked Problems and Climate Change: Restraining the Present to Liberate the Future' (2009) 94 *Cornell Law Review* 1153.

29 See, e.g., Natarajan & Khoday, n. 16, 133.

30 But see Eric Paglia, 'The Swedish Initiative and the 1972 Stockholm Conference: The Decisive Role of Science Diplomacy in the Emergence of Global Environmental Governance' (2021) 8 *Humanities and Social Science Communications* 5 (noting that climate change was among the concerns motivating Sweden to promote the idea of a UN conference

brief reference to the risks associated with climate change.[31] It threatens the very kind of 'massive and irreversible harm to the earthly environment' that the conference sought to prevent[32] and constitutes the very kind of environmental problem that the Stockholm Declaration predicted would 'require extensive co-operation among nations and action by international organizations in the common interest'.[33] I begin by showing that customary international law, while offering some avenues for demanding enhanced harm prevention from states, has not kept pace with the global, intertemporal, and developmental dimensions of climate change. I then offer a brief account of the evolution of the global climate regime launched by the 1992 UN Framework Convention on Climate Change (UNFCCC).[34] As this discussion will illustrate, thirty years later, the regime continues to wrestle with the complexities of the climate challenge, including difficult burden-sharing questions and the fraught relations between North and South referred to above.[35] The 2015 Paris Agreement,[36] which introduced a new approach to international climate governance into the regime, is a response to these complexities. As I hope to show, it offers some hope – or at least our best hope – that we will manage to pull back from the brink.

13.2 CUSTOMARY LAW AND CLIMATE CHANGE: INCHING AWAY FROM THE BRINK

The Stockholm Declaration both reflects the territorial logic of general international law at the time and sketches out a more ambitious conceptual framework, encompassing global, intertemporal, and developmental concerns. In the intervening fifty years, customary international environmental law has seen cautious efforts to push the boundaries of its sovereignty-based core, but it is unclear that it is equipped to avert 'massive and irreversible harm to the earthly environment', like climate change.

on the environment; indeed, it was in that context that climate change was first raised in the UN General Assembly in 1968).

31 See 'Action Plan for the Human Environment', in *Report of the United Nations Conference on the Human Environment*, UN Doc. A/CONF.48/14/Rev.1, 16 June 1972, 27.

32 See n. 10 above and accompanying text; see also Jan Eliasson, 'Foreword', in Lövbrand & Mobjörk, n. 1, viii.

33 See n. 11 above and accompanying text.

34 UN Framework Convention on Climate Change, 1992, 1771 UNTS 107 (UNFCCC).

35 See Linnér & Selin, n. 23, 30–33.

36 Paris Agreement on Climate Change, 2015, 3156 UNTS 79 (Paris Agreement).

13.2.1 THE LOGIC OF TERRITORY

However forthright and visionary the Stockholm Declaration was in highlighting the challenges and tasks the world needed to confront, the document, in strictly legal terms, was rather more modest. Principle 21 encapsulates international environmental law's roots in the balancing of states' sovereign rights to use their territories and their obligations to avoid transboundary harm.[37] The Principle reflects the state of customary law at the time. It may even have been ahead of the law, seeing as it stipulated that states had a responsibility to 'ensure that activities within their jurisdiction or control do not cause harm to the *environment* of other states *or of areas beyond the limits of national jurisdiction*'.[38] The International Court of Justice (ICJ), for example, would not confirm that this proposition was 'part of the corpus of international law relating to the environment' until almost twenty-five years later.[39] The Court has since reiterated this conclusion on several occasions,[40] but further development of the rules of environmental harm prevention has been incremental.

Some commentators have argued that, by emphasizing states' sovereign right to exploit the resources in their territories, Principle 21 'damaged environmental law'.[41] It is obviously true that the world – and not merely international law – remains anchored in a 'logic of territory'[42] and a long distance away from planetary boundary thinking[43] or even a consistent ecosystem-oriented approach.[44] Still, although Principle 21 gave expression to its roots in the sovereignty paradigm, it also sought to constrain sovereignty by giving

37 For a tracing, see Jutta Brunnée, 'Procedure and Substance in International Environmental Law' (2020) 405 *Receuil des Cours* 118.

38 Stockholm Declaration, n. 7, Principle 21 (emphasis added).

39 See *Legality of the Threat or Use of Nuclear Weapons*, Advisory Opinion, 8 July 1996, (1996) ICJ Reports 226, para. 29.

40 See *Gabčíkovo-Nagymaros Project (Hungary v Slovakia)*, Judgment, 25 September 1997, (1997) ICJ Reports 7, para. 41; *Pulp Mills on the River Uruguay (Argentina v Uruguay)*, Judgment, 20 April 2010, (2010) ICJ Reports 14, paras. 55–56, 78; *Certain Activities Carried Out by Nicaragua in the Border Area (Costa Rica v Nicaragua) and Construction of a Road in Costa Rica along the San Juan River (Nicaragua v Costa Rica)*, Judgment, 16 December 2015, (2015) ICJ Reports 665, paras. 705–707.

41 See Anthony Burke & Stefanie Fishel, 'From Human Environment to Post-Human Earth: Troubling the Nature/Culture Divide in the Stockholm Declaration', in Lövbrand & Mobjörk, n. 1, 110–113.

42 B. S. Chimni, 'The Grotian Tradition, Grotian Moment, and Decolonization: A TWAIL Perspective' (2021) 42 *Grotiana* 266.

43 For an overview, see Giovanna M. Frisso & Elizabeth A. Kirk, 'Changing Role of Law-making in Responding to Planetary Boundaries', in Duncan French & Louis J. Kotzé (eds.), *Research Handbook on Law, Governance and Planetary Boundaries* (Edward Elgar, 2021), 147–166.

44 See generally Vito de Lucia, *The 'Ecosystem Approach' in International Environmental Law: Genealogy and Biopolitics* (Routledge, 2020).

contours to states' environmental harm prevention obligations. Until such time as there is a broader shift beyond the sovereignty paradigm, elaborating those obligations remains a key task in the development of general international law.

On the plus side, it is now beyond doubt that international law requires states to protect the environment beyond their borders[45] rather than only sovereign rights over territory 'or the properties or persons therein'.[46] It is also clear that states are obligated actively to take steps to prevent harm,[47] an obligation that 'has its origins in the due diligence required of a State in its territory'.[48] In turn, the due diligence dimension of the harm prevention rule imports a contextual standard of conduct, which becomes more demanding in the face of elevated risks and potential for irreversible harm.[49] Finally, as the ICJ confirmed in its decisions on transboundary environmental impacts, the requirements of due diligence entail substantive as well as procedural duties.[50] Indeed, the Court found that a new procedural duty had emerged, such that 'it may now be considered a requirement under general international law to undertake an environmental impact assessment' where there is a risk of significant transboundary impact.[51]

For efforts to deploy the harm prevention rule in relation to climate change, the aforementioned features hold some promise. Most importantly, the rule's due diligence requirements are triggered by risk of harm. That means that a state seeking to invoke the rule need not demonstrate that activities under other states' jurisdiction or control cause, or will cause, climate-related harm to it. In order to demand that others undertake environmental impact assessments, or emission reductions and other measures appropriate to the risk at

45 See Jutta Brunnée, 'International Environmental Law: Of Sovereignty, Complexity, and Grotian Moments' (2022) 20 *Grotiana* 11.

46 See *Trail Smelter Case (United States v Canada)*, Judgment, 16 April 1938 and 11 March 1941, reprinted in (1905) 3 *Reports of International Arbitral Awards* 1905, para. 1965, http://legal.un.org/riaa/cases/vol_III/1905-1982.pdf; see also *Island of Palmas Case (Netherlands v United States of America)*, Award, 4 April 1928, reprinted in (1928) 2 *Reports of International Arbitral Awards* 829, para. 839, https://legal.un.org/riaa/cases/vol_II/829-871.pdf.

47 See Duncan French, 'Trail Smelter (United States of America/Canada) (1938 and 1941)', in Eirik Bjorge & Cameron Miles (eds.), *Landmark Cases in International Law* (Hart Publishing, 2017), 181.

48 *Pulp Mills*, n. 40, paras. 55–56.

49 See, e.g., ITLOS, *Responsibilities and Obligations of States Sponsoring Persons and Entities with Respect to Activities in the Area*, Advisory Opinion, Case no. 17, 1 February 2011, paras. 43, 46–47, 117, 131–132, www.itlos.org/fileadmin/itlos/documents/cases/case_no_17/17_adv_op_010211_en.pdf.

50 See, e.g., *Pulp Mills*, n. 40, para. 79.

51 *Ibid.*, para. 83; see also *Certain Activities*, n. 40, paras 706–707.

hand, the state must simply demonstrate the existence of the risk of such harm. According to the International Law Commission, the requisite risk can range from 'a high probability of causing significant transboundary harm' to a 'low probability of causing disastrous harm'.[52] Since we now face a high probability of disastrous climate harm – or even an existential risk – it stands to reason that virtually all states are subject to elevated requirements of harm prevention.

A number of other features, however, undercut the harm prevention rule's potential to pull us back from the climate brink. First, invoking due diligence obligations on one state at a time is a cumbersome and slow approach to solving a pressing global problem like climate change. Second, even if some states conclude that we find ourselves so close to the precipice that every small step in the right direction matters, the terrain remains fraught. After all, the harm prevention rule does not prohibit climate harm but instead requires states to exercise due diligence in seeking to prevent such harm.[53] Under general international law, in other words, it continues to be lawful for a state to cause even significant climate harm, so long as appropriate efforts were made to prevent that outcome. Of course, as noted above, given the dire situation in which we find ourselves, it could well be difficult for some states to demonstrate that they meet the arguably now heightened requirements of due diligence.

A third point is worth making: given the global nature of climate change, one might be inclined to think that the most apposite invocation of the harm prevention rule would focus not on transboundary harm but, rather, on the prevention of harm to the environment beyond state jurisdiction. Specifically, it would seem appropriate that all states owe to all others an obligation to prevent harm to the global climate system. Yet, although the obligation to prevent harm to the environment of areas beyond national jurisdiction is firmly established in general international law,[54] the contours of this obligation remain fuzzy. For example, does the obligation apply only to 'areas' beyond national jurisdiction, such as the high seas, or does it apply more broadly to natural systems, such as the global climate system? Natural systems ought to be protected by the rule, but there has been little in the way of state practice that would allow a firm conclusion. Similarly, it stands to reason that the obligation to prevent harm to areas beyond national jurisdiction or control is owed *erga omnes*, such that 'all States can be held to have a legal interest' in

[52] International Law Commission (ILC), *Draft Articles on Prevention of Transboundary Harm from Hazardous Activities*, UN Doc. A/CN.4/SER.A/2001/Add.1, 2001, 151–152, art. 2(a).

[53] See, e.g., *ibid.*, 154, para. 7.

[54] See, e.g., the repeated confirmation by the International Court of Justice (ICJ) in the cases cited in n. 39 and n. 40 above.

compliance with it.[55] But, again, there is little direct practice to support this conclusion.[56] Finally, even assuming the obligation is owed *erga omnes*, it remains unclear who would be entitled to hold states accountable for their failure to take appropriate harm prevention measures. As for the ICJ, although some of its judgments suggest a willingness to contemplate common interest standing for obligations *erga omnes partes*,[57] the Court has not answered the standing question specifically for obligations *erga omnes* arising under general international law.[58]

13.2.2 BEYOND THE LOGIC OF TERRITORY

Notwithstanding the central role of Principle 21, the majority of the Stockholm Declaration's principles actually focused on global, intertemporal, and developmental concerns. However, they were cast as policy statements rather than in legal language. Given the state of international law at the time, this approach was unsurprising and, indeed, sensible. The key question for present purposes is whether, over the past fifty years, general international law has evolved beyond the transboundary harm prevention rule to engage global, intertemporal, and developmental concerns.

In the decades following the Stockholm Conference, there initially were some indications that the conceptual framework of international environmental law might indeed evolve along the lines the Stockholm Declaration had suggested. Most notably, on the occasion of the twentieth anniversary of the Stockholm Conference, the 1992 Rio Declaration on Environment and Development picked up some of the key ideas sketched out in the Stockholm Declaration and cast them into legal language.[59] For example, the Rio Declaration embraced the proposition that global environmental concerns demand collective action, while underscoring that states have 'common but differentiated responsibilities' in this respect.[60]

55 *Barcelona Traction, Light and Power Company, Limited (Belgium v Spain)*, Judgment, 5 February 1970, (1970) ICJ Reports 3, 32, para. 33.

56 Some support for this proposition can be found, in the context of the law of the sea, in the advisory opinion of the International Tribunal on the Law of the Sea's (ITLOS) Seabed Chamber on *Responsibilities in the Area*, n. 49, 51, para. 148.

57 For a detailed analysis, see Priya Urs, 'Obligations *erga omnes* and the Question of Standing before the International Court of Justice' (2021) 34 *Leiden Journal of International Law* 505.

58 See James Crawford, 'Responsibility for Breaches of Communitarian Norms: An Appraisal of Article 48 of the ILC Articles on the Responsibility of States for Internationally Wrongful Acts', in Ulrich Fastenrath *et al.* (eds.), *From Bilateralism to Community Interest: Essays in Honour of Bruno Simma* (Oxford University Press, 2011), 224; see also Urs, n. 57, 524.

59 See 'Rio Declaration on Environment and Development', in *Report of the UN Conference on Environment and Development*, UN Doc. A/CONF.151/26 (Vol. I), 12 August 1992 (Rio Declaration).

60 See *ibid.*, Principle 7; compare Stockholm Declaration, n. 7, Principle 12.

The developmental dimension of environmental protection highlighted in the Stockholm Declaration, along with its intergenerational aspects, also found expression in the concept of sustainable development, which appears throughout the Rio Declaration. For example, the Rio Declaration stipulates that 'the right to development must be fulfilled so as to equitably meet developmental and environmental needs of present and future generations'.[61] Finally, again echoing ideas found in the Stockholm Declaration, the Rio Declaration demanded that 'in order to protect the environment, the precautionary approach shall be widely applied by States according to their capabilities. Where there are threats of serious or irreversible damage, lack of full scientific certainty shall not be used as a reason for postponing cost-effective measures to prevent environmental degradation.'[62]

Alas, none of the more ambitious ideas floated at Stockholm and then articulated in legal terms in the Rio Declaration have ripened into general international law. To be sure, the precautionary approach to environmental protection has made some inroads, through the harm prevention rule's due diligence standard, which is more demanding in the context of serious risks or the potential for irreversible harm.[63] However, the precautionary principle as set out in the Rio Declaration has not emerged as a free-standing norm of general international law.[64] Likewise, the concepts of sustainable development,[65] intergenerational equity, and common but differentiated responsibilities have not acquired customary law status.[66]

As some observers have pointed out, the formal legal status of these principles may be less critical than their 'operational significance'.[67] And, indeed, each of these concepts has been influential in shaping the development of international environmental law, particularly in the context of treaty-based regimes. For example, the UNFCCC invokes these principles both in the preamble and in an operative article on the principles that are to guide parties in pursuing the goals of the treaty.[68]

61 See Rio Declaration, n. 59, Principle 3; compare Stockholm Declaration, n. 7, Principles 1, 2, 3, 5, 14.

62 Rio Declaration, n. 59, Principle 15; compare Stockholm Declaration, n. 7, Proclamation 6, Principle 6.

63 See Rio Declaration, n. 60 and accompanying text; see also ILC, n. 52, para. 155.

64 See Brunnée, n. 45, 13. On the status of the precautionary principle in international law, see also Jacqueline Peel, 'A Southern State of Mind: From Being "Mindful of . . . Effects on Climate" to Climate Litigation in the Global South', in this volume, 357.

65 But see Jorge Viñuales, 'Sustainable Development', in Rajamani & Peel, n. 14, 291.

66 See Brunnée, n. 45, 14.

67 See Rajamani & Peel, n. 24, 14.

68 See UNFCCC, n. 34, art. 3.

13.3 TREATY-BASED CLIMATE COMMITMENTS: EXPERIMENTATION AT THE PRECIPICE

Much as the Stockholm Declaration identified,[69] the enduring challenge for international environmental policy is to guide states with diverse priorities and circumstances towards cooperation. All told, international environmental treaty-making has been quite successful in supporting such collective action. However, notwithstanding the ever-growing urgency of the climate crisis, the global climate regime remains a work in progress.

13.3.1 SUCCESSES

Since the 1970s, states have negotiated a large number of MEAs that deal with regional as well as global issues.[70] The framework-protocol model, premised upon the incremental development of commitments over time, quickly emerged as the approach most conducive to building dynamic, adaptable environmental regimes. It enables states to engage around a problem without waiting for agreement on all of its dimensions, let alone what response action is required. An initial framework treaty sets out a common concern and agreed objective; basic principles for, and commitments to, action; procedural obligations designed to promote information sharing and engagement; as well as rules and institutions for decision-making and subsequent treaty development. Supplementary treaties, typically referred to as protocols, allow for an overarching problem to be broken down into more manageable sub-issues.[71] Protocols are related to the underlying framework in that they adopt its basic goals, principles, and decision-making rules. At the same time, they are separate from the framework in that they have their own sets of parties and therefore entail commitments only for those parties.[72]

Framework-protocol regimes have been remarkably successful in dealing with some aspects of the protection of the atmosphere. For example, the 1979 Convention on Long-Range Transboundary Air Pollution (LRTAP Convention) was able to draw fifty-one states into an expanding regime designed to deal with transboundary pollution the origins of which are 'at

69 See n. 11 above and accompanying text.

70 See Ronald B. Mitchell, 'International Environmental Agreements Database Project, 2002–2022', version 2020.1, *University of Oregon*, iea.uoregon.edu/ (identifying over 1,300 multilateral environmental agreements, including amendments and adjustments to existing agreements, adopted between 1800 and 2020).

71 For an overview, see Dan Bodansky, Jutta Brunnée & Lavanya Rajamani, *International Climate Change Law* (Oxford University Press, 2017), 57–58.

72 See *ibid.*, 86–88.

such a distance that it is not generally possible to distinguish the contribution of individual emission sources or groups of sources'.[73] Multiple protocols served to break the problem down into substance-specific commitment regimes,[74] thereby facilitating significant reductions in sulphur, nitrogen oxide, and volatile organic compound emissions, among others.[75] All told, the regime has been effective in curbing atmospheric pollution in Europe and, albeit to a somewhat lesser extent, in North America.[76] As explained by Phoebe Okowa and Sean O'Reilly, it is less clear how useful a model the LRTAP regime has been for other regions, notably Asia and Africa.[77]

The framework-protocol approach did transfer very well to a major global concern – the depletion of the ozone layer. The 1985 Vienna Convention was supplemented through the 1987 Montreal Protocol, which was then repeatedly amended and adjusted to include a growing range of ozone-depleting substances and to speed up the phase out of these substances.[78] A recent study suggests that the measures catalysed by the ozone regime will lead to the recovery of the earth's ozone layer around the middle of the century.[79] Indeed, the ozone regime is widely seen as one of the – if not *the* – most successful international environmental regimes of all times.[80]

13.3.2 THE CLIMATE REGIME: A WORK IN PROGRESS

In the light of these successes, the framework-protocol model was also deployed to tackle climate change. But this tried and tested approach on its own turned out to be insufficient for overcoming the mismatch between treaty

73 See Convention on Long-Range Transboundary Air Pollution, 1979, 1302 UNTS 217, art. 1(b). For the regime's ratification status, see *United Nations Treaty Collection*, treaties.un.org/Pages/ViewDetails.aspx?src=TREATY&mtdsg_no=XXVII-1&chapter=27&clang=_en.

74 See 'Protocols', *UNECE*, unece.org/protocols.

75 See 'The Convention and Its Achievements: A Common Framework for Transboundary Cooperation on Air Pollution', *UNECE*, unece.org/convention-and-its-achievements.

76 See Elizabeth Moses, Beatriz Cardenas & Jessica Seddon, 'The Most Successful Air Pollution Treaty You've Never Heard Of', *Insights*, 25 February 2020, www.wri.org/insights/most-successful-air-pollution-treaty-youve-never-heard.

77 Phoebe Okowa and Sean O'Reilly, 'Implementing Principle 21 of the Stockholm Declaration: Regional Efforts to Regulate Transboundary Air Pollution', in this volume, 313.

78 See Vienna Convention for the Protection of the Ozone Layer, 1985, 1513 UNTS 323; Montreal Protocol on Substances That Deplete the Ozone Layer, 1987, 1522 UNTS 3.

79 See 'Ozone Layer Recovery Is an Environmental Success Story', *World Meteorological Organization*, 15 September 2021, https://wmo.int/media/news/ozone-layer-recovery-environmental-success-story.

80 See, e.g., Frederike Albrecht & Charles F. Parker, 'Healing the Ozone Layer: The Montreal Protocol and the Lessons and Limits of a Global Governance Success Story', in Paul t'Hart & Mallory Compton (eds.), *Great Policy Successes* (Oxford University Press, 2019), 304–322.

law's moorings in sovereign consent and the need for dynamic and ambitious collective action that could be supported by developed as well as developing countries. The drafters of the UNFCCC were certainly aware of what was required. The Convention's objective was the 'stabilization of greenhouse gas concentrations in the atmosphere at a level that would prevent dangerous anthropogenic interference with the climate system'.[81] It acknowledged 'that the global nature of climate change calls for the widest possible cooperation by all countries and their participation in an effective and appropriate international response'.[82] What is more, it specifically acknowledged that parties ought to cooperate 'in accordance with their common but differentiated responsibilities and respective capabilities' and that developed country parties ought to 'take the lead in combating climate change'.[83] As already noted, the Convention also embraced precaution, intergenerational equity, and sustainable development as principles that would guide parties' implementation and regime development efforts.[84]

The UNFCCC sets out different avenues for the further development of the climate regime, including amendments, protocols, and decisions of the plenary body, the Conference of the Parties (COP).[85] Unfortunately, all of them have been hampered by the inability of parties to agree upon the voting rule in its Rules of Procedure. As a result, the COP has operated on the basis of a general agreement that decisions be taken by consensus.[86] While actual consensus-breaking has been rare, the prospect of a negative vote often suffices to prevent a decision from being put forward in the first place or prompts compromises at a lower level of ambition.[87]

Nonetheless, in 1997, the parties adopted the Kyoto Protocol.[88] Its swift completion is in part due to the fact that the negotiating mandate specifically excluded new commitments for developing countries,[89] thereby bracketing the question of burden sharing between industrialized and developing

81 UNFCCC, n. 34, art. 2.
82 *Ibid.*, preamble.
83 *Ibid.*, preamble, art. 3.2.
84 See n. 68 above and accompanying text.
85 See UNFCCC, n. 34, arts. 7, 15–17.
86 Antto Vihma, 'Climate of Consensus: Managing Decision Making in the UN Climate Change Negotiations' (2015) 24 *Review of European Community and International Environmental Law* 62.
87 See Bodansky, Brunnée & Rajamani, n. 71, 75–76.
88 Kyoto Protocol to the United Nations Framework Convention on Climate Change, 1997, 2303 UNTS 162 (Kyoto Protocol).
89 UNFCCC, *The Berlin Mandate: Review of the Adequacy of Article 4, Paragraph 2(a) and (b), of the Convention, including Proposals Related to a Protocol and Decisions on Follow-up*, UN Doc. FCCC/CP/1995/7/Add. 1, 6 June 1995, 4.

countries for the purposes of the protocol negotiations.[90] In keeping with the negotiating mandate, the Kyoto Protocol reflected the Convention's proposition that 'developed country Parties should take the lead in combating climate change'[91] and the insistence of developing countries that their commitments ought to be differentiated from those of developed countries.[92] The Protocol enshrined emission reduction targets only for parties listed in Annex I to the UNFCCC (that is, developed countries and countries with economies in transition).[93]

However, the Kyoto Protocol stipulated a five-year commitment period (2008–2012) and mandated that an amendment would be required to establish targets for subsequent periods.[94] In other words, Annex I parties did not consent to long-term emission commitments but, rather, ensured that there would be another decision point. The protocol also contained a range of flexibility elements, such as allowing parties to pool and jointly meet commitments or to engage in emissions trading.[95] In order to both backstop the emissions target and ensure the integrity of the flexibility elements, parties also agreed to develop stringent emissions inventory and reporting requirements[96] and to create a compliance mechanism for the Kyoto Protocol.[97] Since these elements required detailed rules in order to be operational, the Protocol empowered its Meeting of the Parties to adopt decisions to flesh out these key parts of the Protocol.[98]

The requisite bundle of decisions, dubbed the Marrakesh Accords,[99] was adopted in 2001. But, given its commitment structure, the Kyoto Protocol's entry-into-force formula required ratification by at least fifty-five parties to the Convention, including Annex I parties accounting for at least 55 per cent of these parties' total carbon emissions.[100] Reaching this emissions threshold proved challenging since the United States, accounting for more than 30 per cent of the relevant emissions, indicated, also in 2001, that it would

90 See Bodansky, Brunnée & Rajamani, n. 71, 105–109.
91 UNFCCC, n. 34, art. 3.1.
92 *Ibid.* For a discussion, see Bodansky, Brunnée & Rajamani, n. 71, 26–30.
93 See Kyoto Protocol, n. 88, art. 3.1, Annex B.
94 *Ibid.*, art. 3.9.
95 *Ibid.*, arts. 3.10–3.12, art. 6 (joint implementation), art. 12 (clean development mechanism), art. 17 (emissions trading).
96 *Ibid.*, arts. 5, 7, 8.
97 *Ibid.*, arts. 18.
98 *Ibid.*, arts. 6.2, 7.4, 8.4, 12.7, 17, 18.
99 See UNFCCC, Marrakesh Accords, Decisions 2–24/CP.7, UN Doc. FCCC/CP/2001/13/Add. 1–3, 21 January 2002.
100 *Ibid.*, art. 25.1 (total emissions in 1990).

not ratify the Protocol.[101] The US retreat meant that every other Annex I party had to join the Protocol for it to enter into force. The emissions share threshold was finally crossed in February 2005.[102] In hindsight, although all of the Protocol's Annex I parties met their emissions targets,[103] the overall impact of the first commitment period was limited, accounting for only 24 per cent of global greenhouse gas emissions.[104]

If bringing the Kyoto Protocol into force was challenging, a much bigger challenge was to develop a more ambitious post-2012 emission reduction regime. In these negotiations, the parties now had to confront the difficult burden-sharing issues raised by global climate action.[105] In view of the emissions trajectories of major developing countries, such as China and India,[106] industrialized countries insisted that any post-2012 emissions regime had to include commitments by developing countries. In turn, developing countries insisted that the Kyoto Protocol, with binding emission commitments for only industrialized countries, ought to be extended for an additional commitment period.[107]

Given the entrenched positions, it proved politically impossible to amend the Protocol to include all states.[108] As part of a multi-pronged effort to break the log-jam in the climate negotiations, the parties did adopt an amendment to the Kyoto Protocol – the 2012 Doha Amendment – establishing a new commitment period for the protocol's industrialized parties.[109] However, because the United States had not joined the protocol, Canada had withdrawn prior to the end of the first commitment period,[110] and Japan and Russia declined to accept new emissions targets, the Doha Amendment ended up applying to parties representing less than 12 per cent of global emissions.[111] By

[101] See Bodansky, Brunnée & Rajamani, n. 71, 107.

[102] See 'Kyoto Protocol to the United Nations Framework Convention on Climate Change', *UNTC*, https://treaties.un.org/Pages/ViewDetails.aspx?src=TREATY&mtdsg_no=XXVII-7-a&chapter=27&clang=_en.

[103] See Michael Grubb, 'Full Legal Compliance with the Kyoto Protocol's First Commitment Period: Some Lessons' (2016) 16 *Climate Policy* 673.

[104] See Bodansky, Brunnée & Rajamani, n. 71, 108, 173.

[105] See *ibid.*, 109.

[106] See *ibid.*, 8, 354 (on China overtaking the United States as the single largest emitter in 2005).

[107] See *ibid.*, 108.

[108] For an overview, see *ibid.*, 108–115.

[109] See Doha Amendment to Kyoto Protocol, UN Doc. FCCC/KP/CMP/2012/13/Add.1, Decision 1/CMP.8, 12 December 2012, https://treaties.un.org/Pages/ViewDetails.aspx?src=TREATY&mtdsg_no=XXVII-7-c&chapter=27&clang=_en (Doha Amendment).

[110] 'Kyoto Protocol', n. 102.

[111] See Bodansky, Brunnée & Rajamani, n. 71, 114.

the time it finally entered into force in 2020,[112] the UNFCCC parties had adopted the Paris Agreement.[113]

Like the Kyoto Protocol, the Paris Agreement operates under the umbrella of the UNFCCC.[114] But recourse to a new treaty enabled parties to deviate from the Protocol's approach and develop a very different mix of substantive and procedural as well as binding and non-binding requirements. This new approach made it possible for the Paris Agreement to establish a commitment regime applicable to both developed and developing countries.[115] A record 175 UNFCCC parties signed the agreement on the day it opened for signature, and it entered into force in less than a year.[116] The Paris Agreement calls upon parties to strengthen the global response to climate change by mitigating emissions with a view to holding global temperature increases 'to well below 2°C [degrees Celsius] above pre-industrial levels and pursuing efforts to limit the temperature increase to 1.5°C'.[117] To this end, all states are to undertake progressively more ambitious efforts.[118] However, each state's contributions to the global response to climate change is 'nationally determined'.[119] These 'nationally determined contributions' (NDCs) themselves are not legally binding under international law.

The NDCs are the most experimental aspect of the Paris Agreement's approach. This feature prompted many observers to describe its approach as 'bottom-up', in contrast to the Kyoto Protocol's 'top-down' reliance on binding targets enshrined in the treaty.[120] As other commentators have pointed out, the Kyoto targets were also ultimately nationally determined since individual parties decided which targets to put forward.[121] The main difference between the Kyoto targets and the Paris Agreement's NDCs is that compliance with the former was owed to the other protocol parties, whereas the Paris Agreement limits itself to obligating parties to 'prepare, communicate and maintain successive' NDCs.[122] While parties, therefore, are free to determine the

112 See Doha Amendment, n. 109.

113 Paris Agreement, n. 36.

114 See *ibid.*, preamble, art. 2.1(a).

115 See *ibid.*, arts. 4.2, 4.3.

116 See 'Paris Agreement', *UNTC*, treaties.un.org/Pages/ViewDetails.aspx?src=TREATY&mtdsg_no=XXVII-7-d&chapter=27&clang=_en.

117 See Paris Agreement, n. 36, art. 2.1(a).

118 *Ibid.*, art. 4.3.

119 *Ibid.*, art. 3.

120 See, e.g., Jessica F. Green, Thomas Sterner & Gernot Wagner, 'A Balance of Bottom-up and Top-down in Linking Climate Policies' (2014) 4 *Nature Climate Change* 1064.

121 See Joanna Depledge, 'The "Top-down" Kyoto Protocol? Exploring Caricature and Misrepresentation in Literature on Global Climate Change Governance' (2022) 22 *International Environmental Agreements: Politics, Law and Economics* 673.

122 Paris Agreement, n. 36, art. 4.2.

content of their NDCs, they are not free to do as they please. Individual parties do have obligations related to their NDCs. Notably, parties 'shall pursue mitigation measures, with the aim of achieving the objectives' of their NDCs.[123] In joining the Paris Agreement, states also consent to maintaining consecutive NDCs.[124]

Furthermore, domestic decision-making is encumbered by a series of collective expectations and other non-binding requirements developed under the auspices of the Paris Agreement. First, the Paris Agreement provides for certain normative expectations, including that each successive NDC 'will represent a progression beyond' the party's current NDC and will 'reflect its highest possible ambition' as well as 'its common but differentiated responsibilities and respective capabilities, in the light of different national circumstances'.[125] The parties' NDCs are also to be pursued 'with a view to achieving the purpose' of the Paris Agreement, including notably the temperature goals it sets out.[126] Second, the parties are subject to a range of reporting and other procedural requirements, designed to ensure accountability for performance.[127] The Paris Agreement's transparency framework, although it does not formally assess compliance with NDCs, will provide for a publicly accessible tracking of parties' progress in the achievement of NDCs.[128] Finally, while individual parties 'may at any time adjust' their existing NDCs, the Paris Agreement specifies that an NDC may be adjusted 'with a view to enhancing its level of ambition, in accordance with the guidance' adopted by the parties.[129]

13.4 CONCLUSION

The 1972 Stockholm Declaration foretold our journey into the Anthropocene and warned that we risked doing massive and irreversible harm to the environment. It sketched a path for international environmental law beyond transboundary pollution to global and intergenerational concerns and highlighted development issues as being integral to environmental protection. Taking stock of our progress in safeguarding the environment for present and future generations is not for the faint of heart. Notwithstanding the exponential growth of international environmental law over the last fifty years, we have

[123] *Ibid.*
[124] See n. 122 above and accompanying text.
[125] Paris Agreement, n. 36, art. 4.3.
[126] *Ibid.*, arts. 2, 3, 4.1.
[127] See *ibid.*, arts. 13–15.
[128] See 'Introduction to Transparency', *UNFCCC*, unfccc.int/Transparency.
[129] See Paris Agreement, n. 36, art. 4.11.

arrived at a precipice, certainly in climatic terms. While 'deep, rapid and sustained reductions in greenhouse gas emissions' can still make a difference, our window for securing a liveable future is rapidly closing.[130] The reasons for our predicament are manifold, and some are found in the conceptual structures and processes of international law.

At the 1992 Rio Conference, there was a great deal of optimism about the development of international environmental law and the potential for international cooperation. The conference, after all, came shortly after the fall of the Berlin Wall and, arguably, was buoyed by a (fleeting, as it turned out) sense that a new world order was emerging. From our perch today, we know only too well that the upswing of multilateralism and international lawmaking in the late 1980s and early 1990s may have been the high point of what was achievable because the shared ground on which to build was much more limited and more fragile than it seemed.[131] In hindsight, it is apparent that the Rio Conference marked the peak of enthusiasm of global environmental lawmaking.[132]

A recent push to rekindle the codification and progressive development of the principles of international environmental law through a Global Pact for the Environment has failed thus far to garner sufficient support.[133] The territorial logic of customary international law, in any case, has proven to be resilient, and, even now, in the face of crisis, rapid paradigm shifts in general international law seem unlikely.[134] This goes for the emergence of rules that would better address the fraught history of North-South relations and recalibrate states' responsibilities for global environmental protection in the light of differential contributions, impacts, and capacities. And, given industrialized and developing states' shared investment in state sovereignty, the emergence of customary rules that prioritize earth systems and their boundaries, rather than international law's current territorial logic, seems even less likely.[135]

130 See Intergovernmental Panel on Climate Change, *Sixth Assessment Synthesis Report: Summary for Policymakers*, 2023, 12, 24, www.ipcc.ch/report/ar6/syr/downloads/report/IPCC_AR6_SYR_SPM.pdf.

131 See Jutta Brunnée, 'Challenging International Law: What's New?' *Opinio Juris*, November 2018, opiniojuris.org/2018/11/13/challenging-international-law-whats-new/.

132 See, e.g., Stacy D. VanDeveer, 'Green Fatigue' (2003) 27 *Wilson Quarterly* 55.

133 See UN General Assembly, *Towards a Global Pact for the Environment*, UN Doc. A/RES/72/277, 10 May 2018; see also, e.g., Jasmin Raith, 'The "Global Pact for the Environment": A New Instrument to Protect the Planet?' (2018) 15 *Journal for European Environmental and Planning Law* 3.

134 See Brunnée, n. 45, 23.

135 See also Giovanna M. Frisso & Elizabeth A. Kirk, 'Changing Role of Law-Making in Responding to Planetary Boundaries', in Duncan French & Louis J. Kotzé (eds.), *Research Handbook on Law, Governance and Planetary Boundaries* (Edward Elgar, 2021), 147–166.

But this does not mean that customary law development has no role to play. Certain, more incremental, but nonetheless meaningful, changes do seem possible. In particular, it is high time to articulate what due diligence requires of states in the face of climate calamity and to push the harm prevention rule much more decisively towards a commons logic.[136] Since the Rio Conference, we have also learned that, although treaty-based cooperation continues to be the most promising arena for international environmental lawmaking efforts, the structures and processes of treaty law can hinder timely progress.[137] This has certainly been true in the climate regime. As the experience with the Kyoto Protocol has illustrated, reliance on binding emissions targets does not guarantee success. In fact, it seems liable to hinder success in a number of ways. Against the backdrop of the burden-sharing stand-off between developed and developing countries, suffice it to point to the decades-long negotiations pertaining to the Kyoto Protocol, the climate regime's consensus gridlock, the lag times to entry into force, and, perhaps most importantly, the fact that any increase in the ambition of binding commitments encounters the same hurdles all over again, without a guarantee that the key parties will agree to join.

The Paris Agreement introduced a more dynamic approach, enabling individual states to make their own policy choices in the light of the Agreement. It is designed not to demand and compel but, rather, to inspire and orchestrate the required shifts towards more ambitious climate action by providing common goals and principles for action as well as processes that facilitate international interaction and accountability.[138] This approach, it turns out, is aimed at precisely the sort of 'extensive cooperation among nations' and 'acceptance of

136 The requests for advisory opinions on states' obligations to combat climate change that are before ITLOS and the ICJ, respectively, have the potential to make significant contributions on these fronts. On the ITLOS proceedings, see 'Request for an Advisory Opinion Submitted by the Commission of Small Island States on Climate Change and International Law (Request for Advisory Opinion Submitted to the Tribunal)', *International Tribunal for the Law of the Sea*, www.itlos.org/en/main/cases/list-of-cases/request-for-an-advisory-opinion-submitted-by-the-commission-of-small-island-states-on-climate-change-and-international-law-request-for-advisory-opinion-submitted-to-the-tribunal/. On the ICJ proceedings, see 'Obligations of States in Respect of Climate Change: Request for Advisory Opinion', *International Court of Justice*, 12 April 2023, www.icj-cij.org/case/187/request-advisory-opinion.

137 See generally Joost Pauwelyn, Ramses A. Wessel & Jan Wouters, 'When Structures Become Shackles: Stagnation and Dynamics in International Lawmaking' (2014) 25 *European Journal of International Law* 733.

138 On the notion of 'orchestration', see Kenneth W. Abbott, 'Orchestration', in Andrew Jordan, Dave Huitema, Harro van Asselt & Johanna Forster (eds.), *Governing Climate Change: Polycentricity in Action?* (Cambridge University Press, 2018), 188–209.

responsibility by citizens and communities and by enterprises and institutions at every level' that the Stockholm Declaration called for fifty years ago.[139]

Can a regime predominantly reliant on non-binding commitments and without enforcement 'inspire countries to deviate from the status quo', such that they would take on the costly policies required to curb greenhouse gas emissions in a meaningful way?[140] A recent empirical study suggests that there is reason for some optimism. It found support for the idea animating the Paris Agreement's design – that 'by making pledges non-binding . . . national governments would be more flexible to reveal what they are willing and able to implement'.[141] Indeed, the study suggests that 'non-binding commitments, with the right supporting institutions, can elicit greater adjustment by countries'.[142]

I want to close by returning to Toby Ord, with whose reflections on this age of existential threats to humanity I began. His book does not in fact 'present an inevitable arc of history culminating in our destruction'. Instead, he explains that 'our choices can still make all the difference'.[143] As I hope to have illustrated, the Paris Agreement offers some hope – or at least our best hope – that we will manage to pull back from the precipice.

ADDENDUM

While the assessment of the international law of climate protection that I offered in my chapter, completed soon after the 2022 Stockholm+50 Meeting, remains largely correct, the ICJ's July 2025 Advisory Opinion on *Obligations of States in Respect of Climate Change* invites some additional observations.[144]

With respect to customary international law, the opinion significantly clarifies and augments the ICJ's previous pronouncements on States' general harm prevention obligations. According to the Court: (i) these obligations are 'not confined to instances of direct cross-border harm',[145] but also apply to 'global environmental concerns', including 'with respect to the climate

139 See nn. 11 and 12 above and accompanying text.

140 See David G. Victor, Marcel Lumkowsky & Astrid Dannenberg, 'Determining the Credibility of Commitments in International Climate Policy' (2022) 12 *Nature Climate Change* 793.

141 *Ibid.*, 798.

142 *Ibid.*

143 Ord, n. 4, 9.

144 *Obligations of States in Respect of Climate Change* (Advisory Opinion of 23 July 2025); at www.icj-cij.org/case/187 [*Obligations of States in Respect of Climate Change*].

145 *Ibid.*, para. 134.

system';[146] (ii) what is more, the salient obligations are owed *erga* omnes;[147] (iii) given the indisputable scientific evidence of urgent risks, 'the standard of due diligence is stringent',[148] requiring States to take measures 'designed to achieve the deep, rapid, and sustained [emission] reductions … necessary for the prevention of significant harm to the climate system;'[149] (iv) whether or not an independently binding principle of international law, 'the 'precautionary approach is … an integral part of the general obligation of due diligence under the duty to prevent significant harm to the environment';[150] (v) likewise, the principle of common but differentiated responsibilities and respective capabilities is relevant to the 'determination of the applicable standard of due diligence in a particular situation';[151] (vi) the fact that risks of harm to the climate system result from the multiple contributions does not relieve individual States from their obligation to take appropriate preventive measures.[152]

The ICJ is clear that the Paris Agreement does not displace these general obligations.[153] Instead, the due diligence requirements under customary international law inform the interpretation of States' 'obligations of conduct' under the Paris Agreement, including their obligations regarding the mitigation of greenhouse gas emissions.[154] Indeed, with respect to parties' nationally determined contributions (NDCs) to emission mitigation, the Court concludes that, 'rather than being entirely discretionary as some participants argued, NDCs must satisfy certain standards under the Paris Agreement' and must be 'capable of realizing the objectives of the Agreement',[155] including remaining within 'the 1.5°C threshold'.[156] The impact of this conclusion on States' attitudes towards existing and new commitments under the Paris Agreement remains to be assessed at a future point. What can be said with certainty now is that customary law provides stringent and remarkably concrete requirements for the conduct of *all* States in the face of the climate crisis.

146 *Ibid.*
147 *Ibid.*, para. 440.
148 *Ibid.*, paras. 137, 138.
149 *Ibid.*, para. 282.
150 *Ibid.*, para. 294 (citing to ITLOS, *Responsibilities and Obligations of States Sponsoring Persons and Entities with Respect to Activities in the Area*, Case No. 17 (Advisory Opinion of 1 February 2011), para. 131).
151 *Ibid.*, para. 137.
152 *Ibid.*, para. 276 (citing ITLOS, *Request for an Advisory Opinion Submitted by the Commission of Small Island States on Climate Change and International Law*, [2024] No. 31 (Advisory Opinion of 21 May 2024), para. 365).
153 *Ibid.*, paras. 162-171.
154 *Ibid.*, e.g. paras. 228-9; 241-2; 78, 245-6; 252; 254.
155 *Ibid.*, para. 249.
156 *Ibid.*, para. 224.

14

A Southern State of Mind: From Being 'Mindful of . . . Effects on Climate' to Climate Litigation in the Global South

Jacqueline Peel

14.1 INTRODUCTION

The 1972 UN Conference on the Human Environment, held in Stockholm, Sweden (and thus known as the Stockholm Conference), has been widely celebrated as the 'beginning' of the modern era of international environmental law.[1] Signature achievements included the 1972 Stockholm Declaration on the Human Environment,[2] an 'ambitious' Stockholm Action Plan comprising 109 recommendations,[3] as well as the establishment of the institutional architecture for the new field, including the UN Environment Programme (UNEP).[4] Assessing the impact of the Stockholm Conference fifty years on, the UN Environmental Management Group described the conference as 'a watershed moment that succeeded in bringing environment to the global stage'.[5]

I would like to express my gratitude to Thea I. R. Shields, Research Assistant, Melbourne Climate Futures and JD Graduate, Melbourne Law School, for her excellent assistance with the research and footnoting for this chapter.

1 See Peter H. Sand, *The History and Origin of International Environmental Law* (Edward Elgar, 2015); Lavanya Rajamani & Jacqueline Peel (eds.), *The Oxford Handbook of International Environmental Law* (2nd ed., Oxford University Press, 2021), 56.

2 'Declaration of the United Nations Conference on the Human Environment', in *Report of the UN Conference on the Human Environment*, UN Doc. A/CONF.48/14/Rev.1, 16 June 1972 (Stockholm Declaration).

3 'Action Plan for the Human Environment', in *Report of the United Nations Conference on the Human Environment*, n. 2, 6 (Stockholm Action Plan).

4 Louis B. Sohn, 'The Stockholm Declaration on the Human Environment' (1973) 14(3) *Harvard International Law Journal* 423.

5 UN Environment Management Group, The Impact of the Stockholm Conference on the UN System: Reflections of 50 Years of Environmental Action, June 2022, 1.

What is less widely appreciated, however, is the role that countries in the global South[6] played in the Stockholm Conference and how the conference and its outcomes reflect Southern approaches to environmental issues, which differ from, and are often in tension with, those of the global North.[7] This Southern perspective on environmental issues focused less on the pollution problems caused by industrialization, which preoccupied the global North at the time of the Stockholm Conference. Instead, Southern representatives participating in preparations for, and negotiations at, the Stockholm Conference emphasized the ways in which poverty and a lack of resources to support development and the thriving of communities contributed to, and exacerbated, environmental threats. On closer inspection, the imprint of this 'Southern state of mind' can be traced in the outcome documents of the Stockholm Conference, along with hints of the emergence of new global environmental concerns, such as climate change. Notably, the Stockholm Action Plan calls on governments in recommendation 70 to 'be mindful of activities in which there is an appreciable risk of effects on climate'.[8]

6 The term 'global South' is one of contested scope and content. See, e.g., R. P. Anand, *International Law and the Developing Countries: Confrontation or Cooperation?* (Banyan Publications, 1987), 120; Elena Fiddian-Qasmiyeh & Patricia Daley, 'Conceptualising the Global South and South-South Encounters', in Elena Fiddian-Qasmiyeh & Patricia Daley (eds.), *Routledge Handbook of South-South Relations* (Routledge, 2019), 1; John Toye, 'Is the Third World Still There?', in Anna Farmar & Mary McEvoy (eds.), *The Developing World: An Introduction to Development Studies through Selected Readings* (Development Education Support Centre, 1988), 1; Joyeeta Gupta, 'Changing North-South Challenges in Global Environmental Politics', in Peter Dauvergne (ed.), *Handbook of Global Environmental Politics* (2nd ed., Edward Elgar, 2012), 97. At the time of the Stockholm Conference, this grouping was simply referred to as 'the developing countries'. Likewise, this chapter, while cognisant of the wider debate about the South-North categorization, understands the distinction to be aligned with the developed/developing country divide that is widely applied in international environmental and climate law scholarship and that underpins the differentiation between Annex I (developed countries and states with economies in transition) and non-Annex I (developing country) parties under the UN Framework Convention on Climate Change, 1992, 1771 UNTS 165 (UNFCCC). Accordingly, major emerging economies such as China, India, Brazil, and South Africa are included as part of the global South on this understanding. See similarly Benjamin J. Richardson *et al.*, 'Introduction: Climate Law and Developing Countries', in Benjamin J. Richardson *et al.* (eds.), *Climate Law and Developing Countries: Legal and Policy Challenges for the World Economy* (Edward Elgar, 2009), 1; Sumudu Atapattu & Carmen G. Gonzalez, 'The North-South Divide in International Environmental Law: Framing the Issues', in Shawkat Alam *et al.* (eds.), *International Environmental Law and the Global South* (Cambridge University Press, 2015), 1.

7 Karin Mickelson, 'The Stockholm Conference and the Creation of the South–North Divide', in Alam *et al.*, n. 6, 109–129.

8 Stockholm Action Plan, n. 3, recommendation 70. This recommendation was included in the section of the Stockholm Action Plan on the identification and control of pollutants of broad international significance. The recommendation goes on to ask that governments 'carefully

The establishment of an international climate change treaty regime came twenty years after the Stockholm Conference with the conclusion of the 1992 UN Framework Convention on Climate Change (UNFCCC), which opened for signature at the follow-up conference to Stockholm – the 1992 UN Conference on Environment and Development, held in Rio de Janeiro (and thus known as the Rio Conference).[9] The UNFCCC ostensibly paid homage, especially in its guiding principles, to the importance of taking account of the needs of the global South and the aim of sustainable development in efforts to safeguard the global climate system.[10] But, in the subsequent development of the international climate regime, during the period between the 1992 Rio Conference and the conclusion of the Paris Agreement in 2015, Southern priorities on climate effects seemed to recede into the background.[11] The 2015 Paris Agreement signalled a potential shift, with the agreement's 'hybrid' approach elevating domestic policy considerations and increasing the focus on domestic enforcement action and litigation to ensure the implementation of parties' nationally determined contributions (NDCs) to the global climate change response.[12] The 2022 report of Working Group III of the Intergovernmental Panel on Climate Change reflects this change in focus, with an extensive assessment of domestic policies and the first-ever discussion of the role of climate litigation in environmental governance of climate change.[13]

In the climate litigation that is emerging globally – which, at the time of the UN International Meeting Stockholm+50: A Healthy Planet for the Prosperity of All – Our Responsibility, Our Opportunity (Stockholm+50 Meeting), totalled more than 2,000 cases, with 88 cases involving global South countries[14] – there is evidence of a divergence in the trajectory of Northern and Southern

evaluate the likelihood and magnitude of climatic effects and disseminate their findings to the maximum extent feasible before embarking on . . . activities [with climate effects]' and 'consult fully other interested states when activities carrying a risk of [climate] effects are being contemplated or implemented'.

9 UNFCCC, n. 6.

10 *Ibid.*, arts. 2, 3.

11 Paris Agreement on Climate Change, 2015, 3156 UNTS 79 (Paris Agreement).

12 Lavanya Rajamani, 'From Stockholm to Johannesburg: The Anatomy of Dissonance in the International Environmental Dialogue' (2003) 12(1) *Review of European Community and International Environmental Law* 23.

13 Priyadarshi R. Shukla *et al.*, *Climate Change 2022: Mitigation of Climate Change (Contribution of Working Group III to the Sixth Assessment Report of the Intergovernmental Panel on Climate Change*', *Intergovernmental Panel on Climate Change* (Cambridge University Press, April 2022), ch. 13.

14 Joana Setzer & Catherine Higham, *Global Trends in Climate Change Litigation: 2022 Snapshot*, policy report (Grantham Research Institute on Climate Change and the Environment and the Centre for Climate Change Economics and Policy, June 2022). A 2023 update issued by the Grantham Research Institute records a total of 2,341 cases as of

jurisprudence.[15] According to Gita Gill and Gopichandran Ramachandran, climate litigation in the global South is driven by 'different mindsets' than pertain in the global North, with a prevailing 'lexicon of "climate language, human and constitutional rights, disaster management, resource conservation, and enforcement of existing environmental and planning legislation"'.[16] In this experience, there are echoes of the different South-North conceptions of environmental threats that were present at the time of the Stockholm Conference. Indeed, developing climate litigation across the global South may provide a new opening for engaging Southern perspectives on the environment that reflect a different understanding of the priorities for climate action and a more integrated approach to the goals of addressing climate change, ensuring environmental protection and achieving sustainable development.

The remainder of this chapter is structured as follows. Section 14.2 goes back to the time of the Stockholm Conference, exploring the Southern perspectives on environmental concerns that emerged in the preparatory sessions and were embedded in the conference outcomes. The emergence of these South-North differences occurred side by side with the efforts of the Stockholm Conference to agree to a global approach to addressing 'pollutants of broad international significance', including those with 'an appreciable risk of effects on climate'.[17] Section 14.3 traces the subsequent development of a body of international environmental law specifically dedicated to addressing climate change. Between 1992 and 2015, this regime largely elevated Northern priorities for addressing the climate-altering effects of industrial pollution over the Southern priorities that had informed the Stockholm Conference negotiations. The 2015 Paris Agreement signalled a turning point in this regard, with a return to an emphasis on Southern environmental concerns and more developed provisions on adaptation, loss, and damage and a means of support

May 2023 with 135 cases in the global South – a significant increase from the previous year. See Joana Setzer & Catherine Higham, *Global Trends in Climate Change Litigation: 2023 Snapshot*, policy report (Grantham Research Institute on Climate Change and the Environment and the Centre for Climate Change Economics and Policy, June 2023).

15 Jacqueline Peel & Jolene Lin, 'Transnational Climate Litigation: The Contribution of the Global South' (2019) 113(4) *American Journal of International Law* (*AJIL*) 679.

16 Gita Gill & Gopichandran Ramachandran, 'Sustainability Transformations, Environmental Rule of Law and the Indian Judiciary: Connecting the Dots through Climate Change Litigation' (2021) 23(3) *Environmental Law Review* 228, 230, citing Shibani Ghosh, 'Climate Litigation in India', in Francesco Sindico & Makane Moïse Mbengue (eds.), *Comparative Climate Change Litigation: Beyond the Usual Suspects* (Springer, 2021), 347–367; Joana Setzer & Lisa Benjamin, 'Climate Litigation in the Global South: Constraints and Innovations' (2020) 9(1) *Transnational Environmental Law* 77; Shibani Ghosh, 'Litigating Climate Claims in India' (2019) 114 *AJIL Unbound* 45; Peel & Lin, n. 15.

17 Stockholm Action Plan, n. 3, recommendation 70.

for developing countries. Section 14.4 explores how the climate litigation that has since emerged globally as a means for ensuring accountability for, and the enforcement of, states' commitments under the Paris Agreement potentially provides new opportunities for a 'Southern mindset' on environmental issues to come to the fore. Section 14.5 concludes with reflections on the broader implications of these developments for the evolution of international environmental law.

14.2 SOUTHERN MINDSETS AT THE STOCKHOLM CONFERENCE

The Stockholm Conference is credited as the foundation of modern international environmental law because of the role it played in raising awareness of the global dimensions of many environmental issues and the need for international cooperation to address them.[18] However, as the history of the preparations for the conference, as well as its outcomes, reveal, differences between the South and the North over how to understand the 'environmental issues' of the time were also salient.

14.2.1 *Differences on Environment in the Lead-up to Stockholm*

The secretary-general of the Stockholm Conference, Maurice Strong, who was appointed in 1970, described one of its central purposes as 'redefining the environmental challenge to determine whether it could serve as a new basis for South-North co-operation'.[19] As Malavika Rao has pointed out, 'this sentiment reveals two interesting aspects about the state of affairs in the run-up to the Conference: (a) that there were conflicting views on what the "environmental challenge" at the time was, and (b) that these tensions arose from differences between the Global South and Global North camps that needed reconciliation at an international level'.[20] These conflicting views and tensions centred on the global North's understanding of international environmental challenges as being those generated by rapid industrialization and the exploitation of natural resources – for instance, acid rain pollution, chemical pollution, and the endangerment of species like whales – and the 'thrust for inclusion' of the global South to help resolve the damage caused by this development in the North.[21]

18 UN Environment Management Group, n. 5, 1.
19 Quoted in Malavika Rao, 'A TWAIL Perspective on Loss and Damage from Climate Change: Reflections from Indira Gandhi's Speech at Stockholm' (2022) 12(1) *Asian Journal of International Law* 63, 69.
20 *Ibid.*
21 *Ibid.*, 71.

At the time, however, environmental challenges that were experienced by the global South were of a different character. The fundamental problem for the global South was conceived as one of underdevelopment, with massive population growth, poverty, and an incapacity to meet the basic needs of peoples driving another kind of crisis than the one emerging in the global North.[22] The stance on development of the different regions also diverged, with the global South focused on the pressing need for development in their countries, while the global North sought limits to growth through development of a global environmental ethic.[23] The South-North tensions over the relationship between environment and development could easily have derailed the Stockholm Conference. Eight months before the conference, numerous developing countries were strong opponents, and several, such as Brazil, voiced plans to boycott.[24] In the end, Prime Minister Indira Gandhi was the only head of government to attend the Stockholm Conference, apart from the Swedish prime minister, Olof Palme.[25]

However, through the complex preparatory process, a majority of these reluctant Southern states were ultimately persuaded to attend the Stockholm Conference in 1972. Indeed, some Southern commentators see the conference as having been 'remarkable for the wide participation of the newly-independent Asian-African states that got a chance from the very beginning to shape the principles that would develop international environmental law'.[26] Historical accounts of the Stockholm Conference's preparatory process give particular credit to Secretary-General Strong in shaping its success. Drawing on his previous role as head of the Canadian International Development Agency, Strong was 'comfortable with the discourse of development [and] knew many of the key diplomatic players',[27] and he was committed to engaging Southern states in the negotiations.[28] At the conference's second preparatory committee meeting in February 1971, Strong proposed a 'radical remake' of the conference agenda that had been approved at the first preparatory committee meeting, with a focus on the integration of environmental

22 *Ibid.*
23 Rajamani, n. 12, 23.
24 Rao, n. 19, 71.
25 *Ibid.*, 71.
26 Parvez Hassan, 'Role of the South in the Development of International Environmental Law' (2017) 1(2) *Chinese Journal of Environmental Law* 133, 144.
27 Mickelson, n. 7, 111.
28 Michael W. Manulak, 'Developing World Environmental Cooperation: The Founex Seminar and the Stockholm Conference', in Wolfram Kaiser & Jan-Henrik Meyer (eds.), *International Organizations and Environmental Protection: Conservation and Globalization in the Twentieth Century* (Berghahn Books, 2016), 106.

considerations with development goals.[29] Strong's inclusion of Southern perspectives in the preparatory process for the Stockholm Conference also extended to non-state actors, such as academics, activist non-governmental organizations, and economists from countries such as Pakistan, Uruguay, and Sri Lanka.[30]

The preparatory Meeting of Experts on Environment and Development convened by Strong and held in Founex, Switzerland, in June 1971 provided a critical forum for the articulation of the environmental interests of Southern states in the lead-up to the Stockholm Conference.[31] The Founex report produced by this meeting[32] reinforced the divergence between Northern concerns about the environment – emerging from production and consumption patterns of the industrialized world – and the environmental problems prevalent elsewhere that 'were a result of underdevelopment and poverty'.[33] The 'formula' that the Founex report proposed for navigating these South-North tensions involved 'treating the environment as an integral dimension of development rather than an impediment'.[34]

In June 1971, the same month as the Founex meeting, Strong was able to secure a commitment from Gandhi, the Indian prime minister, to attend the Stockholm Conference. In his lobbying of the prime minister, Strong stressed that she was uniquely well placed to represent the views of the global South and that, in the absence of developing countries, the industrialized countries could control how environmental issues were addressed internationally.[35] This strategy proved successful in increasing Southern participation in the conference and paved the way for the integrated approach to environment and development, which was at the core of the Founex report, to resonate in the Stockholm Conference itself.[36]

Prime Minister Gandhi's plenary address, popularly referred to as 'Man and Environment', outlined the global South's position on environmental issues and was recognized as a turning point in the representation of Southern environmental concerns in the broader international arena.[37] While Prime

29 *Ibid.*
30 Ignacy Sachs, 'Environment and Development Revisited: Ten Years after Stockholm Conference' (1982) 8(3) *Alternatives: Global, Local, Political* 369, 371.
31 Mickelson, n. 7, 112; Manulak, n. 28, 108.
32 UN Secretary-General, *Founex Report on Development and Environment*, 12 June 1971.
33 Rao, n. 19, 69.
34 Manulak, n. 28, 107. For an extensive discussion of the Founex Conference, see Ellen Hey, 'The Missed Link between International Economic Law and Social and Environmental Issues', in this volume, 87.
35 Mickelson, n. 7, 115.
36 Rao, n. 19, 70.
37 *Ibid.*, 72.

Minister Gandhi's speech is often cited for her famous phrase about the 'poverty of pollution',[38] it more broadly contains 'a perceptive observation of the challenges confronting the Global South at the time', many of which endure in current debates over climate action.[39] She not only reflected the Southern view about the injustice of the developed North asking developing countries to curb their development but also recognized environmental problems as essentially global issues requiring a cooperative solution.[40] Karin Mickelson argues that Gandhi's speech reflected the overall Southern stance at the Stockholm Conference on the emerging international environmental agenda: 'guarded and somewhat sceptical, but at least willing to enter into dialogue'.[41]

14.2.2 *Reflections of Southern Priorities in the Stockholm Outcomes*

The imprint of Southern environmental concerns and priorities can be seen in various outcomes of the Stockholm Conference, including in the final text of the Stockholm Declaration[42] and in the organizational structure of UNEP.[43] Commentators reflecting on the Stockholm Declaration particularly highlight the greater alignment with Southern interests in the way in which the environment and development were conceptualized at the conference. As Parvez Hassan notes, 'environment was perceived as not the only conduit for attaining an appropriate quality of life; it was recognized that it is through the process of development, when properly planned, that the quality of life is ensured. The essential interdependence between environment and development was thus acknowledged'.[44]

The Stockholm Declaration's preambular recital 4 directly reflects the different understandings of the environmental challenge across the South and the North. In respect of 'the developing countries', it cites underdevelopment as the

38 Indira Gandhi, *Speech at the Stockholm Conference 1972*, speech, 14 June 1972.

39 Rao, n. 19, 65.

40 *Ibid.*, 80.

41 Mickelson, n. 7, 117; see also Hassan, n. 26, 144; Rao, n. 19, 71.

42 Mickelson, n. 7, 117; Stockholm Declaration, n. 2.

43 Michael Manulak highlights a further recognition of Southern concerns in the organizational structure of the UN Environment Programme (UNEP) following the conference: 'Furthermore, developing countries secured predominant representation on the UNEP Governing Council and the environmental agenda of the Global South had a prominent place in the UN environmental regime. . . . UNEP's organizational form was a concrete result of the North-South environmental bargain of the Stockholm Conference. . . . The position of the developing world was bolstered further when states voted in the UN General Assembly to locate UNEP's headquarters in Nairobi, Kenya.' Manulak, n. 28, 119.

44 Hassan, n. 26, 142.

major cause of environmental problems and, hence, recognizes that these countries 'must direct their efforts to development, bearing in mind their priorities and the need to safeguard and improve the environment'. 'For the same purpose', Northern countries were called on to 'make efforts to reduce the gap [between] themselves and the developing countries', an early acknowledgement of the need for equity and international cooperation to raise resources to assist developing countries.[45] The preamble recognizes that, in contrast to Southern states, 'in the industrialized countries, environmental problems are generally related to industrialization and technological development'.[46]

Perhaps the most important principle included in the Stockholm Declaration, Principle 21, also bears the hallmarks of Southern interests. While this Principle is best known for its statement on the responsibility of states for transboundary environmental harms – since recognized as customary international law[47] – it also affirms the sovereign right of all states to 'exploit their own resources pursuant to their own environmental policies'. Inclusion of this language, echoing the 1962 Resolution on Permanent Sovereignty over Natural Wealth and Resources,[48] was seen as reaffirming hard-won gains of newly developing states emerging from the previous constraints of colonization.[49] Hence, as Hassan notes,

> when the developing countries joined the international community to internationalize, for the first time, environmental protection across state boundaries in the Stockholm Declaration, they did so in the knowledge that Principle 21 of the Stockholm Declaration echoed the 1962 Resolution on Permanent Sovereignty over Natural Wealth and Resources in declaring the sovereign right of all states to 'exploit their own resources pursuant to their own environmental policies'.[50]

45 Parvez Hassan points to the elaboration of this in principles relating to the transfer of technology and financial assistance (Principle 9), fair pricing for the commodities and raw materials of the developing countries in the international system (Principle 10), resource allocation and international technical and financial assistance to developing countries (Principle 12), and the free flow of technology and experience from the developed to the developing countries on terms 'which would encourage their wide dissemination without constituting an economic burden on the developing countries' (Principle 20). Hassan, n. 26; see also Manulak, n. 28; Stockholm Action Plan, n. 3, recommendations 103(a, b), 107, 109.

46 Stockholm Declaration, n. 2, preamble.

47 *Legality of the Threat or Use of Nuclear Weapons*, Advisory Opinion, 8 July 1996, [1996] ICJ Rep 95.

48 UNGA Resolution 1803 (XVII) on Permanent Sovereignty over Natural Wealth and Resources, 14 December 1962; see also Hassan, n. 26.

49 Hassan, n. 26.

50 Parvez Hassan, 'Environment and Sustainable Development: A Third World Perspective' (2001) 31(1) *Environmental Policy and Law* 36, 38; Sohn, n. 4, 432.

Statements of representatives from the global South made during debates in the plenary session of the conference and in the subsequent discussion of its outcomes in the UN General Assembly (UNGA) expressed some lingering dissatisfaction with the inadequate treatment of the needs of developing countries. For example, the representative of Chile considered that the text of the Stockholm Declaration 'lacked ideological balance', arguing that the United Nations should not attach 'special priorities' to a problem like that of the human environment, which was important only to a limited number of states.[51] However, in many other cases, support was expressed for the Stockholm Declaration. The Indian representative stated that 'the Declaration represented an important milestone in the history of the human race' and that it was 'a starting-point in the task of making the planet a fit place for future generations'.[52] In the UNGA's debate on the decisions of the Stockholm Conference, the representative of Ghana expressed hope that 'the international community would regard itself as committed by the Declaration to resolve the problems of the planet', and he noted the link drawn in the Stockholm Declaration between development and environment, which was of vital importance to the global South.[53]

Overall, the Stockholm Conference, according to Hassan, 'represented an appropriate synthesis of the emerging dichotomy between the interests of the developed world and the developing countries'.[54] Ignacy Sachs reaches a similar conclusion, reflecting that the breakthroughs achieved were more than just rhetorical; rather, 'an intellectual process was started at Stockholm, giving a decisive impulse to the search for new development paradigms'.[55]

14.3 DEVELOPMENT OF INTERNATIONAL ENVIRONMENTAL LAW ON CLIMATE POST-STOCKHOLM

At the Stockholm Conference, environmental problems caused by 'pollutants of international significance' were a key area in the minds of (Northern) negotiators that required a global cooperative approach. The first recommendation in this section of the Stockholm Action Plan foreshadows the development of international environmental law relating to climate change. It recommends that governments

[51] Sohn, n. 4.
[52] *Ibid.*, 432.
[53] *Ibid.*
[54] Hassan, n. 26, 144.
[55] Sachs, n. 30, 371.

be mindful of activities in which there is an appreciable risk of effects on climate, and to this end:

(a) Carefully evaluate the likelihood and magnitude of climatic effects and disseminate their findings to the maximum extent feasible before embarking on such activities;
(b) Consult fully other interested States when activities carrying a risk of such effects are being contemplated or implemented.[56]

However, while scientific concern over pollutants with 'climatic effects' – greenhouse gases (GHGs) – increased during the 1970s and 1980s, the development of a specific international treaty regulating this area did not emerge in international environmental law until twenty years after the Stockholm Conference with the conclusion of the UNFCCC at the Rio Conference on Environment and Development.[57] Framed against the backdrop of the Rio Conference's endorsement of the notion of sustainable development,[58] there were good prospects for the Southern states' approach to climate change – which, as in Stockholm, called for this problem not to be viewed simply as an environmental issue but also as a development issue – to be embedded in the fabric of the new climate treaty.[59]

The text of the UNFCCC offers the promise of such an approach. The UNFCCC's preamble, for example, strongly reflects Southern views, making reference to the need for responses to climate change to 'be coordinated with social and economic development in an integrated manner with a view to avoiding adverse impacts on the latter, taking into full account the legitimate priority needs of developing countries for the achievement of sustained economic growth and the eradication of poverty'.[60] The UNFCCC also gives a central place to equity and the principle of 'common but differentiated responsibilities and respective capabilities' pushed by countries from the South[61] as well as calling for the 'full consideration' of the specific needs and special circumstances of

56 Stockholm Action Plan, n. 3, recommendation 70.

57 Daniel Bodansky, Jutta Brunnée & Lavanya Rajamani, *International Climate Change Law* (Oxford University Press, 2017), 97.

58 See Hassan, n. 26. Hassan views the Rio Declaration as continuing the compromise on both environment and development, which had its origins at Stockholm.

59 *Ibid.*, 145ff.

60 UNFCCC, preamble, recital 21.

61 Julia Dehm, 'Carbon Colonialism or Climate Justice? Interrogating the International Climate Regime from a TWAIL Perspective' (2016) 33(3) *Windsor Yearbook of Access to Justice* 129, 140.

developing countries.[62] However, as the international climate regime evolved, these needs and priorities of developing countries increasingly took second place to a dominant focus on climate change as a pollution problem, principally requiring mitigation efforts (that is, reductions in the emissions of GHGs). Indeed, by the time of the UNFCCC's conclusion in 1992, a 'paradigm shift' could be detected, which began to move away from these Southern objectives.[63]

14.3.1 A *Turn away from Southern Perspectives: 1992–2015*

Although the UNFCCC provided the basis for a more equitable balance to be achieved between the North and the South in addressing the challenge of climate change, the focus turned almost from the outset towards how to strengthen the treaty's obligations relating to mitigation. It was widely recognized that, although the UNFCCC included an 'unenforceable hortatory commitment' for Annex I developed countries to reduce emissions, there remained a need 'to translate this agreement from political will into legal obligations', which became the focus of subsequent conferences of the parties (COPs).[64]

At the first UNFCCC COP in 1995, the parties adopted the 'Berlin mandate', which called on governments to establish specific, legally binding targets and timetables for reducing the emissions of GHGs from developed countries but also directed the negotiations not to consider any new commitments for developing countries.[65] The resulting 1997 Kyoto Protocol

[62] UNFCCC, n. 6, arts 3.1, 3.2. In 1990, a split had begun to emerge between groups of developing countries – particularly between small island states facing existential threats from climate change, and larger developing countries such as India, Brazil, and China, which were concerned about impacts on their sovereignty. These latter countries argued that they were not responsible for creating the climate problem and had more pressing priorities including economic development and poverty alleviation. Bodansky, Brunnée & Rajamani, n. 57, 101. However, during the negotiations for the UNFCCC, these differences were largely set aside in favour of pushing for limited commitments for developing countries and stronger requirements of developed countries to address climate change.

[63] Rajamani, n. 12, 26. Regarding the agenda at the Rio Conference moving away from concerns of poverty alleviation, see also Mickelson, n. 7.

[64] Matthew Coghlan, 'Prospects and Pitfalls of the Kyoto Protocol to the United Nations Framework Convention on Climate Change' (2002) 3(1) *Melbourne Journal of International Law* 19, 22.

[65] *Report of the Conference of the Parties on Its First Session Held at Berlin from 28 March to 7 April 1995*, UN Doc. FCCC/CP/1995/7/, 6 June 1995, para. 4.

embedded this approach,[66] which was seen by some as a victory for the South given that the Protocol recognized strong differentiation between the obligations of developed and developing countries on climate change. However, the single-minded focus of the Kyoto Protocol on emissions reduction marked a distinctive shift from the global goals of supporting sustainable development espoused at the Stockholm and Rio conferences towards an agenda where mitigation and GHG targets for Northern states dominated.

As Julia Dehm and Larry Lohmann have discussed, the Kyoto Protocol's formulation of 'quantified emissions limitation and reduction obligations' for Annex I parties facilitated a reduction of climate action into generalized 'carbon dioxide equivalents' that were substitutable (and tradeable) between carbon market participants. This rendered different actions towards global decarbonization objectives 'commensurable' but overlooked the need for 'different actions in different places' based on their specific social and ecological context.[67] Mitigation efforts that lent themselves to this seemingly more 'global' and 'objective' framing were consequently privileged over questions of adaptation to climate impacts, climate resilient development, and responses to loss and damage that were seen to be more localized in their framing and benefits.[68]

These latter questions, frequently prioritized by Southern states, only began to gain traction at the Bali COP in 2007 following the delayed entry into force of the Kyoto Protocol.[69] The Bali Action Plan adopted at this COP laid the groundwork for negotiation of what would become the Paris Agreement, calling for a 'comprehensive process' to reach an 'agreed outcome' under the UNFCCC that would encompass all aspects of the climate change issue, including mitigation, adaptation, finance, and technology.[70]

66 Kyoto Protocol to the United Nations Framework Convention on Climate Change, 1997, 2303 UNTS 162. Annex B emissions targets in the Kyoto Protocol were developed for developed countries only.

67 Dehm, n. 61, 150; Larry Lohmann, *Carbon Trading: A Critical Conversation on Climate Change, Privatization and Power* (Dag Hammarskjöld Centre, 2006).

68 The only mention of adaptation in the Kyoto Protocol is in respect of the adaptation levy that is part of the Clean Development Mechanism.

69 Lavanya Rajamani, 'From Berlin to Bali and Beyond: Killing Kyoto Softly?' (2008) 57(4) *International and Comparative Law Quarterly* 909.

70 UNFCCC Decision 1/CP.13 on Bali Action Plan, Doc. FCCC/CP/2007/6/Add.1, 14 March 2008.

14.3.2 A New Turning Point: the Paris Agreement in 2015

The Paris Agreement, adopted at COP-21 in 2015, represented another turn in the international climate regime, this time away from the exclusive mitigation focus and developed country-only commitments of the Kyoto Protocol and towards a broader approach.[71] The Agreement's architecture has been described as a 'hybrid' between top-down and bottom-up approaches to climate action.[72] At the heart of the Paris Agreement are its obligations for all parties – across the North and the South – to prepare, communicate, and maintain NDCs to the global climate response,[73] which give parties significant scope to determine their own targets and actions. The desire for the negotiations for the Paris Agreement to take a comprehensive approach and to include developing countries as full participants – a sentiment that had likewise steered the Stockholm Conference's negotiations – saw the re-emergence of Southern perspectives on the nature of the 'environmental challenge' posed by climate change.

The Paris Agreement as a whole, 'in enhancing the implementation of the [UNFCCC]', 'aims to strengthen the global response to the threat of climate change', with aspirational goals laid out in article 2.1 on temperature limits, adaptation, and financial flows.[74] Reflecting Southern perspectives, these 'aims' are set 'in the context of sustainable development and efforts to eradicate poverty'.[75] This context for the implementation of the Paris Agreement is also emphasized in Article 2.2, which states: 'This Agreement will be implemented to reflect equity and the principle of common but differentiated responsibilities and respective capabilities [CBDRRC], in the light of different national circumstances'. Further references are made in the preamble to the principles of the UNFCCC, including CBDRRC, and to the 'intrinsic relationship that climate change actions, responses and impacts have with equitable access to sustainable development and eradication of poverty'. The Paris Agreement's preamble also includes the first ever reference in a climate treaty to human rights, calling on states 'when taking action to address climate change' to 'respect, promote and consider their respective obligations on human rights', including the right to health and the right to development.

71 Lavanya Rajamani, 'Understanding the 2015 Paris Agreement', in Navroz K. Dubash (ed.), *India in a Warming World* (Oxford University Press, 2019).

72 Dan Bodansky expresses this as the Paris Agreement's 'Goldilocks solution'. See Daniel Bodansky, 'The Paris Climate Change Agreement: A New Hope?' (2016) 110(2) *Australian Journal of International Law* 288.

73 Paris Agreement, n. 11, art. 4.2.

74 *Ibid.*, art. 2.1(a)–(c).

75 *Ibid.*, art. 2.1.

While mitigation is a strong focus of the Paris Agreement and was the subject of more detailed obligations,[76] the treaty represents a broader, more South-aligned, perspective on climate action. Beyond the preambular reference to human rights obligations, the Paris Agreement also encompasses commitments on adaptation,[77] loss and damage,[78] and the means of support (finance, technology assistance, and transfer and capacity building) for the implementation of commitments, particularly by developing countries.[79] Article 7 on adaptation, for instance, establishes 'the global goal on adaptation of enhancing adaptive capacity, strengthening resilience and reducing vulnerability to climate change, with a view to contributing to sustainable development and ensuring an adequate adaptation response'.[80] Article 7.2 also recognizes that adaptation 'is a global challenge faced by all with local, subnational, national, regional and international dimensions' and that it is a 'key component of and makes a contribution to the long-term global response to climate change to protect people, livelihoods and ecosystems'. This expression of solidarity on adaptation and recognition of its importance as part of efforts to address climate change is an important departure from the previous Kyoto Protocol. It opens space for a more contextualized understanding of climate action priorities and needs in different countries and communities. Countries of the global South are among the most vulnerable to climate impacts, making adaptation a significant priority for climate action in developing countries.[81]

At the same time, the hybrid structure of the Paris Agreement, centred on self-differentiated NDCs, invites a different approach in ensuring that parties' pledges towards the global climate response are put into action. Unlike the Kyoto Protocol that coupled targets and timetables for (Northern) emissions reductions with a strong international compliance mechanism, the Paris Agreement contains no enforcement mechanism and places no direct legal obligation on parties to achieve the goals that they set for themselves in NDCs.[82] Instead the Agreement's 'enhanced transparency framework' relies on processes of information gathering, review, and collective stocktaking to

76 *Ibid.*, art. 4.
77 *Ibid.*, art. 7.
78 *Ibid.*, art. 8.
79 *Ibid.*, arts. 9–11.
80 *Ibid.*, art. 7.1
81 Hans-Otto Pörtner *et al.*, *Intergovernmental Panel on Climate Change, 2022: Climate Change 2022: Impacts, Adaptation, and Vulnerability. Contribution of Working Group II to the Sixth Assessment Report of the Intergovernmental Panel on Climate Change* (Cambridge University Press, 2022).
82 Shukla *et al.*, n. 13, ch. 14.

illuminate the adequacy of state party actions to address climate change, with the assumption that this gap can be fulfilled by domestic accountability processes, including litigation before domestic courts.[83]

As the next section discusses, the exponential growth of climate litigation since the conclusion of the Paris Agreement – including its emergence in countries of the global South – suggests that this logic is in fact playing out in practice. But, in the process, when this litigation occurs in global South countries, it seems to be emphasizing a different understanding of the climate challenge, one that echoes the Southern perspectives on environment and development that first emerged in the era of the Stockholm Conference.

14.4 NEW OPENINGS FOR A SOUTHERN PERSPECTIVE: CLIMATE LITIGATION IN THE GLOBAL SOUTH

Climate litigation is a growing focus of environmental law scholarship,[84] and it is increasingly recognized for the governance function that it is playing and may play in the international climate regime.[85] Much of the focus of the existing climate litigation literature has been on climate cases taking place in the global North where such cases first emerged and where the majority of cases still take place.[86] As a small but growing number of scholars have begun to discuss,[87] there is an accelerating trend for climate litigation in the global South as well as in the global North, but it reflects different understandings of climate issues than those that are most prevalent in the global North. This phenomenon is of interest as it potentially represents an avenue for feeding back into international environmental law Southern perspectives and priorities on the global challenge of climate change. Global South climate litigation is thus playing a role in keeping such issues on the international climate

83 Thomas Hale, '"All Hands on Deck": The Paris Agreement and Nonstate Climate Action' (2016) 16(1) *Global Environmental Politics* 13; Robert Falkner, 'The Paris Agreement and the New Logic of International Climate Politics' (2016) 92(5) *International Affairs* 1118; see also Robert O. Keohane & Michael Oppenheimer, 'Paris: Beyond the Climate Dead End through Pledge and Review?' (2016) 4(1) *Politics and Governance* 142, 142 ('the Paris Agreement merely creates an opening for effective action on climate change. Political action by organized groups, domestic and transnational, will be essential to make Paris work'). Hale argues that there has been a shift from 'a "regulatory" model of binding, negotiated emissions targets to a "catalytic and facilitative" model that seeks to create conditions under which actors progressively reduce their emissions through coordinated policy shifts' (*ibid.*, 12).

84 See Setzer & Higham, n. 14.

85 Shukla *et al.*, n. 13.

86 Setzer & Higham, n. 14.

87 Peel & Lin, n. 15.

agenda, notwithstanding the ebbs and flows in South-North relations in post-Paris international developments.[88]

A key distinction between much of the climate litigation emerging in the global South as opposed to that in the global North is the 'peripheral' framing of climate issues in the former jurisprudence. In such cases, climate change does not emerge as a dominant motivation or focus of the litigation but, rather, as one of a suite of concerns that span pollution, land use, forestry, natural resource conservation, disaster risk management, implementation of planning frameworks, or environmental justice and rights claims.[89] This framing of climate issues in global South climate cases reflects the lower public policy salience of climate as a self-standing issue in many Southern countries, compared with more pressing social and policy concerns around economic development, poverty alleviation, or public health.[90] This framing aligns with the reality for many litigants in countries throughout the global South – namely, the fact that climate change adds a layer of complexity to, or exacerbates, existing environmental and development challenges rather than presenting as a standalone 'environmental' issue. Climate change is therefore conceptualized as a driver of further harm in addition to existing environmental problems like high levels of air pollution in cities, massive deforestation, land clearing, and rapid biodiversity loss.

Summarizing trends across the case law as a whole, Gill and Ramachandran argue that global North climate litigation is driven by 'different mindsets, [comprehensive] legal and policy frameworks, and climate change challenges',[91] compared with the global South, which is 'experiencing litigation change through the lexicon of "climate language, human and constitutional rights, disaster management, resource conservation, and enforcement of existing environmental and planning legislation"'[92] as well as what they term 'transformative dialogue' around sustainability.[93] A prominent trend across climate litigation in several global South countries has been the use of rights-based arguments as a basis for

88 In this regard, the outcomes of the UNFCCC's twenty-sixth Conference of the Parties in Glasgow seemed to represent a reinterpretation of the objectives of the Paris Agreement to stress the more stringent end of the temperature goal – 1.5 degrees Celsius – and to lessen the focus on the context for implementation based in equity, common but differentiated responsibilities and respective capabilities, sustainable development, and poverty eradication.

89 Peel & Lin, n. 15.

90 *Ibid.*, 693.

91 Gill & Ramachandran, n. 16, 230.

92 *Ibid.*, quoting Ghosh, 'Climate Litigation', n. 16; Setzer & Benjamin, n. 16; Ghosh, 'Litigating Climate Claims', n. 16; Peel & Lin, n. 15.

93 Gill & Ramachandran, n. 16.

climate claims.[94] This is allowing 'real world' application and interpretation in jurisprudence of rights to a clean and healthy environment that are present in greater numbers across the constitutions of countries of the global South.[95] In so doing, these cases are fleshing out the dimensions of the linkages between human rights and climate change and making concrete earlier exhortations in international environmental law, such as Principle 1 of the Stockholm Declaration, of human rights to 'freedom, equality and adequate conditions of life, in an environment of a quality that permits a life of dignity and well-being'.[96]

There is the potential for such global South climate litigation to be overlooked in favour of high-profile Northern cases litigating the adequacy of the emissions reduction targets of industrialized countries. But, in these 'quieter' cases – which are often enforcing environmental laws against deforestation or resource depletion,[97] seeking to enforce constitutional rights to secure livelihoods and a healthy environment,[98] or seeking improved policies (or their implementation) to address critical adaptation challenges[99] – important perspectives are being offered on what is most needed in these countries to ensure climate resilient development in their local contexts. As Joana Setzer and Lisa Benjamin explain, the cases are also serving to chart the best ways forward to 'bind together previously fragmented governance structures in the Global South to ensure that they focus on national climate goals, whether they be mitigation, adaptation, disaster management, or a combination of those aims'.[100]

94 Setzer & Higham, n. 14; see also Supreme Court of Colombia, *Future Generations v Ministry of the Environment and Others*, [2018] STC 4360; High Court of South Africa, *Earthlife Africa Johannesburg v Minister of Environmental Affairs & Others*, Case no. 65662/16, 8 March 2017; Supreme Court of Pakistan, *Rabab Ali v Federation of Pakistan*, Constitutional Petition no. 1 of 2016, 1 April 2016.

95 See, e.g., the constitutions of Brazil, Venezuela, and Colombia, among others.

96 Stockholm Declaration, n. 2, Principle 1.

97 *Future Generations*, n. 94; *Earthlife Africa Johannesburg*, n. 94; *Rabab Ali*, n. 94.

98 See Setzer & Benjamin, n. 16, 19; Lahore High Court, *Public Interest Litigation Association of Pakistan v Government of the Punjab*, Case no. 9137/2012, 8 December 2015; Pakistan Supreme Court, *Shella Zia v WAPDA*, PLD 1994 SC 693 (in which the Pakistan Supreme Court held that the right to life in the Constitution included the right to a healthy environment); Supreme Court of the Philippines, *Minors Oposa*, 33 ILM 173 (1994) (in which the Supreme Court of the Philippines allowed the plaintiffs to sue on behalf of future generations); Court of Sri Lanka, *Faroque v Bangladesh*, Case no. 3, 4–6 July 1997 (in which a broad interpretation of 'aggrieved person' was found under the Bangladesh Constitution).

99 Lahore High Court, *Ashgar Leghari v Federation of Pakistan*, Case no. 25501/2015, 4 September 2015.

100 Setzer & Benjamin, n. 16, 101.

14.5 CONCLUSIONS

South-North 'tensions' over environmental protection are a long-standing feature of international environmental law, the origins of which can be traced back to the earliest discussions of the environment as a global issue of concern at the Stockholm Conference. Such tensions often are portrayed as a battle between a Northern focus on environmental protection and a Southern desire to ensure environmental protections are not used as an unfair constraint on developing countries' efforts to develop, to secure economic prosperity, and to lift their populations out of poverty. As this chapter's revisiting of the negotiations of the Stockholm Conference emphasizes, what lies at the heart of these tensions are different ways of understanding environmental challenges and what is needed to address them.[101] At the Stockholm Conference itself, active efforts made to include Southern perspectives in the preparatory process were successful in brokering a compromise that saw the foundations for international cooperation on the environment established while also respecting the different environmental challenges and development priorities of the global South.

In the fifty years since the Stockholm Conference, we have seen ebbs and flows in the emphasis given to Southern perspectives across different environmental treaty regimes, including over the course of development of the international climate regime. The key treaty of the international climate regime at the Stockholm+50 Meeting – the 2015 Paris Agreement – seems to reflect a 'turning back' to a more nuanced approach in balancing key South-North perspectives and priorities in the fight against climate change. Compared to the focus of the previous Kyoto Protocol on emissions targets and carbon as a generalizable commodity, the provisions and structure of the Paris Agreement provide openings for more context-specific and localized understandings of the climate problem to emerge.

Climate litigation as it takes off across the global South is providing an important avenue for the expression of these perspectives, presenting climate issues as one part of broader sustainable development challenges. This is an important reminder of Southern perspectives on the manifestation of the environmental challenge of climate change, even as the post-Paris implementation efforts seem to be turning towards a more universalizing language of 'keeping 1.5 degrees Celsius alive' and achieving 'net zero by 2050' emissions

[101] Mickelson, n. 7.

reduction targets.[102] Indeed, the persistence of this 'Southern mindset', and its strong consistency over the last fifty years, points to the continuing work that international environmental law needs to do in taking forward global cooperation that addresses environmental challenges not only effectively but also equitably and in the context of sustainable development.

[102] 'Climate Action', *United Nations*, www.un.org/en/climatechange/net-zero-coalition#:~:text=Currently%2C%20the%20Earth%20is%20already,reach%20net%20zero%20by%202050.

15

Trade and Atmospheric Protection at Stockholm+50: Plus ça Change?

Harro van Asselt

15.1 INTRODUCTION

The 1972 Stockholm Conference on the Human Environment (Stockholm Conference) marked a turning point in the relationship between trade and the environment.[1] Until then, trade measures were by and large considered to be a useful way to strengthen environmental protection. In the run-up to the Stockholm Conference, however, concerns began to emerge that such trade measures may also have adverse impacts, particularly on developing countries. The interplay between trade and the environment in the fifty years that followed can be illustrated by the various interactions between measures to protect the atmosphere – tackling the global challenges of stratospheric ozone depletion and climate change – and international trade rules. To prevent free-riding and leakage, the 1987 Montreal Protocol incorporated trade measures in its legal architecture.[2] Although the international climate regime – including the 1992 UN Framework Convention on Climate Change (UNFCCC) and the 2015 Paris Agreement – did not follow suit, countries have begun to adopt an array of unilateral measures that may be at odds with international trade law.[3] With states due to ramp up their climate ambition at different speeds in the pursuit of their nationally determined contributions under the Paris Agreement, trade disputes are likely to intensify. Meanwhile, various international efforts have emerged to ensure that trade rules contribute to environmental protection.

[1] *Report of the UN Conference on the Human Environment*, UN Doc. A/CONF.48/14/Rev.1, 16 June 1972.

[2] Montreal Protocol on Substances That Deplete the Ozone Layer, 1987, 1522 UNTS 3 (Montreal Protocol).

[3] UN Framework Convention on Climate Change, 1992, 1171 UNTS 107 (UNFCCC); Paris Agreement on Climate Change, 2015, 3156 UNTS 79.

This chapter takes stock of the evolution of the trade-environment nexus, focusing on the international legal protection of the atmosphere. The chapter begins by outlining the historical background of the trade and environment debate, centring on the discussions surrounding the Stockholm Conference. Next, the chapter examines: (1) the relationship between the international trade regime and multilateral environmental agreements (MEAs), using the example of the Montreal Protocol's trade measures and (2) the use of unilateral trade measures, as illustrated by climate-motivated measures. Drawing on this analysis, the chapter reflects on the evolution of the trade-environment debate since the Stockholm Conference and offers brief concluding remarks.

15.2 THE TRADE AND ENVIRONMENT DEBATE IN HISTORICAL CONTEXT

15.2.1 *Before Stockholm*

The origins of the trade and environment debate can be traced back to the beginnings of both international environmental law and international trade law.[4] Trade measures such as export licences and import prohibitions were used in some of the earliest environmental treaties, whereas environmental considerations were incorporated in some of the earliest trade agreements. Emerging out of the post-war Bretton Woods conference, the 1947 General Agreement on Tariffs and Trade (GATT) sought to provide regulatory space for environmental measures.[5] The treaty included two exceptions under article XX aimed at measures 'necessary to protect human, animal or plant life or health' and those 'relating to the conservation of exhaustible natural resources'.[6] Notwithstanding these exceptions, environmental concerns did not feature prominently in the negotiations of the GATT nor in the aftermath of its adoption. After the adoption of the GATT, trade measures continued to be included in various conservation-related treaties, and countries began adopting domestic trade-restrictive measures to achieve environmental protection.[7]

[4] Steve Charnovitz, 'Exploring the Environmental Exceptions in GATT Article XX' (1991) 25(5) *Journal of World Trade* 37, 39–41.

[5] General Agreement on Tariffs and Trade, 1947, 55 UNTS 194.

[6] *Ibid.*, art. XX(b), (g).

[7] See, e.g., Lacey Act, 16 USC, ss. 1851ff.

15.2.2 *The 1972 Stockholm Conference*

The Stockholm Conference took place at a time when developing countries became more vocal about the perceived inequities of the international political system. These countries, many of whom gained independence from colonial rule in the wake of the Second World War, came together and expressed their views on the need for self-determination and economic justice. In their demands, developing countries drew attention not only to the unequal trade rules, which were shaped by developed countries, but also to the potential for the environmental measures of developed countries to exacerbate existing inequalities.

As the concerns by developing countries about the upcoming Stockholm Conference grew stronger, the organizers of the conference sought to accommodate them.[8] The secretary-general of the Stockholm Conference, Maurice Strong, consulted with development experts from the global South and organized an expert meeting in Founex, Switzerland, on 4–12 June 1971, to discuss developing country concerns and possible responses.[9] The meeting led to the Founex report, which expresses the fear 'that the insistence of the developed countries on rigorous environmental standards of products exchanged in international trade may well give rise to a "neo-protectionism"' and that 'imports from the developing countries based on less rigorous environmental standards [will] either be taxed or banned'.[10] The report also suggests there is a need for 'appropriate procedures for prior notification, consultation and co-ordination', stressing the role of the GATT in this regard.[11] The Founex meeting also led to an initial study on trade and environment in the GATT context.[12]

The concerns raised in the Founex report also featured in pre-Stockholm diplomacy. In December 1971, the UN General Assembly adopted (by eighty-five votes to two, with thirty-four abstentions) a resolution on development and environment, which stated that any action plan emerging from Stockholm must 'avoid any adverse effects of environmental policies and measures on the

8 Karin Mickelson, 'The Stockholm Conference and the South-North Divide in International Environmental Law and Policy', in Shawkat Alam *et al.* (eds.), *International Environmental Law and the Global South* (Cambridge University Press, 2015), 109.

9 *Report of a Panel of Experts Convened by the Secretary-General of the United Nations Conference on the Human Environment (Founex, Switzerland, 4–12 June 1971)*, UN Doc. A/CONF.48/10, 22 December 1971, Annex I.

10 *Ibid.*, para. 54.

11 *Ibid.*, para. 56.

12 GATT Secretariat, *Industrial Pollution Control and International Trade*, Doc. L/3538, 9 June 1971.

economy of the developing countries in all spheres, including international trade'.[13] The resolution further called on the UN Conference on Trade and Development (UNCTAD), created in 1964, to carry out a study 'on the effects of environmental policies of developed countries which might adversely affect the present or future development possibilities', including through 'a further deterioration in the trading prospects of developing countries by the creation of additional obstacles, such as the new non-tariff measures, which might lead to a new type of protectionism'.[14]

The concerns expressed by developing countries ultimately made their way in the Stockholm outcomes. Importantly, Principle 11 of the 1972 Stockholm Declaration reads:

> The environmental policies of all States should enhance and not adversely affect the present or future development potential of developing countries, nor should they hamper the attainment of better living conditions for all, and appropriate steps should be taken by States and international organizations with a view to reaching agreement on meeting the possible national and international economic consequences resulting from the application of environmental measures.[15]

Although not referring directly to trade measures, the principle's formulation reflects the concerns about green protectionism found in the Founex report.[16] The influence of the report is more readily apparent in the Stockholm Conference's Action Plan for the Human Environment (Stockholm Action Plan), which calls on states 'not to invoke environmental concerns as a pretext for discriminatory trade policies or for reduced access to markets'.[17] Further addressing the risk of environmental protectionism, the Stockholm Action Plan also states that 'uniform environmental standards should not be expected to be applied universally by all countries with respect to given industrial processes or products' and that, 'to avoid an impairment of the access of the developing countries to the markets of the industrialized countries because of differential product standards, Governments should aim at world-wide

[13] UN General Assembly, *Development and Environment*, UN Doc. A/RES/2849(XXVI), 20 December 1971, para. 4(e).

[14] *Ibid.*, para. 10.

[15] 'Declaration of the United Nations Conference on the Human Environment', in *Report of the UN Conference on the Human Environment*, n. 1, Principle 11 (Stockholm Declaration).

[16] Louis B. Sohn, 'The Stockholm Declaration on the Human Environment' (1973) 14(3) *Harvard International Law Journal* 423, 469.

[17] 'Action Plan for the Human Environment', in *Report of the UN Conference on the Human Environment*, n. 1, 26, recommendation 103(a) (Stockholm Action Plan).

harmonization of such standards'.[18] The Stockholm Action Plan underscores prior notification and consultation among states. More controversially, the Stockholm Action Plan also recommends governments to ensure 'appropriate measures for compensation' in case trade restrictions lead to 'negative effects on exports, particularly from developing countries'.[19] In addition, the Stockholm Action Plan points to an important role of international organizations, asking UN organizations to examine 'major threats to exports, particularly those of developing countries, that arise from environmental concerns, their character and severity, and the remedial action that may be envisaged' and recommending that the GATT, UNCTAD, and other international bodies should 'consider undertaking to monitor, assess, and regularly report the emergence of tariff and nontariff barriers to trade as a result of environmental policies'.[20]

A few inferences can be drawn regarding the Stockholm outcomes. First, the Stockholm Action Plan – and, to a lesser extent, Principle 11 – were strongly influenced by efforts to accommodate developing country concerns about the economic injustices caused by environmentally motivated trade measures. Second, procedural steps were seen as an important initial safeguard to address developing countries' concerns about green protectionism. Third, the outcomes underscored the importance of working through international organizations, notably the GATT and UNCTAD. Lastly, however, the outcome documents suggested that developing countries need to be (financially) supported where trade measures lead to negative effects on development.

15.2.3 *From Stockholm to Rio*

Notwithstanding the Stockholm outcomes, the trade and environment debate remained largely dormant until the late 1980s. The main developments in international environmental law were the adoption of several MEAs that employed trade measures, notably the 1973 Convention on the International Trade in Endangered Species and the 1987 Montreal Protocol.[21] In the GATT context, further concerns began to be raised about the impacts of

18 *Ibid.*, recommendation 103(e).
19 *Ibid.*, recommendation 103(b).
20 *Ibid.*, recommendations 104–105.
21 Convention on Trade in Endangered Species of Wild Fauna and Flora, 1973, 993 UNTS 243; Montreal Protocol, n. 2.

environmental policies on trade, in part due to a growing number of environmental policies and in part due to increasing trade flows.[22]

Several developments in the early 1990s significantly increased the political salience of the debate. The first was the rise of trade-environment disputes. Notably, in the *Tuna-Dolphin* dispute, two subsequent GATT panels issued controversial rulings about the legality of unilateral trade measures.[23] Although the panel reports were never adopted, they drew heavy criticism from environmentalists, who saw the narrow interpretation of the GATT's environmental exceptions as confirmation that trade law undermines environmental protection.[24] Second, the 1992 Rio Conference on Environment and Development (Rio Conference) addressed the trade-environment relationship explicitly, with Principle 12 of the 1992 Rio Declaration providing that

> states should co-operate to promote a supportive and open international economic system, ... to better address the problems of environmental degradation. Trade policy measures for environmental purposes should not constitute a means of arbitrary or unjustifiable discrimination or a disguised restriction on international trade. Unilateral actions to deal with environmental challenges outside the jurisdiction of the importing country should be avoided. Environmental measures addressing transboundary or global environmental problems should, as far as possible, be based on international consensus.[25]

Principle 12 supports the idea that an open global economy that facilitates trade will lead to better environmental protection.[26] In the wake of the *Tuna-Dolphin* rulings, the statement that unilateral trade measures should be avoided was not accepted by all countries, with the United States adopting an interpretive statement 'that, in certain situations, trade measures may provide an effective and appropriate means of addressing environmental

22 Aik Hoe Lim, 'History of the Trade and Environment Debate at the WTO', in Panagiotis Delimatsis & Leonie Reins (eds.), *Trade and Environmental Law* (Edward Elgar, 2021), 1; see also 'Evolution of Trade under the WTO: Handy Statistics', *World Trade Organization*, www.wto.org/english/res_e/statis_e/trade_evolution_e/evolution_trade_wto_e.htm.

23 WTO, *United States – Restrictions on Import of Tuna (I)*, (1991) BISD 39S/155 (unadopted) (*Tuna-Dolphin*); WTO, *United States – Restrictions on Import of Tuna (II)*, (1994) 33 ILM 839 (unadopted).

24 Matthew H. Hurlock, 'The GATT, U.S. Law and the Environment: A Proposal to Amend the GATT in Light of the Tuna/Dolphin Decision' (1992) 92(8) *Columbia Law Review* 2098.

25 'Rio Declaration on Environment and Development', in *Report of the UN Conference on Environment and Development*, UN Doc. A/CONF.151/26 (Vol. I), 12 August 1992.

26 Margaret A. Young, 'Principle 12', in Jorge E. Viñuales (ed.), *The Rio Declaration on Environment and Development: A Commentary* (Oxford University Press, 2015) 325, 332.

concerns, . . . subject to certain disciplines'.[27] In subsequent trade disputes, it has become evident that there is scope for such measures, provided that there is a clear 'nexus' between the country adopting such a measure and the environmental problem.[28] The subsequent disputes also confirm the importance of the last sentence of Principle 12 – namely, the need to try and achieve international consensus through negotiation.[29] Third, environment-related issues emerged on the agenda of ongoing trade negotiations. This notably included the Uruguay Round of trade talks, which led to the creation of the World Trade Organization (WTO).

15.2.4 *The WTO*

The creation of a permanent international organization for trade in 1995 marked a turning point in the trade and environment debate.[30] The WTO was established to further the implementation, administration, and operation of multilateral trade agreements concluded under its auspices and serves as a forum for further trade negotiations and for resolving disputes between its members.[31] The 1994 GATT, which largely incorporates the 1947 version, is the main WTO agreement dealing with the trade in goods.[32] Its core rules revolve around non-discrimination, providing market access (for example, prohibiting quantitative restrictions) and preventing unfair trade practices. With regard to non-discrimination, the agreement provides that a country should not discriminate between producers from other countries and domestic producers ('national treatment') and should treat 'like' imported and domestic products as such.[33] Moreover, a country should not discriminate between its trading partners ('most-favoured nation' treatment).[34] Like its predecessor, the 1994 GATT contains two environmental exceptions.

Environmental protection is not listed as a main objective of the organization, but the preamble to the 1994 WTO Agreement suggests that achieving its trade-related goals should allow 'for the optimal use of the world's resources in

[27] *Report of the UN Conference on Environment and Development*, UN Doc. A/CONF.151/26 (Vol. II), 1993, 18.

[28] WTO, *United States – Import Prohibition of Certain Shrimp and Shrimp Products*, Report of the Appellate Body, WT/DS58/AB/R, 12 October 1998, para. 133 (*Shrimp-Turtle*).

[29] *Ibid.*, paras. 166–168.

[30] See Lim, n. 22.

[31] Marrakesh Agreement Establishing the World Trade Organization 1994, 1867 UNTS 154, art. III (WTO Agreement).

[32] General Agreement on Tariffs and Trade, 1994, 55 UNTS 194.

[33] *Ibid.*, art. III.

[34] *Ibid.*, art. I.

accordance with the objective of sustainable development'.[35] Offering a further signal of the mounting prominence of environmental concerns, the creation of the WTO was accompanied by a Ministerial Decision on Trade and Environment, which established a dedicated Committee on Trade and Environment to discuss linkages and issue recommendations on possible modifications to trade rules.[36] The launch of the Doha Round of trade negotiations in 2001 increased attention to environmental issues. The Doha Ministerial Declaration called for new negotiations on the relationship between trade obligations under MEAs and trade rules, procedures for information exchange between MEA secretariats and the WTO, and the reduction of trade barriers for environmental goods and services.[37] However, as the entire Doha Round ground to an almost complete halt in 2008, these negotiations remain uncompleted.

15.3 TRADE RULES AND ATMOSPHERIC PROTECTION

Initially, the interplay between trade and the environment concerned more traditional environmental problems, including the conservation of wildlife, the use of hazardous substances, and industrial pollution. However, the complex and evolving interrelationship between trade and the environment can perhaps best be exemplified with reference to two collective action problems: stratospheric ozone depletion and climate change, two issues that were featured hardly – if at all – in the Stockholm outcomes.[38] Both problems are similar in that: (1) they have a long time horizon; (2) emissions are caused by human-made technologies and occur in all parts of the world; (3) countries cannot solve the problem by acting alone, necessitating international cooperation; and (4) they raise major equity issues as the problems have been primarily caused by developed countries.[39] At the same time, there are also important differences. Most importantly, while technological solutions have been readily available in cases such as ozone depletion, there is no silver bullet to address climate change.

35 WTO Agreement, n. 31, preamble, recital 1.

36 WTO, *Decision on Trade and Environment*, Doc. LT/UR/D-6/2, 15 April 1994.

37 *Ibid.*, para. 31.

38 The only reference to climate is the recommendation to 'be mindful of activities in which there is an appreciable risk of effects on climate'. See Stockholm Action Plan, n. 17, recommendation 70. There is no reference to ozone depletion.

39 Cass R. Sunstein, 'Of Montreal and Kyoto: A Tale of Two Protocols' (2007) 31(1) *Harvard Environmental Law Review* 1, 2–3.

As collective action problems, trade measures have featured in the governance of both ozone depletion and climate change. States opted to include trade measures in the very design of the international ozone regime. While no such measures are provided for in the international climate regime, domestic trade measures have grown in importance. For both types of trade measures, this part looks into three questions: (1) why are they adopted; (2) how do they work; and (3) are they compatible with international trade rules?

15.3.1 *Trade and MEAs: The Case of Ozone Depletion*

Whilst environmental concerns have moved up the trade agenda, trade measures have become part of MEAs on issues as diverse as wildlife protection, genetically modified organisms, and hazardous waste and chemicals.[40] This part will focus on one of the most well-known examples of MEAs that include trade measures: the 1987 Montreal Protocol.[41] The Montreal Protocol is often hailed as one of the big success stories in international environmental law. In the 1970s, the depletion of the stratospheric ozone layer resulting from the release of chlorofluorocarbons (CFCs) was identified as a major cause for concern by scientists.[42] The ozone layer helps shield against harmful ultraviolet radiation, which may have detrimental impacts on human health (leading, among others, to skin cancer). Following the adoption of national measures to cut the production and use of CFCs, negotiations towards a global treaty were launched in 1977.[43] The result was the 1985 Vienna Convention, which as a framework convention did not require parties to undertake measures to reduce CFCs.[44] Quickly after its adoption, however, parties began to negotiate a new treaty that required cuts to CFCs, resulting two years later in the adoption of the Montreal Protocol. Three decades after its adoption, the global consumption of ozone-depleting substances controlled under the Montreal Protocol has declined by more than 99 per cent,[45] the

40 See WTO, *Matrix on Trade-Related Measures Pursuant to Selected Multilateral Environmental Agreements*, Doc. WT/CTE/W/160/Rev.9, TN/TE/S/5/Rev.7, 19 March 2021.

41 Montreal Protocol, n. 2.

42 Mario J. Molina & F. Sherwood Rowland, 'Stratospheric Sink for Chlorofluoromethanes: Chlorine Atom-catalysed Destruction of Ozone' (1974) 249(5460) *Nature* 810.

43 Scott Barrett, *Environment and Statecraft: The Strategy of Environmental Treaty-Making* (Oxford University Press, 2003), 223.

44 Vienna Convention for the Protection of the Ozone Layer, 1985, 1513 UNTS 293.

45 Hannah Ritchie & Max Roser, 'Ozone Layer', *Our World in Data*, https://ourworldindata.org/ozone-layer.

ozone layer is recovering,[46] and an increase in ultraviolet radiation has been prevented.[47]

Trade measures have played a pivotal role in this story. Trade measures against non-parties were initially proposed by the United States to create incentives for countries to participate in and comply with the Montreal Protocol, avoiding the relocation of CFC production facilities to non-parties (that is, preventing 'leakage') and protecting US industry against unfair competition.[48] Likewise, the United States favoured the use of trade measures against non-complying parties when negotiating the 1990 London Amendments to the Protocol.[49] Others, including the then European Community, were suspicious of these motivations, worried that the main reason for the trade measures was to shield US industry, which availed of more advanced technology and could more easily implement the treaty.[50] Ultimately, however, 'there was unanimity that imports from non-parties should be restricted'.[51]

As a consequence, the Montreal Protocol includes several provisions that directly address trade.[52] First, for controlled substances (that is, CFCs and other ozone-depleting substances), the Protocol provides for an import and export ban regarding non-parties.[53] The Protocol also requires parties to ban the import of certain products containing controlled substances from non-parties,[54] whereas for the import of products produced with, but not containing, controlled substances, the Protocol requires parties to study the feasibility of trade restrictions, and, if feasible, adopt such restrictions.[55] The treaty

46 *Ibid.*
47 Richard McKenzie *et al.*, 'Success of Montreal Protocol Demonstrated by Comparing High-Quality UV Measurements with "World Avoided" Calculations from Two Chemistry-Climate Models' (2019) 9 *Scientific Reports* 12332. The Montreal Protocol also made a significant impact on mitigating climate change, given that chlorofluorocarbons (and other substances addressed under the Montreal Protocol) are also greenhouse gases causing global warming. See Guus J. M. Velders *et al.*, 'The Importance of the Montreal Protocol in Protecting Climate' (2007) 104(12) *Proceedings of the National Academy of Sciences* 4814.
48 Richard Elliot Benedick, *Ozone Diplomacy* (Harvard University Press, 1998), 54, 91.
49 *Ibid.*, 183; Adjustments and Amendment to the Montreal Protocol on Substances That Deplete the Ozone Layer, 1991, 1598 UNTS 469.
50 Duncan Brack, *International Trade and the Montreal Protocol* (Earthscan, 1996), 53.
51 Stephen O. Andersen & K. Madhava Sarma, *Protecting the Ozone Layer: United Nations History* (Earthscan, 2002) 76.
52 Other provisions give parties discretion in adopting trade measures. This is the case for the control measures in article 2 that require parties to reduce the consumption of ozone-depleting substances.
53 Montreal Protocol, n. 2, arts. 4(1*sept*), 4(2*sept*).
54 *Ibid.*, art. 4(3)–4(3*ter*).
55 *Ibid.*, art. 4(4)–4(4*ter*).

further discourages the export to non-parties of technology for producing and for utilizing controlled substances.[56] Second, regarding trade with other parties if a party, after a phase-out date for a given substance, cannot cease production of the substance for domestic consumption, it is required to put in place an export ban.[57] Moreover, trade suspensions are possible under the Montreal Protocol's non-compliance procedure.[58] Although such measures have rarely been used in practice,[59] the mere threat of trade suspensions arguably has helped with improving compliance. Third, the Protocol obliges parties to adopt a licensing system for the trade in new, used, recycled, and reclaimed controlled substances to monitor trade flows, including the illegal trade in controlled substances.[60]

There is some (anecdotal) evidence that trade measures have induced some countries (for example, Mexico), to join the treaty.[61] According to Scott Barrett, the Montreal Protocol's trade restrictions created 'a tipping effect. Once enough countries participate in a treaty incorporating trade restrictions, it becomes irresistible for the rest to participate'.[62] However, while trade measures may have contributed to the Protocol's universal coverage, financial support for developing countries provided through the Protocol's Multilateral Fund, as well as access to technologies, have also played a major role.[63] In other words, it was the combination of 'sticks' and 'carrots' that helped make the Montreal Protocol a success.

But are the Montreal Protocol's trade measures permissible under international trade law? In the negotiations on the Protocol, a legal expert from the GATT Secretariat seemed to answer this question in the affirmative.[64] To assess the legality of the Protocol's measures, several distinctions are necessary. First, one needs to distinguish between the measures mandated in the Montreal Protocol and others that are at the discretion of its parties in

56 *Ibid.*, art. 4(5)–4(6).

57 *Ibid.*, art. 4A(1).

58 UN Environment Programme (UNEP), *Report of the Fourth Meeting of the Parties to the Montreal Protocol on Substances That Deplete the Ozone Layer*, UN Doc. UNEP/OzL.Pro.4/15, 25 November 1992, Annex V, C.

59 For an exception, see UNEP, *Decision VII/18, Compliance with the Montreal Protocol by the Russian Federation*, UN Doc. UNEP/OzL.Pro.7/12, 27 December 1995, para. 8.

60 Montreal Protocol, n. 2, art. 4B.

61 Benedick, n. 48, 243–44; Brack, n. 50, 54–58.

62 Scott Barrett, *Climate Change and International Trade: Lessons on Their Linkage from International Environmental Agreements* (Graduate Institute, 2010), 11, https://repository.graduateinstitute.ch/record/296909?ln=en.

63 Brack, n. 50, 56.

64 UNEP, *Report of the Ad Hoc Working Group on the Work of Its Third Session*, UN Doc UNEP/WG.172/2, 8 May 1987, 18.

implementing the treaty (with the latter resembling the unilateral measures discussed earlier in this chapter). Second, a distinction should be made between measures against non-complying parties and measures against non-parties. Third, mandated measures may affect the trade in controlled substances directly, but they may also affect trade in products containing such substances or the trade in products made with, but not containing, such substances. The trade implications of the latter would be the most far-reaching given that controlled substances are used in the manufacture of a wide array of products (for example, electronic equipment).

Although a comprehensive analysis of the different types of measures is outside the scope of this chapter,[65] the Montreal Protocol's trade measures against non-parties – and, where adopted, against non-complying parties – would likely violate the GATT's most-favoured nation treatment rule (article I), given that the restrictions against non-parties (or non-complying parties) are origin based. In addition, the measures would likely be counter to the GATT obligations on national treatment (article III) and quantitative restrictions (article XI).[66] However, it is also probable that the environmental exceptions in article XX of the GATT can assist in justifying such violations.[67] In short, they would have likely been deemed compatible with the GATT rules.

The story emerging from the Montreal Protocol's trade measures appears to be a positive one. Trade rules did not prevent the adoption of the Protocol's multilateral trade measures. These measures became integral to the success of the treaty, contributing to its near universal membership.[68] Moreover, regardless of their compatibility with WTO law, the Protocol's trade measures were never challenged in a trade dispute. The seemingly harmonious relationship between trade and environmental rules in this instance can be explained in part by the inclusion of positive incentives for developing countries to join (notably its Multilateral Fund) and in part by the development of these rules through a multilateral negotiation process. In this way, the Montreal Protocol helped meet some of the concerns voiced by developing countries in the context of the Stockholm Conference. The situation is different in the case of climate change, to which we will now turn.

65 See generally Erich Vranes, *Trade and the Environment: Fundamental Issues in International Law, WTO Law, and Legal Theory* (Oxford University Press, 2009), 353–372; Ann Rutgeerts, 'Trade and Environment: Reconciling the Montreal Protocol and the GATT' (1999) 33(4) *Journal of World Trade* 61.

66 See UNEP, *Trade-related Developments in the Montreal Protocol on Substances That Deplete the Ozone Layer, Communication from the Secretariat of the Vienna Convention and the Montreal Protocol*, Doc. WT/CTE/W/142, 19 June 2000, 9.

67 Rutgeerts, n. 65, 77–81; Brack, n. 50, 14, 20–21.

68 Benedick, n. 48, 91; Barrett, n. 43, 321.

15.3.2 *Unilateral Trade Measures: The Case of Climate Change*

Unlike the Montreal Protocol, the three climate treaties do not provide for trade measures. The UNFCCC includes a general call for coherence, stating that 'measures taken to combat climate change, including unilateral ones, should not constitute a means of arbitrary or unjustifiable discrimination or a disguised restriction on international trade'.[69] The 1997 Kyoto Protocol reaffirms the commitment to 'minimize adverse effects on ... international trade' in the pursuit of its objectives.[70] The Paris Agreement contains no provision on trade whatsoever.

Even without clear normative guidance from the climate change treaties, trade measures have constantly lurked in the background in international climate politics.[71] Climate change mitigation policies include measures that may affect international trade, such as renewable energy support, carbon pricing, product carbon standards, and carbon border adjustments.[72] In implementing their climate commitments, countries have indeed resorted to such measures. Some of these measures – in particular, renewable energy support measures and biofuel policies – have been challenged at the WTO and, in several cases, successfully so.[73] Perhaps most controversial among these climate-motivated measures are unilateral measures that address a product's carbon footprint (that is, the greenhouse gases emitted during the production process), which include the emissions released outside the jurisdiction of the country adopting the measure. Until recently, the debate around such measures was primarily confined to academic circles,[74] but the adoption of a carbon border adjustment mechanism (CBAM) by the European Union

69 UNFCCC, n. 3, art. 3(5).

70 Kyoto Protocol to the UN Framework Convention on Climate Change, 1997, 2302 UNTS 162, art. 2(3).

71 For instance, an early proposal for a carbon and energy tax in the then European Community contained provisions that applied to imports and exports. European Commission, *Amended Proposal for a Council Directive Introducing Tax on Carbon Dioxide Emissions and Energy*, Doc. COM(95) 172 final, 10 May 1995, arts 4, 10.

72 See generally Panagiotis Delimatsis (ed.), *Research Handbook on Climate Change and Trade Law* (Edward Elgar, 2016).

73 Harro van Asselt, 'The Prospects of Climate and Trade Disputes before the WTO: Blocking or Driving Climate Action?', in Ivano Alogna, Christine Bakker & Jean-Pierre Gauci (eds.), *Climate Change Litigation: Global Perspectives* (Brill, 2021), 433.

74 See, e.g., Joost Pauwelyn, 'Carbon Leakage Measures and Border Tax Adjustments under WTO Law', in Denise Prévost & Geert Van Calster (eds.), *Research Handbook on Environment, Health and the WTO* (Edward Elgar, 2013), 448; Kateryna Holzer, *Carbon-Related Border Adjustment and WTO Law* (Edward Elgar, 2014); Michael A. Mehling *et al.*, 'Designing Border Carbon Adjustments for Enhanced Climate Action' (2019) 113(3) *American Journal of International Law* 433.

(EU) means that the relationship between these measures and international trade rules may well be put to the test.[75]

Climate-motivated trade measures can be adopted for a variety of reasons. First, they can help a country collect the necessary information about the greenhouse gas emissions generated in the production of certain goods. Second, trade measures can help mitigate the impacts of carbon constraints on the competitiveness of trade-exposed energy-intensive industries in a country and/or assist such industries in their transition away from energy-intensive production. Third, such measures can help address emissions shifting from one country to another due to differences in climate policy (that is, 'carbon leakage').[76] Fourth, they can provide leverage for other countries to take stronger climate action and thereby counter free-riding behaviour.[77] Last, they can be adopted with a view to influencing the development of a multilateral regime.[78]

The extent to which unilateral trade measures such as carbon border adjustments 'work' depends on the goal pursued with such measures. If the goal is to avoid carbon leakage, it is not entirely clear whether measures such as carbon border adjustments will achieve that goal.[79] Likewise, if the goal is to deter free-riding, the jury remains out about the effectiveness of unilateral trade measures.[80] Discerning the influence of unilateral trade measures on international rule development is also not straightforward.[81] Moreover, even if a trade measure is effective in achieving its intended goals, there are trade-offs

75 Regulation (EU) 2023/956 Establishing a Carbon Border Adjustment Mechanism (2023) OJ L130/52. Indeed, in 2025, Russia requested consultations at the WTO (the step preceding the launch of a dispute) related to the EU CBAM. See WTO, *European Union and its Member States - Carbon Border Adjustment Mechanism - Request for Consultations by the Russian Federation*, Doc. WT/DS639/1, 19 May 2025.

76 See Michael Grubb *et al.*, 'Carbon Leakage, Consumption, and Trade' (2022) 47 *Annual Review of Environment and Resources* 30.

77 William Nordhaus, 'Climate Clubs: Overcoming Free-Riding in International Climate Policy' (2015) 105(4) *American Economic Review* 1339.

78 See Daniel Bodansky, 'What's So Bad About Unilateral Action to Protect the Environment' (2000) 11(2) *European Journal of International Law* (*EJIL*) 339, 343–346.

79 See a discussion of relevant economics literature in Mehling *et al.*, n. 74, 446.

80 Alexandra E. Cirone & Johannes Urpelainen, 'Trade Sanctions in International Environmental Policy: Deterring or Encouraging Free Riding?' (2013) 30(4) *Conflict Management and Peace Science* 309.

81 One could argue, for example, that the International Civil Aviation Organization adopted its international offsetting scheme for international aviation in 2016 due to the European Union's (EU) first adopting a domestic measure covering international aviation emissions in its emissions trading system. See Beatriz Martinez Romera, *Regime Interaction and Climate Change: The Case of International Aviation and Maritime Transport* (Routledge, 2018), 193. However, without a counterfactual (that is, what if the EU had refrained from adopting this measure?), it is hard to offer firm support for this argument.

to consider – for instance, the reaction of other countries. Regardless of their legality, trade measures may lead to retaliation or even risk a trade war.[82]

The compatibility of unilateral trade measures such as carbon border adjustments with international trade law ultimately hinges on the actual design and implementation of a measure. When designing a measure, policy-makers can seek to avoid a violation of the basic rules of the GATT – including most-favoured nation treatment and national treatment – altogether. In that case, they need to ensure at a minimum that the measure is applied to all 'like' products irrespective of their origin (and without reference to country-specific features).[83] Even if a measure violates the core obligations of the GATT, it could still be justified under the GATT's environmental exceptions. Of the two environmental exceptions, the conditions of article XX(g) are the easier to meet. It can likely be argued that a safe climate is an 'exhaustible natural resource'.[84] Moreover, unless the trade measure is only tangentially related to climate protection, it would also likely pass the 'relating to' test.[85] An environmental rationale – for example, tackling carbon leakage or inducing other countries to join international climate change efforts – would thus help prove that a measure falls within the scope of article XX(g). By contrast, an economic rationale – for example, safeguarding the competitiveness of energy-intensive industries – would not be a legitimate objective under article XX(g). To ensure that measures are 'made effective in conjunction with restrictions on domestic production and consumption', any constraints imposed on imports need to be accompanied by constraints on domestic producers of the same goods. This is the case for measures like the EU's CBAM, which functions in parallel to the EU's emissions trading system, which covers domestic producers.

With regard to the *chapeau* of article XX, WTO dispute settlement bodies have suggested, among others, that the country adopting a measure should ensure 'basic fairness and due process' in the application of a measure.[86] This could be achieved, for instance, by allowing the importer to show that the carbon intensity of their product is lower than the emissions benchmark set by the country adopting the measure or by gradually phasing in a measure.[87] Moreover, a country needs to pursue 'serious, across-the-board negotiations

82 See, e.g., Christoph Böhringer, 'Potential Impacts and Challenges of Border Carbon Adjustments' (2022) 12(1) *Nature Climate Change* 22.

83 See Nathaniel Eisen, 'Carbon Emissions as a Physical Property: Ontological Approaches to the WTO Like Products Debate' (2019) 51(3) *New York University Journal of International Law and Politics* 871.

84 Mehling *et al.*, n. 74, 466–67.

85 Pauwelyn, n. 74, 500.

86 *Shrimp-Turtle*, n. 28, para. 181.

87 Mehling *et al.*, n. 74, 468.

with the objective of concluding bilateral or multilateral agreements'.[88] This requirement may be satisfied by the negotiations of (and pursuant to) the Paris Agreement, but it may also be that bilateral negotiations with affected third countries are needed.[89] The measure also needs to be sufficiently flexible in its application to take into account the conditions in third countries. This would preclude a country from requiring other countries to adopt the same measure (for example, carbon pricing) but would not preclude it from requiring the adoption of a measure that is 'comparable in effectiveness'.[90]

Whether measures such as the EU's CBAM are compatible with WTO law remains to be determined.[91] However, compatibility with international trade rules is not the only relevant question when it comes to the legality of trade measures. Another question is whether such measures are consistent with relevant principles and rules in international climate change law. In this regard, a key question is the extent to which trade measures reflect the principle of common but differentiated responsibilities and respective capabilities. For instance, while the EU's CBAM has been designed to be compatible with WTO rules, it can be criticized from the perspective of international climate change law as it does not exempt least developed countries, and revenues from the mechanism are not used to support developing countries in their energy transition.[92]

The potential incompatibility of trade measures such as the CBAM with fairness principles brings us back to the original concerns voiced by developing countries around the Stockholm Conference. Developing countries are still concerned that measures such as the CBAM constitute a form of green protectionism or, updated to the twenty-first century, 'carbon colonialism'.[93] Indeed, the backlash from developing countries can be fierce, as illustrated by

88 *Shrimp-Turtle*, n. 28, para. 166.

89 Mehling *et al.*, n. 74, 468–69.

90 WTO, *United States – Import Prohibition of Certain Shrimp and Shrimp Products (Recourse to Article 21.5 by Malaysia)*, Report of the Appellate Body, WT/DS58/AB/RW, 22 October 2001, para. 144.

91 Initial legal analyses point to several weaknesses, but WTO adjudicators, of course, would have the final word. See, e.g., Ilaria Espa, Joseph Francois & Harro van Asselt, 'The EU Proposal for a Carbon Border Adjustment Mechanism (CBAM): An Analysis under WTO and Climate Change Law' (2022) *Oil, Gas and Energy Law* 1; Gracia Marín Durán, 'Securing Compatibility of Carbon Border Adjustments with the Multilateral Climate and Trade Regimes' (2023) 72(1) *International Comparative Law Quarterly* 73.

92 Alice Pirlot, 'Carbon Border Adjustment Measures: A Straightforward Multi-Purpose Climate Change Instrument?' 34(1) *Journal of Environmental Law* 25; Espa, Francois & van Asselt, n. 91; Marín Durán, n. 91.

93 For a critique, see Arvind P. Ravikumar, 'Carbon Border Taxes Are Unjust', *MIT Technology Review*, 27 July 2020.

the strong negative reactions to the EU's CBAM and other unilateral trade measures aimed at global environmental protection, such as the EU's 2023 Deforestation Regulation.[94] However, while some developing countries have raised their concerns in international forums,[95] including the WTO and the UNFCCC, other countries have begun to adapt to the measure or consider the adoption of measures of their own.[96] This illustrates that not all developing countries perceive and respond to unilateral trade measures in the same way.

15.4 TAKING STOCK OF TRADE AND THE ENVIRONMENT AT STOCKHOLM+50

With reference to the developments in the previous part, the following part reflects on three developments in the trade and environment debate, contrasting these developments with the state of the debate at the time of the Stockholm Conference.

15.4.1 *The Growth of Trade-related Environmental Measures and Trade-Environment Disputes*

A first observation is that the use of trade-related environmental measures has increased significantly since the Stockholm Conference. Although this includes specific measures in MEAs, most of these measures are discretionary measures that states can adopt to implement their obligations under MEAs. According to the WTO, 'there has been a sustained increase in the number of environment-related notifications to the WTO',[97] with the WTO

94 Regulation (EU) 2023/1115 on the Making Available on the Union Market and the Export from the Union of Certain Commodities and Products Associated with Deforestation and Forest Degradation, (2023) OJ L150/206; Alice Hancock, 'EU's Trading Partners Accuse Bloc of Protectionism over Carbon Tax Plan', *Financial Times*, 17 December 2022; Mercedes Ruehl, Alice Hancock & Emiko Terazono, 'EU Deforestation Law Triggers Ire of Its Trading Partners', *Financial Times*, 6 February 2023.

95 See, e.g., the proposal by the 'BASIC' countries (Brazil, South Africa, India, and China) to include a new agenda item on unilateral trade measures at the Dubai Climate Conference in 2023, https://unfccc.int/sites/default/files/resource/COP28_BASIC-Agenda%20proposal.pdf; Abhishek Law, 'India to Raise at WTO EU's Plan to Levy Carbon Tax on Imports', *Hindu BusinessLine*, 27 January 2023, www.thehindubusinessline.com/economy/india-mayraise-eus-carbon-tax-issue-at-wto/article66440036.ece.

96 Alessandro Vitelli, 'EU CBAM Nudges Countries to Establish Carbon Markets', *CZAPP*, 15 November 2023, www.czapp.com/analyst-insights/eu-cbam-nudges-countries-to-establish-carbon-markets; 'India Mulling Its Own Carbon Tax on Exports along the Lines of CBAM', *Business Standard*, 25 September 2023.

97 WTO, *Environmental Database for 2020*, Doc. WT/CTE/EDB/20, 28 January 2020, 3.

Environmental Database listing more than 22,000 environment-related measures by the end of 2025.[98] With the number of trade measures increasing, it is unsurprising that there is also a growing number of trade-environment disputes. The nature of these disputes is also changing. There has been a move away from more 'traditional' disputes focused on conservation measures (for example, *Tuna-Dolphin*, *Shrimp-Turtle*) to disputes that are more about green industrial policy, in which the support measures by states for infant industries in the green economy – such as the renewable energy industry – are challenged.[99] In some cases, these disputes have struck down support measures in emerging economies, with the ruling against India's National Solar Mission's inclusion of local content requirements being a prominent example.[100] Other climate-related disputes, such as the disputes brought by biofuel-producing countries such as Argentina, Indonesia, and Malaysia against the EU,[101] also clearly have a North-South dimension, which brings us to the second observation.

15.4.2 *Persisting North-South Tensions*

Fifty years after Stockholm, North-South tensions continue to form the main backdrop for the trade-environment debate. This is clear from the contested inclusion of a statement to avoid unilateral trade measures in Principle 12 of the Rio Declaration. It is also apparent from the development of the international legal regimes for ozone depletion and climate change. In the negotiations of the Montreal Protocol, some developing countries voiced concerns about trade measures.[102] As noted above, however, these concerns were to some extent addressed by the Protocol's provisions on financial and technological support and the fact that rules were developed multilaterally. In the international climate change regime, developing countries have repeatedly expressed concern about developed countries adopting 'response measures' that could restrict market access for

98 'Environmental Database', *WTO*, https://edb.wto.org/.

99 See Mark Wu & James Salzman, 'The Next Generation of Trade and Environment Conflicts: The Rise of Green Industrial Policy' (2014) 108(2) *Northwestern University Law Review* 401; *Tuna-Dolphin*, n. 23; *Shrimp-Turtle*, n. 28.

100 WTO, *India – Certain Measures Relating to Solar Cells and Solar Modules*, Report of the Appellate Body, WT/DS456/AB/R, 16 September 2016.

101 See Carolyn Fischer & Timothy Meyer, 'Baptists and Bootleggers in the Biodiesel Trade: *EU–Biodiesel (Indonesia)*' (2020) 19(2) *World Trade Review* 297.

102 Benedick, n. 48, 100 (citing a Malaysian negotiator who referred to the measures as 'trade war by environmental decree').

developing countries.[103] Moreover, as noted above, some – though not all – developing countries have protested unilateral climate-motivated measures that are likely to affect their international competitiveness – in some cases, resulting in disputes before the WTO (for example, the disputes targeting EU biofuel policies).

For climate change, in particular, these reactions have to be seen in the light of the broader North-South context. First, various measures are being adopted by developed countries, even though they can be considered to be historically responsible for the problem. Second, there are major differences in the capacity to address the problem, particularly where it concerns the least developed countries. Lower-income countries are hit harder by trade measures, even though they have contributed least to the climate problem, and are most vulnerable to the impacts of climate change. Third, trade measures are adopted by developed countries even though they have not delivered on their obligations to provide financial and other support to developing countries.[104] For these reasons, even if trade measures adopted by developed countries are genuinely aimed at climate protection, they may still be perceived as unfair.

Harking back to the Stockholm Action Plan, the main safeguards put in place by international trade law to address these concerns are procedural, focusing on notification and consultation, ensuring fairness and due process in the design and implementation of measures, and pursuing international cooperation.[105] Such procedural safeguards can help mitigate some developing country concerns about specific measures, but they do not address the broader inequities in addressing global environmental problems. The more radical proposal contained in the Stockholm Action Plan of offering compensation for the negative effects of trade measures seems to be all but off the table. Attempts to revive this idea – for instance, through the proposal by oil-producing states to include in the Kyoto Protocol a 'compensation fund' for lost oil revenues due to developed country implementation measures – have been consistently rejected by developed countries.[106] Although compensation may not be feasible, it may be feasible to flank unilateral trade measures with forms of international cooperation that channel financial and other forms of support to developing countries

[103] Nicholas Chan, 'The "New" Impacts of the Implementation of Climate Change Response Measures' (2016) 25(2) *Review of European, Comparative and International Environmental Law* 228.

[104] Jocelyn Timperley, 'The Broken $100-Billion Promise of Climate Finance – and How to Fix It' (2021) 598 *Nature* 400.

[105] Stockholm Action Plan, n. 19.

[106] Chan, n. 103, 229–230.

to adjust to the impacts of trade measures – for instance, by using revenues of carbon border adjustments to develop energy transition partnerships.[107]

15.4.3 *The Appropriate Forum(s) for Addressing Trade-Environment Interactions*

A third observation is that, after five decades, it is still not entirely clear which forum is best suited to address trade-environment linkages. The Stockholm Action Plan refers to the GATT and UNCTAD, two trade institutions. The lack of a reference to international environmental institutions can easily be explained by the fact that, at the time, there was not yet an international environmental agency (the UN Environment Programme was created in the aftermath of the Stockholm Conference) and that most MEAs had yet to be adopted. Arguably, MEAs – as the main treaties dealing with a given environmental problem – are best placed to resolve a trade-environment dispute within their purview. Yet, as we can see with the climate treaties, MEAs can be silent about trade measures, often because the topic is too controversial to allow for consensus. Still, some environmental treaties, such as the Vienna Convention, include a dispute settlement provision. Resorting to MEA dispute settlement may seem appropriate in case one party adopts trade measures against another.[108] However, dispute settlement provisions in MEAs have rarely been used. Moreover, in the case of trade disputes with non-parties, this route is not available, leaving dispute settlement at the WTO as the default.[109]

Trade dispute settlement has certainly become greener over the years, and the idea of mutual supportiveness has taken hold.[110] At the same time, having trade adjudicators rule on sensitive questions, such as the legality of the EU's CBAM, may put them in a difficult position, as such rulings may affect countries' climate policies, the prospects for international climate cooperation, as well as the external legitimacy of the WTO and its dispute settlement system.[111] More generally, the multilateral trade regime has been unable to

[107] As suggested by Randolph Bell & Elena Benaim, 'Carbon Border Adjustment: A Powerful Tool If Paired with a Just Energy Transition', *OECD Development Matters*, 27 October 2020, https://oecd-development-matters.org/2020/10/27/carbon-border-adjustment-a-powerful-tool-if-paired-with-a-just-energy-transition/.

[108] See WTO, *Report of the WTO Committee on Trade and Environment*, Doc. WT/CTE/1, 12 November 1996, para. 178.

[109] *Ibid.*, para. 38.

[110] See Riccardo Pavoni, 'Mutual Supportiveness as a Principle of Interpretation and Law-Making: A Watershed for the "WTO-and-Competing-Regimes" Debate? (2010) 21(3) *EJIL* 649.

[111] van Asselt, n. 73, 458.

make major advances in developing rules on trade and the environment. An exception was the adoption of the 2022 Agreement on Fisheries Subsidies, which introduces new disciplines for subsidies for unsustainable fisheries, but even this new agreement took several decades to negotiate.[112] Having said that, new initiatives have emerged in the WTO context – though not involving the entire WTO membership – such as the Trade and Environmental Sustainability Structured Discussions, which were launched in 2020,[113] and the WTO Secretariat has become increasingly active in addressing the overlap with environmental challenges, notably climate change.[114] Moreover, through its systems for notifications of trade measures and trade policy reviews, the WTO has come to play an important role in monitoring and discussing environmental measures with an impact on trade.

In the absence of rule development in the multilateral trading and environmental regimes, some states have sought to address the trade-environment overlap elsewhere. This includes in regional trade agreements, through which an increasing number of innovative environmental provisions have been adopted.[115] However, in the area of climate change, such provisions are often hortatory and not backed by an enforcement mechanism (for example, dispute settlement).[116] It may be that a new generation of trade agreements, such as the Agreement on Climate Change, Trade and Sustainability among a group of small trading nations,[117] could overcome these limitations. Yet other initiatives are in the form of limited-membership coalitions, with the Climate Club launched by the Group of Seven in 2023 being a prominent example. Although the Climate Club does not introduce trade measures, it addresses issues closely linked to countries' international competitiveness in a global green economy, such as carbon leakage and comparability of

112 Agreement on Fisheries Subsidies, WTO Doc. WT/MIN(22)/33, WT/L/1144, 22 June 2022; see Bernard M. Hoekman, Petros C. Mavroidis & Sunayana Sasmal, 'Managing Externalities in the WTO: The Agreement on Fisheries Subsidies' (2023) 26(2) *Journal of International Economic Law* 266.

113 WTO, *Communication on Trade and Environmental Sustainability*, Doc. WT/CTE/W/249, 17 November 2020.

114 See 'Trade and Climate Change', *WTO* www.wto.org/english/tratop_e/envir_e/climate_intro_e.htm#wp.

115 Jean-Frédéric Morin, Joost Pauwelyn & James Hollway, 'The Trade Regime as a Complex Adaptive System: Exploration and Exploitation of Environmental Norms in Trade Agreements' (2017) 20(2) *Journal of International Economic Law* 365.

116 Jean-Frédéric Morin & Sikina Jinnah, 'The Untapped Potential of Preferential Trade Agreements for Climate Governance' (2018) 17(3) *Environmental Politics* 541.

117 Agreement on Climate Change, Trade and Sustainability, 2024, https://www.mfat.govt.nz/en/trade/free-trade-agreements/free-trade-agreements-concluded-but-not-in-force/agreement-on-climate-change-trade-and-sustainability-accts.

efforts.[118] Whether initiatives such as the Climate Club are able to strike the right balance between addressing environmental concerns and respecting development priorities remains to be seen. A crucial question for each of these limited membership initiatives ultimately is: who participates? To the extent that developing countries are unable to participate in these initiatives, they may reinforce existing inequities by further restricting market access. This, in turn, may adversely affect international environmental cooperation.[119]

15.5 CONCLUSIONS

This chapter has reflected on the development of the trade and environment debate since the 1972 Stockholm Conference, focusing specifically on the interactions between trade rules and two major problems related to atmospheric protection: climate change and ozone depletion. The main conclusion emerging from this chapter is that, while much has changed at the time of the UN International Meeting Stockholm+50: A Healthy Planet for the Prosperity of All – Our Responsibility, Our Opportunity (Stockholm+50 Meeting) – new international legal regimes have come into being, and many more trade-related environmental measures have been adopted – some things have stayed the same, with North-South tensions continuing to form the main context for trade-environment interactions and ongoing uncertainty about where these interactions should be addressed.

The Stockholm Conference's outcomes suggested the need to avoid trade measures for environmental reasons, and where such measures would negatively impact developing countries, it raised the spectre of compensation. Fifty years later, the evidence shows that such measures are clearly not being avoided, and the question of compensation has all but disappeared due to developed countries' resistance. Instead, procedural requirements – calling for notification, consultation, monitoring, and cooperation, among others – are the main safeguard for developing countries to ensure that developed countries' measures are not just 'green protectionism'.

Concerning trade measures in MEAs, such as the ones in the Montreal Protocol, it is unlikely that they will lead to a major trade dispute, given that they are based on international consensus. And even if they would be

[118] See 'Climate Club', https://climate-club.org/.

[119] In this respect, it should be noted that the Climate Club is intended to be 'inclusive'. For a discussion, see Michael Mehling *et al.*, *Bridging the Divide: Assessing the Viability of International Cooperation on Border Carbon Adjustments* (Climate Strategies, 2023), 19–23.

challenged before trade dispute settlement bodies, it is likely that multilateral trade measures will be deemed compatible with international trade rules. The Montreal Protocol also shows that trade measures can induce participation, but the stick of trade measures should be combined with carrots in the form of financial and technological support.

With regard to unilateral trade measures, it is clear that international trade law offers regulatory space for them, particularly if they clearly contribute to an environmental goal. However, whether they are compatible will depend on the details of design and implementation. Moreover, unilateral trade measures may also be at odds with principles and rules in international environmental law. Last, when it comes to addressing trade-environment linkages, it is rather unlikely at this stage to expect WTO members to come up with an amendment of international trade agreements, but, at the same time, we can see innovations happening through plurilateral and regional initiatives. However, also in the context of these initiatives, it will be important to remain mindful of the genuine concerns expressed by developing countries at Stockholm.

PART V

WATERS

16

The Stockholm Declaration at Sea: Influences on the Content and Context of the Law of the Sea

Richard Barnes

16.1 INTRODUCTION

The 1972 Stockholm Declaration on the Human Environment (Stockholm Declaration)[1] challenged the idea of a state-centric system.[2] It situated humans and human activity within the wider natural environment.[3] It established the environment as central to human well-being and the enjoyment of human rights.[4] And it advanced the need for balance between environmental protection and economic development.[5] The Stockholm Declaration is widely regarded as foundational to environmental law,[6] and many experts note its influence on the law of the sea.[7] However, some fundamental aspects of the law of the sea had developed before the adoption of the Declaration in 1972 and the emergence of international environmental law more generally. This stymied the receptiveness of the law of the sea to wider environmental and human-centric concerns.[8]

[1] 'Declaration of the United Nations Conference on the Human Environment', in *Report of the UN Conference on the Human Environment*, UN Doc. A/CONF.48/14/Rev.1, 16 June 1972 (Stockholm Declaration).

[2] Louis B. Sohn, 'The Stockholm Declaration on the Human Environment' (1973) 14 *Harvard International Law Journal* 423, 513.

[3] Stockholm Declaration, n. 1, 3. The Stockholm Declaration was accompanied by the Stockholm Action Plan. 'Action Plan for the Human Environment', in *Report of the UN Conference on the Human Environment*, n. 1, 6 (Stockholm Action Plan).

[4] Stockholm Declaration, n. 1, preamble, para. 1.

[5] *Ibid.*, preamble generally, and principles 11–13.

[6] Peter H. Sand, 'The Evolution of International Environmental Law', in Daniel Bodansky, Jutta Brunnée & Ellen Hey (eds.), *The Oxford Handbook of International Environmental Law* (Oxford University Press, 2007), 29.

[7] See Myron H. Nordquist, John N. Moore & Said Mahmoudi (eds.), *The Stockholm Declaration and the Law of the Marine Environment* (Brill, 2003).

[8] Richard Barnes, 'Alternative Histories and Futures of International Fisheries Law', in Richard Caddell & Erik J. Molenaar (eds.), *Strengthening International Fisheries Law in an Era of Changing Oceans* (Hart Publishing, 2019), 25.

As we approached the UN International Meeting Stockholm+50: A Healthy Planet for the Prosperity of All – Our Responsibility, Our Opportunity (Stockholm+50 Meeting), there was a growing confluence between the oceans, environmental, and human rights concerns, prompting questions about the relationship between these branches of law. Indeed, this is central to the *Commission of Small Island States* advisory opinion before the International Tribunal for the Law of the Sea (ITLOS), where concerns about rights to a healthy environment and the human rights implications of sea-level rise were raised.[9] In its opinion, ITLOS recognized that climate change represents an existential threat and raises human rights concerns.[10] The confluence between human rights and the environment was endorsed by the ICJ in its *Climate Change* advisory opinion, where the court noted that 'the protection of the environment is a precondition for the enjoyment of human rights'.[11] Specifically: 'The right to a clean, healthy and sustainable environment results from the *interdependence* between human rights and the protection of the environment.'[12]

The precise influence of the Stockholm Declaration on the law of the sea remains ambiguous. Extant scholarship tends to focus on the Declaration's triggering effect or how Principle 7 on marine pollution prevention has been received into the law of the sea.[13] The 1982 UN Convention on the Law of the Sea (UNCLOS) presents multiple opportunities to advance the Stockholm Declaration.[14] However, tracing and assessing the influence of the Declaration on the law of the sea is difficult because the Stockholm principles have become diffused through myriad complex treaty arrangements and other legal relationships. Understanding the relationship between these instruments

[9] ITLOS, *Request for an Advisory Opinion Submitted by the Commission of Small Island States on Climate Change and International Law*, Request for Advisory Opinion Submitted to the Tribunal, Case no. 31, 12 December 2022 (*Request for an Advisory Opinion on Climate Change*). Here, we may note the frequent references to human and environmental rights in the submissions as well as the parallel proceedings initiated before the Inter-American Court of Human Rights. See, e.g., *Amicus Brief Submitted to the International Tribunal for the Law of the Sea by the UN Special Rapporteurs on Human Rights and Climate Change (Ian Fry), Toxics & Human Rights (Marcos Orellana), and Human Rights & the Environment (David Boyd)*, 30 May 2023, paras. 17, 62–63.

[10] *Request for an Advisory Opinion on Climate Change*, n. 9, para. 66.

[11] *Obligations of States in Respect of Climate Change*, Advisory Opinion, 23 July 2025, (2025) ICJ Reports, para 373.

[12] *Ibid.*, para 393 (emphasis added).

[13] See the contributions to Nordquist, Moore & Mahmoudi, n. 7; see also Myron H. Nordquist, Shabtai Rosenne & Alexander Yankov, *United Nations Convention on the Law of the Sea, 1982, vol. 4: A Commentary, Articles 192 to 278 Final Act, Annex V* (Martinus Nijhoff, 1985), 8–9, 36–37.

[14] United Nations Convention on the Law of the Sea, 1982, 1834 UNTS 397 (UNCLOS).

is important in understanding how the law develops. Despite this importance, it has only been considered periodically in the literature.[15]

In this chapter, I trace the Stockholm Declaration's influence through a synoptic review of some ocean instruments. Whilst we can trace some of the genealogy of UNCLOS to Stockholm, especially with respect to the protection of the marine environment, the analysis reveals that much of the shape and character of UNCLOS flows from a wider range of sources and influences. In other words, there is more to the 'nurturing' influence of Stockholm (and other instruments) on the policy and legal environment within which UNCLOS operates than to its direct influence on the textual DNA or 'nature' of UNCLOS. Traditional international law method tends to trace how law develops through modes of treaty negotiation and interpretation or through the jurisprudence of international tribunals. Inevitably, this gives particular weight to a narrow range of material sources – that is, texts. Whilst this is important, it should not blind us to an appreciation of how wider contexts and cultures can shape the law.

16.2 TRACING THE STOCKHOLM DECLARATION'S DNA IN THE LAW OF THE SEA

The 1969 Vienna Convention on the Law of Treaties (VCLT) permits a narrow form of context to be used to ascertain the meaning of a treaty.[16] Context includes treaties 'made between all the parties in connection with the conclusion of the treaty' and any instruments made between 'one or more parties in connection with the conclusion of the treaty and accepted by the other parties as an instrument related to the treaty'.[17] Account also may be taken of subsequent agreements, practice, and any relevant rules of international law.[18] Such context and interpretative material is framed prospectively, referring only to subsequent matters or, at the very least, material consecutive to the conclusion of a treaty. Indeed, even more liberal accounts of interpretation, such as evolutive approaches, tend to focus on how meaning changes prospectively over time.[19] This largely excludes material that is

[15] See Nordquist, Moore & Mahmoudi, n. 7; see also Jonathan I. Charney, 'The Marine Environment and the 1982 United Nations Convention on the Law of the Sea' (1994) 28 *International Lawyer* 879.

[16] Vienna Convention on the Law of Treaties, 1969, 1155 UNTS 331 (VCLT).

[17] *Ibid.*, art. 31(2).

[18] *Ibid.*, art. 31(3).

[19] Eirik Bjorge, *The Evolutionary Interpretation of Treaties* (Oxford University Press, 2014), especially 118ff.

antecedent to the treaty. Supplementary means of interpretation include the *travaux préparatoires* and the circumstances of the conclusion of the treaty,[20] but this too is limited to negotiation texts and contemporary material. The main way that antecedent material becomes relevant is for a treaty to receive the terms of earlier agreements or instruments into its text as either operative provisions or preambular text. An obvious example of this is the reception of the text relating to freedom of the high seas from the 1958 Convention on the High Seas into UNCLOS.[21] Accordingly, there is limited scope to use interpretation as a technique for understanding how instruments like the Stockholm Declaration can influence later agreements.[22]

My point is not to argue for a regressive approach to interpretation that permits historic context to inform treaty texts; rather, it is to highlight the marginalization of important context in how treaty regimes develop. By taking account of a treaty's wider context, one can better perceive how treaty regimes fit together and show the dynamics of how legal developments change over time. From this, one gains a sense of the trajectory within which the more narrowly understood process of treaty negotiations and interpretation occur. Between the Stockholm Declaration and the adoption of UNCLOS in 1982 approximately sixty instruments were negotiated in relation to marine matters. Since then, another 150+ instruments have been adopted. Despite the Stockholm Declaration's significance, explicit reference to it in treaty texts is infrequent and often limited to preambular statements. The Declaration is noted in key general environmental agreements, such as the 1979 Berne Convention,[23] the 1973 Convention on International Trade in Endangered Species,[24] the 1979 Vienna Convention,[25] and the 1998 Aarhus Convention.[26] However, the only marine-specific agreements mentioning Stockholm are the 1992 OSPAR

20 VCLT, n. 16, art. 32.

21 Convention on the High Seas, 1958, 450 UNTS 11.

22 The Stockholm Declaration, n. 1, is cited only once by the International Court of Justice in a decision. *Legality of the Threat or Use of Nuclear Weapons*, Advisory Opinion, 8 July 1996, (1996) ICJ Reports 226, para. 27 (*Nuclear Weapons*). The International Tribunal for the Law of the Sea has not cited it.

23 Convention on the Conservation of European Wildlife and Natural Habitats, 1979, 1284 UNTS 209, para. 8, preamble (noting the call for action in the Stockholm Declaration).

24 Convention on International Trade in Endangered Species of Wild Fauna and Flora, 1973, 993 UNTS 243. The final act of the conference notes Recommendation 99.3 of the Stockholm Conference to convene a conference on wildlife trade.

25 Convention for the Protection of the Ozone Layer, 1979, 1513 UNTS 293, para. 2, preamble (which recalls the Stockholm Declaration, particularly principle 21).

26 Convention on Access to Information, Public Participation in Decision-Making and Access to Justice in Environmental Matters, 1998, 2161 UNTS 467, para. 1, preamble (recalling principle 1).

Convention (and also the 1972 Paris Convention preceding it) and the 1992 Helsinki Convention.[27] The lack of formal reference to the Stockholm Declaration in treaty texts mutes its formal influence on the interpretation of latter rules and obscures its deeper influence on the law. Tracing its influence requires us to look more forensically at how the Declaration's 'DNA' – its specific language and textual concepts – has been inherited by later agreements.

This section traces the Stockholm Declaration's DNA and examines the Declaration's influence on the nature of UNCLOS, the 1995 UN Fish Stocks Agreement (UNFSA),[28] and the 2023 Agreement on Areas beyond National Jurisdiction (BBNJ Agreement).[29] These agreements form the superstructure of the law of the sea and give a strong indication of how the Declaration has informed ocean lawmaking. The twenty-six Stockholm principles are analysed in eight thematic areas:

1. developing the human environment nexus (preamble, principles 1 and 8);
2. protection and sustainable use of natural resources, including habitats (principles 2–5);
3. preventing pollution and environmental harm (principles 6–7) and liability rules (principle 22);
4. improving working conditions (principle 8);
5. sovereignty and differential commitments for developing states (principles 9–12 and 21–23);
6. integrated and rational planning of resource use/activities (principles 13–17);
7. the use and promotion of science and education to protect the environment (principles 18–20); and
8. the cooperation/use of international organizations (principles 24–25).

Table 16.1 shows how the Stockholm Declaration's principles map onto later instruments.

[27] Convention for the Protection of the Marine Environment of the North-East Atlantic, 1992, 2354 UNTS 67 (paragraph 5 of the preamble considers the recommendations of the Stockholm Conference); Convention for the Prevention of Marine Pollution from Land-based Sources, 1972, 1546 UNTS 119; Convention on the Protection of the Marine Environment of the Baltic Sea Area, 1992, 2099 UNTS 197.

[28] Agreement for the Implementation of the Provisions of the United Nations Convention on the Law of the Sea of 10 December 1982 Relating to the Conservation and Management of Straddling Fish Stocks and Highly Migratory Fish Stocks, and Related Instruments, 1995, 2167 UNTS 3 (UNFSA).

[29] Agreement under the United Nations Convention on the Law of the Sea on the Conservation and Sustainable Use of Marine Biological Diversity of Areas beyond National Jurisdiction, 2023, https://treaties.un.org/doc/Treaties/2023/06/20230620%2004-28%20PM/Ch_XXI_10.pdf (BBNJ Agreement).

TABLE 16.1 *Mapping the Stockholm Declaration's principles*

Stockholm Declaration	UNCLOS	UNFSA	BBNJ Agreement
Principle 1: right to healthy environment	n/a	n/a	*preamble; article 7(k)*
Principle 2: safeguard natural resources	article 61	article 2	preamble; article 2
Principle 3: maintain/restore renewable resources	article 61	preamble; articles 2, 5; Annex II	preamble; articles 2, 7
Principle 4: safeguard wildlife and habitats	article 194(5)	article 6(3)(d)	part III
Principle 5: non-renewable resources for benefit of mankind	article 140	n/a	n/a
Principle 6: toxic substances	articles 194(3), 195, 207(5)	n/a	preamble; articles 7(l), 17(c)
Principle 7: sea pollution	part XII	article 5(f)	preamble; articles 7(l), 17(c), 30
Principle 8: social development for better living and working conditions	articles 94(3), (4), 266(2)	n/a	n/a
Principle 9: financial and technological assistance	articles 202, 203	preamble; articles 24, 25, 26	part V
Principle 10: price stability for primary commodities	article 150(h)	n/a	n/a
Principle 11: environmental policies enhance developing countries	article 207(4)	preamble; *articles* 5, 6	preamble; article 2; part IV
Principle 12: resources to preserve and improve environment	articles 202, 203	n/a	articles 40, 43(5)
Principle 13: integrated and coordinated development planning	preamble; articles 272, 276; Part XI	article 5(d), (e)	article 5(f); parts III, IV

Principle 14: rational planning	*articles 199, 206; part XI*	article 6(3)(d)	parts III, IV
Principle 15: planning of settlements	n/a	n/a	n/a
Principle 16: demographic policies	n/a	n/a	n/a
Principle 17: planning institutions	n/a	n/a	n/a
Principle 18: use of environmental science and technology	articles 61, 119, 200, 201; part XIII	articles 5(b), 5(k)	articles 7(i), 19(3), 24(3), 26(5), 31, 35, 37; part V
Principle 19: education	articles 202, 244, 268, 277	n/a	article 44
Principle 20: scientific research	parts XIII	articles 5(j), 5(k), 6(3)(d), 10(g), 14, 25(3)(b)	preamble; article 8(3), 9(c), 14(2)(f); part V
Principle 21: sovereignty over natural resources/non-harmful use	parts V, VI, XII	articles 3, 7(1), 7(2)(f)	preamble; articles 6, 11(4), 18, 22(5), 32(2)(a), 47(7), 60
Principle 22: liability and compensation	articles 139, 232, 235, 263, 304	article 35	preamble
Principle 23: differential commitments	articles 61, 62, 119, 82(3), 82(4); 202, 203, 207; parts XI, XIV	preamble; article 3(3)	articles 7(m), (n), 9, 11(6), 14, 15, 17, 21(8), 25(3), 27(f), 51(5), 52; part V
Principle 24: environmental cooperation	preamble; part XII	articles 5, 7, 17, 20, 21, 24(2); parts III, VII	article 8; throughout
Principle 25: International organizations	articles 207(4), 208(5), 210(4), 211(1), 212(3)	article 7; part III	articles 5, 8; throughout
Principle 26: eliminating nuclear weapons and weapons of mass destruction	n/a	n/a	n/a

Notes: Provisions in italics indicate an implicit/indirect link to the principle rather than direct use of the same text or synonyms.

Some preliminary comments can be drawn from this tabular overview. First, some elements of the Stockholm Declaration appear to be more relevant than others. These include principle 21 on resource sovereignty and non-harmful use, principle 24 on the duty to cooperate in tackling environmental harm, and, of course, principle 7 on preventing marine pollution. Second, the law of the sea remains limited in its reception of the Stockholm Declaration's human-centric concerns around 'rights to a healthy environment' and improving social development (for example, principles 1 and 8). Law of the sea texts remain focused on rules related to resource use or exploitation. This limited reception is also reflected in provisions on planning, which accommodate objectives on rationale use but fall short of setting out more detailed planning measures that necessarily integrate a wider range of social considerations. Third, there is more frequent reference to science, technology, and research (for example, principles 18–20), further reflecting the technical focus of the law of the sea.

16.2.1 HUMAN/ENVIRONMENT NEXUS

Principle 1 states that 'man has the fundamental right to freedom, equality and adequate conditions of life, in an environment of a quality that permits a life of dignity and well-being, and he bears a solemn responsibility to protect and improve the environment for present and future generations'. Principle 1 links environmental conditions to human rights, with principle 8 providing that economic and social development is essential for ensuring a favourable living and working environment. Although the link between the environment and human rights and human well-being is widely acknowledged,[30] it is seldom articulated in a specific set of rights.[31] This suggests that the Stockholm Declaration is part of a wider policy context that has nurtured change rather than instigating specific legal developments. It is only in the year of the Stockholm+50 Meeting that a general right to a healthy environment was

[30] Alan E. Boyle & Michael R. Anderson (eds.), *Human Rights Approaches to Environmental Protection* (Oxford University Press, 1996); Donald K. Anton & Dinah L. Shelton (eds.), *Environmental Protection and Human Rights* (Cambridge University Press, 2011); Anna Grear & Louis J. Kotzé (eds.), *Research Handbook on Human Rights and the Environment* (Edward Elgar, 2015).

[31] See, for example, the preamble of the 2015 Paris Agreement, which is the first multilateral environmental agreement of global scope to refer to human rights. Paris Agreement on Climate Change, 2015, 3156 UNTS 79; see also the preamble and paragraph 91 of the Glasgow Climate Pact, 13 November 2021, reprinted in *Report of the Conference of the Parties Serving as the Meeting of the Parties to the Paris Agreement on Its Third Session*, Doc. FCCC/PA/CMA/2021/10/Add.1, 2021, 2–10.

recognized by the United Nations in July 2022.[32] This achievement was the product of a wider range of contextual factors rather than specific regulatory drivers – hence, the resolution's references to a range of instruments including the Stockholm Declaration, the UN Sustainable Development Goals (SDGs), and human rights instruments, and concepts like the ecosystem approach and sustainable resource use as well as the equitable treatment of vulnerable groups and states.[33]

The human–environment nexus is part of the context that nurtures the law of the sea rather than part of its texts, and so it is not determinative of specific obligations. UNCLOS's preamble speaks of peace, justice, and progress for peoples and their social advancement, but it is otherwise silent on individual rights and responsibilities. The same is true of the UNFSA.[34] According to the VCLT, preambular exhortations may influence the construction of other obligations, but they are not constitutive of specific legal entitlements.[35] Furthermore, the generic language of the preambles of UNCLOS and the UNFSA is capable of being turned to any cause rather than being used as a tool to drive specific human/environmental outcomes.[36]

The BBNJ Agreement marks a significant change in emphasis, with its preambular reference to stewardship: 'Desiring to act as stewards of the ocean in areas beyond national jurisdiction on behalf of present and future generations by protecting, caring for and ensuring responsible use of the marine environment.'[37] The inclusion of stewardship serves to imbue the text (and the DNA) of the agreement with ideas that have hitherto formed only part of the wider regulatory context. Stewardship entails a shift in how duties are framed, to whom they are owed, and the accountability for their implementation.[38] Thus, unlike UNCLOS and the UNFSA, the BBNJ Agreement frames states' responsibilities towards both current and future generations, engaging questions of inter-generational justice. The change in

32 *The Human Right to a Clean, Healthy, and Sustainable Environment*, UN Doc. A/76/L.75, 26 July 2022.

33 See the list of influences in *ibid.*, preamble.

34 UNFSA, n. 28, preambular para. 9.

35 VCLT, n. 16, art. 31(1); see further Rainer Lagoni, 'Preamble', in Alexander Proelss (ed.), *United Nations Convention on the Law of the Sea: A Commentary* (C.H. Beck, 2017).

36 This is reflected in the (limited) use of the preamble in international jurisprudence. See, e.g., ITLOS, *Responsibilities and Obligations of States with Respect to Activities in the Area*, Advisory Opinion, Case no. 17, 1 February 2011, 10, paras. 151, 163 (*Activities in the Area*).

37 BBNJ Agreement, n. 29.

38 See Richard Barnes, 'Stewardship beyond the State: Implications for the Regulation of Marine Genetic Resources in Areas beyond National Jurisdiction', in Niels Krabbe & David Langlet (eds.), *Marine Bioprospecting, Biodiversity and Novel Uses of Ocean Resources: New Approaches in International Law* (Hart Publishing, 2024).

culture is reinforced through discrete provisions that connect specifically to human rights or values, such as article 7(k), which provides that parties shall be guided by: 'The respect, promotion and consideration of their respective obligations, as applicable, relating to the rights of Indigenous Peoples or of, as appropriate, local communities when taking action to address the conservation and sustainable use of marine biological diversity of areas beyond national jurisdiction.'[39] Together these provisions bridge the gap between contextual respect for human/environmental rights and the designation of formal legal obligations.

16.2.2 SUSTAINABLE USE OF RESOURCES AND HABITATS

The Stockholm Declaration sets forth four principles that demand the wise use of resources.[40] Principle 2 requires the planet's natural resources to be 'safeguarded for the benefit of present and future generations'. Principle 3 requires vital renewable resources to be 'maintained and, wherever practicable, restored or improved'. Principle 4 states that 'man has a special responsibility to safeguard and wisely manage the heritage of gravely imperilled wildlife and its habitat'. Finally, non-renewable resources must be used in such a way as to guard against their 'exhaustion and to ensure benefits are shared by all mankind' (principle 5). These principles are not addressed to states – they are general exhortations – and reflected the prevailing concern not to overly restrict the exercise of sovereignty.[41] Although the term is not used explicitly, the language embodies the idea of sustainable use. This idea aligns with states' self-interests, and it has since permeated the law of the sea. As William Edeson notes, a body of law post-UNCLOS has ensured 'that the importance of the long-term sustainable use of marine living resources has been placed at the forefront of any serious analysis of the legal regime'.[42] In this respect one can identify the direct influence of Stockholm on UNCLOS's regime for resource use.

However, when we look more closely at the framing of these commitments, we can detect some resistance to broader ideas of wise use and habitat conservation. This has resulted in a slower than expected evolution of the overarching

39 See also BBNJ Agreement, n. 29, arts. 13, 44(1)(b), Annex II(iii).

40 See also Stockholm Action Plan, n. 3, recommendations 37, 46–50.

41 Sohn, n. 2, 456.

42 William Edeson, 'Towards Long-Term Sustainable Use: Some Recent Developments in the Legal Regime of Fisheries', in Alan Boyle & David Freestone (eds.), *International Law and Sustainable Development: Past Achievements and Future Challenges* (Oxford University Press, 1999).

idea of responsibility into specific textual provisions in subsequent instruments. Although the idea of sustainable use is echoed in the provisions on fisheries conservation and management,[43] UNCLOS does not adopt terminology used in the Stockholm Declaration such as 'ecosystems', 'safeguard', 'careful planning', 'improvement', 'wise use', and 'benefit sharing'. Even 'habitat' is used only once.[44] Indeed, it has been remarked that UNCLOS provides a rudimentary framework for the protection of habitats.[45] UNCLOS places few restrictions on the use of non-living resources other than requiring that rights on the continental shelf do not infringe navigation or other freedoms of the sea.[46] Whereas the Stockholm Declaration emphasized safeguarding, UNCLOS is more pragmatic. Thus, the sustainable use of fisheries is caveated so that economic considerations can be leveraged against conservation concerns. Use is also linked to optimum utilization, and, unfortunately, this often results in catch levels being set too high.[47] The state of the world's fisheries remains precarious and has been since before the adoption of the Stockholm Declaration.[48] It may be observed that this resistance to habitat protection in fisheries permeates into regional and domestic regimes. For example, a significant criticism of the European Union's Common Fisheries Policy is that it excepts itself from habitat protection rules.[49]

Responsible use of resources is more strongly evident in the UNFSA, where the list of general principles includes long-term sustainability, the precautionary approach, the ecosystem-based approach, the explicit alignment of fisheries and marine environmental protection, and biodiversity protection.[50] However, although there are references to ecosystems, this is linked to measures to protect species rather than to the wider protection of habitats per se.[51] The UNFSA retains a pro-exploitation heritage.

43 UNCLOS, n. 14, art. 61(3).
44 *Ibid.*, art. 194(5).
45 Edward J. Goodwin, 'Threatened Species and Vulnerable Marine Ecosystems', in Donald R. Rothwell *et al.* (eds.), *The Oxford Handbook of the Law of the Sea* (Oxford University Press, 2015), 807–808.
46 UNCLOS, n. 14, art. 78(2).
47 Evelyne Meltzer, 'Global Overview of Straddling and Highly Migratory Fish Stocks: The Non-Sustainable Nature of High Seas Fisheries' (1994) 25 *Ocean Development and International Law* 255.
48 Tony J. Pitcher & William W. L. Cheung, 'Fisheries: Hope or Despair?' (2013) 74 *Marine Pollution Bulletin* 506.
49 Thomas Appleby & James Harrison, 'Taking the Pulse of Environmental and Fisheries Law: The Common Fisheries Policy, the Habitats Directive, and Brexit' (2019) 31 *Journal of Environmental Law* 443.
50 UNFSA, n. 28, art. 5.
51 *Ibid.*, art. 5(d), (e).

The protection of habitats, ecosystems, and biodiversity more generally has been driven by the 1992 Convention on Biological Diversity (CBD).[52] Notably, the CBD can trace its heritage more strongly to Stockholm via the 1992 Rio Declaration on Environment and Development.[53] Building on the duty to establish in situ conservation measures, considerable progress has been made under the CBD's marine and coastal biodiversity programmes. Yet it was not until the adoption of the BBNJ Agreement that these wider concerns began to permeate the law of the sea more directly. Indeed, whilst the BBNJ Agreement is an implementing agreement for UNCLOS, it is notable that its heritage can be strongly traced to the CBD.[54] In the CBD, conservation takes a more prominent role in governance than compared to the extractive focus of UNCLOS. Within the BBNJ Agreement, we can see more clearly the strong connections between resource use and environmental protection, with governance mechanisms focusing on spatial management or environmental assessments. Sustainable use permeates all the Agreement's provisions courtesy of article 2, whilst part III is wholly focused on the protection of habitats along with their ecological systems and biological diversity. If nothing else, the BBNJ Agreement shows the importance of cross-fertilization of treaty norms in advancing the environmental reach of the law of the sea. This is achieved not merely through the repetition of textual provisions but also through the structural framing of commitments – and, in particular, the use of obligations of means as well as institutional support mechanisms.

Judicial contributions to the law on sustainable resource use is hamstrung by the exclusion of disputes concerning the exercise of sovereign rights over living resources from compulsory dispute settlement under UNCLOS.[55] In

[52] Convention on Biological Diversity, 1992, 1760 UNTS 79.

[53] 'Rio Declaration on Environment and Development', in *Report of the UN Conference on Environment and Development*, UN Doc. A/CONF.151/26 (Vol. I), 12 August 1992; Dinah Shelton, 'Stockholm Declaration (1972) and Rio Declaration (1992)', in *Max Planck Encyclopedia of Public International Law* (Oxford University Press, 2008); see also Alexandre C. Kiss, 'The Destiny of the Principles of the Stockholm Declaration', in Nordquist, Moore & Mahmoudi, n. 7, 53.

[54] See also Catherine Blanchard *et al.*, 'Three Structural Pillars of the Future International Legally Binding Instrument on the Conservation and Sustainable Use of Marine Biodiversity of Areas beyond National Jurisdiction', in Marta C. Ribeiro *et al.* (eds.), *Global Challenges and the Law of the Sea* (Springer, 2020), 352; Alex O. Elferink & Baine P. Kerr, 'Finding a Home for BBNJ? The CBD, the LOSC and the General Assembly. Complementary Alternatives?', in Vito De Lucia, Alex O. Elferink & Lan N. Nguyen (eds.), *International Law and Marine Areas beyond National Jurisdiction: Reflections on Justice, Space, Knowledge and Power* (Brill, 2022).

[55] See UNCLOS, n. 14, art. 297(3).

the *Sub-Regional Fisheries Commission* advisory opinion, the meaning of sustainable use was confined by ITLOS to a textual construction of 'conservation and development' in article 63 of UNCLOS,[56] reinforcing my argument that wider contextual factors are sometimes muted in how the law develops. Countering this narrow approach, the *South China Sea* arbitration tribunal stated that article 293(1) of UNCLOS and article 31(3) of the Vienna Convention enabled it to take into account the CBD for the purpose of interpreting the UNCLOS provisions on ecosystem protection (that is, article 194(5)).[57] The CBD (and potentially other instruments) are now regarded as relevant rules of international law informing the duty of due diligence to conserve the living resources of the sea.[58] This line of reasoning, which requires states to deploy adequate means, to use best possible efforts, and to exercise vigilance towards achieving commitments to protect and preserve the marine environment, is able to drive integrative practices and so can tap into wider contextual developments in the law of the sea. Indeed, in the *Activities in the Area* advisory opinion, due diligence was framed as a variable concept that may change over time 'as measures considered sufficiently diligent at a certain moment may become not diligent enough in light, for instance, of new scientific or technological knowledge'.[59] This is the essence of context, where changes in the environment within which specific rules operate inform their application and development. It is notable that many states have recently made recourse to both the CBD and the BBNJ Agreement in framing how UNCLOS's commitments to protect and preserve the marine environment should be interpreted as part of the *Commission of Small Island States* advisory opinion.[60]

16.2.3 PREVENTING POLLUTION OR HARM TO THE ENVIRONMENT

The influence of the Stockholm Declaration on UNCLOS commitments to prevent pollution is well documented so there is no need to rehearse

56 ITLOS, *Request for Advisory Opinion Submitted by the Sub-Regional Fisheries Commission*, Advisory Opinion, 2 April 2015, 4, paras. 188–191 (*Sub-Regional Fisheries Commission*).

57 PCA, *South China Sea Arbitration (Philippines v China)*, Award on Jurisdiction and Admissibility, 29 October 2015, para. 176.

58 See ITLOS, *Southern Bluefin Tuna (New Zealand v Japan; Australia v Japan)*, Provisional Measures, Cases nos. 3 and 4, 27 August 1999, 280, para. 70; PCA, *South China Sea Arbitration*, Award, Case no. 2013-19, 12 July 2016, para. 941 (*South China Sea*).

59 *Activities in the Area*, n. 36, para. 117.

60 See, e.g., *Written Statement by New Zealand*, Doc. C31_WS-1-3, 15 June 2023; *Written Statement by Italy*, Doc. C31_WS-1-7, 15 June 2023; *Written Statement by the EU*, Doc. C31_WS-1-9, 15 June 2023; *Written Statement by Singapore*, Doc. C31_WS-1-15, 16 June 2023.

them in detail. The link between the Stockholm Declaration and UNCLOS is explicit in that Recommendation 86 called upon states to participate fully in UNCLOS III with a view to bringing under control all significant sources of pollution within the marine environment.[61] Further, Recommendation 92 called upon governments to endorse a set of principles for pollution assessment as guiding concepts for the Conference on the Law of the Sea.[62] Tullio Treves notes that there was some overlap in delegates at the Stockholm Conference and other fora, which resulted in the cross-fertilization of ideas and approaches.[63] There is evidence of states using the Stockholm Declaration to frame their positions during the negotiation of UNCLOS,[64] so, unsurprisingly, it is generally recognized that the Declaration had an impact upon the scope of UNCLOS.[65] In part, it motivated action; in part, it influenced the shape of commitments, as is evidenced in the text of part XII of UNCLOS.

However, the Stockholm Declaration did not shape the specific rules on pollution control; this was a product of UNCLOS's negotiations and wider political trends. As Jonas Ebbesson notes, the Stockholm principles were largely of political influence.[66] The early 1970s witnessed a boom in multilateral environmental agreements, including the 1972 London Convention on the Prevention of Marine Pollution by Dumping of Wastes and Other Matters,

61 Stockholm Declaration, n. 1, 22.

62 *Ibid.*, 23. These are the principles are set out in *ibid.*, 73–74, Annex III.

63 Tullio Treves, 'Regional Approaches to the Protection of the Marine Environment', in Nordquist, Moore & Mahmoudi, n. 7, 137–154.

64 See positions of Brazil (*Summary Records of Meetings of the Third Committee 6th Meeting*, Doc. A/CONF.62/C.3/SR.6, 17 July 1974, paras. 50, 54); Canada (*Nineteenth Meeting of the Third Committee*, Doc. A/CONF.62/C.3/SR.19, 26 March 1975, para. 57; *Twenty-first Meeting of the Third Committee*, Doc. A/CONF.62/C.3/SR.21, 17 April 1975, paras. 5–7); Germany (*Summary Records of Meetings of the Third Committee 5th Meeting*, Doc. A/CONF.62/C.3/SR.5, 17 July 1974, para. 58); Japan (*Summary Records of Meetings of the Third Committee 5th Meeting*, Doc. A/CONF.62/C.3/SR.5, 17 July 1974, para. 32); Sudan (*Summary Records of Meetings of the Third Committee 5th Meeting*, Doc. A/CONF.62/C.3/SR.5, 17 July 1974, para. 26); Tanzania (*Nineteenth Meeting of the Third Committee*, Doc. A/CONF.62/C.3/SR.19, 26 March 1975, para. 28; see also *The Activities of the Inter-Governmental Maritime Consultative Organization in Relation to Shipping and Related Maritime Matters*, Doc. A/CONF.62/27, 10 June 1974, paras. 136–137); UN Environment Programme (*Communication from the United Nations Environment Programme*, Doc. A/CONF.62/112, 10 April 1981). The link was also made in UN General Assembly Resolution 133 (XXVIII) on the Protection of the Marine Environment, 13 December 1973.

65 Robin Churchill, Vaughan Lowe & Amy Sander, *The Law of the Sea* (4th ed., Manchester University Press, 2022), 604.

66 Jonas Ebbesson, 'Protection of the Marine Environment of the Baltic Sea Area: The Impact of the Stockholm Declaration', in Nordquist, Moore & Mahmoudi, n. 7, 155–164.

and the 1973–78 MARPOL Convention.[67] A significant factor here was the UN Environment Programme's lead in developing a series of regional seas conventions and action plans.[68] These instruments marked several important changes. First, they provided significantly detailed standards of conduct for the protection of the marine environment. Second, they combined to consolidate and expand coastal state jurisdiction over marine environmental protection. Thus, the MARPOL Convention superseded the 1954 International Convention for the Prevention of Pollution of the Sea by Oil[69] and established a more detailed framework for pollution control. It adopted an open-ended approach to jurisdiction to 'be construed in the light of international law in force at the time of application or interpretation of the present Convention'.[70] The broad jurisdictional framework with expanded coastal state responsibilities under part XII enabled an incremental expansion of the jurisdictional reach of the MARPOL Convention, particularly over the exclusive economic zone. Third, they established a model for marine environmental protection based upon the development of generally accepted international rules and standards. This again shows the importance of context in nurturing legal rules.

There is little specific jurisprudence on marine pollution incidents before international tribunals. However, in those few relevant cases, one significant development has been the reception and articulation of obligations of due diligence to protect the marine environment.[71] Arguably, this advances the call in principle 7 to 'take all reasonable steps to prevent' pollution. As discussed in the previous section, this opens up the possibility of states having recourse to a wider range of texts and contextual materials to determine the appropriateness of their actions by rendering diligence contingent on knowledge, consultation, and cooperation.[72]

16.2.4 SOVEREIGNTY AND DIFFERENTIAL COMMITMENTS

Principle 21 of the Stockholm Declaration provides that states have sovereignty over their natural resources and they may exploit them in accordance with

67 Convention on the Prevention of Marine Pollution by Dumping of Wastes and Other Matters, 1972, 1046 UNTS 120; International Convention for the Prevention of Pollution from Ships, 1973, as amended by the Protocol of 1 June 1978, 1340 UNTS 61 (MARPOL Convention).

68 Michael A. Jacobson, 'The United Nations' Regional Seas Programme: How Does It Measure Up?' (1995) 23 *Coastal Management* 19.

69 International Convention for the Prevention of Pollution of the Sea by Oil, 1954, 327 UNTS 3.

70 MARPOL Convention, n. 67, art. 9. It further provided that nothing in the MARPOL Convention would prejudice the content of UNCLOS.

71 See *South China Sea*, n. 58, para. 944; *Activities of the Area*, n. 36, paras. 117–120.

72 *Sub-Regional Fisheries Commission*, n. 56, 207.

national priorities, but that they must not do so in a way that causes harm to the environment of other states or areas beyond national jurisdiction. The principle is long established and recognized as customary international law.[73] The Stockholm Declaration qualified the principle of sovereign equality by calling for differential treatment of, or support for, developing states. This reflected the reality of differences in the capacity to implement commitments but also the wider question of fairness in how burdens should be shared. Thus, principle 9 calls for the transfer of financial and technical assistance to mitigate environmental risks, principle 11 states that environmental policies should advance, not hamper, the potential of developing countries, and principle 12 calls for the provision of resources to protect the environment, particularly that of developing countries.[74] Principle 23 is more explicit in recognizing differences between states. It provides that, when adopting international (or national) standards, 'it will be essential in all cases to consider the systems of values prevailing in each country, and the extent of the applicability of standards which are valid for the most advanced countries, but which may be inappropriate and of unwarranted social cost for the developing countries'.

The idea of differential commitments influenced the negotiation of UNCLOS,[75] and a number of the provisions in UNCLOS articulate this, mainly in the context of pollution control.[76] However, such commitments are invariably framed in hortatory terms, leaving the extent and form of assistance to be determined by the donor states. This reinforces the idea that UNCLOS favours forms of development patronage that undermines true burden-sharing.[77] Even the much-vaunted common heritage regime for the Area suffers from limitations. As well as seeking to establish a more equitable distribution of resource wealth,[78] the common heritage of mankind regime also sought to account for the different capacities of developing states when activities are conducted in the Area.[79]

[73] See *Nuclear Weapons*, n. 22, paras. 27–29; *Gabčíkovo-Nagymaros Project (Hungary v Slovakia)*, Judgment, 25 September 1997, (1997) ICJ Reports 7, para. 53.

[74] Principle 10 recognizes the dependence of developing states on commodities and raw material so flags the need for price stability and adequate earnings. However, this goes beyond the capacity of the law of the sea to address.

[75] Position of Tanzania, cited in *Nineteenth Meeting of the Third Committee*, n. 64; Nordquist, Moore & Mahmoudi, n. 7, 100.

[76] For a more detailed analysis, see Richard Barnes, 'Global Solidarity, Differentiated Responsibilities and the Law the Sea' (2020) 51 *Netherlands Yearbook of International Law* 107; Tara Davenport, 'Differentiated Rights and Responsibilities in Activities in the Area: From Wealth Redistribution to Marine Environmental Protection' (2020) 51 *Netherlands Yearbook of International Law* 147.

[77] Barnes, n. 76, 127.

[78] Davenport, n. 76, 169.

[79] UNCLOS, n. 14, arts. 140, 148.

However, when they were considered in the *Activities in the Area* advisory opinion,[80] a chamber of ITLOS recognized the need to promote the participation of developing states[81] but then emphasized the need for a formal equality of commitments to ensure commercial entities could not exploit the sponsoring state 'of convenience'.[82] This points to structural barriers within UNCLOS to the more equitable determination of states' obligations.

The UNFSA more clearly identifies differential needs of developing states to include vulnerability (that is, economic dependence on fisheries) and needs of subsistence, small-scale and artisanal fisheries, women fishers, and Indigenous people. It also recognizes a disproportionate conservation burden.[83] Support is not intended to redistribute fishing entitlements to catch fish; rather, it is directed at improving developing states' capacity to conserve and manage stocks over which they already enjoy access.[84] However, in the final analysis, there is little evidence that the UNFSA has enhanced developing states' access to high seas fisheries.[85] This is a structural problem: regional fisheries and environmental arrangements tend to ignore differential commitments precisely because such bodies are comprised of states at similar levels of development and capacity, meaning there is little need for more equitable sharing of burdens between such states.

Differential commitments come more strongly to the fore in the adoption of the BBNJ Agreement. Numerous articles provide for account to be taken of developing state needs or participation.[86] It is a matter of general principle[87] as well as the focus of part V on capacity building and technology transfer. Of note is article 15, which requires representation of developing states on the Access and Benefit Sharing Committee, which is charged with developing policies and processes to ensure the fair and equitable sharing of both monetary and non-monetary benefits. Given the strong institutional procedures (for example, the Clearing-House Mechanism, a funding mechanism, and the Conference of the Parties) – which reflects the CBD's strong influence on the BBNJ Agreement – there appears to be greater scope for such provisions to develop teeth in practice.

80 *Activities of the Area*, n. 36.
81 *Ibid.*, para. 156.
82 *Ibid.*, para. 159.
83 UNFSA, n. 28, art. 24, see also art. 3(3).
84 *Ibid.*, art. 25(3).
85 Michael W. Lodge *et al.*, *Recommended Best Practices for Regional Fisheries Management Organizations-Report of an Independent Panel to Develop a Model for Improved Governance by Regional Fisheries Management Organizations* (Chatham House, 2007), 95.
86 See BBNJ Agreement, n. 29, arts. 2, 9, 11(6), 14, 15, 17, 21(8), 25(3), 27(f), 51(5), 52.
87 *Ibid.*, art. 7(m), (n).

16.2.5 INTEGRATED AND RATIONAL PLANNING

Planning now seems a rather benign and obvious function for law, but this was not always the case. In 1972, some states were ideologically resistant to planning because it was associated with socialist economies. Despite this, moderate calls for planning were embodied in principle 13, which called for the rational management of resources through integrated and coordinated planning. This is echoed in principle 14, which presents rational planning as a tool to mediate development and environmental goals. Principle 15 provides that planning must be used to avoid the adverse effects on the environment whilst enabling maximum social and economic development. In the Stockholm Declaration, planning is aligned with reasoned decision-making but shorn of strong ideological leanings. Crucially, planning should be situated in appropriate national institutions (principle 17), thereby qualifying its use and limiting the risk of it becoming part of a wider international agenda.

Although UNCLOS emphasizes the importance of integrated approaches,[88] it does not prescribe the planning of marine activities. UNCLOS is a zoning regime that establishes areas of maritime jurisdiction. It is a starting point for planning rather than a planning regime per se. It contains numerous provisions on managing activities or making decisions. At best, this implies a degree of planning in the general sense of engaging in prospective orientated conduct. Planning in any meaningful sense is left to individual states. For example, article 193 provides that states may exploit their natural resources pursuant to their own environmental policies. Planning is actually inhibited by the sectoral framework of UNCLOS where activities are categorized into discreet regimes such as fisheries or shipping and interactions are managed under sweeping interstitial norms, such as 'due regard'.[89] UNCLOS does not explicitly attach values or priorities to different ocean activities and so structure decision-making. The UNFSA is also largely silent on planning, although a degree of planning is implicit in fisheries management, the adoption of related measures, and the work of regional fisheries management bodies.

Despite the lack of specific planning commitments in UNCLOS, marine spatial planning has blossomed in coastal waters around the world.[90] Much has been done by the Intergovernmental Oceanographic Commission to champion marine spatial planning, but the main emphasis remains on

88 See Richard Barnes, 'The Law of the Sea Convention and the Integrated Regulation of the Oceans' (2012) 27 *International Journal of Marine and Coastal Law* 859.

89 See UNCLOS, n. 14, arts. 56(2), 58(3), 87(2), 142(1), 234.

90 Charles N. Ehler, 'Two Decades of Progress in Marine Spatial Planning' (2021) 132 *Marine Policy* 104134.

developing national practices and then coordinating these between states rather than establishing international planning structures. Arguably, these developments are more a response to intensified use of oceans space and the need to manage conflicting and competing uses of finite space and resources rather than resulting from general international policy prescriptions. The extent and quality of such planning regimes vary considerably in practice, with much being dependent upon local or regional infrastructure and regulatory capacity.[91] Such planning regimes are mainly limited to areas within national jurisdiction because flag state jurisdiction provides a limited basis for any meaningful planning regime.[92] Also, we are more likely to find their heritage in the mechanisms developed under the CBD. For example, in 1998, a programme of work on marine and coastal biodiversity was adopted and then updated in 2004.[93] As outlined in the annexes to the CBD's Conference of the Parties Decision VII/5, there is a range of key actions required of the parties and relevant organizations to implement the CBD in order to conserve and sustainably use marine and coastal biodiversity.[94] There is no comparable driver of planning in UNCLOS, and this parallels the earlier observations with respect to habitats protection that the wider regulatory context has influenced the development of practice.

The adoption of the BBNJ Agreement should enable a higher degree of planning of ocean activities on the high seas because it establishes mechanisms for the adoption of area-based management tools[95] as well as both strategic and activity orientated environmental assessments.[96] Area-based management tools are tools for managing one or several sectors and activities within a spatially defined area. They are thus a form of planning tool, as are environmental impact assessments. For example, article 28 requires parties to conduct environmental impact assessments, and it is accompanied by a series of provisions detailing the threshold and procedures for such assessments as well as mitigation measures and reporting requirements.[97] Although they are tools at the disposal of individual states, they are subject to coordination,

91 Rachel Zuercher *et al.*, 'Narrowing the Gap between Marine Spatial Planning Aspirations and Realities' (2022) 79 *ICES Journal of Marine Science* 600.

92 Jeff Ardron *et al.*, 'Marine Spatial Planning in the High Seas' (2008) 32 *Marine Policy* 832.

93 Decision IV/5 on Conservation and Sustainable Use of Marine and Coastal Biological Diversity, Including a Programme of Work, Doc. UNEP/CBD/COP/DEC/IV/5, 1998; Decision VII/5 on Review of the Programme of Work on Marine and Coastal Biodiversity, Doc. UNEP/CBD/COP/DEC/VII/5, 13 April 2004.

94 See the Annexes of both Decision IV/5, n. 93, and Decision VII/5, n. 93.

95 BBNJ Agreement, n. 29, part III.

96 *Ibid.*, part IV.

97 *Ibid.*

guidance, and oversight by bodies established by the BBNJ Agreement. This institutional structure is important since it provides a space for shared values and approaches to coalesce and for the different interests of states and different ocean users to emerge.

16.2.6 SCIENTIFIC RESEARCH AND EDUCATION

Principle 18 of the Stockholm Declaration provides that science and technology must be applied to 'the identification, avoidance and control of environmental risks and the solution of environmental problems and for the common good of mankind'. This is reinforced by a call in principle 19 for the use of education and mass media to be used to create awareness of environmental issues. Principle 20 calls for the promotion of scientific research nationally and at the international level, along with free flows of information and technical experience, and the provision of environmental technologies to developing states on terms that would not cause an economic burden to developing states. Science and education are at the heart of the Stockholm Declaration.

It is easy to understate the profound influence of science on the law of the sea. It permeates every area of UNCLOS. Science is the main object of part XIII, and it is implicit in the mechanisms for the development and transfer of marine technology in part XIV. Each maritime zone frames rights and duties to conduct scientific research,[98] with many specific commitments dependent on the research and the availability of scientific advice, such as articles 61 and 119 on fisheries conservation and management. It underpins cooperation on the protection of the marine environment through articles 200–202. The UNFSA promotes scientific research and requires conservation and management to be based on best scientific evidence.[99] Science is woven through the entirety of the BBNJ Agreement, and authority for advancing its use is vested in a Scientific and Technical Body.[100] If mere textual references are a marker of the centrality of science to the law of the sea, then the 51 references to science in UNCLOS, the 79 references to 'science'/'data' in the UNFSA, and the 112 references to 'science' in the BBNJ Agreement indicate how rooted science is in the DNA of the law of the sea.

It is perhaps now axiomatic that regulation must take account of science. The UN General Assembly has recognized this fundamental role, initiating the UN Decade of Ocean Science Research for Sustainable Development in

98 See, e.g., UNCLOS, n. 14, arts. 22(1)(g), 40, 56(1)(b)(ii), 87(1)(f).
99 UNFSA, n. 28, art. 5(b), (g); see also, arts. 10, 14.
100 BBNJ Agreement, n. 29, art. 49.

2021.[101] The question is not so much that science should be used but, rather, what science is used and how.[102] This is something that depends upon context, how science develops, how learnings are drawn from other regimes, and how this is accommodated within law of the sea institutions. Answers to such questions are increasingly critical to the law of the sea. They have serious implications for how the law can respond to the threats of climate change. For example, in the *Commission of Small Island States* advisory opinion, a significant feature of ITLOS' opinion was the fining that pollution of the marine environment includes anthropogenic greenhouse gas emissions, and that the work of the Intergovernmental Panel on Climate Change constitutes the best available evidence of the impacts of climate change on the ocean.[103]

16.2.7 COOPERATION AND INTERNATIONAL ORGANIZATIONS

Principle 24 of the Stockholm Declaration calls for cooperation on environmental matters between states on an equal footing, taking due account of the sovereignty and interests of all states. The principle is recognized as customary international law.[104] This aspect of the Stockholm Declaration, albeit not something exclusive to the Stockholm Conference, has had a profound influence on the law of the sea; it is the means by which law develops, and, more specifically, it is a means for bridging between the text of agreements and wider legal developments.

Cooperation is part of the textual code of treaties on the law of the sea: UNCLOS, the UNFSA, and the BBNJ Agreement are replete with commitments to cooperate, both generally and in the development of specific regimes.[105] At the same time, such provisions provide a critical means to engage with the wider influences on the law. Cooperation is generally framed by reference to a context and purpose that shapes the outcomes of cooperation. Cooperation can be used as a vehicle to evolve treaty commitments in a way that is not confined to the specific textual code of the treaty. This evolutive role

101 UN General Assembly Resolution 72/73, 2017, para. 292.

102 See Hilde Woker, 'Interactions between Law and Science within the Law of the Sea: A Systems Theory Perspective', in Nele Matz-Lück, Øystein Jensen & Elise Johansen (eds.), *The Law of the Sea: Normative Context and Interactions with Other Legal Regimes* (Routledge, 2022).

103 *Request for an Advisory Opinion on Climate Change*, n. 9, paras 159–79 and 208.

104 ITLOS, *MOX Plant (Ireland v United Kingdom)*, Order, Case no. 10, 3 December 2001, 95, para. 82.

105 On UNCLOS's cooperative commitments, see Seokwoo Lee & Jeong W. Kim, 'UNCLOS and the Obligation to Cooperate: International Legal Framework for Semi-Enclosed Seas Cooperation', in Keyuan Zou (ed.), *Maritime Cooperation in Semi-Enclosed Seas* (Brill, 2019).

for cooperation has been recognized in a number of cases.[106] The International Court of Justice has held that states parties have a duty to cooperate with the International Whaling Commission (IWC), which included an obligation to give due regard to the IWC's recommendations despite such recommendations not being binding.[107] In its *Activities in the Area* advisory opinion, ITLOS linked the duty to cooperate with control over private actors: thus, a state sponsoring deep sea bed mining 'is obliged not only to cooperate with the Authority in the establishment and implementation of impact assessments, but also to use appropriate means to ensure that the contractor complies with its obligation'.[108] In the *Sub-Regional Fisheries Commission* advisory opinion, ITLOS stated that the duty to cooperate in article 64(1) of UNCLOS is an obligation of due diligence, to be exercised in good faith, through meaningful consultations directed towards the adoption of measures necessary to coordinate and conserve shared stocks.[109] Cooperation does not change the text;[110] rather, it creates a nexus between the text and wider legal developments.[111]

Principle 25 provides that states shall ensure that international organizations play a coordinated, efficient, and dynamic role for the protection and improvement of the environment. As a framework agreement, UNCLOS also makes frequent use of other international organizations, especially the International Maritime Organization to advance more detailed regulation of ocean space.[112] The UNFSA is almost wholly contingent on cooperation through regional fisheries management bodies.[113] Whilst the BBNJ Agreement carries forward a cooperative approach, somewhat paradoxically, the role reserved for regional and international bodies in the BBNJ Agreement has been the object of criticism in respect of the obligation to 'not undermine' existing frameworks and bodies.[114]

106 Margaret Young & Sebastián R. Sullivan, 'Evolution through the Duty to Cooperate: Implications of the Whaling Case at the International Court of Justice' (2015) 16 *Melbourne Journal of International Law* 311.

107 *Whaling in the Antarctic (Australia v Japan: New Zealand intervening)*, Judgment, 31 March 2014, (2014) ICJ Reports 226, paras. 83, 137.

108 *Activities of the Area*, n. 36, para. 50.

109 *Sub-Regional Fisheries Commission*, n. 56, para. 210.

110 See text accompanying n. 56 above.

111 PCA, *Chagos Marine Protected Area Arbitration (Mauritius v United Kingdom)*, Award, Case no. 2011-03, 18 March 2015.

112 See UNCLOS, n. 14, arts. 210, 211, 213, 216, 217, 218; see further James Harrison, *Making the Law of the Sea: A Study in the Development of International Law* (Cambridge University Press, 2011).

113 UNFSA, n. 28, part III.

114 BBNJ Agreement, n. 29, art. 5(2); see Richard Barnes, 'Fisheries and ABNJ: Advancing and Enhancing Cooperation', in Tomas Heidar (ed.), *New Knowledge and Changing Circumstances in the Law of the Sea* (Brill, 2020).

It is not so much the need to ensure cooperation with such bodies that is problematic but, rather, the way in which the BBNJ Agreement may insulate such bodies from the influence of positive legal developments if a robust approach to not undermining is taken , thereby allowing such bodies to resist positive reforms or developments in how they exercise their mandates. This point reaffirms that it is not so much the duty to cooperate but, instead, the contextual framing of the duty and mechanisms through which cooperation takes place that are critical to its effect.

16.3 CONCLUSIONS: THE IMPORTANCE OF TEXT AND CONTEXT

This chapter has shown the difficulty of assessing the influence of the Stockholm Declaration through a mere reading of texts. There are specific examples of direct influence on some treaty provisions in UNCLOS, but much of the Declaration's influence is contextual or indirect. The influence of the Stockholm Declaration has varied considerably, with stronger direct influences on pollution control, cooperation, and the use of science, and more muted influences on human and environmental rights, planning, and differential commitments. One reason for this variable influence is the dominant perception of the oceans as a space that is worked or travelled rather than lived in. Hence, it is of less concern to mainstream human rights discourse.[115] Another reason is that both the textual DNA and regulatory culture of the law of the sea is state-centric and focused on technical aspects of resource governance. Human rights have permeated some areas of the law of the sea, such as duties to render assistance to persons in distress or prevent slavery,[116] but this forms a relatively small part of the law. Human rights operate well in these contexts because the rights in question (for example, rights to life, liberty, and security of person) are sufficiently well defined as to enable their application and because they align with states' duties under the law of the sea.[117] Yet, even in this area, judicial bodies have read human rights concepts into the law of the sea but only to the extent that this is not incompatible with the law of the sea.[118] This shows the priority afforded to text over context.

115 See Richard Barnes, 'Environmental Rights in Marine Spaces', in Sanja Bogojevic & Rosemary Rayfuse (eds.), *Environmental Rights in Europe and Beyond* (Hart Publishing, 2018).

116 Irini Papanicolopulu, *International Law and the Protection of People at Sea* (Oxford University Press, 2018).

117 See A.S., *D.I., O.I. and G.D. v Italy*, Communication no. 3042/17, Views adopted by the Committee under Article 5(4) of the Optional Protocol, Doc. CCPR/C/130/D/3042/2017, 27 January 2021.

118 See PCA, *Arctic Sunrise Case*, Award on the Merits, Case no 2014-02, 14 August 2015, para. 198.

Arguably, the influence of a wider range of human rights and responsibilities, such as conditions of work or adequate standards of living or health, is less clear in the law of the sea because of their open or progressive nature. However, we are witnessing a cultural shift towards embracing a wider set of human rights at sea.[119] This is due to several factors: an increased awareness of people being mistreated at sea;[120] better understandings of the link between poor working conditions and environmental degradation;[121] and the embedding of human rights concerns in a wider range of instruments that influence the way in which law of the sea instruments are understood. These are important contextual considerations. This change in regulatory culture is apparent in the development of the BBNJ Agreement and its focus on stewardship, Indigenous rights, and other human communities.

These trends are paralleled in the way we think about planning. Since the Stockholm Declaration, states' positions on planning have evolved, possibly because the fear of a socialist international order has retreated but, more likely, under the influence of ideas and values drawn from environmental and biodiversity law.[122] In part, this is a response to our better understanding of how natural systems interconnect and how profoundly and extensively human activities impact not just locally but also beyond the narrow confines of national jurisdiction. This demands better planning, which in turn draws wider systemic thinking and practices into the law of the sea. We have entered a period when international law is paying greater attention to its relationship with dynamic, complex planetary systems.[123] This is something that Benedict Kingsbury refers to as infrastructure thinking, which lends itself to planning approaches.[124] However, there remains scope to enhance these approaches. One common critique of marine planning is that it has often failed to deliver properly on social objectives.[125] It thus remains

[119] See Natalie Klein, 'Geneva Declaration on Human Rights at Sea: An Endeavor to Connect Law of the Sea and International Human Rights Law' (2022) 53 *Ocean Development and International Law* 232; 'Special Issue on Applying a Human Rights Lens to the Ocean-Climate Nexus' (2023) 38 *International Journal of Marine and Coastal Law* 403.

[120] Ian Urbina, *Outlaw Ocean* (Bodley Head, 2019).

[121] Jessica L. Decker Sparks & Leslie K. Hasche, 'Complex Linkages between Forced Labor Slavery and Environmental Decline in Marine Fisheries' (2019) 18 *Journal of Human Rights* 230.

[122] W. Michael Reisman, 'International Law after the Cold War' (1990) 84 *American Journal of International Law* 859.

[123] Lous J. Kotzé & Rakhyun E. Kim, 'Earth System Law: The Juridical Dimensions of Earth System Governance' (2019) 1 *Earth System Governance* 100003.

[124] Benedict Kingsbury, 'Introduction to the Symposium on Infrastructuring International Law' (2023) 117 *American Journal of International Law Unbound* 1.

[125] Wesley Flannery & Benedict McAteer, 'Assessing Marine Spatial Planning Governmentality' (2020) 19 *Maritime Studies* 269.

focused on systems of exploitation rather than the pursuit of wider environmental and social goals. In this sense, the wider legacies of Stockholm seem to have been muted.

The increasing availability and use of more human rights-centric ideas, planning techniques, and sensitivity to different contexts within the wider regulatory context of the law of the sea increases the prospects of these approaches feeding into the specific text of formal legal agreements or, at the very least, of making them part of the interpretative matrix used by lawyers and courts to construct the meaning of formal legal texts.[126] This was addressed by the ICJ which has stated that States must 'take their obligations under international human rights law into account when implementing their obligations under the climate change treaties and other relevant environmental treaties and under customary international law, just as they must take their obligations under the climate change treaties and other relevant environmental treaties and under customary international law into account when implementing their human rights obligations.'[127] There are signs of a deeper contextual approach emerging in lawmaking. For example, Resolution 76/147 on the rights of the child expresses profound concern in its preamble for issues including 'sea level rise, coastal erosion and ocean acidification, loss of biodiversity and pollution'.[128] The annual UN General Assembly resolutions on oceans and law of the sea refer to several issues related to the realization of human rights and the right to a healthy environment, such as sustainable livelihoods, biodiversity conservation, and food security.[129] The Voluntary Guidelines for Securing Sustainable Small-Scale Fisheries are explicit in stating how their implementation depends upon, and promotes, a human rights-based approach.[130] And, more generally, the discourse on illegal, unreported, and unregulated fishing is drawing strong connections between illegal fishing and human rights abuses.[131] These semantic and policy links enable

126 On the influence of Stockholm specifically, see Jutta Brunnée, 'The Stockholm Declaration and the Structure and Process of International Environmental Law', in Nordquist, Moore & Mahmoudi, n. 7, 67–84; William Edeson, 'Soft and Hard Law Aspects for Fisheries Issues', in Nordquist, Moore & Mahmoudi, n. 7, 165. More generally, see Natalie Klein (ed.), *Unconventional Lawmaking in the Law of the Sea* (Oxford University Press, 2022).

127 *Climate Change*, n. 11, para. 404.

128 UN General Assembly Resolution 76/147 on the Rights of the Child, UN Doc. A/RES/76/147, 16 December 2021, 5.

129 UN General Assembly Resolution 77/248 on the Oceans and Law of the Sea, UN Doc. A/RES/77/248, 30 December 2022, paras. 208, 228.

130 Food and Agriculture Organization (FAO), *Voluntary Guidelines for Securing Sustainable Small-Scale Fisheries* (FAO, 2015), preface, s. 3.1.

131 Elizabeth R. Selig *et al.*, 'Revealing Global Risks of Labor Abuse and Illegal, Unreported, and Unregulated Fishing' (2022) 13*Nature Communications* 1612.

ideas and practices to occur that can advance a more integrated approach between law of the sea, environmental concerns, and human rights.

The Stockholm Conference was a cautionary moment, so it is useful to finish with some cautions fifty years later. First, in law, context depends upon text so we cannot ignore the importance of striving to ensure that law of the sea instruments embody appropriate language and concepts that allow for the inclusion of more sophisticated human/environment concepts. Given the resilience of established values or approaches in the law of the sea, this points to the importance of period efforts to reset and redirect our lawmaking approaches if we are to address the enormity of environmental challenges that we face. Second, even if we can identify a positive influence of the Stockholm Declaration on the law of the sea, we still need to question whether it has really made a difference. Alas, as Ebbesson observed twenty years ago, it is the difference made to the quality of the environment that matters, and, with few exceptions, the quality of the marine environment has declined.[132] A recent study by Frank Biermann and others, which attempted such an assessment of the UN SDGs provides a similar cautionary tale in that it revealed only limited transformative impacts on livelihoods.[133]

132 Ebbesson, n. 66, 163.

133 Frank Biermann *et al.*, 'Scientific Evidence on the Political Impact of the Sustainable Development Goals' (2022) 5 *Nature Sustainability* 795.

17

Linking International Regimes on Oceans and Fresh Water since the 1972 Stockholm Conference: The Case of Preventing Land-based Marine Plastic Pollution via International Watercourses

Yoshifumi Tanaka

17.1 INTRODUCTION

The 1972 Stockholm Declaration on the Human Environment clearly sets out:

> States shall take all possible steps to prevent pollution of the seas by substances that are liable to create hazards to human health, to harm living resources and marine life, to damage amenities or to interfere with other legitimate uses of the sea.[1]

Since the 1972 Stockholm Conference, environmental norms concerning marine environmental protection have developed both in quality and quantity. Nonetheless, the marine environment is continuously threatened by multiple sources of pollution. Among other things, marine plastic pollution constitutes a serious threat to the marine environment.[2] In fact, according to the UN Environmental Programme (UNEP), 'the amount of plastics in the oceans has been estimated to be around 75–199 million tons' and 'under a business-as-usual scenario and in the absence of necessary interventions, the amount of plastic wastes entering aquatic ecosystems could nearly triple from some 9–14 million tons per year in 2016 to a projected 23–37 million tons per year by 2040'.[3]

Studies suggest that a considerable amount of plastics enter the oceans via rivers.[4] The introduction of plastic litter into the oceans via rivers gives adverse

[1] 'Declaration of the United Nations Conference on the Human Environment', in *Report of the UN Conference on the Human Environment*, UN Doc. A/CONF.48/14/Rev.1, 16 June 1972, Principle 7 (Stockholm Declaration).

[2] UNEA Resolution of 15 March 2019, Doc. UNEP/EA.4/Res.6, 28 March 2019, preamble.

[3] UN Environmental Programme (UNEP), *From Pollution to Solution: A Global Assessment of Marine Litter and Plastic Pollution* (UNEP, 2021), 3, www.unep.org/resources/pollution-solution-global-assessment-marine-litter-and-plastic-pollution.

[4] While figures vary according to studies, one study suggests that 'more than 1000 rivers account for 80% of global annual emissions, which range between 0.8 million and 2.7 million metric

impacts on the marine and freshwater environments, including ecosystems.[5] Accordingly, to prevent land-based plastic pollution, the interaction between the legal regime governing the protection of the marine environment (that is, the marine regime) and that governing the protection of the freshwater environment (that is, the freshwater regime) is of critical importance.[6] Thus, this chapter addresses the interaction between the legal regimes governing the oceans and fresh water, focusing on the prevention of land-based marine plastic pollution.

Following the introduction, section 17.2 reviews the development of international law concerning the protection of the marine and freshwater environment since the Stockholm Declaration. Section 17.3 examines common obligations of the law of international watercourses and international marine environmental law applicable to the prevention of plastic pollution. Section 17.4 addresses the institutional interlink between maritime and freshwater regimes, and section 17.5 offers some concluding remarks.

17.2 DEVELOPMENT OF INTERNATIONAL LAW GOVERNING THE PROTECTION OF MARINE AND FRESHWATER ENVIRONMENTS SINCE 1972

As a preliminary consideration, this section reviews the development of international law with regard to the protection of the marine and freshwater environments since 1972 on the basis of two criteria that are intimately intertwined: the

tons per year, with small urban rivers among the most polluting'. Lourens J. J. Meijer *et al.*, 'More Than 1000 Rivers Account for 80% of Global Riverine Plastic Emissions into the Ocean' (2021) 7 *Science Advances* 1, www.science.org/doi/10.1126/sciadv.aaz5803; see also Christian Schmidt, Tobias Krauth & Stephen Wagner, 'Export of Plastic Debris by Rivers into the Sea' (2017) 51 *Environmental Science and Technology* 12246; Laurent C. M. Lebreton *et al.*, 'River Plastic Emissions to the World's Oceans' (2017) 8 *Nature Communications* 3; Hannah Ritchie, 'Where Does the Plastics in Our Oceans Come From?' *Our World in Data*, 1 May 2021, https://ourworldindata.org/ocean-plastics.

5 For instance, marine plastic may cause mortality or sub-lethal effects when plastic is ingested by animals such as turtles, small-toothed whales, and seabirds. It may also damage critical ecosystems, such as coral reefs, and cause smothering of sediments. *UNEP Year Book 2014: Emerging Issues in Our Global Environment* (UNEP, 2014), 49.

6 In this chapter, the term 'regime' is broadly defined as a complex of norms, non-binding instruments, institutions, and compliance procedures in a particular field of international law. See also Seline Trevisanut, Nikolaos Giannopoulos & Rozemarijn Roland Holt, 'Introduction: Regime Interaction in Ocean Governance', in Seline Trevisanut, Nikolaos Giannopoulos & Rozemarijn R. Holst (eds.), *Regime Interaction in Ocean Governance: Problems, Theories and Methods* (Brill, 2020), 3.

degree of codification and the progressive development of law[7] and the diversification of environmental norms.

17.2.1 *Codification and Progressive Development of Law*

The Stockholm Declaration occupies a crucial place in the codification and progressive development of international law because it includes key elements concerning environmental protection. For example, the no-harm principle, which constitutes a cornerstone of the protection of the environment in customary international law,[8] was formulated in principle 21 of the Stockholm Declaration.[9] Furthermore, principle 24 highlights another basic principle of environmental protection – that is, the principle of cooperation. Principle 2 makes an explicit reference to the safeguard of 'the benefit of present and future generations'. It may be said that principle 2 already reflects the concept of intergenerational equity. Moreover, as quoted earlier, principle 7 of the Stockholm Declaration stresses the need for the prevention of marine pollution.[10]

While the Stockholm Declaration does not refer to plastic pollution, principle 6 states: 'The discharge of toxic substances or of other substances and the release of heat, in such quantities or concentrations as to exceed the capacity of the environment to render them harmless, must be halted in order to ensure that serious or irreversible damage is not inflicted upon ecosystems.' This principle may seem to apply to the prevention of marine plastic pollution. Related to this, Recommendation 55(b)(i) of the Action Plan for the Human Environment states that 'the oceans are the ultimate recipient for the natural and man-made wastes discharged into the river systems of the continents'.[11] Furthermore, paragraph 3 of Annex III to the

7 In practice, the distinction between codification and progressive development is not clear cut. See UNGA Resolution 174(II) on the Statute of the International Law Commission, 21 November 1947, art. 15.

8 *Legality of the Threat or Use of Nuclear Weapons*, Advisory Opinion, 8 July 1996, (1996) ICJ Reports 241, para. 29; *Gabčíkovo-Nagymarous Project (Hungary/Slovakia)*, Judgment, 25 September 1997, (1997) ICJ Reports 41, para. 53; see also Alan Boyle & Catherine Redgwell, *Birnie, Boyle and Redgwell's International Law and the Environment* (4th ed., Oxford University Press, 2021), 152–153.

9 See Section 17.3.1 of this chapter.

10 This principle was further amplified by Recommendations 86–94 of the Action Plan for Human Development. 'Action Plan for the Human Environment', in *Report of the United Nations Conference on the Human Environment*, n. 1 (Stockholm Action Plan).

11 Stockholm Action Plan, n. 10.

Report of the United Nations Conference on the Human Development states: 'States should use the best practicable means available to them to minimize the discharge of potentially hazardous substances to the sea by all routes, including *land-based sources such as rivers*, outfalls and pipelines within national jurisdiction, as well as dumping by or from ships, aircraft and platforms.'[12] It is noteworthy that the interlink between the oceans and rivers, although embryonic, was reflected already in the report of the Stockholm Conference.

Since the adoption of the Stockholm Declaration, a great number of multilateral environmental agreements have been concluded. With respect to marine environmental protection, the 1982 UN Convention on the Law of the Sea (UNCLOS) marked a milestone in the history of international law by establishing a general and comprehensive framework for protecting the marine environment as *lex scripta*.[13] Subsequently, the environmental norms set out in the UNCLOS have been elaborated by global environmental treaties, such as the 1995 Fish Stocks Agreement,[14] and the 2023 Agreement on Biodiversity in Areas beyond National Jurisdiction (BBNJ Agreement).[15]

Unlike UNCLOS, there is no global treaty that establishes a general framework for the protection of the freshwater environment. To a certain extent, however, the obligation to prevent transboundary environmental harm was codified in the 1992 Convention on the Protection and Use of Transboundary Watercourses and International Lakes (Water Convention)[16] and the 1997 UN Convention on the Law of the Non-Navigational Uses of International Watercourses (Watercourses Convention).[17]

12 Recommendations 86–94, n. 10, 73 (emphasis added).

13 UN Convention on the Law of the Sea, 1982, 1833 UNTS 3, part XII (UNCLOS); see also Yoshifumi Tanaka, *The International Law of the Sea* (4th ed., Cambridge University Press, 2023), 362–364.

14 Agreement for the Implementation of the Provisions of the United Nations Convention on the Law of the Sea of 10 December 1982 Relating to the Conservation and Management of Straddling Fish Stocks and Highly Migratory Fish Stocks, and Related Instruments, 1995, 2167 UNTS 3 (Fish Stocks Agreement).

15 Agreement on the Conservation and Sustainable Use of Marine Biological Diversity of Areas beyond National Jurisdiction, 2023, UN Doc A/CONF.232/2023/4.

16 Convention on the Protection and Use of Transboundary Watercourses and International Lakes, 1992, 1936 UNTS 269, art. 2 (Water Convention). Owing to the amendments of 2003, all UN member states are allowed to accede to it.

17 Convention on the Law of the Non-Navigational Uses of International Watercourses, 1997, 2999 UNTS 77, art. 7 (Watercourses Convention).

17.2.2 *Diversification of Environmental Norms*

The development of international law of the environment can also be characterized by the diversification of environmental norms. Here, three points merit attention. First, there is the expansion of the scope of environmental norms. The material and spatial scope of norms concerning the protection of the marine environment has been expanded over time. With respect to material scope, as 'marine pollution' is a generic term,[18] its meaning can evolve over time, covering new forms of pollution, such as plastic pollution. Thus, UNCLOS, along with other particular treaties, regulates a wide range of marine pollution. Furthermore, the protection and preservation of marine species and biological diversity currently constitutes an inseparable part of marine environmental protection.[19] Likewise, the protection of fresh water ecosystems is increasingly provided in treaties governing international watercourses.[20] The spatial scope of environmental norms has also been expanded over time, and environmental norms cover the marine environment as a whole, including the deep seabed.

Second, there is the development of regional treaties. Since 1972, many regional treaties have been concluded with a view to preventing marine pollution.[21] Under the auspices of UNEP, in particular, multiple regional

18 In this regard, see Yoshifumi Tanaka, 'Reflections on Time Elements in the International Law of the Environment' (2013) 73 *Zeitschrift für ausländisches öffentliches Recht und Völkerrecht* 150.

19 International Tribunal for the Law of the Sea (ITLOS), *Southern Bluefin Tuna Cases (New Zealand v Japan; Australia v Japan)*, Provisional Measures, Case nos 3 and 4, 27 August 1999, 295, para. 70; see also ITLOS, *Request for an Advisory Opinion Submitted by the Sub-Regional Fisheries Commission (SRFC)*, Advisory Opinion, 2 April 2015, 37, para. 120; PCA, *South China Sea Arbitration (Philippines v China)*, Merits, 12 July 2016, reprinted in (2020) 33 *Reports of the International Arbitral Awards* 526, para. 956 (*South China Sea*); Yoshifumi Tanaka, *The South China Sea Arbitration: Toward an International Legal Order in the Oceans* (Hart Publishing, 2019), 135–136.

20 See, e.g., Water Convention, n. 16, art. 2(2)(d); Watercourses Convention, n. 17, art. 20; Agreement on the Protection of the (River) Meuse, 1994, (1995) 34 ILM 854, art. 5(d); Convention of Cooperation for the Protection and Sustainable Use of the Danube River, 1994, arts. 2(3)(5), 3(d), 9(1), www.icpdr.org/sites/default/files/DRPC%20English%20ver.pdf (Danube River Convention); Agreement on the Cooperation for the Sustainable Development of the Mekong River Basin, 1995, arts. 3, 7, https://internationalwaterlaw.org/documents/regionaldocs/mekong.html; Convention for the Protection of the Rhine, 1999, 3422 UNTS no. 56710, art. 3 (Rhine Convention); Protocol for Sustainable Development of Lake Victoria Basin, 2003, arts. 4(2)(i)(j), 6(1), https://faolex.fao.org/docs/pdf/mul41042.pdf; Framework Convention for the Protection of the Marine Environment of the Caspian Sea, 2003, art. 14(f), https://faolex.fao.org/docs/pdf/mul63152E.pdf; Niger Basin Water Charter, 2008, arts. 2, 12, www.abn.ne/images/documents/Charte_Eau/niger_basin_water_charter_certified_copy.pdf; Agreement of the Nile River Basin Cooperative Framework, 2011, art. 3(7), https://faolex.fao.org/docs/pdf/mul203276.pdf.

21 Tanaka, n. 13, 370.

treaties and action plans have been adopted with a view to protecting the marine environment.[22] The role of regional treaties is of particular importance in the prevention of land-based marine pollution.[23]

Third, there is the appearance of new concepts and approaches. The development of international law governing the protection of the environment is also characterized by the appearance of various key concepts and approaches. An illustrative example is the precautionary principle/approach. While the precautionary principle/approach was not referred to in the Stockholm Declaration, it was formulated in principle 15 of the 1992 Rio Declaration on Environment and Development.[24] An obligation to apply the precautionary principle/approach has been provided in a number of environmental treaties, including treaties regarding the protection of the marine environment[25] and freshwater environment.[26] Even though the precautionary principle is not explicitly included in UNCLOS, it has been suggested that the provisions of UNCLOS must be interpreted in accordance with this approach.[27]

Overall, it can be observed that the rules of international law governing the protection of the marine and freshwater environments have been significantly developed since the adoption of the Stockholm Declaration. However, traditionally, the development of international environmental law has been dominated by the sectoral approach, thereby ignoring the inter-connectiveness of

22 Further, see 'UNEP Regional Seas Programme', *UNEP*, www.unep.org/explore-topics/oceans-seas/what-we-do/regional-seas-programme.

23 Yoshifumi Tanaka, 'Regulation of Land-Based Marine Pollution', in Malgosia Fitzmaurice, Norman A. Martínez Gutiérrez & Riyaz Hamza (eds.), *The IMLI Manual on International Maritime Law*, vol. 3 (Oxford University Press, 2016), 150–163.

24 'Rio Declaration on Environment and Development', in *Report of the UN Conference on Environment and Development*, UN Doc. A/CONF.151/26 (Vol. I), 12 August 1992 (Rio Declaration).

25 Examples include Convention for the Protection of the Marine Environment of the North-East Atlantic, 1993, 2354 UNTS 67, art. 2(2)(a) (OSPAR Convention); Convention on the Protection of the Marine Environment of the Baltic Sea Area, 1974, 1507 UNTS 168, art. 3(2); Fish Stocks Agreement, n. 14, art. 6(1).

26 Examples include Protocol for Sustainable Development of Lake Victoria Basin, 2003, art. 4(2)(f), www.internationalwaterlaw.org/documents/regionaldocs/Lake_Victoria_Basin_2003.pdf; Niger Basin Water Charter, n. 20, art. 6; Rhine Convention, n. 20, art. 4(a); International Law Commission (ILC), 'Draft Articles on the Law of Transboundary Aquifers' (2008) 2 *ILC Yearbook* 19, art. 12.

27 Aline L. Jaeckel, *The International Seabed Authority and the Precautionary Principle: Balancing Deep Seabed Mineral Mining and Marine Environmental Protection* (Nijhoff, 2017), 135. ITLOS, in its advisory opinion of 2024, clearly stated that 'this obligation [articles 61 and 119 of UNCLOS] requires the application of the precautionary approach and an ecosystem approach'. ITLOS, *Request for an Advisory Opinion Submitted by the Commission of Small Island States on Climate Change and International Law*, Advisory Opinion, Case no. 31, 21 May 2024, para. 441(4)(e); see also paras. 418, 242.

environmental issues.[28] As a consequence, the interlink between the protection of marine and freshwater environments has attracted only limited attention. In response, more focus should be placed on the interaction between these two legal regimes.

17.3 COMMON OBLIGATIONS OF THE LAW OF INTERNATIONAL WATERCOURSES AND INTERNATIONAL MARINE ENVIRONMENTAL LAW

17.3.1 *The No-Harm Principle*

17.3.1.1 The No-Harm Principle in the Protection of the Marine and Freshwater Environments

The first common obligation between the two regimes concerns the principle of *sic utere tuo ut alienum non laedas*. This principle, usually called the no-harm principle, was formulated in principle 21 of the Stockholm Declaration as follows: 'States have, ... the responsibility to ensure that activities within their jurisdiction or control do not cause damage to the environment of other States or of areas beyond the limits of national jurisdiction.'[29] It is of particular interest to note that the formulation requires states to protect the environment beyond the limits of national jurisdiction. It seems to follow that the no-harm principle is no longer bilateral but operates *erga omnes* in relation to areas beyond the limits of national jurisdiction.[30] This formulation is relevant in the prevention of marine plastic pollution because plastic litter can spread widely in marine spaces beyond the limits of national jurisdiction.

In the context of marine environmental protection, the no-harm principle is provided in article 194(2) of UNCLOS. This provision evolved from principle 21 of the Stockholm Declaration.[31] In the context of the law of international watercourses, the no-harm principle is reflected in the Water Convention and the Watercourses Convention. Article 7 of the Watercourses Convention states:

> 1. Watercourse States shall, in utilizing an international watercourse in their territories, take all appropriate measures to prevent the causing of significant harm to other watercourse States.

[28] A similar problem arises in the context of climate change. Boyle & Redgwell, n. 8, 380.
[29] See also Rio Declaration, n. 24, principle 2.
[30] Boyle & Redgwell, n. 8, 162.
[31] Detlef Czybulka, 'Article 194', in Alexander Proelss (ed.), *The United Nations Convention on the Law of the Sea: A Commentary* (Hart Publishing, 2017), 1306.

2. Where significant harm nevertheless is caused to another watercourse State, the States whose use causes such harm shall, in the absence of agreement to such use, take all appropriate measures, having due regard for the provisions of articles 5 and 6, in consultation with the affected State, to eliminate or mitigate such harm and, where appropriate, to discuss the question of compensation.

Article 7(2) seems to suggest that the causing of significant harm is tolerated in the situation where compensation may be possible.[32] However, article 7 must be read in connection to the principle of equitable and reasonable utilization reflected in articles 5 and 6 of the Watercourses Convention.[33] Article 5 provides the principle of equitable and reasonable utilization, and article 6 enumerates several elements for determining equitable and reasonable utilization. These elements include, inter alia, '(d) the effects of the use or uses of the watercourses in one watercourse State on other watercourse States' and '(f) conservation, protection, development and economy of use of the water resources of the watercourse and the costs of measures taken to that effect'. The two elements can be used to effectuate the no-harm principle. Given that article 7(2) contains an obligation to have due regard for the provisions of articles 5 and 6, there may be some scope to argue that the no-harm principle is an integral part of the principle of equitable utilization.[34] On this matter, the International Law Commission's (ILC) commentary states that 'a use which causes significant harm to human health and safety is understood to be inherently inequitable and unreasonable'.[35] Hence, the introduction of plastic litter that may cause 'significant harm' would be contrary to the no-harm principle embodied in article 7(1).[36]

32 ILC, 'Draft Articles on the Law of the Non-Navigational Uses of International Watercourses and Commentaries Thereto and Resolution on Transboundary Confined Groundwater' (1994) 2(2) *ILC Yearbook* 122, para. 4; Salman M. A. Salman, 'The Obligation Not to Cause Significant Harm (Article 7)', in Laurence Boisson de Chazournes *et al.* (eds.), *The UN Convention on the Law of the Non-Navigational Uses of International Watercourses: A Commentary* (Oxford University Press, 2018), 114; Stephen C. McCaffrey, 'Intertwined General Principles', in Stephen C. McCaffrey, Christina Leb & Riley T. Denoon (eds.), *Research Handbook on International Water Law* (Edward Elgar, 2019), 90.

33 For a relationship between the no-harm principle and the principle of equitable and reasonable utilization, see Salman, n. 32, 114.

34 Stephen C. McCaffrey, *The Law of International Watercourses* (Oxford University Press, 2007), 445; Attila M. Tanzi, 'The Inter-relationship between No Harm, Equitable and Reasonable Utilisation and Cooperation under International Water Law' (2020) 20 *International Environmental Agreement* 619, 621–622.

35 ILC, n. 32, 104, para. 14.

36 Attila M. Tanzi, 'The Global Water Treaties and Their Relationship', in McCaffrey, Leb & Denoon, n. 32, 51. McCaffrey argued that 'there is presumably no such thing as an equitable right to pollute'. Stephen C. McCaffrey, 'The Customary Law of International Watercourses', in Mara Tignino, Christian Bréthaut & Laura Turley (eds.), *Research Handbook on Freshwater Law and International Relations* (Edward Elgar, 2018), 164.

Furthermore, article 2(1) of the Water Convention places a general obligation upon the parties to 'take all appropriate measures to prevent, control and reduce any transboundary impact'.[37] Article 2(2)(c) requires the parties to ensure that 'transboundary waters are used in a reasonable and equitable way, taking into particular account their transboundary character, in the case of activities which cause or are likely to cause transboundary impact'. Here, one can find the interlink between the no-harm principle and the principle of equitable utilization.[38] The Water Convention further specifies various principles and standards required when taking measures to prevent transboundary impacts.[39] These principles and standards may provide guidance for the implementation of article 7(1) of the Watercourses Convention. In this sense, one can say that the two conventions are mutually complementary.[40]

17.3.1.2 Challenges in the Application of the No-Harm Principle

While the no-harm principle constitutes a key obligation in the marine and freshwater regimes, its application to the prevention of plastic pollution encounters some challenges.[41] First, it does not absolutely prohibit environmental damage[42] but protects the environment only from significant or substantial damage.[43] Yet there is no established standard for classifying the level of marine pollution, including plastic pollution, in international law. Accordingly, it may be difficult if not impossible to objectively define the threshold of the 'significant or substantial harm' in the particular context of the prevention of marine plastic pollution.[44] Second, the concept of 'due diligence' is at the heart of the no-harm principle because a state is not responsible for damage if it has paid such 'due diligence'.[45] 'Due diligence' is an evolutionary concept,[46] and a reasonable standard of due diligence may change

37 Water Convention, n. 16.
38 Tanzi, n. 34, 621.
39 See Water Convention, n. 16, arts 2(5), 3(1).
40 Tanzi, n. 36, 50.
41 See also Yoshifumi Tanaka, 'Shared Responsibility for Land-based Marine Plastic Pollution' (2023) 12(2) *Transnational Environmental Law* 244, 250–251.
42 Boyle & Redgwell, n. 8, 162.
43 Rüdiger Wolfrum, 'Purposes and Principles of International Environmental Law' (1990) 33 *German Yearbook of International Law* 308, 317.
44 ILC, 'Draft Articles on Prevention of Transboundary Harm from Hazardous Activities with Commentaries' (2001) 2(2) *ILC Yearbook* 152, para. 4.
45 *Ibid.*, para. 30.
46 The evolutionary nature of the due diligence obligation was stressed by ITLOS. ITLOS, *Responsibilities and Obligations of States Sponsoring Persons and Entities with Respect to Activities in the Area*, Advisory Opinion, Case no. 17, 1 February 2011, 43, para. 117 (*Activities in*

with the development of science and technology. Furthermore, since economic and technological capacities vary between states, it would be difficult to set out the same standard of due diligence that should apply to all states.[47] The situation will be exacerbated when marine plastic pollution arises from various sources located in multiple states. Third, the no-harm principle, in itself, offers little guidance with respect to the specific measures that should be taken by each state. Hence, it may be less easy to decide the breach of the no-harm principle.

17.3.2 *Obligation to Protect the Environment*

17.3.2.1 Obligation to Protect the Marine Environment

The second common obligation relates to the obligation to protect the environment. Under article 192 of UNCLOS, 'states have the obligation to protect and preserve the marine environment'. More specifically, the prevention of land-based marine plastic pollution is to be regulated primarily by articles 207 and 213 of UNCLOS. However, the regulation of land-based marine plastic pollution faces considerable challenges. First, the activities that may cause land-based pollution, including plastic pollution, are closely bound up with crucial national programmes for economic, industrial, and social development. The economic costs of measures to regulate land-based pollution inevitably affect economic development. Hence, states are often reluctant to approve any attempts at restricting their economic developments by legally binding instruments.[48] Second, the regulation of land-based plastic pollution is more complex than ocean-based plastic pollution as it involves multiple actors and sources. Each actor and/or source requires different measures to prevent plastic pollution. This requirement makes regulatory measures highly complex.[49] Third, many developing countries do not have adequate technological and financial facilities to prevent marine pollution, including marine plastic pollution. In the light of the economic and technological gaps between developed and developing countries, it is hard to place the same obligations upon developing countries to regulate plastic pollution as are placed on

the Area); *Request for an Advisory Opinion on Climate Change*, n. 27, para. 239; see also Samantha Besson, *La due diligence en droit international* (Brill/Nijhoff, 2021), 138.

47 Timo Koivurova, 'Due Diligence', in Rüdiger Wolfrum (ed.), *Max Planck Encyclopedia of International Law* (Oxford University Press, 2010), para. 19.

48 Tanaka, n. 23, 141.

49 See also Eva van der Marel & Catherine Redgwell, 'Unrealised Ambition or Unattainable Goal? Sustainable Consumption and Production in International Law', in this volume, 205.

developed states at the global level.[50] Thus, there is a need to tailor specific rules preventing land-based marine plastic pollution by taking account of the particular needs and circumstances of the relevant states.

17.3.2.2 Obligation to Protect the Freshwater Environment

Under article 20 of the Watercourses Convention, watercourse states must 'individually and, where appropriate, jointly, protect and preserve the ecosystems of international watercourses'.[51] The obligation under article 20 does not refer to transboundary damage. Nor does it refer to 'significant harm'. It would seem to follow that watercourse states are obliged to protect and preserve the ecosystems of international watercourses, even if pollution does not cause transboundary effect or significant harm.[52] Given that plastic litter may give adverse effects on ecosystems of international watercourses, a discharge of plastic litter into the watercourses could breach the obligation under article 20.

Furthermore, article 21(2) of the Watercourses Convention places an obligation upon watercourse states to 'prevent, reduce and control the pollution of an international watercourse that may cause significant harm to other watercourse States or to their environment'. According to the ILC's commentary, 'the obligation to "prevent" relates to new pollution of international watercourses, while the obligations to "reduce" and "control" relate to existing pollution'.[53] Hence, arguably, watercourse states are obliged to prevent new plastic pollution of international watercourses and to reduce existing plastic pollution in order that significant harm would not occur. While, under article 21(2), state responsibility is limited to 'significant harm', plastic pollution that falls short of causing 'significant harm' could still breach the obligation under article 20 or that under article 23 concerning marine environmental protection.[54] In this regard, the ILC took the view that 'as in the case of article 20, the principle of precautionary action is applicable, especially in respect of dangerous substances such as those that are toxic, persistent or bioaccumulative'.[55] Given that plastic pollution is persistent and bioaccumulative, the application of the precautionary approach is relevant. In fact, article 2(5)(a) of the Water Convention provides the 'precautionary principle' as a guiding principle.

50 See UNCLOS, n. 13, art. 207(4).
51 See also Water Convention, n. 16, art. 2(2)(d).
52 McCaffrey, n. 34, 459.
53 ILC, n. 32, 122, para. 4.
54 *Ibid.*, para. 6; McCaffrey, n. 34, 451.
55 ILC, n. 32, 122, para. 4; see also Boyle & Redgwell, n. 8, 591.

17.3.3 *Obligation to Conduct an Environmental Impact Assessment (EIA)*

17.3.3.1 Obligation to Conduct an EIA in the Watercourses Convention

The third common obligation that merits discussion is the obligation to conduct an EIA.[56] An EIA is a procedure to predict environmental risks and likely impacts of a proposed project and integrate environmental concerns into the decision-making process before authorizing or funding the project.[57] The obligation to conduct a transboundary EIA is part of customary international law.[58]

The Watercourses Convention provides the obligation to conduct an EIA merely as a subsidiary of the obligation of notification.[59] In the light of the customary law character of the obligation to conduct a transboundary EIA, however, one can argue that states are under the obligation to perform an EIA in customary international law in the prevention of transboundary pollution, independent of the obligation of notification.[60] A state cannot deny a breach of the due diligence obligation if it had not conducted an EIA and its activities cause serious environmental harm.[61] Thus, the obligation to conduct an EIA provides a legal procedure for effectuating a due diligence obligation in the protection of international watercourses.[62]

56 By way of example, the Convention on Environmental Impact Assessment in a Transboundary Context, 1991, 1989 UNTS 309, art. 1, para. (vi), defines EIA as 'a national procedure for evaluating the likely impact of a proposed activity on the environment'.

57 Boyle & Redgwell, n. 8, 184.

58 *Pulp Mills on the River Uruguay (Argentina v Uruguay)*, Judgment, 20 April 2010, (2010) ICJ Reports 83, para. 204 (*Pulp Mills*); *Certain Activities Carried Out by Nicaragua in the Border Area (Costa Rica v Nicaragua) and Construction of a Road in Costa Rica along the San Juan River (Nicaragua v Costa Rica)*, Judgment, 16 December 2015, (2015) ICJ Reports 706, para. 104 (*Certain Activities Carried Out by Nicaragua*); *Activities in the Area*, n. 46, 50, para. 145; *Request on Climate Change*, n. 27, para. 355.

59 Watercourses Convention, n. 17, art. 12; see also Komlan Sangbana, 'Notification and Consultation Concerning Planned Measures', in Laurence Boisson de Chazournes, Makane Moïse Mbengue, Mara Tignino and Komlan Sangbana (eds.), *The UN Convention on the Law of the Non-Navigational Uses of International Watercourses: A Commentary* (Oxford University Press, 2018), 177. However, the 1992 Water Convention contains the obligation to perform an environmental impact assessment (EIA). Water Convention, n. 16, art. 3(1)(h); Berlin Rules on Water Resources, 2004, art. 29 (which provide a clear obligation to conduct an EIA. International Law Association, *Berlin Rules of Water Resources* (Berlin Conference, 2004), https://unece.org/fileadmin/DAM/env/water/meetings/legal_board/2010/annexes_groundwater_paper/Annex_IV_Berlin_Rules_on_Water_Resources_ILA.pdf.

60 *Certain Activities Carried Out by Nicaragua*, n. 58, para. 104.

61 *Pulp Mills*, n. 58, para. 204; see also *Certain Activities Carried Out by Nicaragua*, n. 58, para. 104.

62 Yoshifumi Tanaka, 'Obligation to Conduct an Environmental Impact Assessment (EIA) in International Adjudication: Interaction between Law and Time' (2021) 90 *Nordic Journal of International Law* 86, 89–94.

17.3.3.2 Obligation to Conduct an EIA in UNCLOS

In the context of marine environmental protection, the obligation to conduct an EIA is set out in article 206 of UNCLOS:

> When States have reasonable grounds for believing that planned activities under their jurisdiction or control may cause substantial pollution of or significant and harmful changes to the marine environment, they shall, as far as practicable, assess the potential effects of such activities on the marine environment and shall communicate reports of the results of such assessments in the manner provided in article 205.

However, article 206 provides no further precision with regard to the contents and procedures of an EIA. Hence an international court or tribunal may encounter a challenge when deciding a breach of article 206.[63] In the light of the technical nature of an EIA and diversity of state practice, it is hard to expect that the rules of customary international law would develop with regard to the contents and procedures for an EIA in the future. Hence, the realistic road to follow may be to specify the contents and procedures for an EIA by a particular treaty. In this regard, it is noteworthy that the BBNJ Agreement contains detailed rules concerning an EIA in the particular context of the conservation of marine biological diversity in areas beyond national jurisdiction.[64]

17.3.4 *Obligation to Cooperate*

17.3.4.1 Obligation to Cooperate in the Watercourses Convention

The obligation to cooperate is one of the basic principles of international law,[65] and the need for international cooperation in environmental protection was highlighted by principle 24 of the Stockholm Declaration. The statement remains valid in the protection of marine and freshwater environments. In fact, as an international watercourse is a shared natural resource,[66] international cooperation is a prerequisite to protect its environment.[67] Thus,

63 In reality, this issue was raised in *South China Sea*, n. 19, para. 991.

64 See BBNJ Agreement, n 15, part IV; see further Yoshifumi Tanaka, 'Reflections on the Environmental Impact Assessment in the BBNJ Agreement: Its Implications for the Conservation of Biological Diversity in the Marine Arctic beyond National Jurisdiction' (2024) 55 *Ocean Development and International Law* 85.

65 Declaration on Principles of International Law Concerning Friendly Relations and Co-operation Among States in Accordance with the Charter of the United Nations, UNGA Resolution 2625 (XXV), 24 October 1970, principle 4.

66 McCaffrey, n. 34, 466.

67 Berlin Rules of Water Resources, n. 59, 20.

article 8 of the Watercourses Convention provides a general obligation to cooperate. The general obligation under article 8 is further amplified by article 9, which provides an obligation to regularly exchange data and information on the condition of the watercourse, particularly that of an 'ecological nature and related to the water quality as well as related forecasts'. Furthermore, the obligation to cooperate is clearly stated in article 11 of the 2004 Berlin Rules of Water Resources and is further elaborated in Chapter XI of the Rules.[68] Given that a discharge of plastic litter to an international watercourse may affect its ecosystem, arguably watercourse states are obliged to exchange available data and information on the ecological condition of the watercourse, including impacts of plastic litter on the ecosystem of the watercourse.

17.3.4.2 Obligation to Cooperate in UNCLOS

As ITLOS stated in the 2002 *MOX Plant* case, the obligation to cooperate is at the heart of the protection of the marine environment.[69] Under article 207(3) of UNCLOS, states are required to endeavour to harmonize their policies in this connection at the appropriate regional level. States are also obliged to 'endeavour to establish global and regional rules, standards and recommended practices and procedures to prevent, reduce and control pollution of the marine environment from land-based sources' pursuant to article 207(4). The implementation of the obligations necessitates international cooperation between states. However, the obligations set out under article 207(3) and (4) are qualified by the term 'endeavour'. Furthermore, UNCLOS contains no reference to the regulation of specific substances of land-based marine pollution, such as marine plastic litter. In the light of the weak normativity of the obligations regarding the prevention of land-based marine pollution, it may be difficult for an adjudicative body to decide a breach of the obligations regarding land-based marine plastic pollution under UNCLOS, all the more so if multiple states are involved in this type of pollution.[70]

Of particular importance in this context is cooperation between watercourse states and other states. While UNCLOS pays little attention to this

68 *Ibid.*

69 ITLOS, *MOX Plant Case (Ireland v United Kingdom)*, Request for Provisional Measures, Case no. 10, Order, 3 December 2001, (2011) ITLOS Reports 110, para. 82.

70 Yoshifumi Tanaka, 'Land-based Marine Pollution', in André Nollkaemper & Ilias Plakokefalos (eds.), *The Practice of Shared Responsibility* (Cambridge University Press, 2017), 299.

matter, article 2(6) of the Water Convention obliges the riparian parties to cooperate to develop harmonized policies 'aimed at the protection of the environment of transboundary waters or the environment influenced by such waters, including the marine environment'.[71] Article 23 of the Watercourses Convention also obliges watercourse states to cooperate with other states to take measures to protect and preserve the marine environment. An issue that arises here is how one can strengthen the interlink between legal regimes governing international watercourses and those of marine environmental protection. This issue will be discussed in Section 17.4.

17.4 INTERLINK BETWEEN THE PROTECTION OF AN INTERNATIONAL WATERCOURSE AND THE MARINE ENVIRONMENT IN REGIONAL LEGAL REGIMES

As a case study, this section will examine the interaction between the marine and freshwater regimes in the North-East Atlantic and the Black Sea.[72]

17.4.1 *The North-East Atlantic*

The first example that merits discussion concerns the cooperation between the International Commission for the Protection of the Rhine (ICPR) and the OSPAR Commission in the North-East Atlantic. According to one study, it is estimated that the Rhine River transports twenty to thirty tonnes of plastic litter per year to the North Sea.[73] Accordingly, the prevention of plastic pollution via the Rhine is one of the crucial issues in the protection of the environment of the North-East Atlantic. The protection of the Rhine is governed by the 1999 Convention for the Protection of the Rhine (Rhine Convention).[74] To implement the Rhine Convention, the contracting parties must pursue their cooperation within the ICPR.[75] Under article 11(3) of the Rhine Convention, the contracting parties must report regularly to the ICPR on (1) the legislative,

[71] See also Water Convention, n. 16, art. 9(4).
[72] See also Yoshifumi Tanaka, 'International Regulation of Marine Plastic Litter in the North-East Atlantic' in Elizabeth A. Kirk, Naporn Popattanachai, Richard Barnes & Eva R. van der Marel (eds.), *Research Handbook on Plastic Regulation: Law, Policy and the Environment* (Edward Elgar, 2024), 218–220.
[73] Maarten Van der Wal *et al.*, *Identification and Assessment of Riverine Input of (Marine) Litter: Final Report for the European Commission DG Environment under Framework Contract no. ENV.D.2/FRA/2012/0025*, 2015, vi; see also Thomas Mani *et al.*, 'Microplastics Profile along the Rhine River' (2015) *Scientific Report* 4, www.nature.com/articles/srep17988.pdf.
[74] Rhine Convention, n. 20.
[75] *Ibid.*, art. 6(1).

regulatory, and other measures they have taken with a view to implementing the provisions of the Convention and on the basis of the commission's decisions; (2) the results of the measures; and (3) problems arising in the implementation of the measures. On the basis of the report, the ICPR 'may decide that measures will be taken to assist the implementation of the decisions'.[76] Thus, compliance with the Rhine Convention is supervised by the ICPR.

Marine pollution of the North-East Atlantic is regulated by the 1993 OSPAR Convention.[77] Under article 3 of the OSPAR Convention, the contracting parties are obliged to 'take, individually and jointly, all possible steps to prevent and eliminate pollution from land-based sources in accordance with the provisions of the Convention, in particular as provided for in Annex I'.[78] The contracting parties to the Convention include landlocked states surrounding the Rhine – that is, Luxembourg and Switzerland. In accordance with article 3, Luxembourg and Switzerland are required to take measures to prevent and eliminate land-based pollution via the Rhine.

Under article 2(1) of Annex I, 'point source discharges to the maritime area, and release into water or air which reach and may affect the maritime area, shall be strictly subject to authorisation or regulation by the competent authorities of the Contracting Parties'. It appears that waters 'which reach and may affect the maritime area' can include rivers. Under article 2(1) of Annex I, 'such authorisation or regulation shall, in particular, implement relevant decisions of the Commission which bind the relevant Contracting Party'. The OSPAR Commission, made up of representatives of each of the contracting parties, is to draw up plans for the reduction and phasing out of hazardous substances in accordance with article 3(a) of Annex I. Thus, the authorization or regulation by the contracting parties with respect to emissions of such substances is subject to the control of the OSPAR Commission. Furthermore, compliance with the OSPAR Convention is supervised by the OSPAR Commission.[79] Accordingly, marine plastic pollution from land-based sources in the North-East Atlantic is to be collectively regulated by the OSPAR Commission.[80]

76 *Ibid.*, art. 11(4).

77 OSPAR Convention, n. 25.

78 To elaborate this obligation, Appendix 2 of the OSPAR Convention provides a detailed list of priority pollutants. *Ibid.*

79 *Ibid.*, art. 23.

80 The OSPAR Commission adopted the North-East Atlantic Environment Strategy 2030 on 1 October 2021. The Strategy set out the objective that the OSPAR Commission would 'prevent inputs of and significantly reduce marine litter, including microplastics, in the marine environment to reach levels that do not cause adverse impacts to the marine and

Of note is the cooperation between the ICPR and the OSPAR Commission. In this regard, the contracting parties to the Rhine Convention – comprising Germany, France, Luxemburg, the Netherlands, and Switzerland – expressed their awareness in the preamble that 'the restoration of the Rhine is also necessary to conserve and improve the ecosystem of the North Sea'. Indeed, the preamble of the Convention explicitly refers to the OSPAR Convention. Furthermore, the Convention states in article 3(5) that one of its aims is 'to help restore the North Sea in conjunction with the other actions taken to protect it'.

The interaction is clearly reflected in 'Rhine 2040', which is a programme to achieve sustainable management of the Rhine. Noting that 'the OSPAR action plan on marine litter also addresses the rivers as influx pathways, and provides for cooperation with the river basin commissions', Rhine 2040 states that the ICPR 'can provide support to reduce the influx of waste, especially plastic, into the water'.[81] Thus, it sets out a goal to reduce 'influx at source, through the better management of plastics along the value chain, in particular through waste management'.[82] It also states that the ICPR would continue to exchange information with marine organizations, including the OSPAR Commission.[83] Accordingly, the ICPR has observer status to the OSPAR Commission.[84]

17.4.2 *The Black Sea*

The second example that merits discussion concerns the cooperation between the International Commission for the Protection of the Danube River (ICPDR) and the International Commission for the Protection of the Black Sea (ICPBS). The Danube River is protected by the 1994 Danube River Convention.[85] The ICPDR is an organ to implement the Convention.[86] The preamble of the Danube River Convention emphasizes 'the urgent

coastal environment with the ultimate aim of eliminating inputs of litter'. *Strategy of the OSPAR Commission for the Protection of the Marine Environment of the North-East Atlantic 2030*, Doc. OSPAR 21/13/1, 1 October 2021, strategic objectives 4, 10, annex 22, www.ospar.org/convention/strategy.

81 International Commission for the Protection of the Rhine, *RHINE 2040 Programme: The Rhine and Its Catchment: Sustainably Managed and Climate-resilient*, 13 February 2020, 17, www.iksr.org/fileadmin/user_upload/DKDM/Dokumente/Sonstiges/EN/ot_En_Rhine_2040.pdf.

82 *Ibid.*

83 *Ibid.*, 24.

84 'Observers', *OSPAR Commission*, www.ospar.org/organisation/observers.

85 Danube River Convention, n. 20.

86 *Ibid.*, art. 18(1). The Commission is empowered to adopt legally binding decisions. *Ibid.*, annex IV, art. 5(2).

need for strengthened domestic and international measures to prevent, control and reduce significant adverse transboundary impact from the release of hazardous substances and of nutrients into the freshwater environment within the Danube Basin *with due attention also given to the Black Sea*'.[87]

Under article 5(1) of the Danube River Convention, the contracting parties are obliged to 'develop, adopt and implement relevant legal, administrative and technical measures as well as provide for the domestic preconditions and basis required in order to ensure efficient water quality protection and sustainable water use and thereby also to prevent, control and reduce transboundary impact'. To this end, the contracting parties must separately or jointly 'adopt legal provisions for the handling of substances hazardous to water'.[88] In accordance with article 7(1) of the Convention, the contracting parties are obliged to 'set emission limits applicable to individual industrial sectors or industries in terms of pollution loads, and concentrations and based in the best possible way on low- and non-waste technologies at source'. In this connection, Annex II to this Convention enumerates a list of industrial sectors and industries as well as an additional list of hazardous substances and groups of substances, the discharge of which from point and non-point sources shall be prevented or considerably reduced.[89] The list includes 'manufacture and processing of plastics'.[90]

Land-based pollution in the Black Sea is regulated by the 1992 Bucharest Convention[91] and the 1992 Bucharest Protocol.[92] Article 1 of the Bucharest Protocol places an obligation upon the contracting parties to 'take all necessary measures to prevent, reduce and control pollution of the marine environment of the Black Sea caused by discharges from land-based sources on their territories such as *rivers*'.[93] Under article 4 of the Protocol, 'the Contracting Parties undertake to prevent and eliminate pollution of the marine environment of the Black Sea from land-based sources by substances and matter listed in Annex I to this Protocol'. Annex I includes 'persistent synthetic materials which may float, sink or remain in suspension'.[94] Furthermore, 'taking into account that rivers tributary to the Black Sea constitute a major source of

87 *Ibid.*, preamble (emphasis added).
88 *Ibid.*, art. 5(2)(c); see also art. 5(2)(d).
89 *Ibid.*, art. 7(3).
90 *Ibid.*, annex II, para. 5(d).
91 Convention on Protection of the Black Sea against Pollution, 1992, 1764 UNTS 3 (Bucharest Convention).
92 Protocol on the Protection of the Black Sea Marine Environment against Pollution from Land-Based Sources, 1992, 1764 UNTS 18 (Bucharest Protocol).
93 *Ibid.* (emphasis added).
94 *Ibid.*, annex I, para. 8.

pollution of the marine environment of the Black Sea', the contracting parties to the Bucharest Convention decided that they 'will closely follow the activities of the Danube States regarding the improvement of the ecological conditions in the Danube and will endeavour to initiate cooperation including future meetings with them for the purposes of the Convention'.[95]

To achieve the purposes of the Bucharest Convention, the ICPBS was established.[96] The functions of this Commission include cooperation with 'competent international organizations, especially with a view to developing appropriate programmes or obtaining assistance in order to achieve the purposes of this Convention'.[97] It appears that the ICPDR can be regarded as a 'competent international organisation' in this context. In fact, the ICPBS and ICPDR adopted a memorandum of understanding to achieve common strategic goals in 2001.[98] More recently, cooperation with the ICPBS was stressed by the 2022 Danube Declaration, encouraging 'Romania and Bulgaria, the EU member states of the Danube River Basin sharing the Black Sea waters, to continue working on the coordination of the implementation of the Marine Strategy Framework Directive in the Black Sea Region in close cooperation with the Black Sea Commission'.[99]

17.5 CONCLUSIONS

Importantly, the Stockholm Declaration specified some key principles governing environmental protection, such as the no-harm principle and the principle of cooperation. It would be no exaggeration to say that the Stockholm Declaration has been a catalyst for the development of international law of the environment. In particular, it is remarkable that the Stockholm Declaration highlighted, in principle 7, the obligation to 'take all possible steps to prevent pollution of the seas' by harmful substances. This

95 Resolution 2 on the Establishment of Cooperation with Danube States for Promoting the Objectives of the Convention on the Protection of the Black Sea against Pollution, 17 April 2009.

96 Bucharest Convention, n. 91, art. XVII.

97 *Ibid.*, art. XVIII(6).

98 'Memorandum of Understanding between the International Commission for the Protection of the Black Sea (ICPBS) and the International Commission for the Protection of the Danube River (ICPDR) on Common Strategic Goals', Doc. IC/027, 26 December 2001, www.icpdr.org/main/resources/mou-between-icpbs-and-icpdr.

99 Danube Declaration adopted at the ICPDR Ministerial Meeting on 8th February 2022: A Vision for Integrated Water Management in Our Shared Basin: Building a Sustainable Future in the Danube River Basin, 8 February 2022, para. 29, www.icpdr.org/sites/default/files/nodes/documents/danube_declaration_2022.pdf.

obligation is increasingly crucial in a contemporary context of the prevention of marine plastic pollution. It may be said that the Stockholm Declaration constituted a forward-looking instrument. Despite the great wave of treaty making in the field of the protection of the marine and freshwater environments, however, little attention has been paid to the interaction between the marine and freshwater regimes. The lack of regime interaction constitutes one of the fundamental weaknesses of international environmental law on the basis of the sectoral approach. To prevent land-based marine plastic pollution, strengthening the interlink between the two legal regimes at the normative and institutional levels is a prerequisite.

With respect to the normative link, one can identify common obligations applicable to the prevention of plastic pollution in the marine and freshwater regimes. They include:

- the no-harm principle;
- the obligation to protect the environment;
- the obligation to conduct an EIA; and
- the obligation to cooperate.

These obligations provide a common foundation for the prevention of land-based marine plastic pollution in the marine and freshwater regimes. In fact, one can find some instances of institutional cooperation between the marine and freshwater regimes in the North-East Atlantic and the Black Sea. It appears that the normative and institutional link between the two regimes at the regional level provides an alternative that is well worth considering in the prevention of land-based marine plastic pollution.

PART VI

NATURE AND BIODIVERSITY

18

The Progressive Development of International Biodiversity Law from the 1972 Stockholm Conference to the Synergistic Protection of Biodiversity and Human Rights, Including at the Ocean-Climate Nexus

Elisa Morgera

The progressive development of international biodiversity law, from the 1972 Stockholm Conference on the Human Environment to today, is exemplified in the evolving interpretation of the 1992 Convention on Biological Diversity (CBD) towards the protection of human rights.[1] Realizing its transformative potential in addressing the intertwined global planetary crises (climate change, biodiversity loss, and toxic pollution), including at the ocean-climate nexus, requires a significant shift from the sectoral[2] and incremental environmental protection envisaged in the 1972 Stockholm Declaration[3] towards an updated understanding of cosmopolitan cooperation foreshadowed in the Declaration.[4]

18.1 INTERNATIONAL LAW AND NATURE PROTECTION AT THE TIME OF THE STOCKHOLM CONFERENCE

The Stockholm Conference on the Human Environment is traditionally seen as the 'birthday' of modern international environmental law. According to Jutta Brunnée, the resulting Stockholm Declaration 'foreshadowed to

[1] Convention on Biological Diversity, 1992, 1760 UNTS 79 (CBD). As anticipated, to some extent, by the Stockholm Declaration on the Human Environment. 'Declaration of the United Nations Conference on the Human Environment', in *Report of the UN Conference on the Human Environment*, UN Doc. A/CONF.48/14/Rev.1, 16 June 1972 (Stockholm Declaration). See Donald K. Anton & Dinah L. Shelton, *Environmental Protection and Human Rights* (Cambridge University Press, 2011), at 72.

[2] Anton & Shelton, n. 1, 73.

[3] Stockholm Declaration, n. 1.

[4] Jonas Ebbesson & Ellen Hey, 'Introduction: The Sustainable Development Goals, Agenda 2030 and International Law', in Jonas Ebbesson & Ellen Hey (eds.), *The Cambridge Handbook of the Sustainable Development Goals and International Law* (Cambridge University Press, 2022), 26.

a remarkable degree, the framework within which international environmental lawyers operate today',[5] including key concepts such as the common concern of humankind,[6] the common but differentiated responsibility principle,[7] intergenerational equity,[8] precaution,[9] and the human rights-based approach to environmental protection.[10] It has also been argued that the Stockholm Declaration, with its references to living conditions 'for all' and to distributive justice issues,[11] contained the seeds of the integration of development issues and environmental concerns,[12] which was more clearly articulated during the 1992 Rio Conference on the Environment and Development and eventually led to the 'leave-no-one-behind' approach of the 2030 Agenda for Sustainable Development.[13]

Looking back from today's perspective, however, the Stockholm Declaration can also be considered quite traditional in protecting specific sectors of the environment through an end-of-pipeline approach, whereas the developments in international environmental law that followed shifted towards the regulation of sources of harm that could affect more than one sector.[14] In addition, the Stockholm Declaration is seen to have prioritized the national implementation of international environmental law as the role of states, with little attention to the role of other actors.[15] It also largely focused on bilateral approaches to transboundary environmental issues, embodying a 'mutual limitation paradigm' and an attempt to balance

[5] Jutta Brunnée, 'The Stockholm Declaration and the Structure and Processes of International Environmental Law', in Aldo Chircop, Ted L. McDorman & Susan J. Rolston (eds.), *The Future of Ocean Regime-Building: Essays in Tribute to Douglas M Johnston* (Brill, 2009), 43, reprinted in David Freestone (ed.), *Sustainable Development and International Environmental Law* (Edward Elgar, 2018).

[6] Stockholm Declaration, n. 1, proclamation, as discussed in Brunnée, n. 5, 51.

[7] Stockholm Declaration, n. 1, principle 12, as discussed in Brunnée, n. 5, 51.

[8] Stockholm Declaration, n. 1, principles 1, 2, as discussed in Brunnée, n. 5, 51.

[9] Stockholm Declaration, n. 1, proclamation 6, as discussed in Brunnée, n. 5, 52.

[10] Stockholm Declaration, n. 1, principle 1, as discussed in Anton & Shelton, n. 1, 72; see also Dinah L. Shelton, 'Human Rights, Environmental Rights and the Right to Environment' (1991) 28 *Stanford Journal of International Law* 103, 112, 125.

[11] Ebbesson & Hey, n. 4, 26.

[12] Brunnée, n. 5, 42.

[13] 'Rio Declaration on Environment and Development', in *Report of the UN Conference on Environment and Development,* UN Doc. A/CONF.151/26 (Vol. I), 12 August 1992; *Transforming Our World: The 2030 Agenda for Sustainable Development,* Doc. A/Res/70/1, 25 September 2015.

[14] Anton & Shelton, n. 1, 73.

[15] Michael Bowman, Peter Davies & Catherine Redgwell, *Lyster's International Wildlife Law* (Cambridge University Press, 2010), 107.

'competing contemporary interests of States, but not potential inter-temporal impacts of States' activities'.[16]

The Stockholm Declaration contains numerous explicit references to nature protection, which point to precautionary and intergenerational approaches to the protection of species and ecosystems;[17] the conservation and sustainable or wise use of species and habitats, including through the integration of nature protection in development planning;[18] and the protection of marine species through the prevention of marine pollution.[19] In addition, the Stockholm Declaration arguably refers implicitly to biodiversity when it speaks of maintaining and restoring the earth's capacity to produce vital renewable resources,[20] and of guarding against overusing non-renewable resources, if one considers biodiversity's role in the water cycle, for instance.[21] Biodiversity can also be considered implicit in the principle related to ensuring a favourable 'living environment' for humanity through (or despite?) economic and social development and creating conditions on earth that are necessary for the improvement of the quality of life[22] – taking into account ecological processes in ensuring the stability of prices and adequate earnings for primary commodities and raw materials for developing countries in order to contribute to environmental management.[23]

On the one hand, these references underpin the general duty to cooperate enshrined in the Stockholm Declaration with regard to 'safeguarding the ecological balance of the planet as an essential interest of all states',[24] including with regard to the intrinsic value of nature.[25] On the other hand, these references do not yet capture the full range of values of biodiversity as well as the multiple and increasing threats to biodiversity, as we understand them today, although they did underscore the importance of nature protection for broader environmental protection and human well-being in the present and in the future. By way of contrast, the 2019 Global Assessment of Biodiversity and Ecosystems Services

16 Brunnée, n. 5, 43–44, commenting on the Stockholm Declaration, n. 1, principle 21.

17 Stockholm Declaration, n. 1, principle 2 refers to 'flora and fauna and especially representative samples of natural ecosystems' that 'must be safeguarded for the benefit of present and future generations through careful planning or management, as appropriate'.

18 *Ibid.*, principle 4 refers to humankind's 'special responsibility to safeguard and wisely manage the heritage of wildlife and its habitat' and to include in planning for economic development 'nature conservation, including wildlife'.

19 *Ibid.*, principle 7 calls upon states to 'take all possible steps to prevent pollution of the seas by substances that are liable to . . . harm living resources and marine life'.

20 *Ibid.*, principle 3.

21 *Ibid.*, principle 5.

22 *Ibid.*, principle 8

23 *Ibid.*, principle 10.

24 *Ibid.*, principle 24, as discussed in Anton & Shelton, n. 1, 72.

25 'Veiled references' in *ibid.*, principle 4, according to Bowman, Davies & Redgwell, n. 15, 66.

illuminated the role of biodiversity for addressing poverty, hunger, health, water, and climate change and held that 'most of nature's contributions to people are not fully replaceable and some are irreplaceable' as the rate of global biodiversity degradation during the past fifty years is unprecedented in human history.[26]

Perhaps the most striking advance in our understanding of the importance of biodiversity can be found in the evidence on the relationship between biodiversity and human health.[27] It has increasingly been underscored how exposure to biodiverse spaces can improve psychological, cognitive, and physiological health as well as supporting children's development and improving life expectancy.[28] On the other hand, reduced human contact with biodiversity weakens the human microbiome's immune-regulatory role and increases the risk of the onset of non-communicable diseases (type 1 diabetes, multiple sclerosis, inflammatory bowel diseases).[29] Further, for natural resource-dependent human populations, the global decline in various species will present major public health challenges, particularly in low- and middle-income countries (significantly decreasing clinical levels of energy, proteins, certain vitamins, including iron, zinc, magnesium, and fatty acids).[30] And as widely experienced across the globe during the COVID-19 pandemic, human-caused changes in ecosystems are increasing the risk and impact of infectious disease transmission.[31]

Comparing the knowledge at the time of the fiftieth anniversary of the Stockholm Declaration[32] to the state of development of international biodiversity law at the time and immediately after the Stockholm Conference clearly shows that the relevant principles of the Stockholm Declaration and the early treaties on nature protection, while remaining relevant today, were conceived in relatively narrow and fragmented terms.

26 Sandra Diaz *et al.*, *Summary for Policymakers of the Global Assessment Report on Biodiversity and Ecosystem Services of the Intergovernmental Science-Policy Platform on Biodiversity and Ecosystem Services* (Intergovernmental Science-Policy Platform on Biodiversity and Ecosystem Services, 2019), 10.

27 Liz Willetts *et al.*, 'Health in Global Biodiversity Governance: What Is Next?' (2023) 401 (10376) *Lancet* 533.

28 World Health Organization (WHO), *Report by the Director-General: Health, Environment and Climate Change – Human Health and Biodiversity*, Doc. A71/11, 2018.

29 WHO, *Urban Green Spaces and Health: A Review of Evidence*, Doc. WHO/EURO:2016–3352-43111–60341, 2016; WHO, *Urban Green Space Interventions and Health: A Review of Impacts and Effectiveness*, 2017.

30 WHO, n. 28.

31 David R. Boyd, *UN Special Rapporteur on Human Rights and the Environment, Summary of Expert Seminar on the Role of Human Rights and Environmental Conservation in the Prevention of Future Pandemics*, UN Doc. A/HRC/52/44, 2023.

32 Liz Willetts, 'Stockholm+50: What Does It Mean for Global Health?' (2022) 6(5) *Lancet Planet Health* e388.

18.2 INTERNATIONAL BIODIVERSITY TREATIES BETWEEN THE 1970S–1990S

To some extent, the references to biodiversity in the Stockholm Declaration can be explained by previous international initiatives on conservation. These include the 1968 UN Educational, Scientific and Cultural Organization's (UNESCO) Man and the Biosphere Conference and the adoption of the 1971 Ramsar Convention on Wetlands of International Importance,[33] which focuses on the protection of a particular type of habitat and takes a holistic approach to its 'wise use'.[34] In addition, the Ramsar Convention has been considered pioneering for the involvement of civil society in its conception, negotiations, and implementation as well as for the development of its key institutional structure, such as the Secretariat and Conference of the Parties (COP), which have become common features in posterior international environmental agreements.[35]

Due to parallel negotiations under the aegis of UNESCO, delegates in Stockholm refrained from directly mentioning world heritage,[36] whereas the 1972 World Heritage Convention,[37] which was adopted shortly after the Stockholm Conference, fleshed out an intergenerational obligation of conservation within that conceptual framework. In addition, the World Heritage Convention provided, similarly to the Ramsar Convention, 'a material incentive' for developing countries to protect outstanding habitats, while imposing stricter obligations than the Ramsar Convention for listed sites.[38] A new generation of international biodiversity treaties emerged in the aftermath of the Stockholm Conference. These are focused on specific species of international concern – the 1973 Convention on International Trade in Endangered Species (CITES)[39] on species subject to international trade and the 1979 Convention on the Conservation of Migratory Species (CMS)[40] on species whose range crosses national boundaries.

33 Convention on Wetlands of International Importance Especially as Waterfowl Habitat, 1971, 996 UNTS 245; Bowman, Davies & Redgwell, n. 15, 12–13; Louis B. Sohn, 'The Stockholm Declaration on the Human Environment' (1973) 14 *Harvard International Law Journal* 423, 459.

34 Bowman, Davies & Redgwell, n. 15, 416–419; C. Max Finlayson *et al.*, 'The Ramsar Convention and Ecosystem-Based Approaches to the Wise Use and Sustainable Development of Wetlands' (2011) 14 *Journal of International Wildlife Law and Policy* 176.

35 Bowman, Davies & Redgwell, n. 15, 13.

36 Except for the 'fleeting' reference in Stockholm Declaration, n. 1, principle 4: Bowman, Davies & Redgwell, n. 15, 453.

37 Convention for the Protection of the World Cultural and Natural Heritage, 1972, 1037 UNTS 151.

38 Bowman, Davies & Redgwell, n. 15, 453–454, 481.

39 Convention on International Trade in Endangered Species of Wild Fauna and Flora, 1973, 993 UNTS 243.

40 Convention on the Conservation of Migratory Species of Wild Animals, 1979, 1651 UNTS 333.

CITES has reached a very broad membership and is still considered a 'strong' agreement with detailed international obligations and a 'collective retorsion' system that emerged over time to impose trade sanctions.[41] That said, there is an inherent bias towards targeting developing countries through the CITES compliance procedure, albeit in return for technical assistance.[42] Other commentators have noted that the complexities of CITES listings make the task of national enforcement very hard.[43] In comparison, the CMS appears 'thin on substantive commitments' and has attracted a smaller number of parties, particularly from developing countries.[44] Taken together, these two treaties can be considered to have embodied a certain degree of internationalization of listed species in the recognition of their status as shared resources. Their coverage, however, remains insufficient, and their overall approach does not necessarily target the root causes of biodiversity loss.[45]

On the whole, Ramsar, CITES, the CMS, and the World Heritage Convention are all characterized by unprecedented interactions between national and international agencies and procedures.[46] But it remains to be seen, to this day, whether they have contributed to 'dispelling the notion that nature conservation was simply a luxury [that states] could ill afford'.[47]

18.3 THE INNOVATIONS OF THE CBD

18.3.1 *Definitions and Objectives*

The negotiations and adoption of the CBD in the early 1990s revolutionized the international legal landscape on nature protection,[48] with a series of regulatory innovations – new international legal concepts (biodiversity, genetic resources,[49]

41 Elisa Morgera *et al.*, 'Implementation Challenges and Compliance in Multilateral Environmental Negotiations', in Pamela Chasek & Lynn M. Wagner (eds.), *The Roads from Rio: Lessons Learned from Twenty Years of Multilateral Environmental Negotiations* (Routledge, 2012), 222.

42 Peter H. Sand, 'Enforcing CITES: The Rise and Fall of Trade Sanctions' (2013) 22 *Review of European, Comparative and International Environmental Law* 251, 515.

43 Bowman, Davies & Redgwell, n. 15, 533.

44 *Ibid.*, 15.

45 Cyril De Klemm, 'Migratory Species in International Law' (1989) 29 *Natural Resources Journal* 935, 940, 978.

46 Bowman, Davies & Redgwell, n. 15, 14.

47 *Ibid.*, 15.

48 CBD, n. 1.

49 Rosemary Rayfuse, 'Biological Resources', in Daniel Bodansky, Jutta Brunnée & Ellen Hey (eds.), *The Oxford Handbook of International Environmental Law* (Oxford University Press, 2007), 362.

ecosystems[50]) and objectives of international regulation (sustainable use and fair and equitable benefit sharing). The treaty-based definitions of ecosystems and sustainable use, and the subsequent interpretative elaboration of the ecosystem approach represented crucial normative developments to the references to ecosystems and wise use already found in the Stockholm Declaration. And fair and equitable benefit sharing can be seen as a significant elaboration on the vague indications in the Stockholm Declaration on distributive justice and human rights.[51]

Although the CBD is widely criticized in the literature for having an 'anthropocentric bias towards development issues' and for being too vague and heavily qualified,[52] this subsection and the following will reflect on how these and other perceived weaknesses can be considered strengths. The open-ended language of the CBD and its participatory process[53] have allowed the CBD parties to develop evolving interpretations that have supported the flourishing of the seeds contained in the Stockholm Declaration with regard to environmental integration, human rights, the integration of development issues and environmental concerns, and distributive justice.

Biodiversity, rather than nature, was defined as 'the variability among living organisms' across terrestrial, marine and freshwater ecosystems.[54] It refers to diversity within species and between species, including at the genetic level. It also includes the diversity of ecosystems, which are internationally defined as 'a dynamic complex of plant, animal and micro-organism communities and their non-living environment interacting as a functional unit'.[55] It thus provides a much more multilevel and interconnected understanding of nature. It implies that the use of non-living natural resources that may affect biodiversity conservation and sustainable use, including climate change mitigation and adaptation measures, are also falling under the scope of the Convention.[56]

50 Dan Tarlock, 'Ecosystems', in Bodansky, Brunnée & Hey, n. 49, 574.

51 Elisa Morgera, *Fair and Equitable Benefit Sharing in International Law* (Oxford University Press, 2024).

52 Bowman, Davies & Redgwell, n. 15, 17–19.

53 Elisa Morgera & Elsa Tsioumani, 'Yesterday, Today and Tomorrow: Looking Afresh at the Convention on Biological Diversity' (2011) 21 *Yearbook of International Environmental Law* 3, reprinted in Freestone, n. 5.

54 CBD, n. 1, art. 2.

55 *Ibid.*

56 Elisa Morgera, 'No Need to Reinvent the Wheel for a Human Rights-Based Approach to Tackling Climate Change: The Contribution of International Biodiversity Law', in Erkki J Hollo, Kati Kulovesi & Michael Mehling (eds.), *Climate Change and the Law* (Springer, 2013), 350–390.

The Convention's definition of genetic resources also clarified that state sovereignty over natural resources extends to genetic resources.

The three objectives of the CBD, in turn, represent a landmark in international law. While previous international treaties on biodiversity were almost exclusively concerned with conservation, the CBD includes sustainable use as an objective that remains elusive in other areas of international law.[57] The CBD defines it as 'the use of components of biological diversity in a way and at a rate that does not lead to the long-term decline of biological diversity, thereby maintaining its potential to meet the needs and aspirations of present and future generations'.[58] This objective is particularly dependent on the valuation and mainstreaming of biodiversity in different sectors that directly or indirectly affect the use of forests, wetlands, and freshwater (such as mining and infrastructure development, for instance).[59] These can be seen as elaborations of the references in the Stockholm Declaration to the need to integrate nature in development planning.

The third objective has been even more innovative in two respects.[60] First, it concerns fair and equitable benefit sharing from the use of genetic resources in the context of transnational bio-based research and development, which has been spelled out in the legally binding 2014 Nagoya Protocol on Access to Genetic Resources and Benefit-Sharing.[61] But fair and equitable benefit sharing has also emerged under the CBD as a component of the ecosystem approach (discussed below),[62] as arising from the use of Indigenous Peoples' science and local communities' knowledge systems,[63] and as distinctive ecological stewardship practices in traditionally occupied or used territories, shared cultural identity, and customary norms.[64] In this connection, fair and equitable benefit sharing serves as recognition and reward for the distinctive knowledge systems, and customary sustainable management and conservation practices. This interpretation has cross-fertilized with the benefit-sharing

57 Catherine Redgwell, 'Sustainable Use of Natural Resources', in Ludwig Krämer & Emanuela Orlando (eds.), *Principles of Environmental Law* (Edward Elgar, 2018), 103, 115.

58 CBD, n. 1, art. 2.

59 CBD Decision XIV/3, 2018; CBD Decision XIII/3, 2016.

60 This paragraph draws on Elisa Morgera, 'Fair and Equitable Benefit-sharing', in Krämer & Orlando, n. 57, 323–337.

61 Nagoya Protocol on Access to Genetic Resources and the Fair and Equitable Sharing of Benefits Arising from Their Utilization, 2014, 3008 UNTS 3, Annex I.

62 CBD Decision V/6 on Principles of the Ecosystem Approach, 2000, para. 9.

63 *Ibid.*, principle 8; CBD Decision VII/11 on the Refinement and Elaboration of the Ecosystem Approach, 2004, Annex, rationale to principle 4.

64 CBD, n. 1, arts. 8(j), 10(c). See generally Brendan Tobin, *Indigenous Peoples, Customary Law and Human Rights: Why Living Law Matters* (Routledge, 2014).

safeguard that has emerged in international human rights law with regard to the protection of Indigenous Peoples' human rights to property, survival, and culture,[65] depending on their lands, territories, and natural resources.[66]

18.3.2 *The Ecosystem Approach*

The three objectives of the CBD and the new definition of ecosystems, which were already referred in the Stockholm Declaration, provided the basis for another legal innovation under the Convention – the ecosystem approach. First, the ecosystem approach concerns integration: it is aimed at integrating the management of land, water, and living resources as well as balancing the three objectives of the Convention.[67] Hence, this approach fundamentally challenges the long-embedded sectoral and fragmented approach to environmental law-making and implementation at the national and international levels,[68] prioritizing conservation and conditioning sustainable use to the limits of ecosystem functioning and ecological connectivity.[69] Second, the ecosystem approach aims to integrate modern/western science and Indigenous and local knowledge in adaptive management,[70] recognizing that human beings and their cultural diversity are an integral component of many ecosystems. Third, the ecosystem approach emphasizes equity and calls for a decentralized, social process.[71] It underscores the need for understanding and factoring in societal choices, the rights and interests of Indigenous Peoples and of local communities, as well as the intrinsic and tangible and intangible values attached to biodiversity. It also points to the challenge of ensuring the appropriate representation of community interests in the decision-making

65 African Commission on Human and Peoples' Rights, Centre for Minority Rights Development (Kenya), and Minority Rights Group International, *Endorois Welfare Council v Kenya*, Communication no. 276/2003, 25 November 2009; IACtHR, *Case of the Kaliña and Lokono Peoples v Suriname*, Judgment (Merits, Reparations and Costs), 25 November 2015.

66 Namely, United Nations Declaration on the Rights of Indigenous Peoples, UNGA Resolution 61/295, UN Doc. A/61/49, 13 September 2007, arts. 25–26. See *Report of the UN Special Rapporteur on Indigenous Peoples Rights*, UN Doc. A/HRC/15/37, 2010, paras. 76–77; John Knox, *Report of the UN Special Rapporteur on Human Rights and the Environment: Framework Principles on Human Rights and the Environment*, UN Doc. A/HRC/37/59, 2018 (*Framework Principles*) (where benefit sharing is included under Principle 15).

67 CBD Decision V/6, n. 62, para. 1.

68 Froukje Platjouw, 'The Need to Recognize a Coherent Legal System as an Important Element of the Ecosystem Approach', in Christina Voigt (ed.), *Rule of Law for Nature: New Dimensions and Ideas in Environmental Law* (Cambridge University Press, 2013), 158.

69 *Ibid.*, principle 6.

70 CBD Decision V/6, n. 62, principle 11.

71 *Ibid.*, para. 6.

process.[72] This is expected to enhance the responsibility, ownership, accountability, and participation of different stakeholders in achieving the Convention's objectives. From a normative perspective, the ecosystem approach should thus be understood as a consensus-building process, which requires good-faith efforts and a considerable investment of time and resources.[73]

Furthermore, as our knowledge of ecosystem functioning is incomplete, the ecosystem approach is tightly linked with precaution: it is predicated on the application of appropriate scientific methodologies and on the adoption of adaptive management to deal with the complex and dynamic nature of ecosystems. It also calls for a prudent approach in respecting the limits of ecosystem functioning.[74] Finally, the ecosystem approach supports the consideration of ecosystem services[75] – the benefits that humans derive from ecosystems as the result of ecological functions and processes of ecosystems, including the purification of water and air, pest and disease control, pollination, soil fertility, and resilience to climate change.[76] As a result, the ecosystem approach embodies a balancing of economic and non-economic understandings of the relationship between humans and the environment as well as the inherent tensions in this regard, which are also reflected in the concept of fairly and equitably sharing not only economic, but also sociocultural and environmental, benefits arising from biodiversity conservation and sustainable use.[77] As such, the ecosystem approach remains controversial in the literature and in practice.[78]

18.3.3 *Open-Ended yet Legally Binding*

A final novel feature of the CBD concerns its overall design and drafting style. All CBD provisions are framed in open-ended, and often qualified, terms, with a view to supporting common but differentiated responsibility as well as a bottom-up approach to defining the most appropriate implementation

72 *Ibid.*, paras. 9, 11.
73 CBD Decision VII/11, n. 63.
74 CBD Decision V/6, n. 62, paras. 2–4.
75 *Ibid.*, principle 5.
76 Millenium Ecosystem Assessment, *Living beyond Our Means: Natural Assets and Human Wellbeing* (United Nations, 2005).
77 Elisa Morgera, 'The Ecosystem Approach and the Precautionary Principle', in Elisa Morgera & Jona Razzaque (eds.), *Encyclopedia of Environmental Law: Biodiversity and Nature Protection Law* (Edward Elgar, 2017), 70–80.
78 See, e.g., Vito deLucia, *The 'Ecosystem Approach' in International Environmental Law: Genealogy and Biopolitics* (Routledge, 2019).

strategies for the local and national levels. This has allowed a wide margin of discretion in implementation for governments, which, however, can also be followed through with tokenistic or minimalistic approaches. It has also raised doubts about the legally binding nature of the CBD operative text. In particular, in relation to terms such as 'as far as possible and appropriate', the question has been raised as to whether it may in practice be impossible to identify an actual breach of obligations.[79] In the author's opinion, the correct understanding of the status of the CBD content is that all articles therein are legally binding since they are contained in a legally binding treaty and use legally binding language. Their qualifications pertain to how the obligations will be implemented, not whether they need to be implemented. Similar reasoning has been deployed, for instance, by the High Court of Australia when looking at similarly qualified language in the Word Heritage Convention.[80]

It should also be considered that the open-ended nature of the CBD text has been complemented by very intense and original soft law-making activity in the form of decisions made by the COP. Because of its broad coverage and openness to inputs from non-state actors (including representatives from Indigenous Peoples and from local communities), the COP has allowed the CBD to function as a 'catch-all regime', addressing a variety of new threats to biodiversity and the livelihoods and knowledge systems of Indigenous Peoples and local communities, far beyond the expectation of its drafters.[81] The COP has developed a multitude of sub-processes for the further refinement of the CBD provisions,[82] which have led to the intergovernmental development of guidelines for national implementation, often recommending reforms of national laws, policies, and administrative practices. Through these decisions, the CBD has also influenced how other international environmental treaties have been interpreted,[83] including earlier ones discussed in the previous subpart. Some CBD guidelines have been repeatedly recognized by international human rights bodies as relevant interpretative guidance or international standards, as discussed in the next part of this article.

79 See, e.g., Alan Boyle & Christine Chinkin, *The Making of International Law* (Oxford University Press, 2007), 220–222.

80 *Commonwealth v Tasmania*, [1983], HCA 21, 158 CLR 1, para. 24.

81 Morgera & Tsioumani, n. 53.

82 The CBD Conference of the Parties (COP) has established seven thematic work programmes. See 'Thematic Programmes and Cross-cutting Issues', *Convention on Biological Diversity*, www.cbd.int/programmes/.

83 See, e.g., CBD Decision IX/16 on Ocean Fertilization, 2008, para. 89w (catalysed developments under the Ocean Dumping regime, London Convention and London Protocol); Resolution LC-LP.1 on the Regulation of Ocean Fertilization, Doc. LC 30/16, 2008.

18.4 THE EVOLVING INTERPRETATION OF THE CBD AND HUMAN RIGHTS

There has been a growing cross-fertilization between international human rights law and the CBD. This is particularly important because, as the 2019 Global Assessment of Biodiversity and Ecosystems Services noted, biodiversity is generally declining less rapidly in Indigenous Peoples' lands than elsewhere, and, at the same time, the areas of the world projected to experience significant negative effects from global changes in climate and biodiversity are home to large concentrations of Indigenous Peoples and many of the world's poorest communities, where there is less access to social protection mechanisms (including access to health care).[84] For all these reasons, the Global Assessment underscored the need for transformative processes to tackle climate change and biodiversity loss by addressing inequalities, especially regarding income and gender, which undermine the capacity for sustainability; inclusive decision-making, as well as the fair and equitable sharing of benefits arising from the use of biodiversity and its conservation; and the recognition and respectful inclusion of the knowledge and innovations of Indigenous Peoples and local communities in environmental governance.[85]

As discussed above, the Stockholm Declaration foreshadowed the relationship between human rights and the environment, but efforts to develop mutually supportive interpretations of these two areas of international law remained limited until the late 2010s.[86] It was only following decades of progress in including the human right to a healthy environment in national constitutions,[87] the adoption of new treaties on procedural environmental rights,[88] and international human rights case law and jurisprudence[89] that

84 Diaz *et al.*, n. 26, 14–15.

85 *Ibid.*, 16.

86 Fatma Zohra Ksentini, Special Rapporteur to the Sub-Commission on the Prevention of Discrimination and Protection of Minorities, *Human Rights and the Environment: Final Report*, UN Doc. E/CN.4/Sub.2/1994/9, 1994. For a reflection on these efforts, see, e.g., Alan Boyle, 'Human Rights and the Environment: Where Next?' (2012) 23 *European Journal of International Law* 613; Ben Boer (ed.), *Environmental Law Dimensions of Human Rights* (Oxford University Press, 2015).

87 See, e.g., James R. May & Erin Daly (eds.), *Global Environmental Constitutionalism* (Cambridge University Press, 2014).

88 Convention on Access to Information, Public Participation in Decision-making and Access to Justice in Environmental Matters, 1998, 2161 UNTS 447; Escazú Agreement on Access to Information, Public Participation and Justice in Environmental Matters in Latin America and the Caribbean, 2018, 3397 UNTS 195; see, e.g., Jerzy Jendroska & Magdalena Bar (eds.), *Procedural Environmental Rights* (Intersentia, 2018).

89 Summarized in *Framework Principles*, n. 66.

the work of the UN Special Rapporteur on Human Rights and the Environment, created in 2012,[90] finally cleared the way for the international recognition in 2022 of the human right to a healthy environment by the UN General Assembly,[91] which was also recognized under the CBD in its Global Biodiversity Framework.[92]

Even before these developments, however, the CBD had made progress on human rights in an implicit way, focusing on equity as part of the ecosystem approach, through its COP decisions.[93] For instance, the CBD parties agreed that ensuring equity in protected area governance entails appropriate mechanisms for the full and effective participation of Indigenous Peoples and local communities; gender equality; customary tenure and governance systems; transparency and accountability; and fair resolution of disputes or conflicts.[94]

Perhaps the most significant contribution to human rights so far by the CBD is represented by the 2014 Akwé: Kon Guidelines on socio-cultural and environmental impact assessments, which have been relied upon in the international human rights context because they provide concrete and systematic indications on how impact assessments should be conducted to ensure respect for Indigenous Peoples' procedural and substantive human rights.[95] Besides practical guidance to implementation, the Akwé: Kon Guidelines provide hooks for more transformative changes. The integration of fair and equitable benefit sharing as part of the assessment,[96] for instance, arguably helps move away from an exclusive focus on 'damage control' that tends to characterize these exercises.[97] Instead, the consideration of benefits calls for a systematic consideration of positive implications and not only the negative

90 UNHRC Resolution 19/10, 2012 (establishing the mandate of the independent expert on human rights and the environment, which was then repeatedly renewed with the status of the special rapporteur).

91 UNGA Resolution A/RES/76/300, 2022.

92 CBD Decision XV/4, 2022, Annex, para. 7(g).

93 Elisa Morgera, 'Against All Odds: The Contribution of the Convention on Biological Diversity to International Human Rights Law', in Denis Alland *et al.* (eds.), *Unity and Diversity of International Law: Essays in Honour of Professor Pierre-Marie Dupuy* (Martinus Nijhoff, 2014), 983.

94 CBD Decision XIV/8, 2018, Annex II.

95 CBD Decision VII/16 on Akwé: Kon Voluntary Guidelines for the Conduct of Cultural, Environmental and Social Impact Assessments Regarding Developments Proposed to Take Place on, or Which Are Likely to Impact on, Sacred Sites and on Lands and Waters Traditionally Occupied or Used by Indigenous and Local Communities, 2014, section F.

96 *Ibid.*, paras. 34, 40.

97 Elisa Morgera, 'Under the Radar: Fair and Equitable Benefit-sharing and the Human Rights of Indigenous Peoples and Local Communities Connected to Natural Resources' (2019) 23 *International Journal of Human Rights* 1098; see also Neil Craik, 'Biodiversity-Inclusive Impact Assessment', in Morgera & Razzaque, n. 77, 431–444.

impacts (such as potential damage to ways of life, livelihoods, well-being, and traditional knowledge) of proposed developments.[98] Thus, the Akwé: Kon Guidelines focus on elements that support the consideration of benefits from the perspective of Indigenous Peoples, such as food, health, environmental sustainability, and community well-being, vitality, and viability (employment levels and opportunities, welfare, education, and the availability and standards of housing, infrastructure, and services).[99] With this focus, the Guidelines open up assessments to different world-views in order to take into account, in an integrated manner, Indigenous peoples' rights over lands and waters traditionally occupied or used by them as well as their associated biodiversity.[100]

Despite continued tensions among CBD parties about whether to embrace more explicitly international human rights language in COP decisions,[101] the 2017 report of the UN Special Rapporteur on Human Rights and the Environment focusing on biodiversity and ecosystem services provided an authoritative assessment of the CBD as a matter of international human rights law. It offered the unequivocal understanding that the full enjoyment of everyone's human rights to life, health, food, and water depend on healthy ecosystems and their benefits to people.[102] In other words, the protection and realization of basic human rights depend on successful efforts to prevent biodiversity loss.[103]

From a normative perspective, the cross-fertilization between the CBD and international human rights clarifies the limits for states' discretion in implementing the CBD and other international biodiversity obligations, which generally leave significant room for discretion, thereby enhancing their justiciability.[104] For instance, in a case concerning the creation of a protected area of lands traditionally occupied by Indigenous Peoples, the Inter-American Court of Human Rights clarified that states' obligations under the CBD to respect Indigenous Peoples' customary sustainable practices imply the obligation to ensure their effective participation in the creation of

98 CBD Decision VII/16, n. 95, paras. 42–43.

99 *Ibid.*, para. 40.

100 Morgera, n. 97, 1110–1111.

101 As discussed in *ibid.*; see, e.g., CBD Decision XIII/18 on Article 8(j) and Related Provisions, 2016.

102 John Knox, UN Special Rapporteur on Human Rights and the Environment, *Report on Biodiversity*, UN Doc. A/HRC/34/49, 2017, para. 5.

103 *Ibid.*, as discussed in Elisa Morgera, 'Dawn of a New Day? The Evolving Relationship between the Convention on Biological Diversity and International Human Rights Law' (2018) 54 *Wake Forest Law Review* 691.

104 Morgera, n. 97, 1104.

protected areas; their continued access and use of traditional territories, including those within the protected areas; and their sharing in the benefits arising from conservation initiatives. In doing so, the Court emphasized that these obligations are also a matter of respect for Indigenous Peoples' human rights to a dignified life and cultural identity.[105]

From an accountability perspective, this cross-fertilization compensates for the fact that the CBD has yet to develop a systematic and credible system for monitoring implementation by states, so the opportunity to assess compliance with the CBD as part of international human rights monitoring systems has already been identified in the literature.[106] For instance, the Committee on the Elimination of Racial Discrimination underscored that Suriname did not ensure adequate socio-cultural and environmental impact assessments in accordance with the CBD Akwé: Kon Guidelines, as part of its obligations to respect Indigenous and tribal peoples' human rights.[107]

The cross-fertilization with international human rights law can also matter in terms of clarifying the legal status of the CBD guidelines. The CBD parties often emphasize their voluntary nature, but only in two exceptional cases have they expressed the intention to limit their interpretative value (either as subsequent agreement or subsequent practice)[108] in order to pre-empt limitations on states' discretion in developing national legislation.[109] Even in the few exceptional cases in which parties have excluded their value as treaty interpretation tools, the CBD guidelines can arguably be considered as 'best practices' that serve to 'facilitate the implementation' of existing international obligations and should be 'adopt[ed] as expeditiously as possible'.[110] This is because it becomes increasingly difficult for a state to defend any substandard

105 IACtHR, *Case of Kaliña and Lokono Peoples v Suriname*, Judgment (Merits, Reparations and Costs), 25 November 2015, paras. 181, 193 (*Kaliña and Lokono Peoples*).

106 Morgera, n. 97.

107 Committee on the Elimination of Racial Discrimination, *Concluding Observations on the Combined Thirteenth to Fifteenth Periodic Reports of Suriname*, UN Doc. CERD/C/SUR/CO/13-15, 2015, para. 26.

108 Vienna Convention on the Law of Treaties, 1969, 1155 UNTS 331, art. 31(3)(a), (b).

109 CBD Decision XIII/18 on the CBD Mo'otz Kuxtal Voluntary Guidelines for the Development of Mechanisms, Legislation or Other Appropriate Initiatives to Ensure the 'Prior and Informed Consent', 'Free, Prior and Informed Consent', or 'Approval and Involvement', Depending on National Circumstances, of Indigenous Peoples and Local Communities for Accessing Their Knowledge, Innovations and Practices, for Fair and Equitable Sharing of Benefits Arising from the Use of Their Knowledge, Innovations and Practices Relevant for the Conservation and Sustainable Use of Biological Diversity, and for Reporting and Preventing Unlawful Appropriation of Traditional Knowledge, 2016, note 4.

110 Morgera, n. 103, 119–120 (applying by analogy the reasoning in Knox's *Framework Principles*, n. 66).

approach, particularly when the state has joined the consensus in accepting these guidelines after its participation in intergovernmental negotiations. Consensus adoption by 196 parties to the CBD had, in practical terms, a 'powerful law-making effect' with it 'securing widespread support for a text that legitimises and promotes consistent State practice'.[111] An additional argument about the legal value of these guidelines is derived from the legally binding international human rights law, to which the interpretation of CBD decisions is considered relevant. For instance, the Inter-American Court of Human Rights indicated that the creation of specific mechanisms that guarantee fair and equitable benefit sharing from the use of biological resources with Indigenous Peoples, on the basis of the CBD, was a matter of international law on political rights.[112] Along similar lines, the CBD and related COP decisions can also be considered relevant in interpreting the international legally binding obligations of the states that are party to the 1965 Convention on the Elimination of All Forms of Racial Discrimination,[113] the 1966 International Covenant on Economic, Social and Cultural Rights (with regard to everyone's right to health, food, and water),[114] the 1979 Convention on the Elimination of All Forms of Discrimination against Women,[115] and the 1989 Convention on the Rights of the Child.[116]

Finally, as the CBD guidelines are explicitly aimed at influencing not only the conduct of the CBD parties but also private companies, they have been relied upon in international corporate accountability standard-setting and monitoring initiatives, for the purpose of complementing the 2011 UN Framework and Guiding Principles on Business and Human Rights.[117] The CBD decisions therefore represent intergovernmentally approved standards for business responsibility to respect human rights in the context of activities

[111] Boyle & Chinkin, n. 79, 160.

[112] *Kaliña and Lokono Peoples*, n. 105, para. 197.

[113] International Convention on the Elimination of all Forms of Racial Discrimination, 1965, 660 UNTS 195.

[114] International Covenant on Economic, Social and Cultural Rights, 1966, 993 UNTS 3.

[115] Convention on the Elimination of all Forms of Discrimination against Women, 1979, 1249 UNTS 13.

[116] Convention on the Rights of the Child, 1989, 1577 UNTS 3; *General Comment no. 26 on Children's Rights and the Environment with a Special Focus on Climate Change*, UN Doc. CRC/C/GC/26, 2023. This paragraph builds on Elisa Morgera, *Biodiversity as a Human Right and Its Implications for the EU's External Action*, Report to the European Parliament, 2020.

[117] *Guiding Principles on Business and Human Rights to Implement the UN Protect, Respect and Remedy Framework*, UN Doc. A/HRC/17/31, 2011 (adopted by the Human Rights Council in Resolution 17/4), 6 July 2011.

that negatively affect biodiversity conservation and sustainable use, ranging from extractives to climate change response measures.[118]

18.5 THE OCEAN–CLIMATE NEXUS AND TRANSFORMATIVE CHANGE

As mentioned above, the Stockholm Declaration was characterized by a sectoral approach to environmental issues. This remains a characteristic of the vast body of treaty law in this area. However, it has become increasingly clear that the triple planetary crises are interconnected[119] and that efforts to address one environmental issue in isolation from others not only are ineffective but also can lead to human rights violations. This is most prominently the case with respect to climate change response measures.[120] As part of the current efforts to better connect disparate areas of international environmental law, it has also become clear that the protection of the marine environment has lagged behind compared to land-based environmental measures, including with regard to climate change[121] and human rights.[122] The Stockholm Declaration merely pointed to marine pollution, which has been one of the dominant areas in the development of international law on the protection of the marine environment.

In 2024, however, the International Tribunal for the Law of the Sea (ITLOS) clarified that marine pollution include greenhouse gas emissions[123]

118 Elisa Morgera, *Corporate Environmental Accountability in International Law* (2nd ed., Oxford University Press, 2020).

119 *General Comment no.* 26, n. 116, paras. 5, 63–64.

120 See, e.g., Ian Fry, UN Special Rapporteur on Climate Change and Human Rights, *Promotion and Protection of Human Rights in the Context of Climate Change*, UN Doc. A/77/226, 2022; Human Rights Council Advisory Committee, *Impact of New Technologies Intended for Climate Protection on the Enjoyment of Human Rights*, UN Doc. A/HRC/54/47, 10 August 2023.

121 Elisa Morgera *et al.*, 'Ocean-based Climate Action and Human Rights Implications under the International Climate Change Regime' (2023) 38 *International Journal of Marine and Coastal Law (IJMCL)* 411.

122 Nathan J. Bennet *et al.*, 'Environmental (In)Justice in the Anthropocene Ocean' (2022) 147 *Marine Policy* 105383.

123 The notion of marine pollution including greenhouse gas emissions had already been widely supported in the literature. See, e.g., Alan Boyle, 'Protecting the Marine Environment from Climate Change: The LOSC Part XII Regime', in Elise Johansen, Signe Veierud Busch & Ingvild Ulrikke Jakobsen (eds.), *The Law of the Sea and Climate Change: Solutions and Constraints* (Cambridge University Press, 2020), 8; Elisa Morgera & Mitchell Lennan, 'Ensuring Mutual Supportiveness of the Paris Agreement with Other Multilateral Environmental Agreements: A Focus on Ocean-Based Climate Action', in Alexander Zahar (ed.), *Research Handbook on the Law of the Paris Agreement* (Edward Elgar, 2024).

and that the obligations under the law of the sea on the protection and restoration of marine biodiversity are relevant for climate change mitigation and adaptation,[124] ensuring a more integrated interpretation of the international obligations on the protection of the marine environment, biodiversity, and climate change. These clarifications came on the back of a vast area of scholarship and international practice on the need to expand and clarify the law of the sea with respect to biodiversity.[125] The CBD, as a catch-all regime, promptly identified interconnections between environmental issues and has been developing integrated responses since the 2010s. The CBD parties have systematically identified potential and actual threats that climate change and climate change response measures pose to the conservation and sustainable use of biodiversity, along with ways to assess and prevent negative impacts on biodiversity through the mutually supportive interpretation and application of international climate and biodiversity law. These contributions have been based on the CBD ecosystem approach and have (often implicitly) contributed to defining a rights-based approach to climate change adaptation and mitigation, mainly with regard to the human rights of Indigenous peoples and local communities.[126]

For instance, the CBD parties committed to adopting an ecosystem-based approach to climate change mitigation, including when updating their nationally determined contributions and pursuing domestic climate action under the 2015 Paris Agreement, taking into account the importance of ensuring the integrity and functionality of all ecosystems, including oceans.[127] In addition, in 2008, the CBD COP had already emphasized the importance of marine protected areas, inland waters protected areas, coastal resource management, and marine spatial planning in protecting and building the resilience of marine and coastal ecosystems, communities, and infrastructure against the impacts of climate change.[128] In 2010, the CBD COP proposed to integrate climate change-related aspects of marine and coastal biodiversity into relevant national strategies, action plans, and programmes as well as into the design and management of marine and coastal protected

124 ITLOS, *Request for an Advisory Opinion Submitted by the Commission of Small Island States on Climate Change and International Law*, Advisory Opinion, Case no. 31, 21 May 2024 (*Request for an Advisory Opinion on Climate Change*).

125 See, e.g., Louise A. de La Fayette, 'A New Regime for the Conservation and Sustainable Use of Marine Biodiversity and Genetic Resources beyond the Limits of National Jurisdiction' (2009) 24 *IJMCL* 221.

126 Morgera, n. 56; Morgera, n. 93.

127 CBD Decision XIV/5 on Biodiversity and Climate Change, 2018; Paris Agreement on Climate Change, 2015, 3156 UNTS 79.

128 CBD Decision XIII/4 on Biodiversity and Climate Change, 2016, para. 5.

areas.[129] It addressed specific climate change-related issues, such as ocean acidification and coral bleaching, with specific attention to impacts on reef-dependent coastal communities.[130] The COP also developed voluntary guidelines for the design and effective implementation of ecosystem-based approaches to adaptation and disaster risk reduction that are also relevant for the protection of the marine environment.[131]

On the whole, the CBD COP has systematically identified concrete opportunities to integrate parties' initiatives at the national level as well as through international cooperation, recognizing that the effects of climate change are disproportionate for, and require the full and effective participation of, Indigenous Peoples and local communities. More gradually, the CBD COP also called attention to the role of women in climate change mitigation and adaptation and, to a lesser extent, of youth and older people, both in terms of their local-level action and the integration of their strategic needs in the design of ecosystem-based adaptation tools.[132] These developments are particularly significant because, despite the 2022 recognition of the need to address ocean-based climate action under the Paris Agreement[133] and its importance from a human rights perspective,[134] it remains unclear whether the international climate change regime will be able to take timely ecosystem- and human rights-based ocean climate action. This is due to limited public participation in the process as well as the well-documented negative impacts on biodiversity and on the human rights of land-based climate change response measures.[135]

While the extent of the influence of the CBD guidance on implementation practices under the international climate change regime remains a matter of contention,[136] ITLOS has now clarified states' strict due diligence mitigation

129 *Ibid.*, para. 7.

130 CBD Decision XII/23 on Marine and Coastal Biodiversity: Impacts on Marine and Coastal Biodiversity of Anthropogenic Underwater Noise and Ocean Acidification, Priority Actions to Achieve Aichi Biodiversity Target 10 for Coral Reefs and Closely Associated Ecosystems, and Marine Spatial Planning and Training Initiatives, 2014, paras. 8.1.b, 8.3.c–g, 8.8c; CBD Decision XIV/5, n. 127, paras. 9, 10(f).

131 CBD Decision XIV/5, n. 127.

132 *Ibid.*, paras. 3(g), 5(c); see also CBD Decision XIII/4, n. 128, preamble; Victoria Jenkins, 'Gender and the Convention on Biological Diversity', in Morgera & Razzaque, n. 77, 331–345.

133 *Glasgow Climate Pact*, Doc. CP.26/1, CMA.3/1, 2021.

134 Mitchell Lennan & Elisa Morgera, 'The Glasgow Climate Conference (COP26)' (2022) 37 *IJMCL* 137.

135 Morgera *et al.*, n. 121.

136 The lack of cross-reference in decisions taken in the context of the international climate change regime to relevant decisions taken in the context of the CBD has been emphasized by Harro van Asselt, 'Managing the Fragmentation of International Environmental Law: Forests at the Intersection of the Climate and Biodiversity Regimes' (2012) 44 *New York University*

obligations, which are additional to those contained in the Paris Agreement, to conserve and restore marine biodiversity enhancing carbon sequestration, while referring also to 'human rights concerns'.[137] In that connection, the Tribunal's clarification about states' obligation to undertake environmental and socio-economic impact assessment for any planned activity that may contribute to climate change, in accordance with the precautionary and ecosystem approaches, and to take into account climate change impacts on marine ecosystems that will put 'key cultural dimensions of lives and livelihoods at risk',[138] provide entry points for applying international human rights law.[139]

In 2025 the legal value of the CBD and its guidance for the international climate change regime, the law of the sea and human rights[140] has been unequivocally confirmed in the advisory opinions on climate change of the International Court of Justice[141] and the Inter-American Court of Human Rights.[142]

In the near future, the implementation of the innovative obligations to address in a holistic way the objectives of the law of the sea, international biodiversity law, and international climate change law that have been enshrined in the 2023 UN Agreement on Marine Biodiversity of Areas beyond National Jurisdiction may provide further openings for the consideration of human rights.[143]

18.6 CONCLUSIONS

Some of the most forward-looking concepts enshrined in the 1972 Stockholm Declaration have guided the progressive development of international biodiversity law for fifty years, notably the need for cosmopolitan cooperation that

Journal of International Law and Politics 1205, 1240 (referring specifically to decisions on forests).

137 *Request for an Advisory Opinion on Climate Change*, n. 124, paras. 390, 400, 441(3)(b–c), and 66. On the applicability of international human rights law, see the declarations of Judges Infante, Caffi, and Pawlak.

138 *Ibid.*, paras. 414, 410.

139 Elisa Morgera, *Scene-setting Report of the UN Special Rapporteur on Climate Change and Human Rights*, UN Doc. A/HRC/56/46, 2024.

140 See Elisa Morgera, 'One Ocean Hub Submission to the International Tribunal for the Law of the Sea', *ITLOS*, 2023, www.itlos.org/fileadmin/itlos/documents/cases/31/written_statements/4/C31-WS-4-10-OOH.pdf.

141 ICJ, *Advisory Opinion on the Obligations of States in Respect of Climate Change*, 23 July 2025.

142 IACtHR, *Advisory Opinion on the Climate Emergency and Human Rights*, 29 May 2025.

143 Elisa Morgera *et al.*, 'Addressing the Ocean-Climate Nexus in the BBNJ Agreement: Strategic Environmental Assessments, Human Rights and Equity in Ocean Science' (2023) 38 *IJMCL* 447; *Agreement under the United Nations Convention on the Law of the Sea on the Conservation and Sustainable Use of Marine Biological Diversity of Areas beyond National Jurisdiction*, Doc. C.N.203.2023.TREATIES-XXI.10, 19 June 2023.

takes into account distributive justice issues and human rights.[144] At the same time, the sectoral and largely incremental approach of the Stockholm Declaration is no longer fit to address the urgent triple planetary crises that we are facing. Rather, a transformative change has been invoked[145] – a shift away 'from the technocratic and regulatory fix of environmental problems to more fundamental and transformative changes in social-political processes and economic relations'.[146]

International biodiversity law, in its interactions with human rights, can contribute to such transformative change, by focusing on 'environmental and social justice issues'[147] that are interwoven with the ocean in less visible ways than terrestrial biodiversity.[148] It can contribute to ensuring that solutions, including climate change response measures, have sustainable impacts at other scales and in other sectors; and empowering those whose interests are currently not being met and who represent transformative sustainability values. In particular, the CBD guidance is relevant to 'transdisciplinary governance' (the recognition of different knowledge systems and the inclusion of under-represented types of knowledge).[149] This is an element of transformative governance that can contribute to the protection of cultural and procedural rights, thereby addressing, from a legal perspective, the 'politics of transformative change',[150] preventing a shifting of the burden of response onto the vulnerable, avoiding discriminatory decisions, and addressing issues of power and legitimacy.[151]

144 Elisa Morgera, 'SDG 15', in Ebbesson & Hey, n. 4, 376.
145 Bolanle Erinosho *et al.*, 'Transformative Governance for Ocean Biodiversity', in Ingrid J. Visseren-Hamakers & Marcel T. J. Kok (eds.), *Transforming Biodiversity Governance* (Cambridge University Press, 2022), 313–338.
146 Ingrid J. Visseren-Hamakers & Marcel T. J. Kok, 'Introduction', in Visseren-Hamakers & Kok, n. 145, 3.
147 *Ibid.*
148 Bennet *et al.*, n. 122.
149 Erinosho *et al.*, n 146, 314.
150 Visseren-Hamakers & Kok, n. 146, 12.
151 Erinosho *et al.*, n. 145, 328.

19

Aspirations of Developing Countries in Biodiversity Treaty-Making Processes: Dreams Deferred?

Dire D. Tladi

19.1 INTRODUCTION

The modern framework of biodiversity governance is built upon a network of treaties underpinned by the 1992 Convention on Biological Diversity (Biodiversity Convention).[1] These include, in addition to the Biodiversity Convention, the 2000 Cartagena Protocol on Biosafety,[2] the 2014 Nagoya Protocol on Access and Benefit-Sharing,[3] and the 2010 Nagoya-Kuala Lumpur Supplementary Protocol on Liability and Redress.[4] This intricate treaty system on which biodiversity governance is founded was made possible by the 1972 Stockholm Conference on the Human Environment. Of course, there are many other treaties relevant to biodiversity – in particular, wildlife treaties, many of which were adopted in the 1970s in the aftermath of the Stockholm Conference and which, no doubt, form part of the network of treaties. This chapter, however, focuses on the narrow network of treaties based on the Biodiversity Convention because it is that network of treaties on which the modern framework for biodiversity governance is built. The treaties underpinning this framework all aim to protect the environment, and biodiversity, in particular, while paying attention to the specific needs of the environment.

1 Convention on Biological Diversity, 1992, 1760 UNTS 79 (Biodiversity Convention).

2 Cartagena Protocol on Biosafety to Convention on Biodiversity, 2000, 2226 UNTS 208 (Cartagena Protocol).

3 Nagoya Protocol on Access to Genetic Resources and the Fair and Equitable Sharing of Benefits Arising from Their Utilization to the Convention on Biological Diversity, 2014, 3008 UNTS 3 (Nagoya Protocol).

4 Nagoya-Kuala Lumpur Supplementary Protocol on Liability to the Cartagena Protocol on Biosafety, 2010, 3240 UNTS A-30619 (Nagoya-Kuala Lumpur Supplementary Protocol).

The 1972 Stockholm Conference contributed to biodiversity governance in various ways.[5] First, at the institutional level, the Biodiversity Convention, which was the centre piece of this governance network, was the result of a series of decisions adopted at the UN Environment Programme (UNEP), which itself emerged from the Stockholm Conference.[6] Second, the 1972 Stockholm Declaration on the Human Environment set out the fundamental principles underpinning modern international environmental law and biodiversity governance.[7] For example, the Stockholm Declaration is the first global instrument to provide for the principle that 'States have ... the sovereign right to exploit their own resources ... and the responsibility to ensure that activities within their jurisdiction or control do not cause damage to the environment of other States or of areas beyond national jurisdiction'.[8] This principle, together with the principle that 'natural resources of the earth ... must be safeguarded for the benefit of present and future generations',[9] are key elements of the modern global framework for biodiversity governance.[10]

The Stockholm Conference contributed to the modern biodiversity framework in another, more fundamental, way: it was the Stockholm Conference that gave impetus to the rise of sustainable development, the concept that resulted in a fundamental change in international environmental law and

5 On the Stockholm Conference generally, see Dinah Shelton, 'Stockholm Declaration (1972) and Rio Declaration (1992)', in *Max Planck Encyclopedia of Public International Law* (Oxford University Press, 2008).

6 See Dire Tladi, *Sustainable Development in International Law: An Analysis of Key Enviro-Economic Instruments* (Pretoria University Law Press, 2007), 20 ('institutionally, an important consequence of the Stockholm Conference was the establishment of the United Nations Environment Programme'); see also Recommendation 4 of the 'Action Plan for the Human Environment', in *Report of the United Nations Conference on the Human Environment*, UN Doc. A/CONF.48/14/Rev.1, 16 June 1972 (which provided for the establishment of a 'central body' entrusted with 'over-all responsibility' for an 'agreed programme' on the environment). For an accessible history of the UN Environment Programme (UNEP), see Konrad von Moltke, 'Why UNEP Matters' (1996) *Green Globe Yearbook* 55, 56; see also Mark Allan Gray, 'The United Nations Environment Programme: An Assessment' (1990) 20 *Environmental Law* 291, 294.

7 'Declaration of the United Nations Conference on the Human Environment', in *Report of the UN Conference on the Human Environment*, UN Doc. A/CONF.48/14/Rev.1, 16 June 1972 (Stockholm Declaration).

8 See *ibid.*, principle 21.

9 *Ibid.*, principle 2.

10 See, e.g., Biodiversity Convention, n. 1, art. 3, titled 'Principle', which recalls that 'States have, in accordance with the Charter of the United Nations and the principles of international law, the sovereign right to exploit their own resources pursuant to their own environmental policies, and the responsibility to ensure that activities within their jurisdiction or control do no cause damage to the environment of other States or of areas beyond the limits of national jurisdiction'.

policy.[11] At the substantive level, the biodiversity framework is very much a framework founded on the law of sustainable development. The interests, countervailing interests, compromises, and trade-offs that are at the heart of sustainable development discourse, are reflected also in the biodiversity framework. These include questions of equity and addressing concerns of developing countries. At the same time, the 1992 Rio Conference on Environment and Development, the progeniture of the Stockholm Conference, was instrumental in mainstreaming the idea of regimes, built on framework conventions and developed over time. The regimes are built not only through the adoption of protocols but also through the establishment of machinery, in the form of conferences of the parties, that facilitate substantive discussions of gaps and, thus, the elaboration of protocols and other instruments as needed. Of course, this approach to international environmental law-making was not invented at the Rio Conference. Rather, it can also be traced back to the Stockholm Conference, as reflected in the regional 1979 Convention on Long-Range Transboundary Air Pollution and the 1985 Convention for the Protection of the Ozone Layer.[12] Yet the biodiversity and climate change regimes, which are the two main treaty instruments to come out of the Rio Conference, took this idea to a whole new level.

Against this background, this chapter provides some comments on the process of building the biodiversity treaty framework from the perspective of developing countries. In particular, it observes that often, groups of developing countries come into treaty negotiations with particular interests – in fact, sometimes, it is those interests that are the reasons for the launch of negotiations. Yet, at the end of the negotiations, those interests, at times, were the ones that were least accounted for in the treaty concerned. In the next section, I will consider this claim through a survey of biodiversity instruments adopted under the framework of the Biodiversity Convention, in particular, the Cartagena Protocol, the Nagoya Protocol, and the Kuala Lumpur Supplementary Protocol. I will also briefly consider another biodiversity instrument that is outside the Biodiversity Convention family and also just outside the time span of 1972–2022 – namely, the 2023 Agreement on Biodiversity in Areas beyond National Jurisdiction (BBNJ Agreement) under the 1982 UN Convention on the Law of the Sea (UNCLOS), which, it will be argued, shows traces of the same trend.[13]

11 See von Moltke, n. 6.

12 Convention on Long-Range Transboundary Air Pollution, 1979, 1302 UNTS 217; Vienna Convention for the Protection of the Ozone Layer, 1985, 1513 UNTS 323.

13 Agreement under the United Nations Convention on the Law of the Sea on the Conservation and Sustainable Use of Marine Biological Diversity, Doc. A/Conf.232/2023/4, 19 June 2023

A caveat! This chapter is not concerned with the merits or demerits of the positions of any of the protagonists but, rather, with the manner in which the aspirations of developing countries – generally, the largest negotiating bloc – have been dealt with in treaty negotiations.[14] A second caveat! The chapter refers to developing countries without seeking to define what is meant by this concept. In some instances – in particular, in the negotiations of the Biodiversity Convention – the Group of Seventy-seven (G-77) and China represented developing countries. Yet, in the negotiations on the two protocols adopted at Nagoya, developing countries did not adopt unified positions. For example, South Africa and Brazil prevented the formulation of a G77 group position in those treaty negotiations. The position of developing countries was thus carried forward by a group consisting of the Africa group, minus South Africa, and a large proportion of developing countries lead by Malaysia and excluding states like South Africa, Brazil, and Argentina.

19.2 BUILDING THE BIODIVERSITY REGIME WHILE DEFERRING ASPIRATIONS

19.2.1 *Biodiversity Convention and Deferred Aspirations*

As alluded to in the introduction, the Stockholm Conference was critical for the emergence of the current framework of international environmental law generally and, more particularly, the modern governance framework of biodiversity. It is useful therefore to set the context by describing the 'lay of the land' at the time of the 1972 Stockholm Conference. At that time, much of international environmental law was rudimentary and lacked the extensive

(BBNJ Agreement); UN Convention on the Law of the Sea, 1982, 1833 UNTS 397 (UNCLOS).

14 For examples of my views on some of the issues addressed in this chapter, see Dire Tladi, 'The Biosafety Protocol and the Promotion of Sustainable Development: With One Hand It Giveth, with the Savings Clause It Taketh' (2006) 39 *Comparative and International Law Journal of Southern Africa* 83; Dire Tladi, 'Civil Liability in the Context of the Cartagena Protocol: To Be or Not to Be (Binding)' (2010) 1 *International Environmental Agreements: Politics, Law and Economics* (*IEA*) 15; Dire Tladi, 'The Common Heritage of Mankind and the Proposed Treaty on Areas beyond National Jurisdiction' (2014) 25 *Yearbook of International Environmental Law* 113; Dire Tladi, 'An Institutional Framework for Addressing Marine Genetic Resources under the Proposed Treaty for Marine Biological Diversity in Areas beyond National Jurisdiction' (2019) 19 *IEA*485; Dire Tladi, 'Challenges and Opportunities in the Implementation of the Supplementary Protocol: Reinterpretation and Re-imagination', in Akiho Shibata (ed.), *International Liability Regime for Biodiversity Damage* (Routledge, 2014); see also *Sustainable Development in International Law: An Analysis of Key Enviro-Economic Instruments* (Pretoria University Law Press, 2007), 159–203.

network of multilateral treaties that today might be taken for granted. This is not to say that there were no multilateral treaties before the Stockholm Conference. Multilateral treaties concluded earlier than the Stockholm Conference include, for example, the 1900 Convention Designed to Ensure the Conservation of Various Species of Wild Animals in Africa Which Are Useful to Man or Inoffensive and the 1933 Convention Relative the Preservation of Fauna and Flora in Their Natural State.[15] It was also during this era that the 1946 International Convention for the Regulation of Whaling was adopted.[16]

Yet, while there were certainly environmental treaties before 1972, the Stockholm Conference marked the beginning of an explosion in multilateral treaty making. The conference is often credited with the establishment of a multitude of international environmental agreements, including the Regional Seas Programme and other treaty regimes.[17] The treaties that can be traced back to the Stockholm Conference include the 1973 Convention on Trade in Endangered Species and the 1989 Basel Convention on Transboundary Movement of Hazardous Wastes.[18] The Rio Conference, at which the Biodiversity Convention was adopted, was itself a product of the Stockholm Conference. It was on the basis of a recommendation by the Brundtland Commission, which itself was established on the basis of a recommendation by the UNEP Governing Council in 1983, that the UN General Assembly (UNGA) decided in 1989 to convene the conference.[19]

In addition to initiating the process that led to the Rio Conference, which birthed the Biodiversity Convention, UNEP was also at the heart of the elaboration of the Convention itself. In 1987, the UNEP Governing Council, having expressed concern about 'the disappearance of plant and animal species as a result of the destruction of their habitats' and having identified the 'need for adequate protection and preservation of biological

15 See Ulrich Beyerlin & Jenny Grote Stoutenburg, 'Environment, International Protection', in *Max Planck Encyclopedia of Public International Law* (Oxford University Press, 2013), para. 4; see also Edith Brown Weiss, 'International Environmental Law: Contemporary Issues and the Emergence of a New World Order' (1993) 81 *Georgetown Law Journal* 675, 675ff.

16 International Convention for the Regulation of Whaling, 1946, 161 UNTS 72.

17 See Tladi, n. 6, 20ff.

18 Convention on Trade in Endangered Species of Wild Fauna and Flora, 1973, 993 UNTS 243; Basel Convention on the Control of Transboundary Movements of Hazardous Wastes and Their Disposal, 1989, 1673 UNTS 126.

19 See UNGA Resolution 44/228 on the Convening of the Conference, 22 December 1989, para. 1 ('decides to convene the United Nations Conference on Environment and Development, which shall be of two weeks' duration and shall have the highest possible level of participation, to coincide with World Environment Day, on 5 June 1992').

diversity', requested the executive director of UNEP to establish an ad hoc group of experts to consider 'the desirability and possible form of an umbrella convention' to rationalize activities impacting on biological diversity.[20] In 1989, the Governing Council authorized the establishment of an ad hoc working group of legal and technical experts – later renamed the Intergovernmental Negotiation Committee.[21]

The Biodiversity Convention proclaims, as its objectives, three interrelated pillars – namely, the conservation of biological diversity, the sustainable use of its components, and the fair and equitable sharing of the benefits arising from its use.[22] As is the case with sustainable development in general, the Biodiversity Convention concerns both issues of distribution and conservation, which creates schisms along North-South lines.[23] For developing countries, two interrelated issues were of particular importance. The first concerned genetic modification and the risks that it posed to the biodiversity of developing countries. The second issue concerned the equitable sharing of benefits arising from the use of genetic resources. Genetic resources (which are at the heart of the second issue) are raw materials for biotechnology (which is at heart of the first issue).[24] Both of these issues essentially concern the allocation of risks/costs and benefits from the use of biotechnology.[25]

During the negotiations of the Biodiversity Convention, the focus of many states was on rules intended to limit the use of biodiversity in order to preserve biodiversity. Developing countries, however, also sought to include provisions addressing the potential impact of biotechnology and biosafety issues in the treaty being negotiated.[26] While the negotiations on the Convention

20 UNEP Governing Council Decision 14/26, 10 July 1987, para. 1.

21 UNEP Governing Council Decision 15/34, 15 May 1989, para. 6.

22 Biodiversity Convention, n. 1, art. 1.

23 G. Kristin Rosendal, *The Convention on Biological Diversity and Developing Countries* (Kluwer, 2000), 4 ('[w]hile the main bulk of biological diversity is situated in the "South", it is primarily the developed countries that have the economic and (bio)technological capacity to extract the full commercial benefits from these resources … the negotiations on [the Biodiversity Convention] have thus concerned distribution as well as conservation issues').

24 Kristin Rosendal, 'The Convention on Biological Diversity: A Viable Instrument for Conservation and Sustainable Use?' (1995) 71 *Green Globe Yearbook of International Cooperation on Environment and Development* 69, 70.

25 David R. Downes, 'New Diplomacy for the Biodiversity Trade: Biodiversity, Biotechnology, and Intellectual Property in the Convention on Biological Diversity' (1993) 4 *Touro Journal of Transnational Law* 2, 3; see also Rosendal, n. 23, 70.

26 See, e.g., Robert Falkner, 'Negotiating the Biosafety Protocol: The International Process', in Christopher Bail, Robert Falkner & Helen Marquand (eds.), *The Cartagena Protocol on Biosafety: Reconciling Trade in Biotechnology with Environment and Development?* (Earthscan, 2002), 6.

proceeded at a rapid pace – one author describes the process as having been completed 'in near record-time'[27] – the issue of addressing biotechnology emerged fairly early in the process. Indeed, even before the commencement of the negotiations on the Convention in 1985, the UN Industrial Development Organization, UNEP, and the World Health Organization had begun considering the adequacy of safety rules and protocols pertaining to genetic modification.[28]

Developing countries feared that the introduction of genetically modified organisms (GMOs) – or living modified organisms – posed a risk to human health and could impact negatively on socio-economic security.[29] Indeed, while the European Union (EU) also sought to regulate GMOs, the concerns of the EU were mainly based on the potential threat to the environment.[30] Of course, other states, most notably the United States, Japan, and others, did not believe that GMOs posed any risk beyond that posed by other products.[31] The outcome of the negotiations on this issue was that the Biodiversity Convention did not regulate GMOs. Instead, the Convention kicked the issue down the line, deferring it for a later instrument. While biotechnology is addressed in general, non-invasive ways in the Biodiversity Convention, the provision most relevant for the regulation of biotechnology and its potential impact on human health, the environment, and socio-economic conditions in the developing world is Article 19(3): 'The Parties shall consider the need for and

27 Melinda Chandler, 'The Biodiversity Convention: Selected Issues of Interest to the International Lawyer' (1993) 4 *Colorado Journal of International Environmental Law and Policy* 141, 143; see also Catherine Tinker, 'A "New Breed" of Treaty: The United Nations Convention on Biological Diversity' (1995) 12 *Pace Environmental Law Review* 191, 191 (explaining that the rapid pace of the negotiations was due in part to the desire to adopt the Convention at the Rio Conference).

28 Hamdallah Zedan, 'The Road to the Biosafety Protocol', in Bail, Falkner & Marquand, n. 26, 28.

29 For a discussion, see Lakshman Guruswamy, 'Sustainable Agriculture: Do GMOs Imperil Biosafety?' (2002) 9 *Indiana Journal of Global Legal Studies* 461; see also Aarti Gupta, 'Governing Trade in Genetically Modified Organisms: The Cartegena Protocol on Biosafety' (2000) 42 *Environment: Science and Policy for Sustainable Development* 22.

30 Gupta, n. 29, 23. The middle position, occupied by the European Union (EU), is aptly captured by Catherine Tinker, n. 27, 213 ('for years, the United States has strictly maintained that there is no danger at all from biotechnology, and therefore no need for [regulation]. This position has been modified by the OECD countries, generally to that of a gradual approach to the question of regulation, with the EU in support of drawing up short-term technical guidelines on biosafety').

31 See generally David Schnier, 'Genetically Modified Organisms and the Cartagena Protocol' (2001) 12 *Fordham Environmental Law Journal* 377; see also an article that can only be described as unabashed advocacy, Chandler, n. 27, 166 ('first, there is no evidence that biotechnology as a process is in itself a threat to biological diversity. To single it out in the Convention, with no reference to other technologies ... is indefensible').

modalities of a protocol setting out appropriate procedures, including, in particular, advance informed agreement, in the field of the safe transfer, handling and use of any living modified organisms resulting from biotechnology that may have adverse effect on the conservation and sustainable use of biological diversity.'

With respect to the question of the equitable sharing of benefits derived from genetic resources sourced from the territories of developing countries, the aspirations of developing countries were deferred in a different way. The highest proportion of genetic materials necessary for biotechnology is to be found in developing countries.[32] Yet the technological advancement necessary for the profitable exploitation of these genetic materials is to be found in the developed world.[33] Developing countries were concerned about biotech accessing genetic materials from biodiversity rich countries in the South and patenting products derived from such genetic materials.[34] For developing countries, it was unjust and inequitable for entities from developed countries to make profits from genetic materials sourced from the South without any compensation, particularly so when the populations of those developing countries could not afford the products.[35] In many ways, the argument of the developing countries was based on the bedrock principle of the Biodiversity Convention, which had its roots in principle 21 of the Stockholm Declaration – sovereignty over natural resources. For developing countries, therefore, genetic resources could not be treated as 'common heritage', and the principle of sovereignty of resources dictated control over such genetic resources and, therefore, an equitable share in the benefits arising from their exploitation.[36]

Yet, for developed countries, the perspective was different. The point of departure for the position of developed countries was that the intellectual property rights (of entities sourcing genetic materials and patenting the products derived from those materials) should not be violated.[37] From the

32 Rosendal, n. 23, 69.

33 *Ibid.*

34 See Downes, n. 25, 6 ('[developing countries] complained that for too long the North had treated tropic genetic resources as a "common heritage" free to all ... without paying any compensation to the countries from which the genetic resources came. They argued that they deserved to share in the rewards that biotechnology promised to reap from the manipulation of their biodiversity. Having most of the world's biodiversity within their borders, they emphasised the right of sovereign nations to control access to their own natural resources, including genetic resources').

35 *Ibid.*

36 Rosendal, n. 23, 71.

37 For full discussion, see *ibid.*, 72ff.

perspective of developed countries, the protection of intellectual property would serve to safeguard biodiversity, and any undermining of the intellectual property rights would be to the detriment of biodiversity protection.[38] Moreover, addressing this issue would require states to interfere in business transactions of private entities since biotech companies often secured access to genetic materials without the intervention of governments.[39]

The Biodiversity Convention does not defer the question of access and benefit sharing to a subsequent protocol, as is the case with biosafety issues. The matter is addressed in Article 15 but, as with compromise solutions, it is addressed in an ambiguous and ambivalent language. Article 15 provides, first, for the 'sovereign right' of the territorial state.[40] However, this is limited by a duty to 'endeavour to create conditions to facilitate access to genetic resources for environmentally sound uses ... and not to impose restrictions that run counter to the objectives of the Convention'.[41] This 'duty' is littered with qualifiers that essentially erode its content: 'endeavour', 'create conditions', 'facilitate', 'for environmentally sound uses'. Article 15 also provides that access is to be 'on mutually agreed terms' and 'subject to prior informed consent'.[42] None of these provisions sufficiently address the concerns expressed by developing countries. In recognition of this, Article 15(7) requires the parties to take measures 'with the aim of sharing in a fair and equitable way the results of research and development and the benefits arising' from, inter alia, the commercialization of genetic resources with the party providing the genetic resources.[43] This provision makes plain that, under the Biodiversity Convention, the rules governing access and benefit sharing remain, by and large, domestic, with Article 15 providing broad principles. To address the concerns of developing countries fully would require the elaboration of another instrument. In other words, the aspirations of developing countries were once again deferred to other instruments.

19.2.2 *Developing Country Aspirations in Protocols*

Since both the biosafety and access and benefit-sharing concerns of developing countries remained unresolved under the Biodiversity Convention, it was left up to subsequent protocols to address the aspirations of those countries.

38 Chandler, n. 27, 161ff.
39 *Ibid.*
40 Biodiversity Convention, n. 1, art. 15(1).
41 *Ibid.*, art. 15(2).
42 *Ibid.*, arts. 15(4), (5).
43 *Ibid.*, art. 15(7).

The results were three protocols: two on biosafety – the Cartagena Protocol and the Nagoya-Kuala Lumpur Supplementary Protocol – and one on access and benefit sharing – the Nagoya Protocol. Given the importance of the topic of biosafety to developing countries, it was unsurprising that, already at the first Conference of the Parties to the Biodiversity Convention, several states were clamouring for its discussion and arguing for the launching of negotiations.[44] In these negotiations, some developing countries (Argentina, Chile, and Uruguay) were part of a group – the Miami Group – which had opposed the strict regulation of GMOs.[45] Consequently, the G-77 could not negotiate as a bloc, and developing countries formed a group called the Like-Minded Group.[46] This Like-Minded Group, which constituted the largest negotiating bloc, sought a comprehensive instrument that would address all facets of biosafety from genetic modification, including socio-economic impacts, domestic production, and concerns about liability for any damage that resulted from genetically modified organisms,[47] referred to in the negotiations and the consequent treaty as living modified organisms (LMOs). With respect to the latter, the position of the Like-Minded Group was that the Cartagena Protocol should contain a comprehensive civil liability regime setting out who would be liable and the extent of the liability.[48]

Developed countries, in general, opposed the idea of launching negotiations towards a new treaty.[49] The point of departure of the Miami Group was, in the main, that there was no 'evidence of a negative impact' of living modified organisms on biodiversity to justify concluding a treaty that would constrain biotechnology.[50] Once it became clear that a treaty would have to be negotiated, the objective of the Miami Group became to find an instrument that could address 'potential environmental impacts' of LMOs 'through strengthened decision-making processes' that would not unnecessarily restrict trade in LMOs.[51] This meant restricting the instrument to transboundary movements of LMOs and excluding national processes. It also meant excluding from the scope of the agreement socio-economic factors as well as issues of liability for damage. According to Kate Cook, chair of the Working Group on Liability and Redress in the negotiations towards the Cartagena Protocol,

44 See Falkner, n. 26, 6.
45 Gupta, n. 29, 24.
46 *Ibid.*, 26 (for a full constellation of the negotiating blocs, see Table 1).
47 Falkner, n. 26, 9.
48 Kate Cook, 'Liability: 'No Liability, No Protocol', in Bail, Falkner & Marquand, n. 26, 377.
49 *Ibid.*
50 Cathleen A. Enright, 'United States', in Bail, Falkner & Marquand, n. 26, 95.
51 *Ibid.*, 98.

> developing countries expressed the view that an imbalance was emerging in the negotiations: the very inclusion of a number of topics of particular concern to them, in particular liability and redress, socio-economic considerations and capacity-building, was still uncertain. In contrast the inclusion of subjects for which developed countries were pushing ... had moved further along and was generally accepted.[52]

These fears appeared to be realized in that the final instrument did not adopt the comprehensive ambition aspired by the Like-Minded Group. It was limited, principally, to LMOs that are subject to transboundary movement.[53] In particular, the Cartagena Protocol sets forth a procedure – the advanced informed agreement – for the transboundary movement of LMOs.[54] With respect to the aspiration of developing countries, the scope of the Protocol does not cover socio-economic factors.[55] While the Protocol provides that 'risks to human health' will be taken into account, no such mention of socio-economic factors, which were important to developing countries, is made in the scope. Instead, Article 26 simply provides that states 'may', when taking decisions on whether to allow transboundary movement of living modified organisms, 'take into account . . . socio-economic considerations' but that such considerations should be consistent with their 'international obligations'. Thus, first, socio-economic considerations were not an obligatory or core consideration in the decision-making process. Second, the taking into account of socio-economic considerations was subject to the caveat of existing international obligations. Similarly, with respect to the other core issues aspired to by developing countries, the parties decided not to address the question of liability and redress in the event of damage from LMOs at all. Instead, the aspiration of developing countries to address liability and redress are dealt with in Article 27:

> The Conference of the Parties serving as the meeting of the Parties to this Protocol shall, at its first meeting, adopt a process with respect to the appropriate elaboration of international rules and procedures in the field of liability

52 Cook, n. 48, 379.

53 See Cartagena Protocol, n. 2, art. 4 ('this Protocol shall apply to the transboundary movement, transit, handling and use of all living modified organisms that may have adverse effects on the conservation and sustainable use of biological diversity').

54 See Cartagena Protocol, n. 2, art. 7.

55 Rajen Habib Khwaja, 'Socio-Economic Considerations', in Bail, Falkner & Marquand, n. 26, 365 (expressing the hope that the provision amounts to making socio-economic considerations 'part of the Protocol'). Nonetheless, even this optimistic view is laced with a hint of scepticism ('it is now up to the global community to display the requisite degree of will and work together in constructive cooperation to implement the biosafety . . . in letter and spirit').

and redress for damage resulting from transboundary movements of living modified organisms, analysing and taking due account of the ongoing processes in international law on these matters, and shall endeavour to complete this process within four years.

In Article 27, which has been described as 'controversial and ambiguous', the aspiration of developing countries for liability to be addressed was (yet again) deferred to a later process.[56] Cook had already noted, even before the entry into force of the Cartagena Protocol, that, out of all the outstanding issues, 'the issue of liability in the context of biosafety [was] not likely to remain on the back burner for long'.[57] True to this prophecy, even before the first Conference of the Parties serving as Meeting of the Parties to the Cartagena Protocol, the preparatory works for the negotiations on liability and redress had already commenced.[58] In these negotiations, developing countries 'demanded ... an effective civil liability regime'.[59] The EU, however, proposed an administrative approach to liability, modelled on a 2004 EU Environmental Liability Directive – an approach based on the 'allocation of costs of responsive measures and restoration measures'.[60] For the Like-Minded Group, this approach would be acceptable as long as it was accompanied by a civil liability regime.[61]

In the end, the Nagoya Kuala-Lumpur Supplementary Protocol adopted the administrative approach favoured by the EU. With respect to civil liability, the Protocol adopted what one negotiator referred to as 'a single rather vacuous article'.[62] The provision, Article 12, provides that parties are to establish 'in their domestic law' rules to address damage arising from LMOs.[63] This provision envisions that states will apply their domestic law 'including, where applicable, general rules on and procedures on civil liability'.[64] In essence, the provision calls for states to apply their own domestic law, but it does not

56 Akiho Shibata, 'A New Dimension in International Environmental Regimes: A Prelude to the Supplementary Protocol', in Shibata, n. 14, 9.

57 Cook, n. 48, 384.

58 René Lefeber & Jimena Nieto Carrasco, 'Negotiating the Supplementary Protocol: The Co-Chairs' Perspective', in Shibata, n. 14, 53.

59 Gurdial Singh Nijar, 'Civil Liability in Supplementary Protocol', in Shibata, n. 14, 111; see also Elmo Thomas & Mahlet Teshome Kebede, 'One Legally Binding Provision on Civil Liability: Why It Was So Important from the African Negotiators' Perspective', in Shibata, n. 14, 117.

60 Shibata, n. 56, 25; Council Directive (EU) 2004/35 on Environmental Liability with Regard to the Prevention and Remedying of Environmental Damage, (2004) OJ L143.

61 Nijar, n. 59, 121; see also Thomas & Kebede, n. 59, 130.

62 Nijar, n. 59, 117.

63 Nagoya-Kuala Lumpur Supplementary Protocol, n. 4, art. 12(1).

64 *Ibid.*

establish, as was the aspiration of developing countries, an international regime on civil liability. In recognition that Article 12 was not sufficient to meet the aspirations of developing countries, and in keeping with the general theme of deferring developing country aspirations, Article 13 provides for the assessment and review of the effectiveness of the Protocol and, in particular, provides that the 'first review shall include a review of Articles 10 and 12' – the civil liability regimes.

The second issue that was deferred in the negotiations of the Biodiversity Convention was access and benefit sharing, and it also became the subject of a protocol adopted at Nagoya – the Nagoya Protocol. Like the Nagoya-Kuala Lumpur Supplementary Protocol, the Nagoya Protocol emerged from a failure to adopt concrete provisions on an issue of importance to developing countries. Unlike the biosafety issue addressed in the Nagoya-Kuala Lumpur Supplementary Protocol, however, access and benefit sharing was not the subject of an explicit mandate for negotiation. In the period subsequent to the adoption of the Biodiversity Convention, it is reported that there have been several allegations of biopiracy.[65] In response to these allegations of biopiracy, the Conference of the Parties to the Biodiversity Convention adopted a non-binding set of guidelines, the 2002 Bonn Guidelines.[66] Shortly thereafter, at the 2002 Johannesburg World Summit on Sustainable Development, world leaders agreed to launch negotiations for an instrument on access and benefit sharing.[67]

During the ensuing negotiations, developing countries sought a regime on access and benefit sharing that would ensure that developing countries enjoy a share of the benefits derived from their biodiversity. The Nagoya Protocol provides fully for the right of the state from which genetic materials are sourced to share in the monetary and non-monetary benefits arising from the commercialization and other applications of products from such genetic materials. While the aspirations of developing countries were met in the Nagoya Protocol, developing countries proposed in the course of the negotiations that the scope of the Protocol be extended to cover genetic resources sourced in areas beyond national jurisdiction. Unable to arrive at a conclusion, the Protocol includes the following: 'Parties shall consider the need for and modalities of a global multilateral benefit-sharing mechanism to

65 See Reji K. Joseph, 'International Regime on Access and Benefit Sharing: Where Are We Now?' (2010) 12 *Asian Biotechnology and Development Review* 77, 78ff.

66 See Bonn Guidelines on Access to Genetic Resources and Fair and Equitable Sharing of the Benefits Arising out of their Utilization, UN Doc. UNEP/CBD/COP/Dec.6/20, 19 April 2002.

67 Thomas Greiber *et al.*, *An Explanatory Guide to the Nagoya Protocol on Access and Benefit Sharing* (International Union for Conservation of Nature, 2012), 19.

address fair and equitable sharing of benefits derived from the utilisation of genetic resources and traditional knowledge associated with genetic resources that occur in transboundary situations or for which it is not possible to grant or obtain prior informed consent.'[68]

Even, with this 'deferment', the Nagoya Protocol still addresses the concern of developing countries. In part, this was because, unlike in the negotiations in the biosafety context, developing countries were much more united in the access and benefit-sharing negotiations. Yet, as is the case with any negotiation process resulting in compromise, developing countries did not get everything they wished for. For example, the lack of sanctions in the event of non-disclosure or the false disclosure of origins of knowledge associated with genetic resources significantly limits the effectiveness of the Nagoya Protocol.[69] The point, however, is that the issue sought to be addressed was addressed.

19.2.3 *Biodiversity in Areas beyond National Jurisdiction: A 'Post-Script'*

In June 2023, the UNGA adopted the BBNJ Agreement.[70] It is worth making some brief observations about it, in part because it is the most recent addition to the biological diversity family. However, apart from being a recent addition to the biological diversity framework, it is relevant for this chapter for several reasons. First, while the source of the BBNJ Agreement is UNCLOS, whose antecedents were not, at least not directly, connected with the Stockholm Conference, the importance of safeguarding the marine environment and its biodiversity was well recognized at the Stockholm Conference.[71] Indeed, as mentioned earlier, the Regional Seas Programme, a creation of UNEP, was itself a creation of the Stockholm Conference, which is evidence of the concern for marine biodiversity at the conference. Second, and most importantly, the negotiations for the BBNJ Agreement provided an opportunity to test the deferral trends identified in this chapter. Therefore, although the BBNJ Agreement is not an agreement under the Biodiversity Convention and was

68 Nagoya Protocol, n. 3, art. 10.

69 See Joseph, n. 65, 92.

70 BBNJ Agreement, n. 13.

71 See, e.g., Stockholm Declaration, n. 7, principle 7 ('States shall take all possible steps to prevent pollution of the seas by substances that are liable to create hazards to human health, to harm living resources and marine life, to damage amenities or to interfere with other legitimate uses of the sea'); see also Richard Barnes, 'The Stockholm Declaration at Sea: Influences on the Content and Context of the Law of the Sea', in this volume, 403.

concluded after the Stockholm + 50 Conference, some brief remarks should be provided.

The impetus for the BBNJ Agreement included two issues.[72] The first issue pursued by the EU concerned (the lack of) a legal framework for establishing marine protected areas or the so-called area-based management tools issue.[73] The second issue concerned the divergence of views over the legal framework governing marine genetic resources in the deep seabed, referred to in UNCLOS as the Area.[74] In simple terms, the argument of developing countries was that marine genetic resources in the Area should be subject to the common heritage of mankind.[75] While the discussions on these issues began in 2006, the negotiations only officially commenced in 2018 after the adoption of UNGA Resolution 72/249, which established the Intergovernmental Conference.[76] This resolution was preceded by UNGA Resolution 62/292 in 2015, which established a preparatory committee for the elaboration of the treaty.[77] What is relevant is that in neither Resolution 72/249 nor 62/292 does the principle of common heritage of mankind – the principle demand of the G-77– appear. This is in contrast to the concepts of marine protected areas and area-based management tools, which were treated as pillars of the negotiations.[78] Already in 2014, I noted elsewhere that the language of the common heritage of mankind had almost completely been erased from the discussions towards a treaty.[79] That same paper also noted that the issues of marine protected areas and environment impact assessments were far more developed than the marine genetic resources question that brought developing countries to the negotiating table.[80]

Towards the end of the negotiations, however, there appeared to be a regrouping of the G-77 and, as a result, a more vociferous call for the

72 For a discussion of the history of the BBNJ Agreement, see David Freestone, 'The UN Process to Develop an International Legally Binding Instrument under the 1982 Law of the Sea Convention: Issues and Challenges', in David Freestone (ed.), *Conserving Biodiversity in Areas beyond National Jurisdiction* (Brill, 2019), 16–20.

73 For a discussion of this issue, see Kristina M. Gjerde & Anna Rulska-Domino, 'Marine Protected Areas beyond National Jurisdiction: Some Thoughts for Moving Forward' (2012) 27 *International Journal of Marine and Coastal Law* 351.

74 For a discussion, see Fernanda Millicay, 'A Legal Regime for the Biodiversity of the Area', in Myron H. Nordquist, Ronán Long, Tomas Heidar & John Norton Moore (eds.), *Law, Science and Ocean Management* (Brill, 2007), 739–850.

75 Tladi, 'Common Heritage', n. 14.

76 UNGA Resolution 72/249, 24 December 2017.

77 UNGA Resolution 69/292, 19 June 2015.

78 See, e.g., UNGA Resolution 69/292, n. 77, para. 2; UNGA Resolution 72/249, n. 76, para. 2.

79 Tladi, 'Common Heritage', n. 14, 114.

80 *Ibid.*

common heritage of mankind principle. The final text adopted by the UNGA thus includes as a 'guiding principle' 'the principle of the common heritage of humankind'.[81] Yet, this principle is only a 'guiding principle', which is not firmly operationalized in any part of the treaty. Second, and consistent with the observation of deferral, the modalities for the sharing of monetary benefits arising from the exploitation of marine genetic resources are to be addressed through a future process.[82] Nonetheless, while the marine genetic resources section is certainly less well developed than the area-based management tools section of the treaty, developing countries ensured that the deferral would not amount to further negotiations, which could leave them empty-handed. It does so by setting a definitive decision-making process to be adopted in the event that agreement is not reached.[83] More importantly, while the BBNJ Agreement defers decision on the modalities for the sharing of benefits, it does not defer a decision on the principle of sharing benefits.

19.3 SOME (PRELIMINARY) CONCLUSIONS

While there are many things that could be observed from the emergence of the Biodiversity treaty network, this chapter has sought to focus on a single, discrete aspect which, I believe, has not received any attention to date. It is an apparent trend – I say apparent because it is impossible to be conclusive on the basis of what is, admittedly, an anecdotal account – to defer aspirations of developing countries to future negotiations. Given the sheer numerical advantage of developing countries in negotiations, this observed trend is curious. There may be many different reasons for the deferrals (or even complete non-taking up) of negotiating positions of countries. For example, the particular issue may simply not be ripe for inclusion in a treaty. Or the group in question may simply not be sufficiently well-organized, well-coordinated, and/or coherent enough. Power dynamics may also play an important role, impacting on the influence that a group, irrespective of its size, may have on the negotiation process. It may be a combination of all these factors. Whatever the reason, it is worth pointing out that this technique of deferment, in fact, has allowed for the building of consensus over time and the possible emergence of regimes. The complex network of treaties on biodiversity, built since 1992 on the back of

81 See BBNJ Agreement, n. 13, art. 7.
82 See *ibid.*, art. 14(7).
83 *Ibid.* ('if all efforts to reach consensus have been exhausted, a decision shall be adopted by three-fourths majority of the Parties present and voting').

the legacy of the Stockholm Declaration, has emerged in part because of this trend.

In the BBNJ Agreement, we also see patterns of deferral. For example, the main issue called for by developing countries – the common heritage principle – is not explicitly given any operational content but is merely reflected as a guiding principle. Second, the modalities for benefit sharing, which is the other concern of developing countries, are to be subsequently negotiated after the entry into force of the BBNJ Agreement. Yet a closer look at the BBNJ Agreement reveals that developing countries could see it as a win. First, it is remarkable that the common heritage of humankind is reflected at all when, for much of the negotiations, it had become a forgotten child. Second, the Agreement sets forth a definitive decision-making process in the event that there is no consensus to ensure that the deferral does not amount to an empty promise. Finally, in the BBNJ Agreement, what is deferred is not the principle in question but, merely, the modalities.

The legacy of Stockholm is undeniable. The 1972 Stockholm Conference ushered in a 'new' era of international environmental law and policy. For many, modern international environmental law began with the Stockholm Conference. Institutionally, its legacy includes UNEP, which itself has had a deep and enduring impact on international environmental law. Substantively, the Stockholm Conference ushered in an era of unprecedented lawmaking, both in the form of non-binding instruments and in the form of treaty making. Key amongst the treaties with direct lineage from Stockholm is the network of treaties under the 1992 Biodiversity Convention.

20

The Influence of the Stockholm Conference on the Development of Nature Protection Law at an International Level and in Europe

Nicolas de Sadeleer

20.1 INTRODUCTION

Biodiversity faces a major crisis at both the global and European level, the implications of which still have not been fully appreciated. All over the world, most natural or semi-natural, continental, marine, and coastal ecosystems have been subject to significant changes by human activities. The 1972 Stockholm Declaration on the Human Environment has been prompting the adoption of a flurry of multilateral environment agreements (MEAs).[1] This chapter examines and critically assesses the outcome of the 1972 Stockholm Conference on the Human Environment (that is, the Stockholm Declaration and the Stockholm Action Plan) on nature conservation and its influence on international environmental law (IEL) as well as on European Union (EU)[2] secondary law.[3] In doing so, it will also show the dynamics between international and EU law and the role played by the EU in the field of nature conservation at the international level. In this connection, EU law on nature protection should be seen as a case for examining the cross-fertilization between international environmental law and a regional international organization.

In section 20.2, we briefly examine the influence of principles 2 and 4 of the Stockholm Declaration on the development of international rules on nature

1 'Declaration of the United Nations Conference on the Human Environment', in *Report of the UN Conference on the Human Environment*, UN Doc. A/CONF.48/14/Rev.1, 16 June 1972 (Stockholm Declaration).

2 In 1972, the organization was named the European Economic Community (EEC); in 1993, it would change to the European Community (EC), and, in 2009, to the European Union (EU) – thus, the different acronyms in some legislation by the organization. Hereinafter, it will consistently be referred to as the EU.

3 'Action Plan for the Human Environment', in *Report of the United Nations Conference on the Human Environment*, n. 1 (Stockholm Action Plan).

protection and, subsequently, on biodiversity. In section 20.3, we take stock of the contribution of EU law, in the aftermath of the Stockholm Declaration, to the development of international law regarding nature protection between 1972 and 2022. In section 20.4, we look in reverse at the influence exerted by international nature protection law on EU secondary law.[4] Insofar as the EU is bound by its international obligations regarding nature conservation, one can demonstrate the contribution of international law to the development of EU secondary legislation. Finally, in section 20.5, we use a case study to highlight the cross-fertilization between international law and EU law.

20.2 THE INFLUENCE OF THE 1972 STOCKHOLM CONFERENCE ON THE DEVELOPMENT OF INTERNATIONAL NATURE PROTECTION LAW

20.2.1 *A Shift from the Protection of Species and Their Habitats to Broader Instruments*

As a reaction to the devastation caused by the rise of industrial civilization, the first efforts at international cooperation in nature protection were mainly inspired in the nineteenth century by a utilitarian approach. This was reflected in attempts to conserve directly exploited species, such as birds that were 'useful to agriculture', whales, seals, and fish.[5] The twentieth century was marked by the shift from a utilitarian conception of nature to a 'conservationist' ethic – in other words, a shift from an anthropocentric way of perceiving the protection of biological resources to a more eco-centric approach. Aesthetic values were of paramount importance.[6] Perceived as a natural or collective heritage that is necessary to safeguard, wild species were thus protected for their symbolic or aesthetic value.

Although the conventions adopted during the first half of the twentieth century made it possible to save a certain number of species from extinction, they quickly ran up against their limits. Since the nature 'sanctuary' does not fit in well with the dynamic nature of ecosystems, which do not conserve

4 Nicolas de Sadeleer, 'European Union', in Elisa Morgera & Jona Razzaque (eds.), *Biodiversity and Nature Protection Law* (Edward Elgar, 2017), 413–430.

5 Rosemary Rayfuse, 'Biological Resources', in Daniel Bodansky, Jutta Brunnée & Ellen Hey (eds.), *The Oxford Handbook of International Environment Law* (Oxford University Press, 2008), 368

6 See the preambles of the Convention on Nature Protection and Wildlife Preservation in the Western Hemisphere, 1940, 161 UNTS 193, and the African Convention on the Conservation of Nature and Natural Resources, 1968, 1001 UNTS 4.

themselves like the old masterpieces on display in a museum, neither status as a national park or as a natural sanctuary that has been granted to certain enclaves separated from one another by completely de-naturalized environments, nor the status of protected species granted to endangered animal species, has made it possible to counteract the erosion of biological diversity. On the other hand, as far as marine biodiversity is concerned, the perception of the risks created by the intensification of fishing is absolutely non-existent, which explains why international conventions on the law of the sea are focused more on cost-effectiveness than on the conservation of resources.

20.2.2 *Stockholm Declaration: The Birth of Modern Environmental Law and a New Generation of International Nature Protection Agreements*

Of the twenty-six principles in the 1972 Stockholm Declaration, only two of them – principles 2 and 4 – are devoted to the protection of nature. Principle 2 requires the safeguard of 'flora and fauna and especially representative samples of natural ecosystems', whereas principle 4 is more specific in stating that 'man has a special responsibility to safeguard and wisely manage the heritage of wildlife and its habitat, which are now gravely imperilled by a combination of adverse factors. Nature conservation, including wildlife, must therefore receive importance in planning for economic development.' These principles call for several comments. The authors of the Stockholm Declaration thus proclaimed the responsibility that mankind bears for wildlife 'for the benefit of present and future generations' (principle 2). Without bothering to list the flurry of factors that were already contributing to the disappearance of wildlife at the time, principle 4 acknowledged that it was under serious threat. Furthermore, the importance that should be attached to the conservation of nature, including wildlife, should have been addressed in the context of 'economic development', which puts more emphasis on a utilitarian approach. Finally, from an institutional point of view, more attention seems to have been paid to combating pollution than to protecting wildlife.[7]

Have these two principles been more successful than the other principles of the Stockholm Declaration in influencing the development of international environmental law? To answer this question, we must look chronologically at the main international agreements that have progressively fleshed out

[7] The Stockholm Action Plan for the Human Environment does not address nature protection. Stockholm Action Plan, n. 3. Recommendation 43(5)(a) notes that the International Union for Conservation of Nature 'might, logically, be given responsibility for wild species, in co-operation with FAO, the Man and the Biosphere Programme (UNESCO)'.

principle 4, although they do not expressly refer to it in their preambles. In the aftermath of the Stockholm Conference, and also after the 1971 Ramsar Convention,[8] the adoption of four landmark universal conventions marked a turning point in the history of nature conservation. The 1970s thus saw a radical evolution in the legal treatment of nature protection. Since the survival of species was affected more by the maintenance of the quality of their environment than by the regulation of hunting, the safeguarding of their habitats or ecosystems gradually established itself as the cornerstone for wildlife protection during the 1970s. Two of these MEAs related specifically to the protection of natural species, whilst the two others were aimed more particularly at the protection of vulnerable or endangered species.

Due to the irreparable loss for mankind in economic, scientific, and cultural terms caused by the disappearance of wetlands, the Ramsar Convention, for its part, sought to protect lakeland areas that were particularly threatened by human activity. The 1972 World Heritage Convention was an important step in the process of the 'heritagization' of nature.[9] It was adopted to reconcile the protection of cultural heritage with the protection of natural heritage. Accordingly, these sites, features, formations, and monuments form part of the common heritage of mankind that was to be passed on intact to future generations. Moreover, the 1973 Convention on International Trade in Endangered Species (CITES) regulated the international trade in certain wild species whose populations had been put under pressure by the capturing and hunting and the opening up of important markets in the Western world.[10] Finally, by endorsing a universal approach to conservation covering different classes of animals, the 1979 Bonn Convention was adopted with the intention of guaranteeing protection to species of mammals, birds, fish, and even insects a significant portion of the populations of which periodically crossed over the territory of one or more states.[11]

In parallel to the conclusion of these four universal conventions, efforts were made on a regional level to conserve both habitats and their species – in particular, in Europe where the 1979 Bern Convention was drawn up under the aegis of the Council of Europe.[12] This Convention marked a new stage in

[8] Convention on Wetlands of International Importance Especially as Waterfowl Habitat, 1971, 996 UNTS 245 (Ramsar Convention).

[9] Convention for the Protection of the World Cultural and Natural Heritage, 1972, 1037 UNTS 151 (World Heritage Convention).

[10] Convention on Trade in Endangered Species of Wild Fauna and Flora, 1973, 993 UNTS 243 (CITES).

[11] Convention on the Conservation of Migratory Species of Wild Animals, 1979, 1651 UNTS 333 (Bonn Convention).

[12] Convention on the Conservation of European Wildlife and Natural Habitats, 1979, ETS no. 104 (Bern Convention).

the development of nature conservation principles in Europe and had a significant impact on EU nature conservation law. Last, whereas the International Maritime Organization initially privileged a sectoral approach to the fight against marine pollution, which did not make it possible to regulate the conservation of large marine ecosystems, the UN Environment Programme's 'regional seas programme' has promoted the adoption of various agreements on regional seas since 1974. This quickly led to the establishment of regional legal frameworks to regulate the conservation of suitable marine ecosystems.

20.2.3 *The Quest for a New Status for Biological Resources during the 1970s and 1980s*

In the 1970s, it quickly became apparent that the concept of absolute sovereignty was ill suited to guaranteeing the conservation of biological resources that do not recognize national boundaries. Within this perspective, several international treaties on the conservation of species and habitats have gradually established the idea that certain elements of natural heritage must be conserved by states for the benefit of all mankind. Similarly, at the regional level, EU law on nature conservation has recognized since 1979 that the habitats of migratory birds form part of a shared heritage of the union.[13] Accordingly, the management of certain vulnerable resources was to be controlled by an international authority, as a custodian of the world's heritage, to ensure that they not be wasted. This control was to be exercised both on behalf of current generations (that is, through the right of access to these resources) and of future generations (that is, through the right to development).

The dialectical relationship between state responsibility and the common heritage of mankind reflects a reconsideration of the classical concept of states' sovereignty over their biological resources with enhanced participation by representatives of civil society in the implementation of nature protection policies – where each state assumes specific responsibility for all biological resources, including endangered species, located on its territory. According to this argument, the seabed and outer space were classified as the common heritage of mankind. These spaces were accordingly regarded as the common heritage that mankind – which includes not only past and present generations but also future generations – is to administer. The Stockholm Declaration falls short of enshrining the common heritage of mankind. Principle 4 proclaims

[13] Council Directive (EEC) 79/409 on the Conservation of Wild Birds, (1979) OJ L103 (Wild Birds Directive).

the 'responsibility to safeguard and wisely manage the heritage of wildlife', whereas only principles 5 and 18 refer to 'mankind' and the 'common good of mankind'. Although the culmination of this evolution – the 2001 International Treaty on Plant Genetic Resources – is not binding, it is subject to the principle that these resources should remain accessible to all on the grounds that they constitute a common heritage.[14]

20.2.4 *The Rise of International Protection of Biodiversity in the 1980 and 1990s*

Since the start of the 1980s, it has become increasingly apparent that, due to the breadth of the changes to which ecosystems and the species dependent upon them have been subject, protection measures should no longer be limited to certain species or to certain habitats (such as ancient forests or wetlands) but, rather, should apply to all forms of biological diversity. In 1980, the World Conservation Strategy laid the foundation for a global approach to conservation,[15] and, in 1982, the UN General Assembly adopted the World Charter for Nature,[16] which proclaimed that 'every form of life is unique warranting respect regardless of its worth to man' and that nature should be conserved due to its inherent value.

Another major step was taken at the start of the 1990s with the 1992 Rio Conference on Environment and Development and the adoption of the 1992 Convention on Biological Diversity (CBD).[17] For the first time in the history of international law, a universally applicable legal instrument enshrined the concept of biological diversity. Although the question was debated during the negotiations, the CBD did not codify the existing international law on the conservation of species and ecosystems. As a framework convention, it lays the foundations that should underpin all national legislation on the conservation and sustainable use of biodiversity as well as the bases on which access to generic resources and the fair division of the benefits resulting from that exploitation should be regulated. The enshrinement of the eco-systemic approach by the Conference of the Parties (COP) to the CBD marked a radical turning point in the conceptualization and management of natural resources, privileging integrated long-term management grounded on science

[14] International Treaty on Plant Genetic Resources for Food and Agriculture, 2001, 2400 UNTS 303.

[15] International Union for Conservation of Nature, UN Environment Programme, and World Wildlife Fund, *World Conservation Strategy: Living Resource Conservation for Sustainable Development*, 1980.

[16] UNGA Resolution 37/7 on World Charter for Nature, Doc. A/RES/37/7, 28 October 1982.

[17] Convention on Biological Diversity, 1992, 1760 UNTS 69 (CBD).

and with the involvement of local populations rather than a short-term sectoral approach.[18]

Further developments are worthy of note. In the law of the sea, various regional seas agreements emphasize an integrated approach to the protection of the marine environment and biodiversity. This approach to conservation, which is more eco-systemic and regional, also influenced the adoption of the 1991 Alpine Convention, which contains various sectoral protocols, one of which concerns spatial planning, an area rarely included in treaties.[19] Finally, international agreements and other instruments focusing on specific groups of migratory species under annex II of the Bonn Convention have been adopted, resulting in a scientifically appropriate response through innovative legal techniques (action plans and so on) to the problems of the conservation of species whose migratory routes may pass through dozens of states.

20.2.5 *Preliminary Remarks*

Although there has been a shift towards a holistic approach paying heed to the intrinsic value of nature, MEAs addressing biodiversity have never completely departed from a utilitarian conception. In addition, several treaties maintain a mono-specific approach. Thanks to the impetus given by the 1972 Stockholm Conference, IEL has been enriched by a raft of MEAs intended to put a stop to the sinking of Noah's ark.[20] However, the existence of these agreements should not lull us into thinking that all natural components are now well protected. The conservation objectives, the material and territorial scope,[21] and the level of stringency of these MEAs vary from one agreement to the next, such that no harmonization, even on a geographical level, is achieved. It is mainly ignorance, lack of political will, lack of financial and human resources, and growing pressures on ecosystems as a result of the gross domestic product and demographic growth that explain the failure of international nature protection law.

Against this background, I assess in the next section the extent to which the EU has contributed to the development of international nature conservation law. Most commentators acknowledge that the EU has played a leading role in promoting environment issues and, in particular, nature protection on the

18 Decision V/6 COP on Ecosystem Approach, 2024.

19 Convention on the Protection of the Alps, 1991, 1917 UNTS 135.

20 Michael Bowman, Peter Davies & Catherine Redgwell, *Lyster's International Wildlife Law* (2nd ed., Cambridge University Press, 2011).

21 The emphasis has been placed on regimes relating to the protection of predominantly terrestrial species and habitats.

international stage.[22] Several MEAs would not have been possible without the EU's engagement and financial support.

20.3 EU NATURE CONSERVATION LAW IN THE CONTEXT OF THE 1972 STOCKHOLM CONFERENCE

The purpose of this section is to take stock of the contribution of EU law to the development of international law regarding nature protection after the Stockholm Declaration. After briefly outlining the sources of the EU's legal order, it looks at the role that the EU and its member states have played in shaping international nature protection law. This is a difficult exercise insofar as the EU does not exert an exclusive competence in this area. The EU and its member states are involved in the preparatory negotiations and the conclusion of the MEAs whose object is nature conservation. Consequently, the respective roles of the EU and the twenty-seven member states in the course of the negotiations are not easy to assess.[23]

20.3.1 *The EU's Legal Sources Regarding Nature Protection*

The EU's legal order is made up of a set of legal sources, ordered by a principle of hierarchy of norms as precise as in a state's legal order. Although autonomous from the legal orders of the member states, the EU's order has primacy over the latter. The various amending treaties that establish the EU have strengthened the EU's competence in the field of environmental protection: objectives have been laid down (article 191(1) of the 2016 Treaty on the Functioning of the European Union [TFEU]); principles have been set out (article 191(2) of the TFEU); and criteria have been established (article 191(3) of the TFEU).[24] This legal framework has enabled the EU to play a major role in nature protection, both internally (the adoption of different directives and regulations) and externally. Given that the EU cannot conduct its environmental policy in isolation, environmental issues are today at the core of its

[22] See, among other strategies, European Commission, *Stepping up EU Action to Protect and Restore the World's Forests*, Doc. COM(2019)352 final, 23 July 2019; European Commission, *EU Biodiversity Strategy to 2020*, Doc. COM(2011) 244, 3 May 2011; European Commission, *EU Biodiversity Strategy for 2030*, Doc. COM/2020/380 final 4.2, 20 May 2020. The EU has been supporting the conclusion of an ambitious legally binding agreement on marine biological diversity of areas beyond national jurisdiction. It used all of its diplomatic leverage to help broker agreement on the designation of three vast marine protected areas in the Southern Ocean.

[23] In particular, the agreements do not mention in their preamble the contribution of the EU.

[24] Treaty on the Functioning of the European Union, (2016) OJ C202/47, art. 267 (TFEU).

external action. In virtue of article 21(2)(f) of the 2010 Treaty on European Union, the EU commits itself to cooperate with third states and international organizations in order to 'develop international measures to preserve and improve the quality of the environment and the sustainable management of global natural resources'.[25]

In short, EU law on biodiversity and nature protection derives mainly from three distinct normative sources:

- the provisions of primary law – that is, those included in the TFEU, particularly those relating to sustainable development and the environment, which are at the top of the normative pyramid;
- the various international agreements to which the EU and its member states are parties in the areas of biodiversity and nature protection, which rank below primary law but above secondary legislation; and
- the secondary legislation adopted on the basis of the various legal bases assigning specific policies (agriculture, fisheries, environment, and so on) to the EU institutions, which implement the TFEU obligations as well as the various obligations stemming from international nature protection agreements to which the EU and its member states are parties.

In addition, one must take into consideration an array of non-binding sources and the numerous judgments of the Court of Justice of the European Union (CJEU). The CJEU endorses a teleological interpretation, thereby giving precedence to nature conservation objectives over textual interpretations that would restrict the scope of the EU's rules. So far, hundreds of judgments have been delivered on nature protection matters. In particular, many questions have been referred to the CJEU by domestic courts through the preliminary ruling mechanism. Thanks to the doctrines of the *effet utile*, consistent interpretation, and direct effect, the CJEU has played a key role in interpreting the obligations placed on the member states. In particular, the CJEU regularly affirms in its judgments on nature protection the existence of general principles such as the precautionary principle, the principle of prevention, and the principle of a high level of environmental protection.[26] Unlike several international agreements on nature protection,[27] these

25 Treaty on European Union, (2010) OJ C83/13.

26 See Nicolas de Sadeleer, *Environmental Principles: From Political Slogans to Legal Rules* (2nd ed., Oxford University Press, 2020), 181–187.

27 The preamble of the CBD, n. 17, provides that 'where there is a threat of significant reduction or loss of biological diversity, lack of full scientific certainty should not be used as a reason for postponing measures to avoid or minimize such a threat'. Although this statement is not binding, being set out in the preamble to the agreement and not its operative provisions, it is

principles are formulated in a general way without their conditions and modalities of application being really defined in treaty law.

20.3.2 *The Role Played by the EU and Its Member States in Shaping Nature Protection International Law*

Political commitments made by the EU's institutions tend to influence international decisions. This is evidenced by the willingness to curb biodiversity loss. For instance, in 2001, the European Council decided to halt the decline of biodiversity by 2010,[28] whereas, in 2002, the parties to CBD committed themselves to achieve a significant reduction of the rate of biodiversity loss.[29] The influence exerted by the EU on the international political agenda is therefore far from negligible. However, we will confine our discussion to highlighting the participation of the EU and its member states in the adoption and implementation of several MEAs aiming at nature protection.

In the early years of the EU's environmental policy, before the entry into force of the specific provisions on environmental matters in the treaties establishing the EU, it had concluded a significant number of international agreements in the area of nature protection. Given the absence of a specific competence, these agreements were concluded on the basis of the EU's implicit external competences.[30] With only a few exceptions, most MEAs on nature protection provide for the accession of regional economic integration organizations, such as the EU. The following MEAs have thus been concluded both by the EU and its member states:

- CITES;[31]
- the Bern Convention;[32]

not however devoid of legal effects (interpretative function). See CJEU, Case C-67/97, *Bluhme*, [1998] ECR I-8033, paras. 36, 38.

28 European Council, *Presidency Conclusions – Göteborg*, Doc. SN 200/01 REV 1, 15–16 June 2001, para. 31.

29 David Langlet & Said Mahmoudi, *EU Environmental Law and Policy* (Oxford University Press, 2016), 350.

30 The European Community was able to acquire exclusive competence in the environmental field through internal regulation according to the *ERTA* principle. See CJEU, Case 22/70, *ERTA*, [1971] ECR 263; CJEU, Opinion 1/94, *Competence of the Community to Conclude International Agreements Concerning Services and the Protection of Intellectual Property*, [1994] ECR I-5267, para. 77.

31 Council Decision (EU) 2015/45 Concerning the Accession of the EU to the Convention on International Trade in Endangered Species of Wild Fauna and Flora (CITES), (2015) OJ L75.

32 Council Decision (EEC) 82/72 Concerning the Conclusion of the Convention on the Conservation of European Wildlife and Natural Habitats, (1982) OJ L38/11.

- the CBD;[33]
- the 1994 Convention to Combat Desertification;[34]
- the Bonn Convention;[35]
- the 2006 Agreement on African-Eurasian Migratory Waterbirds;[36]
- the Alpine Convention;[37]
- the 1981 Convention on Antarctic Marine Living Resources;[38]
- the 1982 Geneva Protocol;[39]
- the 1995 Barcelona Protocol.[40]

Although the EU is bound by these MEAs, it did not always adopt measures of secondary law to implement them. By way of illustration, there is no framework directive on biodiversity that could flesh out the requirements of the CBD.

The EU is not a contracting party to the 1971 Ramsar Convention, although the 1992 Habitat Directive and 1979 Wild Birds Directive guarantee the conservation of a very large number of wetlands classified as Ramsar sites.[41] Nor is the EU a party to the 1972 World Heritage Convention or the 2000 European Landscape Convention.[42] Although the EU has adopted measures to protect cetaceans, including by restricting cetacean products originating from third countries, it has only an observer status in the 1946 International Convention for the Regulation of Whaling.[43]

[33] Council Decision 93/626 Concerning the Conclusion of the Convention on Biological Diversity, (1993) OJ L309/1.
[34] Council Decision 98/216 on the Conclusion, on Behalf of the European Community, of the United Nations Convention to Combat Desertification in Countries Seriously Affected by Drought and/or Desertification, Particularly in Africa, (1998) OJ L83/1.
[35] Council Decision 82/461 on the Conclusion of the Convention on the Conservation of Migratory Species of Wild Animals, (1982) OJ L210/10.
[36] Council Decision (EC) 2006/871 on the Conclusion on Behalf of the European Community of the Agreement on the Conservation of African-Eurasian Migratory Waterbirds, (2006) OJ L345.
[37] Council Decision 96/191 Concerning the Conclusion of the Convention on the Protection of the Alps, (1996) OJ L61/31.
[38] Council Decision 81/691 on the Conclusion of the Convention on the Conservation of Antarctic Marine Living Resources, (1981) OJ L252/26.
[39] Council Decision (EEC) 84/132 on the Conclusion of the Protocol Concerning Specially Protected Areas in the Mediterranean, (1984) OJ L68.
[40] Council Decision (EC) 1999/80 on the Conclusion of the Protocol Concerning Specially Protected Areas and Biological Diversity in the Mediterranean, (1999) OJ L322.
[41] Council Directive (EEC) 92/43 on the Conservation of Natural Habitats and of Wild Fauna and Flora, (1992) OJ L206 (Habitat Directive); Wild Birds Directive, n. 13.
[42] Council of Europe Landscape Convention, 2000, ETS no. 176.
[43] International Convention for the Regulation of Whaling, 1946, 161 UNTS 72 (ICRW). This does not preclude the Council of the EU to adopt decisions establishing the position to be adopted on behalf of the EU at the Conferences of the Parties of the ICRW with regard to

As mentioned, the external competence in the area of nature protection is not exclusive but, rather, shared between the EU and the member states.[44] Accordingly, all nature protection agreements to which the EU is a contracting party, including those concluded both before and after the entry into force of the 1987 Single European Act, are classified as 'mixed agreements', concluded pursuant to article 191(4) of the TFEU both by the EU and the member states.[45] The mixture of these agreements made it possible to satisfy both the EU and the member states when each of them asserted their own powers. It follows that mixed agreements are negotiated, concluded, implemented, and managed jointly by the EU and the member states 'within their respective spheres of competence'. In particular, the mixed representation at the Conferences of the Parties guarantees the participation of both the EU and its member states in the decision-making process. The member states are represented, in their individual capacity, in the intergovernmental institutions in charge of implementing these agreements.[46]

The EU and the member states are jointly responsible for fulfilling the obligations owed to third states. It is settled case law that 'in ensuring respect for commitments arising from an agreement concluded by the [EU] institutions the Member States fulfil, within the [EU] system, an obligation in relation to the Community, which has assumed responsibility for the due performance of the agreement'.[47] The implementation of mixed agreements requires a coordinated action by the EU and its member states.[48] Moreover, the obligations resulting from the mixed agreement are applicable to the member states, despite the absence of EU secondary rules.

Once environmental mixed agreements have been concluded by the EU, they form an integral part of the EU's legal order. Their status under EU law is identical to that of agreements concluded exclusively by the EU in so far as their provisions fall within the scope of the EU's competence.[49] Given that the

proposals for amendments. The member states may thus present a common position for the EU in the International Whaling Commission.

44 TFEU, n. 24, art. 4(2)(e) (which stipulates that competence over environmental matters shall be shared).

45 Single European Act, (1987) OJ L169, 1.

46 The presence of national representatives in the organs of the TFEU, n. 24, is justified both by the fact that certain matters covered by the mixed agreement fall within the competence of the member states and by the fact that the member states make financial contributions to the operation of the agreement.

47 CJEU, Case 12/86, *Demirel*, [1987] ECR 3719, para. 11; CJEU, Case C-13/00, *Commission v Ireland*, [2002] ECR I-2943, para. 15.

48 CJEU, Case 3, 4 and 6–76, *Cornelis Kramer and Others*, [1976] ECR 1279, paras. 39–45.

49 *Demirel*, n. 47, para 9; *Commission v Ireland*, n. 47, para. 14; CJEU, Case C-213/03, *Etang de Berre*, [2004] ECR I-7357, para. 25.

agreements concluded by the EU have primacy over secondary EU legislation,[50] they bind both the EU and the member states by virtue of article 216(2) of the TFEU. In principle, the compliance of EU secondary law with these international obligations may be subject to review before the EU courts. The possibility for claimants to invoke directly before their domestic courts mixed international agreements is likely to oblige the courts to discard national law that is inconsistent with the international obligations. The ruling in *Etang de Berre* is a case in point.[51] The CJEU held that, as long as it is worded in clear, precise, and unconditional terms, the requirement laid down in the 1980 Protocol on Land-based Sources to subject the discharge of pollutants into surface water to an authorization procedure has direct effect.[52] Interestingly enough, the Court stressed in its judgment that direct effect 'can only serve the purpose of the Protocol . . . and reflect the nature of the instrument, which is intended, *inter alia*, to prevent pollution resulting from the failure of public authorities to act'.[53]

However, the logic of other environmental agreements makes it impossible to recognize many of their provisions as having a direct effect in the EU. In *Lesoochranárske zoskupenie*, a case on habitat conservation, the CJEU held that article 9(3) of the 1998 Aarhus Convention had no direct effect on the grounds that it does not contain 'any clear and precise obligation capable of directly regulating the legal position of individuals'.[54] Nonetheless, with the view of safeguarding rights that individuals derive from the mixed agreement, as well as the EU secondary law implementing it, the Court held that the provision at issue could not be interpreted by national courts in such a way as to make it impossible in practice or excessively difficult to exercise rights (standing) conferred by EU law. Applying the doctrine of consistent interpretation may in such a case lead to a similar result as would have a direct effect. Last, the very fact that a treaty, such as that on biological diversity, contains provisions that do not have a direct effect does not preclude the ability of the EU courts to review compliance with the obligations incumbent upon the EU as a party to that agreement.[55]

50 CJEU, Case C-61/94, *Commission v Germany*, [1996] ECR I-3989, para. 52; CJEU, Case C-311/04, *Algemene Scheeps Agentuur Dordrecht*, [2006] ECR I-609, para. 25

51 *Etang de Berre*, n. 49.

52 Protocol for the Protection of the Mediterranean Sea against Pollution from Land-based Sources, 1980, 1328 UNTS 105; *Etang de Berre*, n. 49.

53 *Etang de Berre*, n. 49, para. 45.

54 Convention on Access to Information, Public Participation in Decision-making and Access to Justice in Environmental Matters, 1998, 2161 UNTS 447; CJEU, Case C-240/09, *Lesoochranárske zoskupenie*, [2011], ECR I-1255, para. 45.

55 CJEU, Case C-437/98, *Netherlands v Parliament and Council*, [2001] ECR I-7079, paras. 53–54.

20.4 THE INFLUENCE OF INTERNATIONAL LAW ON EU SECONDARY LAW

There is a clear link between the Stockholm Conference and the start of the EU's environment policy. The Stockholm Conference, which was held from 5–16 June 1972, was followed in November 1973 by the first EU Environmental Action Programme, which focused primarily on the fight against pollution and ignored nature protection.[56] Consequently, nature protection agreements, rather than political declarations and action programmes, have led to the development of the EU's nature protection policy.

20.4.1 *The Influence of the Council of Europe*

Seeking to overcome the divisions of the Second World War, the EU and the Council of Europe have shared common values of democracy, the rule of law, and human rights. All twenty-seven EU member states are also members of the Council of Europe, while the EU has observer status. Various subjects lend themselves to synergies, such as environmental law, criminal law, the protection of cultural property, and the protection of personal data in the age of new technologies. As far as nature protection is concerned, the Council of Europe has also played a key role in drafting:

- the 1979 Bern Convention;
- the 1998 Convention on the Protection of the Environment through Criminal Law;[57] and
- the 2000 European Landscape Convention.

The Bern Convention, being the first international treaty to protect both species and habitats, influenced the drafting of the Wild Birds and Habitats directives. Although the EU is not a party to the 1998 Convention, Council Directive (EC) 2008/99 probably implements the 1998 Convention by supplementing existing administrative sanction systems with criminal law penalties to strengthen compliance with the laws for the protection of the environment.[58] In 2022, the Committee of Ministers of the Council set up an expert committee entrusted with the elaboration of a new Convention on the Protection of the Environment through Criminal Law.

[56] Declaration of the Council of the European Communities and of the Representatives of the Governments of the Member States Meeting in the Council, (1973) OJ C112.

[57] Convention on the Protection of the Environment through Criminal Law, 1998, ETS no. 172.

[58] Council Directive (EC) 2008/99 on the Protection of the Environment through Criminal Law, (2008) OJ L328.

20.4.2 *The Dual Conservation Approach in International and EU Law*

The various directives and regulations adopted during the 1980s aiming at protecting nature were clearly inspired by the Ramsar Convention,[59] the Bern Convention, and the Bonn Convention. Moreover, EU secondary law must be interpreted, as far as possible, in the light of international law – in particular, where such texts are specifically intended to implement an international agreement concluded by the EU.[60] As mentioned, the Bern Convention has been fleshed out in the Wild Birds Directive and the Habitats Directive, which are the cornerstones of the EU's nature conservation policy.[61] Conservation measures operate along twin tracks. Like the Bern Convention, the two directives simultaneously pursue an ecosystem approach (the protection of vulnerable habitats or habitats of threatened species) and a specific approach (the protection of certain wild species). Contemporary to the Bern Convention, the Wild Birds Directive is in line with this treaty by distinguishing between the protection of the habitats of bird species, on the one hand, and the protection of bird species as such by regulating their taking, on the other.[62] Following the example of the Bern Convention, the Habitats Directive ensures the conservation of particular natural habitats as well as species of wild fauna and flora.[63]

20.4.3 *The Stringency of Habitat Protection under EU Law*

The designation and conservation regimes of protected areas designated under the Wild Birds and Habitats directives are much stricter than under international law. For instance, the Natura 2000 network constituted the first serious attempt in Europe to establish a network of protected sites. The two directives afford specific importance to the conservation of the natural habitats of wild fauna and flora enshrined in two legal instruments: 'special protection

[59] See Wild Birds Directive, n. 13, art. 4(2) (which requires member states to 'pay particular attention to the protection of wetlands and particularly to wetlands of international importance').

[60] *Commission v Germany*, n. 50, para. 52; CJEU, Case C-341/95, *Safety Hi-Tech S.R.L*, [1998] ECR I-4355, para. 20. This is not the case where the agreement has not been concluded by the EU or ratified by the member states. See CJEU, Case C-379/92, *Peralta*, [1994] ECR I-3454, para. 56.

[61] Nicolas de Sadeleer & Charles-Hubert Born, *Droit international et communautaire de la biodiversité* (Dalloz, 2002), 436.

[62] Charles-Hubert Born *et al.* (eds.), *The Habitats Directive in Its EU Environmental Law Context* (Routledge, 2015).

[63] Species that are protected under the Bern Convention, n. 12, are not necessarily protected under the Habitats Directive, n. 41. This is the case with the badger.

areas' intended to protect the habitats of rare bird species as well as migratory species under the Wild Birds Directive and 'special areas for conservation' intended to protect non-bird habitats of EU interest under the Habitats directive. In contrast, few international agreements provide for the obligation to protect habitats.[64]

In addition, in international law, the designation of protected areas is, in principle, a matter for the states. By way of illustration, under the World Heritage Convention, the listing of sites remains under the sovereignty of the state in which they are located.[65] Similarly, under the Ramsar Convention, each party must designate suitable wetlands in its territory for inclusion in the List of Wetlands of International Importance.[66] The choice must be made on the basis of their international significance. In contrast, under the Wild Birds Directive, the discretion of states is limited in regard to both the number and size of areas, which must be large enough to ensure the conservation of threatened species as well as migratory species.[67] The margin of appreciation of the member states is limited because of the objectives of nature protection. Furthermore, the Habitats Directive has introduced a much more sophisticated procedure for selecting EU-specific sites, further reducing the discretion of member states.[68]

EU nature protection law is far from being toothless. If nature conservation rules are incorrectly applied, the European Commission can bring an action for failure against the defaulting member state. In addition, in national cases where secondary EU law is invoked, the domestic courts regularly refer questions to the CJEU for preliminary rulings on the binding scope of the provisions at hand. Table 20.1 highlights the influence of some MEAs and policy documents on the development of EU secondary law and policies on nature conservation.

20.4.4 *The Extraterritorial Scope of the EU's Nature Protection Law*

Almost 80 per cent of the EU's biodiversity is found in the outermost regions and overseas territories. While the Habitats and Wild Birds directives apply to

64 The 1979 Bonn Convention, n. 11, defines habitat as 'any area in the range of a migratory species which contains suitable living conditions for that species'.

65 World Heritage Convention, n. 9, art. 2.

66 Ramsar Convention, n. 8, art. 2.

67 CJEU, Case C-355/90, *Marismas de Santona*, [1993] ECR I-4221, para. 22; CJEU, Case C-44/95, *Lappel Bank*, [1996] ECR I-3805, para. 26; CJEU, Case C-166/97, *Estuaire de la Seine*, [1997] ECR I-1719, para. 38; CJEU, Case C-96/98, *Marais poitevin*, [1999] ECR I-8548, para. 41.

68 Sadeleer & Born, n. 61.

TABLE 20.1 *Milestones of international nature protection law*

Topics	International arrangements/agreements	EU policy and legal commitments
Bases of the environment policy	1972 Stockholm Conference	1972 European Council Declaration on a Community Environment Policy
General framework	1992 CBD	No framework directive
European Wildlife and Natural Habitats	1979 Bern Convention	1979 (and 2010) Wild Birds Directive completed by the 1992 Habitats Directive
Wild birds	1979 Bonn Convention and the related 1995 Agreement on African-Eurasian Migratory Waterbirds	1979 (and 2010) Wild Birds Directive
Protection of species of wild fauna and flora by regulating trade therein	1973 CITES	1996 CITES Regulation
Invasive alien species	1992 CBD	Regulation 1143/2014 on Invasive Alien Species[69]
Access to genetic resources and the fair and equitable sharing of benefits arising from their utilization	2010 Nagoya Protocol on Access to Genetic Resources[70]	Regulation 511/2014 on Compliance Measures for Users from the Nagoya Protocol on Access to Genetic Resources[71]

the Azores, Madeira, and the Canary Islands, as these islands are part of the EU's territory, the other member states' overseas territories are not subject to the EU's harmonization measures. Since article 355 of the TFEU on the territorial scope of the Treaty makes no reference to the territory of the member states, this provision cannot be interpreted as limiting the territorial application of the TFEU only to the territories under the sovereignty of the member states. The scope of application of the TFEU as well as of secondary

69 Council Regulation (EU) 1143/2014 on Invasive Alien Species, (2014) OJ L317, 35–55.

70 Nagoya Protocol on Access to Genetic Resources and the Fair and Equitable Sharing of Benefits Arising from Their Utilization, 2014, 3008 UNTS 3.

71 Council Regulation (EU) 511/2014 on Compliance Measures for Users from the Nagoya Protocol on Access to Genetic Resources and the Fair and Equitable Sharing of Benefits Arising from Their Utilization in the Union, (2014) OJ L150, 231–233.

law may thus extend beyond the territory of the member states to the extent that public international law allows member states to exercise limited jurisdiction. This interpretation is of great importance from the point of view of conservation and sustainable use of biodiversity – in particular, with regard to the continental shelf, fishing zones, and exclusive economic zones. It follows that the EU lawmaker is competent to adopt rules relating to the conservation of biodiversity falling within the scope of article 191 of the TFEU in any area where member states have competence under public international law to protect the environment outside their own territory.[72] However, the exercise of extraterritorial competences in the environmental field must be in accordance with the rules of international law.[73]

20.4.5 *Preliminary Remarks*

One might wonder whether the EU's nature protection policy might be likely to offer better protection for ecosystems and species than a highly variegated international law. Indeed, EU law today extends to twenty-seven member states and probably more in the years to come. As mentioned, the EU is not a toothless legal order and represents a clear advantage over public international law in terms of efficacy. This is seen not least in the specific powers of the European Commission to sue before the CJEU member states that do not apply the nature protection obligations.[74] The enforcement policy has already cut its teeth in this area.[75] As far as the international scene is concerned, it is generally acknowledged that the EU has become the linchpin of international environmental policy. In addition to being a party with its member states to several key international agreements on nature protection without the active engagement of the EU, agreements such as the 2000 Cartagena Protocol on Biosafety would not have been concluded.[76]

Yet the picture is not as idyllic as one might be led to think as the EU still lags behind its purported aspirations. Neither biodiversity nor nature conservation are enshrined in the founding EU treaties. Moreover, the EU's legal order has neither the equivalent of the CBD nor that of the 1982 UN Convention on the Law of the Sea, agreements that laid the foundations for land and marine biodiversity conservation regimes.[77] In the absence of

[72] CJEU, Case C-405/92, *Armand Mondiet*, [1993] ECR I-6176, paras. 31–36.
[73] CJEU, Case C-366/10, *Air Transport Association of America*, [2011] ECR I-13755.
[74] TFEU, n. 24, arts. 258, 260.
[75] CJEU, Case C-510/20, *Commission v Bulgaria*, [2022] EU:C:2022:324.
[76] Cartagena Protocol on Biosafety, 2000, 2226 UNTS 208.
[77] UN Convention on the Law of the Sea, 1982, 1833 UNTS 3.

a framework directive on biological diversity, the EU has found itself forced to fall back upon legislative acts stemming from diverse areas of policy-making, each adopted according to its own specific procedures, pursuing different goals, and elaborated without any general overview.

20.5 CROSS-FERTILIZATION BETWEEN INTERNATIONAL LAW AND EU LAW: THE CASE OF INTERNATIONAL TRADE OF ENDANGERED SPECIES

The object of CITES is to protect certain endangered species of wild fauna and flora by regulating international trade. It lays down different rules on protection for different species, which are divided into three categories, corresponding to the three appendices to the Convention. CITES covers over 38,700 endangered species – about 5,950 species of animals and 32,800 species of plants – against over-exploitation by regulating international trade. In the past, CITES was only open to states and not to international organizations. A 1983 amendment of the Convention, which entered into force in 2013, enabled the EU to become a party to CITES in 2015.[78] The EU is an important region of destination, transit, and origin for many of the species protected under CITES.

At the outset, the EU has applied CITES without being able to ratify it. The first regulation implementing CITES dates from 1982. This regulation was replaced by the 1996 Regulation 338/97 on the Protection of Species of Wild Fauna and Flora by Regulating Trade Therein.[79] In implementing uniformly in all EU member states the provisions of CITES, this regulation considerably broadened the scope of application of CITES within the EU's legal order. The regulation classifies wild animal and plant species under four annexes. The first three annexes of the Regulation (A to C) roughly correspond to the three appendices of CITES (I to III). Regarding these annexes, the Regulation applies in compliance with the objectives, principles, and provisions of CITES. That being said, the regulation has an additional annex (D) that lists species that are not covered by CITES but which are imported into the EU in such numbers as to warrant monitoring.[80]

Regulation 338/97 provides for strict rules to ensure that wildlife products only enter the EU's market if they are of legal and sustainable origin. It

78 Council Decision 98/216, n. 34.
79 Council Regulation 338/97 on the Protection of Species of Wild Fauna and Flora by Regulating Trade Therein, (1997) OJ L61, 1–69.
80 CITES, n. 10, art. 3.

subjects species that are not necessarily included in the CITES annexes to control regimes. For instance, Annex A of the Regulation 338/97 includes several species from annex II of CITES. Accordingly, the discrepancies between the CITES appendices and the annexes of Regulation 338/97 are related to the willingness of the EU to regulate a number of species more strictly. Regulation 338/97 is regularly modified to comply with the decisions adopted by the CITES institutions.

The CJEU has ruled on disputes concerning the detention of parrots, taking into account, as the following examples show, the obligations set out in CITES. In *Tridon*, the CJEU assessed the compatibility of a French regulation prohibiting all commercial uses of captive born and bred specimens of species of macaw found in French Guyana with CITES and with Regulation 338/97. The Court concluded that the CITES appendices do not preclude legislation of a member state that lays down a general prohibition in its territory of all commercial use of captive born and bred specimens.[81] In *Ministerstvo životního prostředí*, the CJEU supported the interpretation that the competent authorities have the power to examine the ancestry of a breeding stock of hyacinth macaw (*Anodorhynchus hyacinthinus*) in the context of an application for an exemption certificate for the sale of specimens born and bred in captivity. The CJEU stressed that the 2006 Regulation 865/2006, which lays down detailed rules for the implementation of the CITES regulation, corresponds to resolutions of the CITES Conferences of the Parties.[82] These resolutions were adopted in view of the concern that much trade in specimens declared as born and bred in captivity remains contrary to CITES and to the resolutions of the COPs and may be detrimental to the survival of wild populations of the species concerned.[83]

20.6 CONCLUSIONS

We have seen to what extent the 1972 Stockholm Declaration has enticed states in Europe and elsewhere in the course of the 1970s to negotiate and conclude a swath of MEAs regarding nature protection. In addition, this declaration undoubtedly encouraged the EU to commence harmonizing national rules on nature conservation at the end of this decade. However, the authors of the Declaration could not have foreseen in 1972 that more

81 CJEU, Case C-510/99, *Xavier Tridon*, [2001] ECR I-7777.

82 Council Regulation (EC) 865/2006 Laying Down Detailed Rules Concerning the Implementation of Council Regulation (EC) 338/97 on the Protection of Species of Wild Fauna and Flora by Regulating Trade therein, (2006) OJ L166.

83 Case C-659/20, *Ministerstvo životního prostředí*, [2022] EU:C:2022:642, para. 55.

holistic concepts (biodiversity instead of nature conservation, and sustainable use instead of protection)[84] were required given the seriousness of the ecological crisis. These concepts, which are more closely related to sustainable development, emerged in 1992 with the CBD.

The 1972 Stockholm Declaration did not put an end to the debate between the utilitarian approach, ensuring a sustainable level of exploitation of natural resources, and the protection of the natural world as a heritage of mankind. At the UN International Meeting Stockholm+50: A Healthy Planet for the Prosperity of All – Our Responsibility, Our Opportunity, the developments of nature protection instruments, at both the international and EU level, still reflect the underlying tensions between, on the one hand, the utilitarian approach, and, on the other, the recognition of the intrinsic value of biodiversity.[85]

84 On these concepts, see Rayfuse, n. 5, 370–371.

85 The preamble of the CBD, n. 17, recognizes the intrinsic value of biodiversity, which is recognized as being the 'common concern of humankind'.

21

Fifty Years of International Lawmaking on the Environment: Women Shaping Legal Principles and Solidarity

Claudia Ituarte-Lima

21.1 INTRODUCTION

The 1972 Stockholm Conference on the Human Environment sowed the seeds of transnational environmental law, with states negotiating commitments towards a healthy environment and explicitly recognizing responsibilities to safeguard and wisely manage nature.[1] It was a watershed moment in understanding the vulnerability of humanity to ecosystems' degradation across the world. Nations acknowledged that 'through ignorance or indifference we can do massive and irreversible harm to the earthly environment on which our life and well-being depend'.[2] In reflecting on the legacy of the Stockholm Conference and looking ahead, Johan Rockström and colleagues argue that, after the Stockholm Conference in 1972, evidence has increased on how social-ecological problems are systemic, with various feedback ranging from the biophysical and social domains, and 'wicked' since those groups disproportionally affected are unlikely to be the perpetrators. Staying within safe planetary boundaries that leave no one behind becomes impossible without radical transformation.[3] While the inequalities among people in various countries and between the global North and the global South are increasingly recognized, the agency of women from the global South in international lawmaking has not been sufficiently visibilized.

The author would like to thank Patricia Kameri-Mbote, Jonas Ebbesson, David Langlet, Christine Evans, Sam Geall, Tang Yingxia, and the participants of Stockholm+50: International Environmental Law in Perspective, which was held at Stockholm University from 15–17 September 2022, for valuable comments to an early version of this chapter.

[1] *Report of the UN Conference on the Human Environment*, UN Doc. A/CONF.48/14/Rev.1, 16 June 1972.

[2] *Ibid.*, para. 6.

[3] Johan Rockström *et al.*, 'Stockholm to Stockholm: Achieving a Safe Earth Requires Goals That Incorporate a Just Approach' (2021) 4 *One Earth* 9.

The methods used in this article are legal interpretation, the analysis of policy documents and academic literature, which were complemented by insights obtained during the participation in events discussing the legacy of Stockholm +50 in 2022, specifically the official in-person UN event 'Stockholm+50: a healthy planet for the prosperity of all – our responsibility, our opportunity' (Stockholm +50)[4] and 'Environmental Law from Below, in China and Beyond' – an hybrid conference held in conjunction with Stockholm+50 jointly organized by The Raoul Wallenberg Institute of Human Rights and Humanitarian Law and Dialogue Earth[5] and the 'Stockholm+50: International Environmental Law in Perspective' Conference organized by the Stockholm Environmental Law and Policy Centre at Stockholm University.[6] This chapter examines the lawmaking dynamics relevant to understanding the positive legacy and limitations of the 1972 Stockholm Conference. The text focuses on women's rights and the agency of women from the global South whose contributions to international lawmaking are often overlooked. Section 21.2 identifies the strengths and weaknesses of the Stockholm Declaration and proposes key conceptual entry points for analysing lessons learned from the past fifty years that can serve to inform the future of international law. Section 21.3 maps women's agency in shaping international human rights law, and section 21.4 tracks advances in multilateral environmental agreements. Section 21.5 focuses on the right to a healthy environment and ecocide – whose seeds were planted in the Stockholm Conference – which hold strong promise for the future of international law.

21.2 WHERE IN THE 1972 STOCKHOLM CONFERENCE ARE RIGHTS AND NATURE

The Stockholm Declaration is often referred to as a Magna Carta for nature protection, reflecting existing customary international law and shaping future legal and policy normative developments.[7] The Stockholm Declaration

[4] See more information here: www.stockholm50.global/.

[5] See more information here: https://rwi.lu.se/wp-content/uploads/2022/06/Environmental-Law-from-Below-Meeting-Report_J2022.pdf. This Conference included the topic of women's rights and environment and preparatory material including Claudia Ituarte-Lima, 'Women's Rights in Environmental Law, from 1972 to Today' Dialogue Earth (2021), https://dialogue.earth/en/justice/womens-rights-in-environmental-law-from-1972-to-today/.

[6] See more at: www.su.se/stockholm-environmental-law-and-policy-centre/about-the-centre/stockholm-50-international-environmental-law-in-perspective-1.596265.

[7] Günther Handl, *Introductory Note to the Declaration of the United Nations Conference on Human Environment (Stockholm Declaration) 1972 and the Rio Declaration on Environment and Development 1992 and Preparatory Documents* (UN Audiovisual Library of International Law, 2012), https://legal.un.org/avl/ha/dunche/dunche.html.

articulates the connections between nature and human rights: 'Both aspects of man's *environment*, the natural and the man-made, are essential to his well-being and to the enjoyment of basic *human rights* – even the right to life itself.'[8] The Stockholm Declaration is relatively progressive in acknowledging how people depend on nature for the enjoyment of human rights and the risks that emerge by the non-wise use of agency and power: 'Man's capabilities, if used wisely, can bring to all peoples the benefits of development and the opportunity to enhance the quality of life. Wrongly or heedlessly applied, the same power can do incalculable harm to human beings and the human environment.'[9]

But while the Stockholm Declaration may have been progressive and innovative at the time, it was gender blind. It made no explicit mention of women, girls, or gender. Instead, women, girls, boys, and non-binary people were subsumed within the category of 'man', as shown in principle 1 of the Stockholm Declaration: '*Man* has the fundamental right to freedom, equality and adequate conditions of life, in an environment of a quality that permits a life of dignity and well-being, and *he* bears a solemn responsibility to protect and improve the environment for present and future generations' (emphasis added). Furthermore, the Stockholm Declaration has an essentialist view of 'man'. It lacks specification of who caused most of the social-ecological damage and, hence, obscures who bears most of the responsibility of the ecological breakdown. It also does not acknowledge that there are certain countries and groups within countries that are disproportionally burdened by the historical process of colonization and patriarchal hierarchies. Universalizing language that fails to situate and account for the level of responsibility risks reinforcing these patterns of injustice.[10]

Yet it would be a mistake to assume that the limitations of the Stockholm Declaration equate to women being passive recipients of men's ideas. Women certainly had agency in the Stockholm Conference: the only head of government present at the Stockholm Conference, other than the Swedish Prime Minister Olof Palme, was his Indian counterpart Indira Gandhi.[11] She delivered a powerful speech on behalf of developing countries and framed the Stockholm Conference not only as a negotiating space reaching limited

8 'Declaration of the United Nations Conference on the Human Environment', in *Report of the UN Conference on the Human Environment*, n. 1 (Stockholm Declaration) (emphasis added).

9 *Ibid.*

10 Natalia Urzola Gutiérrez, 'Gender in Climate Litigation in Latin America: Epistemic Justice through a Feminist Lens' (2023) 16(1) *Journal of Human Rights Practice* 208.

11 Indira Gandhi's full speech can be found at '1972 UN Conference on the Human Environment', *YouTube*, www.youtube.com/watch?v=jKaYPk5YnsU.

agreements but also as an event with a bold aim – namely, 'establishing *peace* and harmony in life among all races and with *Nature*'.[12] She questioned the kind of agency, linked to the concept of 'efficient man', that was promoted under the industrial civilization:

> The industrial civilization has promoted the concept of the efficient man, he whose entire energies are concentrated on producing more in a given unit of time and from a given unit of manpower. Groups or individuals who are less competitive and according to this test, less efficient are regarded as lesser breeds – for example the older civilizations, the black and brown peoples, *women* and certain professions.[13]

Can we envision a world where the interspecies solidarity and intersectional solidarity issues raised by Indira Gandhi fifty years ago are taken seriously; where we make peace with nature; and where the contributions to healthy ecosystems by women, girls, and non-binary people from the global South, Indigenous, Afro-descendant, and rural people are valued and supported everywhere? In order to analyse lawmaking and institutional dynamics associated with the Stockholm Conference, I propose three entry points: vulnerability, agency, and solidarity. Women from the global South are often framed as a vulnerable and oppressed group. In common language, the term 'vulnerability' is commonly equated with weakness and powerlessness. The *Oxford Dictionary* defines 'vulnerability' as 'the *fact of being weak* and easily hurt physically or emotionally'.[14] Research on vulnerability relevant for biodiversity conservation and sustainable use includes studies contextualizing the social-ecological and power dynamics that generate the vulnerability and marginalization in the first place;[15] examining how the divide between the rich and poor is likely to deepen, as the frequency and severity of anthropogenic ecological disasters increase; and analysing power relationships and inequality experienced, for example, by women in community-based resource management in marine protected areas.[16]

12 *Ibid.* (emphasis added).

13 *Ibid.* (emphasis added).

14 *Oxford's Learners Dictionary*, www.oxfordlearnersdictionaries.com/definition/english/vulnerability (emphasis added). A physical and mental impairment such as illness, disability, or other types of physical or mental impairments is often described as a cause of such vulnerability. 'Vulnerable Adults', NHS, www.hanwellhealthcentre.nhs.uk/policies/vulnerable-adults/.

15 See, e.g., Jessy Ribot, 'Vulnerability Does Not Just Fall from the Sky: Toward Multi-scale Pro-poor Climate Policy', in Robin Mearns & Andrew Norton (eds.), *Social Dimensions of Climate Change: Equity and Vulnerability in a Warming World* (World Bank, 2009).

16 Danika Kleiber, Leila Harris & Amanda C. J. Vincent, 'Gender and Marine Protected Areas: A Case Study of Danajon Bank, Philippines' (2018) 17 *Maritime Studies* 163.

Under legal scholarship, vulnerability has been subject to increasing debate.[17] Martha Albertson Fineman proposes vulnerability as a theoretical foundation for legal and political engagements, bringing out both universality and particularity as features of the human condition.[18] Lois Kotzé argues that human rights have been ill suited to address injustices affecting billions of individuals and other non-human beings and proposes to use vulnerability theory to understand the vulnerability of the entire human order and the challenges confronting human rights in the context of the Anthropocene.[19] Milka Sormunen proposes to redefine vulnerability and effective remedies in the climate context because the rights of future generations and nonhuman animals and other natural resources are not adequately represented in current democratic processes.[20] Instead of highlighting vulnerability as a characteristic of human nature, some researchers have focused on the concept of 'vulnerable groups'. For example, Lourdes Peroni and Alexandra Timmer consider that reasoning in terms of vulnerable groups opens the opportunity to move closer to a more robust idea of equality but also carries the risks of essentialism, stigmatization, and paternalism.[21] However, vulnerability in the context of women shaping environmentally relevant international law from the Stockholm Conference to today has escaped scholarly attention.

Complementary to vulnerability, I use agency and solidarity as entry points of analysis. A narrow definition of agency in international law is restricted to states' ability to wage war, dominate treaties, and enforce a certain behaviour of states through compulsory power,[22] largely ignoring forms of non-Western agency.[23]

[17] See, e.g., Alexander H. E. Morawa, 'Vulnerability as a Concept of International Human Rights Law' (2003) 6 *Journal of International Relations and Development* 139; Alexandra Timmer, Moritz Baumgärte & Louis Kotzé, 'The Potential and Pitfalls of the Vulnerability Concept for Human Rights' (2021) 39(3) *Netherlands Quarterly of Human Rights* 190.

[18] Martha Albertson Fineman, 'Equality, Autonomy, and the Vulnerable Subject in Law and Politics', in Martha Albertson Fineman & Anna Grear (eds.), *Vulnerability: Reflections on a New Ethical Foundation for Law and Politics* (Ashgate, 2013).

[19] Louis J. Kotzé, 'The Anthropocene, Earth System Vulnerability and Socio-Ecological Injustice in an Age of Human Rights' (2019) 10(1) *Journal of Human Rights and the Environment* 85.

[20] Milka Sormunen, 'Rethinking Effective Remedies to the Climate Crisis: A Vulnerability Theory Approach' (2023) 24 *Human Rights Review* 171.

[21] Lourdes Peroni & Alexandra Timmer, 'Vulnerable Groups: The Promise of an Emerging Concept in European Human Rights Convention Law' (2013) 11 *International Journal of Constitutional Law* 1056.

[22] Amitav Acharya, 'Global International Relations (IR) and Regional Worlds' (2014) 58 *International Studies Quarterly* 647.

[23] Elise Dietrichson & Fatima Sator, 'The Latin American Women: How They Shaped the UN Charter and Why Southern Agency Is Forgotten', in Rebecca Adami & Dan Plesch (eds.),

Like Elise Dietrichson and Fatima Sator, I am interested in a broader understanding of agency that examines who shapes international law based on ideational capabilities such as various forms of solidarity. Indeed, lawmaking is not restricted only to military and economically powerful states.[24] Like the rise of vulnerability in the international fora, interest in solidarity is also on the rise. For example, in 2023, the UN independent expert on human rights and international solidarity, Obiora Chinedu Oka, presented a revised draft declaration on human rights and international solidarity to the UN Human Rights Council.[25]

Building on the mandate and work of the current and prior UN independent experts on human rights and international solidarity mandate holders, the UN Office of the High Commissioner for Human Rights frames international solidarity as a broader concept than international cooperation and as an expression of unity among individuals, peoples, states, and international organizations as well as a foundational principle underpinning international law for preserving international order and the survival of the international society, including our common ecological habitat for which we are all responsible.[26] While building on discussions at international fora and literature on solidarity both as a legal principle and as a concept,[27] my approach in this article is distinct. I use solidarity as a heuristic tool for a deeper understanding of how women shape international human rights law and environmental law in an interconnected world.

21.3 INTERNATIONAL HUMAN RIGHTS LAW: REVISITING AGENCY AND SOLIDARITY

More than twenty years before the 1972 Stockholm Conference, women from the global South were engaged in transforming women's concerns into lawmaking in the drafting of the UN Charter – the founding document of the

Women and the UN: A New History of Women's International Human Rights (Routledge, 2021).

24 *Ibid.*

25 Obiora Chinedu Okafor, *Revised Draft Declaration on Human Rights and International Solidarity: Report of the Independent Expert on Human Rights and International Solidarity*, Doc. A/HRC/53/32, 2 May 2023.

26 See 'About International Solidarity and Human Rights', *OHCHR*, www.ohchr.org/en/special-procedures/ie-international-solidarity/about-international-solidarity-and-human-rights; 'Independent Expert on Human Rights and International Solidarity', *OHCHR*, www.ohchr.org/en/special-procedures/ie-international-solidarity.

27 See, e.g., Carl Wellman, 'Solidarity, the Individual and Human Rights' (2000) 22(3) *Human Rights Quarterly* 639.

United Nations.[28] The UN Charter, adopted in 1945, is often framed as 'the Constitution of the world'. It mentions the promotion of human rights without distinction of race, sex, language, or religion and repeats this principle in four articles in the Charter. The inclusion of non-discrimination based on sex was proposed by female delegates from Brazil, Uruguay, Mexico, the Dominican Republic, and India.[29] The UN Charter's preamble recognizes the equal rights of men and women; Articles 1, 7, 13, and 15 concern non-discrimination based on sex.[30] Article 8 deals with the equal participation of men and women in the United Nations. The Brazilian delegate Bertha Lutz framed Article 8 as a Latin American contribution to the world, which brings a new perspective to the multifaceted ways in which international solidarity can be expressed, including by contributing to new ideas in lawmaking processes.

According to Dietrichson and Sator, these provisions in the UN Charter involved hard fought battles in a context where the US delegates, followed by the British, were often deeply opposed.[31] Agency in lawmaking processes is connected to institutional developments. In 1946, the formal establishment of the Commission on the Status of Women (CSW), which is seen as one of the first formal recognitions of women's rights in the United Nations, was catalysed by Latin American delegates who proposed that the United Nations follow the precedent of the Inter-American Commission of Women. Through ECOSOC Resolution 11(II) in 1946, the CSW was created with the mandate to prepare recommendations on promoting women's rights in political, economic, civil, social, and educational fields.[32]

While the Stockholm Declaration is seen as the first international environmental law instrument, the 1948 Universal Declaration of Human Rights is considered the foundational international human rights law instrument.[33] India-born Hansa Mehta – the only woman delegate besides Eleanor Roosevelt in the Commission on Human Rights – revised the wording in the Universal Declaration from 'the rights of man' to 'human rights' and from 'all men' to 'everyone' and 'all human beings'.[34] The Universal Declaration has inspired a rich body of legally binding and non-binding international

28 Charter of the United Nations, 1945, 1 UNTS 15.

29 Dietrichson & Sator, n. 23, 8.

30 These articles use the wording of 'distinction' rather than 'discrimination'.

31 Dietrichson & Sator, n. 23.

32 For more on the Commission on the Status of Women (CSW), see 'Commission on the Status of Women', *UN Women*, www.unwomen.org/en/csw.

33 UNGA Resolution 217A (III) on Universal Declaration of Human Rights, 10 December 1948.

34 *Ibid.*

instruments – hence, the relevance of Hansa Mehta translating gender equality concerns into the wording of the Universal Declaration. Both the 1966 International Covenant on Civil and Political Rights (ICCPR)[35] and the 1966 International Covenant on Economic, Social and Cultural Rights (ICESCR)[36] recognize the right to equality between men and women in the rights covered by the respective treaty. In 1968, the Human Rights Commission hosted a high-profile inter-agency conference in Teheran that became a pivotal moment in the revision of the human rights discourse, placing greater weight on economics; women's rights provided a rare subject of agreement, with plans for greater investment in rural agriculture where women's work remained often informal.[37] These legal, institutional, and discourse developments laid the ground for international law on women's rights.

In contrast to the limited attention to women's rights at the Stockholm Conference, the United Nations designated 1975 as the International Women's Year and organized a conference in Mexico City, which resulted in concrete commitments to women's rights, specifically instructing the CSW to finalize the 1979 Convention on the Elimination of Discrimination against Women (CEDAW) specifying women's rights and corresponding state obligations.[38] While the legal obligations that emerge from these international treaties are key, there are other relevant processes at stake in the emergence of norms and institutions. The Mexico City Conference also resulted in the creation of the UN Development Fund for Women (UNIFEM) and the UN International Research and Training Institute for the Advancement of Women (INSTRAW). The outcomes of the Mexico City Conference are evidence of the agency of the global South delegates leading the development of international institutions.[39]

The emergence of INSTRAW is relevant for epistemic justice because it aims to strengthen women's capacities as knowledge generators, not only as research users. Through alliance building not only among UN member states but also with international organizations, academia, civil society, the private sector, and other actors, INSTRAW undertakes action-oriented research from a gender perspective with the aim of having concrete impact on policies and programmes.[40] Annie

35 International Covenant on Civil and Political Rights, 1966, 999 UNTS 171 (ICCPR).

36 International Covenant on Economic, Social and Cultural Rights, 1966, 993 UNTS 3 (UNESCR) (it entered into force six months before the ICCPR).

37 Ellen Chesler, 'Who Wrote CEDAW?' in Adami & Plesch, n. 23.

38 Convention on the Elimination of All Forms of Discrimination against Women, 1979, 1249 UNTS 13.

39 Chesler, n. 37.

40 'United Nations International Research and Training Institute for the Advancement of Women | UIA Yearbook Profile', *Union of International Associations*, https://uia.org/s/or/en/1100063863.

Jiagge, the second woman lawyer in the newly independent state of Ghana, argued at the Mexico City Conference in 1975 that advancing women rights would not only benefit women. She framed the conference's outcomes as a revolution for all humanity with no turning back.[41] The outcomes of the Mexico City Conference, such as the creation of INSTRAW, sheds new light on the understanding of intersectional solidarity and international solidarity, which goes beyond state-to-state relationships. Yet the Mexico City Conference was a missed opportunity to prioritize social-ecological challenges and advance interspecies solidarity and other forms of solidarity.

Like the active contribution of Indira Gandhi and other women at the Stockholm Conference, women from the global South have continued to participate in major global fora shaping international law. CEDAW was initially prepared by the Philippines senator Letitia Ramos-Shahani.[42] While it was adopted after the Stockholm Declaration, CEDAW is the culmination of more than thirty years of work by the CSW. As part of this process, women from the global South have contributed to reframing the global understanding of social and economic inequalities as essential human rights issues. They have advanced the principle of the indivisibility of human rights, arguing, on the one hand, that rights cannot be realized in the absence of resources and, on the other hand, that social and economic investments must respect political freedoms and civil liberties.

Complementary to the lawmaking processes, international conferences such as the Stockholm Conference and the Mexico City Conference were spaces to catalyse intra-generational solidarity. In 1985, the UN Women's Conference in Nairobi was one of the first international forums to stress the importance of gender equality and women's participation for sustainable development.[43] In 1992, China hosted an interregional workshop on the role of women in environmentally sound and sustainable development. International participants to this interregional workshop were encouraged to attend the 1995 Beijing Fourth World Women's Conference. Many women from low- and middle-income countries participated in the interregional workshop, and it was organized by the Task Force on Women in Development from the UN Department of Economic and Social Development, in cooperation with the INSTRAW and in association with

41 Quoted in Chesler, n. 37.

42 Adami & Plesch, n. 23.

43 'World Conference to Review and Appraise the Achievements of the United Nations Decade for Women: Equality, Development and Peace, Nairobi, 15–26 July 1985', *United Nations*, www.un.org/womenwatch/daw/beijing/nairobi.html.

China's State Science and Technology Commission and the All-China Women's Federation of the People's Republic of China.[44]

In contrast to how CEDAW is framed, the proceedings of this interregional workshop placed an emphasis on how to advance women's agency for a green and prosperous earth rather than a focus on advancing gender equality as a human rights issue. The report from this workshop reads: 'In order to make the planet earth green, peaceful and prosperous, the women of China are prepared to work together with women of the world, regardless of what social system they are from, their ethnic origins, religion, and creed, for the common interest of mankind and its future.'[45] Note that reference is made to the 'women of China' with other women in the world rather than to state-to-state cooperation. Like the rippling effect of the Stockholm Conference in environmental law, the 1995 Beijing Women's Conference has had a strong legacy. This conference – which had more than 17,000 participants from 189 governments with a further 30,000 people attending a parallel forum – was another space that provided a fertile ground for discussing the role of women in development and environmental global governance. Delegates prepared a Platform for Action and Point K of this platform made reference not only to women in terms of vulnerability associated with poverty but also to women's agency. Specifically, it highlighted the need for women's active participation in decision-making on matters relating to the environment at every level and called for the incorporation of gender issues into policies and programmes for sustainable development.[46] In the 2020 Beijing+25 Declaration,[47] states committed to intensify the mainstreaming of a gender perspective into policies considering not only the vulnerability experienced by women and girls but also the importance of women's leadership in environmental decision-making. The Beijing+25 Declaration refers to general environmental policies as well as specific climate change and disaster-risk reduction policies.

As we can see in this section, advances on women rights in international human rights law started to emerge as early as the 1940s, with the UN Charter and the Universal Declaration – hence, long before the 1972 Stockholm

44 'Interregional Workshop on the Role of Women in Environmentally Sound and Sustainable Development', *IRC*, www.ircwash.org/sites/default/files/71-INSTRAW92-11140-2.pdf.

45 *Ibid.*

46 United Nations, *Report of the Fourth World Conference on Women*, UN Doc. A/CONF.177/20, 1995.

47 *Political Declaration on the Occasion of the Twenty-fifth Anniversary of the Fourth World Conference on Women*, Doc. E/CN.6/2020/L.1, 2 March 2020, https://digitallibrary.un.org/record/3855071?ln=en&v=pdf; see also 'CSW64 / Beijing+25 (2020), Commission on the Status of Women', *UN Women*, www.unwomen.org/en/csw/csw64-2020.

Conference. Yet it was not until the 1990s that the connections between women's rights and the environment became explicit.

21.4 ENVIRONMENTAL LAW: FROM THE 1972 STOCKHOLM CONFERENCE TO THE 1992 RIO CONFERENCE

The 1972 Stockholm Conference paved the way for the 1992 Rio Conference on Environment and Development. The Rio Declaration on Environment and Development reaffirms the Stockholm Declaration and seeks to build upon it.[48] Yet there are important differences between these two declarations. Unlike the Stockholm Declaration, the Rio Declaration was the first international instrument to recognize the twin realities of women in the global South as especially vulnerable to environmental degradation and as agents of change. The concept of vulnerability is mentioned in relation to those 'most environmentally vulnerable', and it is framed in terms of countries being more or less vulnerable. Principle 6 states: 'The special situation and needs of developing countries, particularly the least developed and those *most environmentally vulnerable*, shall be given special priority. International actions in the field of environment and development should also address the interests and needs of all countries' (emphasis added).

The gender equality and women's empowerment narrative in the Rio Declaration was not only put forward in terms of fundamental human rights issues but also as a pathway for achieving peace and harmony between people, and with nature, as well as for achieving sustainable development.[49] In analysing expressions of intersectional solidarity, principle 20 on women's leadership should be read together with the Rio Declaration's principle 10 on access to information, access to public participation, and access to justice and principle 22 recognizing Indigenous peoples and local communities' traditional knowledge and practice and their vital participation in environmental management and development. Principle 20 reads: '*Women* play a *leading role* in environmental management and in development. For that reason, it is indispensable for them to participate fully if sustainable development is to be achieved' (emphasis added).

At the Rio Conference, Agenda 21 was adopted, and this comprehensive plan of action was to be taken globally, nationally, and locally by organizations of the UN system, and governments and major groups called for mainstreaming women

48 'Rio Declaration on Environment and Development', in *Report of the UN Conference on Environment and Development*, UN Doc. A/CONF.151/26 (Vol. I), 12 August 1992.

49 Handl, n. 7.

rights in environmental governance.[50] Likewise, two international treaties were adopted at the Rio Conference: the 1992 Convention on Biological Diversity (CBD)[51] and the UN Framework Convention on Climate Change (UNFCCC).[52] Like in the Rio Declaration, the term 'vulnerability' is used in the CBD in relation to 'environmental vulnerability' of developing countries such as those with arid and semi-arid zones and coastal and mountainous areas.[53] Among the women who contributed to the drafting process of the CBD is Vandana Shiva, an Indian physicist and social activist. The way in which Shiva places human agency in the context of a complex web of life is useful for revisiting the notion of vulnerability not only of certain countries but also of all humans and beyond human beings. It also helps in rethinking vulnerability coupled with agency, interspecies solidarity, and intergenerational solidarity.

In contrast to the narrative that biodiversity law notions are an imposition of the West and a luxury for global South countries, Shiva highlights the strong efforts that she and others have made for embedding in the CBD the notion that the entire web of life is held together by the relationships between species, and she argues that we need a new human solidarity and a new Earth solidarity.[54] While considering humans as one strand in this web, she also highlights human beings as earth's custodians and argues that 'cultivating and conserving diversity is *no luxury* in our times: it is a *survival imperative*',[55] and she considers that 'we are a *strand* in the web of life and the *web of biodiversity*. We are *custodians*, breeders and producers of seed. Living seed is our living heritage which we have received in diversity and integrity from our ancestors, and which we have a duty to safeguard and pass on to *future generations*.'[56]

50 Agenda 21, UN Doc. A/CONF. 151/26, 13 June 1992. For more on Agenda 2021 and women, see, e.g., 'Agenda 21: An Easy Reference to Specific Recommendations on Women', *UNFEM*, www.gdrc.org/gender/a21/agenda1.html; 'Review of Implementation of Agenda 21', *Sustainable Development*, https://sustainabledevelopment.un.org/content/documents/1126SD21%20Agenda21_new.pdf.

51 Convention on Biological Diversity, 1992, 1760 UNTS 79 (CBD).

52 UN Framework Convention on Climate Change, 1992, 1171 UNTS 107.

53 This reference is included under article 20 on financial resources, referring to developed country parties' obligations to provide new and additional financial resources to enable developing country parties to meet their CBD obligations.

54 Vandana Shiva, 'Transcript: Dr Vandana Shiva on Diverse Expressions of a Living Earth /311', *For the Wild*, 2022, https://forthewild.world/podcast-transcripts/vandana-shiva-on-diverse-expressions-of-a-living-earth-311; see also Vandana Shiva, *Terra Viva: My Life in a Biodiversity of Movements* (Chelsea Publishing, 2022).

55 Vandana Shiva, 'Rights Livelihood Awards Acceptance Speech', *Rights Livelihood*, https://rightlivelihood.org/speech/acceptance-speech-vandana-shiva/ (emphasis added).

56 Vandana Shiva, 'Women's Day 2021: A Message from Dr. Vandana Shiva', *Navdanya International*, 2021, https://navdanyainternational.org/womens-day-2021-a-message-from-dr-vandana-shiva/ (emphasis added).

Unlike the Stockholm Declaration, the CBD refers to the vital role that women play in the conservation and sustainable use of biological diversity as well as the need for their full participation at all levels of biodiversity conservation policy-making and implementation.[57] Two years later, the 1994 UN Convention to Combat Desertification (UNCCD) was adopted in Paris, and this treaty stresses the important role played by women in regions affected by desertification and/or droughts, specially of rural women in developing countries and the importance to ensure the full participation of both women and men in associated programmes at all levels.[58] Promoting awareness and facilitating the participation of local populations particularly of women and youth is mentioned under article 19(1)(a), and educational programmes and opportunities particularly for girls and women are mentioned under article 19(3)(f).[59]

Contrasting the Stockholm Declaration, the CBD's text does not refer to human rights or women rights and, hence, is relatively less progressive in bridging human rights and environmental law than the Stockholm Declaration. When rights are mentioned in the CBD, it is in relation to state-to-state interactions. It took more than twenty years after the Stockholm Declaration for the 1998 Aarhus Convention to recognize the connections between human rights and environment and forty years for an instrument to recognize the linkages between climate change, human rights, and gender equality.[60] Adopted in 2015, the Paris Agreement acknowledges that climate change is a common concern of humankind and makes explicit reference to 'obligations on *human rights*, the right to health, the rights of indigenous peoples, local communities, migrants, children . . . as well as *gender equality*, *empowerment of women* and *intergenerational equity*'.[61]

The momentum in 2015 for connecting human rights, gender equality, and environment also included the adoption of Agenda 2030 and the Sustainable Development Goals and the adoption of gender plans under the CBD.[62] The

57 CBD, n. 48, preamble.

58 UN Convention to Combat Desertification in Countries Experiencing Serious Drought and/ or Desertification, Particularly in Africa, 1994, 1954 UNTS 3, preamble, art. 10(f) (UNCCD).

59 For the UNCCD's Conference of the Parties' decisions relevant to women's rights, see 'United Nations Convention to Combat Desertification', *UN Women*, www.unwomen.org/en/how-we-work/intergovernmental-support/climate-change-and-the-environment/united-nations-convention-to-combat-desertification.

60 Convention on Access to Information, Public Participation in Decision-making and Access to Justice in Environmental Matters 1998, 2161 UNTS 447 (Aarhus Convention).

61 Paris Agreement on Climate Change, 2015, 3156 UNTS 79, preamble (emphasis added).

62 *Transforming Our World: The 2030 Agenda for Sustainable Development*, Doc. A/Res/70/1, 25 September 2015; see Patricia Kameri-Mbote & Nkatha Kabira, 'SDG 5: Achieve Gender Equality and Empower All Women and Girls', in Jonas Ebbesson & Ellen Hey (eds.), *The Cambridge Handbook of the Sustainable Development Goals and International Law*

first gender action was the CBD 2015–2020 Gender Plan of Action, which then inspired its sister conventions – the UNFCCC and the UNCCD – to adopt gender action plans. Yet there are limitations on the way in which human rights are incorporated into the CBD's gender action plan; human rights are only mentioned one time, and instead of recognizing human rights in line with human rights law language, this action plan refers to the 'provision of human rights', such as access to water, which points to a confusion between human rights and the provision of public services. The gender action plan also refers to tenure and use rights but does not connect this issue to international human rights law. Under the 'Possible Actions for Parties', which identifies potential policy obstacles to gender mainstreaming, the gender action plan advises: '2.1. Review relevant policies to identify gender differences, including in policies related to *tenure and use rights*' (emphasis added). The Secretariat of the CBD advised the inclusion of specific activities to tackle gender inequalities and the allocation of adequate funding for efforts to mainstream gender in countries' national biodiversity strategies and action plans.[63] There have been further developments since then, which I discuss in the next part.

In brief, from the 1972 Stockholm Declaration to the 1992 Rio Declaration and beyond, women have shaped international principles and have contributed to a revised concept of vulnerability in international law. A definition coupling vulnerability with women's agency and solidarity is a better fit to advance various forms of solidarity and encourage an interpretation of women rights that is not only in line with international human rights minimum standards but also goes beyond these minimum standards.

21.5 FUTURE OF INTERNATIONAL LAW

21.5.1 Women Shaping the Right to a Clean, Healthy, and Sustainable Environment (Right to a Healthy Environment)

From the Stockholm Conference in 1972 to today, recognizing agency is a crucial dimension of the inherent dignity of every human being. The

(Cambridge University Press, 2022), 140; Claudia Ituarte-Lima & Maria Schultz (eds.), *Human Right to a Healthy Environment for a Thriving Earth: Handbook for Weaving Human Rights, SDGs, and the Post-2020 Global Biodiversity Framework* (SwedBio/Stockholm Resilience Centre, International Development Law Organization, Office of the High Commission of Human Rights-Special Procedures, UN Environment and Natural Justice, 2019), https://shorturl.at/toUvI.

63 Secretariat of the Convention on Biological Diversity, *Review of Implementation of the 2015–2020 Gender Plan of Action*, Doc. CBD/SBI/3/2/Add.3, 14 April 2020.

recognition of the right to a healthy environment by the UN General Assembly in 2022 – an outcome of collective action since 1972 – has provided an opportunity to highlight women's agency in shaping law and solidarity.[64] Among the many women championing this cause is Costa Rica's Ambassador Catalina Devandas Aguilar – part of the core group of countries championing the recognition of this right by the United Nations.[65] The United Nations' recognition of the right to a healthy environment also builds on advances in plurilateral processes. For example, the 2003 Maputo Protocol, which entered into force in 2005,[66] recognizes a wide range of environmental-related women's rights, including article 16 on the right to live in acceptable living conditions in a healthy environment, as well as clarifying the duties of state parties to this protocol in Africa.[67] This treaty also reaffirms the principle of gender equality enshrined in the Constitutive Act of the African Union and recognizes the '*crucial role of women* in the preservation of African values based on the principles of equality, peace, freedom, dignity, justice, *solidarity* and *democracy*'.[68]

The recognition of the right to a healthy environment also builds on environmental democracy treaties that recognize this right, specifically the Aarhus Convention, which emerged as a European treaty but is also open for other countries to join,[69] and the 2018 Escazú Agreement.[70] The Escazú Agreement, like the Aarhus Convention, translates principle 10 of the Rio Declaration into legal obligations. The Escazu Agreement is the first treaty specifying the rights of human rights defenders in environmental matters (article 9) or biosphere defenders[71] and providing an Action Plan on Human

64 UN General Assembly, *The Human Right to a Clean, Healthy and Sustainable Environment*, UN Doc. A/RES/76/300, 28 July 2022.

65 'Access to a Healthy Environment, Declared a Human Right by UN Rights Council', *UN News*, 2021, https://news.un.org/en/story/2021/10/1102582.

66 Protocol to the African Charter on Human and People's Rights on the Rights of Women in Africa, 2003 (Maputo Protocol).

67 Elsabé Boshoff, 'Women's Environmental Human Rights in Africa with Reflections on Key Provisions of the Maputo Protocol', in Michael Addaney & Ademola Oluborode Jegede (eds.), *Human Rights and the Environment under African Union Law* (Palgrave Macmillan, 2020).

68 Maputo Protocol, n. 66, preamble (emphasis added).

69 Aarhus Convention, n. 60. For example, Guinea-Bissau recently became party to this treaty. 'Guinea-Bissau Accedes to the Aarhus Convention, Opening New Horizons for Environmental Democracy in Africa and Worldwide', *UNECE Media*, 25 April 2023, https://unece.org/media/press/377878.

70 Regional Agreement on Access to Information, Public Participation and Justice in Environmental Matters in Latin America and the Caribbean, Doc. LC/PUB.2018/8, 4 March 2018.

71 Claudia Ituarte-Lima, 'Biosphere Defenders Leveraging the Human Right to Healthy Environment for Transformative Change' (2023) 1 *Environmental Policy and Law* 139; Claudis Ituarte-Lima, Maria Andrea Nardi & Liisa Varumo, 'Just Pathways to Sustainability:

Rights Defenders in Environmental Matters in Latin America and the Caribbean.[72] Unlike the Aarhus Convention, the Escazú Agreement also has specific provisions concerning Indigenous peoples and local communities (article 5, paragraph 4; article 7, paragraph 15; and article 7, paragraph 10). At the Escazu Agreement's third Conference of the Parties in 2024, parties adopted a decision on strengthening the gender perspective in implementing the Escazú Agreement and encouraging parties to continue to promote the full and effective participation of women in all their diversity, including Indigenous women.[73] Yet more work needs to be done to implement a gender lens in practice and achieve the objectives of these environmental treaties and unite human rights, women rights, and the environment.

The legal advances that have occurred since 1972 show that the principle of equality goes beyond non-discrimination, which was the initial framing of women's rights back in the UN Charter. The 2020 'Call to Action on Human Rights' by António Guterres, the UN secretary-general, on the occasion of the seventy-fifth anniversary of the United Nations identifies gender equality and equal rights for women in public participation and civic space among key areas that require extra efforts and attention.[74] An enabling environment to spur participation and action towards a healthy biosphere and support the diversity of life on earth is critically important in advancing women's rights. The time for a stand-alone target on access rights and environmental defenders (target 22) and a stand-alone target on gender equality (target 23) with a strong focus on open information and public participation finally came with the adoption of the 2022 Kunming-Montreal Global Biodiversity Framework.[75] This framework was initially proposed by the CBD's Women's Caucus – with strong global South leadership – and was also championed by UN Women (UNIFEM), Costa Rica, and twelve other countries. Target 22 states:

From Environmental Human Rights Defenders to Biosphere Defenders' (2023) 53 *Environmental Policy and Law* 347.

72 Decision III/2 on the Action Plan on Human Rights Defenders in Environmental Matters, 2024, https://acuerdodeescazu.cepal.org/cop3/sites/acuerdodeescazucop3/files/2400669e_cop.ez3_decisions_adopted_6_may.pdf.

73 Decision III/4 on Mainstreaming the Gender Perspective, 2024, https://acuerdodeescazu.cepal.org/cop3/sites/acuerdodeescazucop3/files/2400669e_cop.ez3_decisions_adopted_6_may.pdf.

74 UN Secretary-General, 'The Highest Aspiration: A Call to Action for Human Rights', *United Nations*, 2020, www.un.org/peacebuilding/sites/www.un.org.peacebuilding/files/documents/2020_sg_call_to_action_for_hr_the_highest_aspiration.pdf.

75 *Kunming-Montreal Global Biodiversity Framework*, Doc. CBD/COP/DEC/14/5, 19 December 2022, www.cbd.int/doc/decisions/cop-15/cop-15-dec-04-en.pdf.

> Ensure *gender equality* in the implementation of the Framework through a gender-responsive approach, where all women and girls have *equal opportunity and capacity to contribute* to the three objectives of the Convention, including by recognizing their equal rights and access to land and natural resources and their full, equitable, meaningful and informed *participation* and *leadership* at all levels of action, engagement, policy and *decision-making* related to biodiversity. (emphasis added)

Weaving the right to a healthy environment with international law principles is important because the extent to which women can exercise their right to a healthy environment will heavily depend on whether there is equality in exercising access rights (access to information, public participation, and access to justice) recognized in principle 10 of the Rio Declaration and other international instruments mirroring this principle. The incorporation of the right to a healthy environment and women's rights in the Kunming-Montreal Global Biodiversity Framework provides an entry point for women, girls, and other groups not only to minimize negative impacts on their own health but also to empower them to act as agents of change for ecosystems' stewardship including using law as a means to support the enjoyment of this right for present and future generations and hold accountable those who do not act in line with human rights law and multilateral environmental agreements.

21.5.2 *Women Shaping Ecocide Law*

While this chapter has focused on women's rights in international human rights law and international environmental law, there are other branches of international law such as criminal law that are relevant for safeguarding Earth's life support systems and advancing gender equality. Today, there is a serious accountability gap with impunity for those committing large-scale and irreparable damage to the environment. Instead, the abuse of law and criminalization of people who defend nature and human rights is on the rise.[76] Women journalists and media professionals have been criminally charged, often for defamation[77] with chilling effects that have society-wide impacts.

The Stockholm Declaration calls for the further development of international law bearing on environmental liability. Olof Palme, the Swedish

[76] M. Forst, *Report of the Special Rapporteur on the Situation of Human Rights Defenders*, UN Doc. A/71/28, 13 August 2016.

[77] Margaret Sekaggya, *Report of the Special Rapporteur on the Situation of Human Rights Defenders*, Doc. A/HRC/19/55, 21 December 2011.

prime minister, used the concept of ecocide at the Stockholm Conference.[78] Women continue to use the Stockholm Conference's legacy to shape international law, advancing an understanding of vulnerability that is connected to cultivating peace and harmony among all people and with nature. For example, in 2022, Dior Fall Sow co-chaired an Independent Expert Panel to propose that an ecocide definition be included in the 1998 Rome Statute.[79] Dior Fall Sow is a female UN jurist from Senegal and former prosecutor.[80] As she explained, 'this is the beginning of a difficult but exhilarating adventure that should only end with the introduction into the Rome Statute of this fifth crime of ecocide. Let's dare to do it!'[81]

Another woman member of the Independent Expert Panel proposing the ecocide definition is Syeda Rizwana Hasan from Bangladesh, who is director of the Bangladesh Environmental Law Association. She highlights the need for law to defend both nature and present and future generations, which converges with the notion of vulnerability connected to solidarity. Her statement also resonates with the intra-generational solidarity and intergenerational solidarity issues raised by Indira Gandhi in the Stockholm Conference in 1972, questioning the destructive forms of development. Hasan places emphasis on the situation of people in the global South: 'We, in the global south, are witnessing massive destruction of natural systems in the name of development, against which national legal systems are not responding adequately. … We need recognition of ecocide in international law, to defend Mother Earth, nature and both present and future generations.'[82]

Five decades after the 1972 UN Stockholm Conference, Sweden and Kenya hosted the UN International Meeting Stockholm+50: A Healthy Planet for the Prosperity of All – Our Responsibility, Our Opportunity (Stockholm+50 Meeting). In the final plenary of the Stockholm+50 Meeting, the Stockholm +50 Youth Task Force presented its policy paper following global consultations, including with the contributions of girls and young women from the global South. Its demand to governments is clear both in terms of recognizing

78 'Demand for Ecocide Law Was One of the Big Topics Buzzing in the Halls of UN International Environment Meeting Stockholm +50', *Stop Ecocide*, www.stopecocide.earth/stockholm-50-summary.

79 Rome Statute of the International Criminal Court, 1998, 2187 UNTS 90.

80 'Independent Expert Panel for the Legal Definition of Ecocide', *Stop Ecocide Foundation*, 2021, https://static1.squarespace.com/static/5ca2608ab914493c64ef1f6d/t/60d7479cf8e7e5461534dd07/1624721314430/SE+Foundation+Commentary+and+core+text+revised+%281%29.pdf.

81 This quote appears in the introduction of the panel members at *Stop Ecocide*, www.stopecocide.earth/expert-drafting-panel.

82 'Legal Definition', *Stop Ecocide*, www.stopecocide.earth/legal-definition.

the right to a clean, healthy, and sustainable environment in legal systems at different scales as well as recognizing ecocide as a crime in the Rome Statute for 'holding governments and corporations accountable for their damage to our common planet'.[83]

In contrast to the stereotype of women being weak and vulnerable, women are taking on a daring attitude to contribute to make law work for – and not against – nature and people.[84] Can we not only envision, but also make a reality, the bold proposals from Dior Fall Sow, Syeda Rizwana Hasan, the Stockholm+50 Youth Task Force, among many others – where the law is effectively used to hold accountable those people who commit significant damage to the environment and also where law is a catalyst for the enjoyment of the right to a healthy environment for everyone, everywhere?

21.6 CONCLUSIONS

In this chapter, I have discussed not only innovations but also limitations from the 1972 Stockholm Declaration. In line with the principle of non-regression in human rights law, the Stockholm Declaration was more progressive than the Universal Declaration in connecting human rights to environmental concerns. The 1972 Stockholm Conference was a watershed moment for understanding the vulnerability of humanity to ecosystems' degradation across the world and the irreversibility of harm to the environment upon which the life and well-being of present and future generations of human and other living beings depend. Yet, the Stockholm Declaration failed to adopt a more gender progressive language than the Universal Declaration, the ICCPR, and the ICESCR, despite being adopted more than twenty years after the Universal Declaration and more than five years after both of the covenants. Hence, in contrast to linear phases of international law as a whole, this chapter finds that advances have differed across environmental and human rights law. Likewise, distinct notions of vulnerability exist in human rights and environmental law, and these understandings of vulnerability have also changed through time.

83 'Stockholm+50: Global Youth Policy Paper', *Knowledge Hub*, 2022, www.sparkblue.org/system/files/2022-06/S%2B50%20Global%20Youth%20Policy%20Paper%20-%20Third%20Official%20Version%2C%20May-22.pdf.

84 Other women who currently are shaping discourse on ecocide law and who are part of Stop Ecocide International include Fiame Naomi Mata, prime minister of Samoa, Maureen Colette Payne-Hyman, a senator in Antigua, and Robin Barbuda Gairdner. 'Right Livelihood Award Laureates Call for Ecocide Law: Stop Ecocide International', *Stop Ecocide International*, 3 June 2022, www.stopecocide.earth/new-breaking-news-summary/right-livelihood-award-laureates-call-for-ecocide-law.

International law dynamics are embedded in contrasting narratives on how and by whom international law is shaped. In this chapter, I have shown how decoupling vulnerability from weakness and coupling it with agency and solidarity allows for a deeper understanding of the role of women from the global South in international lawmaking. First, decoupling vulnerability from weakness and powerlessness helps unveil the assumptions behind the narrative of global hegemony with a Eurocentric character that present non-Western countries as passive recipients of global narratives and ideas that originate in the West. Opponents to the United Nations and to feminism as a product of the West use this narrative to challenge international cooperation today and reject the relevance of women rights and feminism.[85] Yet, as Ellen Chesler highlights, the characterization of women's rights as a Western invention, imposed on innocents elsewhere in the world, is not only incorrect but also insulting because this narrative ignores the many years of commitment of women and allies from the global South who have assumed positions of leadership in global and regional fora.[86] In this chapter, I have shown that advances in international human rights law relevant to the environment were significantly shaped by global South women even before the 1972 Stockholm Conference. Environmental law is often subject to the same accusations to those of the United Nations and feminism – for example, framing biodiversity as a luxury for the West to enjoy rather than as a prerequisite for survival for all, especially by those more directly connected to nature for their livelihoods – despite the latter being historically voiced by grassroot movements in the global South.

Second, rather than a narrow interpretation of agency in the context of international law focusing on states' ability to instigate wars, control treaties, and enforce state's behaviour through compulsory power, the broad definition of agency used in this chapter is helpful in mapping key moments of international legal and institutional developments before, during, and after the 1972 Stockholm Conference. Recognizing the positive agency of global South women in environmental lawmaking is not only a matter of getting the facts right but also an issue of epistemic justice – where the global South is acknowledged as a generator of legal ideas and knowledge in international lawmaking and not just a user of ideas imposed by others. In international human rights fora, women have advanced in practice the indivisibility of civil and political rights with economic, social, and cultural rights that apply in the environmental context. Women's advocacy in connecting a wide range of

85 Dietrichson & Sator, n. 23.
86 Chesler, n. 37.

rights was transformed into binding legal provisions in one single treaty – CEDAW – which was adopted in 1979 in spite of the historical emergence of two distinct treaties in 1966 that specified a distinct set of rights (that is, the ICCPR and the ICESCR). Institutional developments on women's rights also preceded the Stockholm Conference, with the CSW being created as early as 1946 with a broad mandate to address a spectrum of rights, again in contrast to the ICCPR and the ICESCR. Furthermore, the CSW was important for later developments such as UNIFEM and INSTRAW in 1978.

However, these developments on women's rights happened in parallel rather than in synergy with the 1972 Stockholm Conference. It was not until the 1992 Rio Conference that women's rights and the environment started to converge. Through these developments and other dynamics involved in international negotiations, I have shown that lawmaking relevant to women rights and biosphere stewardship has not been restricted to economically powerful states. Ideational capabilities also matter in international lawmaking and the development of international institutions. If humanity is to address successfully the systemic social-ecological challenges, the collective action of all needs to be recognized, not least the actions of female international lawmakers.

Third, coupling the notion of vulnerability with women's agency is a first step, but it is not sufficient. Solidarity needs to be placed within the equation in order to demonstrate the multifaceted dynamics of lawmaking. Through the analysis presented in this chapter, I have shown that coupling vulnerability with agency and solidarity is needed if international law is to be up to the challenge of addressing contemporary social-ecological crises. The entry point of solidarity used in this chapter has been useful in visibilizing relationships that often go under the radar when the focus is only on state-to-state international cooperation. Like the Stockholm Conference, international women's conferences such as the one in Mexico City in 1975, followed by the Nairobi Conference in 1985, the Beijing Conference in 1995, and other international conferences that have followed were spaces to catalyse collective action by right holders from various countries towards a peaceful and prosperous earth. In this chapter, I have revealed concrete illustrations of women shaping solidarity in multilateral environmental agreements, human rights instruments, and the emerging ecocide law.

I have provided examples on how women have helped advance the 'five i's of solidarity': intersectional solidarity, interspecies solidarity, intragenerational solidarity, intergenerational solidarity, and international solidarity. As part of these five i's of solidarity, solidarity between women groups and other constituencies is necessary if peace and harmony between all people and with nature is to be achieved. Acknowledging the vulnerability of humanity to biodiversity loss and the degradation of ecosystems is not an act of weakness but, rather, an act of courage that is vital to confronting heads on the planetary polycrises.[87] Evidence of women's agency and solidarity in a context of a vulnerable Earth show the very concrete possibility of transformative change. State institutions as the main human rights duty bearers with obligations to respect, protect, and fulfil human rights can synergize with women-led initiatives for innovative ways to achieve the realization of the right to a clean, healthy, and sustainable environment.

Furthermore, weaving women rights and obligations emerging from multilateral environmental agreements can be a means for catalytic collective action to safeguard healthy ecosystems and biodiversity. Existing practices triggered by women's groups with positive social-ecological outcomes at the national, regional, and international levels are vitally important because these practices demonstrate the feasibility of effective actions in a context of increased vulnerability for humanity as a whole. The time is now to act upon the interdependencies between women rights, biodiversity, and healthy ecosystems for present and future generations to thrive. International lawmakers unleashing values of solidarity is a leverage point for the transformative action needed to address the earth's planetary crises.

[87] Anu Lähteenmäki-Uutela *et al.*, 'Planetary Boundaries Nurturing the Grand Narrative of the Right to a Healthy Environment?' (2024) 54 *Environmental Policy and Law* 15.

ANNEX A

Declaration of the United Nations Conference on the Human Environment[1]

Stockholm 5–16 June 1972

The United Nations Conference on the Human Environment,

Having met at Stockholm from 5 to 16 June 1972,

Having considered the need for a common outlook and for common principles to inspire and guide the peoples of the world in the preservation and enhancement of the human environment,

I

Proclaims that:

1. Man is both creature and moulder of his environment, which gives him physical sustenance and affords him the opportunity for intellectual, moral, social and spiritual growth. In the long and tortuous evolution of the human race on this planet a stage has been reached when, through the rapid acceleration of science and technology, man has acquired the power to transform his environment in countless ways and on an unprecedented scale. Both aspects of man's environment, the natural and the man-made, are essential to his well-being and to the enjoyment of basic human rights – even the right to life itself.
2. The protection and improvement of the human environment is a major issue which affects the well-being of peoples and economic development throughout the world; it is the urgent desire of the peoples of the whole world and the duty of all Governments.

[1] This excerpt is taken from the *Report of the UN Conference on the Human Environment*, UN Doc. A/CONF.48/14/Rev.1, 16 June 1972.

3. Man has constantly to sum up experience and go on discovering, inventing, creating and advancing. In our time, man's capability to transform his surroundings, if used wisely, can bring to all peoples the benefits of development and the opportunity to enhance the quality of life. Wrongly or heedlessly applied, the same power can do incalculable harm to human beings and the human environment. We see around us growing evidence of man-made harm in many regions of the earth: dangerous levels of pollution in water, air, earth and living beings; major and undesirable disturbances to the ecological balance of the biosphere; destruction and depletion of irreplaceable resources; and gross deficiencies, harmful to the physical, mental and social health of man, in the man-made environment, particularly in the living and working environment.
4. In the developing countries most of the environmental problems are caused by under-development. Millions continue to live far below the minimum levels required for a decent human existence, deprived of adequate food and clothing, shelter and education, health and sanitation. Therefore, the developing countries must direct their efforts to development, bearing in mind their priorities and the need to safeguard and improve the environment. For the same purpose, the industrialized countries should make efforts to reduce the gap themselves and the developing countries. In the industrialized countries, environmental problems are generally related to industrialization and technological development.
5. The natural growth of population continuously presents problems for the preservation of the environment, and adequate policies and measures should be adopted, as appropriate, to face these problems. Of all things in the world, people are the most precious. It is the people that propel social progress, create social wealth, develop science and technology and, through their hard work, continuously transform the human environment. Along with social progress and the advance of production, science and technology, the capability of man to improve the environment increases with each passing day.
6. A point has been reached in history when we must shape our actions throughout the world with a more prudent care for their environmental consequences. Through ignorance or indifference we can do massive and irreversible harm to the earthly environment on which our life and well-being depend. Conversely, through fuller knowledge and wiser action, we can achieve for ourselves and our posterity a better life in an environment more in keeping with human needs and hopes. There are

broad vistas for the enhancement of environmental quality and the creation of a good life. What is needed is an enthusiastic but calm state of mind and intense but orderly work. For the purpose of attaining freedom in the world of nature, man must use knowledge to build, in collaboration with nature, a better environment. To defend and improve the human environment for present and future generations has become an imperative goal for mankind – a goal to be pursued together with, and in harmony with, the established and fundamental goals of peace and of world-wide economic and social development.

7. To achieve this environmental goal will demand the acceptance of responsibility by citizens and communities and by enterprises and institutions at every level, all sharing equitably in common efforts. Individuals in all walks of life as well as organizations in many fields, by their values and the sum of their actions, will shape the world environment of the future. Local and national governments will bear the greatest burden for large-scale environmental policy and action within their jurisdictions. International co-operation is also needed in order to raise resources to support the developing countries in carrying out their responsibilities in this field. A growing class of environmental problems, because they are regional or global in extent or because they affect the common international realm, will require extensive co-operation among nations and action by international organizations in the common interest. The Conference calls upon Governments and peoples to exert common efforts for the preservation and improvement of the human environment, for the benefit of all the people and for their posterity.

II PRINCIPLES

States the common conviction that:

Principle 1

Man has the fundamental right to freedom, equality and adequate conditions of life, in an environment of a quality that permits a life of dignity and well-being, and he bears a solemn responsibility to protect and improve the environment for present and future generations. In this respect, policies promoting or perpetuating *apartheid*, racial segregation, discrimination, colonial and other forms of oppression and foreign domination stand condemned and must be eliminated.

Principle 2

The natural resources of the earth, including the air, water, land, flora and fauna and especially representative samples of natural ecosystems, must be safeguarded for the benefit of present and future generations through careful planning or management, as appropriate.

Principle 3

The capacity of the earth to produce vital renewable resources must be maintained and, wherever practicable, restored or improved.

Principle 4

Man has a special responsibility to safeguard and wisely manage the heritage of wildlife and its habitat, which are now gravely imperilled by a combination of adverse factors. Nature conservation, including wildlife, must therefore receive importance in planning for economic development.

Principle 5

The non-renewable resources of the earth must be employed in such a way as to guard against the danger of their future exhaustion and to ensure that benefits from such employment are shared by all mankind.

Principle 6

The discharge of toxic substances or of other substances and the release of heat, in such quantities or concentrations as to exceed the capacity of the environment to render them harmless, must be halted in order to ensure that serious or irreversible damage is not inflicted upon ecosystems. The just struggle of the peoples of all countries against pollution should be supported.

Principle 7

States shall take all possible steps to prevent pollution of the seas by substances that are liable to create hazards to human health, to harm living resources and marine life, to damage amenities or to interfere with other legitimate uses of the sea.

Principle 8

Economic and social development is essential for ensuring a favourable living and working environment for man and for creating conditions on earth that are necessary for the improvement of the quality of life.

Principle 9

Environmental deficiencies generated by the conditions of under-development and natural disasters pose grave problems and can best be remedied by accelerated development through the transfer of substantial quantities of financial and technological assistance as a supplement to the domestic effort of the developing countries and such timely assistance as may be required.

Principle 10

For the developing countries, stability of prices and adequate earnings for primary commodities and raw materials are essential to environmental management since economic factors as well as ecological processes must be taken into account.

Principle 11

The environmental policies of all States should enhance and not adversely affect the present or future development potential of developing countries, nor should they hamper the attainment of better living conditions for all, and appropriate steps should be taken by States and international organizations with a view to reaching agreement on meeting the possible national and international economic consequences resulting from the application of environmental measures.

Principle 12

Resources should be made available to preserve and improve the environment, taking into account the circumstances and particular requirements of developing countries and any costs which may emanate from their incorporating environmental safeguards into their development planning and the need for making available to them, upon their request, additional international technical and financial assistance for this purpose.

Principle 13

In order to achieve a more rational management of resources and thus to improve the environment, States should adopt an integrated and co-ordinated approach to their development planning so as to ensure that development is compatible with the need to protect and improve environment for the benefit of their population.

Principle 14

Rational planning constitutes an essential tool for reconciling any conflict between the needs of development and the need to protect and improve the environment.

Principle 15

Planning must be applied to human settlements and urbanization with a view to avoiding adverse effects on the environment and obtaining maximum social, economic and environmental benefits for all. In this respect, projects which are designed for colonialist and racist domination must be abandoned.

Principle 16

Demographic policies which are without prejudice to basic human rights and which are deemed appropriate by Governments concerned should be applied in those regions where the rate of population growth or excessive population concentrations are likely to have adverse effects on the environment of the human environment and impede development.

Principle 17

Appropriate national institutions must be entrusted with the task of planning, managing or controlling the environmental resources of States with a view to enhancing environmental quality.

Principle 18

Science and technology, as part of their contribution to economic and social development, must be applied to the identification, avoidance and control of environmental risks and the solution of environmental problems and for the common good of mankind.

Principle 19

Education in environmental matters, for the younger generation as well as adults, giving due consideration to the underprivileged, is essential in order to broaden the basis for an enlightened opinion and responsible conduct by individuals, enterprises and communities in protecting and improving the environment in its full human dimension. It is also essential that mass media of communications avoid contributing to the deterioration of the environment, but, on the contrary, disseminate information of an educational nature on the need to protect and improve the environment in order to enable man to develop in every respect.

Principle 20

Scientific research and development in the context of environmental problems, both national and multinational, must be promoted in all countries, especially the developing countries. In this connexion, the free flow of up-to-date scientific information and transfer of experience must be supported and assisted, to facilitate the solution of environmental problems; environmental technologies should be made available to developing countries on terms which would encourage their wide dissemination without constituting an economic burden on the developing countries.

Principle 21

States have, in accordance with the Charter of the United Nations and the principles of international law, the sovereign right to exploit their own resources pursuant to their own environmental policies, and the responsibility to ensure that activities within their jurisdiction or control do not cause damage to the environment of other States or of areas beyond the limits of national jurisdiction.

Principle 22

States shall co-operate to develop further the international law regarding liability and compensation for the victims of pollution and other environmental damage caused by activities within the jurisdiction or control of such States to areas beyond their jurisdiction.

Principle 23

Without prejudice to such criteria as may be agreed upon by the international community, or to standards which will have to be determined nationally, it will be essential in all cases to consider the systems of values prevailing in each country, and the extent of the applicability of standards which are valid for the most advanced countries but which may be inappropriate and of unwarranted social cost for the developing countries.

Principle 24

International matters concerning the protection and improvement of the environment should be handled in a co-operative spirit by all countries, big and small, on an equal footing. Co-operation through multilateral or bilateral arrangements or other appropriate means is essential to effectively control, prevent, reduce and eliminate adverse environmental effects resulting from activities conducted in all spheres, in such a way that due account is taken of the sovereignty and interests of all States.

Principle 25

States shall ensure that international organizations play a co-ordinated, efficient and dynamic role for the protection and improvement of the environment.

Principle 26

Man and his environment must be spared the effects of nuclear weapons and all other means of mass destruction. States must strive to reach prompt agreement, in the relevant international organs, on the elimination and complete destruction of such weapons.

21st plenary meeting
16 June 1972

ANNEX B

Stockholm+50: A Healthy Planet for the Prosperity of All – Our Responsibility, Our Opportunity, Summary Points of Leadership Dialogues and Outcome[1]

Stockholm, 2 and 3 June 2022

III LEADERSHIP DIALOGUES

Summary points of leadership dialogue 1: Reflecting on the urgent need for action to achieve a healthy planet and prosperity for all

1. Resetting our relationship with nature is essential to achieve peace and a healthy planet and prosperity for all. Speakers representing Member States and other participants expressed a real sense of urgency to act, at the required scale, and transform our socioeconomic systems. It was recognized that these transformations require new measures of progress and human well-being, and a fundamental change in attitudes and behaviour.
2. Greater accountability is required to deliver on national and international responsibilities and address the triple planetary crisis in integrated ways. Leadership is essential to drive the sustainability agenda, both in fulfilling existing commitments and to further global cooperation on the climate, biodiversity and pollution agendas.
3. It is recognized that human rights, intergenerational equity and inclusion are all fundamental elements of sustainable development. Action to transform socioeconomic systems can be informed by the human right to a healthy, clean and sustainable environment, as well as by remedying

[1] This excerpt is taken from the *Report of Stockholm+50: A Healthy Planet for the Prosperity of All – Our Responsibility, Our Opportunity*, UN Doc. A/CONF.238/9, 1 August 2022.

the effect that current development impact can have on human rights and the upholding of justice.

4. Restoring trust through effective multilateralism and partnerships can strengthen international cooperation and solidarity. A fair platform is important to accelerate action, bringing together different actors, providing the means to respond to shared challenges and giving every country the right to be heard.
5. Systemic changes in consumption and production systems need to be accelerated, providing for fair transitions in high-impact sectors, including food systems. Action to scale up progress on Sustainable Development Goal 12 includes transforming value chains, addressing resource efficiency and promoting circular economy approaches. Business and multi-stakeholder approaches have an important role to play.
6. Achieving a healthy planet and prosperity for all requires the alignment of financial flows: public and private, domestic and international. The political will and political commitment to drive just transitions, scaling-up sustainable finance and repurposing harmful subsidies, as well as building capacity and sharing technology and knowledge are all critical steps in that process.

Summary points of leadership dialogue 2: Achieving a sustainable and inclusive recovery from the COVID-19 pandemic

1. Global value chains should be strengthened to ensure a resilient global economy; that should include creating access to and enhancing capacities of small and medium-sized enterprises in developing countries, small island developing States and least developed countries.
2. Sustainable consumption and production and the circular economy should be harnessed to accelerate the transformation of global value chains. A global dialogue on sustainable consumption and production should be established that could lead to a global roadmap on the circular economy for all stakeholders.
3. Support should be provided to businesses that are at the forefront of driving the shift to circularity. Such support could be underpinned by a global circularity protocol that would set clear targets and track progress through a transparency mechanism.
4. The influence of consumers in transforming global value chains should be recognized; they should have access to the information they need to make sustainable consumer choices.

5. The importance of the food sector for sustainability and as part of the solution for overcoming the COVID-19 pandemic should be recognized; that will require stopping environmentally harmful subsidies and redirecting those funds into sustainable areas, increasing investment in sustainable practices generally and empowering smallholder farmers.
6. Building back better must include green and energy transitions. Mere commitments are not enough: real climate action is needed, action that 'walks the walk', not only 'talks the talk'.
7. Women and girls play a vital role in advancing sustainable development. They should be involved at all levels, as should young people and vulnerable groups. The knowledge and experience of indigenous peoples and local communities is also of great value. For the contribution of all these groups to be maximized, they will need access to education, capacity-building and the regulatory framework.
8. As the digital economy and solutions for sustainable development, including e-commerce platforms, have grown in importance, the need for an inclusive platform has become ever more essential to address the digital divide and digital illiteracy, while managing the potential negative impact of digitalization on energy consumption.

Summary points of leadership dialogue 3: Accelerating the implementation of the environmental dimension of sustainable development in the context of the decade of action and delivery for sustainable development

1. Access to and the quality and quantity of finance available to developing countries, especially least developed countries, for achieving the Sustainable Development Goals needs to be improved.
2. Mitigation and adaptation action is essential to ensure a balanced, equitable transition, the rights of States and people for development, and gender parity.
3. The finance gap must be bridged to allow environmental action to catch up with aspirations and hopes.
4. Well-designed government action, including green and sustainable budgeting, is needed to start realigning and redirecting environmentally harmful subsidies.
5. Coordination of sovereign debt relief, debt guarantees and the pooling of debt risk in the context of climate financing is needed.

6. Scaled-up access to quality, affordable education and for the promotion of environmentally conscious syllabuses and curricula is urgently required.
7. Cooperation by all actors is essential to accelerate the transfer of knowledge, technology and know-how, and to scale up the availability and access to and affordability of digital goods and services and critical infrastructure in developing countries.
8. All actors should work together to combat inequality within and between nations as an essential step towards addressing environmental and development crises.
9. Existing processes and mechanisms for financing adaptation and sustainable transition in developing countries need to be reinvigorated, with efforts directed at reviving them, rather than establishing new processes and mechanisms.
10. Collective international action is essential to ensure that environmental purposes do not become or are not used as trade barriers or to hamper developmental processes.

V OUTCOME OF THE INTERNATIONAL MEETING

Summary: Recommendations for accelerating action towards a healthy planet for the prosperity of all

In our capacity as Presidents, the following key recommendations emerged from Member States and stakeholders, through the plenary and leadership dialogues at the Stockholm+50 international meeting.

The recommendations reflect the resolve of the participants to urgently accelerate the implementation of commitments for a healthy planet for the prosperity of all, in the context of the decade of action and delivery for sustainable development – including a sustainable recovery from the coronavirus (COVID-19) pandemic – and taking into account the outcomes from the fifth session of the United Nations Environment Assembly of the United Nations Environment Programme and from the special session of the Environment Assembly to commemorate the 50th anniversary of the establishment of the United Nations Environment Programme, held in Nairobi on 3 and 4 March 2022.

Since the United Nations Conference on the Human Environment in 1972, the global community has adopted a wealth of multilateral environmental agreements, as well as other commitments, including the Sustainable

Development Goals and the 2030 Agenda. Fulfilment of the objectives and commitments of all those agreements would take us a long way towards securing a healthy planet for all.

Stockholm+50 has emphasized the global interconnectedness of the environment and the need to collectively address the triple crisis of our common environment – climate change, biodiversity loss and pollution – for present and future generations. Stockholm+50 has also underlined the urgent need for bold and deliberate actions, as well as clear political will to accelerate action on these commitments, strengthen the multilateral system, increase ambition and solidarity, and set us on a credible path towards a healthy planet for all, leaving no one behind.

The discussions during Stockholm+50 reaffirmed the importance of local realities and national implementation, and the need for a combination of incentives and policies, finance and capacity support to achieve sustainable development. We have heard the following recommendations for actions to accelerate implementation:

1. **Place human well-being at the centre of a healthy planet and prosperity for all**, through recognizing that a healthy planet is a prerequisite for peaceful, cohesive and prosperous societies; restoring our relationship with nature by integrating ethical values; and adopting a fundamental change in attitudes, habits and behaviours to support our common prosperity.
2. **Recognize and implement the right to a clean, healthy and sustainable environment**, through fulfilling the vision articulated in principle 1 of the 1972 Stockholm Declaration.
3. **Adopt a system-wide change in the way our current economic system works to contribute to a healthy planet**, through defining and adopting new measures of progress and human well-being, supported by economic and fiscal policies that account for the value of the environment; investing in infrastructure, developing effective policy and encouraging a global dialogue to promote sustainable consumption and production; and promoting the phasing-out of fossil fuels while providing targeted support to the poorest and most vulnerable, in line with national circumstances and recognizing the need for financial and technical support towards a just transition.
4. **Strengthen national implementation of existing commitments for a healthy planet**, through enhancing national environmental legislation, budgets, planning processes and institutional frameworks; promoting evidence-based policymaking, including by enhanced collaboration

between academic disciplines and thematic scientific panels, drawing on insights and expertise from indigenous and traditional knowledge; and scaling up capacity support and development, access to and financing for environmentally sound technologies.

5. **Align public and private financial flows with environmental, climate and sustainable development commitments**, through developing and implementing well-designed policies to repurpose environmentally harmful subsidies; redirecting, mobilizing and scaling up the availability of public and private financial flows to support economic diversification; and adopting recovery and stimulus measures, blended sources of capital and de-risking instruments that augment financial flows.
6. **Accelerate system-wide transformations of high impact sectors, such as food, energy, water, building and construction, manufacturing and mobility**, through adopting and implementing policies to promote circularity, resource efficiency, regenerative production approaches and nature-based solutions in value chains, and adopting frameworks that enhance and reinforce transparency and accountability by business; promoting just transitions through support for impacted youth, labour and local communities by strengthening capacity and skills for the creation of green jobs and for micro-, small and medium enterprises; and transforming food systems by promoting regenerative farming and fisheries approaches that provide healthy diets and minimize food waste, including investments in the ocean economy.
7. **Rebuild relationships of trust for strengthened cooperation and solidarity**, through recognizing the importance of developed country leadership in promoting sustainability transitions; supporting capacity-building and technology transfer for national efforts by developing countries to implement internationally agreed environmental agreements, taking into account national circumstances, including honouring the commitment to mobilize $100 billion every year for climate finance for developing countries; and enabling all relevant stakeholders, including youth, women, rural communities, indigenous peoples, interfaith groups and local communities, to participate meaningfully in policy formulation and implementation at both the national and international levels.
8. **Reinforce and reinvigorate the multilateral system**, through ensuring an effective rules-based multilateral system that supports countries in delivering on their national and global commitments, to ensure fair and effective multilateralism; strengthening the environmental rule of law, including by promoting convergence and synergies within the United

Nations system and between multilateral environmental agreements; and strengthening the United Nations Environment Programme, in line with the UNEP@50 political declaration.

9. **Recognize intergenerational responsibility as a cornerstone of sound policymaking**, through engaging with the Stockholm+50 Global Youth Task Force and its policy paper; highlighting the important need to build the capacity of young people to engage with financial institutions; recognizing the critical role of young people in environmental action, highlighting the fact that progress has been made in fostering the meaningful engagement of youth, and calling upon multilateral environmental funds to include youth-inclusive parameters in their funding schemes and take further steps to ensure ease of access to funds for environmental action by youth-led organizations.
10. **Take the Stockholm+50 outcomes forward** through reinforcing and reenergizing the ongoing international processes, including a global framework for biodiversity, an implementing agreement for the protection of marine biodiversity beyond national jurisdiction and the development of a new plastics convention; and engaging with relevant conferences, such as the 2022 United Nations Ocean Conference, the high-level political forum on sustainable development, the twenty-seventh meeting of the Conference of the Parties to the United Nations Framework Convention on Climate Change, and the Summit of the Future.

Index

For EU product safety concerns, contact us at Calle de José Abascal, 56–1°, 28003 Madrid, Spain or eugpsr@cambridge.org.

www.ingramcontent.com/pod-product-compliance
Ingram Content Group UK Ltd.
Pitfield, Milton Keynes, MK11 3LW, UK
UKHW021817051026
15470UKWH00026B/1404
* 9 7 8 1 0 0 9 4 4 5 7 7 1 *